AF844019

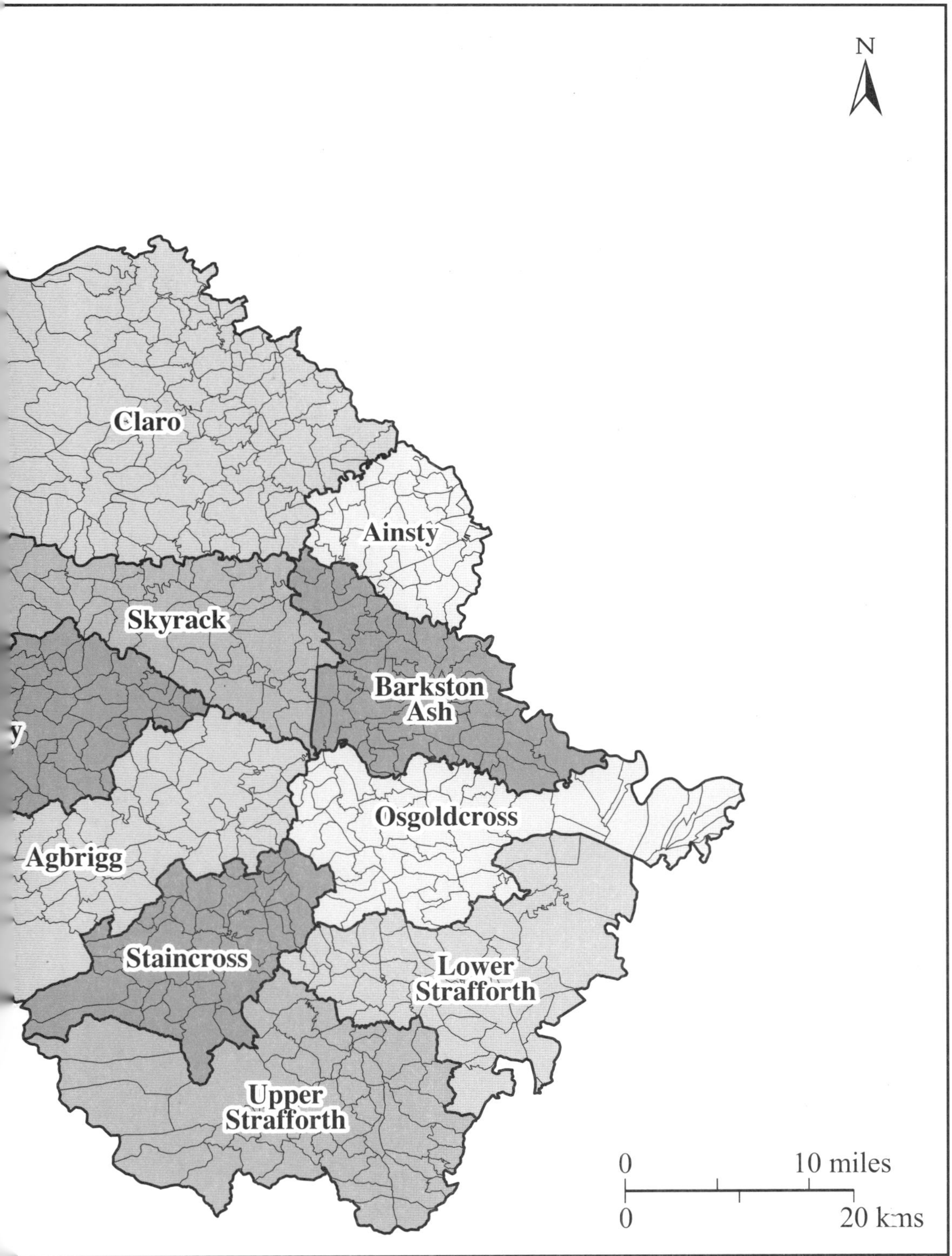
N
Claro
Ainsty
Skyrack
Barkston Ash
Osgoldcross
Agbrigg
Staincross
Lower Strafforth
Upper Strafforth
0
10 miles
0
20 kms

THE BRITISH RECORD SOCIETY
PROFESSOR MARGARET SPUFFORD, O.B.E., LITT.D., F.B.A.
General Editor, Hearth Tax Series

Editorial Committee:

PATRIC L. DICKINSON, M.A., *Honorary Secretary*; ELSE CHURCHILL, B.A.;
PROFESSOR PETER SPUFFORD, PH.D., LITT. D., F.B.A., *Chairman*;
SARAH PEARSON, B.A., F.S.A.; JOHN STRINGER, *Honorary Treasurer*
CLIFFORD WEBB, M.A., F.S.A., *General Editor, Probate Series*

BRITISH ACADEMY HEARTH TAX PROJECT
& CENTRE FOR HEARTH TAX RESEARCH
ROEHAMPTON UNIVERSITY LONDON

ANDREW WAREHAM, PH.D., F.R.HIST.S., *Director*
JOHN PRICE, B.A., *Project Manager*

YORKSHIRE WEST RIDING
HEARTH TAX LADY DAY 1672

Issued by
THE BRITISH RECORD SOCIETY
[INDEX LIBRARY 121]
HEARTH TAX SERIES VOLUME V

in association with the
BRITISH ACADEMY HEARTH TAX PROJECT

Jacket Information for Hearth Tax Volumes

General

The fireplaces illustrated on the jacket come from various parts of England and Wales and reflect a wide social spectrum from the major gentry (Little Moreton Hall) to yeoman farmhouses (Valley Farm, Glencoyne). Unfortunately, few seventeenth-century fireplaces in small, single-hearth houses and cottages survive unaltered, and it has proved impossible to find suitable illustrations of them. However, the simple timber chimney and fireplace of Ty-Mawr, the brick one at Valley Farm, and the cooking hearth of Glencoyne, are typical of the period and could have been found in many smaller houses and cottages.

Descriptions

Front jacket

Top Left
Little Moreton Hall, Cheshire. Decorative fireplace in the chamber over the porch. The house was owned by the powerful Moreton family, whose wealth was based on land. The fireplace is part of the late sixteenth-century additions to the medieval house. By the seventeenth century there were around twenty fireplaces. © Jeremy Milln.

Top Right
Wickens, Charing, Kent. Fireplace with plaster overmantel in the chamber over the parlour. The house was built around 1600 by the Dering family, who were minor gentry. Six hearths were charged in the hearth tax of 1664. © Sarah Pearson.

Bottom Left
Valley Farm. Flatford, Suffolk. A late-medieval yeoman's house; in the sixteenth century a brick fireplace and ceiling (now removed) were inserted into the open hall. By the late seventeenth century a second stack with one, or possibly two, fireplaces had been added to heat the adjacent cross wing. © John Walker.

Bottom Right
Ty-Mawr, Castell Caereinion, Montgomeryshire. An open-hall house built in 1461. In the sixteenth century a half-.timbered fireplace was added, and later an upper floor inserted (now removed). Ty-Mawr means 'great house', and although probably a long-house, with animals at one end, and only one hearth in the 1660s, this was a dwelling of high status in the region. © Peter Smith.

Outside Back jacket

Glencoyne Farm, Ullswater, Cumbria. A rare surviving open fire, complete with hearth furniture, set within a typical northern firehood. The large space was lit by its own window, to the right of this photograph of *c.1900.* The house received its present form in 1629. It was owned by a family called Harrison, one of whom was taxed on three hearths in 1674. Reproduced by courtesy of the Museum of Lakeland Life, Kendal, Cumbria.

YORKSHIRE WEST RIDING HEARTH TAX ASSESSMENT LADY DAY 1672

Edited by
David Hey, Colum Giles,
Margaret Spufford and Andrew Wareham

Assisted by
Simon Best, Duncan Harrington, Alasdair Hawkyard,
Christine Leighton, John Price, Mike Shand and Sue Stearn

Published by The British Record Society
c/o Patric Dickinson
The College of Arms
Queen Victoria Street
London EC4V 4BT

ISBN 978-0-901505-48-4

© British Record Society 2007

All rights reserved. No portion of this publication may be reproduced, stored in a retrieval system, or transmitted in any form or by any means, mechanical, electronic, photocopying, recording, or otherwise, without prior permission, in writing, from The British Record Society

Typeset by Cambrian Typesetters, Camberley, Surrey
Printed in Great Britain

Contents

Plates

Figures

Tables

Maps

ACKNOWLEDGEMENTS

The British Academy Hearth Tax Project depends upon the goodwill of its volunteers who dedicate their spare time to the transcription of these records. In this instance the work was undertaken by Gwyn De Jong, Mary Fraser, Anne George, Averil Harper-Smith, Thomas Jackson, Claire Jarvis, Chris Potter and Laurie Woods, and the Project wishes to express its gratitude to them. The Project would also like to express its thanks to Alasdair Hawkyard and Christine Leighton for completing the palaeographical checking of the text, and to Duncan Harrington for his work on the exemption certificates. Sue Stearn and Mike Shand have demonstrated the wonders of email in working together to produce the statistical tables and maps, and Simon Best compiled the personal and place name indexes. Peter Spufford has done an immense amount of work while Margaret was hospitalised with a crushed ankle for what seemed an eternity, and has steadfastly kept her end of the enterprise moving.

The Project has been extremely fortunate in recruiting David Hey and Colum Giles to write the introductions to this text. All local and social historians know and have been helped by David Hey's work. He also has a particular interest in the distribution of surnames, so family historians also follow his writing. Colum Giles, who is head of Urban Research at English Heritage, is also very well known for his work on the vernacular buildings of Yorkshire as any who have read his previous work know. Brian Roberts provided the topographical maps, and the Project is grateful to him for his cartographical assistance.

The Hearth Tax Project is a collective exercise, and colleagues in the School of Arts and the Research Office at Roehampton University provided advice and assistance on numerous historical and technical matters in the preparation of this volume, most notably John Price, Trevor Dean and Keith Tritton. Elizabeth Parkinson, Senior Research Fellow, has continued to give us advice on the hearth tax documents as well as writing the section on the administration of the tax. Sarah Pearson, our other Senior Research Fellow, has continued to advise us on buildings and those most expert on them, as well as reading drafts.

Without the support of the Project's funders, it would not be possible to bring these important texts into the public domain, and thereby to enrich understanding of communities and households, including those beneath the taxation threshold in later Stuart England. On this occasion generous assistance has been provided by the Marc Fitch Fund, as part of a project on 'The Hearth Tax County Returns and Regional Comparisons', and the Aurelius Trust, while The British Academy continues to provide advice and support. The Project wishes to express its gratitude for the support received, leading to the publication of *Yorkshire West Riding Hearth Tax Returns Lady Day 1672.*

Andrew Wareham, Ph.D., F.R.Hist.S.
Director of the British Academy Hearth Tax Project
and Roehampton University Centre for Hearth Tax Research
Roehampton University London
Feast of the Assumption, 2007

The Determinants of the Hearth Tax Project

by Margaret Spufford

The British Record Society is proud to present the fifth volume in the Hearth Tax Series, which we are publishing in collaboration with the British Academy Hearth Tax Project.

I was aware, when I began on the Hearth Tax Project, of its enormous size, since I wanted to print, analyse and map the best surviving hearth tax return of every county which did not already have one in print. I therefore knew it would take a very long time. I was not fully conscious of just how long and slow it would be. I had not previously directed a scheme that depends upon the goodwill and enthusiasm of volunteers who give up their free time to transcribe historical texts. The only other such scheme of which I was aware was the work of the Cambridge Group for the History of Population and Social Structure, which used volunteers to analyse the parish registers of England from 1538, for nearly two decades before E. A. Wrigley and R. S. Schofield were able to produce their magisterial *Population History of England* in 1981. Their first tabulations had been made in 1964. They managed to complete 404 analyses of parish registers to their satisfaction. These contain three and a half million names. I knew therefore that our analysis would take a very long time to carry out, if we managed to do pieces of work which satisfied our requirements. The hearth tax of 1662 to1689 was the last great tax of medieval and early modern England which had not been fully analysed. Since I wrote my first paper on it in 1962 I had been aware of this need. From Domesday Book to the 1334 subsidies to the Great Subsidy of 1524–5, brave people had tackled and mapped the figures, and the poll taxes of the 1370s and 80s have been added since. But the hearth tax returns were just too big for any but a sizeable team of people to work on. So I too began to think of using volunteers in a similar way.

The tax was levied twice a year, at Michaelmas and Lady Day from 1662 to 1689. A county for which all the returns have survived, as they do uniquely for Warwickshire, had therefore eight county returns, as well as a series of "exemption certificates" for those who had a house with a rental value of 20 shillings a year or less, and had land or goods worth £10. (See below, Elizabeth Parkinson, pp. 553–4) Very few lists of these exempt people have been indexed or listed and as a result, we know much less about those who were "poor" in the eyes of the hearth tax assessors, even though there is more available about the "poor" in the hearth tax than there is in any tax which precedes it. C. A. F. Meekings printed one appendix on the Dorset exemption certificates, and we have paid particular attention to those exempt in County Durham in the Project's last volume. This proved so fruitful that the Project has continued this policy in this volume, and are actively seeking funds to index and count the numbers covered in the remaining mass of exemption certificates in the National Archives. Until the Project has obtained a grant to do this work the Project's analysis of the hearth taxes will remain incomplete.

Speed remains a daunting problem. We are working on a score of further counties. The Project's volunteers are put in pairs so that they may exchange problems and notes. But I did not initially realise that transcribing each county might take up two years, depending on its size. I was aware that each transcript would need checking by a professional palaeographer, but not aware that this checking of lists of names and numbers would be one of the grimmest jobs that could befall a palaeographer, since each name on a list to be checked lacks any context to provide clues. It is merely a list. A palaeographer can therefore only work for one day a week on the data. This was, of course, a step which was not necessary for the Cambridge Group since they were only counting the numbers of people baptised, married or buried in each parish by the year. They were not recording the names of heads of households taxed. I had at least realised that after the initial transcript was made by the volunteers the Project would need to employ professionals for the other tasks before publication. A further handicap was that despite the size and importance of the Project, or perhaps because of it, funding bodies with some shining exceptions, did not wish to contribute and I have had constant financial anxiety about covering the following set of consultants' fees. Another two years can easily be spent on the vital task of accuracy. The next task for another professional, after we had our accurate texts, is the production of the tables revealing the totals of households with different numbers of hearths in each township or other taxation unit. These are produced by our statistician. Lastly, and crucially, the results for each unit had to be mapped on the base which the Project's GIS cartographer had been working on to have ready for the figures. It is impossible to read the tables of results and produce maps in one's head. Spatial data needs to be displayed on a spatial base. Since I had taken great care in devising the "bands" of householders with significantly different numbers of hearths, from one hearth upwards to ten hearths and over, these can be mapped as percentages and densities across all areas of a county. These, when mapped across all areas of a county, and then across all other counties also, will show us social comparisons from county to county, as well as density of households and wealth and poverty.

Our task is enormous, but our volunteers are making steady inroads into the mass of material that awaits them. Two sets of county total figures exist, probably based on the hearth tax of 1689, one for Davenant's *Essay After the Ways and Means of Supplying the War* and one from John Houghton's 1693 broadsheet, *An Account of the Acres and Houses, with The Proportional Tax, etc., of each County in England and*

Wales. The totals reached by both these men can be compared.[1] From our point of view the most encouraging mark of our progress is that the two highest figures in these lists are for London, Middlesex and Westminster at 111,215 and the three Ridings of Yorkshire plus York and Hull at 121,052. The Project's volunteers have completed a transcription of the London and Middlesex Lady Day return for 1666. We have complete transcripts of returns for all three Ridings of Yorkshire and these are in palaeographic hands for the North and East Ridings. As this volume shows, work on the West Riding is triumphantly concluded. The Project was drawn towards completing the West Riding first because it stood out as "different" from the other northern counties where we had already worked, as David Hey and Colin Giles discuss in their Introductions. David provides a characteristically masterful survey of the West Riding in the later Stuart age, bringing to life the households and environments depicted in the Hearth Tax data.

Colum uses a case study methodology to examine and contrast two areas of the West Riding, one to the west on the edge of the Pennines and one to the east on the flatter, richer, more gentrified soils. He illustrates the very different societies which grew up in these 'pays' and shows how careful the historian must be in determining such local regions. He also illustrates the way different building styles manifested themselves in their different 'countries'.

We are encouraged by D V Glass's comment in his conclusion to his first paper on Gregory King "It must be emphasised that the analysis of hearth tax material is difficult and labourious and it is in any case unlikely that any absolute set of statistics for the whole country could be obtained, but what could be done is to use the available records to build up a more consistent statistical account, and work in this direction should be encouraged."[2] We seem to have been rather slow on the uptake, but we appear to be fulfilling this request made in 1965.

One of the main objects of our research has been to investigate the prosperity of the inhabitants of England between the 1660's and the 1680's, measured in terms of their numbers of hearths, and indeed, to try and set all these hearth numbers into the appropriate vernacular houses. So far, we have worked down from Northumberland through Durham, from Westmorland through part of Lancashire, the three Yorkshire Ridings and parts of the West Midland counties, as well as Northamptonshire, Huntingdonshire and Cambridgeshire. We have also begun a ring of counties round London, which gives us Kent, approximations for Surrey and large parts of Essex,[3] as well as London and Middlesex themselves. The Project has therefore made considerable progress in the task we have undertaken, and all this, though still very incomplete, is enough to give us strong hints of the ultimate pattern. The histograms below which we have constructed

[1] D. B. Glass and D. E. C. Eversley, eds, *Population in History: essays in historical demography* (1965, London), table 12, 218.

[2] *Ibid.*, 219

[3] These two counties are not yet covered in full, and therefore there are no histograms for them yet.

from the counties we have worked on in full show clearly the extreme poverty measured in numbers of hearths of the north-west and its gradual diminution and the growth of prosperity as we approach the south-east.

In 2005 Leigh Shaw-Taylor published an article on 'Family farms and capitalist farms in mid nineteenth century England'[4] which, very improbably has some bearing on our work. He ends it by a reworked version of maps derived from 1086, 1334 and 1524–5 compared together and showing 'above average wealth per mile' and 'low wealth per mile' and so on, distributed and compared through the counties of England. It seemed extraordinary, and very welcome to me, that I have not yet been able to identify any area in which the pattern of wealth was radically different from the pattern of the distribution of hearths in the hearth tax. It is true that there were fluctuations over time from county to county. One of them, the increasing prosperity of parts of the West Riding, is demonstrated in this volume. Dr Shaw-Taylor puzzles over the picture he reveals, which pays little or no attention to what one would suppose were obviously relevant in dictating this pattern, agricultural regions, early or late enclosure, or arable or pasture farming. He concludes 'When the maps produced here [ie within his paper] are compared with the relative distribution of wealth and poverty across the medieval and early modern periods … rather more straightforward similarities are apparent. Those areas where family farming thrived in the mid-nineteenth century correspond closely to those which were poor between the eleventh and the sixteenth centuries. Those areas where large-scale capitalist farming predominated in the nineteenth century were the areas which were consistently the most prosperous between the eleventh and sixteenth centuries. To some degree both sets of patterns reflect the quality of the agricultural land. The areas which were poor before 1600 and where family farms remained significant in the mid-nineteenth century are notable for the general absence of good soils and the general prevalence of poor and medium quality soils. The south-east, where agrarian capitalism was most intense in the mid-nineteenth century and which was consistently the most prosperous part of the country from the eleventh through to the nineteenth century, had very extensive areas of good soils but it also contained large tracts of medium quality and poor soils. Although soil quality was clearly a major determinant of regional wealth levels in the medieval and early modern periods, other factors were also important, not least the proximity to London and to European markets and the distance from border warfare.'[5]

We will have laboured for a long time, but I think we have almost enough to change his wording from 'the eleventh and sixteenth centuries' to 'the eleventh

[4] L. Shaw-Taylor, 'Family farms and capitalist farms in mid nineteenth century England' *Agricultural History Review*, 53 (2005), 158–91.

[5] Ibid., 191

to the late seventeenth centuries'. The hearth tax, like its predecessors, followed the same pattern of relative distribution of poverty and wealth within England. Our findings for Northumberland add something to his picture of the importance of border warfare. Soil was a major determinant, but Dr Shaw-Taylor correctly identifies other determinants like home and foreign markets. The pulling power of the London market was enormous. The late seventeenth century, despite the disruptions of that century, did not break a pattern of prosperity which had been established by Domesday.

Wealth and Poverty in Six Counties

Histograms by John Price

In her Preface Margaret Spufford emphasised the regional patterns of wealth that can be seen from the distribution of hearths in the hearth tax. These histograms demonstrate very clearly the differing proportions of people living in one hearth houses in different parts of the country. The graphs have been arranged in order of this – starting with Westmorland where four fifths of householders lived in one hearth houses and ending with Kent where only a third of householders did so. Two hearth houses multiplied as the proportion of one hearth houses shrank. In the West Riding they had already reached 22% of households and in the relative comfort of the Isle of Ely as many as 30% of those taxed. In two hearth houses in the West Riding the hall or 'housebody' always had one of them and the cooking was done there. The second hearth in such West Riding houses was most commonly in the parlour. At the other end of the scale it will be seen how high a proportion of the householders of Kent lived in larger houses, and how small a proportion did so in Westmorland.

It must of course always be borne in mind that as well as those who appear in the Hearth Tax, whether as payers, exempted non-payers, or the poor, who are fortunately so often listed in the West Riding, (we have assumed that the poor householders listed were in one hearth houses), there is an invisible underclass who were poorer than poor. They were to be found everywhere, but many of those on poor relief at the bottom of society had no hearths of their own, since they were not householders, but lodgers (see pp. 15, 592–3, 596), often with their rent paid by the overseers. The proportion of such people cannot be known, but does not influence these graphs of householders. What does alter the graphs is that whilst in the West Riding the numbers of poor householders are often given, in other counties they are much less commonly given. This means that the proportion of one hearth householders in the West Riding is therefore inflated in comparison with the other counties, and the proportion of those in larger houses consequently diminished, so that the West Riding was in reality proportionately richer than it appears at first sight.

We have deliberately chosen not to amalgamate the figures of those exempt from the tax in certificates for places where data is lacking in the assessments we have printed, with those in the rolls themselves. We chose not to do this because the exemption certificates were not dated necessarily to exactly the same collection as the main assessments we have analysed, and radical changes could take place in very short periods of time, as Keith Wrightson has shown for the Durham coalfield. For particular places exemption certificates can enormously

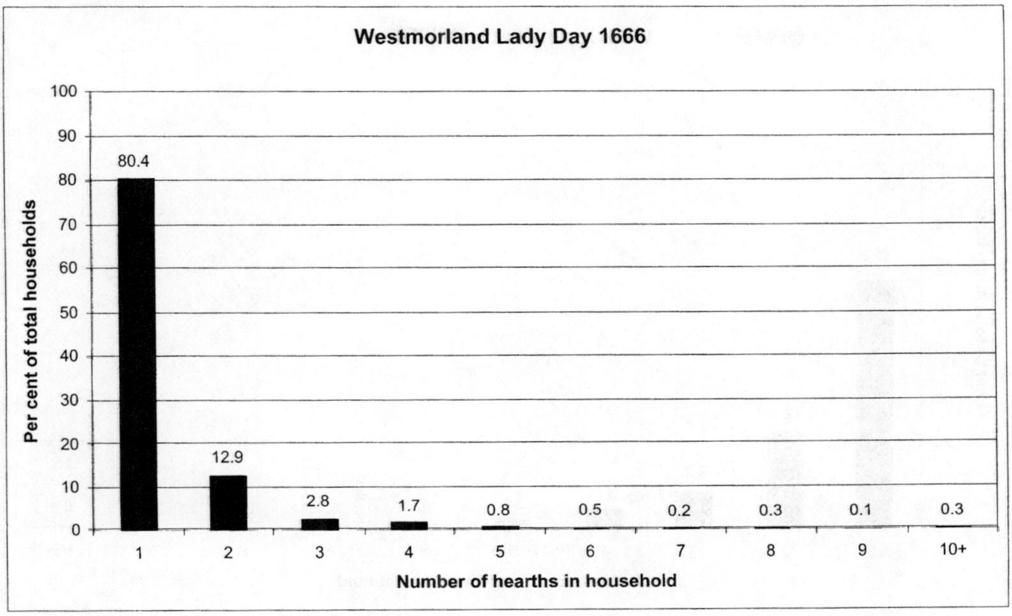

Figure 1 Distribution of households assessed on differing numbers of hearths in Westmorland

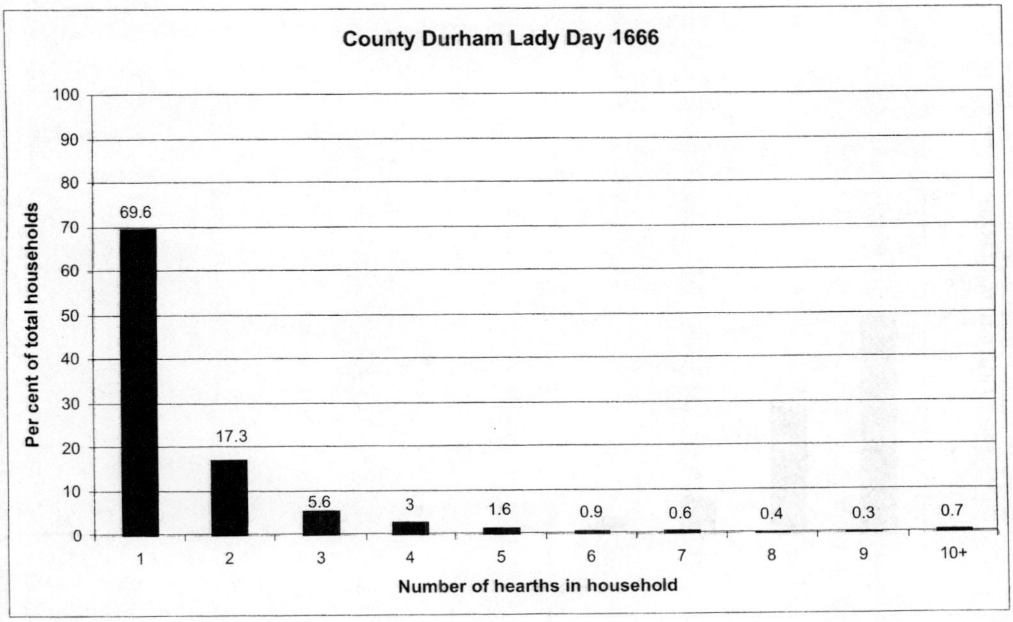

Figure 2 Distribution of households assessed on differing numbers of hearths in County Durham

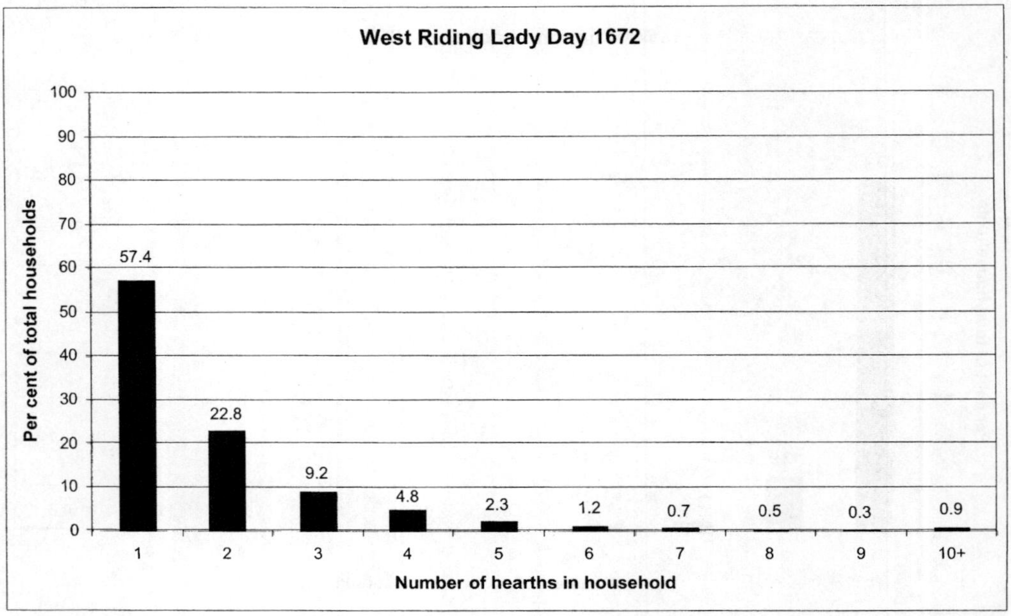

Figure 3 Distribution of households assessed on differing numbers of hearths in Yorkshire, West Riding

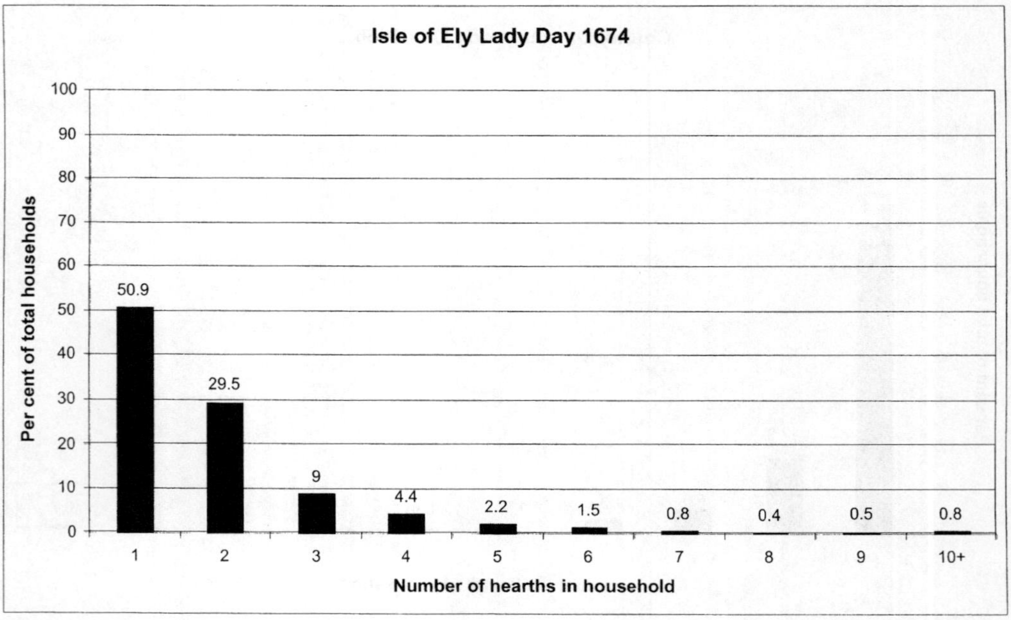

Figure 4 Distribution of households assessed on differing numbers of hearths in Isle of Ely

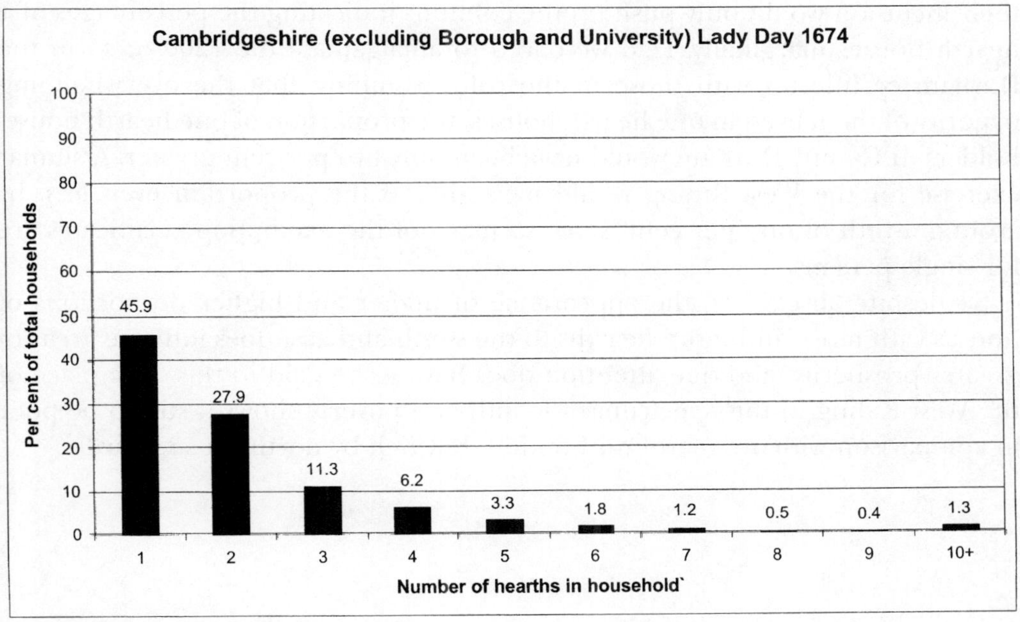

Figure 5 Distribution of households assessed on differing numbers of hearths in Cambridgeshire

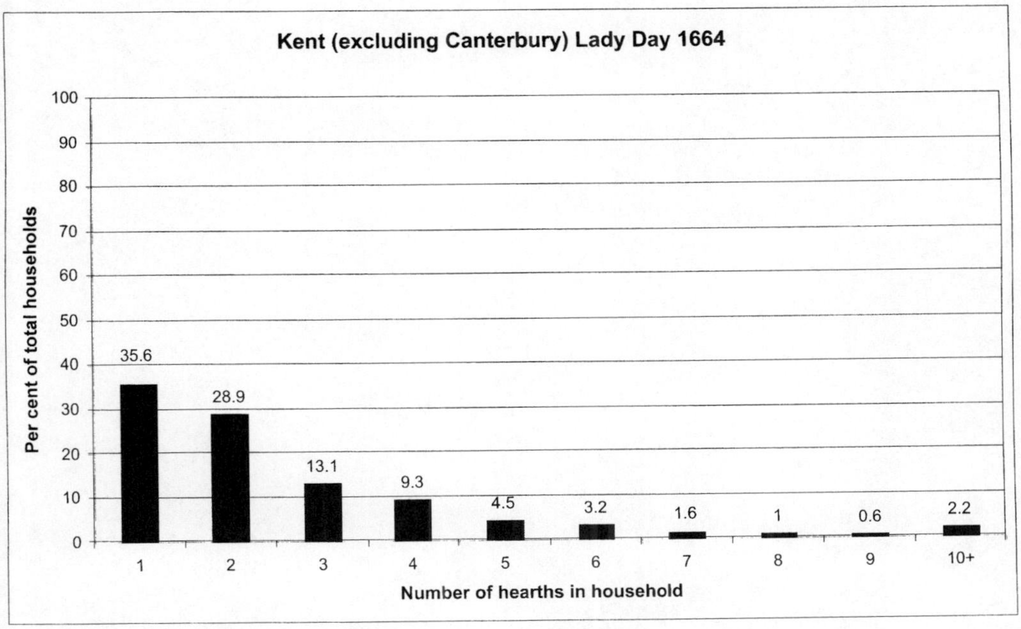

Figure 6 Distribution of households assessed on differing numbers of hearths in Kent

change our perceptions as at Barnard Castle or Halifax, but at a county level their inclusion would only push up the columns indicating the percentages of 1 hearth houses marginally. Had we dared to amalgamate the 1200 or so in the Durham certificates with those in the rolls, assuming that the overwhelming majority of them lived in one hearth houses, the proportion of one hearth householders in County Durham would have been only two per cent greater. A similar exercise for the West Riding would have altered the proportion even less, by around a fifth of one per cent, since so many of the exemption certificates are for single persons.

So despite all caveats, the appearance of higher and higher proportions of houses with more and more hearths to the south and east does indicate areas of greater prosperity, and due attention does have to be paid to this. The place of the West Riding in this spectrum of wealth and poverty shows it still to be poor in comparison with areas around London, but rich by northern standards.

THE WEST RIDING IN THE LATE SEVENTEENTH CENTURY

by David Hey

Not only was Yorkshire by far the largest of the ancient counties of England, at 1,709,307 acres, but the West Riding alone exceeded in size every other county except Lincolnshire. The word riding is derived from the late Old English 'thrithing' or 'thriding', itself adapted from an Old Norse loan word, meaning a third part. Wapentake, similarly derived, was the equivalent of the Anglo-Saxon hundred, and came from the symbolic flourishing of weapons to signify agreement when decisions were made in open-air assemblies at convenient sites, such as a river crossing or by a stone cross.[1] The wapentakes continued to see to the levying of taxes, the raising of the militia and the maintenance of law and order and did not finally disappear until the reorganisation of local government in 1974. The West Riding was divided into eleven wapentakes: Ainsty, Agbrigg, Barkston Ash, Claro, Ewcross, Morley, Osgoldcross, Skyrack, Staincliffe, Staincross and Strafforth. The Ainsty, bounded by the rivers Ure, Ouse and Wharfe, had been annexed by Henry VI (d. 1471), king of England, to the city of York, as the county of the city, which was independent of all three ridings, but it was still considered to be a West Riding wapentake.

The wapentakes were divided into townships, the vills of medieval documents. In the eastern parts of the West Riding many townships were coterminous with the ecclesiastical parishes and were referred to as parishes in the hearth tax returns, but the large moorland parishes in the west contained numerous townships. Penistone parish had eight townships, Bradford parish had thirteen, and the huge parish of Halifax was divided into twenty-three. At the local level, the township, or 'constablery', was the unit that mattered until urban and rural district councils were created in 1894.

It is a difficult task to define the precise boundaries of all the townships at the time of the hearth tax returns. Those that followed watercourses as far as possible are the easiest to perambulate, but in most cases we have no maps on a sufficiently large scale to plot boundaries accurately before the nineteenth century, by which time some new townships had been formed and some names had changed. Fortunately, for present purposes, small-scale maps with approximate boundaries suffice, but defining township boundaries is an important task for local historians. Farming systems were organised at township level and it was not unusual to find that one township had a different character from that of its neighbours. In the parish of Sheffield, for example, Attercliffe township was

[1] K. Cameron, *English Place-Names* (London, 1996), 61.

farmed on a three-field system, with a common, around a planned village, with hardly a tree in sight, yet immediately across the river Don the township of Brightside Bierlow consisted of scattered farmsteads and hamlets with irregular-shaped closes, no open fields, and several, well-defined coppice woods.

The divisions of the large moorland parishes are sometimes recorded in the hearth tax returns as 'quarters' rather than townships. Haworth had two 'quarters', Ecclesfield had four, and to the west of the urban township of Huddersfield stretched the five 'quarters' of Quarmby – Lindley, Longwood, Golcar, North Crosland and Scammonden – each of which lay in the parish of Huddersfield. Further south, that part of the manor of Wakefield that was known as the Graveship of Holme lay partly within the parish of Almondbury, partly within Kirkburton. At the time of Domesday Book the graveship was already divided into units named Cartworth, Holme (two), Austonley, Thong, Wooldale, Hepworth and Fulstone, each of which was a township in the nineteenth century, but the collectors of the hearth tax placed all the inhabitants of the graveship under the heading of Holmfirth, the alternative name for the Graveship of Holme. In the far north-west of the riding the returns for the parish of Dent were gathered together under seven separate 'bills', but no district names were given.

Townships varied enormously in size. The largest were frequently sub-divided into hamlets, a term that was used not in the present sense but to mean a defined small district, often with its communal townfields, common pastures and moorland. Some units in the hearth tax returns, such as Dikesmarsh in the parish of Thorne, were probably hamlets, for they were never recorded as townships. These hamlets have left few, if any, records, yet surprisingly some of them were fixed firmly enough in local memory for their names and boundaries to be plotted on the first edition of the six-inch Ordnance Survey maps of the mid-nineteenth century.

Most of the West Riding's market towns were uncomplicated administratively. The returns for Halifax, Huddersfield and Rotherham, for example, are straightforward lists of the names of householders, like those of rural townships, and Sheffield was recorded in just two parts. Bradford was divided into Kirkgate and Westgate, and Wakefield into Kirkgate, Northgate and Westgate. All these towns had extensive parishes that included many rural townships; none was divided into numerous parishes like York. Away from the Pennines, the medieval town of Tickhill was in decline, but its former status was hinted at by its subdivisions: Westgate, Northgate and Sunderland. Its fellow Norman new town, Pontefract, continued to flourish and the tax collectors distinguished between Micklegate, Neat Market, New Market, Ropergate, Castle & Park and Baileygate. Two other important medieval towns still dominated their surrounding districts. In the north of the riding, Ripon's four divisions consisted of All Hallow Gate, Crossgate, Westgate and Skelgate (though exemption certificates also mention Horse Fair and Stammergate), and in the south Doncaster's tax payers were placed in Market Place (twice), French Gate (twice), St George's Gate, Marsh Gate, Fisher Gate, Baxter Gate, Hall Gate, High Street & Scot Lane, St Sepulchre, and St Sepulchre without the Bar, names that are redolent of the Middle Ages. By 1672, however, the riding's leading town was Leeds, which was divided into North, East and South Parts, and into Kirkgate, Briggate, Headrow and Mill Hill or Boars Lane.

Collecting the tax

The hearth tax return used in this volume is mostly the exchequer duplicate for Lady Day 1672, which appears to be the most comprehensive return to survive amongst those for the West Riding in the National Archives.[2] There are, however, two exceptions to this; namely for Ainsty and Osgoldcross wapentakes.

By good fortune, the sheriff's copy of the same return also survives at Wakefield Metropolitan District Council Library, as the *Nomina Villarum*.[3] As the exchequer copy of the return for Ainsty wapentake is in poor condition, the sheriff's copy has been preferred for transcription. The whole of the sheriff's copy has been published elsewhere in a series of booklets covering each wapentake.[4] A comparison of the two copies reveals numerous minor discrepancies, with the omission of some details in the exchequer copy, but no major changes. The sheriff's copy is likely to be the most reliable as far as the spellings of surnames is concerned, because of local knowledge. Variations in the spellings of the same name in the two copies suggest that exchequer clerks called out the names to the transcriber. It is clear that many errors were made, but normal transcription practice has been followed in leaving the names as they were written even when it is clear that the clerk had misheard a name or had made a careless error. Family historians need to be aware that an ancestor might be there in the return under an unfamiliar phonetic form of the name or under a clerk's misspelling.

In relation to Osgoldcross neither the *Nomina Villarum* return nor the 1672 Lady Day return are adequate.[5] The *Nomina Villarum* return is incomplete and

[2] TNA, E179/210/400 (Claro), 210/410 (Staincross), 210/413 (Agbrigg & Morley), 210/415 (Osgoldcross), 210/417 (Skyrack), 210/418 (Staincliffe & Ewcross), 262/14 (Barkston Ash), and 262/15 (Strafforth). Appendix II, pp. 557–64 lists the surviving West Riding Hearth Tax Documents. J. D. Purdy, *Yorkshire Hearth Tax Returns*, Centre for Regional and Local History, University of Hull, Studies in Regional and Local History 7 (Hull, 1991) also includes a descriptive list. These returns are plentiful and in most part are in good condition.

[3] Wakefield Metropolitan District Library (WMDL), Wakefield Hearth Tax Return for 1672.

[4] The returns for Skyrack wapentake are published by in *Miscellanea*, ed. J. Stansfield (Thoresby Society Publications, II, 180–204, Leeds, 1891) and ibid., (IV, 17–36, 1895). The Ripon Historical Society and the Ripon, Harrogate & District Family History Society have published booklets covering Claro (1992), York City & Ainsty (1992), Agbrigg & Morley (1992), Staincliffe & Ewcross (1992) and Barkston Ash & Osgoldcross (1994). Strafforth & Staincross wapentakes are covered in *The Hearth Tax Returns for South Yorkshire, Lady Day 1672*, ed. D. Hey (Division of Continuing Education, University of Sheffield, 1991).

[5] TNA, E179/210/415; WMDL, Wakefield Hearth Tax Return for 1672.

the National Archives return for Lady Day 1672 is in a poor condition.[6] In order to provide comprehensive coverage in relation to names of people and data on hearth tax obligations, the return from Lady Day 1674 has been used.[7]

As with all taxation documents, we need to consider whether some people managed to avoid payment of the tax. Local studies suggest that the returns are reasonably comprehensive. Dr Denis Ashurst found that four long-established Worsbrough families that were recorded in the baptism register at the time do not appear in the list of taxpayers or in the exemption certificates, but these formed a small minority amongst 100 householders.[8] The tax collectors and constables were authorised to enter houses in order to check the number of hearths, and it is unlikely that they missed many households. It is noticeable, however, that in some townships the constable who attested the accuracy of the return did not appear in the list of taxpayers.

In a study of the Hallamshire cutlers, Dr Joan Unwin noted the names of all the fathers in the Sheffield baptism register between January and December 1672 and compared these with the Lady Day 1672 hearth tax return.[9] She found 65 per cent of the 216 fathers. The majority of the other 35 per cent had distinctive Hallamshire surnames, so it is unlikely that they were itinerant craftsmen. Were they lodgers, or were they living with parents? Of the 71 Cutlers' Company masters who took apprentices in 1671 and 1672 only nine did not appear in the Lady Day 1672 return, where they were easy to spot because their smithies were recorded. But when Dr Unwin looked at the names of the 176 men who completed an apprenticeship in 1671 or 1672, she found that only 110 became freemen immediately and another 23 became freemen several years later. In other words, 43 never became freemen but presumably worked as journeymen or at another job. It is unlikely that many of these left Hallamshire, for there were few opportunities to practise their craft elsewhere, but only three were householders in the Lady Day 1672 return. This pattern is unlikely to have been confined to Hallamshire. It may help to explain why Sheffield had large numbers of households with more than one domestic hearth. The great majority of the metalworkers of rural Hallamshire had only one or two domestic hearths and a single industrial hearth, but in Sheffield township, where the skilled work was carried out, three-quarters of the craftsmen had more than one domestic hearth and 38 had four or more.

6 TNA, E179/262/17.

7 TNA, E179/262/13.

8 Personal communication; D. Ashurst, 'Worsbrough: Change and Continuity in the Society, Economy and Buildings of a South Yorkshire Township, 1600–1851' (unpublished PhD, University of Sheffield, 1994).

9 M. J. Unwin, 'The Hallamshire Cutlery Trades in the late seventeenth century: a study of the hearth tax returns and the records of the Cutlers' Company' (unpublished PhD, University of Sheffield, 2002).

The Exempt

The poorest section of society were exempt from payment of the hearth tax. In the sheriff's copy they are noted either as 'poor' or as 'ced', meaning that they had an exemption certificate. Large numbers of these certificates are held in the National Archives and have been transcribed for the present study. The householders who were exempt from paying tax were not just those in receipt of parish poor relief. They also included those who paid less than 20 shillings rent per annum on their properties. A clear distinction between the two groups was made in the township of Hutton Wandesley, alias Long Marston, on 7 October 1672, when five people were said to 'receive relief out of the poor mans boxe' and another five were listed as paying rents under £1 but 'do not receive relief'.[10] Likewise, at Rawcliffe in 1671 39 householders were 'discharged by certificate' and another 18 were 'omitted by reason of poverty'.[11]

Unfortunately, however, the distinction between the two groups is not usually made in the returns. Exemption certificates often state that they are for poor people, without explaining what is meant by 'poor'. At Acomb the five exempted householders were 'poore folks all',[12] at Rufforth the 'names of the poore' amounted to five,[13] and at Sykehouse 'poore persons' numbered twelve.[14] There is no way of arriving at overall figures to distinguish paupers from those who were exempt because of the low rents that they paid, but it is clear that all the exempt were considered to be poor by the standards of the time, even if they were not paupers in receipt of parish relief. In some places, such as Attercliffe with Darnall, marginal comments show that care was taken to decide whether or not a person claiming exemption was legally entitled to do so.

A petition from the churchwardens and other leading figures in Tadcaster to the Lord Mayor of York supported the case of 'a poore man' who should not have been taxed because of the low rent that he paid. It reads:

> 'Att the request of the bearrer hearof Anthony Wisse of the East Part of Tadcaster for certefying the true vallue of what he farmeth: we do humbly certefy that he is a poore man and that the poore cottadge he lives in which is all that ever he farmes in all the world is but six shillings eight pence per annum; and being of lait charged with the duty of Harth mony: contrary to the Actt in that behalph he humbly beggs your lordships best help and assistance for acquitinge him heareof and he will as in duty bound ever to pray for you: to the truth hearof we set to our hands this sixth of Decemr 71'.[15]

[10] TNA, E179/350/327.
[11] Ibid., E179/350/3/344.
[12] Ibid., E179/349/322.
[13] Ibid., E179/350/325.
[14] Ibid., E179/350/264.
[15] Ibid., E179/350/336.

It seems reasonable to conclude from cases such as this that we may speak of 'the exempted poor in the hearth tax returns' as long as we do not equate them with parish paupers. Even so, the figures are difficult to interpret. In the first place, the surviving lists do not coincide neatly with the returns for Lady Day 1672, but are often a year or two out. Secondly, lots of townships have no surviving certificates, so we are left with the problem of whether there truly were few or no exempted poor in these places or whether large numbers are missing. Thirdly, the sheriff's copy, which has marginal annotations that identify the exempt, in some cases matches exactly the number of exemption certificates in TNA, but in other cases has discrepancies, some of them huge.

The township of Worsbrough (Staincross wapentake) illustrates the difficulties of interpretation. The sheriff's copy has five 'ced' but no 'poore' amongst its 100 householders. TNA exemption certificates for 2 November 1671 (which would still be in force at Lady Day 1672)[16] number 26, including the five in the sheriff's copy. Dr Ashurst found most of these 26 names in the Worsbrough chapelry register. They include many long-established families; five of them paid poll tax in 1660 and many appeared in the burial register for the late seventeenth and early eighteenth centuries. They were decidedly not transient poor.

The neighbouring township of Barnsley had only one 'ced' and two 'poor' householders listed among the 132 householders in the sheriff's copy of the return. The exemption certificates for 7 December 1672[17] name just six 'inhabitants of the cottages'. Yet in 1670 the West Riding justices of the peace heard that Barnsley people had wandered into neighbouring parishes to beg, for 531 inhabitants needed relief and only 'a few able persons' in Barnsley were able to support them.[18] Of course, petitions often exaggerated their case and this desperate situation might have improved by Lady Day 1672, but our suspicions are that the hearth tax returns did not list all the exempt. These suspicions increase when we find that in the whole of Staincross wapentake only 56 householders were listed as 'poor' or 'ced', that is only 3.46 per cent, a much lower figure than in other wapentakes.

In the case of Halifax, the discrepancies between the number of exempt in the final return and those listed by name in the bundles of exemption certificates are glaring. In the return which we print, Halifax has 313 payers and 39 exempt, plus 17 empty houses and 111 poor.[19] This gives the impression of a town of around 370 households including houses temporarily empty. However, the Halifax exemption certificates dated 10–13 October 1670, also printed here, name 179 people, suggesting a huge number of extra households. A later bundle of exemption certificates, dated 3 March 1672/3, records 143 individuals, of whom only 49

16 Ibid., E179/350/372.
17 Ibid., E179/350/78.
18 West Yorkshire Archives, Wakefield, quarter sessions records.
19 'Omitted by reason of poverty iii' to be read as 111; see below, 81.

were listed as exempt in 1670. Even if we add a few others who may have been members of the same family, the high turnover of names amongst those who were exempt from payment is striking. The sheriff's copy of the return for Ladyday 1672 confirms a high number of exempt, with 71 names recorded as 'poor' and a further 37 with a certificate.

Exemption certificates were usually signed by the minister, churchwardens, or overseers of the poor and ratified by Justices of the Peace (JPs), or in the case of the Ainsty by the Lord Mayor of York. Sometimes, it was necessary to petition the authorities on behalf of poor people who were being harassed by the tax collectors. A petition to the JPs on 22 November 1672 on behalf of William Machin of South Kirkby noted that he 'hath a wife and six children, being a very poore man, lives in a roome of Kirkby Hall upon the charity of Sir John Digby and others without paying any rent'.[20] A petition to the Lord Mayor of York from Tadcaster on 6 December 1671 reads:

> 'We whose names are hear subscribed out of bowell of compassion in the behalph of one widdow Langton within that part of Tadcaster within your lordships libertee being a very poore woman having eight small children: seaven whearof not caipable of releveing themselves: but laime and distempered in boddy so that we are forst to releve them by a weekly allowance out of the poore mans box: yet not with standing the Act for payment of harth mony do acquitt such from paying: yet of laitt in her husbands time the collectors forst him to pay allthough the cottadge she lives in is but eight shillings yearly rent and being all that ever she farmes in all the world: we humbly begg in her behalph: for she is not able to came her selfe …'.[21]

Surviving accounts of the parish overseers of the poor show that the old, the infirm, the sick and orphans were on the whole treated sympathetically by their neighbours, though the 1662 Act of Settlement had encouraged hard-hearted attitudes to paupers who were legally settled elsewhere. At meetings of the quarter sessions JPs found that their time was increasingly taken up with resolving settlement disputes.

Population

The number of householders in a township's hearth tax returns has often been used as a basis for estimating population levels by using a multiplier of between 4.25 and 4.75, as a notional average size for a household. The accuracy of the figures that are arrived at by this method depends on the comprehensive recording of the exempted poor. Unfortunately, the West Riding has many populous townships with no recorded poor. For example, a group of moorland townships

[20] TNA, E179/350/205.
[21] Ibid., E179/350/337.

in Agbrigg wapentake, comprising Cumberworth Half, Farnley Tyas, Shelley, Slaithwaite and Thurstonland, have no lists of the exempt, nor have Dales townships such as Barden Forest, Bentham, Cawton, Cracoe, Grassington, Hanleth, Hartlington and many others in Ewcross and Staincliffe wapentakes, while in neighbouring townships the figures are suspiciously low, often only one or two. Nowhere are the numbers of exempted poor as high as in many other parts of England. This is undoubtedly partly due to under-recording in numerous townships, yet it might also reflect the modest prosperity of ordinary families in the emerging industrial districts. The West Riding had been overshadowed by the East Riding during the Middle Ages but by the later seventeenth century it had become the most populous and enterprising part of Yorkshire, with about half the county's estimated 350,000 to 430,000 inhabitants.

The difficulties of estimating population levels are illustrated by the example of the six townships of the huge parish of Sheffield. In 1616 the population of the urban township was counted at 2,207 and in 1736 at 10,121.[22] Judging by the recorded annual numbers of baptisms and burials in the parish register, most of this marked increase occurred during the early eighteenth century. What level had been achieved by 1672? The sheriff's copy of the hearth tax returns names 27 people with certificates and 37 who were receiving poor relief, a total of 64. TNA exemption certificates include 50 that were issued for the urban township in February 1672/3 and 61 on 31 March 1674.[23] The names of 42 of the 61 can be identified in the sheriff's copy of the returns for Lady Day 1672, when 13.3 per cent of the householders of Sheffield township (and 15 per cent of the whole parish) were listed as exempt. Do we accept these figures at their face value, on the grounds that the cutlery industry was booming, or do we inflate the figures to allow for omissions, say perhaps by 30 or 40 per cent, which has been suggested as a national average? The Compton ecclesiastical census of 1676[24] gives the round figure of 3,000 people who were old enough to receive communion in the whole of the parish and an analysis of the parish register suggests that population growth, in line with national trends, was sluggish at the time. It seems likely that the whole of the parish contained some 4–5,000 people in the 1670s and that about half of these lived in the central township, but we cannot be more precise than this.

In the late seventeenth century the national population was overwhelmingly rural. Three out of four people lived in the countryside and many urban families dwelt in small market towns which were essentially rural in nature except on market day. The county town, York, had only about 12,000 inhabitants in the 1670s, but it remained by far the largest town in Yorkshire. The dramatic increase

[22] D. Hey, *The Fiery Blades of Hallamshire: Sheffield and its neighbourhood, 1660–1740* (Leicester, 1991), 62–5.
[23] TNA, E179/350/394; E179/350/2/292.
[24] *The Compton Census of 1676: A Critical Edition*, ed. A. Whiteman, British Academy: Records of Social and Economic History, N.S. 10 (London, 1986).

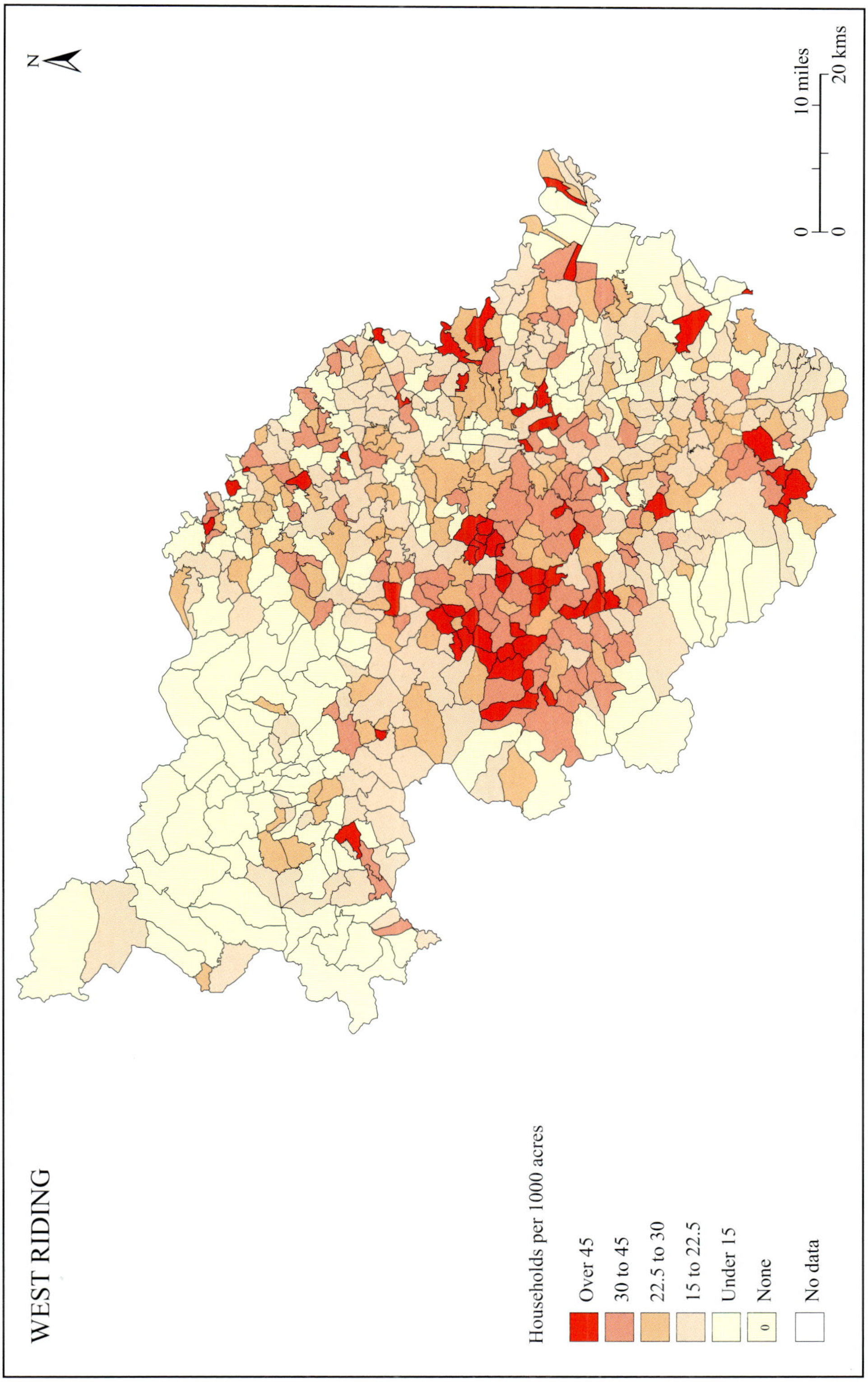

Map 1 West Riding: households per 1000 acres

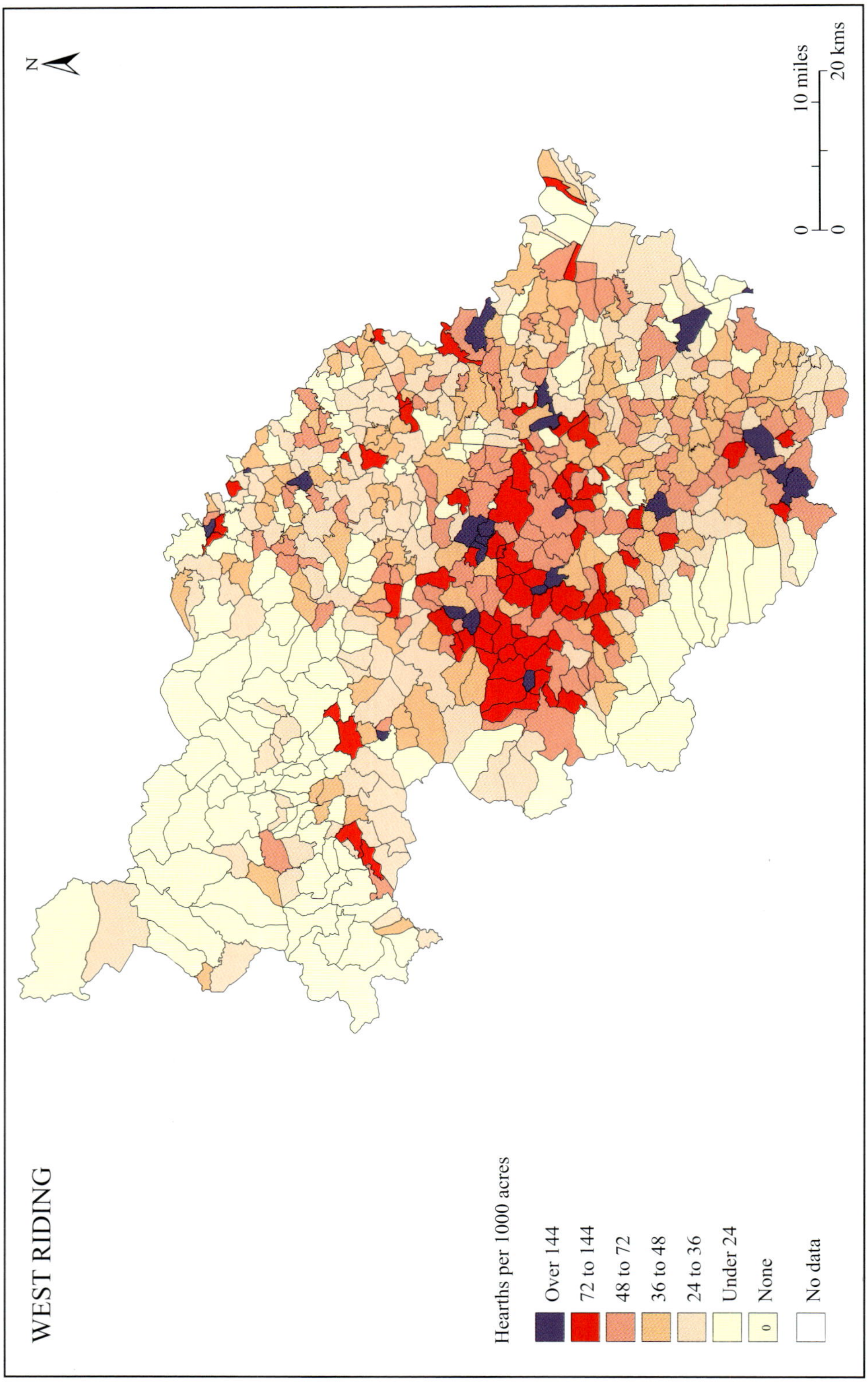

Map 2 West Riding: hearths per 1000 acres

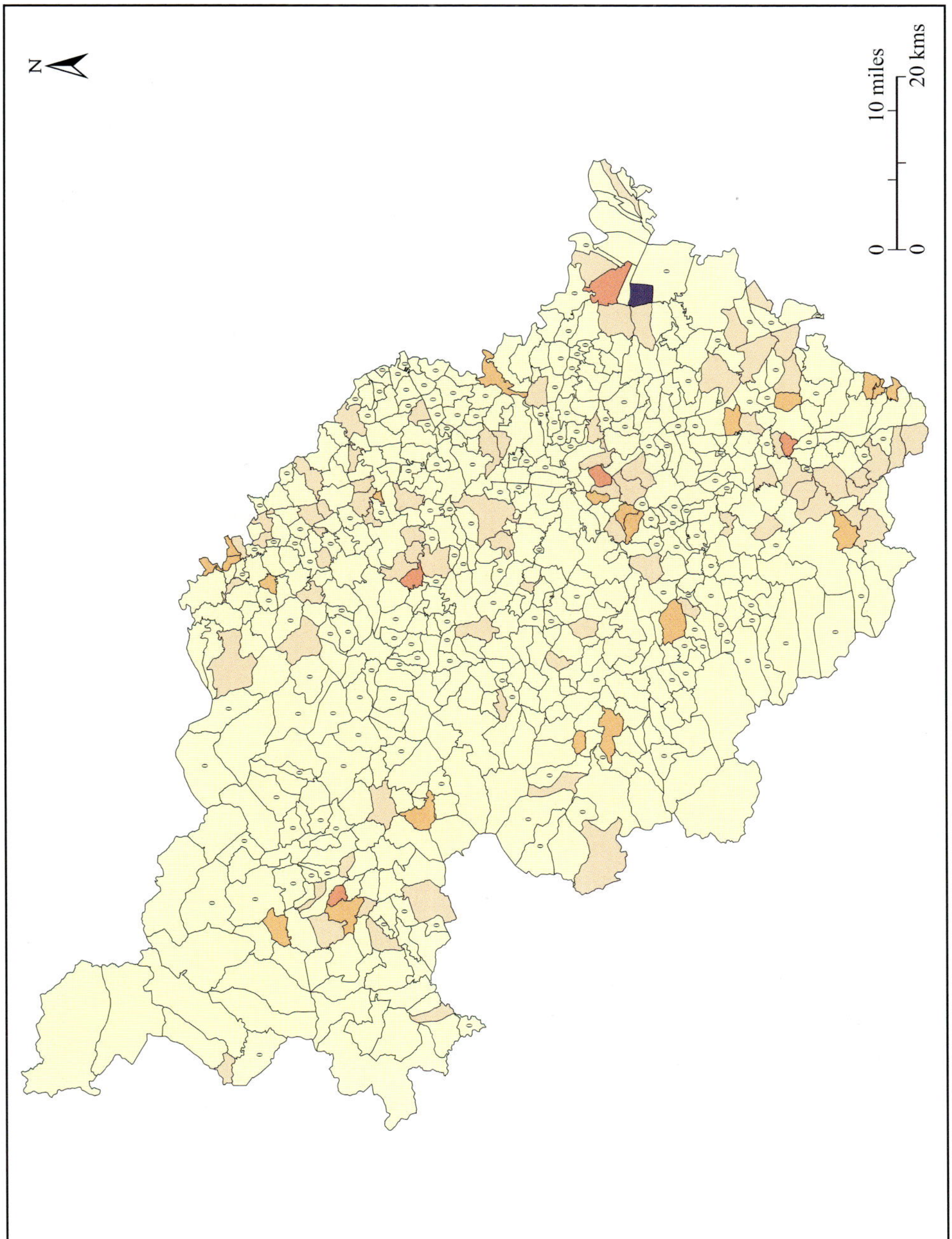

Map 3 West Riding: percentage of exempt households

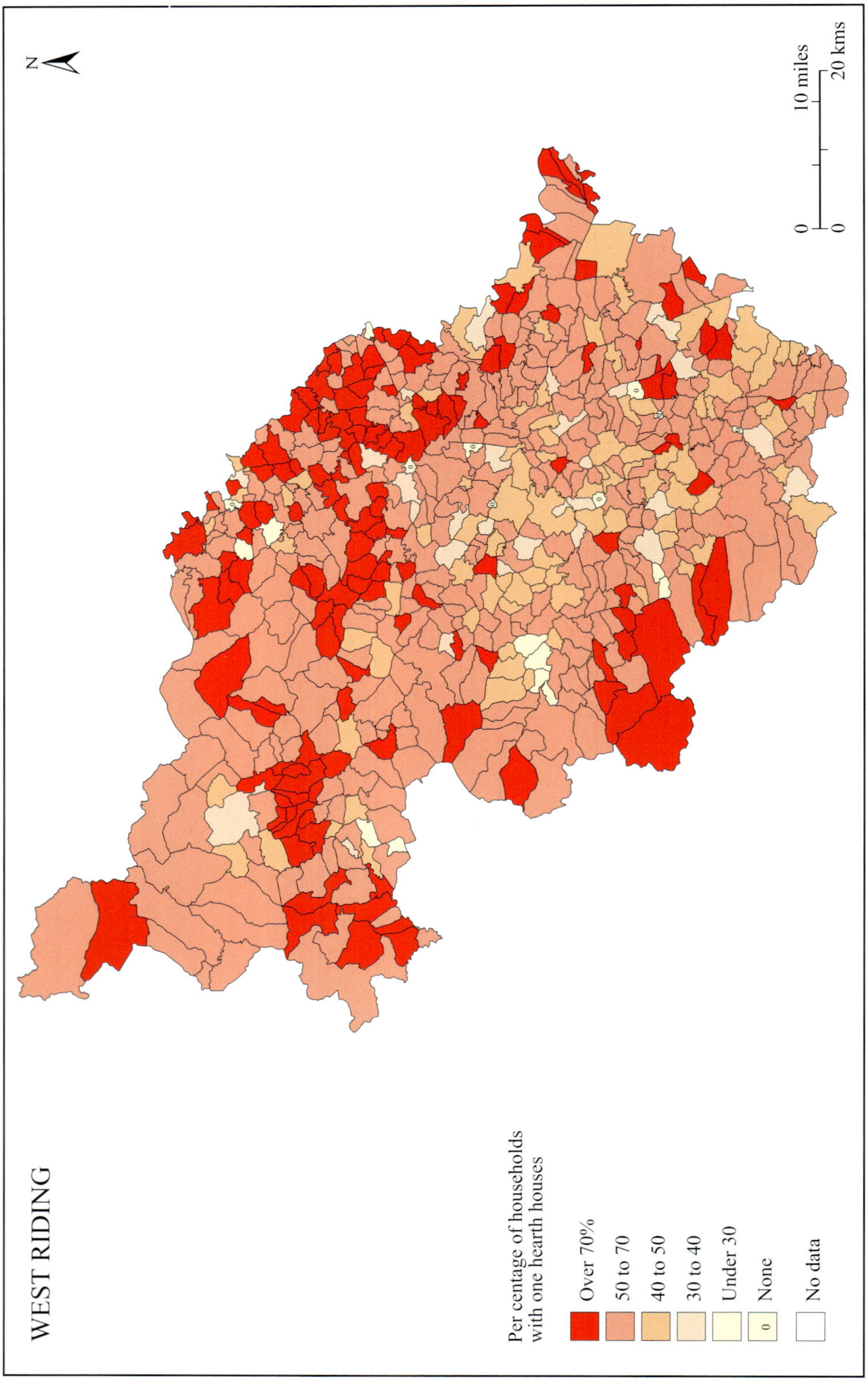

Map 4 West Riding: percentage of households with one hearth houses

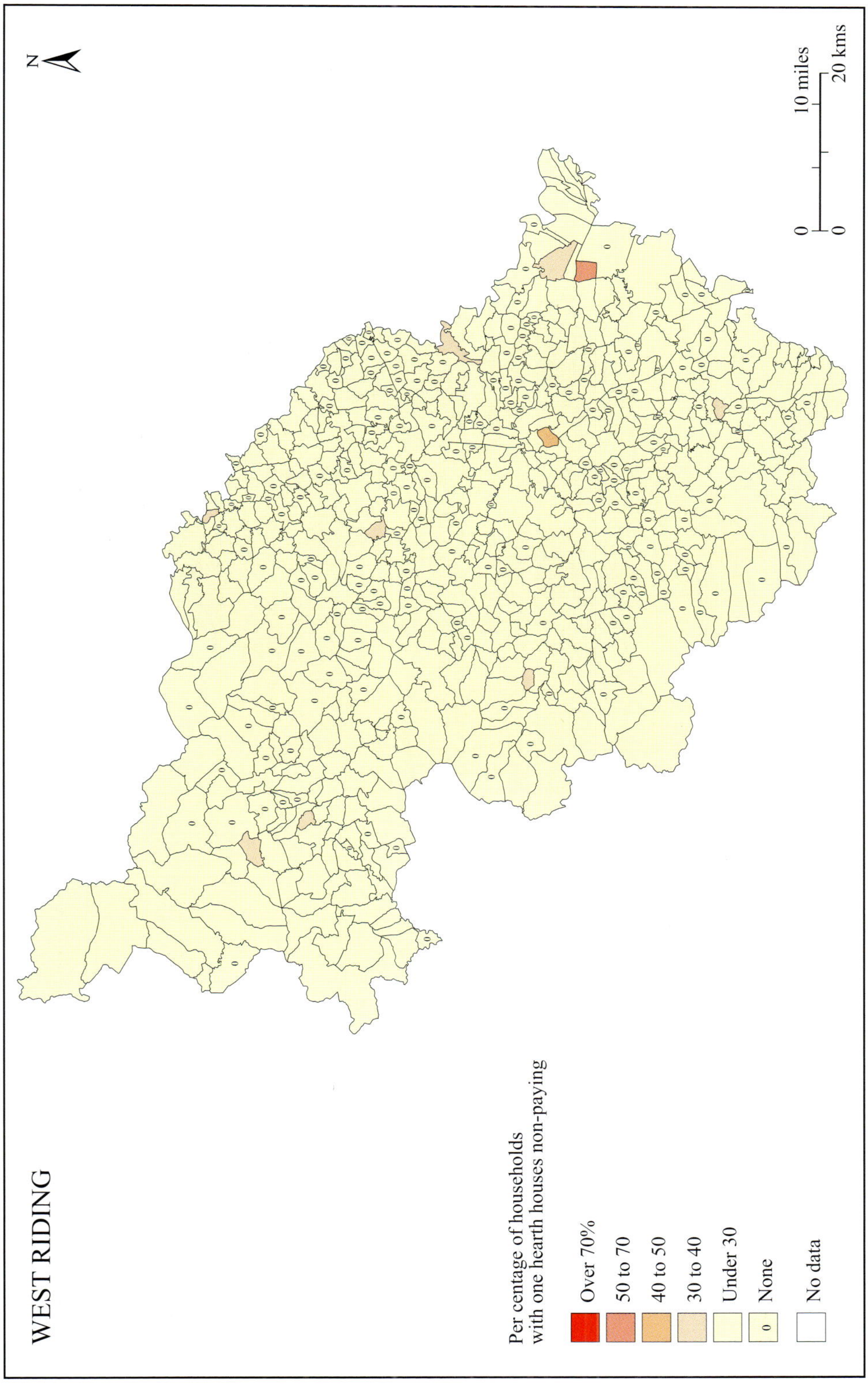

Map 5 West Riding: percentage of households with one hearth houses non-paying

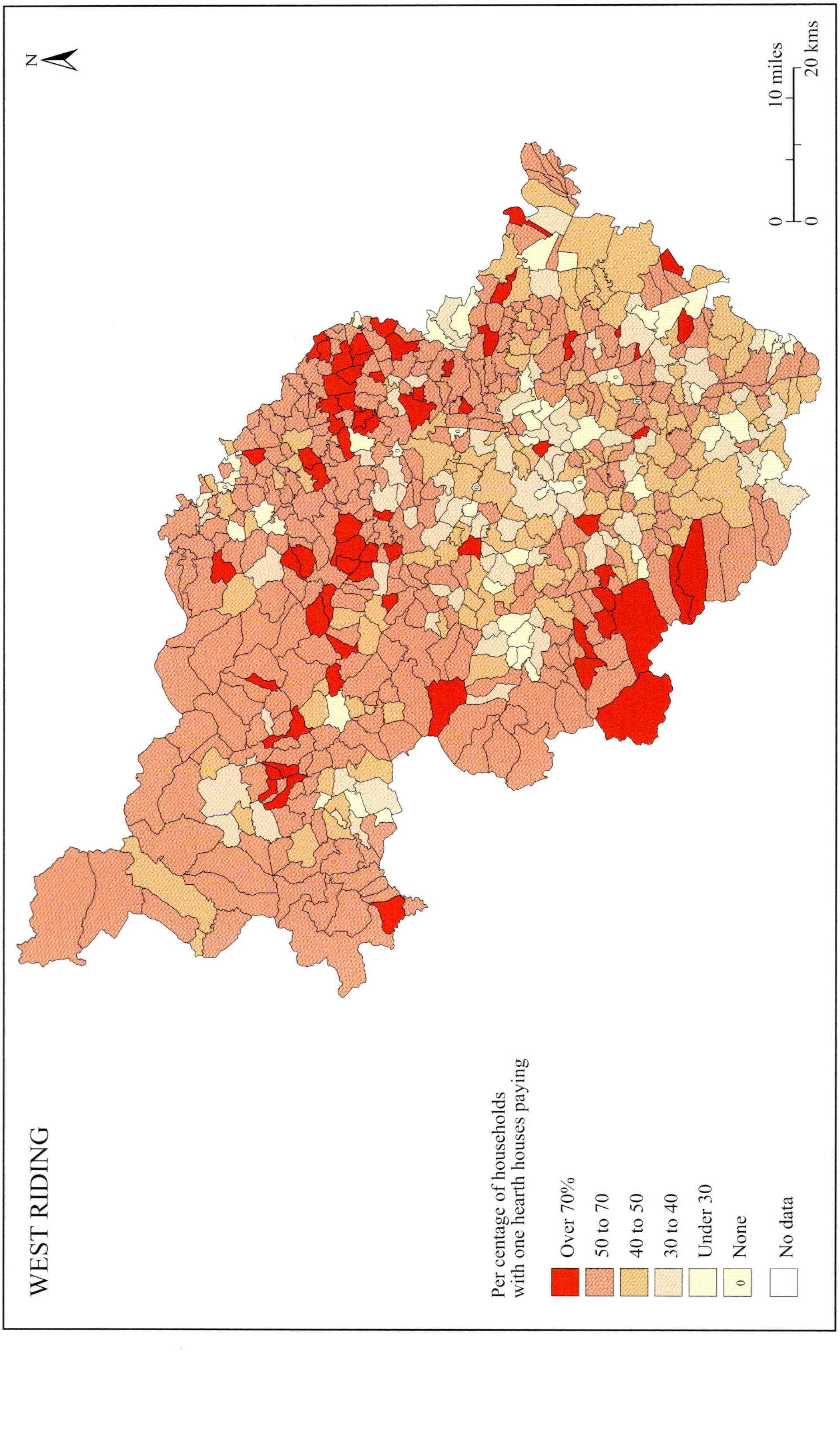

Map 6 West Riding: percentage of households with one hearth houses paying

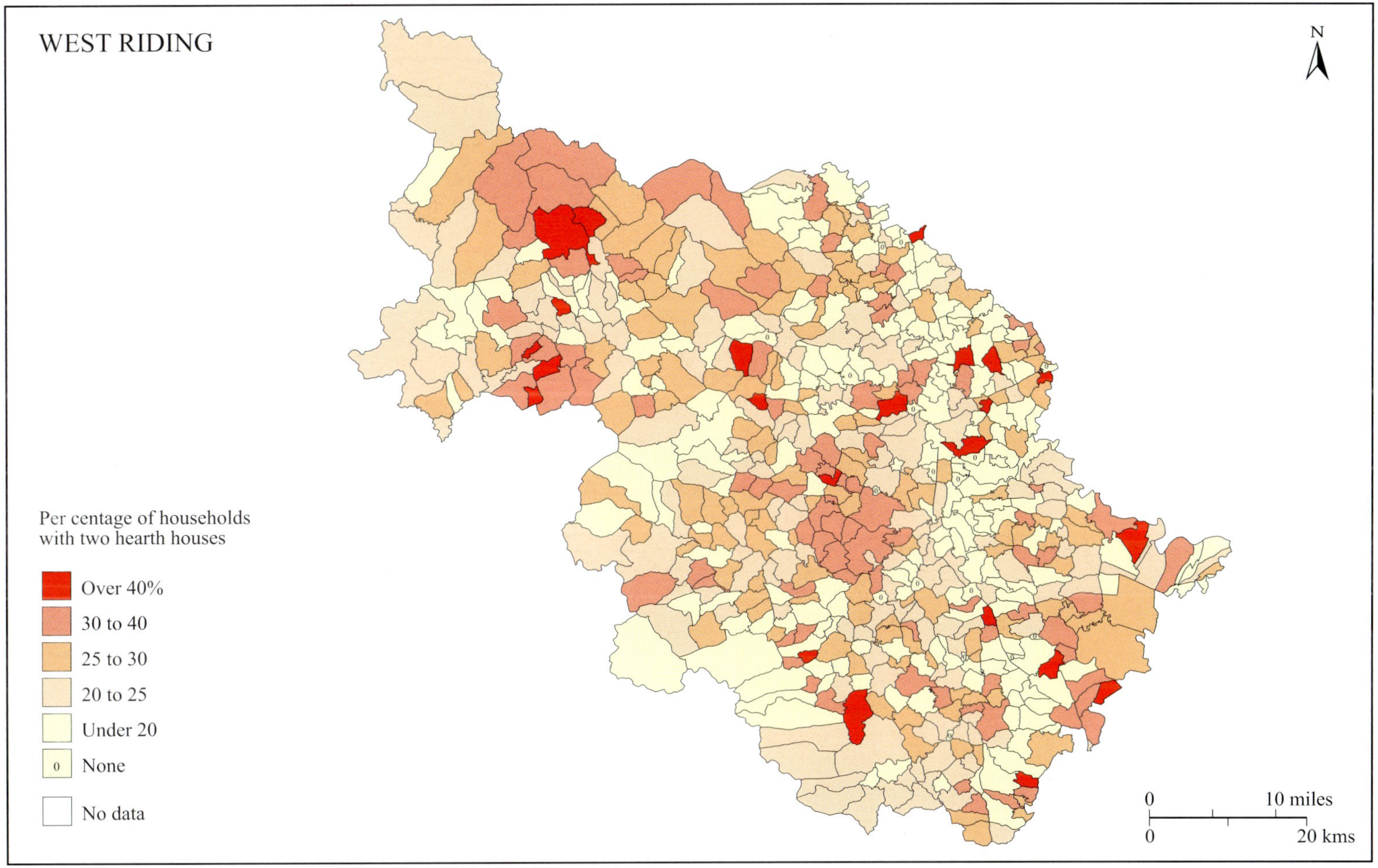

Map 7 West Riding: percentage of households with two hearth houses

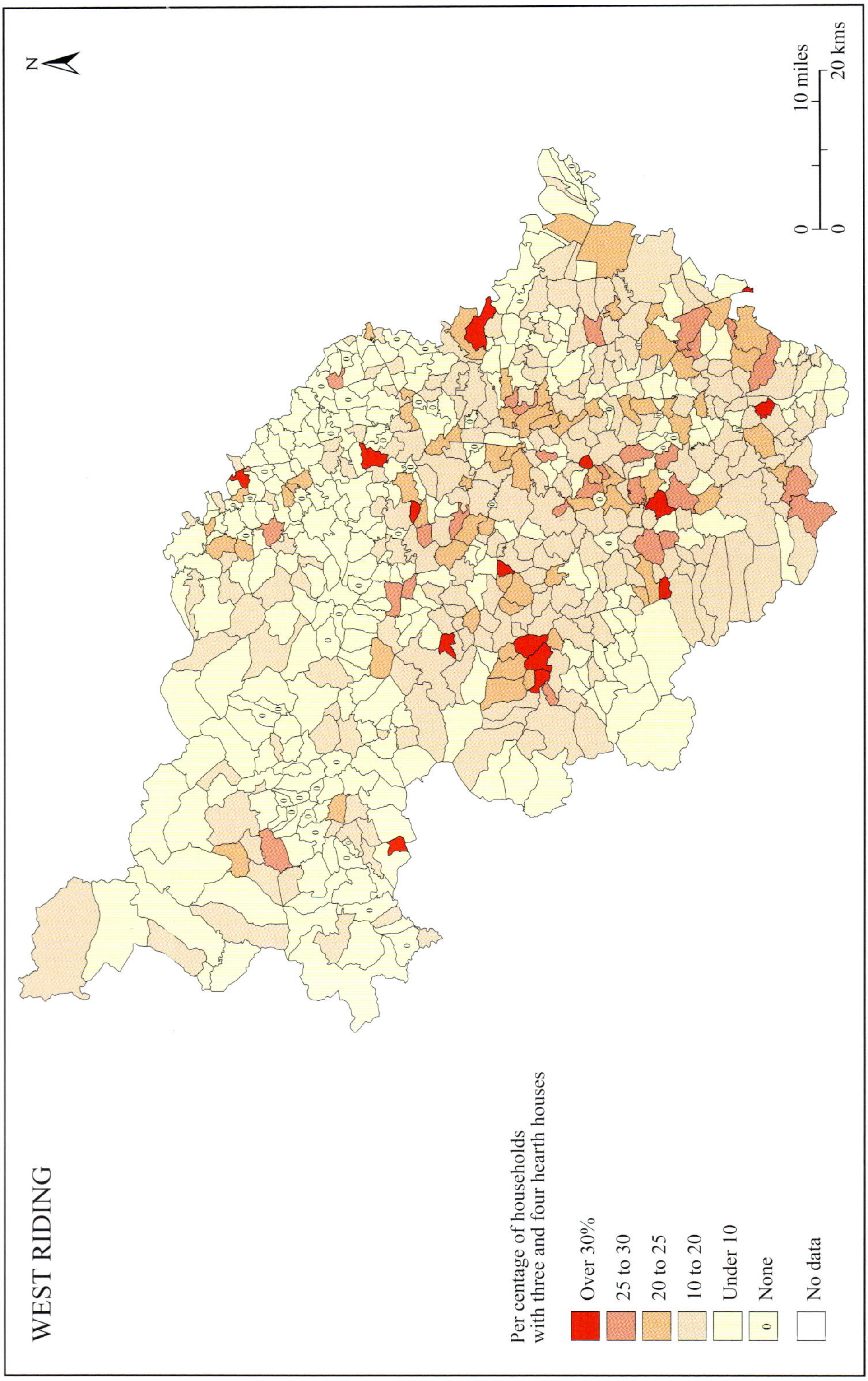

Map 8 West Riding: percentage of households with three and four hearth houses

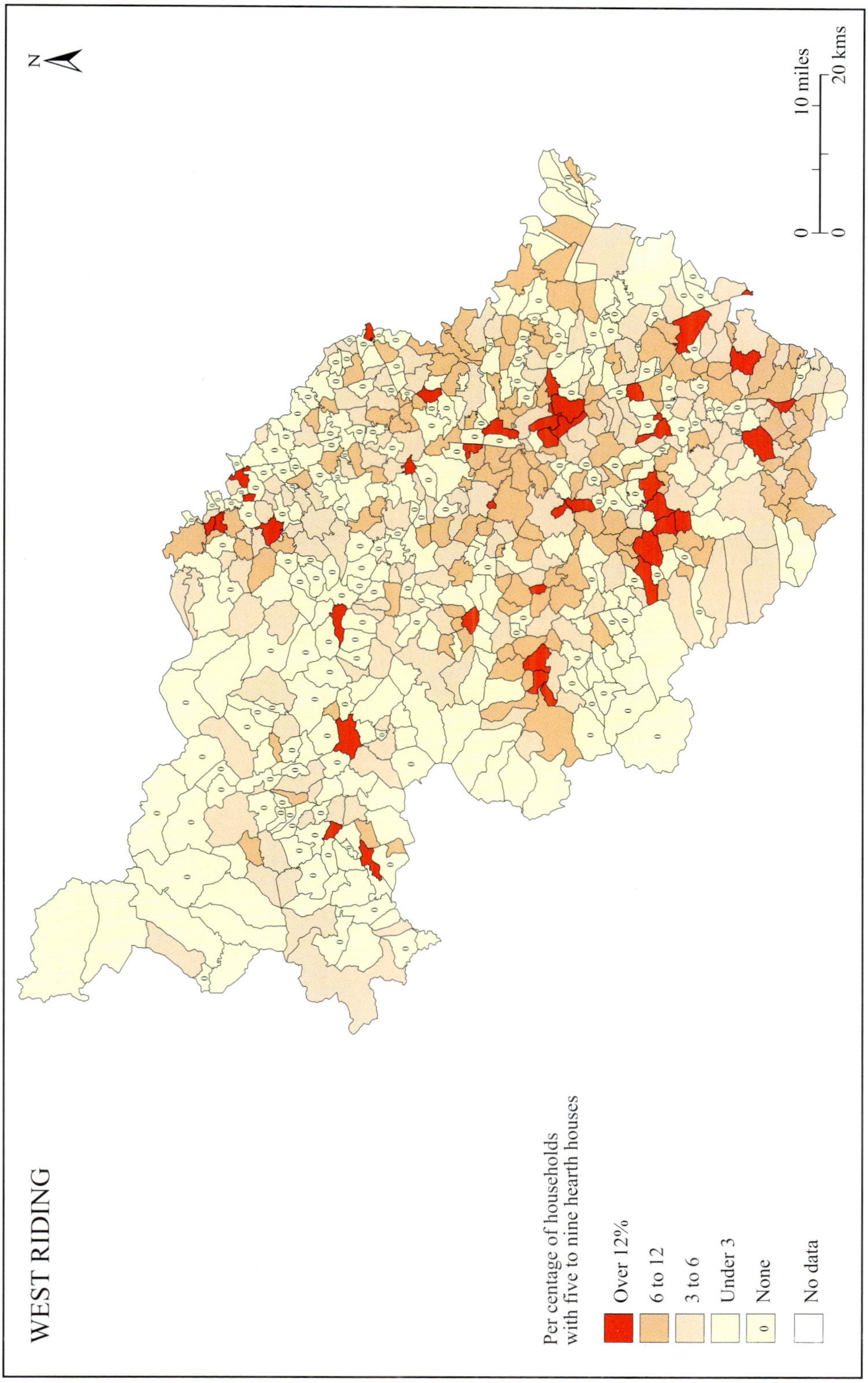

Map 9 West Riding: percentage of households with five to nine hearth houses

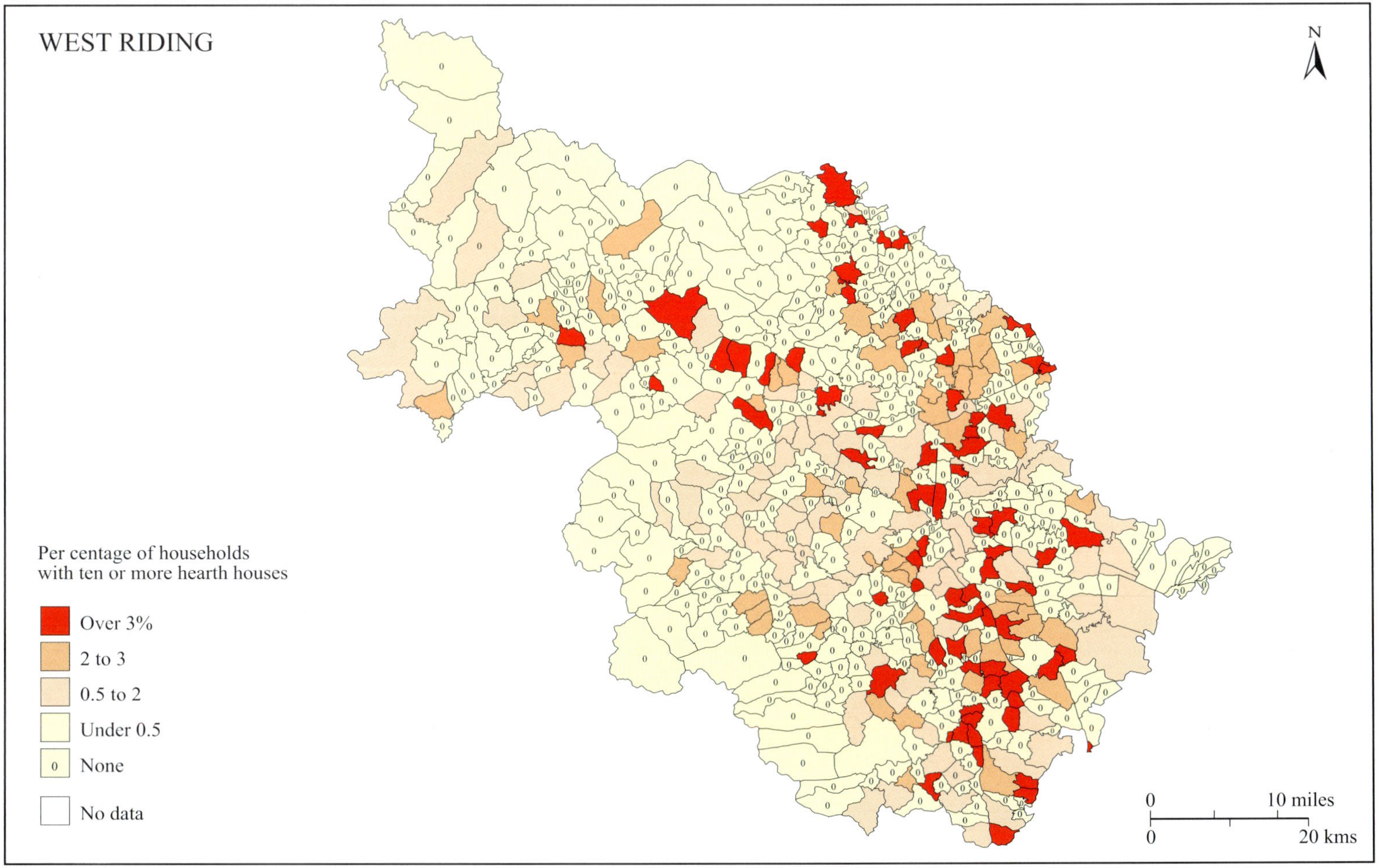

Map 10 West Riding: percentage of households with ten or more hearth houses

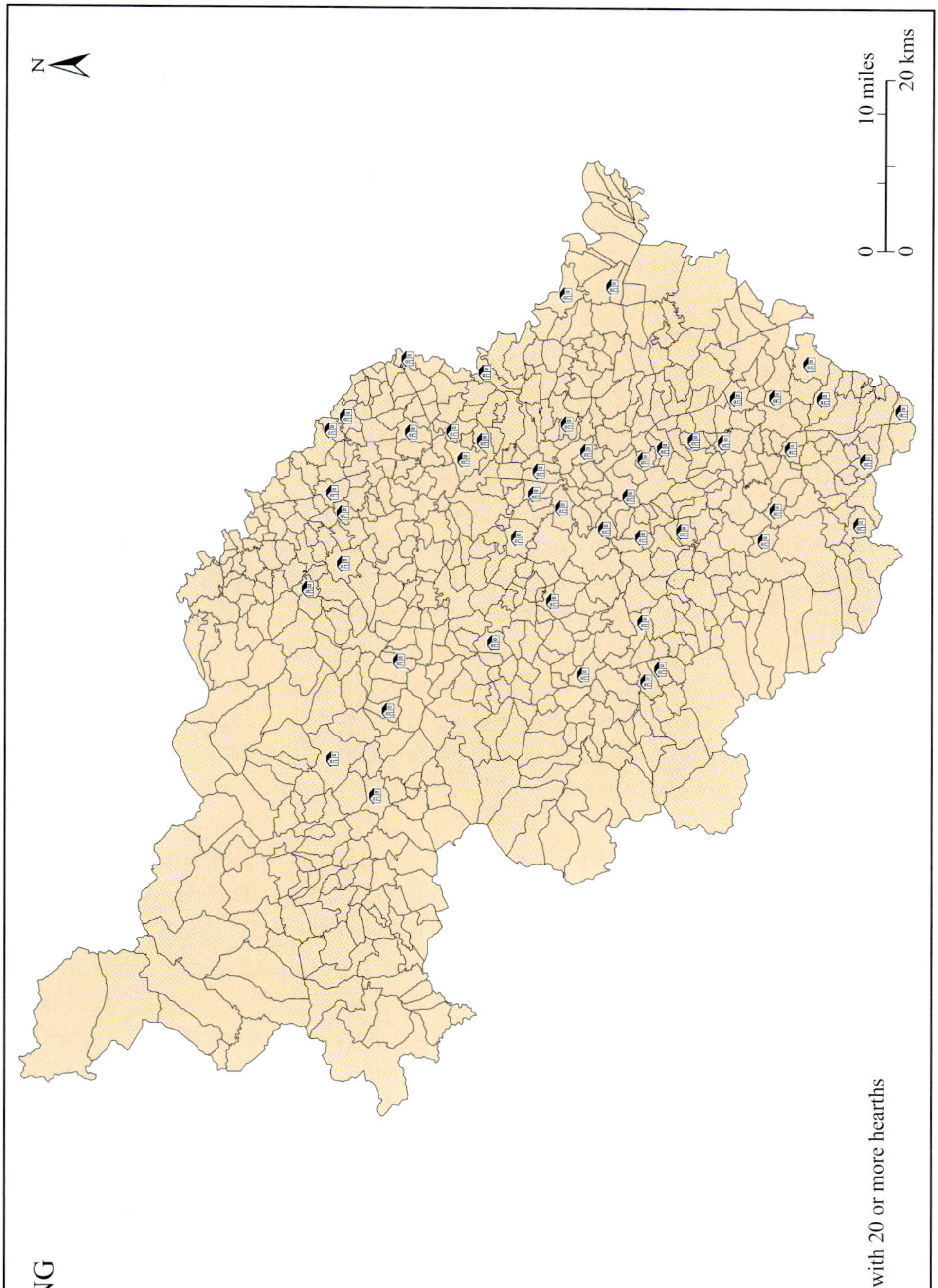

Map 11 West Riding: households with 20 or more hearths

in the West Riding's urban population lay in the future. Nevertheless, the drift from the countryside to the towns and the industrial rural parishes had already begun. By the middle of the eighteenth century those parishes that relied entirely on agriculture were in decline. It has been estimated that between 1664 and 1743 some 3,000 people moved away from the rural parishes of mid-Wharfedale.[25] Lowland farming villages further east fared no better, for this was a time when villages that had shrunk in the Middle Ages were finally deserted. Wharfedale parish registers consistently reveal a surplus of baptisms over burials, so the loss of population can be explained only by emigration. People were moving in search of better economic opportunities.

Most of the immigrants into the industrial districts travelled short distances. We have the evidence of the apprenticeship registers of the Cutlers' Company of Hallamshire from 1624 to 1799 which reveal that two out of every three boys came from within 21 miles of the centre of Sheffield and that less than one in ten came from places more than 41 miles away.[26] Here, as elsewhere, the labour force was overwhelmingly local in origin. Men and women chose their marriage partners from within the neighbourhood with which they were familiar, and poor law settlement papers show that after the Act of Settlement (1662) paupers were reluctant to move far from the place where they were legally settled and if they tried they were liable to be sent back. London was the great exception to the rule that most mobility occurred over short distances, for the capital city attracted young people from all over England. In 1680 Sir John Reresby, who was taxed at Thrybergh on 22 hearths, observed that London 'drained all England of its people'.[27]

The hearth tax returns come halfway between the period of surname formation and the present day and so are an invaluable source for the study of the distribution of names and thus of population movement. A large number of distinctive names have been analysed in David Hey and George Redmonds, *Yorkshire Surnames and the Hearth Tax Returns of 1672–73*,[28] so only a few brief comments are necessary here. The West Riding is particularly rich in the number and variety of its distinctive surnames, many of which were derived from Pennine farmsteads and hamlets, names such as Ackroyd, Barraclough, Gaukroger and Murgatroyd, which originated high in the Calder Valley, or Hallamshire names such as Broomhead, Creswick, Dungworth and Staniforth. But all classes of surnames are represented; those derived from personal names such as Oddy (which has a single-family origin in the Ribblesdale township of Rimington),

[25] M. F. Pickles, 'Labour migration: Yorkshire, c. 1670–1743', *Local Population Studies*, 57 (1996), 29–49.

[26] E. J. Buckatzsch, 'Places of Origin of a Group of Immigrants into Sheffield, 1625–1799', *Economic History Review*, 2nd ser., 2 (1950), 303–6; Hey, *Fiery Blades*, 75–9.

[27] A. Browning, ed., *The Memoirs of Sir John Reresby* (Glasgow, 1936), 376.

[28] D. Hey and G. Redmonds, *Yorkshire Surnames and the Hearth Tax Returns of 1672–73*, University of York Borthwick Paper 102 (2002).

from nicknames such as Shillitoe or Sillitoe (from Featherstone), and from occupations such as Frobisher (a polisher of armour, from Altofts). Each seem to have had a single ancestor and had remained close to their points of origin.

Many of these intensely local names had ramified during the sixteenth and seventeenth centuries and had become more characteristic of their native districts than ever before. The hearth tax returns illustrate this time and time again. Distinctive surnames were concentrated in neighbourhoods, close to their point of origin, neighbourhoods that were bounded by the nearest market towns and which local people referred to as their 'country'. The sense of belonging to both a particular place – a town or a rural parish or township – and to a wider district or 'country' was stronger in the seventeenth century than it is now and most families inhabited a world of limited horizons. The cutlers of Hallamshire had little in common with the weavers of the Calder and Colne valleys and they knew nothing about the farmers of the dales or the Vale of York. The whole way of life for ordinary Yorkshire men and women was peculiar to their particular 'countries'. The gentry families were sometimes linked by marriage at the county level, but ordinary families were not. The sense of being Yorkshire folk came much later.

Towns

Yorkshire's towns can be ranked in importance as market and communications centres in the decade after the hearth tax returns of Lady Day 1672 by returns to the War Office in 1686 which recorded the number of guest beds and stabling facilities that were available in each place throughout the land.[29] The county town was still by far the most important urban centre in Yorkshire with 483 guest beds and 800 stables; then came Leeds with 294 and 454 respectively; Wakefield with 242 and 543 respectively; and Doncaster with 206 and 453 respectively, before the leading East Riding towns of Malton, Hull and Beverley. A less important group was formed by Halifax with 130 guest beds and 306 stables; Sheffield with 119 and 270 respectively; Ripon with 118 and 422 respectively, and the North Riding towns of Thirsk and Richmond. The West Riding towns that had between 50 and 100 guest beds were Pontefract (92 guest beds and 235 stables); Barnsley (64 and 109 respectively), Rotherham (63 and 72 respectively); Selby (58 and 89 respectively); Bawtry (57 and 69 respectively) and Tadcaster (50 and 72 respectively). In each of these towns, many of the people who were taxed on a large number of hearths were inn-holders. The inns provided opportunities for social and economic advancement that were largely absent in the countryside. This difference is evident from the hearth tax returns, which reveal relatively few rural houses with numerous hearths below the level of the gentry, whereas the

[29] TNA, WO 30/48.

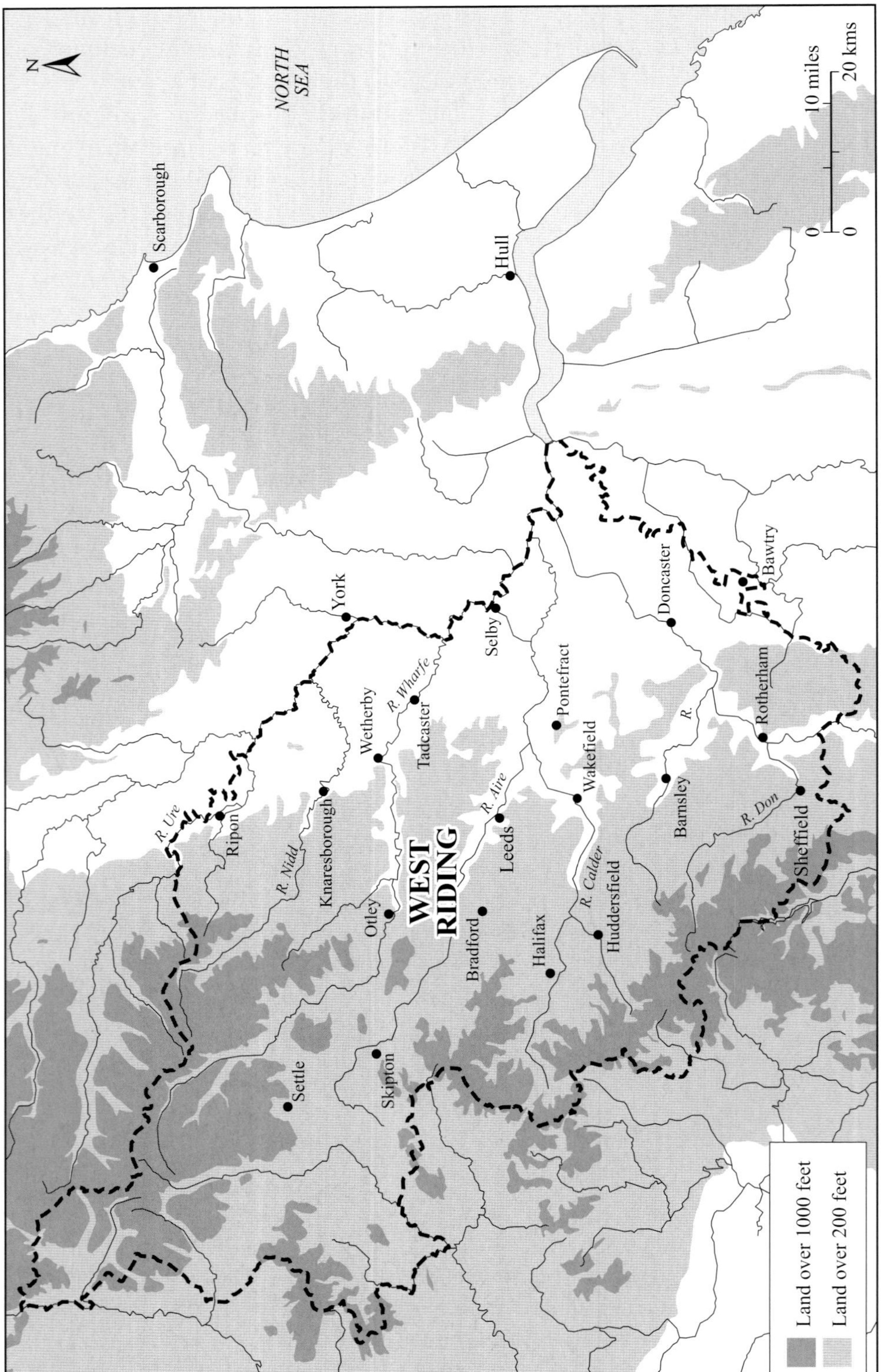

Map 12 West Riding Topography and Towns

central streets of the most prosperous towns had buildings with large numbers of hearths, many of which were inns.

In 1698 Celia Fiennes wrote, 'Leeds is a large town, severall large streets clean and well pitch'd and good houses all built of stone, some have good gardens and steps up to their houses and walls before them; this is esteemed the wealthyest town of its bigness in the Country ... they have provisions so plentifull that they may live with very little expense and get much variety'.[30] The borough extended over the 21,000 acres of the parish, yet two out of every three of the 9–10,000 inhabitants lived in the urban township that was no more than half a square mile in size. The finest houses were in Briggate, but in all parts of the town the rich lived alongside the poor and the craftsmen's workshops. The poorest part was the eastern district from Mabgate to Marsh Lane, where the dyehouses and fulling mills were situated. If the hearth tax returns are to be believed, Leeds had relatively few paupers. About two in five of the inhabitants had one hearth, a similar proportion had two or three hearths, and one in five had more.[31]

The market place was the hub of any town. At Wakefield it lay by the churchyard and was surrounded by inns and filled with booths and stalls on market days. Old names such as Shambles, The Cross, Bull Ring and Hog Market defined the central area. Doncaster was largely confined within its medieval limits and the tax collector wound his way in and out of the central streets and into the market place. Doncaster could be reached by river as well as by the Great North Road and it remained a great regional market centre. Ripon, too, was famous for its horse fair, two great cloth fairs, wool fair and leather market. Celia Fiennes thought it had 'the finest and most beautiful [market] square that is to be seen of its kind in England'.[32] Selby and Bawtry were flourishing river ports and Tadcaster was 'a very good little town for travellers, mostly Inns and little tradesmens houses'.[33]

The other thriving town in the textile district was Halifax, which was described by a visitor in 1639 as 'a pretty well built town of stone'.[34] Judging by the number of householders recorded in the hearth tax returns, its population reached well over 2,000 and the rural townships of its enormous parish were growing quickly as the weaving trade became one of the wonders of the age. Bradford, however, was still a small market town, its population no more than 1,000–1,200, within a vast and thinly populated parish, and Huddersfield's Tuesday market had been established only in 1671 by John Ramsden, lord of the manor, 'for the buying and selling of all sorts of Cattle, Goods and Merchandise'.[35] By the following year Huddersfield had a mere 600–700 inhabitants.

30 *The Illustrated Journeys of Celia Fiennes, c.1682–c.1712*, ed. C. Morris (London, 1984), 182.
31 *A History of Modern Leeds*, ed. D. Fraser (Manchester, 1980), 18.
32 *Celia Fiennes*, 95–7.
33 Ibid., 90.
34 John Aston, quoted by J. Hargreaves, Halifax (Lancaster, 1999), 64–5.
35 G. Redmonds, *The Making of Huddersfield* (Barnsley, 2003), 12.

Sheffield was the leading provincial centre of cutlery manufacture, but London excelled in the production of high-class wares. Sheffield's central streets were arranged around its medieval market place, but the townsmen were no longer dominated by their feudal lords, for the castle had been demolished at the end of the Civil War and the dukes of Norfolk were non-resident landlords. Since 1624 the cutlers had organised their trade through their own company rather than the manor court. About 60 per cent of the workforce were involved in the cutlery trade and beyond the Market Place and the High Street many a house had a cutler's smithy attached to it or one in a back yard.

It is usual to find in the returns that market towns, however small, had more houses with two or more hearths than did townships in the countryside. In Skyrack wapentake, for example, Otley held a Tuesday market for corn and provisions and two annual fairs. Of its 118 recorded householders, 37.2 per cent had only one hearth, whereas in the rural parts of the parish the figure was 62.6 per cent. The townsmen had a much higher proportion of households with three to five hearths.[36] The division between town and countryside was far from obvious, however. Towards the end of the seventeenth century the village of Hatfield was said to be 'not dignify'd either with a market or fair, yet it stands so conveniently that it is not far off of any', having Doncaster, Bawtry and (since 1659) Thorne nearby, but indeed it was itself 'so well furnished with one or two of almost every trade, as butchers, mercers, chandlers, joyners, cutlers, chirurgians, etc, that other places stands in more need of them than the latter of the former'.[37]

Much of the trade of the West Riding was via the river ports and down the Humber to Hull, but improvements to the navigable rivers still lay in the future. The Aire and Calder Navigation was the first, in 1699.[38] Only two of the important national highways that were marked on John Ogilby's road maps of 1675 came through the West Riding.[39] In the east, the Great North Road entered the county at Bawtry (which could be reached from London in three days), and proceeded via Doncaster on its way north through the Vale of York. The alternative route from London came via Mansfield and Rotherham and then veered north-west to Barnsley, Huddersfield, Halifax and on to Richmond. Weekly carrying services connected the West Riding with London and, through linked services, with the leading provincial towns. The regional highways that became turnpike roads in the mid-eighteenth century were already well-established routes that linked the market towns and the increase of trade encouraged local authorities to build stone packhorse bridges to replace the old wooden ones and

[36] D. E. Smith, 'Otley: a study of a market town during the late seventeenth and eighteenth centuries', *Yorkshire Archaeological Journal*, 52 (1980), 153–6.

[37] For Abraham de la Pryme's manuscript history of Hatfield, see BL, Lansdowne MS, 898.

[38] B.F. Duckham, *The Yorkshire Ouse: The History of a River Navigation* (Newton Abbot, 1967), 37.

[39] J. Ogilby, *Britannia* (London, 1675), plates 7, 8, 48, 49.

to lay causeys across the moors to facilitate horse traffic. A team of packhorses could travel, on average, 30 miles a day.

Farming regions

The West Riding was a county of great physical contrasts, ranging from the wet and windswept summits of the Pennine moors to the equally lonely wastes of the Humberhead levels, which were only a few feet above sea level. By the time of the hearth tax returns the market system was so reliable that farmers were able to concentrate upon whatever their soils and climate enabled them to do best.[40] On the Pennine foothills, for example, yeomen and husbandmen concentrated on livestock, especially dairy cattle, because their profits from industrial by-employments paid for the bread corn and malt that they purchased from badgers or in the market place. Oats was still grown where townfields survived in the Pennine hamlets, but many farmers had abandoned cereal production. In the dales most of the arable townfields had been enclosed by the end of the seventeenth century. Inventories of the personal estate of Wensleydale farmers that were taken between 1670 and 1700 show that only one in seven farmers in the lower parts of the dale and as few as one in 20 in the upper parts grew cereals. The dale bottoms were lined with small meadows and pastures, which were grazed by milk kine and young beasts that were being fattened for the butcher. Large, stinted pastures on the fell sides provided summer grazing for cattle and year-round nourishment for sheep; beyond lay the extensive wastes.

Partible inheritance was a common form of tenure on the manors of the northern Pennines, so farms were small and farming families survived only through dual occupations and generous common rights. Many Wensleydale farmers were part-time weavers, for farms had been reduced in size, and cottagers were increasingly dependent for most of their living on linen weaving, which was replacing the manufacture of woollen cloth as the main trade. In Dentdale many farms were only three or four acres in extent and few were larger than eight or nine acres. Since Elizabethan times the knitting of coarse stockings had been an essential by-employment for men, women and children alike. On the lead fields of the carboniferous limestone extensive exploration took place in the early modern period and the scale of mining operations was beginning to grow in the late seventeenth century, but most miners were still part-time farmers. Further south, though, arable farming was still taken seriously. In 1664 the farmers of Wharfedale and Airedale told the Georgical committee that on the hill sides they planted wheat or maslin in winter and black oats in the spring; they limed their clay lands, and then followed a rotation of fallow, barley, beans or

[40] This section is based on D. Hey, 'Yorkshire and Lancashire' in *The Agrarian History of England and Wales, V:I: 1640–1750*, ed. J. Thirsk (Cambridge, 1984), 59–88.

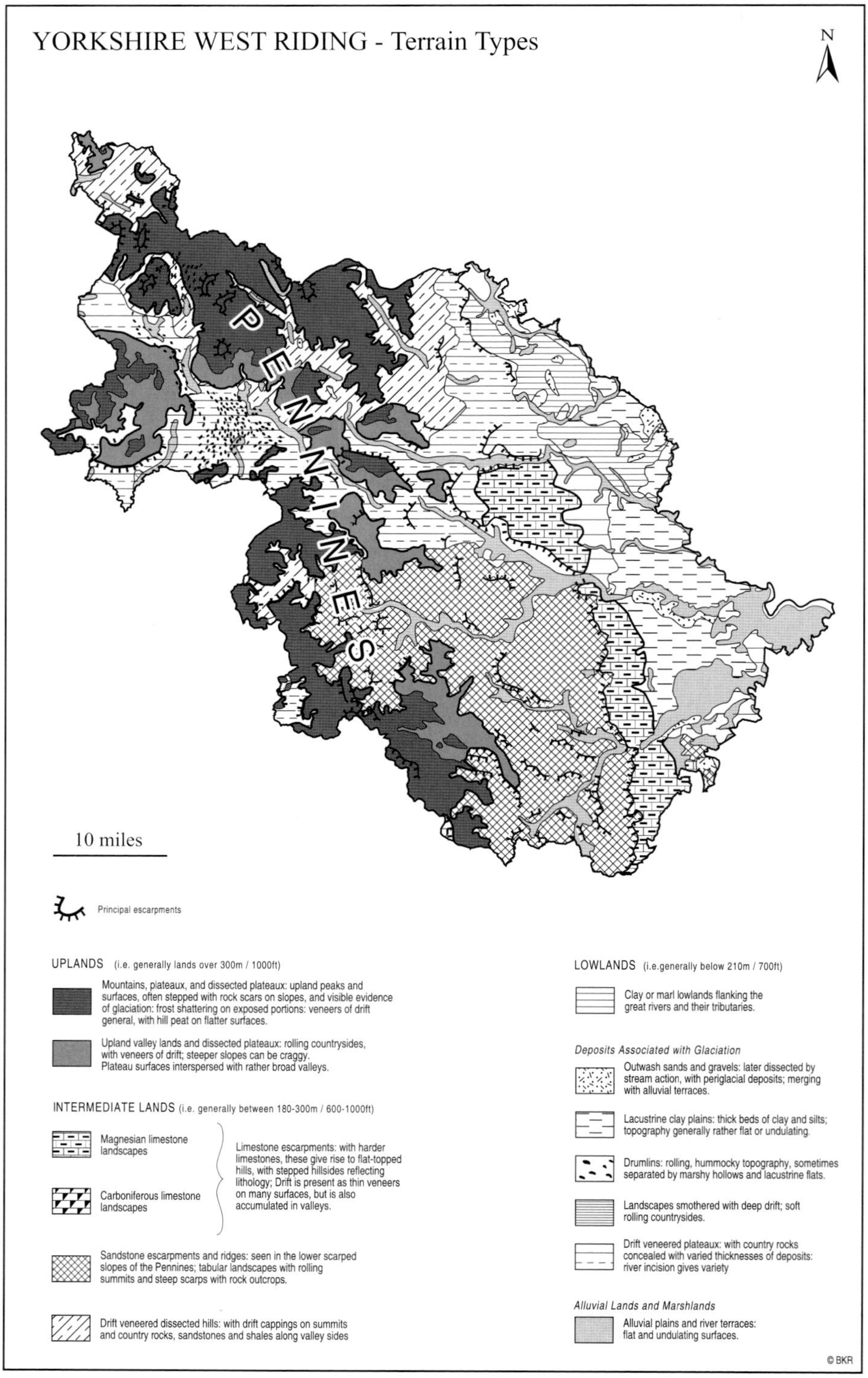

Map 13 West Riding Terrains (by permission of Brian Roberts)

oats, and wheat; on their most fertile ground their course was wheat, barley, beans and fallow. They improved their land with lime, dung and marl, and they bought seed from 'the more champion country' near Wetherby and York.

All the way along the Pennine edges, hay meadows and generous grazing rights on the commons were of prime importance. In a case heard before the Court of Chancery in 1676 Humphrey Bray, a Hepworth copyholder of £10 per annum who paid tax on one hearth, claimed that without the common pastures it would have been impossible to manure his farm and support his flock of sheep.[41] In the huge manor of Wakefield, which included much of the moors of west Yorkshire, and further south in Hallamshire, copyholds were secure and manorial policy allowed the enclosing of new intakes from the extensive wastes and commons. Day-to-day decisions on communal farming activities were still being taken at township or hamlet level.

Each Pennine township also regulated the right to dig peat for winter fuel on the moorland wastes. The great extent of these activities can still be seen on the ground, where sledge ways from individual farms and hamlets lead up to areas that have been stripped of turf in an organised manner, with vertical edges and regular depressions. The 1679 probate inventory of Edward Barker of Ronksley, on the Yorkshire-Derbyshire border, noted '2 peat sleds, 2 pair of peat sides, a sled rope and 3 pairs of sled legs', presumably runners.[42] Peat was brought down from the moors in springtime and stacked and dried at the farmstead. Manorial records for Hallamshire note moorland farms with peat houses in 1637 and a dispute between neighbouring townships in 1724 which involved 'digging turffs in Moscarr'.[43]

In the wood pastures of the coal-measure sandstones east of the Pennines and south of the river Wharfe, industry and agriculture were inseparable. Gentlemen and yeomen profited from their investments or from their organisational roles in industrial enterprises, whilst most of the clothiers, metalworkers and other craftsmen combined their trade with farming. Some of these craftsmen were poor cottagers or smallholders, but many others gained an adequate living, and the yeomen-factors were often substantial men. In 1697 Celia Fiennes described the land on the coal-measure sandstones between Leeds and Elland as 'good grounds for feeding cattle and for corne', where the inhabitants 'are so well provided that together with their industry they needs be very rich'. In the late seventeenth century agreements were made to abandon communal agriculture by enclosing open fields and sometimes also the commons, but many townships retained their common fields. In this region, although there were poor sandy soils on the hills and ill-drained clays on the flatter surfaces, many fertile sandy

41 TNA, C5/448/19.

42 Lichfield Joint Record Office, Archdeaconry of Derby wills and inventories.

43 Ibid.; J.G. Ronksley, ed., *An Exact and Perfect Survey and View of the Manor of Sheffield, with other Lands, by John Harrison, 1637* (Sheffield, 1908); Sheffield Archives, ACM S60.

Plate 1 Ledston Hall had thirty-one hearths in 1672, six recorded as 'not yet finished', indicating that Sir John Lewis was in the middle of an extensive programme of improvements. (Copyright English Heritage)

Plate 2 Barkisland Hall, Barkisland, in the west of the county, built in 1638 and possibly the house recorded as having fourteen hearths in 1672. (Copyright Colum Giles)

Plate 3 Rose Farm, Walton, a substantial yeoman house of the mid 17th century in the east of the county of West Yorkshire. (Copyright Colum Giles)

Plate 4 Wood Lane Hall, Sowerby, built by John Dearden, gentleman, in 1649. It was assessed at eight hearths in 1672. (Copyright Colum Giles)

Plate 5 Peel House, Warley, probably rebuilt in stages from the late 16th century and including, to the right of the entrance porch, a workshop. (Copyright Colum Giles)

Plate 6 Restoration of a house at Carlton Husthwaite, North Yorkshire, revealed a surviving firehood: the view shows the firehood rising through the first floor chamber to the apex of the roof (Crown Copyright National Monuments Record)

Plate 7 Birks, Slaithwaite: the open housebody in a single-storeyed house, probably typical of smaller houses of the Middle Ages and later. (Crown Copyright National Monuments Record)

Plate 8 Bankhouse, Skircoat: a late-medieval aisled house, with the housebody heated by a fire-hood. (Copyright Colum Giles)

Plate 9 Flailcroft, Todmorden: a mid-17th century house with a heated housebody: the fire area is lit by the small two-light window. The stack on the far gable is probably an addition providing heating for the parlour. (Copyright Colum Giles)

(a)

(b)

Plate 10 East Riddlesden Hall, near Keighley: a: the 1648 block provided many heated rooms, including a kitchen, parlours and chambers; b: the dining parlour. (Copyright National Trust)

(a)

(b)

Plate 11 Lower Old Hall, Norland: a: exterior view; b: the housebody, with decorative fireplace and plaster overmantel. (Copyright Colum Giles)

Plate 12 Roebucks, Warley: the housebody, showing the bressumer beam over the original fire area, and the 18th or 19th-century fireplace which replaced the firehood. (Copyright Colum Giles)

loams supported a mixed farming economy of dairying and arable. The numerous coppices were carefully managed to provide fuel for the charcoal iron industry, pit props for the coal mines, bark for the tanners, and all the usual products such as fences, hurdles, gates and tool handles.

Farming practices in the Vale of York varied according to the nature of the great variety of soils that were found in each township. The calcareous, loamy and freely-drained, red-brown soils that overlie the narrow band of magnesian limestone that rose to the east of the coal-measures provided the best arable land in the North. Here were small, nucleated villages, many of which had shrunk or decayed since medieval times. The parishes normally consisted of a single township and were the smallest in the north of England. Few had any woodland and the crafts were only those that supported agriculture. The more populous parishes retained their open fields and common pastures, but elsewhere a squire had enclosed all. This was a district of mixed husbandry where farmers paid equal attention to livestock and crops. On the sands and Keuper marls to the south-west of Hatfield Chase husbandmen placed equal emphasis upon corn and cattle and kept more sheep than their neighbours in the marshlands. In the eastern parts of the Vale of York ill-drained lands could be used only for grazing.

Plate 13 Heaton Royds Farmhouse, Heaton: the house is dated 1634, and the large arched fireplace in the kitchen is likely to belong to this period. (Crown Copyright National Monuments Record)

Plate 14 Glenesk Farm, Morton, a late-17th century house (perhaps post-dating the Hearth Tax): the housebody has a large fireplace in a stone stack which also provided heating for the adjacent parlour. (Crown Copyright National Monuments Record)

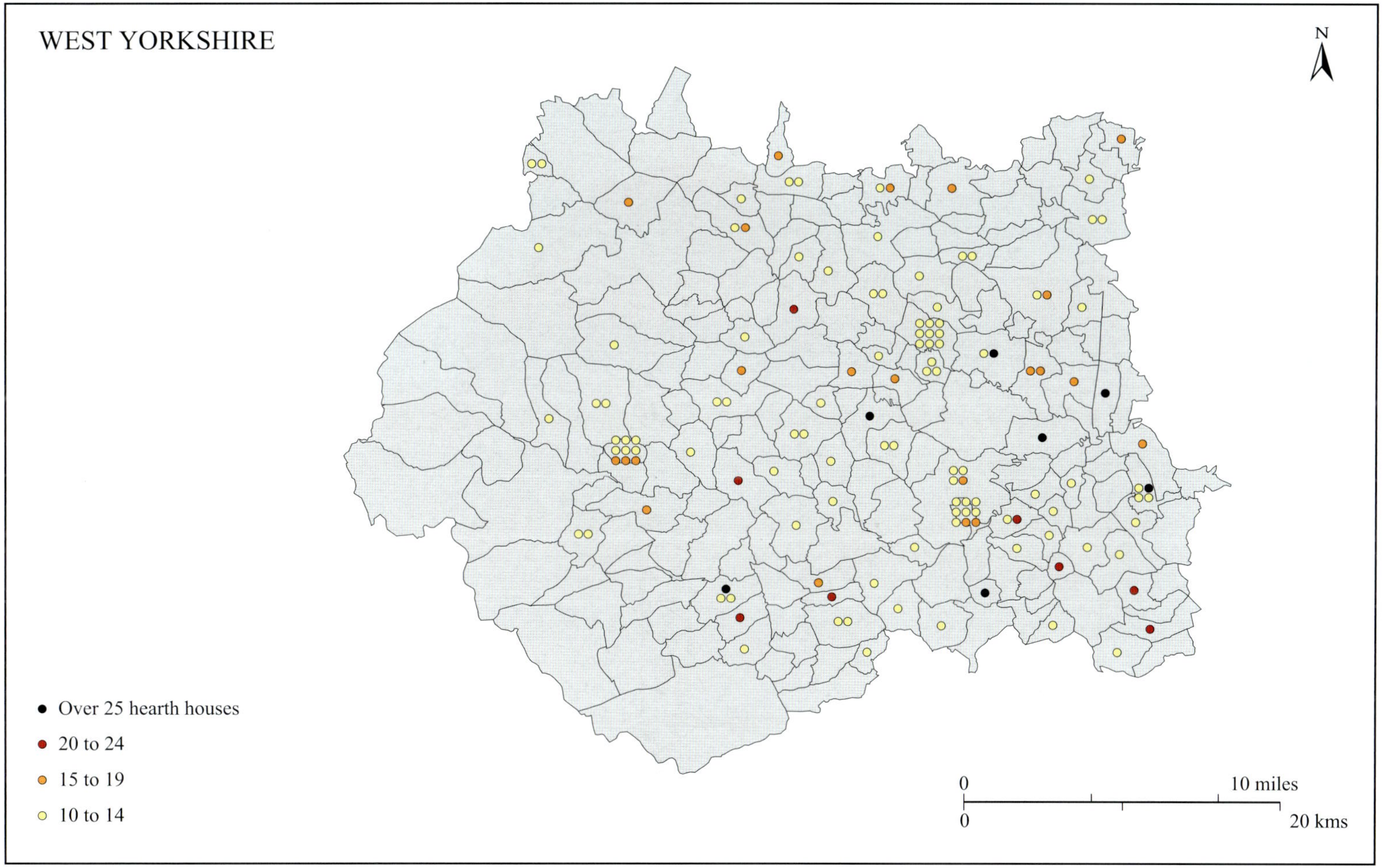

Map 14 West Yorkshire: distribution of households with ten or more hearth houses paying

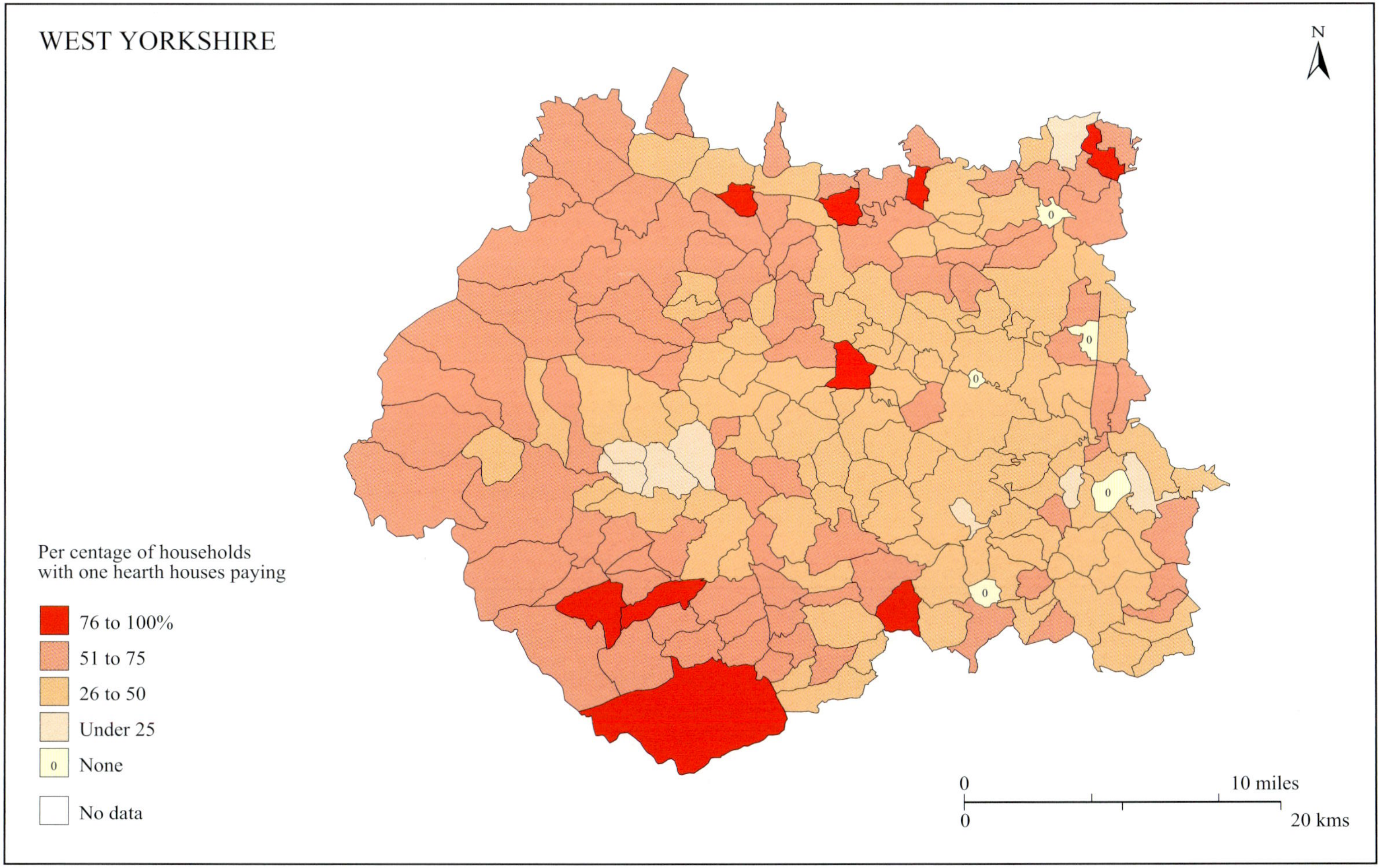

Map 15 West Yorkshire: percentage of households with one hearth houses paying

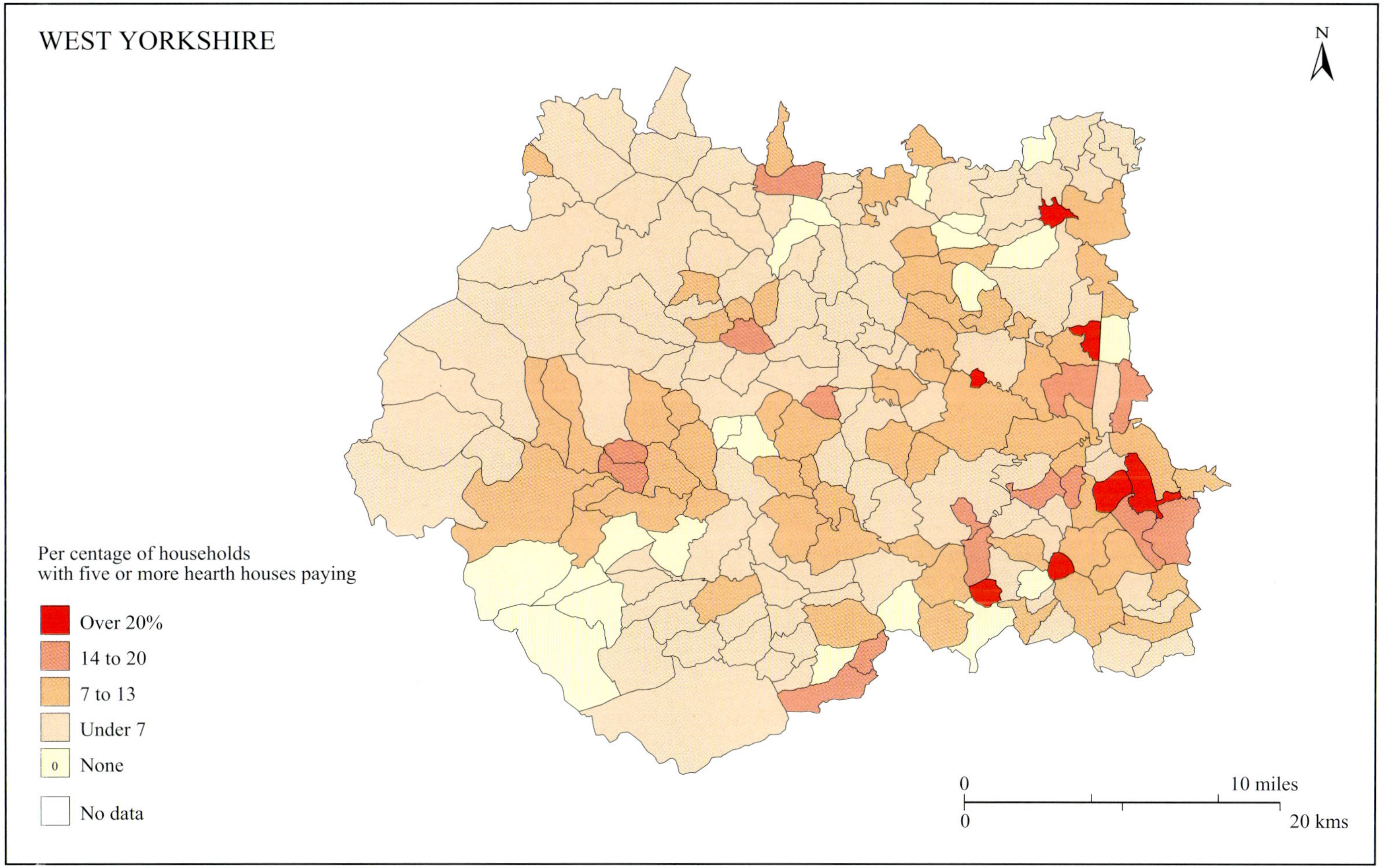

Map 16 West Yorkshire: percentage of households with five or more hearth houses paying

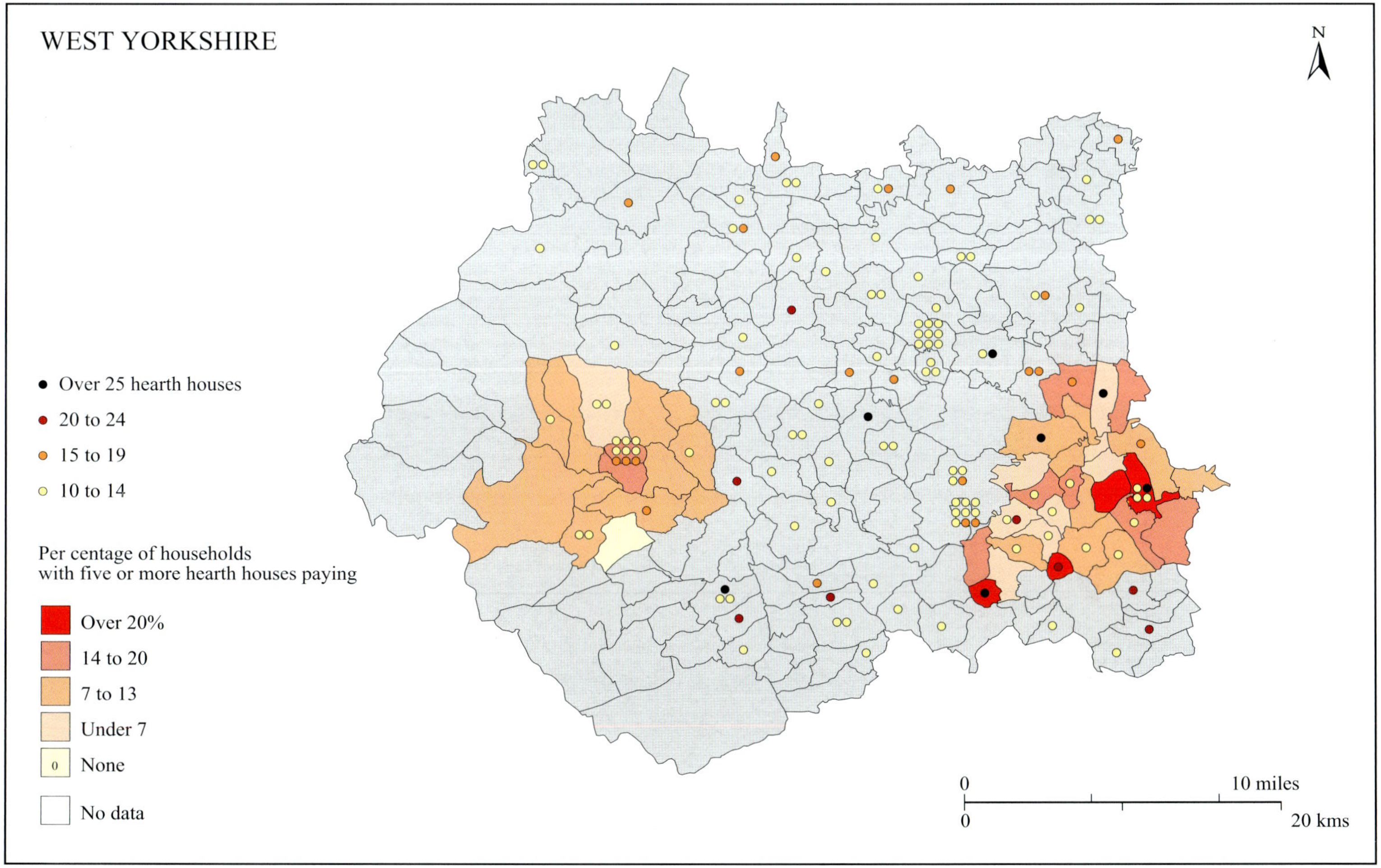

Map 17 West Yorkshire: distribution map of east and west sample areas

Pasture closes and sometimes meadows were more extensive than arable fields. By 1672 some townships on the heavy clay soils were fully enclosed and in others the open-fields had been adapted to a system of convertible husbandry; however the use of closes for grazing meant that some of the larger commons remained unstinted. Rearing and fattening cattle were the most profitable lines, though most farmers also grew cereals. Around Selby, Snaith and Sykehouse they often grew a few acres of flax and in Hatfield Chase, which had been partly drained by Vermuyden's company in the late 1620s, Dutch and Flemish settlers had improved much of the new land by warping in order to grow oats, winter corn and rapeseed. Hatfield Park was divided up in the 1660s and converted to tillage and each township had a small area of common fields, surrounded by closes and ings, beyond which lay extensive common pastures and turf moors. Many Thorne inventories speak of 'turves on the moors', either for a farmer's own use or for sale down the river; William Middlebrooke, sailor (1726) had 'turves paid for, deliver'd and undeliverd,' worth £10. York was a major market and as far back as 1597 the citizens there had declared that turves were 'nowe the greatest parte of our fewell'.[44]

Small farms did not necessarily lead to conservative husbandry practices, for farmers in many parts of Yorkshire were willing to try new ideas to improve the quality of crops and livestock. For example, in 1664 the Georgical committee of enquiry found that farmers in the liberty of Ripon pared, dried and burned their pastures and worst sorts of ground to yield three or four good crops, after which they spread lime, dung, or marl, mixed with dung to make good pastures. Throughout the West Riding, family farms were held on secure tenures or as small freeholds and were often less than 20 acres in extent, though with associated grazing rights on the commons.

Industry

At the time of the hearth tax returns, York still played an important role as a textile marketing centre, Doncaster's woolstaplers were importing good-quality wools, and Ripon's cloth fair remained well attended. But by then, the cloth markets at Leeds and Wakefield had outpaced their ancient rivals and were indisputably the most eminent in Yorkshire. Despite foreign competition and the Anglo-Dutch wars, the West Riding textile industry not only captured much of the home market but exported many of its products to Holland and Germany and thus expanded steadily long before the great stimulus of the opening of the Aire and Calder Navigation in 1699. After the Restoration the manufacture of worsteds began to rival that of woollens, providing the West Riding textile district with a unique and strong combination. By the end of the seventeenth century

[44] D.M. Palliser, *Tudor York* (Oxford, 1979), 273.

the parish of Halifax was not only the leading centre of kersey manufacture but also of worsted shalloons. Worsted manufacture gradually spread beyond the upper valleys of the Calder and Aire, as far north as Haworth and Keighley and as far east as Bradford (the later centre) and even to Leeds and Wakefield. Kerseys and other narrow cloths were made in Pennine townships stretching south from Halifax to Huddersfield and Penistone, while broad cloths were made in the district bounded by Leeds, Wakefield, Huddersfield, Halifax and Bradford, and white or undyed cloths were made in the Calder Valley and coloured cloths were produced in the parish of Leeds and in the villages immediately to the west and the south.[45] Both the hearth tax returns and the surviving vernacular architecture demonstrate that the wealth provided by trade and industry differentiated the flourishing textile districts from purely agricultural communities.

The West Riding lay well away from its export markets and had no advantage over its competitors in terms of wool supplies, which were largely imported. Nor were its labour costs significantly different. Contemporary opinion was that the West Riding owed its success to the peculiar structure of its industry, which provided opportunities for men of enterprise and initiative. Its domestic system of organisation was radically different from that of its ancient rivals in East Anglia and the West Country, where manufacture was dominated by wealthy merchants and clothiers who employed numerous outworkers for wages. In the West Riding countryside the typical enterprise in the woollen industry was the family farm where everyone helped to make one piece of cloth each week for the local market. Little capital was needed and the industry was able to expand enormously, simply by spreading into neighbouring townships. Leeds merchants dominated only the finishing and marketing processes. The variety of woollens and worsteds that were made within the same district meant that manufacturers could switch products relatively easily as fashion demanded. The West Riding textile industry concentrated on the cheaper end of the market with cloths offering value for money to the rising population.

The Hallamshire cutlery industry was organised on a similar basis.[46] It could not yet compete with London at the top end of the market but it had triumphed over its provincial rivals, such as Salisbury and Thaxted, largely because its rivers could be dammed to provide water power and the local sandstone was ideal for making grindstones. Between 1660 and 1740 the number of water-powered sites on the local streams and rivers rose from 49 to 90, about two-thirds of which were used for grinding cutlery, and the number of wheels at each unit rose appreciably. No other place in England used so much water power. In his *Worthies of England* (1662), Thomas Fuller wrote that most of the common knives of English

[45] On the West Riding textile industry see H. Heaton, *The Yorkshire Woollen and Worsted Industries from the Earliest Times up to the Industrial Revolution* (Oxford, 2nd edn, 1965); Hargreaves, *Halifax*, 25–67.

[46] The following account of the Hallamshere cutlery industry is based on Hey, *Fiery Blades*, 93–145.

country people were made in and around Sheffield and that 'One may justly wonder how a knife may be sold for one penny'.[47] By the time of the hearth tax, some high-quality cutlery was being made and the growing fashion for forks was encouraging a new craft, alongside other specialisations such as file making. The steel that was necessary for sharp cutting edges had long been imported from Spain, Germany and Sweden. The incorporation of the Cutlers' Company of Hallamshire in 1624 had freed the industry from manorial control. By the middle of the seventeenth century about 60 per cent of the adult male workforce in the township of Sheffield were employed in the cutlery trades.[48]

The hearth tax returns provide a unique insight into the cutlery and other secondary metal trades at this time, for industrial hearths were listed separately alongside domestic ones while the Cutlers' Company were engaged in a protracted battle at law. In the sheriff's copy of the returns, smithies were recorded alongside domestic hearths, but here they were placed in separate lists of cutlers who had 'deposited the duty for theire forges but refused to pay the Money without a Tryall at Law'. The Cutlers' Company went to considerable expense in hiring counsel and sending a former Master Cutler and their clerk to lobby in London, York and other places before asking Sir John Reresby, JP, of Thrybergh Hall to use his influence at Court. Reresby noted that 'the corporation of cutlers had spent near £200 in law … without bringing it to any certain issue'. He was well entertained at the Cutlers' Feast in 1677 and was successful in having the tax demands set aside for a while. In 1682 the Company tried another time-honoured method by bribing 'Mr Trueman, Collector of the Hearth dutie to forbear distreineing of Smyths Forges till further consideration' and in the following year by presenting him with some good-quality cutlery 'for his civilities to the towne.' Similar methods were employed with equal success three years later.[49]

The filesmiths, awlbladesmiths and scythemakers joined the Cutlers' Company during this long struggle to exclude industrial hearths from payment of the tax. The hearth tax returns are a major source of evidence for the size and distribution of the various metalworking trades in and just beyond Hallamshire. In 1672 about 600 smithies were recorded in south Yorkshire and adjacent parts of north Derbyshire. Sheffield township had 224 smithies, that is one to every 2.2 houses, but even more Sheffielders were employed in the cutlery trade than this figure suggests, for the most skilled men worked in their chambers hafting and finishing the best-quality knives. Probate inventories suggest that one in every four cutlers had work chambers but no smithies. The grip of the trade on the town was remarkable. Sheffield was an ancient centre of cutlery manufacture long before it became Steel City.

[47] *Fuller's Worthies: Selected from The Worthies of England by Thomas Fuller*, ed. R. Barber (London, 1987), 423.
[48] *Mesters to Masters: A History of the Company of Cutlers in Hallamshire*, eds C. Binfield and D. Hey (Oxford, 1997), 12–39.
[49] Hey, *Fiery Blades*, 136–9; Purdy, 23–30.

The small workshop worked by a 'little mester' with an apprentice and perhaps a journeyman or two remained the typical unit of production in both the town and the countryside. At this time, filemaking was an urban craft, scissorsmiths were at work in the townships of Sheffield and Attercliffe, scythe-making was the distinctive craft of the north Derbyshire parish of Norton, whilst their neighbours in Eckington parish made sickles, 'common wares' were made in the outlying townships of Hallamshire, and the nailmakers lived and worked further north in the villages, hamlets and scattered farmsteads near the slitting mills at Wortley and Masborough. Like the weaver-farmers of the Calder and Colne valleys, the rural metalworkers had a dual occupation, with their smithies standing next to the cow shed and the barn.

Most of the steel that the cutlers required for their cutting edges still came from abroad. The first reference to a cementation steel furnace in south Yorkshire is from 1642 when parliamentary soldiers wrecked one recently built by Charles Tooker of Moorgate Hall, Rotherham.[50] The next reference comes in the sheriff's copy of the 1672 return for Kimberworth, where 'Willm Hellefeild or Mr Copley' were taxed on four hearths 'per Steele Furnish'. Mr Copley was Lionel Copley, the leading gentleman-ironmaster in south Yorkshire. These early steel furnaces were erected in the countryside near Sheffield and Rotherham; the urban township of Sheffield did not have one until the early years of the eighteenth century. Fuel for these furnaces and the cutlers' smithies came from the exposed coalfield, which had been mined for centuries. Before the age of the railways the landlocked position of the Yorkshire coalfield prevented it from competing in national markets with Northumberland and Durham, which had ready access to the sea. The local demand for coal as a domestic fuel grew considerably in the seventeenth century, however, for the price of firewood soared when the ironmasters bought up the coppice woods to ensure their supplies of charcoal for their blast furnaces.

During the seventeenth century the English glass industry migrated to the midland and northern coalfields and by the later decades furnaces were at work at Gawber, Glass Houghton and Silkstone.[51] The John Pilmay, who was taxed on four hearths at Silkstone with his stepson, Mr Scott, had established his works there by 1658. He was descended from an immigrant glassmaker from Lorraine who had moved to southern England during the reign of Queen Elizabeth (d. 1603). Another prominent immigrant family who had not yet arrived in the West Riding were the Fenneys; later on Henry Fenney leased Glass Houghton; while Joshua Fonney was at Rothwell Haigh, and other members of the family built glasshouses at Bolsterstone and Catcliffe.[52]

50 D. Hey, 'The South Yorkshire Steel Industry and the Industrial Revolution', *Northern History* 42 (2005), 91–6.

51 D. Ashurst, *The History of South Yorkshire Glass* (Department of Archaeology & Prehistory, University of Sheffield, n.d.), 19–44.

52 Ibid., 27–8.

Contrasting 'countries'

As the hearth tax was collected by county it is natural to make comparisons at this level, but an analysis of the West Riding returns shows much variety between sub-regions, the neighbourhoods that people once spoke of as their 'countries'. Daniel Defoe, for example, spoke of 'the country called Hallamshire', the ancient estate that became a Norman lordship tucked away in the south-western corner of Yorkshire.[53] The physical geography of Hallamshire, the preservation of its name by the Cutlers' Company, the unique nature of the work, the vernacular nature of the buildings (especially the smithies), the long residence of its core families, whose distinctive surnames were coined locally, local speech (much of it derived from the cutlery trade), and the strong Dissenting tradition set it apart from its neighbours.

Since the pioneering work of Joan Thirsk and Alan Everitt,[54] agricultural historians have been accustomed to think in terms of *pays* (the French form of 'country'), where farming practices, settlement patterns, local economies and even social structures were deeply influenced by the topography of a sub-region. In the West Riding, to take but two contrasting examples, life in a nucleated village under the control of a squire on the magnesian limestone belt, where the rich soils produced fine crops of cereals in the communal open fields, was very different from life in a moorland township high in the Calder Valley. There families were more likely to live in scattered farmsteads or hamlets than in a village, with no landlord or parson living close by. In such areas making a weekly piece of cloth was perhaps more important than farming a smallholding.

But even when we get down to the level of a 'country' we find that the quality of housing might vary considerably from village to village, even in the richest districts. The different 'countries' were not uniformly wealthy or poor. Even in the Upper Calder Valley the inhabitants of some of the outlying townships struggled to make a living. It is usual in an analysis of the hearth tax returns (and earlier taxation lists such as the medieval lay subsidies) to rank townships according to the amount of tax paid per 1,000 acres. As this allows a rough-and-ready comparison to be made across the kingdom, maps have been constructed on this basis here, even though this distorts the true picture in the western townships of the West Riding, which consisted mostly of extensive moorland wastes. In Staincross wapentake, for example, 6,522 of the 8,116 acres of the township of Thurlstone were classified as commons and wastes at the time of their enclosure in 1812–16; the wastes had been even more extensive at the time of the hearth tax returns. The inhabitants of an average moorland township were better-off than figures based on total acreages imply. In particular, the townships in the

53 D. Defoe, *A Tour through the Whole Island of Great Britain* (London, 1962), 181.

54 *The Agrarian History of England and Wales, IV: 1540–1640*, ed. J. Thirsk (Cambridge, 1967).

vicinity of Halifax had a high proportion of large, vernacular houses which compared favourably with the best yeomen's dwellings across England.

It is nevertheless true that much of northern England was poorer than the south. This is testified by the disgruntled pleas of auditors who were paid for transcribing the rolls at the rate of a halfpenny for twenty hearths. In 1662 Richard Aldworth, Esq., the auditor for Yorkshire, Durham and Northumberland claimed that he was underpaid 'by reason of the pooreness of the buildings and fewnes of chimneys in each house generally in those parts'.[55] Another petition reads:

> 'Sirs, May it please your lordshipps to be humbly informed by Joseph Seymour that there is a great difference between the hearth roll in the North of England and the more western and southern parts, for there are maney rolls in the Northern parts wherein conteyned to every line in that roll but 1, 2 or 3 hearths and generally but one, whereas in Mr Auditor Phelips Office and Sir Edmund Sawyers and others that have great citties and townes, and populous counties there is scarce in any roll but that every line hath 7, 8, 10 or 12 or more chimneys ...'[56]

His complaint was that he was getting a smaller financial reward for his pains than the auditors of more prosperous regions. The 'countries' of the West Riding where industry was profitably combined with agriculture should not be included in this general view of a backward North. Well before the classic period of the Industrial Revolution, the West Riding had emerged as more dynamic and prosperous than Yorkshire's other two ridings.

The Compton ecclesiastical census

In 1676, just four years after the compilation of the Lady Day 1672 hearth tax returns, ministers made returns of the number of communicants, 'Popish Recusants' and 'Other Dissenters' in their parishes.[57] Although the numbers were often approximations, they provide a rough guide to the geographical patterns of dissent. In the West Riding archdeaconry, dissenters of all kind amounted to only 3.4 per cent of the 75,501 recorded persons; 574 of these were Catholics and 2,013 belonged to Protestant dissenting congregations. They were a small, but often influential minority. Rural gentlemen and urban tradesmen helped to preserve dissent during the years of repression between 1662 and 1689. Many ejected ministers served tiny congregations in a discreet manner, particularly in remote parts of the countryside where patrons provided meeting places and offered some protection from the law. In contrast, dissent was easily suppressed in estate villages where resident lords ensured that their communities remained dependent upon the estate for tenancies and employment. It was a

[55] TNA, E179/3544.
[56] Ibid., E179/359.
[57] *Compton Census, passim.*

different matter where the lord was a dissenter himself. The largest Catholic congregation was the 80 who lived in the small parish of Burghwallis that was dominated by the Anne family. The next largest Catholic congregations were in central and eastern parts of the riding at Pontefract (57), Wakefield (57), Spofforth (51), Barwick-in-Elmet (40) and Saxton (37).

The strongholds of Protestant Nonconformity were in the growing industrial parishes and the moorland chapelries that were remote from a parish church. Wakefield had about 300 (12.5 per cent), Sheffield and Birstall both had 300 (10 per cent), but the 150 dissenters in each of the large parishes of Halifax and Leeds amounted to little more than 1 per cent. Other parishes in the textile district, with between 50 and 109 dissenters, included Batley (11.7 per cent), Kirkburton (3.75 per cent), Woodkirk (3.0 per cent), Dewsbury (6.25 per cent) and Bradford (2.5 per cent). Economic and topographical considerations favoured the spread of dissent but did not automatically produce it and it is the lack of any urban pattern that is striking at this time. Rotherham had been strongly puritan during the Civil War and its large parish contained numerous metalworkers, but it had only three dissenters among 750 communicants. Barnsley had only seven dissenters out of 638 communicants, despite the fact that it had a flourishing market and a wire-drawing industry and was merely a chapel-of-ease of Silkstone parish. In Doncaster, where only eight of an estimated 3,000 communicants were dissenters, the mayor and corporation claimed five years later that, 'We can truly say without boasting that we have neither in our town or corporation one dissenter from the present government in church and state'.[58]

In the Vale of York, the highest number of dissenters were at Hampsthwaite (10.6 per cent), Tadcaster (8.6 per cent) and Pontefract (3.75 per cent). Much larger numbers were recorded in the marshland parishes in the southeast. The parish of Fishlake (including its chapelry of Sykehouse) had 136 dissenters (24.3 per cent) and the neighbouring parish of Thorne (including Dikesmarsh) had 103 (20.6 per cent). However, the adjacent parish of Hatfield had only six dissenters amongst its 642 communicants. The immigrant Dutch and Flemish families who had drained Hatfield Chase and settled in the area may partly explain the high number of dissenters in Fishlake and Thorne, but ecclesiastical court books record numerous prosecutions against people with English names, 'for not being obedient to the Church of England in anything'.[59]

The Great Landholders

Neither the Civil War nor the Restoration had serious long-term affects on the general pattern of landholding in the West Riding. By recording the number of

[58] D. Hey, 'The Pattern of Nonconformity in South Yorkshire, 1660–1851', *Northern History* 8 (1973), 86–119.
[59] Borthwick, R.VI.E.2. The Flemish and Dutch immigrants worshipped just across the Lincolnshire border.

hearths in the greatest houses, the tax returns of Lady Day 1672 help to capture an old pattern of landownership before the creation of large estates after the 1688 revolution. The number of recorded hearths include those in lodgings and outbuildings – at High Melton and Wadworth Halls the sheriff's copy even noted heated dog kennels – but they nevertheless allow us to construct an order of ranking. The West Riding had 41 houses that had at least 20 hearths.

At the top of the list with 60 hearths was Skipton Castle, which had been partially demolished at the end of the Civil War but then lovingly restored from 1659 by the formidable Lady Anne Clifford, Countess of Pembroke. The Honour of Skipton stretched from Airedale over much of Staincliffe wapentake into Wharfedale, where she also restored Barden Tower (27 hearths), which had been built by her ancestor during the reign of King Henry VIII (d. 1547). The other great feudal lordship that still formed a single estate was Hallamshire, but the Howards, dukes of Norfolk, were non-resident landlords. Sheffield Castle had been demolished and the Manor Lodge, which had been extended into a great country house in the sixteenth century by the Talbots, earls of Shrewsbury, on the site of the old hunting lodge in the deer park, was now divided between the lord's two chief officers, Mr Ratcliffe (36 hearths) and Mr Nevill (21 hearths). The deer were soon to be withdrawn, the huge park was divided into farms, and in 1708 or shortly afterwards the lodge was demolished. Continuity with the medieval past was also evident in the archbishop of York's palace at Bishopthorpe (Ainsty), which had 38 hearths, and less so at Tickhill Castle (24 hearths), where the second of three Ralph Hansbys had built a gabled house that still stands within the bailey walls.

The West Riding had some of England's finest 'prodigy houses', built in Elizabethan and early-Stuart times by men who had prospered through government office and who had built up large estates in Yorkshire. Sir Arthur Ingram, a native of Rothwell who had long served as James I and Charles I's finance minister, had enlarged the Darcys' old house at Temple Newsam (45 hearths), which was now owned by his grandson, Viscount Irwin. The Ingrams had extensive estates in other parts of Yorkshire, for Sir Arthur had been steward and master of game in the Forest of Galtres and had built a magnificent town house behind York Minster, now held by Lady Ingram (33 hearths), as well as other properties in Lincolnshire, Derbyshire and Suffolk. At Wentworth Woodhouse (43 hearths), William, the second Earl of Strafford, lived in the house that his father, Sir Thomas Wentworth, had built on his ancestral estate before his execution in 1641. In the eighteenth century, Sir Thomas Watson-Wentworth, first Marquess of Rockingham, enlarged the park until it was nine miles in circumference, built up a 17,200 acre estate, and erected the largest Palladian house in England. The Wentworths also owned Tankersley Hall (25 hearths), a great Elizabethan house that was demolished in the late 1720s, and Sir Thomas had been largely responsible for the present appearance of Ledston Hall (31 hearths), which was added to and was now owned by Sir John Lewis, an East India merchant.

The various branches of the Saviles, a minor gentry family in Norman times who by Henry VIII's reign had become stewards of Pontefract Castle, sheriffs, and members of the Council of the North, also benefited from the spoils of public office to become great landowners in west Yorkshire.[60] Howley Hall (44 hearths), Morley, which was built for Sir John Savile in the 1590s, was the most impressive of these 'prodigy houses' at 60 yards square.[61] Methley Hall (43 hearths), erected by another Sir John from 1588, was famous for its large expanse of glass windows.[62] Both have been demolished. Nor is there much evidence of the former status of Nun Appleton Hall (40 hearths), owned by George Villiers, second Duke of Buckingham, the son of the court favourite of King James I (d. 1625), and himself a great public figure. He was lord lieutenant of the West Riding from 1661 to 1667 and retired to his Yorkshire estates in 1686. The house was on the site of a former Cistercian nunnery and was depicted in the 1720s by Samuel Buck[63] as a tall, gabled building, three bays square. Other public figures who erected grand houses in the riding included Sir Richard Hutton, a judge in the Court of Common Pleas, who had built Goldsborough Hall (29 hearths), and Sir Thomas Osborne, later Earl of Danby and Duke of Leeds, who had succeeded to a baronetcy and south Yorkshire estates in 1647. These were centred on Kiveton Hall (26 hearths; rebuilt in the 1690s to the designs of William Talman) and Thorpe Salvin Hall (20 hearths; an Elizabethan structure now in ruins). His star was in the ascendancy during the reign of William (d. 1702) and Mary (d. 1694).

Hickleton Hall (32 hearths) was occupied by the fourth Sir John Jackson, the first having bought the estate when he was an attorney at the Council of the North. The Whartons had been prominent Yorkshire gentry since Sir Thomas Wharton, a leading supporter of Henry VIII in Cumberland and a member of the Council of the North, had acquired the Healaugh Priory estate at its dissolution. In 1672 Healaugh (28 hearths) was occupied by Phillip, fourth Lord Wharton, a parliamentarian and Independent in religion, and in south Yorkshire Edlington (21 hearths) was the home of his brother, Sir Thomas. Other converted monastic estates included that of Roche Abbey at Sandbeck (30 hearths, where the Saundersons were now Viscounts Castleton), the Cistercian nunnery at Kirklees (24 hearths, Sir John Armitage baronet), Nun Monkton (21 hearths, a former Benedictine priory now held by George Paler), and Denby

60 R.B. Smith, *Land and Politics in the England of Henry VIII: The West Riding of Yorkshire, 1530–1546* (Oxford, 1970), 148, 217–18.

61 M. Girouard, *Robert Smythson and The Elizabethan Country House* (New Haven & London, 1983), 142.

62 Ibid., 276; L. Ambler, *The Old Halls and Manor Houses of Yorkshire* (London, 1913), 57.

63 *Samuel Buck's Yorkshire Sketchbook: reproduced in facsimile from Lansdowne MS 914 in the British Library, with an introduction by Ivan Hall* (Wakefield, 1979), 324.

Grange (20 hearths), which the Kayes of Woodsome Hall (22 hearths) had purchased at the dissolution of Byland Abbey). Their neighbour, William Ramsden, had also done well out of the dissolution of the monasteries and his descendant and namesake still lived at Longley Hall (25 hearths).

The leading West Riding gentry included two ancient families that remained staunch Catholics: the Annes of Burghwallis (41 hearths), who were descended from a fourteenth-century constable of Tickhill Castle, and the Middletons of Middleton and Stockeld (41 hearths). Other long-established West Riding gentry included the Neville family, who had been at Chevet (33 hearths) since the thirteenth century and had long since removed the village to extend their park, the Darcys of Aston (27 hearths), the Dawneys of Cowick (26 hearths), the Malleverers of Allerton (24 hearths), the Ingilbys of Ripley (24 hearths), the Vavasours of Weston (24 hearths) and Hazelwood (20 hearths), the Slingsbys of Moor Monkton (23 hearths) and the Copleys of Sprotborough (21 hearths).

It is clear from these lists that the West Riding had numerous substantial houses that ranked amongst the finest in the land and that leading families played important roles in national affairs. At a lower social level, the modest prosperity of those districts where trade and industry flourished, in combination with agriculture, was reflected in the number of hearths on which householders were taxed and the quality of their vernacular architecture. The West Riding had a number of thriving towns, specialist urban and rural industries, and varied agricultural regions that set it apart from most of the rest of the North. It is true that, like every part of England, a large proportion of the inhabitants lived in one-roomed houses, especially in those districts where industries had not taken root. It is also true that the extent of poverty is underplayed in the hearth tax returns. But it is clear that the West Riding should not be included in sweeping statements about 'the backward North'. The maps in this volume reveal a very different picture to County Durham,[64] where the only major industry at the time was coal mining (which produced a very different social and economic structure). Forthcoming volumes on the hearth tax returns of other northern counties will also reveal the distinctiveness of the West Riding. Within Yorkshire, the vernacular architecture of the East and North Ridings makes a poor contrast with that of the West Riding, whose wealth generated by trade, industry and agriculture distinguished it from the rest of Northern England. The West Riding's economy was thriving long before the great industrial changes of the late eighteenth and nineteenth centuries.

[64] A. Green, E. Parkinson and M. Spufford, eds, *County Durham Hearth Tax Assessment, Lady Day 1666* (British Record Society, 2006).

Wealth Distribution, the Hearth Tax and Housing

by Colum Giles

The evidence for evasion and the doubts about exemptions notwithstanding, it is a reasonable assumption that the proportions and numbers of householders paying tax on different numbers of hearths represent a fair view of the distribution of wealth in a township and, when broader patterns are analysed, in wider areas. Despite the deficiencies of and uncertainties about the hearth tax returns, the source undoubtedly provides the student of seventeenth-century society with the broadest view of how communities were structured, both within counties (in, for example, the 'countries' by which the inhabitants identified themselves) and nationally, where broad differences, for example, between north and south, can be detected.[1] The West Riding hearth tax returns offer great scope for a study of county society, for the riding contained marked geographical variations, strong contrasts in landholding patterns, clear farming regions, and locally dominant industries of considerable scale and importance. All of these characteristics are evident in the returns.

The township

At the level of the individual township there is much variety in the composition of society. In a few places, a single aristocratic family dominated the local scene. At Chevet, the Nevile family lived in splendid isolation in its great house. Other leading families, while certainly dominant, lived in populous townships: in Wentworth, for example, William Strafford, occupying his chief seat of Wentworth Woodhouse (assessed at 43 hearths), was the pre-eminent local figure, but the township had 70 households assessed for tax, one at 10 hearths, two at six hearths, and a dozen at three or four hearths. Temple Newsam was even more populous: the Ingrams lived in splendour in their great house (45 hearths) set within its park, but the township also contained 125 other households, with a wide spread of liability for tax. In other townships the leading family was of gentry rather than aristocratic rank, but its local influence may have been no less complete. In Farnley Tyas, the Kayes of Woodsome Hall (22 hearths) were clearly dominant: of the 39 households in the township, they alone occupied a

1 N. W. Alcock, *People at Home: Living in a Warwickshire Village 1500–1800* (Chichester, 1993), 202 shows, for example, how, in the proportions of single-hearth houses, Warwickshire differed considerably from east Sussex and east Devon, which had lower proportions of one-hearth houses, and from North Yorkshire, where a higher proportion was recorded; see also *Houses and the Hearth Tax: the later Stuart House and Society*, eds. P.S. Barnwell and M. Airs, 18–21.

house of more than four hearths, and 36 households had just one or two hearths. Some townships had more than one titled family: in Almondbury, William Ramsden, Esquire, with 25 hearths, and Mr Ashton, with 10, were the leading figures.

Not all townships had a resident gentry or noble family. In Norland (Agbrigg and Morley) none of the 58 households was of gentry status, but there was, however, a modest spread of taxable wealth: the two largest houses had only six hearths, but there were in all 22 further households assessed at betwen three and five hearths. Many agricultural townships were much poorer. In the Vale of York, Acaster Malbis (Ainsty) had 40 households: 29 paid tax on a single hearth, and 11 on two hearths. In the northern dales, Hebden (East Staincliffe) had 25 households assessed on a single hearth, 11 on two hearths and one exempted household. And in the southern coal measures, none of the 19 households in Little Houghton (Lower Strafforth) paid tax on more than two hearths.

The hearth tax returns thus describe a great variety of communities, from the aristocratic township, through townships with a considerable range of wealth and many social gradations where gentry and yeomen intermingled, to townships teeming with numerous households of widely differing status and wealth, and finally to townships unadorned by titled families where the large majority of people existed at the lower end of the social scale. The returns, therefore, provide strong evidence for the effect of landholding and occupational practices on the structure of local society.

Sub-regional patterns: a study of West Yorkshire

Something of the variety within the West Riding can be illustrated in more depth through a closer examination of a substantial part of its central area. The modern county of West Yorkshire was created in 1974, but was largely dismantled for administrative purposes in 1986. It survives, however, as an authority offering joint services to its constituent districts. In its short life the modern county was the subject of a number of archaeological, architectural and historical studies which provide a strong evidence base for the examination of sub-regional variety. In general, its topography reflects that of the West Riding as a whole: it has high Pennine moors to the west, cut by river valleys (the principal rivers are the Wharfe, Aire and Calder); the rivers cross a central area largely made up of coal measures sandstones; and in the east are lower lying lands together with a narrow belt of magnesian limestone. The contrasts in agricultural practice within the county mirror those of the Riding as a whole (although West Yorkshire contains no extensive fen area to match Hatfield Chase), and the area embraces both districts where farming was the principal support for the local population and districts where industry was of great significance. The county's principal towns in later Stuart England were Leeds, the great marketing centre for both agricultural produce and the products of the textile industry; Wakefield, an important market town with a significant role in the supply of wool to the region's cloth manufacturers; Pontefract, a market town lying just off the Great North Road; and Halifax, a market for the local woollen and worsted manufacturing districts.[2]

The distribution of large houses: the countryside

It may be assumed that large houses were built and occupied by families of substance and that the numbers of hearths in a house, especially at the upper end of the scale, are a reasonable barometer of a family's standing in the community. There are almost certainly instances where this is not the case, for example where, at the time of the hearth tax assessment, a wealthy family inhabited an outmoded house, perhaps an unimproved medieval dwelling. The converse might also be the case, for families fallen on hard times might well occupy a house built by a more fortunate generation. Furthermore, wealth, as expressed in the number of hearths for which a family was liable, did not always correspond closely to the family's titular status, for many families on the rise and already by 1672 occupying new-built or modernised houses, might not yet have gained the status to which, perhaps, they aspired. The hearth tax returns and their status descriptions record only a point in time in an age of considerable social mobility. Another difficulty in interpreting the numbers of hearths for which a family was liable as an accurate indication of the size of its dwelling lies in the uncertainty about quite what the individual assessments include. Did some of the hearths heat outbuildings or provide heat for industrial purposes? We have little detailed understanding of this, although it might be noted that in just one place there is a hint of the complexity that might lie behind the assessments: in North Elmsall, in Osgoldcross wapentake, Lady Wentworth was assessed at twenty-one hearths plus a further hearth 'more for the dog kennel'.[3] Nevertheless, all these exceptions and considerations are unlikely to have been important enough to distort the overall correspondence between wealth and high hearth tax liability, and for the purposes of the present discussion any house of 10 or more hearths may be taken to indicate the existence of a family of at least local significance.

In the area of West Yorkshire in 1672 there were 132 houses of 10 or more hearths (see Map 14). Nearly three quarters of them (95 or 72 per cent) had between 10 and 14 hearths; 22 (16 per cent) had between 15 and 19 hearths; 8 (6 per cent) had between 20 and 24 hearths; and seven (6 per cent) wealthy men paid tax on 25 or more hearths – William Ramsden, Esquire, of Almondbury (25

[2] For a discussion of West Yorkshire towns in the Middle Ages, see G. Sheeran, *Medieval Yorkshire Towns: People, Buildings and Spaces* (Edinburgh, 1998).

[3] Manuscript volume, hearth tax, Lady Day 1672, Wakefield Metropolitan District Library (WMDL). TNA, E179/262/13, m 93v (presented here p. 355) suppresses this detail and simply records Thomas Wentworth, Esquire, as assessed on 22 hearths.

hearths); Sir John Lewis at Ledston (31 hearths) (Plate 1: Ledston Hall, Ledston);[4] the un-named occupier of the New Hall at Pontefract (34 hearths); Mr Sandford Nevile at Chevet (33 hearths); John Savile at Methley (43 hearths); Lord Brudenell at Howley, Morley (44 hearths); and the Lord Erwin at Temple Newsam (45 hearths). Virtually all the houses were occupied by titled families, from Lord Irwin at Temple Newsam, the knightly families at Ledston, Whitley, Farnley Tyas and elsewhere, the numerous 'esquires', to the most common group, the plain 'Mr's. Some families owned land in different parts of the county (and also outside it), and maintained more than one house: Sir John Kaye, for example, had residences of 22 and 20 hearths, in Farnley Tyas and Flockton.

At the extremes of our scale of large houses, there is a general, but not an absolute, correlation between title and size of house. At the top of the county rankings were two lords (Erwin and Brudenell), and, at the bottom end of our scale, among those families occupying houses with 10 or 11 hearths, were concentrated the minor gentry and the wealthiest yeomanry. Two other heads of noble families – Lady Jane Bland at Kippax (15 hearths) and Lady Ann Fairfax at Walton in Ainsty (17 hearths) – occupied only medium-sized residences. While John Savile, Esquire, paid tax on 43 hearths for his house at Methley, many other esquires only just crept into the category covered by this analysis: William Farrer of Midgley was assessed at 11 hearths and Thomas Burley of Chapel Allerton at only 10 hearths. Of the knightly families, Sir John Lewis led the field, with his large mansion of 31 hearths at Ledston, but Sir Lionel Pilkington of Stanley (14 hearths) and Sir Thomas Gascoigne of Parlington (12 hearths) occupied much more modest residences. Mr Sandford Nevile, at Chevet, paid tax on 33 hearths, but this was exceptional for someone with this title and might reflect Nevile's age (a minor?). For the rest, Mr Edward Starkie at East Riddlesden (16 hearths) and Mr Lindley at Bowling (19 hearths) stood out from the bulk of men of this title, who paid tax on between 10 and 15 hearths. The few entirely untitled individuals (Richard Peele of Gomersal, William Green of Liversedge and others) in the group lay at the bottom end of our scale, all, except a townsman, John Ingham of Halifax (17 hearths), paying tax on just ten or eleven hearths.[5]

The range within status groups was wider than the study of individuals assessed for tax on ten or more hearths has revealed. Nothing at the time of the hearth tax provided a cut-off point, at ten hearths or at any other point on the scale. There were a number of titled individuals assessed for tax on less than 10 hearths: Sir John Tempest of Tong (8 hearths), Sir Francis Gotherick of Altofts

[4] The document printed here, p. 330, lists only 25 hearths, but the manuscript volume in Wakefield includes 6 hearths 'not yet finished' WMDL. *Nomina Villarum*

[5] Thomas Stringer of Sharlston was assessed at 14 hearths: although lacking a title in the returns, Stringer was from an established gentry family, and the omission of a title in the returns is here treated as an oversight. This, of course, raises the question of how many other individuals of gentle status were given either no title or an incorrect title by the assessors.

(9 hearths), John Greene of Liversedge, gentleman (6 hearths), Nicholas Moore, Esquire, of Austhorpe (8 hearths), and Phillip Hamerton, Esquire, of Purston Jaglin (5 hearths), all fall into this category. For most men in this group, the assessment related to their principal or only residence and thus described a relatively modest way of life. We know that Nicholas Moore rebuilt his house at Austhorpe in 1694, and the Tempests did the same eight years later at Tong, so it is likely that in these cases, and doubtless in others as well, the hearth tax assessors were describing houses that were already old and outmoded.

The distribution of large houses within West Yorkshire was, as might be expected, uneven. There were few in the upland part of the county and those that existed were relatively modest in scale: west of Bradford and Huddersfield, only the Starkies at East Riddlesden (16 hearths) and Madam Thornhill at Fixby (15 hearths) had more than 14 hearths. In the central and eastern areas, the pattern was more even: the Aire valley, from Hawksworth in the north west to Methley and Ledston in the east, had a large number of substantial houses, as did the townships to the east of Wakefield. The eastern half of the county had all but one of the seven largest houses, and five of these lay east of Wakefield and Leeds.

The distribution of large houses: West Yorkshire's towns

West Yorkshire's towns had few very large houses in 1672. The wealthiest families in the county, whose fortunes were based on landed income or the profits of office, built their houses in the countryside at the centres of their estates. Among the county's largest houses, only the New Hall at Pontrefract lay close to a town, and this could not in any way be considered to be a town house. There is little evidence that county families maintained a house in a town, as happened in York in the eighteenth century and perhaps earlier.[6] Leeds, the town most likely to attract the gentry of the area, was a mercantile centre, with a growing professional class. When John Cossins came to depict it in 1727, the subscribers to his map and the owners of the houses shown on it were overwhelmingly either merchants or professional men.[7]

Topographical considerations – fitting in to the restricted burgage plots in the centres of towns – and a generally modest level of wealth placed a limit on the size of building which townsmen might construct. Large buildings might be either houses or inns, the hearth tax assessors making no distinction between them: it is thought that some of the largest buildings recorded in the Leeds hearth tax returns were inns, something borne out by the evidence of later rate

[6] RCHME, *An Inventory of the Historical Monuments in the City of York: Vol III, South-West of the Ouse* (London, 1972), 76, 85; RCHME, *An Inventory of the Historical Monuments in the City of York: Vol V, The Central Area* (London, 1981), 112; J. Harvey, *York* (London, 1975), 73–4, 85.

[7] H. Murray, *Scarborough, York and Leeds: the Town Plans of John Cossins 1697–1743* (York, 1997), 66–7.

books.[8] The largest building recorded in a West Yorkshire town was the 18-hearth house of Dr Maude in Halifax. John Ingham in Halifax and Mrs Bromley in Wakefield Westgate were each assessed at 17 hearths. Leeds, Wakefield and Halifax each had nine houses or inns with 10 or more hearths. Pontefract had four (including the New Hall) and Otley two. Street names are given in the hearth tax assessments for Leeds, Pontefract and Wakefield, and this allows a clear hierarchy of streets to emerge. In Leeds, the largest buildings were concentrated in Briggate, Milne Hill and Headrow, and Westgate stood out as the premier location in Wakefield.[9] What these streets were like in 1672 is difficult to judge: it is likely that they were still lined largely by timber-framed houses, jettied to the front, but brick was introduced to Leeds as early as 1628, and the process of transforming the appearance of the best streets was probably underway by 1672.[10]

The townships surrounding the more important towns had a high number of large houses. Hunslet (three), Wortley (one), Headingley cum Burley (two), Chapel Allerton (one) and Potternewton (one) lay adjacent to Leeds, and Stanley cum Wrenthorpe (four) and Warmfield cum Heath (two) lay to the north and east of Wakefield. It is possible that the 1672 hearth tax assessments capture an early stage in the mercantile flight from the crowded town centres, but perhaps more likely that they record the wish on the part of some wealthy landed families to be near to the facilities of these commercial, administrative and cultural centres. The village of Heath, known as the 'village of mansions', has an especially close physical relationship to Wakefield, perched on the river cliff above the town: by the eighteenth century it boasted three major houses, but only one existed at the time of the hearth tax.[11]

Patterns of wealth in rural West Yorkshire: the evidence of Hearth tax and houses

The hearth tax returns and the evidence of surviving houses are valuable sources for the study of material culture, but their interpretation is by no means straightforward. There is, furthermore, a developing view that they cannot be taken as crude indices of wealth. The existence of a pattern of high hearth tax assessments and of large surviving houses may certainly be taken to indicate the desire and ability on the part of their occupiers to build substantial, comfortable dwellings, whether in a spirit of emulation or for other reasons. The absence of such a pattern elsewhere, however, might not always be reliable evidence of lower

[8] M. W. Beresford, 'East End, West End: the face of Leeds during urbanisation 1684–1842', *Publications of the Thoresby Society*, 50–1 (131–2) (1988), 23, 84.

[9] Ibid., 15

[10] Ibid., 32

[11] D. Linstrum, *West Yorkshire, Architects and Architecture* (London, 1978), 72–3.

levels of personal wealth. Cultural differences and the type of wealth commonly present (and therefore its availability for investment in housing) may have been important influences on families' decisions not to build anew or improve an existing house. The gathering of evidence from different regions and from different sources will help to inform this debate about the interpretation of documentary and architectural evidence relating to the development of a consumer society.[12]

Critical to the use of surviving houses as historical evidence is awareness of the degree to which the examples remaining to us, or known through records made before demolition, represent earlier patterns with tolerable accuracy. The hearth tax returns provide an indication of where substantial houses are likely to be found, or at least of where they once existed, but the picture of survival of pre-1672 houses within West Yorkshire is extremely uneven. The expansion of the county's towns in the nineteenth and twentieth centuries led to widespread destruction of rural landscapes with their early housing, and industrial development, particularly the mining industry, caused further losses. It is now, for example, impossible to get an accurate idea of the extent of good permanent housing of pre-1672 date in the environs of Leeds: there are a few good surviving vernacular houses of this date, but many more are likely to have been demolished as the city engulfed the adjacent townships. Only the hearth tax returns give an indication of the extent to which the inhabitants of these townships had been able to provide themselves with housing above the minimum standard before the late seventeenth century. Elsewhere in the county, however, losses have been less severe: not all the eastern area was overrun by mines and expanding towns, and in the western hills much of the post-medieval landscape survives remarkably well. There is, therefore, sufficient material in terms of surviving housing, and confidence that this survival represents earlier conditions reasonably accurately, to allow the hearth tax returns and houses to be used together to study the distrubution of wealth in the late seventeenth century.

Two maps of the distribution of taxable wealth in West Yorkshire give the starting point for the study of sub-regional patterns of wealth (Maps 15 and 16). The patterns indicated by the distribution of single-hearth households and of households with more than four hearths tell different sides of the same story. In much of the western part of the county, in the Pennines and their fringes, there were high levels of single-hearth houses and few larger houses, and this pattern extended across much of the northern part of the centre and east of the county:

[12] M. Overton *et al*, *Production and Consumption in English Households 1600–1750* (London, 2004) use the evidence of probate inventories for Kent and Cornwall to point up striking differences in the patterns of personal wealth and cultures of consumption in the two counties; see especially 'Conclusions', 170–7. For a discussion of the reliability of the documentary sources – hearth tax returns, probate inventories and surviving houses – commonly used to study the distribution of wealth in the seventeenth century, see also P.S. Barnwell, 'Houses, Hearths and Historical Inquiry' in *Houses and the Hearth Tax*, 177–83.

in upland Haworth, for example, 76 per cent of chargeable houses had only a single hearth, and in Bramhope, on the moor above the Wharfe valley, the proportion was 82 per cent. In a band across the centre of the county, broad in the east where it embraced the townships around both Leeds and Wakefield, tapering in the west in the townships around Halifax, there were few 'poor' townships where half or more of households were assessed at a single hearth. A number of townships in this area, for example, Skircoat, near Halifax (16 per cent), Gomersal, in the central area (13 per cent), and Darrington, in the east (14 per cent), had a significant proportion of houses with more than four hearths.

The hearth tax assessments may be taken, at one level, as strong evidence for the degree to which the population of West Yorkshire had, by 1672, engaged in a process of rebuilding their houses or improving them in line with contemporary ideas on what their dwellings should provide. This 'Great Rebuilding', first drawn to the attention of modern historians by W. G. Hoskins, and subsequently taken as a starting point for the study of vernacular houses, largely involved the replacement of simple medieval dwellings by houses of more sophisticated form (having, for example, large numbers of rooms, some of them heated, with increasingly specialised functions) and more durable materials.[13] So the hearth tax assessments might reasonably be taken to indicate the extent to which complex, comfortable, 'modern' dwellings had been constructed by 1672. The surviving houses of this rebuilding also, of course, contribute to the debate, and allow a more rounded picture of this important social and economic phenomenon.

The question of the extent to which different areas within the West Riding had witnessed a substantial rebuilding or improvement of its housing stock may be tested through closer examination of two areas – western and eastern – of similar size within West Yorkshire. The hearth tax returns indicate that the townships around Halifax had generally high levels of wealth as represented by the proportions of large houses (those with more than four hearths), and similar proportions can be found in the area to the east of Wakefield (Map 17). The two areas show many contrasts. The western area is more naturally defined, forming part of the upper Calder valley and having clear boundaries in the watersheds to north and south. In terms of terrain and land use, thin and poor soils made cultivation difficult and many townships had large expanses of open moorland, useful only for grazing and for attracting peat for fuel.[14] The eastern area is something of an artificial construct, being defined more to include townships with high levels of wealth than to comprise a discrete geographical region, but there was within it sufficient cohesion to provide useful points of comparison with the

[13] W. G. Hoskins, 'The Rebuilding of Rural England 1570–1640', *Past and Present*, 4 (1953), 44–59.

[14] S. A. Moorhouse, 'Communications', in *West Yorkshire: an Archaeological Survey to A D 1500, Volume 3 The Rural Medieval Landscape*, eds. M. I. Faull and S. A. Moorhouse (Wakefield, 1981), 624–5.

Table 1: Eastern and western sample areas: house size

		Hearths (%)								
	Acreage	1	2	3	4	5	6	>6	Exempt	Total
Eastern area	42982	472	270	131	79	36	22	47	155	**1212**
		39	*22*	*11*	*7*	*3*	*2*	*4*	*13*	***101***
Western area	43072	736	440	239	154	79	34	38	119	**1839**
		40	*24*	*13*	*8*	*4*	*2*	*2*	*6*	***99***
West as % of East	100	156	163	182	195	219	154	81	77	**151**

Acreages taken from Ordnance Survey first edition 6" maps, c.1840–50.

Halifax district. It was more favoured in its land, being low-lying and including the lower reaches of both the Aire and the Calder, and it was a well-farmed area with little waste and with good access to local market towns.

Table 1 and Map 17 present the evidence of the hearth tax for the two areas. Overall, the composition of society, as represented by the proportions of householders assessed for tax on different numbers of hearths, appears remarkably similar: in the east, for example, 39 per cent of householders were assessed on a single hearth, while the west had 40 per cent in this category, and there are no significant differences throughout the scale except amongst those exempted from tax: 6 per cent in the west and 13 per cent in the east.

A closer look at the two areas begins to reveal some important distinctions. There were some exceptional townships in the east where proportions were distorted by the dominance of a large house: in Chevet, Mr Sandford Nevill's house (33 hearths) was the only dwelling, and Nostell Priory (24 hearths) was one of only three houses in the township of Foulby. Leaving aside Pontefract, there were fifteen houses with ten or more hearths but not all dominated their townships in similar fashion. Kippax, Methley and Ledston each had a great house, but the hearth tax returns in these townships show a wide range of assessments from single-hearth households through the middling ranks to the large houses of five or more hearths. Some townships without a great house, like Walton and Sandal Magna, had a high proportion of householders with assessments ranging from three up to six hearths and more. Significantly, 8.9 per cent of all assessed heads of households in this eastern area had titles, most of them simply 'Mr', and in the category of houses with more than four hearths two thirds were occupied by titled heads (Table 2). The hearth tax returns for the eastern townships describe an area where great houses were a powerful influence; where titled families were common, especially among the occupiers of the larger houses; but where society contained a modest number of non-titled households of some standing. The

Table 2: West Yorkshire Hearth Tax, 1672: east and west sample areas: titled heads of household (excludes widows)

	Total households	Titled heads (%)	Total households with > 4 hearths	Titled heads (%)
Eastern area	1212	108 (*8.9*)	105	68 (*65*)
Western area	1839	45 (*2.5*)	151	26 (*17*)

social make up is not the stereotypical image of a population of great families on the one hand and a servile tenantry on the other, but nevertheless the dominant influence was clearly that of the numerous titled families.

When the western area is examined, a very different picture begins to emerge. There were no great houses in the rural area around Halifax: the largest house was that of Mr Thomas Horton of Barkisland, with 14 hearths, and the town of Halifax excepted, there were only six houses with 10 or more hearths (Plate 2: Barkisland Hall). Resident titled families were similarly little in evidence, making up only a sixth of the occupiers of houses with more than four hearths and only 2.5 per cent of all assessed heads of households. In the absence of a resident aristocracy, and with only weak representation by the gentry, the yeomanry was the dominant group in society. In Norland, all seven houses of more than four hearths were occupied by untitled families, and in Northowram only two out of 18 houses with more than four hearths were occupied by people with titles. The proportion of exempted households is low in this area, suggesting that poverty was less of an issue here than in the east.

The eastern and western areas are very different in the types, numbers and dates of their surviving houses. In the east, surviving houses include, as one might expect given the evidence of the hearth tax, aristocratic and gentry houses. Some gentry houses had, by the late seventeenth century, grown around a medieval core: Sharlston Hall, for example, had expanded in many phases to the point where, in 1672, it had fourteen hearths, some in the medieval hall-and-cross-wings house, others in added wings and extensions.[15] There are, in addition, a modest number of yeoman houses built in the seventeenth century and probably recorded in the hearth tax. Some new seventeenth-century houses were timber-framed: the wing at Nook Inn, Oulton, bears the date 1611.[16] Most, certainly by the mid-seventeenth century, were built in stone. The new or improved yeoman houses were generally simple in form. They commonly had

[15] *Inventory of the Historical Monuments in the City of York*, 212

[16] RCHME, *Rural Houses of West Yorkshire 1400–1830* (London, 1986), 117.

either a linear plan with three rooms in line, with heating in the housebody, parlour and perhaps also the kitchen; others had the main heated rooms at the front and unheated service rooms to the rear. A good example of a substantial mid-seventeenth century yeoman house in the east of the county is Rose Farm, Walton: well built of stone and with a good finish externally and internally, it had three heated rooms to the front and service rooms in a rear outshut (Plate 3: Rose Farm, Walton).[17] Using the evidence of surviving buildings, it is possible to suggest that, at the time of the hearth tax assessment in 1672, the east of the county had a good range of modern or improved dwellings, some at least built by yeoman-farmers but many others by the gentry and aristocracy.

In the western area the pattern of surviving houses describes a very different society. As noted above, the great house is absent, but there were gentry families of modest status. Many of these had, by 1672, constructed solid houses showing many of the features of sophisticated planning and comfort characteristic of gentry houses elsewhere in the country. The best example is Wood Lane Hall, Sowerby, built in 1649 by John Dearden, a first-generation gentleman risen from clothier origins (Plate 4: Wood Lane Hall). In 1672 Dearden was assessed on eight hearths, and the house shows a mix of the traditional – the hall rising through two storeys – and the modern – the proliferation of heated parlours and chambers and the incorporation of an internal kitchen. Vastly outnumbering the gentry houses in the west, however, are surviving houses built by yeomen. By 1672, the rebuilding or improving of medieval timber-framed houses by the wealthier yeomen was largely complete in the upper Calder valley: over 150 houses with datestones recording building activity from before 1670 are known in the valley as a whole.[18] As well as being numerous, these yeoman houses are varied in character and complexity: towards the upper end of the scale of wealth and sophistication are houses like Peel House, Warley, with a hall-and-cross-wing plan, a central rear kitchen wing and heating in the housebody, the kitchen, the parlour and probably the chamber over the parlour (Plate 5: Peel House). In 1672, the probable occupier, Widow Waide, was assessed on five hearths. Other new or remodelled houses were smaller: the two-cell house with housebody and parlour to the front and service rooms in an outshut to the rear, was common.[19]

Two principal questions arise from this picture of contrasts. The first concerns the apparent conflict between the evidence of the hearth tax returns and of surviving houses. It has been established (Table 1) that eastern and western areas show remarkably similar proportions of individuals assessed for tax at different levels, evidence which might lead one to the conclusion that society was similarly constituted in the two. It has also been established that the numbers and types of

[17] For a fuller discussion of the pattern of building in the east of the county, see ibid., 116–21; for Rose Farm, Walton, see ibid., 219

[18] Ibid., 109

[19] For a discussion of upper Calder valley houses, see ibid., 107–12

surviving seventeenth century houses are very different in the two areas, and, although allowance must be made for the distortions created by later loss of evidence, this pattern may be taken to suggest real contrasts in the ability or desire of individuals in east and west to invest in improved housing. The resolution of the apparent conflict is straightforward. Two aspects of the evidence stand out as important. First, although similar in proportions, the hearth tax assessments for the two areas show telling differences in social composition. In the east an extraordinary proportion of the houses, especially the larger houses, were occupied by titled families, while in the west the yeomen were the dominant social group. It is therefore not surprising that the rebuilding and improvement of yeoman dwellings should have been so much more advanced in the west.

The second explanation for the apparent conflict between the sources lies in absolute numbers rather than in the proportions of individuals assessed for tax at different levels. Table 1 reveals that, in the two sample areas of approximately equal size, the townships around Halifax supported half as many households again as those to the east of Wakefield, with particular dominance in houses of between two and five hearths. These are precisely those most likely to have been built and occupied by families of yeoman status. The populous nature of the area is especially remarkable given the low productivity of the land. The large number of surviving seventeenth-century houses in the upper Calder valley confirms and refines the conclusion to be drawn from the hearth tax returns that the yeomanry here was, by 1672, numerous, prosperous and able to express its economic power in the concrete form of improved housing of some sophistication. Conversely, the relative scarcity of yeoman houses in the east of the county demonstrates that here significant numbers in this social group had either not attained the levels of wealth which permitted investment in improved living conditions or developed the desire to use spare capital for this purpose.

The second principal question arising from the picture of sub-regional variety which has emerged from study of the hearth tax returns and of surviving early houses relates to the underlying causes of the observed pattern. The regional differences result principally from the nature of the economy in the two areas. The east was an agricultural district, probate inventories and estate records revealing that cereal cultivation and livestock husbandry were the main props in the local economy. Open-field cultivation was still common in this period, and many of the improvements dependent on enclosure were not introduced until the eighteenth century.[20] The fact that the land was a finite resource, virtually fully exploited by the late seventeenth century, meant that relatively few could gain a comfortable living from it. Gentry and aristocratic landowners led the way in the development of commercialised agriculture and gained most from their

[20] For the Bright family's management of their Badsworth estate, see P. Roebuck, *Yorkshire Baronets 1640–1760: Families, Estates and Fortunes* (Oxford, 1980), 212–38.

ownership of the land. Thomas Stringer of Sharlston, from a long-established gentry family, sold more than £330 worth of cereals and legumes in the five years 1638–42 and also derived an income from his rent roll. The evidence of the larger yeoman houses indicates that the more substantial yeomen played a part in a commercial agricultural economy, but for most farmers income and profits were doubtless less. For these families, surplus capital was limited and very closely devoted to the needs of the agricultural economy, leaving only modest amounts to invest in new and improved housing.[21] Valuable mineral rights, especially for the working of coal, were controlled by the landowners, who sometimes exploited their own mines, sometimes took leases from other landowners, and sometimes granted leases for others to extract coal. While not as finite a resource as land, minerals were not open to profitable exploitation by all, and gentry control restricted the degree to which coal mining could contribute to the creation of a numerous and prosperous yeoman group in society.[22]

The high population of the west of the county, and in particular of the Calder valley, was not sustained by agriculture. As already remarked, much of the cultivable land here gave a poor return and the area was dominated by huge expanses of moorland. Agriculture here provided a valuable supplementary source of income, but brought wealth to very few. Nor was mineral extraction the cause of great wealth among either the gentry or the yeomanry of the Pennines, although again coal was commonly worked and gave an income to some. The primary source of income and wealth in the upper Calder valley was, of course, the production of woollen and worsted cloth, and both gentry and yeomanry benefited from it. For landowning families, ownership of fulling mills provided useful income, but their control ceased there.[23] For the rest, the profits of industry were generated by both merchants and manufacturers, the former based mainly in the region's towns, the latter in the countryside in a large area to the west of Leeds and Wakefield and stretching up into the Pennines. The wealth revealed in the 1672 hearth tax returns in this area was principally derived from textiles: Gomersal and Liversedge in central West Yorkshire and Skircoat and Sowerby in the upper Calder valley were manufacturing townships, part of Defoe's 'noble scene of industry'. Despite trade fluctuations, engagement in cloth production brought sustained economic benefit, both for the master manufacturers and for the spinners and weavers working for them. Unlike agriculture, textiles production could support a large population, and Defoe

[21] K. Wrightson, *Earthly Necessities: Economic Lives in Early Modern Britain 1470–1750* (London, 2000), 53–5 discusses the precarious nature of the agricultural economy, with modest surpluses even in good years, in the late medieval period. Wrightson moves on to describe the development of a commercialised agricultural economy, which brought wealth principally to the gentry and leading yeomen.

[22] For gentry control of agriculture and mineral extraction, see J. T. Cliffe, *The Yorkshire Gentry from the Reformation to the Civil War* (London, 1969), 49–66; Cliffe gives details of Thomas Stringer's income from his Sharlston estate.

[23] Ibid., 52–3

remarked on how, in the area between Halifax and Leeds, 'the whole country is infinitely populous'.[24]

What Defoe witnessed in the early eighteenth century was true also of the late seventeenth century. Many prosperous yeoman-clothiers had, by the time of the hearth tax, built large houses, the centre both of their domestic life and of their business operations, for these houses commonly included a shop or workshop filled with the tools of their trades and with stocks of wool and cloth. Below the level of the master-manufacturer were smaller operators, again able to build permanent and substantial houses although on a more modest scale. And below these were the hundreds or thousands of households which derived a living, often an uncertain one, by working for the manufacturers. The high population of the textiles area was supported by its engagement in different aspects of production: there were handsome profits for many and work for the rest. The contrast between the area's harsh terrain and its large population and prosperity was noted by early commentators, for in the early seventeenth century it was remarked how the Halifax district showed the truth of the old saying that 'barraine places give a good edge to industry'.[25]

Hearths and living standards in late seventeenth-century West Yorkshire

The evidence of the hearth tax returns is one-dimensional, simply quantifying the number of hearths in a house. They therefore give little impression of the ways of life which were conducted in dwellings of different sizes and degrees of sophistication. A more rounded view of seventeenth-century living standards emerges when the quantitative material of the returns is considered alongside more of the qualitative evidence provided by two principal sources, the surviving houses of the period and contemporary probate inventories. Houses are complex artefacts: they are made up of more than hearths, and the numbers, features and uses of their rooms. The relationship between spaces within a dwelling, gives a better three-dimensional view of the living conditions hinted at by the hearth tax returns. Probate inventories are a familiar source to historians of material culture: full of traps for the unwary, they have been widely used to demonstrate changing living standards, but in recent years a more rigorous approach to their analysis has been developed so as to avoid the distortions that can so easily result from indiscriminate use.[26] For the West Riding, few probate

[24] D. Defoe, *A tour through the Whole Island of Great Britain*, ed. P. Rogers (London, 1971), 500.

[25] Camden, W., *Britain, or A chorographicall description of the most flourishing kingdomes, England, Scotland, and Ireland, and the Islands adjoyning, out of the depth of antiquitie: : beautified with mappes of the severall shires of England* (London, 1637), 692. For the early history of the West Riding textile industry, see P. Hudson, *The Genesis of Industrial Capital: a study of the West Riding Wool Textile Industry c.1750–1850* (Cambridge, 1986), and for a fuller discussion of the link between industry and housing in West Yorkshire, see *Rural Houses of West Yorkshire*, 106–32.

[26] For further discussion, see *Production and Consumption*; L. Weatherill, *Consumer Behaviour and Material Culture in Britain 1660–1760* (London, 2nd edn, 1996).

inventories survive from the period of the hearth tax, but good survival from 1688 allows a picture to emerge which, in all probability, closely conforms to the conditions which obtained in 1672.

The vast majority of houses recorded in the hearth tax returns had just a single hearth. This heated the housebody, the West Riding term for the hall. The room was the all-purpose living area of the house, used for cooking. In many, perhaps even most, of the single-hearth houses counted in the returns, the housebody was open to the roof. Heating was provided by a hearth set within a large fire area. The smoke from the fire was drawn up into a firehood, a cavernous timber and plaster flue supported by a heavy timber bressumer beam over the fireplace and rising through the roof covering (Plate 6: Carlton Husthwaite). At one end of the housebody might be a small, unheated parlour (used principally as a bedroom) with a chamber over, and at the other end might be a workshop or, in some parts of the West Riding, a byre for the shelter of animals. Ralph Roades of Thornhill, yeoman, died in 1689, and his house consisted of a housebody, with all the paraphernalia required for cooking as well as tables, forms and chairs; a parlour, clearly an unheated bedroom used also for storage of cereal crops; and a chamber, again a bedroom used also for storage.[27] Houses of this type, revealed both by surviving houses and inventories, represented a perpetuation of the way of life common to the majority of the population in the Middle Ages (Plate 7: Birks). A considerable number of the houses may indeed have been a century or more old at the time of the assessment, but others were more recent versions of the established form. Some houses of this type survive today, although in much altered form and severely under-representing their former ubiquity: others were noticed by antiquarians as curiosities in the nineteenth and twentieth centuries.[28]

Not all single-hearth houses, however, should be regarded as the primitive homes of the poorest levels of society. As far as can be determined from fragmentary surviving evidence, the substantial timber-framed yeoman houses of the area, dating from the late Middle Ages, had just a single hearth. However, their solid construction, generous scale and some of their features – such as the dais canopy commonly found at the upper end of the housebody – marked them out as the homes of families of substance, at least in a local context (Plate 8: Bankhouse). The provision of additional heated rooms was central to the process of housing improvement in the seventeenth century and later, but it was not the

[27] Borthwick, inventory of Ralph Roades, Thornhill, Pontefract Deanery, May 1689.

[28] A small cottage in Baildon, for example, was observed in some detail in 1884: the cottage was 'of singularly primitive construction. The rock … had been bared and levelled, and in it were sunk four holes … Four massive oak timbers, shaped something like a boomerang … were inserted into the holes, two and two, so that each pair met at the top. … A wall has been built round, and a fireplace and chimney in the middle completed the cottage. I saw this picturesque and interesting building in 1884; it was pulled down shortly afterwards' W. P. Baildon, *Baildon and the Baildons* (3 vols., privately printed, 1912–27), II, 48–9; *Rural Houses of West Yorkshire*, 42, 191.

only way in which houses might reflect changing living standards. Better quality construction and the adoption of the full two-storeyed dwelling, dispensing at last with the open housebody, were other aspects of the process. Flailcroft, in Todmorden, may have been built with just a single hearth, heating the housebody, and indeed it is at the smaller end of the scale of surviving seventeenth-century houses (Plate 9: Flailcroft). But its building materials and its provision of chambers over all the ground-floor rooms demonstrate that the one-hearth houses recorded in the hearth tax assessments were by no means all of unimproved character and occupied by the poor. We do not know who built Flailcroft, but clearly the family was far above the poverty line.[29]

If single-hearth houses were easily the most common house type in late seventeenth-century West Yorkshire, larger and more elaborate dwellings were nevertheless present in substantial numbers. It is in these houses that improved living standards are most clearly expressed. A yardstick for measuring this improvement is provided by the houses of the area's gentry families, for all our sources – hearth tax assessments, probate inventories and surviving buildings – testify to the fact that, by 1672, the West Yorkshire gentry fully shared in the national movement which created complex and sophisticated houses with many heated rooms of increasingly specialised function.[30] A good local example is East Riddlesden Hall, near Keighley: although it shows many peculiarities, it displays in the partial rebuilding of 1648 many of the chief themes in the development of the seventeenth-century gentry residence (Plates 10a, 10b: East Riddlesden Hall, exterior and interior). Whether consciously in a spirit of emulation, or simply out of more utilitarian and practical considerations reflecting changing ways of life, the middling ranks of the county's society went in the same direction, albeit generally with more modest means and ambitions.

After the single-hearth house, dwellings with two hearths were the most common in the hearth tax returns. Surviving houses and probate inventories indicate that, in these more complex houses, the housebody remained the general purpose living and cooking room, still usually heated by a firehood. The second heated room was most commonly a parlour, used generally as the best bedroom and often, in addition, as a sitting room or storeroom. Timothy Sutcliffe, yeoman, of Northowram, who died in 1689, had a dwelling with a housebody for cooking, living and dining; a heated parlour for sleeping and sitting, furnished with a bed, chairs, tables and a glasscase; a second parlour for meal storage; a buttery; and chambers over the two main ground-floor rooms.[31] The parlour fireplace was invariably set within a stone chimney stack and might

[29] *Rural Houses of West Yorkshire*, 218.

[30] For a full discussion of this process, see N. Cooper, *The Houses of the Gentry 1400–1680.* (New Haven and London, 1999). For a summary of the West Yorkshire evidence, see C. Giles, 'The West Riding Hearth tax Returns of 1672: what do they tell us about the Great Rebuilding?', in *Houses and the Hearth Tax*, 132–43.

[31] Borthwick, inventory of Timothy Sutcliffe, Northowram, Pontefract Deanery, June 1689.

have a simple moulded surround. The modest investment required to provide a second heated room does not adequately reflect the significance of the new domestic arrangements: the parlour fireplace introduced, at quite modest levels of society and in admittedly diluted form, some of the ideas of household living common among the contemporary gentry: the heated parlour might have acted as a private sitting room and certainly provided a degree of comfort not present in simpler houses.

Greater sophistication and more specialisation in room use are evident at the level of the three-hearth house. Many of these houses demonstrate a significant development, that is, the removal of all or most of the cooking to a kitchen. This allowed a more 'polite' use for both the housebody and the principal heated parlour, although the opportunity was apparently not always taken. In 1693 Daniel Thorpe of Sharlston died with a house where both housebody and kitchen were used for cooking, but the 'new parlour' was a well furnished heated sitting and dining room, not used also as a bedroom; and John Hanson, of Warley, had a housebody, a heated kitchen with spits and cooking pans, and a heated dining parlour, again not used as a bedroom.[32] Beds had been banished to the first floor, an important step on the road to modern ways of living. Rose Farm, Walton (see Plate 3), is a well-built example of the three-hearth house dating from the middle decades of the seventeenth century: the heated rooms – kitchen, housebody and parlour – line the main front, and service rooms are contained within an outshut at the rear. Kitchens were commonly heated by a fire beneath a firehood, for the large fire area allowed room for working, but the housebody, released from some at least of the cooking tasks, could have a fireplace within a stone chimney stack: at Rose Farm, a single stack provides heating for housebody and parlour.

In houses of three or fewer hearths, the advances made in heating before the late seventeenth century were confined to the ground floor. Houses with two or three heated ground-floor rooms might have had a full range of chambers, but these were very rarely heated. The low status of first-floor rooms is indicated by probate inventories, which show that they were used for sleeping for lesser members of the household and for storage: in Michael Gragg's house in Knottingley in 1693, there were four chambers: none was heated, only one contained a bed, and two, including the best chamber, were used for cereals storage. The best bedroom was an unheated ground-floor parlour.[33]

The hearth tax returns demonstrate that, in 1672, a significant number of non-titled families occupied houses with more than three hearths. Inventories and surviving buildings show that the larger yeoman houses could be both well

[32] Borthwick, inventories of Daniel Thorpe, Sharlston, and John Hanson, Warley, Pontefract Deanery, December 1693, August 1693.

[33] Borthwick, inventory of Michael Graggs, Knottingley, Pontefract Deanery, June 1693.

appointed and furnished, even rivalling some of the houses of the lesser gentry. By the late seventeenth century, larger yeoman houses might have more than one heated parlour and, a significant innovation at this social level, one or more heated chambers. Thomas Brook's house in Liversedge had, in 1693, a housebody used as a dining room and furnished with tables, forms and chairs; a kitchen for cooking; a heated best parlour for dining, with a table and fourteen chairs; a heated little parlour for sleeping and withdrawing; a heated best chamber; and other rooms including unheated sleeping chambers, service rooms, and a workshop, stocked with a clothier's trade goods.[34] In these large yeoman houses, the housebody and best parlour could be decorated with carved fireplaces, plaster overmantels, panelling, and in a few houses, plaster ceilings similar to those common in contemporary gentry houses (Plates 11a and b: Lower Old Hall, Norland). In rare cases, the best chamber might also have some decorative features.

Increasingly by the late seventeenth century, the use of a firehood was restricted to the kitchen, all other hearths being provided in stone or brick chimney stacks. By then, and perhaps more commonly thereafter, houses which had been built with a firehood in the housebody, but which also had a kitchen, were updated by replacing the firehood by a fireplace within a smaller chimney stack (Plate 12: Roebucks, Warley). At High Bentley, Shelf, this alteration took probably took place in the 1660s, when the medieval timber-framed house was cased in stone, and at Peel House, Warley, the new fireplace bears the date 1691. In both houses, the kitchen retained its firehood to serve the cooking hearth. In some large yeoman houses, therefore, the housebody lost its old range of functions, and the decorative nature of the new fireplaces indicates that the room now had a more refined use as a reception area, similar to that of the hall in a gentry house. A few mid and late seventeenth-century houses abandoned the firehood altogether, even in the cooking hearth, for which wide, stone-arched fireplaces were increasingly used: at Heaton Royds Farmhouse, Heaton, the fireplace in the kitchen dates probably from 1634, while that in the housebody at Glenesk Farm, Morton, is of late seventeenth-century date (Plates, 13, 14).

Summary

The hearth tax returns are a source of major importance for the study of seventeenth-century society, and their value is increased when their evidence is set alongside that of other sources, both documentary and architectural. The returns and the surviving houses demonstrate with vivid clarity the existence within the West Riding of highly distinctive 'countries'. The particular identity of these countries was made up in part, of course, by the character of the different

[34] Borthwick, inventory of Thomas Brook, Edderscliffe, Liversedge, Pontefract Deanery, May 1693.

natural landscapes found within the county. But while geography might have provided one of the primary determinants, it was the different ways in which the people of the county built their society and their livelihoods which lay at the heart of local character. The varied nature of landholding patterns and the different economic opportunities open to people throughout the West Riding shaped the fortunes of the population over many centuries. The hearth tax records the effects of these influences by demonstrating how society had developed in different parts of the county, with some areas characterised by aristocratic and gentry dominance within a largely agrarian economy and others by a more socially diverse society profitably employed in industrial or commercial activities. The surviving houses provide further evidence for distinctive 'countries'. They display strong vernacular features giving local character to areas across the county, in both the Pennine west and lowland east. And, more important in relation to the hearth tax, they also demonstrate clear differences in the degree to which key social groups in different parts of the county had invested in improved 'modern' housing by the late seventeenth century. While the pattern of surviving houses supports and refines what we learn of this process of rebuilding from the hearth tax, the physical evidence of the houses reveals something of the reality of what that improvement involved in terms of changing living standards. The two sources together make a major contribution to our understanding of how people at different social levels, and in the different 'countries' within the West Riding, lived in the late seventeenth century.

The Documents Used In This Edition

by Duncan Harrington

The core of this edition was once a large roll for the West Riding, compiled for the collection due at Lady Day 1672, which formed the twentieth collection of the hearth tax. This roll has since been divided and now forms a number of separate smaller rolls in the National Archives within the E179 series of 'subsidy rolls', the large section of Exchequer records devoted to direct taxation. These smaller rolls each concern one or two wapentakes within the West Riding, E179/210/400 (Claro), E179/210/412 (Staincross), E179/210/413 (Agbrigg and Morley), E179/210/415 (Osgoldcross), E179/ 210/417 (Skyrack), E179/262/14 (Barkston Ash), E179/262/15 (Strafforth and Tickhill)) and E179/210/418 (Staincliffe and Ewcross). Further details can be found in the special section of the National Archives web-site dedicated to this category of Exchequer documents: <www.nationalarchives.gov.uk/E179/>. Here Dr Jonathan Mackman, the cataloguer of E179 documents for Yorkshire, comments that, "The stitching marks clearly show that the present piece was once arranged as one continuous roll, with the membranes stitched end-to-end, and it would seem likely that all the pieces listed above were once joined together as one huge roll." The returns, in their present state, suggest that the original large roll was dismembered by modern 'conservators' who misplaced several of the membranes when restitching them. For the purposes of this edition the original sequence has been reconstructed, with explanations given where the modern numeration no longer progresses normally.

The compiler used only the fine inner side of the parchment. To join the membranes the ends were folded about 10mm at the top and bottom and hooked to the next membrane. The individual membranes were pinned at their four corners preparatory to being ruled, generally in pencil, but sometimes in ink. It is not possible to say at what point the membranes were sewn together, before the compiler entered the information on them, or after. Some clumsiness in the modern restitching has obscured a number of the entries. For instance, in the Claro wapentake roll, E179/210/400, entries are written along the folds created between membranes 18 & 19 and membranes 68 & 69. Careful scrutiny of such entries has enabled us to give these entries correctly and in full. The membranes are approximately 130mm to 140mm wide and vary in length from approximately 745mm to about 900mm. The documents currently comprise two membranes, joined as above, and stitched through at their upper end to form a number of rotulets.

In the case of E179/210/412 the scribe ruled the first nine membranes up in ink and then reverted to pencil returning to ink later in the document. It is not safe to assume that this was the convenient number of membranes joined together before being written upon and subsequently joined to the section above. Because the membranes are now only joined in their original format in pairs it is very difficult to make any judgement on the procedure the scribe employed in transcribing and joining this colossal document.

The whole return for the West Riding was written by one clerk – quite a feat. He was methodical in correcting his errors with hearth numbers, by writing the correct figure in words next to the corrected Arabic number. So he put 'three' next to '3'.

The compiler of the West Riding return sometimes, but not invariably, wrote 'ii' when he meant 11 (eleven) and 'iii' when he meant 111 (one hundred and eleven). At no point did he wish to convey either two or three when he used these forms. Occasionally he wrote 'i' for 1 (one). It was thought best just to treat the practice as a mannerism of the compiler. All the figures are now given in Arabic numerals. This avoided superfluous footnotes. The compiler was not using Roman numerals, only quirky Arabic ones.

The return for the wapentake of Claro (E179/210/400) is exceptional in having a heading. This creates a strong presumption that it was the first return in the roll as delivered into the Exchequer. The heading explicitly states that the piece forms the return of James Collins, collector in the West Riding of the Lady Day 1672 payment. As well as the generic title 'Ebo[rum] Westrideing ending att lady 1672', it also has on the reverse of this first membrane in Latin that, 'It was delivered by the hand of John Peables clerk of the peace within written the sixth day of December in the 27th year of the reign of Charles the Second' [1675]. Written by one of the Exchequer clerks it probably demonstrates that this membrane was on the outside of the roll. It appears that not only was this handed to the Exchequer over three years after the return was made, but also with at least one other document, E179/210/399 which was a return for the whole riding for Michaelmas 1671 and Lady Day 1672 giving the 'old view' and 'new view' and giving details of increases and decreases in taxable hearths in each settlement: hearths demolished, new built, fallen down and those now empty. It looks as if the two documents were produced as part of the same process, possibly during an investigation into arrears. E179/210/399 was presumably compiled to provide an explanation to the Exchequer of the differences between the Lady Day 1672 collection and previous payments. It is possible that an undated schedule of defaulters for the West Riding was also handed in at the same time.

Equally, we can surmise that the last wapentake in the original roll was Barkston Ash wapentake (E179/262/14), since its last membrane has the subscription of three justices of the peace and the clerk of the peace. Furthermore this last membrane only has stitching marks at its head. The following assessment, that for Lady Day 1673, also began with Claro wapentake and

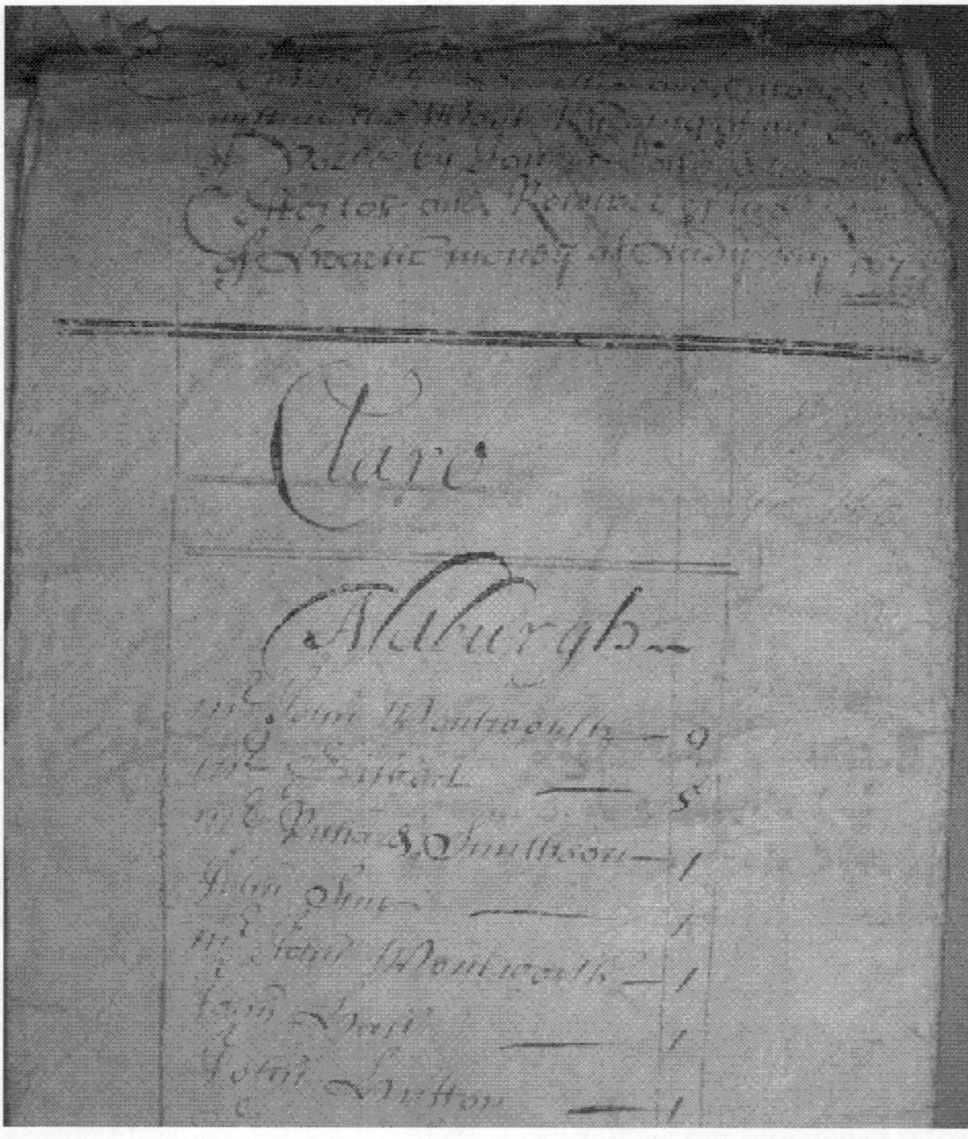

Plate 15 The original beginning of the Lady Day 1672 assessment roll for the West Riding. Now the first membrane of the Claro Wapentake assessment. National Archives E179/210/400 m.1. See transcript p. 137, and comment p. 81.

ended with Barkston Ash. The order of the intervening wapentakes was Agbrigg and Morley, Staincliffe, Strafforth and Tickhill, Osgoldcross, Staincross, and Skyrack. The assessment for Lady Day 1672 may also have followed this order. However, since we cannot tell whether this was so, the separate rolls for each wapentake or pair of wapentakes have been arranged geographically from north to south for the purposes of this edition.

Ainsty

Since no Lady Day 1672 return for the Ainsty wapentake appears to have survived in the National Archives, the return for the Ainsty has been taken from the sheriff's return now at Wakefield Metropolitan District Council Library, as the *Nomina Villarum.*[1] This return comes from an earlier stage in the accounting process than the Exchequer copy, and indeed the Exchequer copy is most probably derived from this return, or both may derive from some now lost roll kept by the receivers. The Wakefield document differs in some respects from the copy delivered to the Exchequer by the clerk of the peace. These differences show by comparing the transcription of the assessment for his wapentake with that of the others. In the Wakefield document, the hearths of properties that were empty, or were discharged by certificate, are shown individually as the lists were compiled, whereas in the Exchequer returns these households were consolidated into blocks. Furthermore, the Wakefield return names the poor, whereas the Exchequer returns merely give their total numbers, and their names are simply 'omitted by reason of poverty.' Sheriff returns survive for other wapentakes as well, labelled '*Nomina Villarum*'. However, no attempt has been made to collate these transcripts with the Exchequer records, although, where necessary reference, has been made to certain missing entries, which are noted in the footnotes.

Osgoldcross

We have not used the part of the gigantic Lady Day 1672 roll devoted to Osgoldcross wapentake, since it is very fragmentary and in a very poor state. Twenty-six membranes survive in E179/210/415, twelve other membranes at four different call numbers, and some of it does not survive at all. For details, see the list of surviving West Riding hearth tax documents in Appendix II. The return used for Osgoldcross E179/262/13 therefore comes from the next surviving return for the whole of the West Riding, that for the year 1673 and Lady Day 1674. Here the membranes are approximately 350mm wide and 600mm in length written on both sides of the parchment in three columns. The back of the parchment is written in the reverse direction to the front to make reading easier. The membranes are folded approximately 10mm from the end and are sewed through the fold in fours onto four cords to create a spine which has then been glued. As such there appears to have been an outside sheet of parchment creating a cover which has now been lost. The scribe numbered the membranes on the fold and these numbers can be found in the binding and sometimes on the spine, indicating that none of the 125 membranes has been lost. The last membrane shows that John Peables, the Clerk of the Peace, delivered this particular document into the Exchequer on 6 December 1675 on exactly the same date as the earlier returns. The scribe of this return would be delighted to know that

[1] WMDL, Wakefield Hearth Tax Return for 1672.

the format of his presentation and binding has ensured that it has remained intact for well over 300 years, a situation that has not befallen the earlier returns.

Editorial Method

The separate rolls for each wapentake have been arranged geographically from north to south for the purposes of this edition. For convenience of reference a map of the wapentakes will be found on the Front End Paper and at p. 446. Within each wapentake the transcript published here follows the order of the original, that is to say, alphabetically by township. In the original the text was written in a single column, apart from the Osgoldcross wapentake taken from the 1673–4 return which was written in three columns. Here it is entirely printed in three columns. The text should not be read across, but down the left hand column, and only then across to the central column and down, and finally to the right hand column. The original membrane numbers are given at the appropriate place in the text, and also with column numbers for Osgoldcross.

Editorial comment has been relegated to footnotes, except extensions which appear in square brackets eg. Ebo[rum] or ten[an]ts. To indicate that there was a gap in the original, e.g. no hearth number [blank] has been used. Names and numbers illegible due to membrane damage are represented by … The original punctuation has not been retained because of the difficulties of interpretation and the problems of distinguishing between a mark and ink showing through.

Place names

The place names are printed in bold. Where the modern form is different from the original, it has been added in brackets.

Personal names

It has not been possible to replicate the seventeenth-century script, superscript or some of the abbreviations. The names are written as found whether they are in an abbreviated form or variant spellings. For certain letters it is not always easy to distinguish between 'n', 'u' and 'v' . In these instances, the modern version such as in David has been used. The reader should also be aware that, in compiling the Exchequer copy, the clerk has introduced his own spellings and errors. In a number of cases the editors have examined the sheriff's return, and this is noted in the footnotes. However they have not collated the text entirely and in cases of doubt it may be necessary to examine the sheriff's text as well.

Status

Abbreviations giving title or status are also written as found. Many of them have several variations such as widdow which appears as widd, wid and the Latin form of *vid.*

Lady Day Assessment 1672

Staincliffe and Ewcross Wapentakes

The National Archives, E179/210/418

m 1]

Staincliffe … Ewcross (Staincliffe and Ewcross Wapentakes)

Adingham (Addingham)

Mr Alex Kippax	2
Mr Ingram F[1]…	3
Rich Holmes	1
Arthur Utley	2
Antho Atkinson	1
Tho Tebbs	1
Tho Holdsworth	1
Tho Utley	1
Chrofer Rishworth	1
Tho Utley	1
John Hodgson	1
Edward Clarkson	2
Nicholas Wetherhead	2
Tho Teale	1
Tho Shackleton	1
Tho Hudson	2
Willm Cockshott	1
Henry Netherwood	1
John Cockshott	1
Tho Foster	1
Tho Wall	1
Ri Spencer	1
Thomas Smith	1
Willm Lister	2
Willm Bramley	1
Willm Watson	2
Rich Wilkinson	2
Will Lister	1
Tho Feildhouse	1
Ri Shackleton	2
Willm Wetherhead	1
Robte Squire	2
Widd Squire	1
Willm Spencer	1
Charles Walmsley	1
John Feildhouse	1
Fran Holmes	1
Tho Blofeild	1
John Sandwith	2
Willm Lund	1
Grace Harrison	1
John Holmes	2
John Parkinson	1
Widd Spencer	3
Widd Bowcocke	1
Widd Holmes	1
Fr Janson	1
Samll Whitley	2
Willm Blakey	2
Rich Brogden	1
Willm Stead	2
Chr Hodgson	1
Willm Brogden	1
Robte Smith	1
John Barker	1
Willm Waineman	1
John Gibson	2
Tho Bland	1
George Spencer	4
Willm Ward	1
Stephen Armistead	1
Willm Stones	1
Rich Lund	1
John Wilson	2
Rich Dawson	1
Geo Windsor	1
Tho Topham	2
Chr Smith	1
Willm Scott	3
John Auswicke	2
Tho Currer	4
John Greene	5
Tho Brashaw	1
Robt Cowing	2
Anth Myers	3
Widd Wilkinson	1
Samll Lister	1
John Bowcocke	1
John Turnor	1
Willm Bolton	1
Geo Gawthropp	1
Geo Brogden	1
The Mill	1
Tho Aireson	1
Ri Clarkson	1
	133

Empty & noe distress to be had

Chr Pickard	1

m 2]

Robert Husband Collr
Willm Scott Const

[1] The letters following F might be read as Franck, which is confirmed by the *Nomina Villarum*.

Appletreewicke (Appletreewick)	
Anne Inman	1
Antho Bumby	1
Geo Bland	1
Will Inman	1
Chr Hewitt	1
Robt Ellis	1
Robte Hebden	2
Geo Bland	1
Antho Bumby	1
John Gill	1
Chr Lawson	4
Robt Heigh	1
Mary Dawson	2
John Hey	2
Willm Barker	1
Lanc Preston	1
Antho Bland	1
Will Hunter	2
Tho Barker	2
Will Preston	2
Will Hunter	1
Eliz Hunter	1
Mr Tho Craven	1
Robte Nussey	2
Ri Jackman	1
Margar Nursey	1
Row Lambert	1
Tho Lascells	1
Tho Joy	1
John Joy	1
John Topham	2
John Beecroft	1
Will Young	2
Tho Beecroft	1
John Bell	3
Antho Horner	1
Mr John Winterburne	7
Tho Winterburne	2
Geo Bland	1
Mr John Preston	7
Ri Spurritt	3
John Walters	2
Widd Beecroft	1
Robte Inman	1
Francis Kidd	1
Chr Pickard	1
Tho Young	1
	88[2]
Omitted by reason of poverty	2
Robt Husband Collr	
Thomas Joy Const	

Airton	
Robte Lund	3
John Hall	1
Henry Preston	1
Willm Preston	1
Willm Young	2
Willm Younge	1
Tho Preston	1
John Petty	2
Henry Bateman	2
Alice Foster	4
John Remington	1
John Squire	1
Anne Younge	1
m 3]	
John Hartley	1
Henry Spencer	1
Chr Tatham	1
Henry Baldwin	1
Tho Lund	1
John Armitstead	1
John King	1
Hugh Iveson	1
Willm Parkinson	1
Tho Parkinson	1
Chr Simpson	1
John Dawson	1
Henry Wilkinson	1
Henry Hall	1
Tho Atkinson forge	1
Henry Lambert	1
George Cryer	1
Henry Atkinson	1
	39
Omitted by reason of poverty	3
Robt Moore Collr	
Will Younge Const	

Armecliffe (Arncliffe)	
Mr Lambert	4
James Burton	2
Chrofer Hamond	2
John Hamond	2
Tho Topham	2
John Silson	2
Edm Bolland	1
Hen Fish	1
Hen Bucke	2
John Stephenson	3
John Atkinson	2
Antho Richardson	1
Tho Abraham	1
Widd Ellis	2
Hen Bradshaw	2
Ri Windser	1
John Kidd	1
Arthur Coldcole	1
Ralph Atkinson	1
Ri Johnson	1
Widd Sedgwicke	1

[2] There is a scribal error since the total is 77, but it needs to be noted that there is a small dot with the number, following the name Mr Thomas Craven, perhaps suggesting 12 hearths, thereby reconciling the figures with the total.

Tho Deman 1
Robte Atkinson 2
38

Empty & noe distress to be had
John Hebden 1

These persons followeing are discharged by certificate
John Brooke and forge 2
Brian Nelson 2
Widd Brookes 1

Robert Husband Collr
Arthur Colcole Const

Austwicke (Austwick)
Mr Ralph Beane 4
Willm Jackson 2
Rich Jackson 3
Widd Downham 1
James Johnson 2
Robt Heaton 1
Tho Grainger 1
Mich Nelson 1
Will Jackson 1
Tho Ash 2
Tho White 1
Tho Remington 2
Roger Lupton 2
Edmond Greene 2
Chrofer Richardson 2
Fr Richinson 1
James Jackson 1
Ri Jackson 1
John Spalton 1
Tristram Tayler gen 7
Willm Jackson 3
Chr Bentham 1
Willm Battersby 2
Willm Beecroft 5
more a forge 1
Robte Johnson 1
Tho Banckes 2
Willm Johnson 3
Laur Waite 1
Robte Walker 1
John Lawson 2
James Remington 1

m 4]

James Spalton 1
Thomas Walker 1
Charles Ingelby Esqr 3
John Bentham 2
John Jackson 1
James Hartley 1
Tho Jackson 1
Stephen Walker 1
Thomas Tennant 1
John Hartley 1
Lawr Staleman 2
George Jackson 2
Robert Grainger 1
Will Downham sen 2
Will Downham jun 1
Edw Ellis 1
John Downham 1
Willm Knipe 1
John Blackhouse 1
Will Baynes 2
John Johnson sen 2
John Johnson jun 2
Widd Clapham 1
James Nayler 1
Geo Place 2
Antho Downham 1
Will Walker 2
Tho Bentham 2
Tho Armistead 2
Ri Foster 2
Will Leach 1
Widd Franckland 1
Collumbus Ingram gen 1
James Harthenwaite 1
Roger Chapman 1
Robert Ratcliffe 1
Henry Marshall 2
Tho Johnson 1
Widd Salmon 1
Widd Hawson 1
Chr Capestocke 1
Geo Capestocke 1
John Leeming 1
Madam Mary Ingleby 11
Henry Peele 4
Tho Dawson 1
Rich Hargreave 2
John Lupton 1
Margarett Wilkinson 2
Agnes Wilkinson 1
Mr John Tompson 2
Agnes Tennant 2
James Lawson 1
Mich Lawson 2
Lawr Peacocke 1
Tho Chapman 1
Tho Ludforth 1
Widd Prockter 1
Will Lupton 1
Leonard Carr 1
Chr Lawson 1
John Houghton 2
Willm Bateman 1
John Ash 1
Agnes Ash 2
Willm Banckes 1
Robt Slackhouse 2
Robt Banckes 2
Tho Ash 1
Jane Ash 1
Willm Tayler 1
Chr Tatham 1
Michaell Bradley 2
James Carr 2
Tho Broadley 2
John Moore 7
Agnes Foster 1
Cuth Gray 2
Chr Nicholson 2
Henry Mayden 2

Henry Bullocke	1
Tho Stockdale	1
Mr Ingleby	1
Robt Bankes	1
John Walker	1
Antho Prockter	2
Tho Wilkinson	1
Antho Wilkinson	2
Wm Norwill	1
Robt King	1
m 5]	
Will Nicholson	1
Cuth Peele	1
Tho Prockter	4
John Bradley	1
Chr Carr	2
Tho Carr	2
Antho Wiglesworth	1
Widd Combe	1
Rich Bradley	1
Will Bradley	2
Tho Bradley	1
John Guy	1
James Overend	1
John Guy gen	5
Anne Prockter	1
Willm Chapman	1
James Banckes	1
Willm Johnson	2
Peter Atkinson	2
Robert Chapman	2
Tho Yeadon	2
James Tennant	1
Willm Yeadon	1
Edw Moore	1
Chr Hancocke	1
Edw Capestocke	1
Peter Fairbancke	1
Francis Allon	1
John Read	2
Widd Halton	1
Chr Spalton	1
John King	1

John Yeadon	1
Edw Lund	1
Rich Armitage	1
Chr Johnson	1
Troylous Atkinson	1
	254
Empty & noe distress to be had	
Mrs Guy	1
Robte Chapman	1
Robte Carter	1
Omitted by reason of poverty	9
Robt Moore Collr	
Will Tayler &	
Will Jackson Const	
Barnoldswicke (Barnoldswick)	
Willm Drake esqr	14
John Hartley gen	8
Widd Hartley	5
Willm Edmondson	9
Chr Waite	3
James Dickinson	4
John Jackson	4
Chr Edmondson	3
Chr Ellis	3
Rich Ellis	2
Tho Wilkinson	1
Chr Higgin	2
Rich Higgin	1
Chr Hargreaves	1
Willm Higgin	1
Rich Hanson	2
John Stephenson	2
Will Lowcocke	2
Thomas Edmondson	3
Willm Hudson	2
Widd Leigh	1
John Edmondson	1
Ri Broughton	2
Widd Monkes	1

Tho Edmondson	2
Tho Kirke	2
John Ellis	3
Rich Dickinson	2
John Tayler	2
Henry Dugdale	2
Nicholas Dugdale	1
John Slater	1
John Watson	2
Rich Brogden	2
Stephen Deane	1
m 5]	
Chr Dickinson	2
John Watson	1
John Briggs	2
Agnes Parker	2
Charles Bannister	2
Miles Walker	2
Lawr Leigh	2
Allon Edmondson	2
Tho Sawley	2
Ri Lowcocke	2
Chrofer Windle	2
Tho Redyhouse	2
Tho Lowcocke	1
James Greenes	1
Chr Hartley	1
Ri Boothman	2
Ri Edmondson	1
Hen Hartley	1
Rich Robinson	1
Chr Bullocke	2
John Clayton	2
Tho Preston	2
Chr Bracewell	1
Henry Hartley	1
Allon Admondson	2
Willm Bracewell	1
John Bullock	1
Tho Higgin	1
Mr Hartley	1
Ri Bullocke	2
Chr Brogden	2

John Baldwin	1
John Cockshott	1
John Baildon	1
Ri Edmond sen	1
Ri Atturneley	1
John Walker	3
John Greenwood	2
Willm Atkinson	1
Will Hudson	2
John Hudson	2
Chr Ellis	2
Tho Hudson	1
Samuell Atkinson	1
Roger Hartley	2
Willm Lowcocke	3
Chr Dickinson	1
Ri Emmitt	1
Rich Thomas	2
James Dickinson	1
Rich Harrison	1
Rich Reyley	1
The mill	1
James Greenwood	1
Chrofer Bridges	2
James Hartley	1
Henry Higgins	1
	183

The person following is discharged by certificate

Chr Tayler	1
Omitted by reason of poverty	17

Robt Corner Collr
John Ellis Const

Bradley

Robt Cowling	2
Tho Havill	1
Tho Smith	1
Jonah Gill	1
Willm Watkinson	1
Tho Burton	1
Willm Watkinson	3
Willm Juryson	2
John Atkinson	1
Hugh Watson	2
Willm Wade	2
Geo Poole	2
John Cowper	3
Samuell Horrax	2
John Lupton	3
Rich Cowper	1
John Tennant	1
Mary Jackson	1
Willm Watkinson	1
John Atkinson	1
John Atkinson jun	1
Henry Overend	3
John Gill	1
Willm Smith	1
Jonath Gill	2
John Watkinson	2
Will Atkinson	1
Henry Smith	1

m 6]

John Craven	2
John Currer	2
Matthew Lupton	6
John Whitwhang	2
Edward Whitwhang	2
Willm Stirke	1
Robert Barrott	1
Robert Bolton	1
Willm Cockshott	1
Tho Peele	1
Willm Smith	1
Tho Runwicke	1
	65

Empty & noe distress to be had

The Smith	1
Omitted by reason of poverty	7

Robert Corner Collr
Richard Cowper Const

Buckden

Chro Parker	3
Widd Lodge	2
Robte Lodge	3
Lawr Hebden	1
Jeffr Parker	2
Oswald Metcalfe	1
John Lodge	1
Fr Stringer	2
Widd Prockter	2
Tho Tayler	2
John Parker	1
Widd Tennant	1
Chr Tennant sen	2
Adam Jaques	1
Henry Lodge	1
Chr Tennant jun	1
John Lodge	2
Anne Fisher	1
Widd Williamson	1
John Slinger	1
Adam Lodge	1
Antho Simpson	2
Widd Tennant	1
Tho Jaques	1
Tho Prockter	1
Jeffr Lodge	1
John Parker	1
Chr Langstroth	1
Robt Tennant	2
Matth Mayson	2
James Tennant	3
Fran Todd	4
Tho Russell	1
John Johnson	1
Matt Slinger	1
Anth Stonay	1
Tho Lambert	2
John Parker	1
George Wilson	3
John Jaques	2
John Graveson	2

James Lobley	1
John Tennant	1
John Coates	1
John Tennant	2
Tho Slinger	2
John Tennant	2
Antho Knowles	2
John Fawcitt	2
Chr Tennant	2
Henry Robinson	1
Rich Wilson	1
Willm Slinger	1
James Tennant	1
Tho Tongate	1
John Nicholson	1
Rich Tennant	1
Rich Graveson	1
Widd Tennant	1
Robte Dawson	1
Henry Falshay	2
Willm Wilson	1
Widd Slinger	2
John Tennant	1
Antho Knowles	1
Widd Metcalfe	2
	99

m 8]

Omitted by reason of poverty	2

Rich Pickard Collr
John Tennant Const

Bracewell

Tho Clarke	6
Tho Hay jun	2
John Robinson	3
Stephen Kendall	2
Alice Armistead	1
Tho Lee	2
James Lockwood	2
John Crosley	1
Hen Crosdall & Tho Hay	2
Tho Hay	1
Widd Browne	3
Robte Jackson	5
Ralph Coore	2
Rich Armistead	2
Abra Greenwood	3
Willm Bealdon	2
Henry Baley	2
Ri Hudson	2
John Stevenson	1
Tho Nunwicke	2
John Wilkinson	1
John Wood	2
Willm Hudson	3
Mr Wilkinson	6
John Hartley	2
John Browne	1
Robte Ingham	1
	62

Rogert Hardcastle Collr
Stephen Kendall Const

Bashaw (Bashall)

John Ferrer Esq	14
John Walmsley	1
Robert Chippendale	2
Tho Cottam	1
Rich Mason	1
John Clayton	1
John Towers	1
John Usherwood	2
Ri Ecles	1
Will Dugdale	1
Ri Dugdale	2
Tho Chapman	2
Robt Potter	1
Robt Gyles	2
Henry Salisbury	2
Tho King	2
Oliver Wilkinson	1
John Kidd	1
Brian Talbott	1
Tho Towers	1
Tho Eccles	1
Tho Aleston	1
Hen Butterfeild	1
Nicholas Turner	1
Robert Walmsley	1
Eliz Tomlinson	1
Tho Walmsley	1
Robert Ridges	1
Ri Butterfeild	1
Edward Eccles	1
Edw Chippendall	2
Arthur Eccles	2
Willm Atkinson	1
Willm Towers	2
Willm Monkes	1
Edward Kitchin	1
Rich Woodroofe	1
Ri Brunum	1
Ri Alestead	1
Tho Broughton	1
Tho Turner	1
Tho Shereburne	1
	65

These persons following are discharged by certificate

Alice Broughton	2
James Cliffe	1
Tho Parpoynt	…

Omitted by reason of poverty	…

Ri Pickard Collr
Tho Austin Const

m 9]

Bentham

John Foster	1
Robt Overend	1
John Marshall	3

Geo Wildman	1
Willm Wildman	1
Willm Davison	1
Mr Robt Baines	6
Willm Clarke	1
John Clarke	1
Willm Thirkin	1
Willm Armistead	1
Tho Tennant	2
Tho Baines	3
Stephen Wildman	1
Henry Wildman	1
John Wildman	1
Widd Wildman	1
Arthur Townson	1
Widd Mason	2
Rich Chapman	1
John Tomlinson	1
John Chapman	2
James Downham	1
Tho Wildman	1
Willm Brashawe	1
Chr Ellershaw	2
Willm Thornton	1
Chr Hathornwhite	1
John Hodgson	1
Francis Wildman	1
James Clapham	1
Willm Greene	1
Lawr Tomlinson	1
Nath Ward	1
Tho Wildman	1
Andrew Overend	2
Edw Overend	3
John Wildman	3
Widd Overend	1
John Knowles	2
Mr Hen Slinger	2
James Bradley	1
James Wilkinson	1
Willm Prockter	1
Rich Hewley	1
Tho Yeadon	1
Robt Mason	1
Antho Overend	2

Roger Carr	1
Leonard Harlin	1
Rich Jackson	1
Miles Readman	1
Math Greenfeild	1
Tho Marshall	1
James Pearson	3
Oliver Tennant	2
John Prockter	1
Arthur Bateman	1
Rich Hall	1
James Place	2
Willm Thornton	2
John Wilson	1
Jeffrey Bentham	1
James Balderston	1
Willm Walker	2
Eliz Remington	1
John Wray	2
Martin Carr	1
Laur Remington	1
Bartho Tenant	2
Tho Overend	2
Tho Baines	4
Lanc Tunstall	1
Robt Remington	1
Matth Walker	1
Fran Johnson	1
Edward Carr	1
Widd Tennant	2
Ellis Tennant	2
John Warding	1
John Cumberland	4
Willm Edmondson	2
Robt Overend	1
Matth Overend	1
Tho Cumberland	1

m 10]

Tho Bancks	2
Mr Husband	6
Alex Warding	1
Tristr Ray	1
Ri Easterby	2

John Robinson	1
Rich Guy	2
Rich Grainger	2
Mr Farrar	4
Tho Gibson	1
Tho Baines	2
Robt Kendall	1
Geo Bland	1
Willm Readman	1
Westend house	2
Tho Baitson	2
Rich Hall	1
John Freckleton	1
Widd Bland	2
John Bond	1
Will Greene smithy	1
John Ellershaw	3
John Walker	2
Willm Bartley	1
Mr Lupton	5
Ri Freckleton	1
Widd Geldart	2
Chr Procter	1
Will Robinson	1
Tho Bradley sen	1
Tho Bradley jun	1
Widd Holmes	1
Leo Windor	1
Math Walker	1
James Bentham	1
John Kendall	1
Widd Longstroth	1
Willm Cumberland	1
John Tomlinson	1
Mr Parkinson	2
Brian Winder	1
John Parker	1
John Remington	1
Robte Barton	1
Miles Foxcroft	1
James Wildman	1
	195

Robert Bennett Collr
John Parker Const

Banck Newton
(Bank Newton)

Nicholas Towneley Esq	6
Tho Habor Esq	12
Willm Jolley	2
Mr Hen Curray	3
Widd Currer	2
Willm Wiglesworth	3
John Wiglesworth	3
Willm Baildon	1
Henry Holgate	1
Willm Dewitt	3
John Drake gen	4
Hen Colthirst	2
John Watkinson	2
Rich Rotheray	1
Antho Wardman	1
Will Hay	1
Fran Walton	1
John Wharfe	1
Chr Wise	1
Nich Hardiker	1
	51

Omitted by reason of poverty	2

Tho Middleton Collr
Christ Wise Const

Broughton

Sir Stephen Tempest	19
Mr Yorke	2
Widd Tempest	2
Mr John Tempest	3
Robert Mitchell	3
John Iveson	1
Richard Ellis	1
Antho Lund	2
Stephen Ellis	1

m 11]

Rich Leach	1
Chro Sugarr	1
Widd Sugarr	1
John Briggs jun	1
Willm Bishop	1
Bridgett Loftus	1
Widd Baxter	2
Willm Clough	1
Willm Wiglesworth	2
John Blenbrough	2
Mr Tempest	2
Henry Hanson	5
Robt Clough	2
Henry Clough	1
Chr Loftus sen	2
Hen Swinden	1
John Bridge	2
Steven Clough	1
The Viccaridge	3
James Oxnard	2
Tho Hooke	1
Robt Roberts	1
Chr Johnson	1
Widd Constantine	1
Henry Loftus	1
John Driver	1
Robte Bishop	1
Henry Maullam	2
Robt Walton	1
Chr Loftus	1
Fr Bell	1
Rich Lund	1
Geo Smith	2
Jero Wilkinson	1
Tho Squire	1
Stephen Smith	1
Edward Walton	1
John Mitton	1
James Walton jun	1
Will Ellis	1
Fra Chapman	1
Willm Peele	1
John Higgin	1
Fran Tompson	1
Susan Lund	2
Fr Ellis	1
John Tillisson	2
Fran Atkinson	1
Tho Wilkinson	1
John Ellis	1
	102

Empty & noe distress to be had

Chr Loftus	1

These persons following are discharged by certificate

Widd Watterworth	1
George Butler	2
Widd Clough	1
Hen Costantine	2
Hen Atkinson	1
Tho Loftus	1
Laur Walton	1

Robt Corner Collr
John Ellis Const

Bolton nigh Bolland
(Bolton by Bowland)

John Wiglesword	5
Rich Broxup	2
John Bowcocke	1
Tho Ryley	4
Tho Walker Rector	3
Mr John Walker	3
Mrs Anne Walker	2
Mr Tho Tellow	2
Robert Battersby	3
Laur Robinson	2
Geo Bolland	1
Will Butterfeild	2
Stephen Carr	1
Antho Carr	1
Tho Preston	2
Ri Whitacre	2
Tho Ainsworth	1
John Billington	1
John Geldart	1

m 12]

Tho Peele	1
Widd Walmsley	1
Fra Atkinson	1
Widd Howgill	2
Fr Franckland	1
John Hudson	2
Tho Parkinson	1
Geo Battersby	1
John Hindle	1
Robte Robinson	1
John Walker	2
Rich Broxupp	1
Hen Walton	1
Widd Harrison	1
Rich Charnley	1
John Greenwood	3
Matthew Aynsworth	2
Thomas Walker	1
Willm Hill	1
James Barritt	1
Tho Ryley	2
Tho Bowcock	6
Geo Foster	2
John Preston	2
John Wriglesworth	2
Tho Peele	1
Widdow Scott	1
John Hindle	2
Widd Atkinson	1
Tho Butterfeild	1
John Battersby	2
John Walker	2
Edward Walker	1
Tho Boococke	2
Hen Lawson	1
John Parkinson	1
Geo Harrison	1
Robt Brooke	1
Ambrose Witton	1
Antho Carr	1
Robte Scott sen	1
Willm Charnley	1
Agnes Marsden	2
Edward Billingham	2
John Preston	1
Hen Franckland	1
Roger Butterfeild	1
Widd Atkinson	1
Antho Ellis	1
Roger Baxter	1
Mr Tho Tellow	1
Willm Burwell	1
Hen Scott	1
John Cawdery	1
Widd Franckland	2
	116

Empty & noe distress to be had	
Coll Ambros Pudsey	8

Omitted by reason of poverty	12

Tho Middleton Collr
Matt Answorth Const

Bradford West (West Bradford)

Willm Walker	5
Tho Tayler	4
Giles Thorneber	2
Nicholas Tayler	1
Robt Siddall	1
Tho Hanson	1
Rich Clough	2
Edw Charnley	1
Willm Hargreave	1
Robert Franckland	2
Ri Waddington	1
Robert Calvert	3
Rich Bashall	1
Nichol Gyles	1
Edm Holt	1
Mary Slater	1
Mr Robt Parker	3

m 13]

Alex Gyler	2
Willm Thornbrough	1
Rich Gyles	1
John Chew	2
Tho Tomlinson	1
Edw Hoyle	1
Hen Baley	2
Tho Dale	2
Mr Calverley	2
Hen Hayhirst	2
Henry Knowles	3
John Slater	1
Nich Thornbrough	2
Hen Mercer	1
Tho Whitacre	1
Ra Avison	1
John Porter	2
Arthur Blackburne	1
Tho Tayler	1
Mr Ro Parker	1
Hen Leeming	1
	62

Empty & noe distress to be had	
Tho Whitacrees	1

Omitted by reason of poverty	1

Roger Hardcastle Collr
Robt Franckland Const

Barden Forrest (Barden Forest)

The Countes of Pembrooke	27
John Chippendale	3
Tho Atkinson	1
Geo Demayne	2
Humphr Holmes	1
Willm Bumby	1
Stephen Lambert	1

Geo Demaine	2
Chr Walters	1
Willm Atkinson	2
Tho Miller	1
John Simpson	2
John Lowcocke	1
John Lambert	1
Humphr Parker	2
James Holmes	1
Henry Simpson	2
Willm Holmes	1
Willm Holmes	1[3]
Ri Howden	1
Jane Smith	1
Henry Addison	2
Fran Holden	1
Lyonell Holmes	1
Tho Metcalfe	2
John Holmes	1
John Holmes	1
John Harrison	1
Tho Simpson	1
	65

Robt Husband Collr
Tho Atkinson Const

Bolland Forrest
(Bowland Forest)

Tho Parker Esqr	9
John Cromlam	2
John Crosdall	3
Thomas Crosdall	1
Hen Waddington	2
Willm Crosdall	2
Thomas Feaster	1
Thomas Towers	1
Thomas Crosdall	1
Edward Austen	1
John Parkinson	2
Robert Austin	1
Eliz Walker	1
Bernard Howson	2
John Parker	1
Chr Salisbury	1
John Walbancke	1
John Firbancke	1
James Driver	1
Widd Dobson	2
Widd Carwicke	1
Willm Siddall	1
Tho Parker Esqr	7
Tho Parker	2
Robte Dobson	3
John Hewson	1
Tho Smith	1
Rich Swinglehurst	1
Robt Dilworth	1
Mr Geo Townson	10

m 14]

Widd Wilcock	2
Tho Parker	2
Widd Parker	2
Tho Rathmell	2
Tho Turner	1
Ri Badger	1
Widd Newson	1
Chr Martin	1
John Sower	1
Tho Bond	1
Chr Singlehirst	3
John Wider	1
Tho Bond sen	2
Willm Swinglehirst	2
Widd Parker	2
Mr James Moore	6
Tho Brewer	2
Robt Crosdale	2
Robt Peele	1
Widd Tomlinson	1
Robte Hawkeshead	1
John Porter	1
Joseph Jackson	1
Stephen Wilkinson	1
Tho Carr	2
John Holden	3
Hen Burrow	1
Willm Clayton	2
Tho Brenard	1
John Walbancke	1
Rich Simonds	1
Widd Simonds	1
John Brenard	1
John Holden jun	1
Willm Hurst	1
Rich Hodgson	3
Mr Cuntcliff	1
John Harrison	1
Geo Harrison	1
Jo Osberderston	1
James Davy	1
Mich Armistead	1
Widd Parkinson	1
John Bond	1
Robte Brenald	1
Robt Swinglehurst	1
Robt Parkinson	1
John Parkinson	1
Rich Hurst	2
Robt Hurst	1
John Martin	1
Rich Hurst sen	1
Robt Whittendale	2
Willm Huntingden	1
James Hotherwood	1
Oliver Martin	1
Mr Roger Parker	3
John Hurst	3
Hen Knowles	1
John Hirst	1
Willm Hirst	1
Willm Martin	1
Willm Martin	3
Robt Standing	1
Edward Clarke	1
	159

[3] sic.

Empty & noe distress to be had	
Mathhew Crosdale	1
Rich Hawthorne	1
Eliz Sharpe	1
Robt Sharpley	1

These persons following are discharged by certificate

Willm Martin	1
Tho Harrison	1
Hen Walmsley	1

Richard Pickard Collr
Robert Dobson Const

Burnsall

Mr Lancaster	6
Mr James Tennant	5
Tho Tennant	2
Jonas Bland	1
Antho Bland	1
Tho Kidd	1
Lowrance Tennant	3
Laur Favill	2
Agnes Favill	3
John Coulton	1
John Williamson	2

m 15]

John Ellis	1
Chr Bland	1
Geo Bland	2
Tho Smith	1
Peter Alcocke	3
Tho Bland	1
Willm Bland	1
Bartho Bland	1
Susann Inman	1
John Kay	1
Willm Wharton	1
John Inman	2
John Hawson	2
Chr Hargreaves	1
Nicholas Tennant	1
John Symm	2
Matthew Metcalfe	1
John Robinson jun	1
John Battey	1
Tho King	2
Alice Martin	1
Tho Raynard	2
John Richardson	1
John Wraythy	2
Robert Symm	3
Ri Stuckard	1
Nicholas Blackburne	2
Roger Bumby	1
Willm Batty	1
Simond Bolland	1
Antho King	1
John Robinson	2
Tho Ellis	2
	74

Empty & noe distress to be had	
Robt Hardcastle forge	1
Omitted by reason of poverty	5

Robert Husband Collr
John Williamson Const

Burton

Willm Tatham	4
Burton Hall	3
John Knowles	2
John Ellershaw	1
Geo Lupidge	3
John Marriner	3
John Huginson	1
John Clough	2
Nicholas Huginson	2
George Topham	1
James Husband	2
Chr Beamont	2
Rich Tatham	2
Willm Brogden	1
Robt Marriner	2
Geo Overend	2
Mr Birkhead Cler	1
Fr Browne	1
Rich Barker	1
Tho Yates	2
Geo Beckitt	1
Rowl Beckitt	1
John Hall	2
Roger Carr	1
Anne Thornton	1
Anne Batty	1
Isaack Mellin	1
Willm Croft	1
Robt Stockhouse	1
Mr Farra mill	1
Tho Foxcroft	1
John Butterfeild	1
Ri Husband	1
	52

Empty & noe distress to be had	
The Courthouse	1
Omitted by reason of poverty	10

Ri Pickard Collr
Robt Dobson Const

Clapham

Arthur Ingleby Esqr	4
Will Foster gen	4
Geo Jackson	2
Willm Batty	3
Robte Carr	2
Widd Foster	2
Stephen Wilson	1
Leonard Walker	1
Jonas Clapham	2
Anne Staleman	1
Laur Wildeman	1

Tho Carr	2
Tho Bentham	1
Leo Wetherhead	1
Mr Place	4
John Harrison	1
Mr White tents	2
John Prockter	1
Chr Jackson	3
Ellin Esh	1
Tho Toogood	2
James Artham	2
Ri Jackson	1
John Wilcocke	1
John Nicholson	3
Rich Harling	1
Hen Ratcliffe	1
Chr Squire	3
Robt Jackson	2
Tho Prockter	1
Mr Tho Watson	6
Mrs Margt Richardson	1
Willm Jackson	1
John Thomson	1
Mr Tho Watson	2
Tho Jackson	1
Widd Jackson	1
Jo Shaw	1
Chr Foster	1
Julyas Clapham	2
James Gifford	1
Eliz Lawson	1
James Lawson	1
Rich Wilcocke	1
Rich Carr	1
Antho Hawson	3
James Armistead	2
Tho Carr	1
Mr Geo Ashton	2
Mr Willm Clapham	1
Ri Coulton	1
Marma Frickleton	1
John Prockter	1
John Banckes	1
Widd Wildman	1
Jo Atkinson	2

Tho Rawthorne	1
Will Bradley	2
Rich Wiglesworth	2
James Hawson	2
Widd Chapman	1
John Chapman	1
Bryan Robinson	1
Rich Burnitt	1
Willm Buckle	1
Robert Harling	1
	107

Omitted by reason of poverty	8

Robert Moore Collr
Chr Jackson Const

Cowlinghead
(Cowling Head)

Widd Jackson	2

m 17]

Widd Bannister	1
Robt Raikes	1
James Briggs	2
Willm Nelson	1
Robt Smith	2
Peter Prockter	1
John Harrison	1
Tho Wilson	1
Henry Walton	1
Willm Emmott	1
John Emmott	4
Chr Smith	2
Peter Harrison	1
John Walton	1
Widd Deane	1
John Smith	3
Peter Smith	1
John Lacocke	1
Alverah Smith	1
Willm Nayler	1
Robt Shackleton	1

Laur Scarbrough	2
Will Smith	2
Bernard Blake	2
Antho Moore	2
Edward Lacocke	3
Will Jackson	1
Hen Hargraves	1
Geo Smith	2
Geo Emmott	2
James Ambler	1
Will Woller	1
John Walton	1
Mich Smith	1
Edmond Robinson	1
Geo Smith	2
Hugh Smith	1
Joseph Hutchinson	1
Robt Laycocke	1
John Smith	1
James Wooler	1
Matth Garforth	1
Peter Hudson	3
Chr Emmott	2
James Emmott	1
Tho Hargreaves	1
Peter Lacocke	1
Chr Smith	2
Tho Moorehouse	1
Miles Hargreaves	1
Alvera Lacocke	1
John Lacocke	1
Widd Smith	2
Will Pickles	1
Widd Starkey	1
John Harrison	1
Laur Mitchell	2
Tho Fould	2
Tho Tillotson	1
Edward Lacocke	2
Fardinand Scarbrough	1
Willm Baldwin	1
John Driver	1
Robert Tillotson	2
Willm Tillotson	1
Peter Hargreave	1

Margarett Calverley	1
John Booth	1
Robert Wilson	1
Robte Wilson	1
John Lacocke	2
Willm Hargraves	3
Willm Hargraves	1
Tho Scarbrough	2
Willm Stowe	2
James Lacocke	1
Willm Garforth	1
Willm Waineman	3
Henry Lacocke	1
Willm Windle	2
Peter Lupton	2
Widd Wilson	1
Hugh Kendall	1
Hugh Smith	1
Edw Smith jun	1
Stephen Tillotson	1
Nath Pickles	1
	124

Omitted by reason of poverty	1

Roger Hardcastle Collr
Willm Hargreaves Const

Connystone (Conistone)

Cuthbert Waide Esq	10
Rich Ayrson	2
Anne Lealand	3

m 18]

Will Lambert	2
Tho Ibbotson	2
Willm Halliday	2
Robt Pullen	1
Edward Hartley	2
Laur Constantine	1
Chr Lambert	2
Mr Tho Ward	6
Robt Sedgwicke	1
John Hartley	1
Mr Willm Tennant	5
Leo Lealand sen	2
Robt Slinger	1
John Horner	2
John Lealand jun	2
Willm West	1
Willm Shaw	1
Rich Tompson	1
Tho Hebden	1
Geo Tennant	1
Willm Dent	1
Ri Constantine	4
Hen Constantine	1
Roger Franckland	2
Robt Wiglesworth	2
Robt Constantine	1
Mich Settle	1
Hen Hewitt	1
Ri Franckland	1
Geo Geldart	1
Geo Bramham	1
Ri Todd	1
John Rogers	1
Augustine Stoney	1
	71

Omitted by reason of poverty	2

Robert Husband Collr
John Winsor Const

Connystone Cold (Coniston Cold)

Joseph Ward gen	4
John Mawham	2
Willm Wharfe	2
Hen Whitacrees jun	2
John Rycroft	2
Tho Hardy	3
James Nelson	3
Nicholas Dawson	2
James Stackhouse	1
John Dawson	1
John Blakey	1
Chr Whitacrees	1
Tho Tayler	2
Tho Rycroft	2
Tho Lingarth	1
Hen Grindrig	1
Hen Whitacrees sen	1
Willm Whitacrees	1
Margarett Tomlinson	1
Tho Blakey	1
Robte Deane	1
John Greene	1
Roger Eccles	1
Ambrose Carr	1
Arthur Anderson	1
Row Raikes	2
Robt Hardy	2
James Jarrett	1
James Smith	1
Geo Tomlinson	1
John Wilson	1
Geo Preston	1
	48

Omitted by reason of poverty	5

m 19]

Robert Moore Collr
Tho Hardy Const

Carleton

Mr Edward Price	2
Mr Tho Parsonson	11
Mr Edward Tempest	2
Widd Bumby	4
John Walton	1
Antho Robinson	2
John Baxter	5
Widd Hargreaves	2
John Calvert	1
Robt Wilson	2
Tho Midlebrough	1

Widd Browne	1
John Cowgill	1
Jonath Cowgill	1
Tho Moone	1
James Gawthrope	1
Tho Lealand	1
James Moone	1
Barnard Hartley	1
Arthur Roberts	2
John Roberts	1
Robert Smith	1
Eliz Midlebrooke	1
Edward Cowgill	2
Mrs Eliz Hargrave	2
Edward Cowgill	2
John Smith	2
Mrs Anne Coates	2
Laur Scurbrough	5
John Sugden	2
Willm Gawthrop	4
Willm Midlebrough	1
Mr John Hargreaves	6
Edward Cowgill	1
Willm Robinson	1
Robert Woodworth	1
Lau Scarbrough	2
Robert Moorehouse	1
Robert Greene	1
John Midlebrough	2
Widd Baxtor	1
Chr Parker	1
Geo Horner	2
John Shrigley	6
Tho Barrett	1
John Tillotson	3
John Constantine	1
Widd Tillotson	2
Peter Scarbrough	1
Simon Tillitson	1
Rich Hindle	2
John Lacocke	1
Robert Smith	1
Stephen Shepheard	1
Antho Hardacres	1
Willm Hewitt	3
Wilfrid Heaton	1
Edward Moore	1
John Robinson	3
Timo Hall	1
John Tillotson	1
Chrofer Pickles	1
Widd Shackleton	3
Tho Smith	1
Arthur Hustler	3
Stephen Rawlin	3
Peter Smith	1
Henry Rycroft	2
Will Northend	1
John Tillotson	1
James Smith	2
John Tillotson	1
Henry Tillotson	1
John Baxter	2
James Dawtry	1
Robert Deane	1
John Heaton	1
Edward Sharpe	1
Edward Hartley	1
Tho Hall	1

m 20]

Mr James Stead	2
James Smith	2
Tho Fell Smithy	1
Tho Dale	2
John Cowgill	1
Hen Hewgitt	1
Edward Banckes	1
Mary Tillotson sen	1
James Tillotson jun	1
Ambrose Hawkes	1
	159
Omitted by reason of poverty	12

Robert Corner Collr
John Smith Const

Cawton

Mr Claxton	9
Tho Fish	1
Widd Preston	2
Hen Wilson	2
Henry Knowles	1
Chr Tatham	1
Rich Kitchin	1
Widd Birtwizle	1
Rich Birtwizle	1
Rich Tompson	1
Hen Lund	1
Willm Nelson	1
Willm Shackleton	1
Geo Nelson	1
Willm Wilson	1
Ri Tompson	1
	26

Tho Midleton Collr
Tho Birtwizle Const

Draughton

Mr John Ramsden	2
Fr Waineman	2
Tho Waineman	2
Willm Wall	1
Chr Wetherhead	1
Will Wall	1
Robt Read	1
Fr Wall	1
Rich Wall	3
Rich Heelas	1
Eliz Tonge	4
Fr Wall	1
Tho Sperritt	1
Tho Robinson	1
John Winterburne	1
John Middleton	1
Tho Simpson	1
Tho Ward	1
Willm Wall	1
John Wilson	1
Agnes Whitingham	1
Widd Gibson	1

Tho Craven	1
Fr Whitacres	1
Chr Lister	1
John Oldfeild	1
Willm Holmes	1
Henry Moorehouse	1
Tho Waineman	1
Tho West	1
Martin West	1
Hen Lanthorne	1
Tho Wall	1
Tho Simpson	1
	42

Omitted by reason of poverty 2

Ri Pickard Collr
Tho Spurrit Const

m 21]

Dent 1st Bill

James Broadley	1
Math Buckle	4
Widd Sedgwicke	1
Geo Mason	3
Row Hodgson	2
John Ward	1
John Noddell	1
Rich Lake	2
Geo Holme	2
Robt Hide	2
John Burton	1
Tho Willam	2
John Burton	3
Willm Trotter	5
James Burton	1
Widd Mason	1
Tho Hodgson	1
Willm Hodgson	1
Rich Hodgson	2
Widd Willam	3
Alex Thistlethwaite	2
Widd Thistlethwaite	2
Miles Prockter	2
Rich Willam	2
Row Harper	1
Henry Crag	1
Widd Capestock	1
Rich Crag	1
Geo Willam	1
Jeffrey Petty	1
Edmond Fawcitt	1
James Holme	1
Hen Sidgwicke	1
	56

Robt Husband Collr
Willm Hodgson Const

Dent 2nd Bill or Deepdall (Dent 2nd Bill or Deepdale)

Widd Waddington	1
Geo Waddington	1
Willm Masson	2
Edward Bainbridge	1
John Capestocke	1
Fr Thistlethwaite	3
Geo Mason	1
Oliver Masson	1
John Ratcliff	1
John Sill	1
Widd Sill	1
John Lamb	1
John Burton	2
James Brathwaite	1
Willm Middleton	1
Geo Masson	1
Rich Robinson	1
Chr Wood	1
John Cragg	1
Widd Haggarth	1
Peter Bunnow	1
Miles Mason	1
Rich Petty	1
Rich Robinson	1
Tho Middleton	1
Ri Middleton	2
Willm Capestock	1
Rich Hodgson	2
Tho Thistlethwaite	1
Jeffrey Holme	1
Leonard Willam	1
Tho Winn	1
Willm Willam	1
Willm Walker	1
Widd Smithwaite	1
John Capstocke	1
Rich Baley	1
Tho Capestock	1
Tho Capestock	1

m 22]

Ralph Burton	1
Leo Burton	1
Widd Willam	1
Rich Whitton	1
John Burton	3
Widd Brathwaite	1
Willm Tennant	1
Geo Mayson	1
Widd Willam	1
Widd Nettleton	1
John Hodgson	1
Tho Wilson	1
John Brathwaite	1
Peter Capestocke	1
Geo Haigarth	1
Willm Smirthwaite	1
Widd Wittan	1
James Chamley	1
Tho Braithwaite	1
Tho Tennant	2
Geo Yates	1
Robte Lund	1
Geo Yates	1
Willm Hodgson	1
Henry Burton	1
Vincent Morthwaite	1
Tho Lund	1
The mill	1
John Ustenson	1
	77

Omitted by reason of poverty	1
Robte Husband Collr	
John Thistlethwaite Const	

Dent 3rd bill

Tho Shaw	1
Widd Trottor	1
Robte Atkinson	1
Rich Heblethwaite	2
Tho Greenwood	2
Robt Jackson	1
Tho Wilkinson	1
Willm Goulthropp	1
Tho Brabann	2
Alex Heblethwaite	2
John Huginson	2
Agnes Fawcitt	2
Alex Thistlethwaite	1
Phil Thistlethwaite	1
Geo Greenwood	3
Widd Greenwood	2
Joseph Cragg	1
John Atkinson	2
John Cragg	2
Widd Archer	1
Tho Archer	2
John Cragg sen	2
	35

George Waineman Collr	
John Atkinson Const	

Dent 4th bill

Rich Hodgson	1
James Spicer	2
John Capestock	3
Edmo Sedgwicke	2
James Smorthwaite	3
Marma Smorthwaite	2
Widd Sedgwicke	1
John Sedgwicke	4
James Moone	4
Antho Fawcitt	2
Leonard Linsley	1
Cuthbert Hodgson	1
Chr Tennant	3
John Willon	1
James Capestocke	1
Geo Capestocke	1
Rich Capestock	1
Laur Hodgson	1
James Yates	2
James Burton	2

m 23]

Widd Hodgson	1
John Burton	2
Edward Moore	2
James Cragg	2
Chr Wood	1
James Hodgson	1
Ri Moyser	1
Marma Hodgson	1
John Bland	1
John Hodgson	1
Mary Tompson	1
Roger Cragg	1
James Capestocke	2
Willm Even	1
Rich Petty	2
Edward Moore	1
John Linsley	1
Richard Mason	1
Thomas Midleton	1
John Yates	1
Tho Walker	1
Henry Tatham	1
John Smorthwaite	5
Tho Winter	1
Marke Petty	2
Chr Tennant	3
Nichol Waterman	5
John Sedgwicke	1
John Browne	2
Alice Sedgwicke	1
Phillip Winster	1
Row Linsley	1
Ralph Linsley	1
James Fawcitt	2
John Sedgwicke	1
	91

Empty & noe distress to be had	
Widd Thistlethwaite	2
Miles Thistlethwaite	1

These persons following are discharged by certificate	
Eliz Linley	1
John Robinson	2
Omitted by reason of poverty	2
Robt Husband Collr	
John Linsey Const	

Dent 5th bill

Edward Thomson	1
Chr Blades	2
John Blades	1
James Nelson	1
Tho Nelson	1
James Thomson	3
John Guy	3
Chr Sedgwicke	2
James Nelson	4
John Trotter	1
Widd Parrington	1
Giles Mason	1
Willm Harrison	1
James Gray	1
John Stockdall	2
John Docker	1
Edm Wilson	1
Jeffrey Guy	4
Will Wilson sen	1
The occupier of Bellow	2
John Rawe	1
John Linsley	1

Alex Guy	2
Will Goldington	1
George Fawcitt	1
Gyles Mason	1
John Langstaff	1
John Fawcitt	1
John Baines	1
Tho Nerby	1
John Guy	1
Edward Holmes	1
George Trotter	1
George Blathorne	1
Widd Guy	1

m 24]

John Dawson	1
Mary Wilson	1
Tho Harper	1
Geo Ewbancke	2
Miles Ewbancke	1
Edward Guy	2
John Dixon	1
Brian Clarke	1
John Fawcitt	2
Willm Nelson jun	1
Widd Parrington	1
Jer Nelson	1
John Warriner	1
Tho Tomlinson	1
Brian Langstaff	1
Chr Blades	1
Gilb Blathorne	1
Willm Shepheard	1
Edward Parrington	1
Tho Owram	1
Mr Lawson	4
Widd Currer	1
James Darby	1
	79

Geo Waineman Collr
Tho Owram Const

Dent 6th bill

Robte Aikeroyde	1
Tho Winn	1
Edward Winn	1
Tho Winn	1
John Windle	3
Edward Dent	1
George Masson	1
Margery Dent	1
Reynold Wynn	1
Robte Dawson	1
John Fothergill	1
Rich Dawson	1
Chr Knowles	1
Willm Masson	1
Will Masson	1
Rich Wilkinson	1
Rich Wilson	1
Geo Holland	1
Tho Masson	1
Rich Harrison	2
Willm Nelson	1
Brian Nelson	1
Chr Wilkinson	1
Jeffrey Atkinson	1
John Dawson	1
Robt Dawson	2
Issabell Collinson	2
John D…son[4]	1
Antho Nelson	2
Miles Thistlethwaite	1
James Dawson	2
Eliz Atkinson	4
Tho Nelson	2
Rich Shaw	2
Gilbert Guy	1
Alice Dawson	3
Edward Morland	2
Antho Nelson	1
Willm Atkinson	2
… Hanley	1
John Cockeronn	1
John Lambert	1

John Nelson	1
John Metcalfe	2
Jer Perkins	1
Widd Dawson	1
John Nelson	1

m 25]

Will Hodgson	1
Robert Row	1
John Forrest	1
John Nelson	1
John Shaw	1
Willm Rowe	1
Mich Dent	1
	71

Robert Husband Collr
Willm Dent Const

Dent 7th bill

Rich Thistlethwaite	1
Jeffrey Thistlethwaite	3
Jeffrey Petty	2
John Thistlethwaite	1
Leo Haggarth	2
Leo Sidgwicke	2
Joseph Hoblethwaite	1
Chr Waddington	1
Rich Haggarth	1
Antho Hodgson	2
Tho Haggarth	1
Leo Sidgwicke	1
Tho Mason	1
Miles Thistlethwaite	1
Will Thistlethwaite	2
Tho Cennes	1
Geo Burton	2
Widd Sidgwicke	1
James Burton	2
Chr Wood	1
Will Haggarth	2
Tho Haggarth	2

[4] Possibly Dawson or Denison.

Miles Mason	1
Thomas Dawson	1
James Haggarth	3
Rich Mason	2
Miles Mason	1
John Mason	1
John Thornton	2
John Sidgwicke	2
Antho Mason	1
George Mason	1
Thomas Mason	1
Edmond Dawson	3
Chr Mason	2
Rich Castocke	2
John Thistlethwaite	1
Ri Thistlethwaite	3
James Sidgwicke	2
James Haggarth	1
John Burton	3
Willm Mason	2
Widd Burton	1
James Burton	1
George Greenbancke	1
John Greenbancke	1
Francis Moore	1
Fran Allon	2
Antho Mason	1
Willm Tompson	2
Willm Burton	1
George Mason	1
James Burton	1
James Benes	1
John Mason	1
John Hacker	1
John Haggarth	2
James Hodgson	1
Henry Mason	1
Ralph Sidgwicke	3

m 26]

Wilfrey Burton	1
Ellin Burton	1
Miles Thistlethwaite	2
Thomas Garthwaite	2
Miles Burton	1
John Burton	1
Ephr Grathwaite	1
John Capestocke	1
John Capestocke	1[5]
Widdow Bones	1
James Capestocke	1
Will Midleton	1
Jerom Thistlethwaite	2
Luke Bonnes	1
Edw Bainebridge	1
Rich Sill	1
Rich Willin	1
Chr Mason	1
	112

Robt Husband Collr
Miles Burton Const

Easington

Will Johnson Esq & his mill	7
Adam Hatfeild	3
Nichol Baley	2
Willm Myers	1
Allon Phillipson	1
Reynold Dickinson	1
Tho Tayler	1
Mrs Bannister	4
Mrs Slinger	5
Rich Wilson	1
John Coates	2
Robert Burrow	1
Willm Clayton	1
Willm Guy sen	1
John Guy	1
Willm Guy jun	1
Hugh Claphamson	2
Will Swainson	1
John Howden	1
John Clayton sen	1
John Clayton jun	2
James Brogden	2
John Butterfeild	1
Willm Prockter	4
Rich Shaw	3
Tho Brenand	1
Tho Coare	2
Widd Harrison	1
Will Day	1
Tho Brenand	1
Tho Elliott	1
Rich Thornton	1
Rich Sutton	1
Rich Mullinax	1
John Bond	2
Hen Briggs	4
Tho Stoute	1

m 27]

Widd Carr	1
Tho Parkinson	1
Robert Blesserd	2
John Peele	1
Chr Fort	1
Nicholas Franckland	1
Edward Beckitt	2
Fr Peele	1
John Hodgson	2
Ri Brearerd	1
Hen Robinson	1
Antho Huddleston	1
Tho Shaw	1
Cuth Hirst	2
Will Brewer	1
Fr Howden	1
Stephen Carr	1
Geo Parkinson	1
Willm Jackson	1
Widd Hodgkinson	1
Tho Parkinson	1
Will Bradley	1
The schoolehouse	1

[5] sic.

Geo Shaw	1
Willm Sutton	1
Tho Brogden	1
Jonath Scott	1
	98

Omitted by reason of poverty 3

Geo Waineman Collr
Tho Brogden Const

Emsley

Fran Demayne	2
John Morritt	3
Rich Watkinson	1
Willm Alcocke	4
Widd Wadsworth	1
Charles Bradforth	2
Robt Waineman	1
Tho Moseley	3
Rich Westwood	1
Mary Settle	2
Rich Colton	1
Will Gawthrop & forge	2
Will Waineman	2
Tho Bolton	3
Agnes Bolton	1
Richard Coates	1
Tho Jackman	3
Willm Atkinson	1
Ri Jackman	1
Robt Jackman	2
Tho Chippendale	1
Will Waineman	4
Will Masson	3
Rich Jackman	2
James Metcalfe	1
Mr Gregson	1
	49

These persons following are discharged by certificate

Tho Waineman	1
Jane Inman	1
John Holmes	1
James Bland	1
John Dickinson	1

George Wainman Collr
Thomas Jackson Const

Eastby

John Petty	1
Nichollas Bolton	1
Margret Chipendale	2
Peter Chipendale	3
Thomas West	2
Richard Mason	1
Peter Fish	1

m 28]

Willm Wainman	1
Willm Burtwisle	1
Thomas Mason	2
Willm Moorehouse	2
Henry Mosley	1
Willm Jolley	1
Thomas Hogson	2
Peter Jackson	1
Thomas Whoatherhead	2
Willm Chipindale forge	1
	25

Empty & noe distress to be had

John Benson 1

The person following is discharged by certificate

Christo Jolly 1

Omitted by reason of poverty 1

Robert Husband Collr
Thomas Chipindale Const

Eashton (Eshton)

Mr John Blackhouse	2
Mr John Wilson	7
Thomas Settle	2
Willm Parkinson	1
Robert Tatham	1
Mary Tatham	2
John Hitchin	2
Jennett Raikes	1
Willm Raikes	1
Eliz Whitwham	1
Geo Brogden	1
Hen Beecroft	1
Bartho Parkinson	1
Tho Wiglesworth	1
Tho Bucke	1
Geo Willand	1
Margar Armistead	1
Willm Simpson	1
Tho Fort	1
Tho Thoneborr	1
Roger Blackburne	1
Jaine Areton	2
	33

Omitted by reason of poverty 7

Robt Husband Collr
Peter Cowin Const

Flaxby cum Winterburne (Flasby with Winterburn)

Mrs Farrand	7
Hugh Currey	2
Will Waineman	2
Mr Robte Pickering	2
Rich Tunstall	1
Widd Howson	1
John Howson	1
Antho Graveson	1
Samll Briggs	1
John Tayler	1
Tho Croft	1

Tho Fairbanck	4
Robte Smithson	1
Tho Kitchin	1
Martin Dickinson	1
Anne Warde	1
…ry[6] Story	1
Willm Howson	1
Rich Dickinson	1
Henry Dickinson	1
Mr John Parker	11
Roger Whaley	7
Willm Parkinson	2
John Wilkinson	1
Widd Remington	2
James Winsley	1
Henry Hill	2
Lanc Oldman	1

m 30]

Henry Mason	1
Tho Hodgson	1
John Constantine	1
Issabell Wharfe	1
Thomas Thorne	2
Stephen Oldfeild	2
Adam Wilkinson	1
Tho Grayson	1
Rich Hargreaves	1
John Tayler	1
Nicho Briggs	1
	72[7]

Omitted by reason of poverty 6

Thomas Middleton Collr
Tho Fish Const

Farnhill

Thomas Harracks	3
Rich Watkinson	1
John Haracar	1
Edward Walsh	2
John Haracar	2
Rich Batty	4
Willm Harrax	2
Tho Greene	2
Rich Overend	2
Willm Barrott	2
Rich Hudson	3
John Skelton	1
Mich Turner	1
Robt Townsend	1
Robt Parkinson	1
Farnhill mill	1
Geo Wilson	1
Mr Samll Squire	4
Willm Sawley	3
Tho Boodwin	2
James Bradley	2
Laur Roberts	1
Hen Sawley	2
Edward Sawley	4
John Bradley	1
Edward Boodwin	1
Will Baxter	1
Hen Gawthropp	1
Will Lister	3
Stephen Hargreave	1
James Gawthrop	1
Tho Robertshaw	1
Hugh Foster	4
Widd Young	1
Henry Smith	2
Edward Walsh	1
Peter Lacock	2
John Smith	2
Willm Lacock	1
Willm Bawdin	2
Tho Bradley	1
Edward Walsh	1
John Bradley	1
Henry Dixon	1
Robt Baxter	2
Edward Welsh	1
Samuell Browne	1
Tho Lacocke	2
John Spench	1
Robt Greenwood	1
John Whitehead	1
	86

Omitted by reason of poverty 7

Robt Corner Const[8]
Tho Greene }
Peter Lacocke }Const

Gigleswicke (Giggleswick)

Antho Lister	4
Mr Tho Claphamson	5

m 31]

Hugh Slackhouse	6
Willm Paley	4
John Gregson	1
Marg Heckett	1
Hugh Claphamson	2
Hugh Claphamson	1
Lawr Lawson	4
Rich Gryne	2
Willm Bancks	4
Robt Overend	2
Tho Brashaw	1
Tho Watkinson	2

6 The forename is perhaps to read as Henry.
7 This is a scribal error as the total is 73, yet the entry for Martin Dickinson's number of hearths is inconclusive, and could be read as one, thereby reconciling the difference.
8 sic.

James David	2
Robt Cookson	1
Mr Coogill	2
Rich Wayden	2
Mr Robt Bancks	6
John Armistead	2
Marg Bond	1
Robert Carr	2
Antho Harrison	2
Rich Roome	1
John Coates	1
Mr Catterill	3
Geo Anderson	1
Eliz Armistead	1
Allen Carr	1
John Sory	2
Tho Brashaw	2
Hen Wilkinson	1
John Winser	2
Widd Foster	4
Fardinand Nicholson	1
Tho Carr	1
Rich Burton	3
Tho Wilson	1
Tho Wright	1
Willm Ash	2
Henry Bland	1
Tho Slackhouse	1
Willm Banckes	2
John Banckes	1
Tho Harrison	2
John Foster	1
Rich Franckland	1
Tho Clapham	1
John Tompson	1
Tho Carr	1
Geo Atkinson	2
Richard Carr	1
Widd Wilson	1
Mr Tho Clapham	5
Mr John Berry	3
Tho Wilson	2
Widd Eaglin	1

Fran Read	4
Willm Browne	1
Mr Willm Paley	5
Math Foulthrop	1
Margt Tayler	1
Henry Tayler	1
Roger Tayler	1
Richard Carr	1
John Midlebrooke	2
Susan Rheynoldson	1
Richard Midlebrooke	1
Rich Rheynoldson sen	1
Willm Midlebrooke	1
Antho Hardwicke	1
Oliver Slackhouse	1
James Newhouse	1
Tho Lawson	1
Stephen Franckland	4

m 32]

More *pro* schoolehouse	1
The Mill	1
James Johnson	1
Roger Preston	1
Rich Ackringley	1
Antho Harrison	2
	150
Omitted by reason of poverty	8

Robert Bennett Coll
John Winsor Const

Glusburne (Glusburn)

Mrs Coates	6
Robert Holmes	4
Edmond Bawdon	6
Stephen Smith	1
Anne Peele	2
Widdow Tillotson	1

Robert Holmes	1
Widd Scott	2
John Spencer	1
John Scott	1
Willm Spencer sen	1
John Rycroft	1
John Bolton	1
Robert Lacock	1
Jonas Heelas	1
Richard Spencer	1
Widd Laycocke	4
Willm Jenings	1
Tho Horracks	2
Tho Horracks[9]	1
Peter Barrett	1
Willm Parkinson	1
John Laycocke	1
Roger Peele	1
Richard Spencer	1
Peter Rycroft	1
Willm Booth	1
Henry Hudson	2
James Tillitson	1
Willm Spencer	1
Willm Overend	1
Henry Spencer	1
John Barrett	1
	53
Omitted by reason of poverty	14

Robt Corner Collr
Willm Overend Const

Grindleton

Willm Earnshaw	1
Tho Shires	2
Tho Hanson	2
Ralph Horner	1
John Swinglehurst	2
Tho Hodgson	2
Thomas Slater	1

[9] sic.

The Coeheires of John Hanson	2
Henry Wallis	1
Wilfray Swinglehirst	1
John Shires	1
Tho Briggs	2
George Horner	2
Thomas Illinworth	1
Edward Greenwood	1
John Leeming	1
Rich Hodgson	2
Tho Illingworth sen	1

m 33]

Ralph Horner	1
Rich Sharpe	1
John Tayler	1
Robte Tomlinson	2
Mr Parker	1
Tho Forrest	1
Rich Horner	2
Tho Chapman	1
Tho Lawson	1
Chr Harrison	1
Widdow Tomlinson	1
Henry Lund	1
John Leeming	1
The hill house	2
John Wetherhead	1
Willm Shires	2
Richard Core	2
Richard Sanderson	1
Henry Scott	1
Ralph Hargreave	1
Henry Tomlinson	1
John Towne	1
Rich Ingskipp	1
Robert Illingworth	1
Stephen Carr	1
John Robinson	1
Henry Birkitt	1
Willm Preston	1
Richard Robinson	1
Thomas Tayler	1
Gyles Parker	1
Francis Wignell	1
Richard Slater	1
Edmond Usherwood	1
George Cotham	1
William Burnitt	1
Mr Parker	1
Tho Clapham	1
Willm Caley	2
	71

Empty & noe distress to be had

Mr Sheareburne	2
Richard Walker	2
Jerome Rathmell	2

Omitted by reason of poverty	8

Robert Carrier Collr
John Swinglehurst Const

Gisburne Forest (Gisburn Forest)

John Ellis	3
Ralph Dobson	2
Tho Swinglehurst	2
Robert Jackson	3
John Swinglehurst	3
Laur Rawsthorne	1
Robert Turner	1
Tho Carr	2
Thomas Clough	1
Henry Geldart	1
Richard Clough	1
Widdow Ellis	1
Robert Battersby	1
Thomas Harrison	1
James Wilcocke	1
Robert Arthington	1
Thomas Simpson	1
Stephen Holgate	1
Willm Hamerton	1
Thomas Geldart	1
Richard Rawsthorne	2

m 34]

Richard Hall	1
William Coore	1
Stephen Smith	1
Richard Carr	2
Willm Bullocke	1
Willm Carr	2
Anthony Ellis	2
Laurence Hartley	1
Robert Geldart	1
John Tomson	1
Anthony Ellis	1
Christopher Lund	2
Henry Lund	1
Robert Butterfeild	3
John Kendall	1
Willm Carr	1
Thomas Carr	1
John Jackson	1
Catherine Clarke	1
John Clarke	1
Henry Holden	2
Oliver Carr	1
Stephen Holden	2
Michll Wood	1
George Holden	2
Rich Holden	1
James Bullocke	1
John Bullocke	1
John Woodworth	1
Stephen Lee	1
George Bullocke	1
James Lee	1
Oliver Carr	1
Rich Abotson	1
Robert Harrison	1
Widdow Knowles	1
Willm Ellis	1
Thomas Guy	1
Edward Billington	1
Widd Ramsdall	1

Thomas Geldart	1
John Watkinson	1
Roger Barker	1
John Barker	1
Martin Haworth	1
Widd Emley	1
Jerome Gregson	1
Edward Gregson	1
	88

Omitted by reason of poverty 3

Robert Husband Collr
Jerome Gregson Const

Gisburne (Gisburn)

Henry Marsden Esq	11
Laur Fearnside	3
Willm King	1
Antho Scott	5
Willm Squire	4
Annis Watson	1
Henry Lund	5
Christo Tidswell	1
Richard Ellin	2
Edward Hodgson	1
Henry Beecroft	2
Widdow Brogden	1
John Ayreton	1
Widdow Ayreton	2

m 35]

Tho Dancer	1
Willm Hallgate	3
Tho Swartbridge	2
Henry Marsden Esq	3
John Hartley	4
Widd Atkinson	3
Tho Smith	2
Ann Scott	3
Tho Ayrton	2
Rich Armistead	5
Rich Sargison	2
Widd Brogden	2
Willm Dancer	1
Willm Tippin	4
Joseph Bridge	2
Willm Dancer	1
Willm Armistead	1
Tho King	1
Edward Chew	2
Tho Armistead	2
Mr John Lister	7
John Hartley	3
Edmond Armistead	2
Thomas Prockter	9
Chrofer Bridge	1
Robert Airton	7
John Pickhard	3
Mr Franc Lister Clerke	5
Mr Lister	1
	124

Empty & noe distress to be had
Nicholas Hargreaves 4

Omitted by reason of poverty 4

Robert Bennett Collr
Tho King Const

Gisburne Grainge Mare (Gisburn Grange)

Matthew Coarre	5
Willm Hartley	5
John Lister	2
Tho Hall	1
Willm Baldwin	4
Will Scott	3
Henry Armistead	2
Widd Cooke	2
Rich Blackbrough	1
Rich Brigg	1
	26

Richard Pickard Collr
Tho Hall Const

Gargrave

Mr Edward Garforth	3
Hen Colthurst	5
Adam Nevill	1
Willm Markindall	1
Francis Tompson	2
Willm Masson	2
Edward Bryans	1
Edward Blakey	1
Widd Watson	1
Chr Thomson	1
Widd Robinson	1
Henry Thomson	1
Mr Wate	2

m 36]

Willm Madelove	2
Robert Markendale	3
Chr Edmondson	2
Rich Andrew	1
James Smithson	1
John Ayreson	1
John Hall	2
Tho Tomlinson	2
Jane Wilcocke	2
Willm Smith	1
Hugh Currer	3
Willm Browne	1
Henry Parkinson	2
Widdow Hargreave	2
Henry Bolton	1
Chr Hall	1
Willm Slater	1
Chr Carr	2
John Tomlinson	1
John Stowes	1
Roger Kitchin	1
Roger Ellis	1
Willm Tomlinson	5
Widd Smith	1
Widd Wilson	1
Rich Browne	1
Tho Carr	2
Willm Arthington	1

Roger Smith	1
Willm Shutt	2
Tho Ellis	3
James Waineman	1
Richard Andrew	1
Willm Parkinson	2
John Stowery	1
Willm Lightfoot	2
Tho Parkinson	1
Christo Paley	1
Tho Smithson	1
John Tattersall	1
John Waineman	1
George Browne	1
Christo Smith	1
Hugh Croft	1
Rich Tomlinson	1
Widd Wade	1
Widd Smith	1
Rich Smithson	2
Abra Robinson	1
Richard Browne	1
Tho Greene	1
Leonard Brashaw	1
	97

Omitted by reason of poverty	5

Richard Pickard Collr
Henry Parkinson Const

Grissington (Grassington)

John Lupton	3
Robert Wrath	1
Tho Kidd	1
Tho Browne	3
John Lealand	1
Widd Wilcocke	2
Thomas Clarke	1
Hen Lealand sen	1
Willm Franckland	1
Fran Wrathall	1
Willm Topham	2
Thomas Marshall	2

m 37]

Geo Heelas	2
Geo Franckland sen	2
John Hewitt	1
John Wrathill	1
Robert Peart	1
Willm Peart	1
Rich Willinson	1
Geo Franckland jun	2
Willm Wrathill	3
Willm Peart	2
Ralph Marshall	1
Laur Deane	1
Stephen Browne	1
John Peart	2
Robert Peart	1
Hen Lealand sen	2
Willm Topham	2
Willm Ibbotson	1
Matthew Hewitt	2
Willm Roberts	1
Stephen Ibbotson	1
Anne Blackburne	1
Robte Ibbotson	2
Joseph Ellis	1
Tho Smithson	1
Mr Willm Newton	2
Tho Watson	1
Widd Oddy	1
Tho Robinson	1
Pearcy Topham	3
Rich Peart	1
Richard Ibbotson	1
Widd Stooke	1
Robt Browne	1
John Smith	1
Geo Browne	1
Geo Maugham	1
Willm Peart	1
	71

Geo Waineman Collr
Joseph Ellis Const

Horton in Craven

Mr Rich Waddington	7
John Lister	1
Thomas Wilkinson	1
James Mitchell	2
Mr Sam Waddington	2
John Mitchell	1
Antho Wilkinson	2
John Wales	1
Widd Armistead	2
Francis Carter	2

m 38]

Michaell Lackland	2
Tho Thornberr	1
James Holt	2
Robt Holt	2
Hen Peele	1
John Wilkinson	2
Widd Wilkinson	1
	32

Geo Waineman Collr
Robt Holt Const

Halton West (West Halton)

Talbut Shepheard	4
Henry Lund	2
Edmond Cooke	3
Edmond Browne	1
John Wilkinson	2
John Lund jun	2
Rich Bancke	2
Leonard Clarke	2
Rich Robinson	1
Henry Lund	1
Henry Lund[10]	1
Willm Shepheard sen	1

[10] sic.

Will Shepheard jun	1
Willm Cooke	1
Stephen Barden	1
John Iveson sen	1
Willm Atkinson	2
Eliz Armistead	1
Antho Cooke	1
Robert Lund	1
John Clarke	1
John Lund	1
Richard Lund	1
John Iveson jun	2
Hen Arthington	1
Richard Bancks	1
	38

Empty & noe distress to be had
Christo Howgate 1

Omitted by reason of poverty 4

Tho Midleton Collr
Edmond Browne Const

Halton East (East Halton)

John Petty	2
Mr Robt Benson	5
Tho Bradley	1
Mr Christo Benson	5
Richard Atkinson	1
Tho Lowlock	1
James Glover	3
Thomas Petty	3
Widdow Glover	5
Thomas Smith	1
Christo Johnson	2
Robert Browne	1
John Bumby	1
Francis Benson	4
John Birch	1
Richard Gott	2
Christo West	1
Willm West	3
Francis West	1
Widd Waineman	1

m 39]

Tho Thompson	1
The Earl of Burlington	9
Willm Greene	4
Widd Carr	2
Richard Croft	2
John Drab	4
John Widdrupp	2
Willm Phillipps	3
Laur Laycocke	2
Tho Turnbull	1
Willm Wright	1
Tho Ward	1
Richard Smith	2
Humphrey Read	1
Willm Waineman	1
Widdow Waite	1
Rich Gibson	1
Willm Kendall	1
Geo Leigh	1
	84

Omitted by reason of poverty 5

Robert Husband Coll
John Birch Const

Hanleth (Hanlith)

Roger Broughton	1
Henry Lawson	1
John Kay	1
John Blackburne	1
Richard Fish	2
Richard Sargison	2
Edward Wilson	1
Roger Sargison	1
Tho Lawson	1
Willm Preston	1
Christo Preston	1
Henry Preston	1
Christo Brayshaw	1
Richard Lund	1
Thomas Townson	1
Thomas Hird	1
Thomas Walker	1
Henry Hall	1
Anthony Clarke	1
Thomas Anderson	1
Willm Atkinson	1
	23

Tho Middleton Collr
Willm Atkinson Const

Hebden

Antho Younge	1
Richard Constantine	1
Richard Constantine	1
Adam Lofthouse	1
Robert Wray	1
Willm Kidd	1
Thomas Rathmell	2
John Browne	1
Jane Topham	1
Robert Topham	2
Thomas Topham	1
Henry Bland	1
George Wray	1
Peter Bland	2
John Ibbotson	1
Willm Topham	2

m 40]

James Ibbotson	2
Richard Tennant	1
Geo Browne	1
Robert Layland	2
George Knight	1
Robert Rothwell	1
Anthony Ibbotson	2
Richard Stainforth	1
Robert Simpson	1

William Fletcher	2
John Layland	1
William Lupton	1
Lyonell Franckland	2
Thomas Younge	2
William Kidd	2
Widd Verrity	1
Robert Kidd	1
John Horner	1
Thomas Fletcher	1
Robert Ibbotson	1
	47

Omitted by reason of poverty	1

Robert Husband Collr
Robert Kidd Const

Hartlington

Francis Hebden	1
Edmond Bland	1
Tho Pawson	1
Tho Pawson jun	1
James Watters	1
James Topham	1
John Watters	1
William Walter	1
William Stamford	1
Robert Shaw	1
Margarett Slackhouse	2
Robert Mawlam	1
Matthew Langstaff	1
Henry Topham	2
Thomas Rycroft	2
John Kidd	1
George Wilson	1
John Younge	1
William Overbrigg	1
Eliazer Squire	1
Wm Broughton	1
Robert Laydland	1
Lawrence Beecroft	1
Widdow Holgate	1
Richard Bolton	1

William West	1
John Richardson	1
Henry Walker	1
Thomas Buckle	1
John Franckland	1
James Craven	1
John Haber	1
William Pagett	1
Thomas Inman	1
John Sheilding	1

m 41]

	38

Empty & noe distress to be had	
Henry Tayler	1

Robert Husband Collr
James Craven Const

Hellifeild (Hellifield)

Mr Stephen Hamerton	10
Henry Holgate	2
Nicholas Banckes	1
Mary Mawson	2
Lawr Camine	1
Henry Walker	2
Robert Armistead	1
Richard Browne	1
Richard Ayrton	1
John Lund	1
John Clarke	1
Tho Camine	1
Henry Hardacrees	2
Lawrence Kay	2
John Kay	1
Henry Kendall	1
Henry Kay	2
Rich Midleton	1
John Preston	1
Richard Armistead	1
William Snell	1

Robert Anderson	2
Lawrence Kay	1
John Woodward	1
John Hamerton	1
John Shaw	2
John Smith	1
Henry Tompson	1
Henry Hall	1
	46

Omitted by reason of poverty	10

Tho Midleton Collr
Willm Bancks Const

Heaton cum Boardley (Hetton with Bordley)

John Franckland	1
Thomas Knowles	1
Willm Blackburne	1
Henry Keighley	1
Thomas Keighley	1
Chrofer Moorehouse	1
Henry Elsworth	1
Christopher Elsworth	1
Mary Franckland	1
John Sharpe	1
Robert Johnson	1
Marke Smith	1
Antho Westwood	1
Willm Wiggin	1
Willm Ellis	1
John Ellis	1
Richard Somerscales	1
Elizabeth Somerscales	1
Willm Pickard	2
John Settle	2
John Scott	1

m 42]

Willm Franckland	1
Simon Topham	2
John Topham	2

Thomas Carlile	1
John Franckland	1
Willm Bootham	1
Thomas Broughton	1
William Darwent	1
Richard Blackburne	1
Thomas Topham	1
Mr Wade	1
Edward Thomson	1
Anthony Prockter	1
Peter Baxter	1
Richard Wharfe	1
Mr Prockter	4
Francis Topham	1
Henry Carrier	2
Simon Wilkinson	2
Thomas Prockter	2
Simon Wilkinson jun	2
Thomas Kidd	2
Simon Wilkinson sen	2
Roger Sargison	1
	58

These persons following are discharged by certificate

Richard Sumerscales	1
Thomas Cockitt	1
Jennet Cockitt	1
Robert Sumerscales	2

Omitted by reason of poverty 2

Robert Husband Collr
John Ellis and John Garforth Const

Hawkeswicke
(Hawkswick)

John Smith	4
Willm Calvert	2
Robert Coldcoate	2
Mr Willm Tennant	3
Rich Fairebridge	1
Willm Nicholson	1
James Scott	1
Henry Knowles	2
James Armistead	2
John Tompson	2
Thomas Wilson	1
Simon Thompson	1
George Armistead	1
Thomas Wilson	1
George Tennant	1
Thomas Preston	1
Tobias Sparke	1
Lawrence Armistead	1
Cuthbert Tompson	1
	29

Robert Bennett Collr
Tho Wilson Const

Horton in Riblesdale
(Horton in Ribblesdale)

Mr Thomas Wilson	4
John Tayler	2
Richard Prockter	4
Anne Armistead	1

m 43]

Edmond Tayler	2
Adam Broadley	1
Antho Tayler	2
Robert Foster	1
Thomas Barton	2
Lancelott Smithson	2
Thomas Lawson	1
Robert Lupton	1
Robert Foster	2
Thomas Howson	1
William Atkinson	1
Lawrence Buton	2
Brian Greene	2
Francis Howson	4
Thomas Eglin	1
John Ward	1
Anthony Eglin	1
John Burton	1
Stephen Eglin	1
Francis Armistead	1
Willm Foster	2
Willm Lilly	1
Thomas Bateman	1
Thomas Lylly	3
John Prockter	2
Widd Prockter	1
Robert Clarke	1
Widd Walker	2
John Clarke	2
George Clarke	1
Thomas Moore	1
Richard Armistead	1
Lawrence Wharfe	1
John Armistead	2
Leonard Dickinson	1
William Howson	1
Christo Lyton	1
Lawrence Swaineson	2
Thomas Foster sen	1
Thomas Foster	1
John Hesleden	2
Thomas Hesleden	1
Francis Howson	1
Lawrence Tunstall	1
Christopher Burton	2
David Dawbikin	2
Widdow Tunstall	2
Anthony Prockter	1
William Bentham	2
Edward Coates	2
Christo Langstroth	2
John Armistead	2
Robert Prockter	1
Edmond Greene	3
Richard Greene	1
John Prockter	1
Willm Hawson	2
Anthony Hesledine	2
John Feildhouse	1
Simon Battersby	4
Robert Burton	1
Stephen Bentham	1

John Jackson	2
Christopher Jackson	1
John Wriglesworth	1
Thomas Moore	1
William Bentham	1
John Bentham	2
William Wildman	2

m 44]

Robert Deane	1
Marmad Burton	2
John Sedgwicke	3
Christo Burton	2
Matthew Wildman	2
Anthony Tayler	2
Willm Moore	1
Anthony Moore	1
Thomas Moore	1
Stephen Moore	3
Stephen Moore	1
William Wetherhead	3
Antho Prockter	2
Thomas Prockter	1
John Prockter	3
Willm Prockter	1
Thomas Wetherhead	1
Peter Battersby	1
Thomas Battersby	1
John Greenbancke	1
Leonard Sedgwicke	2
Margarett Lodge	1
James Waller	1
William Bentham	1
Thomas Lister	2
John Prockter	1
Stephen Sutton	1
Robert Bentham	1
John Lister	1
Richard Langcaster	2
John Metcalfe	2
Francis Prockter	4
John Prockter	2
John Bulton	1
Stephen Tayler	1
John Moore	1
Thomas Knowles	1
John Redman	1
	175

The person following is discharges by certificate

Stephen Howson	1

Omitted by reason of poverty	2

Robt Husband Collr
Tho Moore Const

Ingleton

Anthony Bouch Esq	14
Richard Gibson	1
Leonard Lamb	1
Thomas Lamb	1
Robert Geldart	1
John Sedgwicke	1
Robert Clarke	1
Willm Prockter	2
Thomas Guy	2
John Hazlam	2
Richard Wilcocke	2
Thomas Hodgson	4
John Redman	1
Willm Willcock	2
Lancelott Dowbikin	3
Edmond Sanderson	2
Thomas Sedgwicke	2
William Witton	1

m 45]

Edward Lamb	1
Richard Redman	3
Leonard Redman	1
James Richardson	2
Widdow Babthorpe	2
Elizabeth Tatam	1
The heires of James Simpson	1
John Redman	1
Thomas Prockter	2
Elizabeth Craven	3
Thomas Firbancke	2
John Cocken	2
Robert Walker	1
Richard Walker	2
Henry Wigglesworth	1
Francis Croft	1
Issabell Craven	3
Christo Thurnbancke	1
John Hall	1
Robert Wilkinson	2
Robert Balderson	3
James Skirreth	1
Thomas Walker	1
Christo Oldfield	1
Anne Redman	1
Leonard Hird	1
John Richmond	2
Charles Smith	1
Gyles Redman	1
Christopher Walker	2
Wiliam Lamb	2
Willm Craven	2
Christopher Hird	1
Marmaduke Johnson	1
John Witham	1
Thomas Wilson	1
Anthony Prockter	1
Thomas Hall	1
	100

Empty & noe distress to be had

Laur Butterfeild	1

Omitted by reason of poverty	19

Rich Pickard Collr
Antho Prockter Const

Ingleton Fell Quarter
(Ingleton Fells Quarter)

Stephen Moore	1
Miles Foxcroft	4
Gyles Foxcroft	3
Nathaniell Parker	1
Francis Wetherell	1
Thomas Wetherell	1
William Foxcroft	1
Richard Battersby	2
Thomas Calvert	2
John Johnson	1
Widdow Batty	1
Leonard Prockter	2
Thomas Prockter	1
Stephen Atkinson	1
Thomas Prockter	3
Leonard Foxcroft	1
Thomas Foxcroft	1
John Cansfeild	1
Anthony Prockter	2
Alexander Prockter	1

m 45]

William Wetherhead	2
John Prockter	1
William Bentham	1
Edmond Litton	1
John Burton	1
Anthony Leake	1
Mr Baines	4
James Burton	2
James Wetherell	1
Thomas Prockter	1
Stephen Battersby	1
Anthony Calvert	1
Leonard Calvert	1
Jeffrey Leake	1
Thomas Howson	2
John Langstrath	1
	53

Richard Pickard Collr
James Burton Const

Twisleton & Coldcoates or a member of Ingleton (Twisleton and Cold Cotes)

Mr Anthony Bouch	6
Mr Richard Beesley	6
Anthony Prockter	2
Simon Dawney	2
Andrew Bricke	2
Thomas Greenbanck	2
Leonard Greenbancke	2
Isabell Craven	1
John Wood	1
Elizabeth Wetherhead	2
Robert Nicholson	4
John Prockter	2
Hugh Arnistead	2
Richard Butterfeild	2
Thomas Braithwaite	1
Christo Remington	1
Geo Huginson	1
Thomas Gregson	1
Alice Banckes	1
Rowland Glover	2
Henry Greenwood	2
Willm Thirnbecke	1
Tho Redman	1
Adam Paley	1
John Redman heires	2
James Remington	2
Anthony Battersby	1
Robert Laburne	1
	54

Robert Husband Collr
Marma Redman Const

Kirby Mallandale
(Kirkby Malham)

Tho King jun	3
Widdow King	1
Widdow Horner	1
Richard Masson	1
Richard Wetherell	2
Willm Wetherell	1
Adam Adinson	1
John Husband	1
Widdow Sargison	1

m 47]

John Anderson	1
John Slater	1
Mrs Walton	1
Laurence Hodgson	1
Henry Walker	2
Henry Atkinson	1
Thomas King sen	2
Abraham Kidd	2
John Bentham	1
Adam Atkinson	1
Widdow Hurstley	1
John Parker	1
Willm Atkinson	2
John Atkinson	1
Richard Parker	1
The Freeschoole	1
Cuthbert Kidd	1
	33

Omitted by reason of poverty	2

Richard Pickard Collr
Tho King Const

Kildwicke
(Kildwick)

Hugh Currer gen	14
Mr Robert Collins	3
Mr John Coates	10
Roger Carrocks	2
Jane Netherwood	2
Tho Waterhouse	2
Thomas Coates	1
Rich Holmes	7
Hugh Hudson	3
Henry Briggs	1
Henry Wood	1
Michael Turner	1

Henry Wilson 1
George Emmott 1
Henry Scott 2
Henry Scott 1
Edward Wilson 1
George Baxter 1
Henry Smith 1
Richard Briggs 1
Widdow Hardacrees 1
Robert Smith 1
Michaell Clough 1
59

Empty & noe distress to be had
George Ellmott for the Freeschoole 2
Thomas Jenkinson 1

Omitted by reason of poverty 1

Robert Corner Collr
Henry Briggs Const

Kettlewell
Thomas Messenger 1
James Coates 1
John Stauney 2
Thomas Ryley 2
John Smithson 2
Humphrey Little 1
Christopher Settle 2
Robert Hardcastle 1
Mr Hewett 2
John Ibbotson sen 2
Humphrey Coates 1

m 48]

Roger Bolland 2
Robert Clarke 2
Edward Horsman 1
William Maulby 1
Widd Topham 1
William Coates 1
Christopher Coates 2
John Ibbotson jun 1
John Bolland 2
Widd Prockter 1
Augustine Staney 2
Willm Fawcitt 3
Thomas Coates 2
James Smithson 1
Oswald Stapper 1
John Linsley 1
John Ibbotson 1
Willm Weereing 1
Willm Settle 1
Humphrey Fawcitt 1
Edmond Tennant 1
James Hinde 1
Tho Ripley 1
Mr Tho Mortley 2
Thomas Stauney 2
James Ripley 1
Humphrey Snell 1
James Hulley 2
Willm Coates 1
James Nelson 1
Richard Armistead 1
Vincent Fawcitt 2
Laur Lodge 2
James Stoney 1
John Calvert 1
Willm Calvert 3
Rich Ratcliffe 1
Robert Mitton 2
Robert Calvert 1
Thomas Snell 2
John Strickland 1
John Fletcher 1
Tho Hawley 3
John Coulton 1
John Stonea 2
Chr Simpson 2
Thomas Tatham 1
Widdow Fletcher 1
Willm Fulshaw 2
Guy Colson 1
Christopher Coates 1
William Hardy 1
Lister Simonson sen 1
John Simonson sen 2
Willm Sedgwicke 1
Willm Pearson 1
Christo Simondson 2
Lister Simondson 1
Tho Kidd 1
Tho Dronfeild 1
Thomas Tattersall 1
Mr Robinson 1

m 49]

Henry Ward 2
105

These persons followeing are discharged by certificate
Humphrey Topham 1
Widd Ripley 1
Miles Burton 1
Eliza Ripley widd 1
John Williamson 1

Omitted by reason of poverty 7

Robert Husband Collr
Will Settle and
John Stauney Const

Keighley
Willm Ashton 1
Robert Belton 1
Tho Clapham 1
William Smith 1
John Townesman 2
Geo Clapham 2
Francis Watters 1
Henry Clapham 4
Widdow Hartley 3
John Holdsworth 1

Stephen Parkinson	1
Tho Moore	1
Mr George Keighley	1
John Shuttleworth	1
George Smith	1
Mr Jeremy Craven	1
Widd Beeston	2
John Lupton	1
Thomas Brooke	2
John Hoyle	2
Anthony Hatch	1
John Bawdon	2
Mr Richard Browne	2
Anne Sowden	2
John Steele	1
John Scott	2
John Robinson	2
Anne Poole	1
Willm Potterton	3
Christopher Rhoades sen	1
Willm Mawde	4
John Hole	2
Mr Tho Browne	12
Ellin Phillips	7
Matthew Wilman	2
John Happer	1
Mrs Mary Currey	2
John Ramsbotham	6
Willm Denbigh	1
Chrofer Clapham	1
John Wilkinson	1
Thomas Pearson	1

m 50]

Geo Denbigh	5
Margar Steele widd	1
Richard Denbigh	2
Tho Knowles	4
Tho Wilkinson	2
Thomas Smith	2
John Learoyd	6
Elizabeth Hudson	3
Thomas Jenings	2
Richard Rawlin	3
Widd Drake	4
Anne Lawe	5
John Harrap	1
John Carridus	1
John Drake	3
Francis Fowler	2
John Denby	4
Geo Hudson	4
Geo Dixon	2
Dinnis Steele	1
Willm Clough	4
John Keighley	3
William Smith	3
William Denton	1
John Waddington	1
John Widdop	2
Francis Pasley	1
Avaray Barraclough	2
Mr Thomas Denby	7
John Waddington	1
William Brooke	2
John Wheelewright	2
John Rishworth	1
John Moore	1
Peter Hudson	1
Chrofer Holmes	1
Abraham Firth	1
Stephen Firth	1
John Firth	1
Widdow Holmes	1
William Tillitson	1
Abraham Binns	1
John Shackleton	1
Grace Holmes	1
John Holmes	1
Richard Wheelewright	2
John Wright	1
Walter Wilkinson	1
William Hanson	1
Samuell Midgley	1
Thomas Midgley	1
John Holdsworth	1
Thomas Pickles	3
Henry Pickles	4
William Sharpe	1
Francis Holmes	1
Timothy Dixon	1
Nathaniell Dixon	1
Matthew Holmes	1
Willm Midgley	3

m 51]

Joseph Midgley	1
Willm Midgley	1
Richard Greenwood	1
Edward Moore	1
James Smith	2
Joseph Midgley jun	1
Edmond Hutchinson	2
Robert Tayler	2
Willm Oxnard	1
John Heaton	1
Jonas Rawson	1
Peter Heaton	1
William Binns	2
Richard Sharpe	1
John Wright	3
John Clough	1
William Heaton	1
John Bynn	1
Michaell Tayler	1
Benjamine Tatham	3
John Binns	1
Geo Holdsworth	1
Robert Clough	2
John Heaton	1
Roger Shackleton	2
John Shackleton	2
Robert Hall	3
Willm Sharpe	1
Christopher Eltoft	1
Widd Ickermgill	1
Widd Sharpe	1
Richard Newsam	1
Antho Sharpe	1
Henry Newson	1
Willm Cryer	1
Thomas Bartle	1

John Hanson 1
William Clarke 1
John Shackleton 1
Widd Smith 2
Thomas Sharpe 1
Henry Wright 1
Robert Craven 1
Dinas Cockshott 1
John Shackleton 1
Anthony Wright 2
Robert Ambler 1
Robert Wright 1
John Brooksbancke 2
Geo Sugden 1
Thomas Clough 1
John Steele 3
John Lacocke 1
John Wright 1
Widd Widdop 1
Jonas Townson 2
William Cooke 1

m 52]

Thomas Steele 1
Thomas Bridge 1
Tho Steele jun 1
Willm Widdop 1
Thomas Briggs 2
Thomas Bothamley 1
Christopher Smith 3
John Boothman 1
Willm Hill 1
John Lupton 2
John Smith 1
Willm Denbigh 1
Thomas Barwicke 1
John Denbigh 1
Christopher Hird 2
John Foster 1
John Smith 3
Willm Smith jun 1
Francis Smith 2
Willm Smith sen 1

Willm Bolton 1
John Clapham 1
Samll Craven 1
Samuell Saltenstall 1
Widd Beanland 5
Thomas Pickles 1
Joseph Beaneland 2
Francis Widdop 1
Willm Clapham 3
Richard Shackleton 3
Joseph Leach 1
Edward Moore 1
Matthew Wildman 1
Willm Smith 1
Thomas Clapham 1
William Leach 2
Willm Clapham jun 1
Willm Sugden 1
John Beaneland sen 1
Edward Beanland 1
Willm Blakey 1
Widd Robertshaw 1
Tho Pickles 1
Willm Wright 1
Richard Moore 1
Thomas Tattam 1
John Raper 2
John Hanson 1
John Midgley 1
Anthony Sharpe 1
John Beaneland jun 1
John Sharpe 1
Francis Sharpe 2
John Sugden 2
Nicholas Wright 3
Widdow Sugden 1
Christopher Smith 1
Robert Lancaster 1
Henry Sharpe 2
Chrofer Clarke 2
John Sugden 2
John Clough 2
Edward Moore 1

Jonas Robertshaw 1
John Wright 1

m 53]

Michaell Driver sen 2
Michaell Driver jun 1
Widdow Driver 1
John Barrett 1
John Shackleton 2
Robert Wright sen 3
John Shaw 3
Thomas Tayler 2
Widd Clapham 1
Thomas Hird 4
Robt Smith 2
Willm Hird 2
Thomas Watters 1
Joseph Craven 1
Richard Wooler 2
John Sharpe 1
William Sharpe 1
Simon Sharpe 1
John Browne 1
John Bothomley 2
John Barston 1
Thomas Clough 1
Thomas Briggs 2
Thomas Briggs 1
Widdow Cleward 1
Roger Tatham 1
Francis Sowden 2
William Denton 1

410[11]

Empty and noe distress to be had

Fran Pashley *pro* Tompson 1

These persons followeing are discharged by certificate

Abraham Tilson 1
Isaack Greene 1

[11] This is a scribal error as the total number of hearths is 420.

Omitted by reason of poverty	1
Roger Hardcastle Collr	
John Harper Const	

Linton

Mrs Christo Lancaster	4
Matthew Hewitt Cler	4
Thomas Topham	2
Robert Prockter	2
John Aickroyde	1
Anthony Deane	1
Christo Wilson	1
Thomas Lightfoote	1
John Lightfoote	1
Dennis Prockter	2
Richard Cooke	1
William Bolland	2
George Hewitt	2
Thomas Lupton	2
James Atkinson	1
Ralph Hargreaves	2
Robert Welsh	1
Willm Fountaines	1
John Prockter	1
Henry Currier	2
Willm Wilson	2
	36

Robt Husband Collr
Robt Deane Const

m 54]

Lytton (Litton)

John Prockter	2
Mr Marmad Drake	2
John Atkinson jun	1
Miles Knowles	1
Henry Knowles	1
George Townesend	1
John Clarke	1
Widdow Knowles	2
Gabriell Knowles	2
James Knowles sen	4
Tho Prockter	1
Richard Metcalfe	2
Chrofer Lambert	2
John Winterburne	2
Mr Jonas Dawson	3
James Ellison	1
Lyonell Knowles	2
Willm Wilson	1
Christo Dawson	1
Francis Todd	1
Stephen Frankland	2
Geo Knowles sen	1
Thomas Wetherhead	3
Mr Edward Ward	3
John Lownsbrough	2
James Ellison	2
Willm Preston	2
John Atkinson sen	2
Willm Atkinson	2
Edward Ellison	2
Christopher Preston	1
John Symms	2
George Knowles	1
Thomas Ellison	1
Christopher Tennant	1
Widdow Tennant	1
Laurence Ward	1
Robert Ayreton	1
Thomas Ayreton	1
Thomas Nicholson	1
John Wetherhead	1
John Moppitt	1
James Foster	2
Widdow Knowles	1
Marmaduke Knowles	1
Willm Bentham	1
John Metcalfe	1
John King	2
	75

Robert Husband Collr
James Ellison Constable

Langcliffe

Willm Carr	3
Widdow Kidd	1
Thomas Geldart	1
Jonas Dawson	5
Lawrence Swainson	5
Willm Carr jun	1
Robert Iveson	1
Richard Armistead	3
Anthony Armistead	3
Hugh Coart	1
John Paley	3
Richard Lawson	2
Christopher Rydas	1
Thomas Armistead	1
Thomas Clapham	2
Richard Brashaw	1
Richard Peacocke	1
Robert Wildman	1

m 55]

William Carr	1
Margarett Iveson	1
Willm Clapham	2
	40

Empty & noe distress to be had	
Stephen Robinson	1
Omitted by reason of poverty	9

Robert Moore Collr
Tho Clapham Const

Long Preston

Mr Robert Windle	4
Thomas Knowles	2
Nicholas Bullocke	1
Willm Lawson	2
Thomas Wilson	2
Richard Rycroft	1
John Ryley	1

Simon Bullocke	2
Richard Tayler	2
John Wilson	1
Thomas Wilson jun	1
Thomas Wray	1
Thomas Allon	1
John Preston	2
Jane Clarke	1
Robert Clarke	1
Thomas Hartley	2
Richard Wilkinson	1
Richard Wilkinson	1
Edmond Clarke	1
Thomas Clarke	1
Richard Clarke	1
William Moone	1
Richard Moone	1
Jane Knowles	1
John Knowles	2
Richard Hardacres	1
John Briggs	1
Richard Tayler	1
William Preston	1
Richard Preston	1
Willm Wigglesworth	2
Richard Hartley	1
Christopher Rycroft	1
Edmond Hall	2
Thomas Settle	1
Richard Kayley	1
Thomas Hall	1
Thomas Carrow	2
John Lambert	1
John Clarke	1
Thomas Hewitt	1
Henry Wiggleworth	3
Thomas Anderson	1
Robert Lund	1
Elizabeth Tayler	1
Thomas Snell	1
Stephen Maudesley	1
Robert Batman	1
Roger Prockter	1
Widdow Wigglesworth	1
Thomas Bullocke	2
Austin Wray	2
Annis Maudley	2
Willm Middleton	1
John Clarke	2
Christopher Holgate	2
Henry Snell	1
Issabell Preston	1
Francis Parker	1

m 56]

Michaell Hardacrees	2
Widdow Sargison	1
Lawrence Camin	1
Thomas Caley	1
Robert Batman	1
John Settle	1
Richard Batty	1
Thomas Clarke	2
Richard Tayler	1
Widdow Tayler	1
Alice Moore	1
	94

Empty and noe distress to be had

John Settle	1
Omitted by reason of poverty	17

Robert Moore Collr
Francis Wilkinson
& Edward Hall Const

Mitton

Mr Samll Feildgall	3
Thomas Hall	5
Henry Hall	2
John Hall	4
Alexander Towers	3
John Pilkinton	2
John Read	1
Widdow Read	1
Rosamond Robinson	2
John Dewhirst	1
Francis Dewhirst	1
Robert King	1
Elizabeth King	1
Thomas Nicholson	1
Robert Cotham	2
James Turner	2
John Thorpe	1
Henry Walmesley	1
John Hayton	1
Christopher Beesley	1
Willm Cowill	2
John Ward	2
Henry Yeates	1
Richard Cotham	2
Willm Cowgill	1
Edward Leeming	1
Robert Hindle	1
James Pilkington	3
Widd Parkinson	1
Henry Bleasdale	1
Willm Hindle	1
John Blackburne	1
Cuthbert Crowley	1
James Battersby	1
	55

Empty & noe distress to be had

Tho Tetterington	1

Robert Bennett Collr
Edward Leeming Const

Marton

Mr Thomas Haber	12
Mr Richard Haber	4
Mr Christophe Grandridg	5
Hugh Baldwin Jnr	3
Walter Gleadston	2
Willm Sawley Senr	1
Robert Stockdall	2
Anthony Hartley Junr	3
John Baldwin	2
Ellin Knight	1

Toby Ryley	1
Robert Fort	1

m 59]

Willm Mitchill	1
Widdow Hartley	1
Henry King	3
Henry Hartley	1
Thomas Hall	2
Edmond Sqire	2
Richard Mitchell	3
Robert Munckes	1
John Wilstock	2
Henry Walton	1
Hugh Bawden	2
Widdow Squire	2
Richard Wilson	2
Roger Grimshaw	1
Robert Tempest	3
Isabell Robert	2
Thomas Arnold	2
John Peele	2
John Bawdin Junr	1
Richard Boulton	1
John Pulman	2
James Ellis	1
John Singleman	1
Mr Slearburne	5
Henry Colthrupp	2
Willm Sawley Junr	3
Henry Peele	1
George Forte	1
	88

These persons following are discharged by Certificate

John Baldwin Ser	1
Willm Briggs	1
Willm Measing	2
Easter Bradley	1

Omitted by reason of poverty	2

Robert Corner Collr
Roger Grimshaw Const

Malme Towne
(Malham Town)

Henry Hammon	4
Henry Lealand	2
Thomas Atkinson	2
Thomas Fish	2
Henry Atkinson	2
Thomas Lawson	2
Christopher Lawson	2
Willm Lawson	2
Willm Brashaw	1
John Midlebrooke	1
Willm Atkinson	1
Allice Lawson	1
Grace Hall	3
James Davison	2
James Dixon	1
Thomas Knowles	1
John Shakleton	1
Henry Hall	3
Henry Hill	1
Christopher Walker	1
Widdow Preston	1
Thomas Preston	1
Henry Bradley	1
Thomas Knowles	1
Widdow Bramshaw	2
Thomas Bolland	1
John Anderson	1
Thomas Fird	2
Thomas Brashaw	2
Widdow Knowles	1
Christopher Thompson	1
Richard Hartley	1
Richard Hird	1
Widdow Hill	2
Willm Thompson	2
Robert Hill	1
Christopher Metcalfe	2
Jennet Preston	2
Robert Hodgson	1

m 58]

Thomas Hill	1
Richard Lawson	1
Allice Hill	1
Mathew Knowles	1
Olliver Lawson	1
Henry King	1
Thomas Anderson	1
James Mawson	2
James Thompson	1
	71

Empty and noe distress to be had

John Redman	1

Robert Husband Collr
John Anderson Constable

Mallm Moore
(Malham Moor)

Ralph Buck Senr	2
Widdow Buck	1
John Buck	4
Henry Lighton	2
Richard Hall	2
Ralph Buck Jnr	1
Henry Maudsley	2
Widdow Hartley	2
John Beckwith	2
Marmaduke Browne	1
Thomas Ellinson	2
John Fish	3
Martin Knowles	4
Willm Smith	1
Thomas Tennant	2
Henry Wilkinson	2
Mr Busfeild	3
Peter Buxton	2
Thomas Airton	2
Robert Pickhaver	2
George Knowles	3
Mr John Fish	6
Thomas Warfe	2

Thomas Calie	1
Thomas Whitfeild	4
Thomas Ledgwick	1
James Peacock	2
Thomas Kidd	1
Richard Whitfeild	1
Henry Preston	1
John Walker	1
Francis Topham	1
Robert Paley	1
	67

Robert Husband Collr
Henry Preston Const

Middop

Willm Watterwort	3
Stephen Watson	2
Henry Rawden	6
Willm Watson	2
Mathew Watson	2
Christo Bawden	2
Daniell Lambert	2
John Jackson	3
Michaell Tattersall	2
Henry Deane	3
James Crooke	1
Allexander Hartley	1
John Watterworth	3
	32

Robert Bennett Collr
Henry Bawden Const

Nappa

Henry Arthington	4
Stephen Pickhaver	2
Thomas Wilkinson	1

m 59]

John Wilkinson	1
Henry Atkinson	1
John Wilson	1
Willm Lankaster	1
John Wilkinson	1
Ellin Holmesley	1
Richard Wilkinson	1
	14

Thomas Midleton Collr
Richard Wilkinson Const

Newsholme

Willm Baldwin	1
Thomas Corlas	2[12] two
Stephen Hodgson	1
John Coare	2
Christopher Gregson	1
Thomas Loundall	2
John Sawley	2
Robert Dodgson Jnr	2
Hugh Lownsdall	2
Martin Dickinson	2
Henry Corlas	1
Stephen Atkinson	1
John Arton	1
	21

Thomas Midleton Collr
John Sawley Const

Newby cum Clapham
(Newby with Clapham)

Mr Henry Slinger	3
Thomas Bradley	2
Richard Wildman	1
Robert Bradley	1
Robert Remington	3
Willm Thomlinson	2
Thomas Remington	2
Robert Hawson	1
Christopher Foster	2
Bryan Carr	2
Thomas Harrison	1
Richard Benson	1
James Pearson	2
Thomas Yeaden	1
Henry Battersby	1
Mr Christopher Robingson	3
Widdow Prockter	2
Widdow Bradley	1
John Bradley	1
James Battersby	1
Richard Breadley	1
Christo Wildman	2
Anthony Battersby	1
James Bersby	2
Thomas Guy	2
Widdow Battersby	1
Henry Greenfeild	2
Anthony Prockter	2
Henry Walker	2
John Prockter	1
Widdow Armistead	1
Thomas Knowles	3
Robert Thornton	1
James Foster	1
John Foster	1
Christo Guy	1
Jane Redman	1
Willm Lupton	1
Thomas Foster	3
Widdow Wildman	1
Thomas Foster	1
Christo Foster	1
John Lupton	1
Lawrence Lupton	1
John Tennant	1
Agnes Wildman	1
Lawrence Foster	1

m 60]

John Wildman	1
Robert Lupton	1
	72

[12] Written over 3.

Omitted by reason of poverty 2

Robert Moore Collr
James Battersby Const

Newton in Bolland (Newton formerly Newton in Bowland)

Tempest Slinger Esqr 8
The occupiers of Crawshaw of Crashaw 2
Widdow Stainbridge 1
Widdow Witton 1
John Maisters 2
Richard Shuttleworth 1
Stephen Harrison 1
Leonerd Leigh 2
Edward Turner 1
Scarbrough house 1
Edmond Day 1
Christo Raingill 2
John Driver 1
John Parker 1
Edward Hodgkinson 4
Ralph Faber 4
Henry Parker 2
Nichollas Clough 1
Edmond Walbank 2
Widdow Standing 1
Richard Hurst 1
Occupiers of Standing yates 1
James Rudd 1
Widdow Rudd 1
James Lee 2
Robert Walbank 1
Richard Hurst 2
James Hill 1
Occupiers of Heaks tent 1
John Heake 1
Thomas Clarke 2
Thomas Scott 1
John Beckitt 3
Robert Huntington 1
John Slackhouse 2
Willm Birkitt 2
Occupiers Chapelworth 1
Widdow Turner 1
Edward Clough 1
John Parker 1
Ellen Scott 1
Giles Parker 1
John Singlehurst 1
Mark Brogdon 1
Willm Standing 1
Robert Standing 1
Mr Edward Parker 3[13] Three
Christopher Slator 1
John Slayter 1
Henry Batson 1
Richard Leich 2
John Turner 1
Thomas Turner 2
Cuthbert Hirst 1
James Rudd 1
Thomas Bond 1
Widdow Turner 1
Robert Turner 1
Richard Sharples Jnr 1
Richard Warren 1
90

Empty and noe distress to be had
Edward Clough 1

The person following are discharged by Certificate
Ellin Skiner 1

Omitted by reason of poverty 3

m 61]

Thomas Midleton Collr
Edward Clough Const

Otterburne (Otterburn)

Mr Wadington 7
Richard Roberts 1
Thomas Hird 1
Willm Kendall 1
Adam Preston 1
Willm Roberts 1
John Hill 1
Henry Atkinson 1
Christopr Tatham 1
Thomas Preston 1
John Atkinson 2
18

Empty and noe distress to be had
John Atkinson 1

Omitted by reason of poverty 6

Willm Midleton Collr
Willm Kendall Const

Playthorne (Paythorne)

Willm Lister 5
Willm Clarke 1
John Geldart 2
Thomas Wiggleworth 2
Ralph Browne 2
John Browne 2
John Browne 2
John Hawson 1
Anthony Wilcock 2
Henry Hewitt 2
Christopr Browne 2

[13] 3 written over 1.

Willm Mattock	1
Thomas Lancaster	1
Willm Wilkinson	1
Widdow Carlas	1
George Airton	2
Robert Dodgson	2
Henry Allen	1
John Airton	1
Edward Sergison	2[14] two
Thomas Airton	1
Willm Reddihough	1
John Geldard	1
Henry Carr	1
Henry Hewitt	1
Thomas Airton	2
Willm Browne	1
Peter Wilson	1
Widdow Brogton	1
	45

Omitted by reason of poverty 7

Robert Moore Collr
Willm Geldart Const

Ryleston (Rylstone)

Mr Francis Stireing	6
Mr Watkinson	3
Richard Taylor	1
James Coniers	1
John Ripley	1
John Foster	1
Vicktor Milner	1
Richard Bolton	2
Lawrence Gregson	1
John Kithin Senr	1
Anthony Garforth	1

m 62]

Arthur Wild	1
John Prockter	1
John Scott	1
Thomas Clarke	1
Richard Ibbitson	1
Richard Scott	1
Richard Ellisworth	1
Richard Burton	2
Henry Keighley Jnr	1
Willm Airton	1
Richard Ibbeson	1
John Blackburne	1
John Cooke	1
John Kithin Jnr	1
Thomas Ripley	1
Thomas Telforth	1
Richard Hill	1
Richard Gray	1
Thomas Scott	1
Thomas Bramley	1
John Scott	2
Margrett Dickinson	1
Henry Keighley Senr	1
Richard Dickinson	1
Robert Smith	1
Mathew Woolmer	1
	47

Empty and noe distress to be had

Christopr Blackburn 1

Omitted by reason of poverty 1

Robert Husband Collr
Richard Balden Const

Remington (Rimington)

John Lister	16
John Sawer	2
Christopr Metcalfe	1
John Atkinson	1
James Oddy	2[15]
Robert Baldwin	2
James Burtwisle	1
Ellizabeth Oddy	1
Willm Wilkinson	1
Willm Wilkinson	3[16] three
Widdow Parkinson	4
George Shuttleworth	4
Willm Oddy	2
John Oddy	2
Willm Baldwin	3
James Varley	2
John Shuttleworth	1
Widdow Hartley	1
Robert Chapman	1
James Dewhirst	1
Willm Brearley	3[17] three
Richard Brearley	1
John Baxter	1
Widdow Dancer	1
John Whittacris	2
Richard Ellinthorp	1
Widdow Spencer	1
Henry Hall	1
John Browne	1
Richard Hall	1
George Shutleworth	2
Henry Ellett	2
Thomas Bradley	2
James Holt	1
Henry Read	1
Lance Hartley	2

[14] 2 written over 1.
[15] 2 written over 1.
[16] 3 written over 2.
[17] 3 written over 1.

Willm Blaybrough 2
John Shaw 1
Stephen Hargravs 1
Willm Hargraves 1
Edward Craven 2
James Dickinson 3

m 63]

Thomas Oddy 2
Jonath Watson 1
John Varley 2
Richard Fort 2
John Oddy 2
Willm Dancer 1
Robert Emott 3
James Brearley 2
Richard Hornby 2
Willm Robinson 2
Willm Hartley 2
Henry Read 1
John Dancer 1
Henry Hall 1
Thomas Calverley 1
John Speak 1
Willm Fort 1
John Speake 2
Peter Watson 1
James Holt 1
Christopher Blabrough 1
Mathew Robinson 1
Jonathan Wofendall 1
Edward Crossdall 1
119

Omitted by reason of poverty 5

Robert Corner Collr
Willm Broadley Const

Ratmell
(Rathmell)
Charles Nowill Gent 7
Anthony Foster 4
Thomas Armistead 2
Francis Duckitt 1
John Armistead 3
John Browne 2
Willm Craven 3
Richard Frankland 3
John Swainson 1
John Swainson 1
Richard Walbank 1
Robert Standing 1
Robert Carr 1
John Browne 1
Olliver Bradley 1
John Browne 1
John Moore 5
Edward Blackburn 1
Willm Atkinson 1
Robert Wetherill 1
Willm Bankes Junr 1
Willm Bankes Senr 2
Henry Walmley 1
John Armistead 2
Willm Knight 1
John Foster 3
Christopr Browne 1
Roger Carr 1
Henry Clark 3
Henry Clarke 2
Mr Knipe 2
Willm Ash 1
Margret Settle 2
Christopher Tatham 3
James Howton 1
Ralph Buck 1
Willm Currey 3
Willm Torpin 1
Margeritt Howton 1
Thomas Carr 2
Thomas Knowles 2
Richard Armistead 3
Richard Voughton 1
John Swainson 1
James Carr 2
Christopr Armistead 1
Thomas Bullock 1

m 64]

Willm Dickinson 1
Thomas Mason 1
John Carr 1
89

Empty and noe distress to be had 1
John Longstroth 1

Omitted by reason of poverty 7

Thomas Midleton Collr
Richard Armistead Cons

Sutton
Henry Horsfeild 7
Willm Barrett 4
Willm Emott 1
Peter Blackey 1
Robert Thompson 2
Adam Barett 1
John Brookesbanke 1
John Dransfeild 2
Thomas Driver 2
Edward Shakleton 2
Richard Swift 1
Thomas Huller 1
Richard Shackleton 1
John Shakleton 1
Robert Barrat 1
Willm Jackson 1
Thomas Bothemley 2
Jonas Heaton 2
Averah Jackson 1
John Clough 1
John Driver 2[18]
two

[18] 2 written over 1.

Richard Driver	2[19] two
Lawrence Briggs	1
Widdow Dixon	3
Edward Wilson	1
Arthur Hudson	2
Robert Jackson	2
Robert Harpes	4
Thomas Briggs	1
Willm Briggs	2
Thomas Barrot	2
Hugh Smith	2
Widdow Briggs	2
Thomas Hague	3
Abram Barret	1
John Barrott	2
Willm Craven	3
John Smith	1
John Craven Junr	2
John Shakleton	1
John Barrot	3
Willm Smith	2
John Barrot	2
John Barret Carpenter	1
Widdow Barrett	1
Peter Barret	1
Robert Scott	2
Edward Hartley	1
Henry Hudson	1
Christopr Bridge	1
Christopr Tillison	1
	90

Omitted by reason of poverty 2

Robert Corner Collr
Richard Swift Const

Slaydburn (Slaidburn)

Richard Marsden	4
Widdow Hide	3
Mr John Brodill	4
Willm King	3
Christopher Bremond	3

m 65]

Robert Wilkinson	3
Henry Ramskill	3
James Floyd	2
John Battersby	2
Widdow Bankes	3
Robert Ramskill	1
John Comb	1
Willm Baxter	1
Robert Battersby	1
Robert Parker	2
Willm Atkinson	2
John Pearson	1
Henry Row	1
Willm Harrison	1
Thomas Scott	1
Widdow Gregson	1
Richard Sharpas	1
John Bullock	1
Samuell Stackhouse	1
Leonard Lee	1
Francis Frankland	1
John Crossdall	1
James Parkinson	1
Thomas Cutler	1
Willm Swinglehurst	1
Widdow Hide	1
Shaw house	3
Willm Carter	4
Robert Hide	3
Thomas Mitton	3
Willm Prockter	2
Willm Bankes	1
John Atkinson	1
John Smithson	1
John Stephenson	1
John Bankes	1
John Beamond	1
Willm Smithson	2
Jane Yeaden	1
Widdow Crofft	1
Leonard Lee	3
John Bullock	2
Ambrose Parkinson	1
Samuell Leeming	1
Edward Battersby	2
Widdow Bond	1
Ralph Newsham	1
Christopher Woodworth	2
Richard Taylor	1
Sager Hill	1
Henry Shaw	1
Ralph Walker	1
John Hide	1
Thomas Battersby	1
Robert Brinald	1
Henry Atkinson	1
	99

Empty and noe distress to be had
Baite Hall 2

Omitted by reason of poverty 9

m 66]

George Wainman Collr
John Hide Const

Silsden

Thomas Rushforth	1
John Rushforth	3
Richard Whitfeild	1
Widdow Eastbarne	2
Richard Cromack	1
Martin Johnson	2
John Cockshott	1
Willm Mortiman	1
Thomas Jackson	1

19 2 written over 1.

John Cooling	1
Robert Mithill	2
Thomas Sawley	2
Thomas Whitfeild	1
Widdow Walsh	1
Willm Engleworth	1
George Lambert	5
Isaack Widdop	1
Thomas Hardcastle	1
Abram Booth	1
Willm Booth	1
Peter Phillips	2
John Hanson	2
Robert Smith	2
John Waid	1
Dines Amber	2
Hugh Watkinson	2
John Barrett	3
Widdow Scott	2
Robert Blackey	2
Jonathan Waid	2
Joseph Ambler	1
John Cryer	1
Thomas Cryer	1
Willm Cryer	1
Widdow Sumerscales	2
Widdow Wadsworth	1
Henry Wilkinson	1
Robert Blackey	1
Edmond Coates	1
Richard Wilkinson	1
Widdow Parkinson	2
Widdow Briggs	1
Willm Watson	3
Henry Stirk	2
George Scott	1
George Snaw	1
Mathew Wilkinson	1
Joseph Wilkinson	1
Thomas Hardy	1
John Foster	2
Henry Wilkinson	2
Willm Blackey	1
Widdow Peacock	1
Peter Lambert	2

Thomas Fowler	3
Willm Cromack	1
Thomas Hustler	1
Edmond David	1
George Stirk	1

m 67]

Widdow Stones	1
John Boulton	1
Joseph Wilkinson	1
Robert England	1
Thomas Cockshott	2
Samuell Stones	1
Willm Gott	1
John Stones	1
John Netherwood	1
John Willysey	3
Georg Wilson	1
John Watkinson	2
Edmond Watkinson	2
John Tayler	1
Thomas Cryer	1
Willm Smith	2
Willm Cockshott	1
Widdow Jennings	5
Jonas Laycock	2
Willm Mitchill	2
Anthony Whitfeild	1
Willm Forton	1
Henry Barrett	2
Willm Ambler	1
Arthur Cryer	2
Edmond Witham	2
James Gill	1
Edmond Gill	1
Peter Horne	2
Thomas Forton	2
John Whittingham	2
Widdow Teale	1
Richard Towsend	3
Widdow Hustler	1
Robert Gott	1
George Blackey	1
Thomas Waid	2

Thomas Booth	3
Willm Bradley	2
Willm Potterton	1
Isaacc Denbigh	2
Thomas Bramley	1
Thomas Ealburne	1
Richard Gill	2
Widdow Gill	1
John Waid	2
John Dilson	1
Thomas Ealburne	2
John Taylor	3
Henry Withham	2
Robert Reynard	1
Willm Wilson	2
Mr Jeremiah Craven	8
Francis Start	2
John Hustler	1
Widdow Crawshaw	1
John Robinson	1
Willm Ambler	1

m 68]

Widdow Ambler	3
Robert Hudson	1
Willm Smith	1
Stephen Hargrave	1
Edward Cromack	1
Robert Lambert	1
Richard Waid	1
Richard Welsh	1
Edward Collins	1
Lawrence Midlebrough	1
Willm Eatburne Cler	2
Thomas Dixon	1
Willm Eshburne	2
Henry Hardy	1
Peter Barritt	1
John Teale	1
Peter David	1
	208

Empty and noe distress to be had

Edward Bawdwine	1

The person following is discharged by Certificate
Christopr Broadley 2

Omitted by reason of poverty 6

Roger Hardcastle Collr
Peter David Const

Skipton
Anne Countess of Pembroke 60
Willm Jenkinson 1
Dorothy Hodgson 6
Nicholas Goodgeon 2
Robert Rowell 1
Anthony Wade 3
Willm Sutton 6
Thomas Oddy jun 4
Francis Catterson 8
John Wardman 5
Widdow Wardell 4
Henry Goodgeon 3
Robert Farmer 6
Robert Aston 8
Mr Robert Squire 3
Thomas Kitchin 2
Thomas Tayler 1
Robert Goodgeon 3
William Foster 4
Mr Thomas Parcivall 8
Mr Thomas Wells 4
Mr Goodgeon 5
Jane Bolton 2
Willm Goodgeon 2
Thomas Wilkinson 2
Christopher Corke 1
John Lambert 1
Thomas Whitakers 1

m. 69]

Robert Moore 1
Mr Tho Barker & schoole 4
Widd Lowcocke 2
Dorothy Hodgson p[ro] Newby 3
Willm Deane 1
Christopher Corke 3
John Barnsey 1
John Wilkinson 1[20]
John Scott 1
Widd Holegate 2
Richard Wardman 1
John Catten 1
Christopher Allenson 1
Thomas Pearson 2
Henry Mitchell 10
Robert Mitchell 6
Edward Greenwood 7
Christopher Benson 3
John Mitchell 3
John Cowper 2
Jane Bowcocke 1
Henry Wilson 1
Christopher Robinson 1
Widd Calvert 1
James Thackhurst 1
Thomas Halliday 1
Thomas Waller 1
Anne Waller 1
Willm Goodgeon 3
James Younge 1
Robert Johnson 1
The Walke mill 2
Christopher Younge 1
Edward Barras 1
Willm Deane 1
Mr Wharfe 2
Mr Bowcocke 5
Mr Robert Squire 3
Willm Browne 3

Mr John Jackman 3
Margarett Tiffins 2
Mary Oldfeild 4
Thomas Ayreton 4
Samuell Squire 6
John Bowcocke 2
Samuell Mitchell 5
Richard Dixon 2
Timothy Bancke 5
Willm Stephenson 2
Willm Hodgson 2
Willm Austwicke 1
Thomas Goodgeon 1

m 70]

Roger Swire 4
Samuell Green 6
Widd Surr 4
Edward Oddy sen 5
Roger Robinson 2
Willm Burtwisle 4
John Tompson 3
Mr Fenwicke 8
Mr Edward Barker 4
Chropher Aucocke 4
Thomas Iveson 1
Thomas Tayler 2
Francis Oldfeild 2
Edward Goodgeon 3
James Patefeild 1
William Smith 1
John Haworth 1
Thomas Wilson 5
Mrs Anne Greene 3
John King 2
John Heelas 2
Willm Currer 2
Thomas Johnson 1
Widd Morras 3
John Morras 2
Willm Morras 1
John Lupton 2

[20] In the *Nomina Villarum* John Wilkinson is described as a smithy, with three hearths.

James Barritt 1
Robert Barritt 1
John Paley 1
Samuell Greene 1
Willm Sumerhope 1
Willm Squire 2
Thomas Wells 1
Thomas Goodyeare 1
377

Empty & noe distress to be had
Mr Wharfe 1
Chrofer Geldart 1
Willm Summer 1
Robert Mawlam 1
Thomas Whitacres 1

Omitted by reason of poverty 29

Richard Pickard Collr
Robt Squire Const

Sawley & Towneside (Sawley and Tosside)
Nathaniell Hartley 3
James Briggs 2
John Briggs 2
Thomas Briggs 1
Henry Briggs 1
Widd Core 2
John Hanson 1
Widdow Hanson 1
John Duckworth 1
Thomas Ellis 1
James Banckes 2
Henry Ellinthorpe 1
Nathaniell Halstead 5
John Ingham 1
Widdow Ingham 1
Widdow Heake 1
Henry Wilkinson 1
Hugh Baldwin 3
John Walker 1
John Hoyle 1

m 71]

Richard Kendall 1
Thomas Briggs 1
Widdow Handcocke 1
Mathew Robinson 1
Thomas Swinglehirst 1
Widdow Spencer 1
Thomas Slater 1
Widd Hinde 2
Thomas Hargreaves 2
John Scott 2
John Oddy 1
Widdow Gibson 1
John Chew 1
Robert Emmott 1
John Robinson 2
Henry Preston 2
John Bullocke jun 1
James Woolfindale 1
George Bolland 3
John Bullocke 1
Geo Robinson 2
Willm Holmforth sen 2
Willm Geldart 1
George Robinson 2
John Usherwood 1
Robte Usherwood 1
John Usherwood 1
John Shepheard 1
Willm Bullocke 1
John Bullocke 4
Henry Walker 1
Widdow Carr 2
Laurence Robinson 1
John Robinson 1
Ralph Jackson 1
Willm Robinson 1
Nicholas Walker 1
William Pinder 1
James Wood 1
Nicholas Hindle 1
Thomas Parkinson 1
John Stothard 2
Margarett Chew 1

Widdow Baldwin 1
Thomas Hindle 1
John Harrison 2
Thomas Geldart 1
John Lawson 1
Richard Bridge 1
97

Omitted by reason of poverty 2

Robte Moore Collr
John Bullocke Const

Swinden
Henry Wiglesworth 6
Willm Wilkinson 4
Michaell Wise 2
Lawrence Kay 6
Thomas Hargreaves 3
Stephen Clarke 2
Issabell Wise 2
Richard Dawson 1

m 72]

George Lambert 1
Willm Higgins 1
28

Omitted by reason of poverty 3

Tho Midelton Collr
Chrofer Clarke Const

Scawsthropp (Scosthrop)
Thomas King 1
Christopher Preston 1
William Preston 2
Francis Lund 1
Robert Carlile 1
John Younge 2
Robert Lund 1

Henry Grime	1
Robert Lawson	1
William Settle	1
Robert Greene	1
Anthony Remington	2
John Lawson	1
John Iveson	2
Thomas Benson	1
Stephen Holgate	1
	20

Empty & noe distress to be had	
John Myers	1
Omitted by reason of poverty	4

Robert Moore Collr
John Rawson Const

Steeton

Mr Willm Garforth	8
Henry Craven	2
Thomas Mossen	1
John Mitchell Jun	1
Christo Craven	2
Willm Hustler	1
William Tompson	1
Dinnis Waide	1
Richard Davies	2
John Mitchell sen	2
John Lowcocke	1
Jerome Hustler	1
Richard Jackson	2
Richard Metcalfe	2
Thomas Theaber	1
Thomas Hodgson	2
Matthew Smith	2
William Davie	2
Michaell Greenwood	1
William Anderson	1
John Bordgatt	1
Richard Hall	1
Robert Hudson	1
Jerome Lacocke	1
Richard Hustler	1
John Jackson	1
Anthony Holmes	2
Ralph the Miller	1
John Hudson	1
Peter Tempest	1
Richard Hustler	1
Dinnis Barrett	1
Hugh Currer	1
James Lund	4
John Wilson	2
Stephen Moorehouse	3
John Parkinson	3
Richard Ripley	1
Stephen Parkinson	1
Henry Ripley	1
Peter Bawden	2
Henry Ripley	4
Henry Ripley	2
Willm Parkinson	1
Richard Jackson	1
Abraham Smith	1
	76

Robert Bennett Collr
Stephen Morehouse Const

m 73]

Stainforth

Samuell Watson & mill	6
Chrofer Dawson	4
Joseph Dawson	2
John Paley	3
William Clapham	3
John Armistead	2
James Cooke	1
Hugh Armistead	3
Thomas Armistead	3
William Foster	4
Francis Lupton	3
John Hodgson	2
Francis Clapham	2
Antho Clapham sen	1
Antho Clapham jun	2
Widd Franckland	1
Willm Readman	2
Joseph Preston	1
Richard Fulthropp	1
William Hartley	2
Richard Wharfe	3
Roger Armistead	2
Robert Twisleton	2
William Paley	2
Chrofer Browne	2
Josias Dawson	1
Thomas Armistead	1
Richard Ayreton	1
Robert Lakeland	2
James Foster	3
James Armistead	2
Richard Foster	2
Bridgett Swainson	2
Thomas Craven	2
William Armistead	3
Robert Kidson	1
Thomas Moorehouse	1
Laurence Tompson	2
Isaack Wood	1
William Foster	3
Richard Iveson	1
William Paley	1
Thomas Preston	1
Widdow Iveson	1
John Gibson	1
Alice Husband	1
James Davy	1
	93

The person following is discharged by certificate	
Henry Leakland	1
Omitted by reason of poverty	2

m 74]

Tho Midleton Collr
Tho Murras Const

Settle

William Carr	2
John Kidd	2
George Craven	2
Richard Armistead	2
John Robinson	1
William Armistead	2
John Hall	2
Anthony Prockter	1
William Birkitt	1
John Sidgwicke	1
Hugh Hall	2
Roger Armistead	3
John Greenwood	1
Richard Armistead	1
John Relfe	1
Chrofer Armistead	3
Willm Windle	3
Huhgh Lawson	1
Henry Cundall	1
John Harrison	1
Richard Armistead	3
John Kidd	2
John Carr Clerke	3
Willm Deane	3
George Carr	2
William Carr	3
Francis Slackhouse	2
William Tennant	3
John Richardson	3
Thomas Dawson	3
William Prockter	3
Mr Walker	2
John Wildman	4
Richard Wright	5
Anthony Wright	3
Roger Cooke	1
Thomas Kidd	2
Allon Carr	4
Richard Ash	2
Robert Chamberlane	3
John Lupton	2
Issabell Atkinson	2
John Tennant	2
Roger Ashton	1
Robert Parkinson	2
William Newhirst	2
William Colson	1
William Lupton	1
Chrofer Laton	1
Adam Eglin	1
William Preston	2
Elizabeth Lawson	1
Catherine Hawson	5
Henry Towler	3
John Winson	3
Agnes Altham	3
John Batty	3
Henry Howton	2
Henry Sparke	2
Henry Lund	2
John Robinson	7

m 75]

James Cookson	10
Brian Cookson	6
John Moore	3
Thomas Redihough	3
William Rayley	2
The mill	1
John Ellis	1
Anthony Hall	4
Robert Armistead	3
Robert Greenwood	1
Widdow Foster	5
Adam Browne	3
William Tayler	3
Richard Atkinson	1
William Atkinson	1
Thomas Prockter	1
Richard Preston	3
Henry Knowles	2
Anthony Knowles	2
Robert Lawson	1
John Barton	2
Thomas Wright	1
Richard Carr	1
Thomas Lawson	2
Thomas Tompson	1
Michaell Preston	1
John Armistead	1
William Waide	1
George Paley	1
Robert Wilson	1
Margarett Iveson	1
Edward Young	1
Lawrence Tayler	1
	208

Empty & noe distress to be had

Mr Walker	1
John Carr	3

Omitted by reason of poverty 6

George Waineman Collr
Robert Kidd Const

Sturton (Stirton)

Hosen Bradforth	1
Anne Bradforth	1
Chrofer Bowcocke	2
Robert Croft	1
Francis Domaine	2
Ellin Grime	1
John Bowcocke	1
Mary Atkinson	1
Thomas Atkinson	1
Henry Atkinson	1
Thomas Oxnard	2
Richard Ellis	1
Anne Harrison	1
Jennett Gleadston	1
Anthony Robinson	1
Willm Tompson	2
Alice Domaine	2

George Myers	1
John Oldfeild	2
William Brogden	2
Willm Catterall	1
Thomas Snell	1
John Hird	1
Robert Myers	1
John Austwicke	1
John Pearson	1
Widdow Harrison	1
Widdow Jennings	1

m 76]

	35
Omitted by reason of poverty	4

Tho Middleton Collr
Willm Brogden Const

Sedbergh first bill Marthwaite Qurtr (Sedbergh, first bill Marthwaite Quarter)

Doctor Fawcitt	1
Henry Bland sen	2
Henry Bland jun	3
James Bland	2
Thomas Burton	1
Francis Blaykling	1
John Branthwaite	1
Thomas Crowther	2
William Harrison	1
Christopher Banckes	1
John Atkinson	1
Sarah Shaw	1
Elizabeth Crowther	2
Richard Hobson	1
Richard Corney	2
George Parke	1
Willm Corney	4
Christopher Corney	1
Thomas Tayler	2
Richard Willan	4
James Rownson	2
Margarett Mann	2
John Tomlinson	2
John Langstaff	2
Christopher Heblethwaite	3
John Otway Esq	11
Richard Speight	1
John Dawson	1
Charles Atkinson	1
Richard Robinson	2
Anne Atkinson	1
Mr Ottway	1
Richard Willan	1
Willm Singleton	2
Margarett Dawson	1
Robert Handley	1
Robert Handley	1
John Bland	2
Robert Hodgson	2
Jeffrey Fawcitt	2
Mr Fell	4
Mabell Shaw	1
George Rannson	1
Willm Corney	1
John Heblethwaite	2
Christopher Croft	1
John Croft	1
Thomas Holme	1
Thomas Bowland	1
Robert Moore	2
Thomas Gabetus	1
Richard Wadson	1
Richard Wadson	2
Doctor Leighton	1
John Haydon	1
John Watkingson	1
Anne Winter	1
Anne Etherington	1
John Farey	1
	100
Omitted by reason of poverty	2

Robert Husband Collr
Thomas Collins Const

m 77]

Sedbergh Stoolebancke (Sedbergh, Soolbank)

Mabell Farey	2
Anthony Willam	3
Thomas Shaw	3
John Rawlinson	2
Richard Wadeson	1
Richard Thistlethwate	2
John Chevie	4
Nicholas Corner	2
Henry Breare	4
Nicholas Corner	2
Henry Holmes	3
Thomas Croft	1
Francis Bird	1
Robert Moore	2
Henry Gesling	1
James Holmes	2
Mr Leonard Burton	5
John Grisdale	1
Mr John Mayres	6
Mr John Cowper	7
Mr Thomas Cowper	3
Mr Richard Garthwaite	1
Mr Edward Fell	3
Edward Faucett	2
Richard Holmes	1
Edmond Bland	1
John Robinson	2
Thomas Rigg	1
Christopher Bland	1
John Harrison	1
Thomas Walton	1
Chrofer Garthropp	2
Anne Guy	1
Henry Guy	1
John Harrison	2
John Bland	1
John Holmes	3
Henry Guy	2

Richard Speight	1
Richard Speight	2
Mr Gabatus milne	1
James Simpson jun	2
James Simpson sen	3
John Atkinson	2
James Tompson	2
James Smorthwaite	1
John Tompson	1
James Wilton	1
John Nelson	1
John Dickinson	1
John Bland	1
Elizabeth Busfeild	3
Willm Adamthwaite	1
Freeschoole	1
Edward Trotter	3
Benjamine Nelson	1
William Gesling	1
James Edgson	3
John Langton	1
Miles Harrison	1
Brian Howgill	1
Mr John Cowper	2
John Fawcitt	1
Thomas Borrett	2
Mabell Shaw	1
William Inman	1
Thomas Tennant	1
James Harrison	1
Anne Thornbury	1

m 78]

Edmond Davy	1
Anne Saunderson	1
John Smith	1
	131

Omitted by reason of poverty 7

Robert Husband Collr
James Eddyson Const

Sedbrgh 3rd bill (Sedbergh, 3rd bill)

Widdow Holmes	1
Thomas Robinson	1
Roger Cocke	1
Robert Backhouse	1
Francis Lupton	1
James Bland	1
Miles Bland	1
Widdow Cocke	1
Robert Dickinson	2
Robert Helme	3
Nicholas Cowper	1
Richard Fawcitt	1
Rhenold Cooke	1
Willm Ward	1
Widdow Fawcitt	1
James Fawcitt	1
Henry Fawcitt	1
John Smorthwaite	2
Willm Harrison	1
Thomas Cross	1
Richard Fawcitt	1
Widd Pearson	1
Thomas Harrison	1
John Harrison	1
Robert Fawcett	2
John Scaife	1
Widdow Vary	1
James Bayley	1
Christopr Bland	1
Willm Farrar	1
John Faucitt	2
Mr George Fothergill	3
John Dent	3
James Linsey	2
Thomas Lupton	2
Willm Faucet	2
James Mackeroth	2
Widdow Blades	1
James Linsey	1
Robert Mackeroth	1
Willm Bodkin	2
John Cooper	3
Robert Mackeroth	1
John Towson	3
James Wadrson	2
Francis Spicer	1
Henry Denison	2
Francis Ratcliff	1
Thomas Dixon	2
Edward Fawcett	1
Michaell Fawcet	1
Ambrose Clerton	2
Edward Birkbeck	1
John Adamthwaite	1
Georg Pickering	1
James Winter	1
Anthony Winn	1
Sarah Newby	1
Henry Hall	2
James Ward	1

m 79]

Mr George Fothergill	1
Michael Fawcett	1
Richard Fisher	1
	87

Robert Husband Collr
Henry Holmes Const

Sedbergh Howgill Quarter (Sedbergh, Howgill Quarter)

Thomas Sim	1
Mr John Robinson	7
John Ward	2
Anthony Singleton	1
John Blackling	4
Edward Brantwhaite	2
Edward Brantwhate	1
Henry Bland	1
Thomas Inman	1
Richard Riding	4
James Holmes	2
James Bland	1
John Holmes	1
Richard Bland	1
John Holmes	1

Thomas Crowther	1
John Atkinson	1
Edward Docker	1
James Wilkinson	1
Edward Atkinson	2
Richard Atkinson	1
John Atkinson	1
Anthony Atkinson	1
Willm Ryding	2
Widdow Atkinson	2
John Wilson	2
Edward Inman	1
Richard Branthwaite	4
Edward Ward	5
Henry Inman	1
Henry Washington	4
John Atkinson	1
Henry Inman	1
Francis Robinson	1
Thomas Atkinson	1
Anne Atkinson	1
James Holmes	1
	66

Robert Husband Clr[21]
James Bland Const

Thornton in Lownsdale (Thornton in Lonsdale)

The Lady Redman	5
Mr Edward Foxcroft	4
Widdow Bateman	2
Robert Camfeild	1
The heires of Sir John Canfeild	8
John Aickroyde Cler	2
William Craven	3
Widdow Foxcroft	2
Thomas Tatham	1
James Fleeming	1
Thomas Wildman	3
Thomas Addison	1
Mr Edward Foxcroft	1
Richard Tatham	1
Widdow Holmes	1
Mr Willm Husband	3
John Redman	2
John Hodgson	3
James Balderston	1
Willm Balderston	1
John Balderston	1
Mabell Smith	1
m 80]	
Widdow Burrow	1
John Topham	2
Nicholas Garnitt	2
Richard Hodgson	1
Richard Story	1
Robert Burrow	2
James Prockter	3
Margarett Turner	2
Edmond Foxcroft	3
Widdow Cuming	1
Richard Bonas	4
Thomas Waller	2
Leonard Tatham	1
James Butterfeild	1
Chrofer Tatham	1
Widdow Foxcroft	1
Thomas Waller	2
Thomas Huginson	1
John Whittendale	1
James Coming	1
Margarett Coming	1
Robte Fairebancke	1
Robte Fairbancke	1
Nicholas Wilson	1
Agnes Tatham	1
Robert Whittendale	1
Jeffrey Wildman	1
John Lewis	1
Thomas Gibson	1
Christopher Prockter	1
	91

Empty & noe distress to be had
Nicholas Wilson 1

Omitted by reason of poverty 2

George Waineman Collr
John Lewis Const

Thornton in Craven

Mr Edmond Hough	6
Robert Watson	4
Henry Emmot	2
Robert Walton	1
John Watson	2
Richard Murter	2
John Hartley	2
Henry Mitchell	2
William Wilson	1
Henry Towne	2
Thomas Whitacre	2
Margarett Eastwood	1
Willm Browne	2
John Wright	2
John Browne	2
John Hall	2
Michaell Shepheard	2
Francis Wilkinson	3
John Browne	1
John Mitchell	2
John Wilson	1
Joseph Cowgill	1
Richard Cowgill	1
Jose Dodgson	1
John Windle	2
Samuell Robinson	3
Mr Drakehouse	2
Robert Windle	2
Chrofer Robinson	2
Chrofer Wingell	2
Barney Smith	1
Nicholas Wilkinson	2

21 Hole in ms.

John Witham	2
Henry Grandridge	2
Henry Craven	1
William Grandridge	1
James Browne	1
John Berritt	2

m 81]

William Turner	1
Michaell Crabtree	1
John Hall	2
Marmad Browne	1
Joseph Grandridge	4
Mrs Hargreaves	3
Edmond Mitchell	2
William Craven	2
John Turner	2
Thomas Willian	1
James Walton	1
William Waling	1
James Cowgill	1
James Atkinson	2
Joseph Witham	1
William Witham	1
William Windle	2
Richard Wilkinson	1
William Rycroft	1
William Atkinson	2
William Northend	2
Thomas Higson	2
William Slater	2
Thomas Mitchell	1
Brian Moorehouse	1
Christopher Cowgill	1
John Snowden	3
William Shackelton	1
Henry Walton	1
James Shackleton	2
John Tattersall	1
Robert Watson	1
John Shackleton	1
John Driver	1
Willm Hartley	2
Thomas Ackernley	2
Laurence Atkinson	1
John Tayler	1
James Ackernley	1
John Higson	1
John Slater	3[22]
	three
James Browne	1
Henry Womersley	1
John Manknowles	2
Henry Wilkinson	4
William Story	1
John Bowden	1
William Hartley	1
Thomas Higson	1
Stephen Tempest	2
William Watson	1
Roger Squire	2
Adam Waddington	1
John Emmott	2
Mr Raikes	2
William Hartley	2
Chrofer Briggs	1
Benjamine Parker	1
James Driver	1
John Tayler	1
Lawrence Oxnard	2
John Carter	1
Widdow Hargreave	3
Richard Witham	1
John Browne	1
Robert Browne	1
	172

Empty & noe distress to be had	
William Roberts a forge	1
Omitted by reason of poverty	4

Robert Moore Collr
Robert Walton Const

Threshfeild (Threshfield)

Mr Thomas Hamond	8
Matthew Hewitt	[4][23]

m 82]

James Deane	2
William Gill	2
William Wrathall	1
Francis Stamper	2
Nicholas Daron	2
Thomas Halley	2
John Hewitt	1
William Bumby	2
Richard Gysley	1
William Hodgson	2
Edward Deane	1
William Tempest	1
Anthony Ibbotson	2
Christopher Ratcliffe	2
George Clarke	2
Widdow Hardcastle	1
William Wilkinson	1
William Constantine	2
Richard Tompson	1
Tho Scott	1
Thomas Wilkinson	1
William Airton	2
Thomas Kidd	1
Widdow Pooleman	2
Widdow Aire	1
Robert Ayre	2
Robert Ayreton	2
William Aray	1
James Peart	1
Widdow Ibbotson	1
John Ibbotson	1
William Sawley	1

[22] 3 written over 1.
[23] There is a hole in membrane, but the *Nomina Villarum* indicates an assessment of 4 hearths.

Thomas Ayreton	1
William Kitchin	1
Robert Aireton	1
Richard Peart	1
James Ibbotson	1
	64

Robte Husband Collr
James Deane Const

Waddington

Chrofer Wilkinson Esq	5
Richard Crosdale	8
Henry Crosdale	1
James Lond	2
Richard Bridge	2
Roger Farrand	2
William Crosdale	1
Thomas Crosdale	1
John Farrand	3
William Whitehead	1
John Barrand	1
James Harrison	2
Widdow Tattersall	1
Thomas Tayler	1
Widdow Prockter	1
John Leeming	2
Gyles Dodgson	1
Marke Langfeild	1
John Witton	1
Roger Westwood	1
Stephen Emley	1
Edward Harrison	1
Roger Parker	1
Edward Colthirst	2
John Bradshaw	1
Thomas Parkinson	2
Richard Crosdale	2
John Chapman	1
John Thornbarr	1
George Crombleholme	1
George Hirst	1
Roger Blackburne	1

m 83]

Edmond Dugdale	1
Simond Chapman	1
Thomas Walmsley	1
John Twist	1
Lawrence Tomlinson	1
Widdow Bradshaw	1
Widdow Ellis	1
Widdow Parker	1
Widdow Hancocke	1
Thomas Hanson	1
Richard Bond	1
Widdow Winter	1
Widdow Holme	1
John Booker	1
James Gregory	1
John Briggs	1
Henry Walmsley	1
	70

Empty & noe distress to be had

William Wawne	1

These persons following are discharged by certificate

John Harrison	1
Thomas Spencer	1
William Crosdale	1
Edmond Colthirst	2
Robert Faber	1
John Blackburne	1
Widdow Spencer	2
William Prockter	1
Nicholas Ancocke	1

Omitted by reason of poverty	2

Robert Bennett Collr
Richard Crosdale Const

Wiglesworth (Wigglesworth)

Mr Shereburne	12
Stephen Harrison	3
Francis Duckworth	2
Widd Clarke	3
Thomas Moreley	1
Willm Wiglesworth	2
Leonard Clarke	2
John Hargreaves	3
John Haworth	3
Richard Hargreaves	2
Stephen Woodworth	2
Widdow Cooke	2
William Knowels	2
Thomas Armistead	1
Henry Burton	2
John Cooke	2
Chr Wiglesworth jun	1
Roger Armistead	1
John Smith	1
Thomas Hamerton	2
Stephen Barton	2
Robert Cockett	1
John Geldart	1
John Linsley	4
Willm Nelson	2
Willm Robinson jun	1
Edward Harrison	2
Richard Lund	2
Stephen Armistead	1
William Robinson	1
Widdow Butterfeild	1
Nicholas Bullocke	2
John Carr	1
William Shepheard	2
Edward Harrison jun	1
Thomas Carr	3
Willm Robinson sen	1
John Eglin	2
Richard Smith	2
Thomas Leach	2

m 84]

Christop Middlebrooke	2
John Cooke	1
Thomas Preistley	2
Thomas Wigglesworth	1
John Middleton	1
John Woodworth	1
Widdow Broadley	2
James Wilkinson	1
George Holgate	1
Robert Browne	1
Richard Woodworth	1
William Duckett	2
John Harrison	1
Robert Carr	2
Thomas Bond	1
Widd Bullock	1
Thomas Shepheard	1
John Lee	1
Widdow Wilkinson	1
Margarett Browne	1
James Fletcher	1
Thomas Wilkinson	1
	110

Omitted by reason of poverty	7

Thomas Middleton Collr
Richard Smith Const

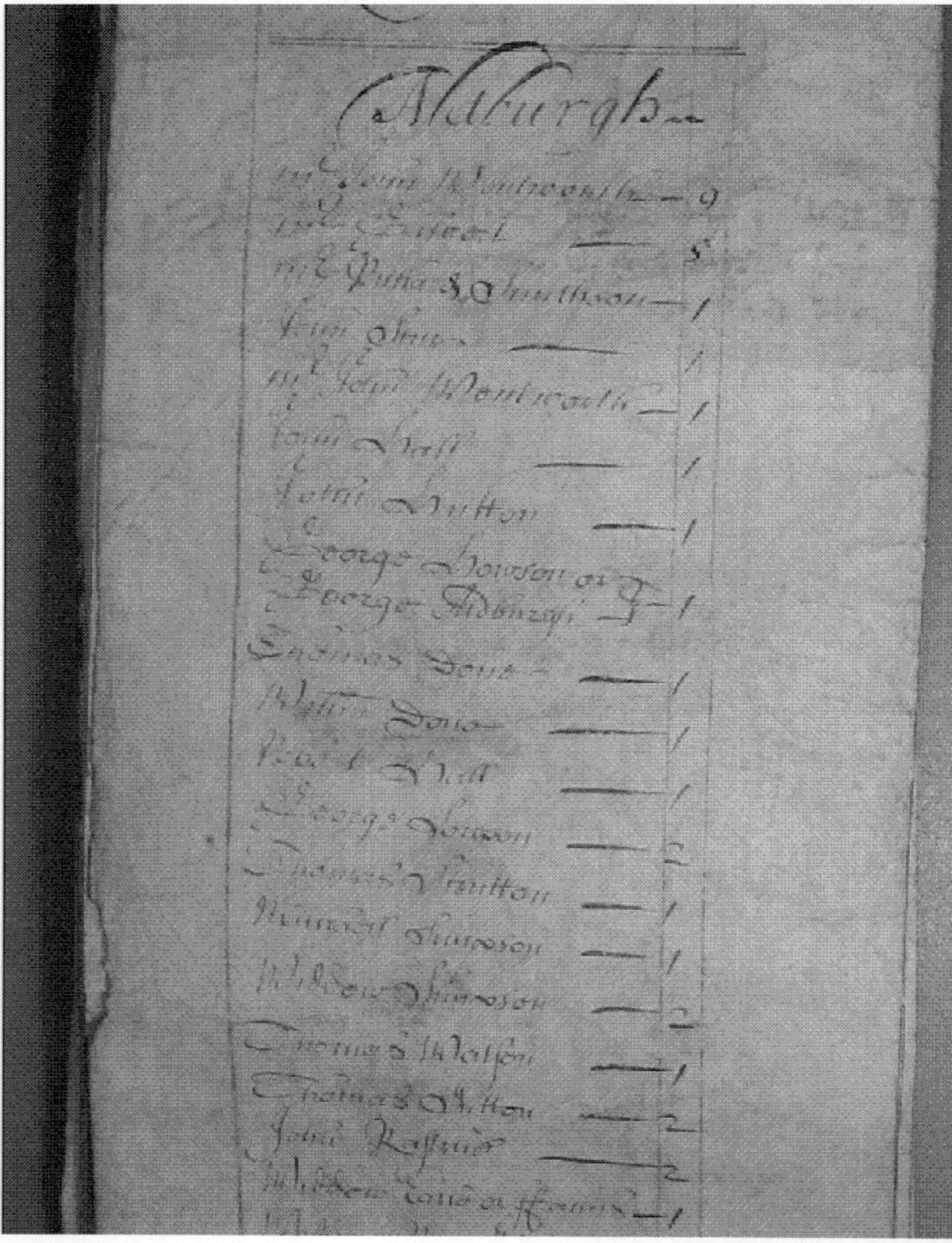

Plate 16 Part of the assessment of individuals in the township of Aldborough. This is typical of the way individuals were listed in a long single column at Lady Day 1672. National Archives E179/210/400 m.1. See transcript opposite

Claro Wapentake

The National Archives, E179/210/400

m 1 dorse]

Deliveratr per manu Johannis Peables clerici pacis infrasc' sexto die Decembr Anno xxvijmo Regni Regis Caroli secundi Ebo[rum]

m 1]

A perfect View of all the Chimneys Hearths and Stoves within the West Rydeing of the Cyttye of Yorke by James Collins his [Maties][24] Collector and Receiver of his Revenues of Hearth money at Lady day 1672

Claro

Aldburgh (Aldborough)

Mr John Wentworth	9
Mr Gilbert	5
Mr Richard Smithson	1
John Scur	1
Mr John Wentworth	1
John Hall	1
John Hutton	1
George Howson or	
George Aldburgh	1
Thomas Done	1
Willm Done	1
Robert Hall	1
George Lowson	2
Thomas Scrutton	1
Michaell Simpson	1
Widdow Simpson	2
Thomas Watson	1
Thomas Sutton	2
John Rastrick	2
Widdow Earle or Francis	1
Widdow Rawlin	1
Peter Hill	1

Robert Myers	1
Thomas Tompson	1
Robert Scruton	1
Thomas Brigham	2
Thomas Hill Jun	1
Richard Hall	1
Christopr Mautas	1
Robert Hall	1
Robert Simpson	2
Peter Scruton & }	
Arthur Simpson }	3
Robert Scur or }	
Peter Blackburne }	1
John Bradley or}	
James Rawling }	1
Robert Browne	1
Thomas Foster	1
Peter Foster	1
Anne Clarke	1
Ellizabeth Robinson	2
Richard Prance	1
Peter Matterson	1
Richard Scruton	1
John Marke	1
Peter Thearsby	1
Willm Dickinson	1

Robert Hutton	1
Humphrey Johnson	1
John Barnard	1
Richard Blackburne	2
George Inglish	1
Thomas Inchbald	1
Edward Inchbald	1
John Thorpe	2
John Dickinson	1
Widdow Dawson	1
Mathew Catton	1
Willm Dickinson	1
John Coultas	1
Richard Bickerdike	1
Widdow Scruton	1
James Dickinson	1
Willm Scruton	1
Jane Sanderson or Enid Catton	1

m 2]

Nichollas Smithson	1
Thomas Smithson	2
	88

[24] Maties is hardly visible under ultra-violet light reading, but the reading can be inferred in the light of the rubric in E179/262/13.

These persons following are discharged by Certificates

Anne Scruton	1
Richd Scur	2
Widd Scur	1

Omitted by reason of Poverty	8

Robt Corner Collr
Richd Webster Const

Askwith

Widdow Illingworth	1
George Whitacres	2
John Newsom or Sonne	2
John Wardman	2
George Newsham	1
Willm Roberts	1
John Richardson	1
John Harper	2
George Booth	4
Peter Dale	2
Thomas Ingland	1
James Atkinson	1
Edmd Greenwood	2
John Mawson	1
Thomas Kendall	2
Willm Shutt and Sonne	2
Willm Watters	1
Willm Thackerey	1
John Horner	1
Anthony Fell	1
Willm Mushamp	2
Widdow Latham	1
Widdow Ward	2
Thomas Foster	2
Anthony Fell	2
Thomas Foster	1
Steven Brathwaite	2
Thomas Foster	2
Mr Willm Cooke	4
Anthony Whitfeild	1
Willm Sowden	3
John Crooke	2
John Smith	1
Willm Bainton	2
Willm Browne	1
Martin Rowlin	1
Margret Silson	1
Willm Shutt	1
John Pawson	1
John Browne	1
Widd Gill	1
Willm Foster	1
Maior Smith	3
Willm Pickard	1
Abraham Coates	1
Thomas Ratcliffe	2
Willm Richardson	2
Willm Hardcastle	1
Richard Wadington	2
Willm Robinson	1
John Mawson forge	1
Willm Mawson	1
Lawrence Kendall	1
Thomas Pawson	1
	83

These persons following are discharged by Certificates

Cuthbert Hodgson	1
Christopher Harrison	1
James Hodgson	1

Robert Husband Collr
Thos Foster Const

m 3]

Arkendale

Willm Pulleine	2
Mr John Simpson	3
Henry Steele	2
Willm Allenson	3
Willm Pulleine	2
Jonas Clarkson	3
Richard Browne	2
Roger Dodgson	1
Robert Browne	1
Richard Towland	1
Willm Dodgson	1
Thomas Wilson	1
Jane Easby	1
Willm Bell	1
John Hagget	1
Widdow Browne or Peter Akers	1
Widdow Akers	1
Thomas Outhwaite	1
Simond Outhwaite	1
Henry Steele	1
Mr John Simpson	1
Jonas Wright or George More	1
Dinis Towland	2
Barnard Dickinson	1
Richard Brice	1
Willm Simpson	1
Willm Ketlewell	1
John Jesbrough	1
Edmond Browne	1
Robert Stead	1
Richard Pallister	1
Robert Anderson	2
Henry Dodgson	1
Richard Browne	1
Richard Earsby	1
Ellizabeth Russell or Steven Brass	1
Marmaduke Kay	1
Henry Dodgson	1
Peter Inchbald	3
Willm Browne	1
Richard Randall or Nichollas	1
Thomas Steele	1
Anthony Simpson	1
Marmad Towbeard	1
Widdow Browne	1
	59

These persons following are discharged by Certificates
Edmond Scary 1
Roger Baxter 1
George Pallister 1
John Smith 1

Omitted by reason of poverty 4
Roger Hardcastle Collr
Richd Browne Const

Allerton cum Flasby (Allerton with Flaxby)
Sir Richard Malliverer 24
Peter Smithson 2
Widdow Sisson 1
John Allinson or Robert Richardson 2
Willm Barras 7
Richard Gibson 3
John Newsom 1
Robert Sisson 2
John Clarke 2

m 4]

Richard Warrington 2
Robert Akers 1
Willm Staineburne 1
John Schoales 1
Robert Lawson 1
Thomas and Edwd Tompson 2
John Linley 2
Francis Webster 1
Christopr Lowson 1
Thomas Cundall 2
Charles Garbutt 3
John Atkinson 1
Francis Clarke 1
Thomas Calvert 1
James Norton 1
Christopr Duffield 1
Thomas Benson 1
Willm Lawson 1
Richard Lawson 1
Abrah Flowton 2
Widdow Tompson 1
72

Omitted by reason of poverty 5

George Wainman Collr
Richd Gibson Const

Audfeild (Aldfield)
George Aislasby 15
Mr Charles Elsley 3
Mr Abraham Smith 4
George Wreakes 6
James Wreakes 2
John Hodgson 1
Richard Linton 1
Thomas Smith 1
Willm Linton 1
George Piper 1
John Linton 1
Richard Heblethwaite 1
Thomas Hobden 1
Willm Mawtas 2
Gilbert Mawtas 1
Marmad Mawtas 2
John Hawksbey 1
John Marshall 1
John Scowthrop 1
Richard Brathwaite 1
Edward Pearson 1
John Smurthwaite 1
Rachell Hunter 3
Leonard Metcalfe 1
Thomas Wicliffe 1
54

Omitted by reason of poverty 3

Richard Pickard Collr
George Wreakes Const

Averah Parke (Haverah Park)
Richard Clint 1
Widdow Faucitt 1
Thomas Dewman 1
Thomas Simpson 1
Thomas Simpson 1
Mr John Cooke 4
Willm Simpson 2

m 5]

Thomas Stubbs 2
Willm Benson 1
Willm Benson 2
Widdow Clint 1
17

Omitted by reason of poverty 1
Robt Corner Collr
John Cooke Const

Azorley (Azerley)
Mr Dawson 9
Mr Lister 9
Anthony Beck 2
John Atkinson 2
Willm Simpson 2
Francis Smith 2
Anne and Peter Todd 2
Abraham Smith 1
Ellizabeth Horner 1
Willm Smith 2
Anne Robinson 1
Mathew Shepherd 1
Dorothy Dibbs 2
Robert Bell 1
Widdow Lee 1
Thomas Bird 1
Christopr Coates 2
John Duffield 1
Marke Baxsby 1
Richard Edyson 1

Thomas Geldart	2
Willm Bradwith	1
Widdow Bell	1
Robert Geldart	2
John Pickersgill	1
John Pickersgill	2
Willm Wilson	1
Willm Langstaff	1
Thomas Vanlaugh	2
John Pickersgill	1
Miles Shepherd	2
Francis Umphrey	1
John Kirby	2
Tristrum Duffield	3
Willm Steele	2
Thomas Bramley	1
George Myers	1
George Day	1
Francis Browne	1
Anthony Fisher	1
Widdow Wells	2
George Cowley	2
Tristram Wells	1
Charles Duffield	2
Henry Duffield	1
Lambert Duffield	1
John or Willm Atkinson	1
Willm Theakstone	1
John Thirkill	1
Willm Thirkill	1
Marmaduke Pratt	1
Henry Wells	2
Charles Richmond	1

m 6]

John Wells	1
George Wood	1
Mr Abraham Favor	2
John Cowley	1
Anne Parker	1
Thomas Spence	2
Thomas Bell	1
The Milne	2
Thomas Shaw	1
Anne Steele	1
Edward Woodhouse	1
Ellizabeth Tennant	1
	105

Omitted by reason of poverty	7

George Wainman Collr
Willm Bell Const

Bishopside

Henry Rydeley	1
Henry Wilkinson	1
John Darnbrooke	2
Anthony Colyer Gent	2
Thomas Smith de Green	1
Willm Burniston	2
Mary Stott	1
Richard Lupton & } Thos Wood }	2
Augustine Burnistone	3
Steven Lupton	3
Anthony Colyer	2
Lambert Tayler	2
Francis Brigges	1
Sampson Lupton	1
Thomas Knipe	1
Widdow Sharpe	1
Thomas Smith	2
John Rhoades	2
Thomas Leeming	6
Thomas Sharpe	1
Anthony Rounder	3
Marmaduke Graing	1
John Bradley	2
Willm Colyer	1
Anne Day or Temple	3
Martin Wheelas Jun	1
Martin Wheelas Sen	2
John Barber	2
Widdow Barber	1
Thomas Shaw	1
John Shaw	1
Thomas Bradley	1
John Bradley	1
Henry Wood	3
James Horner	6
John Darnbrooke	3
Henry Settle	2
John Simpson	1
Thomas Garthwaite	1
Mr Kilvington	4
George Barwicke	5
Mr Richardson *pro* millne	1
Henry Settle	4
John Carlisle	3
Thomas Lupton	1
Francis Lupton	1
Ellin Lupton	1
Willm Holden	4
David Lupton	1
Thomas Jackman	1
John Lupton and Ten[an]ts	2
Widdow Hebden	1

m 7]

Leonard Lupton	2
Francis Darnbrooke	2
Thomas Scaife	3
Sampson Lupton	1
Willm Barrick	2
John Lupton	1
John Lupton[25]	1
Anthony Wood } and Mother}	4
Willm Buck	2
Francis Buck	3
George Buck	1
Willm Shepherd Jun	1
Thomas Horner	3

[25] sic.

Willm Hudson	1
Marmaduke Shepherd	2
Christopr Jackson	1
Robert Myers	2
John Oddy }	
and Mother }	4
Michaell Inman	3
Willm Coates	2
Robert Myers	1
Willm Theakstone	1
Willm Taylor	1
Nicholls Hudson	2
Widdow Inman	1
Peter Inman	3
Thomas Kirby	1
George Atkinson Sen	1
George Atkinson Jun	1
Leonard Lupton *pro* Cliffehouse	1
Willm Day	2
Willm Shepherd	2
Math Hudson	1
Thomas Lupton	1
Mary Caruill	1
Widd Scaife	2
Robert Glew	1
Willm Day	1
Marmaduke Yates	2
	169

Empty	
John Oddy or Metcalfe	2
Robert Bell	1

Omitted by reason of poverty	6

Robt Husband Collr
Anthony Colyer Const

Blubberhouses

George Thorpe	1
Richard Beecroft	2
Richard Watkinson	1
Willm Lister	1
Henry Hawkswell	1
Robert Richinson[26]	1
Willm Wardman	2
Thomas Iles	1
Thomas Beecroft	1
Thomas Tiplady	1
Willm Suttle	2
Widdow Butler	1
George Driver	1
Brian Morehouse	1

m 8]

John Newton	1
Thomas Theaker	1
Thomas Watson	1
John Barritt	1
Widdow Wrayth	1
	22

Robert Husband Collr
Thomas Iles Const

Bishopton cum Clutheram (Bishopton with Clotherholme)

Sr Richard Grime	2
Widdow Wreakes	2
Richard Lambert or Mawtas	3
Mr Sampson Smirke and mill	5
Christopr Yates	1
Francis and Widd Carlisle	6
Willm Wright	1
George Harrison	2
Willm Ingram	2
Christopr Yates	1
Wilfrey Day	5
Willm Atkinson	2
Christopr Pinckney	3
Thomas Pinckney	2
Christopr Hodgson	2
Henry Nicholson	1
Marmaduke Hodgson	1
Willm Horner	1
Thomas Hodgson	1
George Moore	3
John Horner	1
Ralph Loftus	1
John Heward	1
Thomas Tinsley	1
Edward Coates	1
	51

Empty and no distres to be had	
Willm Ingram and Math Sinckler	2

These persons following are discharged by Certificates

Jane Tate	1
Francis Shepherd & forge	2

Omitted by reason of poverty	5

George Wainman Collr
John Heward Const

Bishop Mountaine (Bishop Monkton)

Mr Pulleine	3
Mathew Waide	2
Peter Simpson	1
Roger Richinson	1
John Clarke	1
Widdow Parker	3
Christopher Rooth	1
Lawrance Keighley	1

26 'Ri' is written over a letter, with the scribe then starting the name Richardson again.

Henry Abbot 1
Robert Ryther or
Robert Pollard 1
Thomas Cundall 2
Thomas Parker 1
Peter Cundall 1
George Browne 1
Michaell Cundall 2
John Hardcastle 1

m 9]

Lawrance Keighley 1
George Burditt 2
John Grainger 2
Roger Cundall 2
Peter Wells 1
Robert Pollard 1
Thomas Browne 1
John Waide 1
Willm Waide 1
Arthur Grainger 3
Willm Smithson 1
Willm Smithson Jun 1
Thomas Jaques 1
John Abbot 1
Widdow Grayson 2
John Ryles 1
Edward Parker 1
Christopr Simpson 2
Mrs Cooke &
Marma Jackson 1
Henry Haukswell and
Robert Ryther 1
Luke Jepson 1
George Watkins mill 1
Steven Metcalfe 1
Widdow Allenson 1
Thomas Cundall 1
Lawrance Keighley 1
Thomas Fawber 1
Mathew Waide 1
John Abbot 1
John Topham 1
Edward Cundall 1
Christopr Booth 1
Willm Duffeild 1
Willm Smith 2
John Cundall 2
67

Omitted by reason of
poverty 7

George Wainman Collr
Willm Smith Const

Burrowbridge
(Boroughbridge)

John Abbot 4
Henry Savill 2
Willm Daggitt 9
Mr George Loope 8
Mrs Jackson 8
Robert Burnet 3
Willm Henlock 3
Charles Linton 2
George Smith 1
Ralph Clarke 3
Willm Bell 3
Mr Francis Calvert 6
Widdow Tompson 2
Robert Potter of Leeds 1
Willm Aldburgh 2
Charles Catton 2
Mr Leeming 2
Mrs Anne Geldersome 4
Ralph Smithson 1
Isaac Pickles 2
John Stainthrope 3
Henry Lumley 8
Richard Catton 3
John Hardcastle 3

m 10]

Widdow Shepherd 3
Mathew Townley 4
John Atkinson 1
Willm Burnad 3
John Robinson 1
Mr James Hamerton 9
Willm Stainthrop 1
Sr Willm Tanker 6
Sr Richard Maliverer
mill 1
Willm Scriven 2
Richard Skerray 1
Robert Skeldon 1
Mr Thomas Wilkinson 10
128

Empty and no distres
to be had
Sir Richard Malliverer 1

Omitted by reason of
Poverty 10

Roger Hardcastle Collr
Wm Beckwith Const

Beamsley

Mr Sheafeild Clapham 14
Thomas Watkinson
jun 1
Thomas Watkinson
Sen 1
John Johnson 1
Francis Tompson 1
Willm Roberts 1
Widdow Pettey 3
Henry Sheldon 2
Francis Fountaines 1
Ingram Browne 1
Robert Whitacres 1
George Demaine &
forge 3
Richard Moone 2
Ingram Holmes 1
Martin Wardman 1
George Wilkinson 4
Henry Winterburne 2
James Petty 1
Willm Phillips 1

George Paggitt	2
George Petty	1
Thomas Thompson & forge	3
Robert Moone	1
George Croft	1
Richard Shires	1
Peter Watkinson	2
William Moone	1
George Johnson	1
Stephen Longthorne	3
William Becroft	2
James Thompson	3
Thomas Waite	1
Tho Battersby	2
Thomas Cryer	1
John Holmes	1
Henry Waite	1
Thomas Wardman	1
William Judson	1
Edward Hudson	1
Thomas Myers	1
William Knipe	1
Nichollas Croft	1
Richard Smith	2
	two
James Young	1
Thomas Lowcocke	2
Widd Boulton	1
John Geare	2
Thomas Tennant	1
Thomas Smithson	2
Peter Currer	1
Willm Rhoades	1
George Croft	2

m 11]

Willm Holmes	1
Widdow Holmes	1
Francis Wilson	1
Thomas Holmes	1
Christopr Holmes	2
Lawrance Lawcocke	3
Willm Gill	1
Widdow Pettey & Tenants	2
Lawrance Johnson	1
Margret Falshawe	1
Richard Holmes	1
Samuell Robinson	1
James Phillips	1
	107

Roger Hardcastle Collr
Francis Tompson Const

Burstwith (Birstwith)

John Midgley Sen	1
Widdow Hewicke	1
Willm Farnill	1
Willm Stubbes or Steven	1
Willm Andrewes	2
John Midgley Jun	1
Robert Pullene	1
Willm Jeffrey	3
Samuell Midgley	4
Francis Waite	1
John Walker	1
Thomas Fentiman	1
Willm Waite	2
Thomas Lake	1
Thomas Walker	1
Christopr Smith	3
Ignatious Atkinson	2
John Lumley	1
Samuell Walker	1
John Fairburne	1
Widdow Hardisty & sone	3
Willm Hardisty	2
Mary Roundell	1
Richard Midgley or Mr Franckland	4
Miles Bramley	2
John Walker	1
Widdow Milner	1
Willm Bilton	2
Abraham Askwith & Bradfeild	1
Margret Bramley	2
Thomas Parker	1
John Parker	1
Widdow Snow or Tents	2
Miles Waite	1
Willm Shutt	2
Robert Snow	1
Willm Blackburne	1
Wilfrey Ingleson	1
Willm Umpleby	1
Leonard Atkinson	2
Willm Askwith	1
Miles Andrewes	1
Henry Jeffreyes	2
Thomas Farnill	1
Christopr Harrison	1
John Umpleby	1
Thomas Andrewes	1
Thomas Bucke	1
Christopr Shutt	1
Cuthbert Broake	1
John Ingleson	1
Thomas Smith	3

m 12]

Marmaduke Bramley	1
Peter Parker	1
John Preist	1
John Grayson	1
Miles Waite	1
	82

Robert Corner Collr
Marmad Bramley Const

Brearton

Christoopher[27] Ripley	4
Mr Marmaduke Clarke	3

[27] sic.

John Yates	2
Christopher Parker	2
Francis Parker	2
Richard Hebden	2
Widdow Yates	2
George Wheelas	1
Sir Sallom Swaile or } Richard Simpson }	1
Thomas Baxter & forg	2
Sampson Simpson	2
Richard Syser	1
Widdow Jackson	1
Willm Maude	1
Edward Cooper	1
more a forge	1
Widdow Thorpe	1
Anthony Parritt	1
Christopher Parker	1
Christohpr Parker & tent	1
Robert Pretious	1
Michaell Whealas	1
Widdow Cooper	1
Edward Cooper	1
	36

Roger Hardcastle Collr
Sampson Simpson Const

Bishop Thornton

Mr Peter Ingleby	8
Richard Richmond	2
Mr Steven Sutton	4
John Gill	3
George Linton	1
Mr Thomas Brearey sen	8
Edward Williamson	1
John Joy	2
Mr Longe Milne	1
Willm Colbecke	1
Margret Joy	2
Willm Atkinson	1
John Colbeck	2
Jane Hawksworth	1
Willm Markinfeild	2
John Burras	1
Willm Whitelock	1
Willm Leadom	2
John Stevenson or Hardcastle	1
Richard Wright Gent	1
James Wheelas	2
Willm Wilkinson	1
Mr Willm Wheatley	8
Thomas Shaw	2
Willm Shaw	3
Thomas Kettlewell	1
Francis Kendill	1
Hugh Gill	1
Thomas Allinson	2
Peter Holmsley	1
George Pallister	1
James Lowcock or Ralph	1
Willm Markinfeild	1
Rheynold Tompson	1
John Story	1
Edward Dixon or Francis Burne	1
John Fletcher	1
Marmaduke Mease	1
Thomas Stevenson	1
Richard Bundall	1
Thomas Ballance	3
John Ellis	1
David Richmond	1
Thomas Snowden	2
John Browne	1
John Rheynold forge	1

m 13]

Thomas Browne	7
Samuell Kendall	1
Willm Whitelock	2
	96

Empty and no distress

Thomas Wilkinson	1

George Wainman Collr
Wm Wikinson Const

Burton Leonard

Mr Thomas Wise	4
Mr Wright	2
Mr John Fox	5
Mr Ralph Wise	5
Richard Spence	2
John Smithson	1
Willm Steele	1
John Macnadam	1
Richard Armistead	1
Mr Wise Milne	1
John Thirske	1
Willm Penington	1
Christopr Coates	1
Thomas Cundall	2
Willm Barker	1
Francis Sadler	1
George Addyson	1
John Dickinson	2
John Smith and forge	2
Robert Armistead	1
Christopr Smithson	1
George Atkinson	2
	two
Willm Young	2
George Atkinson	1
Anne Wadington	1
Thomas Smith	1
Christopr Nicholson	1
Christopr Parker	1
George Knowles	1
Ellin Smith	1
Thomas Penington	3
George Barker	1
Thomas Barwicke	2
Anne Smithson	1
Francis Duffeild	1
Charles Watson	1
George Browne	1
John Barker	1
John Browne	1
Ralph Watson	1

Thomas Normavill	1
George Knowles	1
Mary Wright	1
George Parker	1
	65

These persons following are discharged by Certificate

George Smith	2
Anne Yates	2

Omitted by reason of poverty	4

Robert Corner Collr
George Atkinson Const

Bewerley

Christopher Darnbrooke	2
Thomas Horsman	1
Christophr Darnley	2
Marmad Lupton	1
Willm Darnbrooke	1
Richard Darnbrooke	2
Marmad Foster	4
John Darnebrooke	3
Richard Simpson	1
Christopr Darnbrooke	3
Christopr Colyer	2
Thomas Colyer	1
John Dawson	1
John Steele & Jackman	4
John Burmston	4
Peter Ody	2
John Partridge	3
Roger Grainge	1
Henry England	2

m 14]

Widdow Myers	1
Ralph Hardcastle	1
John Tayler	1
Willm Darnbrooke	2
Widdow Colyer	1
Adam Simpson	2
Widdow Richardson	1
John Wrathby	2
Peter Mawer	1
Henry Simpson	1
Robert Fryer	2
Robert Fryer[28]	2
Willm Simpson	2
David Joy	1
Widdow Graing	2
John Barwicke	2
Francis Hidd	2
Anthony Holgate	1
Willm Rodwell	1
Willm Hide	1
Richard Weatherhead	1
Widdow Inman	1
Widdow Colyer	1
Thomas Weatherhead	1
Richard Grainge	1
Marke Woodroope	1
Thomas Rycroft	1
Richard Firth	1
Robert Marden	1
Martin Brendais	1
James Shaw	1
Anthony Gell	3
Edward Downes	1
Robert Waite	1
Mr Johson	1
Peter Mawer Mill	1
Robert Ellis	1
Thomas Holme	1
	89

Roger Hardcastle Collr
Marmad Foster Const

Casley (Castley)

Thomas Wood	6
James Wray	1
Willm Wood	1
Francis Atkinson	1
John Waide	1
Martin Thornton	4
John Milner	1
Beckwith Hartley	1
Thomas Harison	1
Mary Colyer Widd	1
Thomas Johnson	1
John Bradley	2
John Browne	1
Henry Holmes	2
Francis Linley or Robert King	2
	26

Omitted by reason of poverty	2

Robert Husband Collr
Henry Holmes Const

Cattall Magna (Great Cattal)

Lancellot Scott	1
Edward Otter	1
Henry Fuller	1
Henry Daniell	1
Willm Grafton	1
Thomas Nelson	1
Willm Falkingham	1
Clement Wood	1
John Wadington	1
Widd Sturdy	2
Jane Abbey	1
Thomas Raine	1
Thomas Haukes	1
Lawrance Lake	2
Richard Peirson	1
Widdow Hill	2
Richard Dickinson	2
John Oyle	2
Willm Hornby	1

[28] sic.

Leonard Haukes 1
Thomas Armistead 1

m 16][29]

Richard Thackerey 1
John Hill 2
Leonard Hill 1
Richard Daniell 1
Willm Cooper 2
Richard Tompson 1
John Tossimond 1
Caleb Daniell 1
Roger Procter 1
Marke Abbey 1
38

Omitted by reason of poverty 4

George Wainman Collr
John Wadington Const

Cowthrop (Cowthorpe)

Willm Hill and Willm Carrock 12
Mr Henry Flint 3
Richard Clough 1
Robert Parkinson 2
Mrs Flint 3
Edward Petty 1
Boswell Chapman 2
John Gell 1
Robert Shaw 1
Caleb Sharpway 1
John Clough 1
Henry Thackeray 2
Willm Bealby 1
Henry Pettey 1
John Tompson 1
33

These persons following are discharged by Certificates
Willm Binkes 1
Richard Alderson 1

Omitted by reason of poverty 4

George Wainman Collr
John Gell Const

Clint

Sir Sallomon Swaile 2
Thomas Simpson 2
Willm Shann 4
Peter Shann 1
John Milner 1
Ellizabeth Yeoman 4
Willm Whaley 2
James Kilvington 1
John Kendall 2
John Tompson 2
Ellin Elsworth 2
Thomas Catton 4
Thomas Bowes 2
Sir Sallom Swaile & } Leadman } 2
Widdow Baines 1
Willm Ramill 1
John Ellerton 1
Richard Buck Junr 2
James Speakman 2
John Lewley 1
Thomas Wilkinson 1
John Reynold 1
John Farnell 2
Mathew Reynold 2
Thomas Hardcastle 2
Thomas Farnill 2
James Thompson 2
Robert Joy 1
Thomas Stevenson & forge 2
Guy Hudson 1
Willm Whealas 1
Sir Sallom Swaile 1
Robert Wintergill and Oven 3
Ellizabeth Howgill 2
Edward Wells 1
Willm Carrier 1
Thomas Kendall 1
Willm Wilson 1
Miles Hardcastle 1

m 17]

Willm Graues 1
Francis Reynold 1
more *pro* Leo Umpleby 1
Edward Barker 1
Willm Ramill 1
Robert Buckle 1
Widdow Cooke 2
Andrew Dixon 1
Mr Longe 2
Ellizabeth Coates 1
Francis Fish 1
Peter Dixon 1
Christopr Mawlas 1
John Tompson 1
Leonard Luty 1
Richard Buck & forge 2
86

Omitted by reason of poverty 7

Robert Corner Collr
Thomas Kendall Const

Copgraue (Copgrove)

Mr John Richardson 2
Thomas Wilkes 7
Anne Dickinson 2

[29] Membrane 15 is the old cover joined to the bottom of membrane 14.

Samuell Dickinson	2
John Tompson	2
John Thorpe	1
Edward Raife	1
Willm Eltoft	1
Willm Hudlestone	1
Henry Hudlestone	1
Tomasin Cooke	2
Randall Snowden	1
more a forge	1
Thomas Baxter	2
Robert Browne	4
John Corker	3
Alice Wilden	1
Anne Wilden	1
Ellizabeth Roundell	1
Christopr Baxter	1
	37

George Wainman Collr
Thomas Dickinson Const

Connystrop (Coneythorpe)

George Garbutt	2
George Tireman	1
John Atkinson	1
Francis Benson	1
Francis Widford	1
Henry Catterton	1
Thomas Baker	1
Richard Askwith	2
Richard Lane	1
Edward Rawlin	1
Richard Harington	1
Robert Hudson	1
Richard Bruce	1
Willm Leafe	1
Richard Fewsdale	1
Richard Gibson	3
Richard Simpson	1
Richard Catton	1
Henry Simpson	1
	23

Omitted by reason of poverty	4

Roger Hardcastle Collr
Richd Browne Const

Cattall Parva (Little Cattall)

Richard Weston Esqr	19

George Wainman Collr
John Waddington Const

Dacre

Sir Willm Ingleby	9
Willm Wheatley	2
Thomas Wood	1

m 18]

Willm Darnbrough & Sons	1
John Wheatley	1
Leonard Oddy	2
John Wood	2
Christophr Moone	1
Willm Oddy	3
Widdow Metcalfe or Fr	2
Christophr Yates	2
Robert Hardisty	1
Willm Metcalfe	1
Anthony Bake	1
Leonard Grainge	1
Thomas Pulleine	2
Robert Benson	2
Christopher Umpleby	1
Widdow Atkinson	1
Ralph Robinson	1
Willm Robinson	1
Willm Donghill	1
Willm Gill	1
Thomas Abbot	2
Peter Hall	2
Hugh Grime	1
Widdow Gill	1
George Gill	1
Thomas Wilkes	1
Widdow Hall & Thomas	2
Richard Brearley	2
Thomas Gunthwaite	1
Joseph Hardisty	1
Edward Yates	1
John Craven	1
Robert Wilkes	3
John Metcalfe	1
John Benson	2
Thomas Morehouse	3
more	1
Miles Oddy	1
Peter Oddy and Robert Myers	2
John Oddy	1
Francis Scaife	1
Robert Wiglesworth	1
Francis Oddy	1
John Bayocke	3
John Smith	1
Peter Inman	1
George Wikes	2
Miles Metcalfe	2
Robert Darlew	2
John Benson	2
Willm Hardcastle	5
Widdow Wood	1
Mr Lacon or Mr Wood	7
Christopr Yates	2
Thomas Hardcastle Junior & forge	3
Thomas Hardcastle Sen	2
Samuell Atkinson	1
Willm Hardcastle	2
Widdow Bilton	1
John Colyer	3
Widdow Atkinson	2
Willm Hardwick } *pro* Norwood }	2
Samuell Hardcastle	1

Willm Elsworth mill	1
Widdow Dawson	1
Thomas Oddy	2
Willm Gill	1
John Hardcastle	1
	124

Roger Hardcastle Collr
Marmad Foster Const

m 19]

Dunsforth

Mr Thomas Dodsworth	6
John Inchbald	2
Richard Burnand	1
Peter Henlocke	3
Thomas Kay Gent	4
Willm Abbot	2
James Richardson	1
Robert Bentley	1
Richard Metcalfe	1
Robert Fewsdale	1
Willm Fidler	2
Thomas Shaw	2
Willm Wrightson	2
Thomas Lawman	1
George Casse	2
Peter May	1
Willm Staineburne	1
Randolph Hodgson	1
Willm Mayson	1
Willm Stobbart	1
Widdow Metcalfe	1
Robert North	1
Robert Inchbald	1
George Wrightson	1
Abraham Masson	1
& stove	1
	42

Empty and no distress to be had

Barnard Dickinson	1

George Wainman Collr
George Henlocke Const

Dunkeswicke (Dunkeswick)

Henry Barrot	5
Christopher Bainton	7
Thomas Duckett	1
Richard Hanson	1
John Pulleine	1
John Collingworth	1
Willm Forrest	1
John Brearcliffe	1
Robert Wycliffe	1
Robert Sawer	1
Willm Baitson	1
Willm Sawer	1
John Cragg	1
Mathew Harrison	1
Michaell Harrison	1
Widdow Clarkson	1
Mathew Wright	3
Widdow Wood	1
Anthony Bateman	1
John Sawer	1
Richard Tompson	1
Widdow Mallary	1
Anthony Wriglesworth	3
Widdow Wriglesworth	1
	38
Omitted by reason of Poverty	13

Robert Husband Collr
John Brearcliffe Const

Denton

The Lord Fairfax	19
Mr Willm Thornton	4
Walter Blakey	1

m 20]

John Blakey	2
Willm Illingworth	2
Charles Harpham	2
Willm Jepson	1
Willm Stainforth	1
Willm Helmsley	1
Robert Laine	1
Richard Gill	1
Francis Hall	1
George Harrison	2
Thomas Foster	2
James Ward	1
Thomas Hudson	1
Widdow Ratcliffe	1
Thomas Colton	1
Thomas Hebden	2
John Taylor	2
Willm Scawbrough	1
Charles Clapham	4
Richard Wharfe	2
Peter Parkinson	2
John Smith and forge	2
Thomas Oxley	2
	61

Roger Hardcastle Collr
John Smith Const

Follifoote (Follifoot)

Mary Tate	2
Widdow Brigham	1
Widdow Procter	1
John Ryther	1
Willm Browning or } Mr Wilson }	1
Nichollas Hall	1
Widdow Lambert	2
Richard Hall	2
Willm Wright	1
Robert Taylor *pro* Lacock	1
Willm Girstwell	1
John Bucktroute	1
Richd Hardwick *pro* Griswick	3
John Godfrey	3

Willm Shaw	1
John Griswick	1
John Simster	1
John Bucktroute	3
Robert Marshall	2
Thomas Gowland	2
Thomas Laycocke	1
Marmaduke Steele	2
Richard English	1
James Johnson	1
Willm Bolton	1
Thomas Rhoades	1
Richard Winterburne	2
John Swaile	1
Willm Massie	2
Anthony Procter	2
Thomas Bilcliffe	4
Thomas Tompson	1
James Collingworth	4
Willm Graues	2
Francis Leatham	1
John Procter	2
Marmaduke Procter	1
Willm Ellis	2
Willm Baitson	1
Thomas Lawson	1
John Procter	1
John Procter[30]	1
Mr Thomas Lawson *pro* mill	1
George Johnson	1
Anthony [blank] *pro* Barbr	1
Willm Laycocke	1

m 21]

William Clapham	1
Willm Wright	1
Richard Slator	1
Widdow Milner	1
Peter Allen	1
	75

These persons following are discharged by Certificates

Widdow Deighton	1
Margt Crooke	1
Widdow Bilbrough or Crosby	1
Thomas Anikins	1
Robert Burton	1
Willm Richardson	1

Roger Hardcastle Collr
James Collingworth Const

Farnham

Mr Crathorne	6
Richard Jackson	2
Robert Porrett	1
Edward Sharpe	1
Mr Nichols Bickerdike	3
Ellizab Lassells	2
George Bootle	2
James Boggard	1
Thomas Oastler	3
Nichols Bickerdike	2
Henry Midleton	3
John Cundall	2
Dorothy Flint	1
Willm Eminson	2
Henry Todd	1
Willm Newbuilt	1
George Barker	1
Robert Pickard & forg	2
Jane Wincobb and } Barbara Bickerdike }	3
Thomas Midleton	3
Willm Scaife	4
Widdow Flint	1
George Dawson	1
George Barber	1
	49

Omitted by reason of poverty	1

George Wainman Collr
George Dawson Const

Fensclife (Felliscliffe)

Willm Hardisty	3
Richard Maude	1
Willm Shepherd	1
Christopr Halliday	1
Willm Atkinson	2
	two
Thomas Gratian	1
Peter Simpson	1
Francis Bilton	2
Thomas Emitt	2
Thomas Simpson	1
Samuell Midgley	3
Robert Whester	1
Widdow Marsden	1
Leonard Randall	1
Roger Tompson	1
Widdow Risdall	1
Francis West	1
Barbara Hill	1
John Tompson	2
Hercules Simpson	1
Ro Humpleby	1
Christopher Smith	1
John Richmond	2

m 22]

Thomas Parker	1
Mr Tayler	2
Thomas Tompson	1
Dinis Maunby	2
David Bilton	1
Thomas Baitson	1
Robert Harrison	1
Thomas Halliday	1

[30] sic.

Christopr Harison	1
Robert More	1
Joseph Leadom	1
Anne Beane	1
Francis Holmes	1
Miles Waite	2
Thomas Hutchinson	1
Thomas Iles	1
John Stead	1
Miles Hutchinson	1
Thomas Hutchinson	1
John Parker & forge	2
John Beeston	1
Richard Hudson	1
Steven Smith	2
Widdow Wilson or }	
Francis West }	1
John Atkinson	1
John Halliday	1
	one
Thomas Umpleby	1
John Shutt	1
Willm Benson	1
Willm Atkinson	1
Thomas Halliday and }	
Richard More }	2
Thomas Scaife	1
Willm Boococke	1
Robt Randall	1
John Faireburne	1
Widdow Kendall	1
Miles Wilkinson	1
Widdow Lumbe	1
John Kendall	1
Anne Greatwood	1
Willm Moorehouse	1
Widdow Batson	1
John Scaife	1
Willm Grumock	1
Willm Knowles	1
Miles Umpleby	1
	84

Robt Corner Collr
Thos Iles Const

Fountaines Abbey
(Fountains Abbey)

Mr Messenger	11
Widdow Hudson	1
Mrs Margory Yeoman	2
Marmad Wainman	2
Edward Ingram	2
James Wilkinson	3
Mr Steven Wilkes	5
Widdow Hawksby	1

m 23]

Leonard Ketlewell	4
	31

George Wainman Collr
Mr Messenger Const

Firrinsby
(Ferrensby)

Mr Thomas Collins	3
Mr Willm Knarsbrough	4
Willm Fountaines	3
Richard Knarsbrough	3
John Waide	1
Jerem Strickland	2
Ellin Syser	1
Phillp Hall	1
John Jeff	1
Peter Mould	1
Ellizabeth Beiforth	2
John Wray	1
Marmaduke Darley	1
Widdow Piper	1
John Lowson	1
	26
Omitted by reason of poverty	3

Roger Hardcastle Collr
Richd Browne Const

Farnley

Mrs Mary Fawkes	15
Francis Suttill	1
Lawrance Bradley	1
Jane Morritt Widdow	1
Nichollas Dunwell	1
Anthony Dunwell	1
Ellizabeth Dunwell	1
Francis Jackson	1
Thomas Faukes	2
Nichollas Rhoades	2
Samuell Linley	3
Simon Smith	1
Lawrence Browne	1
Willm Jackson	2
Thomas Dale	2
Henry Snowden	2
Thomas Dunwell	2
Thomas Bradley	1
Robert Brogden	1
Widdow Pawson	1
Willm Pulleine	1
Francis Umpleby	1
Henry Page	1
Grace Dale	1
Willm Waite	1
Anthony Whitehead	1
Willm Whitehead	1
Widdow Pawson	1
Thomas Whitehead	1
Widdow Jackson	1
Nichollas Dunwell	2
Lawrance Bradley	1
Thomas Jackson	1

m 24]

Thomas Pope	1
James Atkinson	1
Nichollas Grunwell	1
Edmond Whitehead	1
Nichollas Pawson	1
Thomas Pawson	1
Richard Bradley	1
John Chippendale	1

John Franckland	1
Christopr Jackson	1
Richard Bradley	1
Lawrance Holmes	1
Christophr Daid & forg	1
John Daide	1
John Browne	1
Katherine Pawson	1
	72

Robert Husband Collr
Lawrance Bradley Const

Fountaines Earth
(Fountains Earth)

Christopr Hanley or Roger Sloney	2
Steven Horner	1
Willm Baine	3
John Craven	2
Willm Craven	1
John Oddy	1
Willm Sutle or Widd	3
Widdow Suttle	2
Thomas Craven	1
Peter Craven	1
Mr Dawson heires	4
Edward Thackeray	1
Thomas Craven of Loftus	1
Thomas Craven	1
Richard Baine	1
Christophr Clarke	1
Mr John Horner	4
Willm Craven	1
John Loftus	3
Willm Horner	2
Edmond Dent	2
Roger Inman	3
Roger Reynold	1
Richard Tompson	1
Miles Benson	1
Hugh Thackerey	1
Richard Smurthwaite	2
John Inman Jun	2
Henry Inman	2
John Topham	2
Thomas Horner sen	1
Thomas Horner jun	1
Thomas Burrill	2
John Topham	1
Mr Plaine	1
Widdow Brigges	1
Thomas Topham	2
Willm Brigges	1
Christopr Morehouse	2

m 25]

Mr John Plaine	5
Willm Baine	2
	72

Robert Husband Collr
Alice Suttle Const

Goldsbrough
(Goldsborough)

Richard Hutton Esqr	29
Mr Stables	4
Thomas Tompson	1
John Mawson	1
John Hodgson	1
Thomas Whitacres	1
Ellin Sawnby	1
Willm Lister	2
Richard Catterton	1
Thomas Aikers	1
Richard Baxter	2
Susan Clementshawe	1
Thomas Simpson	1
John Walker	1
Joseph Pollard	1
John Beckwith	1
Willm Barber	1
Willm Hamond	1
John Bywatter	1
John Winder	1
Jennet Colyer	1
Richard Gibson & forge	2
Anne Ouzeman	3
Richard Slater	1
John Smith	1
Christopr Higgin	1
Willm Hawckrigg	1
John Robinson	1
Willm Johnson	1
Thomas Clementshaw	1
Thomas Walker	1
	67

Robert Husband Collr
Robert Clementshaw Const

Giveingdale
(Givendale)

Ralph Parker	2
Willm Heavisides	2
	4

George Wainman Collr
Willm Heavisides Const

Grewelthorp
(Grewelthorpe)

Willm Buckle	1
Richard Baine	2
Willm Jackson & forge	2
Willm Botchby	1
John Wilkes	1
Edward Dixon	2
Christopr Walker Jun	1
John Walker	2

m 26]

Christopher Gregson	1
Leonard Burmstone	1
Margret Danby	3
Dorothy Danby	1
Willm Atkinson	1
Widdow Wainman	1
John Hardcastle	1
	one
Gabriell Loadsman	1

George Spence	1
Thomas Pybus	2
Mathew Akers	1
George Dawson	1
Leonard Mirfeild	2
Margret Walker	1
Willm Baine	1
John Inman	3
Thomas Hemsley	1
Thomas Pybus sen	2
Leonard Gugion	1
Margret Lambert	2
Willm Cooke	1
James Wilkinson	2
Thomas Cundall	1
John Cotton	1
Gilbert Mawlas	1
Christophr Jaques	2
Grace Dawson or }	
John Walker }	1
Robert Richmond	2
John Holdsworth	4
Thomas Allenson	1
John Man	1
Mr Richard Baine	8
John Smith	1
George Ripley	2
John Garth	1
Anthony Walker	2
Mr John Baine	6
Widdow Holdsworth	1
Thomas Ripley	1
Willm Ripley	1
John Ripley	1
John Lye	1
John Richmond	2
Mr Richard Baine	4
Francis Brathwaite	1
Samuell Wilson	1
John Cundall	1
Thomas Dallowe	1
Christopr Dawson	2
John Heblethwaite	2
Willm Baine	2
George Crakill	2
Willm Steele	2
Willm Horner	2
Anne Steele Widd	1
Widdow Grainge	2

m 27]

Charles Watson	1
Willm Pearson	1
Michaell Jackson	1
Widdow Duffeild	1
Willm Smith	1
Leonard Watson	3
John Hague	1
John Thirkill	1
Mr Johnson	1
Thomas Walker	1
George Goodson	1
Jane Atkinson	1
Nichollas Metcalfe	1
Mr Willm Man	5
Richard Dawson	2
Charles Dawson	1
Widdow Dawson	1
Leonard Leadley	1
Willm Eadon	1
George Prentice	1
	134

Omitted by reason of poverty	6

George Wainman Collr
Wm Atkinson Const

Grantley cum Eversone
(Grantley with Eavestone)

George Marshall	3
Willm Hebden	1
Widdow Duffield	1
Christophr Duffield	1
Francis Beacham	1
Willm Stevenson	1
Georg Clarke	3
Leonard Bramley	2
Willm Leeming	4
more a forge	1
Thomas Horner	2
John Mawer	2
Michaell Leeming	1
Mr Ellias Hodgson	1
John Boggett	1
Marmaduke Carter	1
George Maultus	1
Thomas Kirby	4
John Crow	3
Thomas Lumley	1
John Richmond	1
Widdow Wells	1
Steven Kirby	1
Thomas Mawer	1
Mathew Swaile	1
Richard Leeming	2
John Grainge	1
Richard Leeming	1
Barthollo Leeming	1
Edward Richmond	1
Marke Theakstone	1
James Grainge	1
Widdow Smith	1
John Thackeray	1
John Richmond	1
Thomas Stevenson	3
Thomas Popleton	1
Christopr Hebden	1
Willm Rhoades	1
Thomas Leeming	1
Richard Walker	1
Phillip Ibbitson	1
Richard Richmond	2
Thomas Cowley	1
Grantley Mill	1

m 28]

Nichollas Butler	1
John Grainge	1
Widdow Topham	1
	67

Omitted by reason of poverty	2

Robert Corner Collr
Corner Collr
Francis Beacham Const
Beacham Const

Greenehammerton (Green Hammerton)

Mr John Atkinson	9
Mr Leonard Weddell	6
John Bryon	1
Christophr Wilkinson	1
Thomas Squire	3
Brian Jenings	1
Willm Wirdill	1
Willm Bedforth	1
Thomas Johnson	1
Francis Wincobb	1
John Warren	1
Francis Bedford	1
Thomas Dickinson	1
Joseph Clarke	1
Brian Marshall	2
more *pro* Nottingham	1
Richard Shearewood	1
Thomas Ketlewell	2
Robert Lupton	1
Thomas Rawlinson } heires }	2
Christophr Burton	1
Widdow Jane Dickinson	5
Willm Abbey	1
John Slater	1
Thomas Coates	2
Lawrance Clarke	1
Barbar Butler	1
Oswald Langwith	1
Willm Ayre	1
John Longley	1
Guy Marshall	1
	54

Empty and no distress to be had	
Widdow Dickinson	3

Omitted by reason of poverty	3

George Wainman Collr
Francis Wincobb Const

Hunsingore

Richard Browne	1
Widdow Wilson	1
Richard Hulley	1
Richard Bell	1
Richard Hunter	3
Thomas Wincob	2
Willm Munckton	1
Widdow Hawkes	1
John Shafton	1
Richard Wincobb	1
Richard Pulleine	1
John Haukes	3
Thomas Allenson	1
Mr Bonnell	3
Richard Peirson	1
Christophr Bell	1
Thomas Dawson	1
Willm Tompson	2

m 29]

Richard Browne	4
Willm Pulleine	1
Robert Pulleine	2
Francis Benson	2
James Fletcher	2
John Wincobb	2
John Mountaine	1
Richard Wright	1
Bartholl Pulleine	1
Roger Dobson	2
Thomas Stainburne	1
Roger Dobson	1
Henry Bell	1
Willm Pulleine	1
Sir Henry Gootherick	1
	49

These persons following are discharged by Certificates

Ellizabeth May	1
Anthony Flint	1
Sir Henry Gotherick puld downe	10

Omitted by reason of poverty	3

Robt Corner Collr
Willm Pullan Const

Hopperton a member of Arkindale (Hopperton a member of Arkendale)

John Blayd	1
Thomas Bigland	2
Henry Lazonby	2
Willm Porter	1
Henry Hudson	1
Widdow Ingham	1
	8

Omitted by reason of poverty	2

Roger Hardcastle Collr
Richd Browne Const

Humberton cum Milby (Humburton with Milby)

Roger Wright	1
Sir Jerem Smithson } *pro* Cloffehouse }	2
Henry Todd	1
Willm Wilkinson	3
Ralph Tabb	1

Thomas Ibeson 2
Willm Wood 2
12

George Wainman Collr
Roger Wright Const

Hamsthwaite (Hampsthwaite)
Mr Sugon 4
Daniel Hitch 4
Willm Smith or }
Widd Hardisty } 4
Thomas Hardcastle 3
John Pullan 3
Mathew Procter 2
Willm Allenson 1
Thomas Tompson 1
Thomas Umpleby 2
John Birkhead & forge 2
Robert Reynold 1
George Cork 1
Silvester Hebden 1

m 30]

Thomas Kidd 1
Francis Spence 2
Henry Beane & Asquith 2
John Falkiner 2
Ellizabeth Hardisty 1
Willm Pott 1
Christopr Stubb 1
John Simpson 1
Dorothy Hardisty 4
Willm Shann 1
Willm Harrison 2
Thomas Simpson 1
Anthony Hallady 1
Richard Hardacres 1
Edward Steele 1
Willm Harrison 1
Willm Spence 1
Willm Hardcastle 2
Willm Smith and forge 2
Peter Hardisty 1
Nathanll Calverley 1
Mary Tompson 1
Philip Wilkes or }
Willm Smith } 1
61

Empty and no distres to be had
Mr Joseph Ibetson 2

Richard Pickard Collr
John Pullan Const

Harrowgate (Harrogate)
Willm Stockdale Esqr 22
Sir Willm Ingleby 10
Widdow Mathew 1
Willm Hutton 1
John Harrison 1
Mathew Hogg 1
Silvester Atkinson 1
Gilbert Strickland 1
John Benson 2
Francis Kearsby 7
Mr John Hill 7
Ellin Beck 2
Willm Plumpton 1
John Candler 2
John Hogg 1
Michaell Cooke 2
Ellin Surgante 3
Thomas Wild 1
George Baxter 3
John Allon 1
John Eltofts 1
George Waide 2
Peter Benson 3
Phillp Hall 3
John Stevenson 5
George Davy 2
Mr Faucitt 6
Peter Hogg 3
Francis Patricke 1
Jane Wharfe 1
Willm Dobson 2

m 31]

Edward Wharton 2
George Bradley 2
Thomas Wyley 2
John Marston 1
Edward Plumpton 1
Willm Walker 1
Hellin Plumpton 1
Richard Marston 1
Joseph Tompson 1
John Tayler 2
John Lewis 2
Francis Tayler 2
Thomas Squire 1
Robert Younge 1
Francis Beck 1
Hellin Pattrick 1
Edward Atkinson 1
Thomas Wilden 1
Thomas Grimston 1
James Beck 2
John Flint 1
John Spence 2
Lawrance Benson 1
one
Edward Stevenson 1
Willm Benson 2
Roger Tompson 1
Richard Burton 1
John Marston 2
Widdow Murfitt 1
Mr Dickinson 1
Willm Lobley 1
Thomas Robinson 1
George Stainer 2
John Wilkes 1
Willm Benson Long Lands 1
145

Empty and no distres	
Mr Stockdale	1
Mr Carr	2
Omitted by reason of poverty	7
Robt Husband Collr	
John Stevenson Const	

Hewick cum Hewick

Willm Straker	4
Widdow Young	1
Edward Bell	1
Christophr Lund	1
Chr Brafitt and Oburon	2
Thomas Robinson	2
Willm Artas	1
John Carlin	2
Martin Brafitt	1
Widdow Artas	1
George Wass	1
John Smith Jun	1
Robert Wray	1
Robert Hutton	1
Thomas Hunter	1
Tristram Duffield	1
Lawrance Holegate	1
	23
Omitted by reason of poverty	6

m 32]

George Wainman Collr	
Christophr Lund Const	

Hewick Bridge (Bridge Hewick)

Willm Wetherill	3
John Smith	1
John Boggitt	1
Richd Brafitt	2
	two
Willm Myers	3
John Brewster	2
Roger Browne	3
Willm Brooke	2
Mathew Exley	1
John Butterey	1
Widdow Nelson	1
George Webster	1
Edward Drewrey	1
Willm Wethernbye	1
	23

These persons following are discharged by Certificates

John Bell or Garthwaite	1
Thomas Rainforth	1
Widdow Horsman	1
George Wainman Collr	
John Brewston Const	

Hartwith cum Winsley (Hartwith with Winsley)

Mr Brathwaite	5
Mr Jenings	4
James Wheelehouse	3
Henry Crosby	1
Richard Fireman or Horsman	1
John Slee	1
George Calverley sen	2
George Calverley Jun	1
Joseph Jackson	1
Isabell Scaife	1
Ellin Scaife	1
John Lupton	5
Christopr Yates	2
Mrs Anne Constantine	3
Richard Midgley	1
Anne Longstaffe	1
Gabriell Grainge	1
Richard Longbotham	3
John Donghill	2
Richard Oddy	3
Samuell Hardcastle	2
Willm Knightson	2
Marmaduke Bramley	2
Nichollas Wood	2
Robert Wood	2
Thomas Haxsby	3
John Day	3
Robert West	2
Peter Hardcastle	2
James Buck	1
Samuell Hardcastle	1
Thomas Hardcastle	2
Peter Hardcastle	1

m 33]

Robert Hardcastle	3
John Dawson	1
John Smith	1
John Dawson	1
Thomas Harrison	2
George Horsman	2
Lawrance Dawson	2
Cuthbert Brooke	1
John Midgley	2
Henry Dinncore	2
Mr Robert Long	4
Thomas Farnill	1
Mathew Burnitt	2
Miles Reynold	1
John Kendall	2
John & Mary Hardcastle	3
Thomas Slee	1
John Asquith	1
Willm Elory	1
Henry Jackman	1
James Maudes	1
Willm Wheelehouse	1
Anne Scaife	3
Willm Scaife	3
	109
Omitted by reason of poverty	11

Robert Husband Collr
Richd Oddy Const

Ingerthorpe

Mr Richard Norton	9
George Ward	1
John Ellis	2
Edward Madson	1
Richard Bickerdike	1
John Taylor	1
Thomas Deane	1
Nichollas Hudson	1
Thomas Browne	1
Peter Hodgson	2
Henry Bell	1
John Burnitt	1
Willm Howson	1
Michaell Hewby	1
Henry Bell	1
	25

Omitted by reason of poverty 6

Georg Wainman Collr
John Ellis Const

Killinghall

Mr Bowill	3
Richard Wilkes	2

m 34]

Francis Wood	1
Mr Chamley	4
Peter Cooke	1
George Clandwell[31]	1
John Viccars	7
Willm Clandwell[32]	1
Judith Burton	1
Thomas Veepin	2
Capt' Atkinson	4
Edward Bilton	5
Willm Hardisty	3
Robt Pullan } Daniell Shaw or } Thomas Flint }	1
Willm Hodgson	2
Richard Crosby	1
John Wood	1
Willm Turpin	2
Edward Hardisty	1
Willm Browne	2
Widdow Knightson	1
Willm Clarke	1
Arthur Burton	3
Thomas Bradfeild	1
Willm Farnill	1
Ralph Williamson	1
Richard Hardisly	2
Francis Browne	1
Willm Cooke	1
Widdow Wardman	1
Thomas Wardman	1
Richard Carr	5
Robert Lund	1
Arthur Hodgson	1
John Barber	1
Christopr Knightson	1
Francis Robinson	2
James Pickard	2
George Hardisty	2
Steven Brearcliffe	1
Francis Burton	1
Willm Wise	1
Sir John Hewley or } Edward Bainebridge }	1
Arthur Burton *pro* mill	1
John Waine	1
Francis Kirby mill	1
Thomas Luty	2
Thomas Cryer	1
Dinis Shaw	1
	85

Empty and no distress to be had

Francis Robinson	4
Willm Browne	3
Willm Simpson	1

Omitted by reason of poverty 2

George Wainman Collr
Thomas Cryer Const

Kirby Hall

Mr Thomas Dickinson	15
John Abbey	3

m 35]

Adam Haire	4
Widdow Butterfeild	1
Major Watters	6
	29

Omitted by reason of poverty 1

Richard Pickard Collr
Willm Steele Const

Kirby Malzard (Kirkby Malzeard)

Thomas Sharples	2
Mr Timothy Horsman	7
Willm Tompson	2
Thomas Pybus	1
Thomas Ripley	1
Christopr Walker	1
Willm Armistead	2
Lawrance Armistead	2
Henry Newton & } Willm Outhwait}	4
Widdow Richmond	2

[31] Alternatively Claudwell.
[32] Alternatively Claudwell.

Thomas Richardson	3
John Ripley	1
Francis Nickson	1
Dorothy Smith	1
Leonard Abbotson	1
Richard Wass	1
Anthony Fothergill	1
Thomas Beckwith	2
Anthony Procter	4
George Wood	2
John Faubert	2
Willm Holland	1
Mr George Wood	3
George Binslay	1
John Snawden	2
Edward Skelton	1
George Fisher	1
Bryan Fisher	1
Willm Browne	1
Widdow Harrison	1
Thomas Elder	1
Willm Haxby	1
Willm Smith	1
Wilfrey Day	1
Francis Whitton	1
John Ripley	1
John Thackeray	1
John Fish	1
John Beckwith	2
Christopr Buck	1
Thomas Fawber	3
Margret Billington	2
Thomas Kidd	1
Edmond Craw	1
Richard Steele	1
John Ripley	4
Mr Browne Rector	8
John Kirby	1
Edward Richmond	1
John Sanderson	1
John Smith	1
John Browne	1

m 36]

Simond Wrayther	4
Widdow Wallis	1
Willm Atkinson	1
Thomas Horsman	2
Samll Elsley	2
Willm Atkinson War'	1
	102

Omitted by reason of poverty	9

Georg Wainman Collr
Samuell Ripley Const

Kirke Deighton (Kirk Deighton)

Mr Thomas Thornton Cler	7
Mr Willm Ketlewell	7
Willm Brownridge	4
Willm Spinke	2
Francis Clarke	1
Robert Dalby	1
Richard Cromack	1
Sallom: Rawson	1
Widdow Wright	1
Oswald Brownridge	1
Thomas Brownridge	1
Willm Mountaine	2
Joseph Mountaine	1
Edward Wright	2
John Adcock	1
Peter Mountaine	1
Peter Walker	1
Michaell Dunwell	1
James Swaile	2
John Mowson	1
Robert Deighton	1
John Dunwell[33]	1
Marke Mawson	1
Roger Armistead	1

Mary Hebden	1
Robert Tasker	1
Thomas Tayler	1
	46

Empty and no distres to be had	
Duke of Buckingham	2

Omitted by reason of poverty	1

Roger Hardcastle Collr
Willm Brownridg Const

Knarsbrough Tentergate (Knaresborough, Tentergate)

Mr Thomas Richardson	7
Richard Bussie	3
Richard Hill	4
Francis Hill	1
Ralph Waddy	1
Willm Broadbelt	2
Richard Lister	2
Willm Howden	1
Richard Ellis	2
Edward Benson	5
Richard Broadbelt	2
John Inman	2
Daniell Hodgson	1
John Bransby	1
Robert Redshawe	2
Thomas Craven	2
Thomas Hill	2
Widdow Hill	1
Robert Bransby	1
Widdow Adamson	1
Francis Peirson	1
John Day	2
Thomas Thorp	2
John Kirkman	2
Widdow Carter	1

[33] Hole. Reading uncertain.

m 37]

Widdow Mathewes	1
Mathew Tompson	1
George Cooper	1
Richard Craven	1
Willm Halliday	2
Willm Steele	1
Widdow Peirson	1
Widdow Hunter	1
Widdow Roundell	2
Willm Keighley	1
Dinis Clementshawe	20
John Maw	2
John Keighley	1
Robert Tunstall	1
Widdow Sikes	2
Willm Thorpe	2
Widdow Waddington	1
Simond Holegate	1
	75
Omitted by reason of poverty	2

Roger Hardcastle Collr
Thomas Owram Const

Knarsbrough (Knaresborough)

Mr Grayson	1
James Shepherd	2
Willm Brownridge	6
Richard Fishwick	4
Robert Wilson	2
Widdow Harrison	1
Willm Luis	3
Willm Johnson	3
Richard Cundall	2
Thomas Beane	2
Marmaduke Scott	3
Widdow Dungley	2
Widdow Hill	1
Boswell Midleton	4
Willm Fead	1
Francis Horner	1
Aron Lowcocke	3
Thomas Feild	2
Henry Cass	3
Willm Robinson	1
Widdow Daine	2
Willm Carter	2
Mr Best	2
Mr Wise	1
Widdow Slater	2
Mathew Nutbrowne	3
	thre
Mr Bickerdike	4
John Bell	1
Gilbert Haires	1
George Exley	1
Mr Wilkinson	7
	seaven
John Bell	3
Widdow Burgan	3
Willm Burton	4
John Bickerdike	1
Robert Empson	4
Willm Hopper	3
Nichollas Salmond	3
Timothy Cundall	4
Phillip Hall	2
Widdow Anderson	3
Mr Richard Rhoades	5
Mr Francis Barrowby	6
Edward Benson	3
George Bentley	1
Peter Farnham	1
Francis Richardson	1
Mr Hilton	1
Willm Flaskett	2

m 38]

Thomas Plumbley	1
Richard Richardson	1
Richard Norfolke	3
Francis Lister	1
Willm Savidge	2
Richard Yeadon	2
John Broughton	1
John Harrison	1
Widdow Carleton	1
John Simpson	1
Thomas Dauy	1
John White	1
John Maunby	1
Thomas Porter	1
Willm Inman	3
Willm Watters	1
Widdow Shafte	1
Mr Levitt	3
Mr Simon Warrener	2
Willm Inman	1
Robert Wyrill	1
Robert Hardcastle	1
Mr Simon Warrener	4
George Watkins	3
The Mill	1
Thomas Akam	1
Widdow Scott	3
Robert West	2
George Cass	2
Richard Palley	1
John Palley	2
Thomas Latham	1
Widdow Wilson	1
Thomas Bucke	4
Widdow Lucas	3
John Emerson	2
John Benson	2
Willm Band	3
Mary Roundell	2
Mr Kendall Schoole	2
Widdow Winterburne	1
Henry Bullocke	1
Willm Benson	2
Widdow Butler	5
Robert Hill	5
Marmaduke Inman	4
Mr Bucke	1
Thomas Turner	2
Francis Hill	1
John Hill	1
Mary Roundell	5

Thomas Howden 4
Thomas Hodgson 2
Thomas Askericke 1
Peter Bateson 2
Widdow Slater 1
Mr Wincopp 7
Widdow Norfolke 2
Mr Rhoades 6
Willm Watters 4
Jacob Shaun 2
Willm Hill 4
Thomas Atkinson 3
Hugh Lewis 3
George Lucas 6
George Walker 2
Francis Brunton 1

m 39]

Robert Leay 1
Widdow Butterfeild 2
Henry Latham 3
George Jefferson 3
George Cass 1
Willm Bateson 2
Widdow Peirson 2
John Tomlinson 3
Willm Myers 1
John Crawshawe 1
Thomas Smith 1
Thomas Dobson 3
Willm Dickinson 1
Willm Tompson 1
Thomas Howden 1
John Mush 2
Richard Broxup 1
Anthony Cass 1
Thomas Bland 1
Willm Dodgson 1
Thomas Simpson 2
Thomas Simpson 1
James Shepherd 2
Brian Fleeming 1
George Casse 1
Richard Coates 1
Mary Harrison 1
Thomas Bussey 2
Richard Webster 1
Dinis Coates 2
Sir John Hewley 6
John Swaile 2
Christopr Gibson 1
Simond Holegate 1
Widdow Smith 1
Thomas Gibson 3
Mr Edward Conyers 3
Richard Tompson 1
Franc Brounton 1
Widdow Wright 1
Richard Cass 1
Richard Broadbelt 1
Willm Holden 1
Richard Winterburne 1
Henry Clarkson 1
Burnall Hall 4
Robert Wyrill 1
George Cass 2
Willm Grafton 4
Robert Hayes 2
355

Empty and noe distres to be had
Mr Browne 2
Jasper Godsey 1
Mr John Cogill 3
Mathew Dickinson 2

Omitted by reason of poverty 15

Roger Hardcastle Collr
Richd Casse Const

Kirby Overblow (Kirkby Overblow)

Mr Gaile 7
Thomas Dodgson 9

m 40]

Willm Bowman 9 nine
Robert Goodson 3
Richard Easterby 1
Thomas Abbey 1
Thomas Collingworth 1
Richard Goodson 1
Marmaduke Robinson 1
Anthony Poole 1
George Wimble 1
Miles Poole 1
Robert Watson 1
Robert Hall 1
John Spencer 1
Miles Wright 1
Anthony Poole sen 2
Widdow Moore 2
George Spacy 2
Francis Ingle 4
Willm Wood 1
Willm Hall 1
John Atkinson 1
John Abbey 1
Mr Brewerton 1
George Easterby 1
Peter Whitehead 1
Richard Wood 1
Francis Rhoades 1
Thomas Poole 1
Richard Wimble 1
Ellizabeth Earle 1
Richard Richardson 1
Willm Tunstall 1
64

Omitted by reason of poverty 11

Robert Husband Collr
Anthony Poole Const

Kirby cum Netherby (Kearby with Netherby)

Mr Steele	8
Dr Beachill & }	
Mr Killingbecke }	8
Francis Wardropp	1
Edward Barker	1
Anthony Moss	1
Willm Moss	1
Steven Brearcliff	2
Willm Wetherill	1
Richard Jarmine	3
Willm Leeming	1
Jane Redman	1
Grace Flather	1
Andrew Birdsall	1
Willm Mursh	1
Widdow Saxton	3
Francis Jackson	3
Thomas Wiglesworth	1
Richard Knapton	1
Widdow Leadbeater	1
Willm Jeffrey	1
Robert Young	1
Richard Birdsall	2
	44

m 41]

Empty and noe distres to be had

Widdow Broadbelt	3
Omitted by reason of poverty	4

Robert Husband Collr
Francis Jackson Const

Kirke Hamerton (Kirk Hammerton)

Mr Stockdale	8
Thomas Tasker	1
Willm Wilson	1
John Wilson forge	1
Thomas Wardell	1
Thomas Abbey	2
Willm Ellis	1
Willm Palferman	1
John Dickinson	1
Jane Abbey	1
John Haw	1
Willm Lake	2
Richard Dickinson	1
Henry Elsworth	1
John Abbey	1
Thomas Tasker sen	1
John Sanderson	1
Richard Haw	1
John Pape	1
Christopr Sanderson	1
Jane Hardcastle	1
Edmd Burley	2
Richard Wilfoote	1
Willm Smith	1
John Fewston	1
Willm Wadington	2
Richard Abbey	1
Richard Nelson	1
Willm Pinder	3
Mr Atkinson	2
Robert Abbey	1
John Pickersgill	1
Willm Britton	3
Peter Johnson	1
	50

These persons following are discharged by Certificate

Robert Plackett	1
Margret Dickinson	1
Omitted by reason of poverty	6

Robert Corner Collr
Edward Dickinson Const

Leathley

Mr Henry Hitch	11
Mr Dinneson	3
John Moyses	1
Robt Moyses	3
Robert Proctor & Antho	3
Thomas Walker	2
Thomas Forrest	2
Richard Hill	6
Parsibell Foster	1

m 43]

Mathew Wright	1
Thomas Lambe	1
Thomas Barber	1
John Barber	1
John Lupton	1
Jonas Wright	1
Thomas Peters	2
John Forrest sen	1
Willm Forrest	1
Willm Walker	1
Willm Moody	1
Thomas Squire	2
Thomas Shipindale	1
John Procter	1
Anthony Tomlinson	1
Thomas Snawden and }	
Robert Moses }	2
John Bradley	1
George Forrest	1
Lawrance Eltofts	1
Henry Bacock	1
Mathew Thornhill	2
Richard Aldridge	1
John Gill	1
Willm Moore	1
Richard Broadbelt	2
Thomas Emott	1
Christopr Waide	1
Margret Domvell	1
Thomas Todd	1
John Wogden	1
Willm Lupton	1

Thomas Walker Jun 1
Henry Waide 1
Christopr Bradley 1
John Walker 1
Michaell Jackson 2
two
Richard Waite 1
John Forrest Jun 1
Willm Barber 1
Richard Lambe 1
Thomas Squire 1
Willm Pickard 1
80

These persons following are discharged by Certificates
Christophr Chipendale 1
Widdow Bradley 1

Robert Husband Collr
Willm More Const

Linton
Simond Swaile 5
Richard Thorp 2
Willm Wright 3
Willm Rhynolds 1
Willm Parker 1
John Wilson 1
Willm Ward 3
Robert Daleby Jun 1
Robert Daleby Sen 2
Robert Daleby Jun[34] 1
Willm Wilson 1
John Wheelehouse 2
James Pearson 2
John Jarmin 2
27

m 43]

Omitted by reason of poverty 2

Robert Husband Collr
Robert Dalbey Const

Linley (Lindley)
Willm Palmes Esqr 15
Willm Emott 1
Christopr Turner Sen 1
Francis Turner 1
Willm Maude 1
Guy Mercer 2
John Bainebridge 1
Peter Ketlewell 1
Christopr Turner Jun 1
Widdow Tompson 2
Thomas Hebden 1
Francis Mountaine 1
Parcevell Browne 2
Widdow Tompson 1
Francis Lambe 1
Nichollas Mountaine 2
Willm Mercer 1
Parcevell Mountaine 1
36

Roger Hardcastle Collr
Peter Kettlewell Const

Larton (Laverton)
Mr Willm Hardcastle 6
George Rhynold 1
Thomas Jackson 1
John Theakston 2
Willm Haw 2
Christopr Rhynold 1
Barnaby Scowthrop 1
Willm Tompson 1
James Thackerey 1
Willm Russell 1
Nichollas Metcalfe 1
Edward Bickerdike 1
Steven Duffeild 1
Christopher Rocliffe 1
Widdow Wilkinson 1
Willm Waberan 1
Christopr Atkinson 1
John Cragill 1
George Rheynold sen 1
John Russell 1
George Duffeild 2
John Rheynold 1
Bartholl Iles 1
John Dodgson 1
John Richmond sen 1
Richard Richmond Jun 2
John Richmond Jun 1
Edward Dareley 1
Steven Kirby 1
Willm Carlisle 3
Francis Theakston 1
Christopr Wood 1
John Allenson 1
John Allenson[35] 1
Thomas Grainge 2

m 44]

Mary Clarke 1
Godfrey Watson 1
John Ripley 4
Willm Horner 1
Francis Atkinson 1
Thomas Holdsworth 2
Willm Grainge 2
Willm Mitchill 2
Charles Baxter 1
John Nicholls 1
Anthony Fawber 1

[34] sic.
[35] sic.

Thomas Gregg	1
Widdow Burniston	2
Willm Beckwith	2
Willm Outhwate	1
John Beareper	1
John Coulthrust	1
Willm Horsman	1
Edward Horsman	1
Francis Brathwaite	1
John Stewart	2
John Beareper	1
James Beckwith	1
John Raynford	1
John Gibson	1
Chr Wells	1
George Wilson	1
Richard Brathwaite	1
John Brathwaite	1
	85

Omitted by reason of poverty	13

Robert Corner Collr
George Rhynold Const

Marton cum Grafton (Marton with Grafton)

Mr Willm Morrill	1
Mr Richard Browne	4
Robert Steele	1
Richard Walker	2
Robert and Richard Dickinson	2
Thomas Dickinson	1
Thomas Simpson	1
Richard Dickinson	4
Thomas Pretious	2
Richard Spinke	1
Richard Dickinson	1
Thomas Shepherd	2
Anne Snowden	1
Thomas Dewes	2
Edmond Winde	1
Ellizabeth Wheelehouse	2
Robert Dewes	2
Robert Turritt	1
Thomas Hodgson	1
George Hodgson	1
Richard Bell	1
Richard Bickerdike	1
James Smith	1
Leonard Dixon	1
Willm Dewes	2
John Catton	1
Widdow Martin	1
Richard Dewes Tanner	1
Ellizab Metcalfe	1
Robert Randall	1
Willm Tompson	1
Richard Aislaby	1
Abraham Smith	1
Christopr Nottingham	1
Willm Birdsall	1

m 45]

Thomas Hebden	1
Robert Popleton	1
George Scruton or } John Waite }	1
James Scruton	1
Robert Harley	2
Richard Hanley	1
Thomas Courtious	1
Willm Benson	2
Robert Bickerdike	1
Christopr Pick	1
Willm Steele	1
Richard Smeaton	1
	63

Empty and noe distres to be had

Richard Haburne	1

Omitted by reason of poverty	6

Robert Corner Collr
Richd Bickerdike Const

Minskipp (Minskip)

Widdow Earle	1
Widdow Lowry	2
Willm Maultus	1
Thomas Hodgson	1
John Smith	2
Widdow Gilbertson	1
Henry Earle	1
John Maultas	1
Christopr Maultas	1
Christopr Tompson	1
Thomas Young	2
Richard Ward	1
Edward Brigham	1
John Ross or } Edwd Hodgson }	1
Willm Wright	1
John Sturdy	1
Peter Simpson	1
James Simpson	1
Widdow Maultas	1
Willm Browne	1
Widdow Parkins	1
Thomas Ward	1
Willm Tomlinson	1
Anthony Axler	1
Widdow Ward	1
Widdow Prince	1
Willm Gilbertson	2
George Wright	1
John Marke	2
Willm Lawry	1
Roger Houseman	1
Richard Houseman	1
John Ross	2
Richard Hodgson	1
Richard Earle	1
Widdow Parker	1
	42

Omitted by reason of poverty	4

George Wainman Collr
Thomas Dickinson Const

m 46]

Markinthwaite cum Wallathwaite (Markington with Wallerthwaite)

Sir Henry Gootherick	5
Mr John Dodsworth	3
Willm Dixon	2
Anthony Rendall	1
Francis Steele	2
Mr George Usher	4
John Wright Sen	1
Widdow Kay	1
Mr Thomas Hinckes	4
Thomas Wright Jun	1
John Halliday	1
Robert Brewes	1
Willm Hodgson	2
Mr James Singleton	1
Willm Hanson	2
Willm Laycock	2
Christopr Berrey	1
Thomas Whiker	2
John Atkinson	2
Francis Burton	1
Martin Wadington	1
Mr Willm Markinfeild	8
Mary Ward	2
Robert Askwith	1
John Brigges	1
John Darley	1
Thomas Burnett	2
Willm Sweetin	1
Willm Wright	1
Mrs Margt Barne	2
Mr Peternell Markinfeild	2
Willm Hodgson	2
Thomas Wrightson	1
Francis Mawtas	1
John Allen	1
Thomas Robinson	1
Willm Ketlewell	1
Willm Cawthrey	1
John Mawson	1
	70

The person undernamed is discharged by Certifte

Thomas Hering	2

Omitted by reason of poverty 5

Georg Wainman Collr
John Atkinson Const

Midleton cum Stockill (Middleton with Stockeld)

m 47]

John Midleton Esqr	41
Henry Currer	2
Willm Rickerd	2
Edward Wharton sen	1
Willm Robinson	1
Christopr Hodgson	1
Edmond Wharton Jun	1
Richard Anderson	1
Willm Gill	1
Abraham Atkinson	3
Thomas Hawkesworth	1
Willm Hudson	1
Mathew Hudson	1
Ellizabeth Hardwick	3
Christopr Hodgson	2
Lawrence White	1
Arthur Beeston	2
Thomas Harrison	2
Christopr Holmes	1
Mathew Hawkesworth	2
Peter Hodgson	1
John Wilton	1

[End of membrane torn away. Redeposited at E179/368/8, part 7]

Richard Mann	1
Christoph Wharton	1
Arthur Robinson	1
Edmond Wharton	1
	76

Omitted by reason of poverty 3

Robert Husband Collor
Arthur Beeston Const

Menwith cum Darley (Menwith with Darley)

William Lowly	5
John Mires	2
John Beckwith	1
Arthur Bagock	1
Willm Umpleby	1
James Hearefeild	1
Steven Umpleby	1
Leonard Umpleby	1
Thomas Parker	1
John Myers	2
Edward Whyte	2
Richard White	1
Francis Wilkes	2
Edmond Halliday	1
Richard Pullan	1
John Horner	2
John Coates	1
	cne
Thomas Rhoades	1
Robert Haxsby & mother	2
John Coates	2
Peter Pulleine	2
John Metcalfe	1
Miles Lolley	1
George Gill milner	1
Nichollas Wood	2
Abraham Atkinson	2
Thomas Watterton	1
Anthony Metcalfe	4
John Myers	2

Thomas Atkinson	2
William Metcalfe	3
Henry Buck	1
Lawrance Buck	1
John Dibbs	2
Willm Inglesant	1
Willm Hudson	1
Thomas Mires	2
Francis Day	3
Willm Groues	1
Willm Taskerd	1
Widdow Roundell	2
Robert Metcalfe	1
Arthur Myres	2
Richard Robinson	2
Willm Lolley	3
John Waite	1
Thomas Umpley	1
Willm Metcalfe	1
Thomas Marston	1
John Wray	1
Thomas Mires	1
Richard Snow	2
John Spence	1
Richard Scruton	1
Ellin Ireson	1
Thomas Umpleby	1
Barbara Waite	1
Miles Metcalfe	1
Miles Hardcastle	2
John Pulleine	3
Robert Anderson	1
John Waite forge	1
Robt Haxby forge	1
Robert Metcalfe	1
	98

Omitted by reason of poverty 7

Richd Pickard Collr
Arthur Bavock Const

[end E179/368/8, part 7; continuation of m. 48 from E179/210/400]

Nunmountaine (Nun Monkton)

George Paler Esqr	21
John Peckit	1
Richard Sanderson	1
Robt or Richd Sanderson	1
Roger Hanley	1
John Sanderson	3
Thomas Foster	1
Henry Spinke	2
George Ketlewell	1
Henry Haire	1
Thomas Webster	1
Christopr Carr	1
Henry Day	2
Richard Midgley	2
Guj Watterson	2
Willm Savidge Jun	1
Robert Gray	1
John Silversides	1
Willm Wilkinson	3
Christopher Faucett	1
John Topham	2
Richard Beane	1
John Sanderson	1
Willm Maude	1
Thomas Swaile	2
Willm Wilkinson	3
Mr Peter Woodhouse	2

m 49]

Willm Dalton	1
Christopr Dalton	1
Willm Watson	1
Edward Ewing	4
Willm Gray	1
John Thomas	1
Guy Silversides	1
Roger Hanleth	2
John Leeds	1
Robert Campleshon	1
Guy Haire	1
Willm Savidge sen	1
Willm Foster	2
Widdow Hawkesworth	1
Henry Barber	1
Widdow Gray	1
Ellizabeth Silversides	1
Robert Ketlewell	1
Mr Lambert	4
Richard Stead	1
John Pulleine	1
Willm Sanderson forge	1
	90

Omitted by reason of poverty 6

Robt Corner Collr
Robt Campleshon Const

Norwood cum Clifton (Norwood with Clifton)

John Jeffrey	2
Willm Hoalas	2
Mr Willm Hardisty	2
Willm Caltheray sen	1
Wilfrey Harrison	1
Robert Bell	1
Thomas Brigges	1
John Watkinson	2
Ellizabeth Hardisty	2
Walter White	2
Henry Pulleine	1
John Pulleine	2
John White	2
Widdow Gill	2
John Atkinson	1
Thomas Bentley	1
Widdow Smithson	1
Richard Bradley	1
Willm Hardisty	1
Henry Pulleine	2
Moses Hobson	1
John Beane	1
George Stead	1
Allexander Pallner	2
Anthony Morritt	3
Henry Wilkinson	1

John Hebdin	1
John Allenson	1
Willm Cooper	1
Robert Gray	2
Joseph Watterworth	1
Parcibell Wray	1
Walter Holmes	1
Henry Wakefeild	1
Widdow Apleyard	1
John Scaife	2
Joseph Smithson	2
Willm Bell	1
Robert Umpleby	1
John Fletcher	1

m 50]

Richard Ellis	1
Willm Walker	1
Willm Iles	1
Willm Turner	1
Thomas Harper	1
Richard Mathew	1
Henry Jeffrey	2
Francis Tasker	1
Miles Umpleby	1
Widdow Jeffrey	2
Widdow Atkinson	1
Richard Walker	1
Willm Simpson	1
Steven Simpson	1
Leonard Askwith	1
Thomas Ward	1
Thomas Turner	1
Widdow Faucitt	1
Willm Taylor	2
Lancellot Jeffrey	1
Willm Jeffrey	1
Robert Dibb	1
Willm Simpson	2
Willm Jeffrey	1
Widdow Jeffrey	1
John Simpson	1
Edward Gill	1
John Walker	1
Widdow Turner	1
	90[36]

Omitted by reason of poverty	7

Roger Hardcastle Collr
Henry Pullan Const

North Staineley cum Slening Ford (North Stainley with Sleningford)

Mr Mathew Beckwith	11
Mr Miles Staveley	7
John Ullithorne	5
Richard Ullithorne	2
John Wilson	1
Henry Ings	1
Christopr Hanson	1
John Cuthberd	1
Edward Reeves	1
Hugh Todd	1
Christopr Sanderson sen	1
Robt Walker	2
George Walton	1
Richard Metcalfe	1
George Carter	1
George Barne	1
Mary Pickersgill	1
Richard Bell	1
Mr Staveley	2
George Pickersgill	1
Francis Metcalfe	1
John Stapleton	1
Martin Binsley	1
Thomas Lay	1
Francis Browne	1

m 51]

Henry Atkinson Esqr	13
Mr Thomas Wise	5
Charles Duffeild	3
Edward Atkinson	1
Thomas Doughlas	1
Willm Batty	1
John Milner	1
John Bell	1
Mr Warcoppe	3
Thomas Browne	3
Ralph Wilson	1
Willm Gant	1
Thomas Lee	1
Richard Sanderson	1
Thomas Lund	2
Thomas Williamson	1
	87

Empty and noe distres to be had	
Widd Clint	2

Omitted by reason of poverty	5

Georg Wainman Collr
John Wilson Const

Newill cum Cliffton (Newell with Clifton)

Thomas Cliffton	5
Wilfrey Scurrey	2
John Marshall or Simon Thackerey	3
Henry Marshall	1
David Settle	1
Thomas Garvitt	1
Jane Marshall	1
Richard Darwent	2
John Cryer	2
John Wilson	1

[36] There is a scribal error since the total is 89.

John Hardisty 1
Ralph Gill 2
two
Richard Tompson 1
Mr England 1
Francis Whitehead 1
Willm Pearson 1
Richard Cooke 1
Mr John Hardisty 16[37]
Mr Banton 2
Thomas Whitehead 1
Anthony Whitehead 2
Thomas Wells or }
Willm Sherrow } 1
Thomas Hardwick 2
Mr Lancellot Wall 2
Christopr David 2
Thomas Bailden 3
Mr Toby Lambert 5
Samuell Ward 1
Samuell Ward[38] 1
Mr George Burnit 4
Alice Clapham 1
Widdow Whitacres 1
Richard Cook 1
Robert Hardcastle 1
Thomas Chapman 1
74

m 52]

Robert Husband Collr
Thomas Garnit Const

Nesfeild
(Nesfield)
Mr Thomas Farrand 3
Mr Willm Farrand 5
Willm Petty 1
Francis Wall 5
Willm Wall 1
Willm Wharton 1
Thomas Winterburne 1
Widdow Mayson 1
Bryan Mayson 1
Bryan Cryer 2
Thomas Lister 1
Timothy Briggs 1
Mathew Hudson 2
Robert Maskew 1
Widdow Currer 1
Thomas Lister Jun 1
Thomas Robinson 1
George Knowles 1
John Holmes 1
Michaell Hudson 1
Edward Milner 1
Andrew Hardwick 2
Jonathan Hudson 1
Thomas Jackson 2
Thomas Beestin 1
Mrs Anne Coates 4
Christopr Lister 2
Thomas Robinson 1
Willm Hudson 1
Richard Asquith 1
Richard Kendall 1
Willm Robinson 1
Thomas Robinson sen 1
John Lister Old Hall 1
Mr Farrand Milne 1
Willm Rushworth 1
John Bowling 1
55

Omitted by reason of poverty 1

Robert Husband Collr
Brian Mason Const

Nidd
Francis Traps Esqr 7
Mr Robert Browne 1
John Robinson 1
Thomas Cooper 1
Ralph Dearloue 2
Edward Thorpe 2
Thomas Wilks 1
Christopr Wilkinson 2
Francis Wilkes 1
Robert Benson 3
William Wilkes 1
Richard Allen 4
John Hardcastle 1
John Hardcastle 2
Ralph Atkinson 1
Richard Dearloue 1
Peter Shutt 2
Thomas Wilkes 1

m 53]

Peter Wilkes 2
Willm Smith 1
James Farnill 1
Lawrance Parsons Esqr 10
48

Omitted by reason of poverty 2

Robert Corner Collr
John Walker Const

North Deighton
Sir Willm Ingleby 10
Mrs Anne Wilson 7
Willm Chambers 3
James Hickman 3
John Duffeild 1
Leonard Pullan 1
Richard Pulleine 2
Willm Robinson 2
Thomas Lowry 2
John Winde 1

[37] 'sixteene' follows 16.
[38] sic.

Willm Maude	1
George Jepson	2
Willm Langfeild	1
John Burton	1
Richard Snawden	1
Thomas Mountaine	1
George Atkinson	1
Robert Browne	1
	41

Empty and noe distres to be had

Willm Maude	1
Richd Maude	1

Robt Husband Collr
John Burton Const

Nunwick cum Holgraue
(Nunwick with Howgrave)

Mr Thomas Binsley	4
Widdow Barugh	1
Richard Watson	1
Mr Thomas Binsley	1
Thomas Beckwith	1
Christopr Walker	2
	10

Empty and noe distres to be had

Mr Geo Aislaby	1

The person following is discharged by Certificate

Tomasin Dale	1

Omitted by reason of poverty	1

George Wainman Collr
John Palliser Const

Nuby cum Mulwith
(Newby with Mulwith)

Lady Crosland	12
Thomas Duffeild	2
Edward Newsholme	1
Willm Parker	3
	18

Omitted by reason of Poverty	1

m 54]

George Wainman Collr
Willm Corey Const

Osmonderby cum Bongate
(Aismunderby with Bondgate)

Mr John Atkinson	7
Thomas Todd	2
Mr Abraham Smith	6
George Browne	1
Samuell Rawlinson	1
Mr Willm Raper	2
Margret Bellerby	1
Willm Farnill	2
Anne Pickard	1
Mr Ralph Robinson	1
John Walker	2
Widdow Grant	1
Willm English	1
Willm Gill	2
Michaell Toare	1
Mr Christopr Duffeild	5
George Smith	1
Thomas Dawson	2
Markinfeild Mannor	16
John Wright	1
Thomas Dawson	3
Ralph Foxton	1
Widdow Nicholson	1
Sir Edmond Jenings	3
Mr Henry Tompson	7
Mr Longe	1
	72

Empty and no distres to be had

Thos Vevars	1
John Holmes	1
Widd Ragister	1

George Wainman Collr
Georg Smith Const

Pannell
(Pannal)

Mr Thomas Wescoe	7
Mr Harbutt	9
Nichollas Webster	2
Widdow Henlock	2
Mary Roundall	1
Willm Varley	1
Robert Winterburne	1
Willm Bentley	2
Willm Prentice	2
Steven Kitchin	1
Mr Oswald	8
Widdow Bentley	1
Simon Polland	1
Willm Ingle	1
Joseph Waite	2
Edward Webster	2
George Winterburne	1
Henry Hardisty	2
Peter Tupin	1
Richard Newsome	1
Michaell Pearson	1
Ralph Rheynold	1
Robert Cheldray	1
John Cheldray	2
Francis Waugh	1

m 55]

Richard Wray	2
Richard Heathorne	2
Henry Burne	4
Mr Calverley	2
Henry Shutt	1
Willm Kirke	1
Mr Calverley	4

Robert Childray	3
Anne Hill	2
Richard Knowles	2
George Scruton	2
Richard Carr	1
Willm Childray	2
Thomas Deighton	4
Thomas Abbey	1
Barnard Broadbelt	1
John Prentice	1
Willm Winterburne	1
Martin Slator	1
John Allan	1
Robt Hill	2
George Jackson	1
Robert Carr	1
Joseph Holmes	1
Mr Hudson	1
Henry Hill	2
Thomas Knowles	1
Willm Bentley	3
Thomas Benson	1
Simond Reynold	1
Henry Bentley	2
Anne Roome	1
Willm Swaine	1
Willm Swaine[39]	1
Richard Rowlinson	2
Willm Leeming	1
Richard Broadbelt	4
Robt Smith	2
Henry Clint	3
Widdow Leeming	2
Richard Roome	1
Willm Benson Sen	2
Willm Benson Jun	1
Richard Russell	2
Willm Redshawe	3
Nichollas Mountaine	1
Willm Knowles	2
Willm Russell	1
Willm Smirfitt	1
Thomas Deighton	1
John Wells	1
Richard Pearson	1
Mr Willm Bethell	9
John Nicholson	1
Widdow Collingworth	1
Miles Poole	1
Widdow Bentley	1
Charles Carr	1
Willm Marston	1
Katherine Moore	1
John Atkinson	1
Robert Browne	1
Grace Gatton	1
John Watson	1
John Forrest	1
John Hogg	1
Thomas Baynton	1
Richard Coare	3

m 56]

Francis Ingle	1
Robert Redshawe	1
	170

These persons following are discharged by Certificates

Robert Linthwaite	1
Richard Hardwick	1
Richard Kidson	1
Widdow Swan	1
Willm Holmes	1
George Turpin	1

Omitted by reason of poverty	7

Roger Hardcatle Collr
Richd Robinson Const

Plumpton (Plompton)

Mrs Anne Plumpton	11
John Swaile Sen	1
John Swaile Jun	3
Anthony Tayler	2
George Spacy	1
George Gowland	2
Willm Maunby	2
George Inchboard	1
Willm Bickerdike	5
John Parker	1
Willm Bickerdike	1
Thomas Craven	1
Willm Hudson	1
Thomas Lazonby	1
Thomas Hudson	1
John Trowton	1
Richard Fysicke	2
John Robinson	1
Mr Edward Plumpton	1
Margret Smithson	1
George Manings	1
Dais Garthwaite	1
John Knowles	1
Willm Beecroft	1
John Cass	1
John Coates	1
Joseph Walker	1
George Dickinson	1
Willm Greene	1
Robert Hardcastle	1
Richard Lee	1
Faith Flagot	1
Thomas Fleeming	1
George Watkin mill	1
	54

These persons following are discharged by Certifts

Robert Brigs	1
Widdow Anderson	1

Empty and noe distres to be had

Robert Plumpton Esqr	1

[39] sic.

Omitted by reason of poverty	1

Roger Hardcastle Collr
Richard Lee Const

Ribston Parva (Little Ribston)

m 57]

Robert Peacock	2
Richard Buck sen	1
Brian Hardcastle	1
Thomas Lacon	1
Willm Atkinson	1
Henry Pullan	2
John Hinckes	1
Ellizab Stainburne	1
Francis Earle	1
Widdow Atkinson	1
Richard Hudson	3
Richard Maunby	1
Richard Lazonby	1
Willm Hodgson	1
Willm Dawson	1
Roger Brownridge	1
Richard Thwaites	1
Thomas Maunby	2
Miles Wines	1
Charles Sanderson	1
Joseph Baines	1
Robert Webster	1
Mathias Ward	2
John Hargraues	1
George Simpson	1
	31

These persons following are discharged by Certificate

John Cowburne	1
Christopr Rhynold	1
Isabell Hardcastle	1
John Baitson	1
Mary Parke	1

Roger Hardcastle Collr
Willm Hudson Const

Rocliffe (Roecliffe)

Nichollas Yates	1
Sr Willm Tonkard	2
Richard Atkinson	1
Willm Wray	1
Jonathan Dale	1
Widdow Gilbertson	2
John Wilson	1
Simon Toes	1
Charles Ward	3
Richard Earle Sen	2
Widdow Earle	2
Richard Adam	2
Anne Marshall	1
George Ibbetson	1
Widdow Reives	1
John Sanderson	1
Simon Todd	1
Margret Todd	1
Anne Younge	2
Anne Younge	1
Judeth Trees	1
John Burnham	2
John Buckle	1
John Yates	2
John Ward	1
Richard Gilbertson	3
John Catton	2
Thomas Jackson	2
Lancellot Younge	1
Richard Barwicke	1

m 58]

John Surr	1
Widdow Topham	2
Isabell Ward	1
Gawen Clitheroe	1
Willm Hudlestone	1
Richard Robinson	1
	51

Omitted by reason of poverty	3

George Wainman Collr
John Younge Const

Ripley

Sir Willm Ingleby	24
Mr John Kershaw Rector	5
Thomas Pallister	2
Willm Kendall Sen	1
Willm Reynold Jun	1
Mr Constantine	2
Bartholl Reynold	1
Peter Tompson	1
Francis Gailes	1
John Browne	1
Sir Willm Ingleby	1
George Pickard	2
Thomas Nursay	1
Lawrance Hodgson	2
Willm Eadson	2
John Haire	2
Mr Henry Darley	6
Willm Wright	3
Thomas Browne	2
Thomas Garforth	4
Mr Edward Hinckes	3
George Pallister	2
Thomas Hardcastle	1
Roger Coates	2
Willm Hornby	1
Willm Hay	5
Thomas Pallister Jun	4
Thomas Garforth	2
Henry Willis	2
Mathew Elsworth	3
Jane Goldsmith	2
George Browne	1
Willm Barwick	1
Widdow Cooke	2
Widdow Syser	1
Widdow Atkinson & forge	4
Richard Parker	2

m 59]

George Metton	1
	103

Omitted by reason of poverty	9

Robert Corner Collr
Wm Reynold Const

Rigton

Francis Ingle	2
Willm Atkinson	1
Ralph Cande	1
Christopr Tompson	1
Francis Wilkes	1
Willm Luty	1
Francis Casle	1
Willm Smith	1
Willm Moore	1
Thomas Howne	1
John Newsholme	1
Widdow Scaife	1
Thomas Wilkes	1
Willm Ingle	1
Richard Jackson	2
Timothy Tompson	2
Peter Tasker	1
Willm Ingle	1
James Stables	1
Thomas Clapham	1
Widdow Coare	1
Willm Scaife	1
Robert Ellis	2
Mr Bethill	1
Willm Wriglesworth	2
Simond Bayles	1
Richard Hardisty	1
John Bayley	1
Thomas Atkinson	1
Phillip Tate	4
Timothy Smith	1
Richard Russell	1
Richard Ellis	3
Thomas Coare	1
Francis Darley	2
Brian Marshall	2
Mr Willm Calverley	1
Ellizabeth Shutt	1
Henry Ellis	1
Willm Wainman	1
Edward Knightson	1
Widdow Shutt	1
Robert Redshawe	1
Willm Wid	1
John Tompson	1
George Watson	2
Robt Widd	1
John Nicholson	1
John Knightson	1
John Garnet	1
John Mawson	1
	64

Omitted by reason of poverty	3

Robt Husband Collr
John Knighston Const

m 60]

Rippon Allhallowgate (Ripon Allhallowgate)

Sir Edmond Jenings	14
Sir Willm Mettam	11
Mrs Strickland	12
Jonathan Jenings Esqr	11
Francis Wyvill Esqr	6
Mr Henry Redshawe	8
Mr Oxley	4
Mr Drake Sub Deane	12
Mr Willm Stevenson	6
Mr Stursakers	2
Thos Frewerdale	2
Ralph Maltus	4
Thomas Parker	1
Willm Lumley	2
Robert Harrison	1
Edward Hodgson	5
Willm Browne	3
Zachar Jepson	2
Mr Tompson	3
John Browne	1
Anthony Burman	1
Steven Owram	1
Mr Waite	1
Richard Wilden	1
Thomas Watson	3
David Lake	2
Richard Greggs	1
John Grennill[40]	2
Peter Craven	3
James Neveson	1
Christopr Lee	1
Thomas Burnitt	1
Mrs Wild	4
Mrs Moody	3
Mrs Burton	4
Christopr Atkinson	2
Richard Whittell	2
Ralph Barkor	3
Henry Brigs	3
Richard Kendall	1
James Nevison	2
Thomas Horner	2
James Wrightson	2
Benjam Norcliff Esqr	5
Christopr Lee	1
Mrs Bickerdike	2
Miles Jaques	1
Christopr Tyreman	1
John Bainbridge	2
Willm Milner	3
Mr Hewson	4
Christopr Doe	1
John Briggs	1
Thomas Child	1
Owen Briggs	1

[40] Alternatively Grenuill.

Willm Briggs	1
Anthony Atkinson	4
Richard Richardson	1
Anthony Burman	1
Leonard Hinde	1
Marke Simpson	2
Willm Wilson	1
John Sanderson	1
The East Milnes	1
John Dawson	1

m 61]

Thomas Emson	1
Richard Markham	1
Mr Anthony Leadom	6
The Schoolehouse	1
Robert Mangewell	1
Christopr Cooke	2
Thomas Rymer	1
Christopr Mitchill	1
Steven Duffeild	1
James Floxton	1
	209

Empty and noe distress to be had

Mrs Chambers	3
The Comon Hall	1

These persons following are discharged by Certificates

Widdow Jaques	1
Mrs Margret Norton	1
Steven Dixon	1
Thomas Sarvant	1
Miles Morris	2
George Tompson	1
Thomas Sissons	1

Omitted by reason of poverty 13

George Wainman Collr
Steven Dixon Const

Rippon Crosgate (Ripon Crossgate)

Michaell Murgetroyd	2
Willm Ripley	3
Anne Apleby	1
Willm Walker	2
John Harrison	2
Thomas Jackson	5
Martin Bulmer	1
Mr Francis Wood	4
Robert Raine	4
Thomas Wright	4
John Biggins	3
Willm Hesletine	5
Mr John Spence	4
Ninion Warwick	3
Martin Bulmer	3
Christopr Apleby	1
James Coates	6
Mr Brathwaite	5
Cutbert Haggitt	2
Alderm Hebden	9
Widdow Craven	4
Roger Wright	6
Thomas Bradley	5
Alderm Gibson	6
John Watterall	6
Francis Walker	1
Widdow Ripley	5
Alderm Craven	4
Mr Thomas Burton	6
George Garbutt	2
Lancellot Williamson	1
Mrs Holmes	7
Anthony Fauber	6
Mrs Horner	8

m 62]

James Broocke	1
Peter Hodgson	1
Thomas Charnocke	1
Roger Browne	5
Widdow Leadom	2
Robert Thackrey	2
Edward Harrison	6
Willm Tirrie	3
Michaell Dawson	1
Richard Coates	1
Mr Hamond	3
Willm Cundall or }	
Mr Graues }	6
Mr Waite	2
Richard Cant	2
Richard Rooksby	3
Mr Bardon	1
Judeth Pearson	1
John Peighney	2
Willm Fell	1
John Pallister	2
Mr Henry Spence	3
John Daggitt	2
Steven Hunter	1
Richard Sweeting	1
Thomas Newsholme	3
John Pallister	1
Thomas Greene	5
Thomas Topham	1
Edward Dyson	5
Willm Lumley	3
Willm Cundall	3
Thomas Maskie	1
Simon Morthrop	3
Willm Crosby	1
Leonard Clarke	1
George Sharpe	1
Mathew Bogg	2
Simond Graive	1
Mathew Bog	1
Marby Lake	4
John Craven	4
Mr Taylor	3
Peter Johnson	3
John Outhwaite	1
Thomas Thurland	2
Willm Jaques	5
Christopr Walker	3
Peter Hayes	2
Thomas Hebden	6
Richard Porter	8

Alderman Kirby	7
	seauen
Mrs Anne Busfeild	8
Mr Robert Atkinson	4
Mrs Chaytor	6
Alderman Chambers	4
Jeffrey Theakston	3
Richard Shaw	2
John Struther	5
Alderman Catton	4
Mr Chambers	2
Alderman Craven	7
Henry Topham	4
Alderman Milner	6
James Dobbey	4
Steven Parvin	4
Mr Pyat	2
Widdow Faucitt	3
John Browne	2
Christopr Atkinson	5
George Smith	1

m 63]

Michael Murgetroyde	1
Thomas Sowerby	5
Francis Murk	2
Simon Brathwaite	2
Mrs Naylor	6
Thomas Done	1
Robert Webster	2
Willm Myers	4
Willm Beane	1
Thomas Walker	1
Willm Cash	2
Mr Browne	1
George Smurthwaite	4
Ralph Watson	1
Willm Craven	3
Capt Topham	3
Peter Craven	4
Wilfrey Bucke	8
Willm Chapman	1
John Broadley	1
Wilfrey Chayse	2
Widdow Parker	1
Wilfrey Daniell	1
Mary Scotton	1
Simon Brafitt	1
Mr Mountaine	1
Willm Ketlewell	3
Peter Hodgson	1
Richard Tyreman	1
	410

These persons following are discharged by Certificates

Simon Browne	1
Widdow Ripley	2
John Turpin	1
Willm Cowlin	1
Willm Wheatley	1
Willm Horner	1
Samuell Wildman	1
Thomas Milnes	1
Christopr Doe	1
John Webster	1
John Kendall	1

Empty and no distres to be had

Richard Milnes	2
Willm Cass	2
Marmad Bramley	5
Mr Thos Redshaw	4
Willm Pybus	4
Gilbert Halliday	1
John Todd	2

Omitted by reason of poverty 12

Georg Wainman Collr
Christopr Hunter Const

Rippon Westgate
(Ripon Westgate)

Rowland Brathwaite	4

m 64]

Willm Wright	3
Willm Gratian	3
Mr Catton	4
George Batty	4
Willm Hunter	1
Richard Myers	3
Thomas Cunny	1
Marmaduke Warwick	3
Thomas Hamond	1
Widdow Heath	1
Mr Brathwaite	1
Willm Roundthwate	1
George Foster	1
John Inman	2
George Milner	6
John Peace	1
Willm Shepherd	1
Edward Hutton	1
Christopr Snelgate	1
Peter Crauen	3
Henry Thornton	1
Widdow Pickersgill	3
John Heavisides	3
Robert Farnill	1
John Rooth	1
Mr Newill	3
Mr Daggitt	5
Willm Pyper Jun	1
Bartholl Farnell	3
Willm Inman	2
Francis Pickersgill	2
George Pickersgill	1
Henry Clarke	1
Willm Spence	1
Mr George Pinckney	4
Willm Tirrie	3
Thomas Blackburne	1
	82

Empty & no distres to be had

Barthol Farnill	2
Mr Hardcastle	1

Mr John Ann 7
James Simpson 2

Omitted by reason of poverty 6

George Wainman Collr
John Rooth Const

Rippon Skelgate (Ripon Skellgate)

John Buck 3
Widdow Redshawe 6
Thomas Horner 4
Mr Hogg 7
seauen
Mathew Jepson 3
James Tirrey 1
John Tompson 1
Mathew Green 2
Henry Green 2
Widdow Cundall 1
Mr Markinfeild 2
Willm Weepin 3
Mathew Day 2
Alderman Lister 7
Widdow Pickersgill 2
George Smith 2
John Foster 3
Anne Smith 4

m 65]

Widdow Hopwood 3
Richard Bell 2
Anne Grayson 2
Willm Faudington 5
Roger Cooke 2
Lawrance Hornby 2
Anthony Burton 1
John Metcalfe 1
Thomas Dobby 2
Henry Watson 2
George Bowes 1
Willm Bainbridge 2
John Hewitson 2
Thomas Dunn 2
Richard Topham 1
Thomas Hutton 1
Christopr Horner 1
John Lambert 1
John Ostler 4
John Wright 3
Thomas Turner 2
Thos Melmerby 1
Leonard Hodgson 2
John Page 1
101

The person following is discharged by Certificate
Barbar Gamble 2

Geo Wainman Collr
John Wright Const

Sharoe (Sharow)

Willm Bainbridge 5
Richard Tirrie 2
Willm Dixon 3
Ralph Tirrie 1
Rich Allonson 2
Lawr Tirrie 1
Robert Kay 1
Roger Browne 2
Horatio Allenson 2
Steven Allenson 2
George Allenson 1
Willm Cooke 1
Richard Browne 1
Richard Cooke 2
Ralph Gibson two 2
28

Omitted by reason of poverty 8

Georg Wainman Collr
Robert Browne Const

Staineley cum Catton (Stainley with Cayton)

Sir Sallomon Swaile 18
Mr Harrison 8
Robert Wright 2
Michaell Maude 2
Willm Browne 3
Henry Swaile Esqr 6
Mr Booth 4
Thomas Milner 1
Henry Beane 3
Willm Walker 4
Francis Allon 2
Richard Baine 2
55

Omitted by reason of poverty 2

Robt Husband Collr
Willm Browne Const

m 66]

Studley (Studley Roger)

Mr Henry Redshaw 4
Thomas Roundthwate 4
Willm Ullithorne 4
Richard Cooper 2
John Kirby 1
Richard Smirke 3
John Sedgwick 2
John Steele 1
John Vaunt 2
Willm Ullithorne 1
John Outhwaite 1
John Wycliffe 1
Thomas Tunstall 1
Simon Wilson 1
Thomas Watson 1
John Kirby 2
John Roundthwaite 1
Abraham Tunstell 2
Abraham Whaite 1
35

Omitted by reason of poverty	1

Geo Wainman Collr
John Kirby Const

Scriven

Sir Thomas Slingsby Bart	7
Widdow Andrewes	2
Robert Turnball	2
Richard Gibson	1
John Hayes	2
Henry Calvorley	1
Richard Pickard	1
Ralph Dickinson	1
Richard Pretious	2
Willm Roundall	1
Francis Broadbelt	1
Richard Andrewes	1
Marmaduke Turnball	1
Willm Roundall	2
Jonath Inchbald	1
Hugh Smith	1
John Andrewes	2
Peter Keighley	1
Willm Gibson	1
Richard Lambert	2
	33

Roger Hardcastle Collr
Henry Claverley Const

Skelton

George Parker	4
James Parker	2
Michaell Beane	2
John Bell	3
Thomas Newsome	1
John Knowles	1
Mathew Sherlock	1
Henry Mathew	1
John Chapman	1
John Peele	1
Richard Mountaine	2
Willm Wheelehouse	1
John Roper	2

m 67]

George Roper	1
Thomas Newsome	1
Widdow Allenson	2
Widdow Steele	1
George Parker	2
Widdow Pulleine	1
Anne Pearson	1
Willm Gray	1
Widdow Dickinson	1
John Clifforth	1
Widdow Dixon	1
Willm Moore	1
John Peele	1
John Rigg	1
Thomas Fothergill	1
Anne Render	1
Willm Greenehouse	1
John Day	1
John Newsome	1
George Parker	1
Francis Hallidous	1
	45
Omitted by reason of poverty	6

Georg Wainman Collr
Thomas Fothergill Const

Staueley (Staveley)

Robert Foswick	4
Mr Fish	6
Edward Steele	1
John Leadom	1
Steven Burnitt	1
James Hardy	1
Francis Myers	1
Widdow Dickinson	1
Marke Wright	2
John Tomlinson	1
Richard Popleton	1
Thomas Armistead	2
Willm Bolton	1
Thomas Popleton	1
Edward Dickinson	2
Richard Whitfeild	2
	two
Edward Fletcher	2
Thomas Pensick	2
John Popleton	1
Thomas Baines	2
Widdow Keighley	2
John Clarins	1
Edward Popleton	1
Thomas Dixon	1
Edwd Morreton	1
Thomas Wyrill	2
John Dickinson	2
Richard Browne	1
Willm Dickinson	2
Francis Langley	4
Willm Baines	1
Robert Shaw forge	1
	54

George Wainman Collr
Willm Keighley Const

Sicklinghall

Robert Harling	9
Robert Pullan	3

m 68]

Edward Clough	2
Widdow Stead	1
Willm Cobb	2
Widdow Reynard	1
John Saxson	3
Richard Bilbrough	1
Richard Saxson	1
Robert Wyley	1
Thomas Hodgson	1
Michaell Reynard	1

Widdow Shutt	1
Willm Ellison	1
Mathew Elsworth	1
Martin Archer	1
Miles Lawriman	1
Thomas Elsworth	2
John Lowry	1
Thomas Wray	1
John Elsworth	1
Willm Stainburne	1
Oswald Ketlewell	1
Richard Everson	1
John Hawling	1
Richard Staineburne	1
Thomas Rowles	1
Widdow Saxon	1
Thomas Browne	1
Thomas Stead	1
Henry Wray	1
Cuthbert Idle	1
	47

The person following is discharged by Certificate

Widdow Bateson	1

Omitted by reason of poverty	8

Robert Husband Collr
Richd Bilbrough Const

Spofforth

Mr Knightbridge	12
Mr Chamley	9
Mr Burgone	4
Mr Thomas Lawson	10
Thomas Beane	3
John Hunshawe	1
Ralph Simster	1
Robert Bowman	3
Richard Newsome	2
Willm Allinson	1
Martin Archer	1
Edward Archer	2
Robert Crosby	1
Willm Tate	1
Richard Steade	1
James Deighton	1
Willm Bentham	1
Willm Elsworth	1
Richard Bowman	1
Mathew Holmes	2
Leonard Newsholme	1
John Pullan	2
James Pullan	1
Edward Bowman	1
John Foster	2
John Williamson	1
Mathew Popleton	1
Jennet Mathewes	2
Richard Spinke	1
Richard Burley	2
Henry Cromack	1
Willm Ellis	1
Christopr Tompson	1
Robert Earle	1
John Outhwate	2
Richard Wright	1
Mathew More	1
Hugh Buslard	1

m 69]

Willm Tompson	1
Richard Smith	2
John Clarke	1
John Beane	1
John Clough	2
Edward Archer	3
John Deighton	1
John Simister	2
Anthony Deighton	2
John Shaw	1
Anthony Robinson	1
Richard Bowman	1
Willm Andrew	1
Christopr Cawood	1
Willm Greaues	1
Thomas Greaues	1
Robert Joy	1
Thomas Fall	3
Thomas Wright	1
Edward Cragg	1
Richard Hall	2
Richard Thwaites	1
Widdow Wood	2
Willm Pulleine	1
John Hill	3
Widdow Allinson	1
Thomas Dobson	2
John Norsey	1
Richard Smith	2
James Stringfall	1
Widdow Hebblethwate	1
Richard Wright	3
Richard Greaues	1
Thomas Outhwaite	1
Willm Smith	1
John Norsay	1
Thomas Ward	1
John Daniell	2
Willm Gibson	1
Widdow Easterby	1
Willm Tompson	1
Mr Chamley	1
Robert Nursey	1
Willm Burley	1
Grace Webster	1
James Pulleine	1
	144

Omitted by reason of poverty	2

Roger Hardcastle Collr
Willm Oate Const

Staineburne (Stainburne)

Griffin Wright	2
Willm Thackeras	1
Willm Mercer	1
Susan Dunwell	1
Thomas Dunwell	1

Thomas Emley	1
Ellizab Boulton	2
Willm Dunwell	1
Willm Rycroft	1
Willm Horner	1
Willm Hindle	1
Walter Thackeras	1
Thomas Grayson	1
John Thackeras	1
Major Bradley	1
Brian Watson	1

m 70]

Thomas Rogers	2
Thomas Hutton	2
Willm Hutton	1
Willm Gill	1
Thomas Waid Jun	1
Thomas Dunwell Cler	3
George Hardisty	1
Brian Bayley	1
Willm Thackeras	1
Grace Thackeras	2
	two[41]
Robert Dibbey	1
Francis Dixon	1
Thomas Rodwell	1
Abrah Bradley	2
John Daccars	1
Parcabell Emsey	1
Thomas Waid Sen	1
	41

Empty and no distress to be had

Willm Palmer	3

Robt Husband Collr
Franc Dixon Const

Stainebeck Upp
(Stonebeck Up)

Mr John Conyers	1
George Horner Sen	2
George Horner Jun	3
Thomas Horner	1
Christopher Horner	1
George Horner	1
Christophr Horner Jun	2
Anthony Watson	2
John Watson	1
Thomas Horner	1
Widdow Watson	1
Steven Atkinson	1
George Horner	1
Thomas Horner	2
Roger Horner	1
George Horner	1
Widdow Baines	2
Thomas Hanley	2
Richard Downer	1
Thomas Beckwith	4
John Tully	1
Thomas Horner	1
Thomas Yeoman	1
Steven Watson	1
John Ripley	1
John Loftus	1
Richard Baines	3
John Horner	1
Thomas Tomlin	1
Roger Horner	2
	two
John Faucitt	2
Francis Gill	2
Widdow Horner	2
Thomas Brabner	1
Leonard Scott	2
Thomas Sowerby	1
Willm Spencer	2
Willm Waide	2
Widdow Loftus	2

Christopr Craven	2
Thomas Scott	1

m 71]

Thomas Loftus	2
Richard Kidd	2
Willm Horner	1
John Waide	2
Miles Benson	1
	71

Robt Husband Collr
Thomas Yeoman Const

Stainebeck Downe
(Stonebeck Down)

John Joy	2
Widdow Joy	1
George Yates	1
Willm Joy	1
Willm Smith	1
Robert Joy	1
John Eaton	1
Humphrey Joy	2
Thomas Topham	2
Robert Freer	3
Marmaduke Chapman	1
Willm Ward	1
Nichollas Darwin	1
James Grainge	1
Robert Atkinson	1
Widdow Craven	1
Marmaduke Lufton	1
Peter Grainge	1
Robert Moore	3
Thomas Burton	1
Willm Midleton	3
Widdow Colyer	2
Thomas Wilkinson	1
Francis Grainge	2
Robert Freer	1
Widdow Spencer	1

[41] 2 written over 1.

Thomas Browne 2
John Browne 1
Marmad Horsman 2
Willm Grainge 2
John Grainge 1
Francis Langcaster 1
Thomas Freer 1
Richard Reynold 1
John Gill 1
Christopr Gill 1
Lambert Thackeray 2
Willm Langcaster 1
Michaell Geldart 2
Widdow Buckle 1
Willm Duffeild 1
Francis Topham 1
Christophr Clarke 2
Margret Baine Wid 1
John Craven 3
Miles Scowthrop 1
Christopr Hebden 2
Christopr Lawson 2
Thomas Hardcastle 2
Francis Paley 1
Francis Foster 1
Widdow Kinge 1
Thomas Spence 2
John Scaife 1
Willm Topham 2
Ralph Thackeray 1
The Lady Yorke 8
Robert Graing 1
Anthony King 1
Ingram Lolly 1
Mr Umphre Topham 1
John Coape 1
Willm Baine 1
John Fryer 1

m 72]

John Grainge 1
Mary Wray 1

Robert Leathley 1
Francis Lancaster 1
John Rheynold 1
Thomas Topham 1
Robert Brooksbanke 1
Marmaduk Lupton 1
103

Empty and noe distres to be had
Marmaduke Horsman 1
Willm Langcaster 1

Omitted by reason of poverty 2

Georg Wainman Collr
Thomas Craven Const

Sawley
Welbury Norton Esqr 7
Christopr Nicholls 5
Mr Willm Lacon 7
Willm Elsley 1
Willm Coates 2
Widdow Hebden 1
John Scaife 1
Christopr Hebden 1
Willm Iuison 1
Richard Leeming 1
Willm Exleby Jun 1
Willm Dawson 2
Anthony Ingleby 1
Robert Robinson 1
Widdo Newill 2
Willm Lonnsdall 1
Thomas Graing 2
two
James Thackeroy 3
Thomas Coates 2
Marmaduke Burnitt 1
Anthony Lumbe 2
two[42]

Gilbert Theakstone 1
James Cossentine 1
Christopr Outhwaite 1
Willm Haxby 2
Willm Exleby Jun 1
Christopr Lumley 1
Peter Theakston 1
Willm Roundell 1
Widdow Haxby 2
Thomas Ingleby 1
Robert Kendall Jun 1
John Ingleby 1
Thomas Wood 1
Edward Dixon 1
Ralph Walker 1
Thomas Robinson 1
John Palliser 1
Willm Dixon 1
Gilbert Theakston 1
Thomas Turpin 1
Henry Baley 1
Christopr Walker sen 1
Widdow Fairelas 1
Widdow Richmond 1
John Rutter 1
Steven Coates 1
Michaell Inman 4
Simond Pawson 3
Willm Pulleine 1
Robert Myers 1
Robert Hardcastle 1
Mr Henry Procter 3

m 73]

Thomas Hodgson 2
Willm Gatill 1
Willm Simpson 1
Willm Hodgson 1
Claudius Procter 1
George Simpson 1
Joseph Buck 1
Henry Buck 1

[42] 2 written over 1.

John Metcalfe	1
John Beecroft	1
Robert Hebden	1
Christopr Walker Jun	1
Willm Boddy	1
Pressilla Empson	1
Widdow Russell	1
Martin Ingle	1
	103

Omitted by reason of poverty	7

Robt Corner Collr
Henry Bayly Const

Scotton

Ralph Bainbridg	4
Peter Deareloue	1
Willm Preston	1
Willm Buckle	3
Marmad Buckle	2
George Watkinson	8
Peter Blakey	1
	one
Robert Howard	2
Willm Wilson	1
Willm Lingard	3
James Lingard	1
Thomas Dauy	2
Willm Clementshawe	2
Henry Spinke	1
Walter Buckle	1
John Hill	1
Peter Deareloue	1
Walter Buckle	1
George Plumer	1
Willm Wyrell	1
Franc Clementshaw	1
John Wilkes	1
John Slater	1
Willm Wilson	1
John Wilson	1
Henry Spinke	1
Mathew Browne	1
John Cooper forge	1
Willm Lingwood	1
	47

Empty and noe distres to be had

Willm Peck	1
Richard Crosby	1

Omitted by reason of poverty	7

Robert Corner Collr
Henry Spinke Const

Timble Parva
(Little Timble)

Mr John Robinson	8
Mr James Sikes	5
James Roundell	1
Willm Bradley	1
Ralph Gill	1
George Gill	1
Richard Jakes[43]	1
Widdow Howden	1
	19

Roger Hardcastle Collr
Richd Jakes Const

Timble cum Fewston
(Great Timble with Fewston)

m 74]

Thomas Holmes	1
Willm Cooke	1
John Pullan	2
Steven Cass	1
John Jeffrey sen	1
John Jeffrey Jun	1
John Yates	1
Anthony Pullan	2
Richard Snell	1
John Lambert	1
Widdow Snell	1
Jerem Snell	1
John Wood	1
John Ward	1
Robert Wilson	1
George Harrison	1
Daniell Woodhead	1
Widdow Slayden	1
Thomas Roberts	1
John Foster	1
Thomas Dunnill	1
Thomas Richardson	2
Widdow Watson	1
John Gamlin	1
John Richmond	1
Willm Stockdale	1
George Spence	1
Robert Whitacre	1
John Simpson	1
Samuell Saxton	1
Robert Irish Sen	1
Thomas Morehouse	1
Robert or Thos Umpleby	1
John Bramley	1
John Beecroft	1
Robert Irish Jun	2
Richard Beecroft	2
Mr Willm Barker	1
Willm Gill	2
Robert Smith	5
Widdow Holmsley	1
Willm Simpson	1
Willm Iles	1
Francis Croft	1
John Parker	3
George Coates	2
Samuell Linley	2

[43] Corrected from 'Sikes'.

Mr Richard Williamson 6
John Williamson 2
Robt England 2
Widdow Thackeray 1
George Lister 1
Thomas Oddy 3
Richard Metcalfe 2
Steven Hardisty 1
Henry Jeson 1
Francis Hardisty 2
two
Widdow Banister 1
Henry Simpson 1
Richard Oddy 2
Thomas Sugden 1
Francis Watson 1
John Ward 1
John Roundell 1
Henry Hatton 1
George Brigg 1
Willm Thackerey 2
Brian Saxton 1
Willm Hardisty Sen 1
Willm Hardisty Jun 1
John Hobson 1

m 75]

George Stead 2
Thomas Stead 2
Willm Hawkeswell 1
Thomas Roulstone 3
John Iles 1
107

Empty and noe distresse to be had
John Cowburne 1

Omitted by reason of poverty 3

Robert Husband Collr
Thomas Ward Const

Thriscrosse (Thruscross)
Christopr Hardisty 1
Thomas Gill 1
Edward Taylor 2
Robert Whitacres 1
Thomas Gill sen 1
Robert Harrison 1
Thomas Gill 1
George Slingsby 1
Willm Coaleman 1
Ralph Gill 1
John Inman 1
Richard Birtwisle 1
John Gill 1
Steven Hawkswell 2
Richard Graues 1
John Oxnard 2
Lawrence Lowcocke 2
Robert Baocke 1
Widdow Lowcocke 2
George Pullan 2
Arthur Jallup 1
Christopr Hardisty 1
Nichollas Fentiman 1
Thomas Wiglesworth 2
John Skirrett 2
Joseph Pullan 2
Walter Holme 2
Gilbert Bake 1
Willm Shepherd jun 1
Willm Shepherd Sen 2
Mr Feilding 1
Christopr More 1
Marmad Roundell 1
Willm Rhynold 1
John Atkinson 3
Steven Gill 2
Mathew Gill 2
Edward Gill 1
John Shepherd 1
Willm Hill 1
John Gill 1

John Shepherd 1
Willm Hill 1
John Gill 1[44]
Ralph Gill 1
Willm Faucitt 1
Robert Wiglesworth 2
Walter Waite 1
Edward Yates 2
Robert Gill 1
Willm Day 2
Walter Waite Jun 1

m 76]

Francis England 2
Willm Atkinson 1
John Wright 2
two
Willm Hardwicke 2
John Rheynold 3
Mr Bland 1
Marke Wright 1
Mathew Holmes 1
Widdow Holmes Sen 2
George Holmes 1
Francis Holmes 2
John Holmes skiner 1
John Holmes 1
Christopr Yates 1
Anne Hall 2
George Holmes 1
Willm Wright 1
John Metcalfe 2
George Waite 1
Widdow Parker 3
Widdow Parker 1
Edward Plumpton 1
John Gill 1
Widdow Slingsby 1
Widdow Hall 1
Thomas Smith 1
Willm Holmes 1
Steven Gill 1

44 Line inserted.

Widdow Breakes	1
Robert Simpson	2
Willm Bilton	2
Willm Holmes sen	2
	116

Robert Husband Collr
Willm Holmes Const

Usburne Magna (Great Ouseburn)

George Bradshaw	1
Willm Mawlas	1
Marmaduke Abbey	1
Margret Aireton	1
George Lund	1
Robert Tompson	2
Anne Benson	3
Thomas Popleton	2
Thomas Atkinson	2
John Ward	1
Thomas Browne	1
Richard Beck	1
George Cass	1
Widdow Benson	2
George Cass	2
Mr Carr Cler	4
Mr Anthony Clarke	4
John Burniston	2
Willm Simpson	1
Robert Hunter	2
Anne Pickles	1
Joseph Fidler	2
John Dickinson	2
Robert Daniell	1
Christopr Nicholson	1
Guy Pallister	2
George Scurr	2
Willm Lake	1
Peter Siddall	1

m 77]

Willm Watson	1
Francis Johnson	3
Robert Hunter	1
Willm Howson	1
Thomas Rawson	1
John Hodgson	1
George Cass	1
Willm Hunter	1
Richard Hudson	1
James Dickinson	1
John Plumer	1
Henry Thorp	1
Richard Abbey	1
Charles Abbey	1
John Knightson	2
Robert Pick	3
Martin Simpson	1
	70

These persons following are discharged by Certificates

Thomas Bronton	1
Robert Marsingall	1
Anne Abbey	1
Ellin Rainforth	1
Anne Palliser	1
Robert Horner	1
Thomas Pretious	1
John Sigsworth	2
Richard Crosby	1
Thomas Brampton	1

Robert Corner Collr
John Rigston Const

Usburne Parva (Little Ouseburn)

Mr Keighley	3
Edward Pick	1
Widdow Sharp	2
Mallit Taylor	1
Thomas Steele	2
Thomas Tompson	1
Widdow Tompson	1
John Abbey	2
Robert Hanley	1
Gilbert Campie	2
Willm Orton	1
Bryan Mann	2
Widdow Leedom	2
John Wright	1
Francis Fitling	1
Widdow Watson	1
Humphrey Russell	1
Anne Marmaduke	1
Anne Child	1
Thomas Holmes	1
Francis Shepherd	1
Edward Child	1
Edward Tompson	2
	two
Willm Olliver	1
	33

Omitted by reason of poverty	4

Robt Corner Collr
Edward Childe Const

Westwick

Mr George Hardcastle	7
Willm Horner	1
	8

Richd Pickard Collr
Peter Earle Const

Walshforth cum Ribston (Great Ribston with Walshford)

Sir Henry Goodrick Bt	9
Mr John Haxby	3
Willm Widington	1

m 78]

John Slater	2
Widdow Pullan	2

Widdow Simonds	1
John Lake	1
Thomas Dickinson	1
Widdow Wincobb	1
Richard Pullan	1
A Smithy	1
	23

Empty and noe distress to be had

Robert Husker	3

The person following is discharged by Certificate

Widdow May & Smith	3

Omitted by reason of poverty 1

Geo Wainman Collr
Willm Waddington Const

Weston

Maior Vavasour Esq	24
Willm Hitch	5
Samuell Ward Viccar	4
Joseph Lowcock	1
John Stead	1
Thomas Butler	1
Thomas Foster	2
Willm Mawson	1
James Stead	2
John Foster	1
Thomas Acombe	1
Thomas Bradley	1
Willm Sowdon	2
Widdow Pearson	1
Henry Tompson	2
Henry Tompson[45]	2
Leonard Snell	2
Thomas Taylor	1
Thomas Stead	1
John Curtis	1
Mr Anthony Fell	2
Willm Browne	1
Margerey Bradley	2
	two
Thomas Scott	1
Thomas Vavasour	1
Willm Stead	1
Thomas Browne	1
	65

Robt Husband Collr
Willm Stead Const

Whitcliff cum Thorp (Whitcliffe with Littlethorpe)

Sir Edmond Jenings	1
Mr John Redshawe	6
Mr Thomas Redshaw	9
Willm Gregson	2
James Buttrey	1
George Walker	1
John Allenson & forge	2
Richard Mountaine	2
Willm Topham	4
George Grainge	3
Mr Thomas Redshawe	2
Lawrance Watters	1
Willm Goule	1
Mary Mountaine	2
Lawrance Cant	1
Ninian Allinson	1
Ralph Inchbald	2
Mary Crow	2
Widdow Allonson	1
Anthony Jefferson	2
Christopr Newton	1
Edward Roundthwaite	1
Miles Allonson	1
	49

Omitted by reason of poverty 4

m 79]

George Wainman Collr
Willm Gowle Const

Wetherby

Mr Thomas Wood	5
Richard Ward	2
Mr Willm Tompson	4
Mr John Simpson	8
John Wood	4
Mr John Cotterall	4
John Richardson	3
Robert Barker	4
Richard Olliver	3
Willm Drougie	4
Francis Sayer	2
Robert Robinson	1
John Towtall	3
Henry Wood	1
John Ogle	2
John Browne	1
Widdow Wilbor	8
John Weetman	2
Widdow Adieson	2
George Wakefeild	1
Widdow Hudson	2
Thomas Mathewes	4
James Rhoades	3
Lawrance Wilson	3
John Burley	2
Peter Strickland	3
Thomas Kay	3
Mr Mason	4
John Wilson	3
John Brownridge	2
Willm Wright	4
Joseph Clapham	2
Henry Spencer	2
Francis Hopwood	2

45 sic.

Christopr Hardcastle	4
Widdow Bankes	1
Willm Daniell	3
Willm Robinson	3
Joseph Johnson	1
Christopr Ingle	3
Richard Gibson	2
Willm Lister	3
Thomas Coates	2
Richard Laverack	2
Robert Tompson	2
Widdow Holme	2
Jonas Chapman	2
Christopr Barker	1
Mr Taylor	3
Widdow Cowley	3
Henry Keighley	1
Widdow Allonson	2
Willm Shaw	2
Henry Spence Jun	1
Ellizabeth Holgate	2
Francis Lister	2
Edward Franck	2
	152

Omitted by reason of poverty 12

Robert Husband Collr
Richd Gibson Const

m 80]

Whixley

Charles Tankerd Esqr	11
The Minister	1
John Bilbrough	3
Mr Weddall	2
Mr Willm Atkinson	3
Willm Daniell	2
John Burman	2
Willm Bedforth	5
Richard Wrightson	1
John Haire	1
Thomas Daniell	1
Marmaduke Oliver	2
Abraham Clough	2
Peter Ketlewell	2
Andrew Hinckes	1
Thomas Ketlewell	1
Thomas Thirley	1
Thomas Dawson jun	2
Sallom Webster	1
Robert Smeaton	1
Willm Cass	1
Brian Pick Jun	1
Roger Dawson	1
Christopher Ketlewell	1
Ketlewell Dawson	1
Edward Browne	1
Steven Gilbanke	1
Thomas Dawson sen	1
Thomas Fowler	1
Francis Tompson	2
John Cromack	2
Dorothy Yates	1
Widdow Ketlewell	1
Robert Dawson	1
Christopher Bramley	1
Widdow Ketlewell	1
John Fesdale	1
Michaell Dawson	1
Mrs Mann	7
Mr Willm Mann	8
Mr Richard Browne	5
George Wrightson	2
Willm Tompson	2
Willm Hill	2
Thomas Mann	1
Thomas Stainburne	1
Richard Blythman	3
Isaac Spencer	1
Thomas Newsholme	4
John Ellerbecke	1
Henry Thomas	1
Willm Browne	3
John Cooper	1
Willm Headley	1
Guy Watterson	1
Henry Thomas	2
Thomas Savidge	1
Willm Gowland	4
	fower
Willm Wood	1
S[i]r Richd Malliverer	1
Richard Lumbley	2
Robert Shipton	1
Mr Mann	1
Charles Gill	1
Francis Sharper	1
Robert Clarkson	1
Charles Gill	1
	126

Omitted by reason of poverty 8

George Wainman Collr
Thomas Daniell Const

m 81]

Weeton cum Hewby (Weeton and Huby)

Thomas Foster	3
Thomas Taylor	3
Henry Waite	1
Willm Mercer	2
Brian Tosh	1
Widdow Cane	1
Robert Pickard	1
Jerem Wilkinson	3
John Wray	1
John Sutle	2
Willm Pickard	3
Richard Lee	2
Willm Pickard Jun	1
John Burton	1
Willm Waide	1
Parsivell Swaile	1
Richard Swaile	1
Francis Robinson	1
Willm Dibb	1
John Crowther	1
Richard Harrison	1

Anthony Stead	1
James Stables	1
Willm Harrison	1
John Wittey	2
Henry Atkinson	3
Willm Watkinson	1
Barnard Dickinson	2
Willm Harrison	2
Mathew Rothere	1
Rich Midgley	1
Henry Milner	2
Rowland Wray	1
Christopr Tompson	1
Francis Nicholson	1
	52

Empty and noe distres to be had

John Bradley	1
John Wyley	2

These persons following are discharged by Certfies

Robert Wood	1
Christopr Hunter	[blank]
Willm Knapton	1
Widdow Smith	1
John West	1

Robert Husband Collr
Henry Atkinson Const

Westrideing ending att lady 1672

The Wapentake of Ainsty

Wakefield District Metropolitan Archive, *Nomina Villarum* hearth tax assessment[46]

f 360]

The Weapontacke of Ainsty (The Wapentake of Ainsty)

f 360r c 1]

Acombe (Acomb)

Mr Thomas Newarke 9
Mr Willm Burdas 2
Mr Taylor of Melburn 2
Empty
Thomas Scadlock 2
Willm Gowland 2
John Bawmbrough 1
Joseph Lambe 1
John Blyth 1
Mrs Mary Blyth 2
Thomas Hill 2
Phillp Eberington 2
Robt Stadlock 1
John Hartley 2
George Crow 2
Mathew Wharton 1
Robert Ray 1
Mr Blanshard 7
James Abbey 2
George Nicholson 1
Wm Mealby 1
Willm Mealby 1
new erected
John Staineley 1
Mrs Darcy 1
one more erected since Mich's Last
Ralph Dewesberry 1
Robert Walker 2

c 2]

George Shaw 1
Math Leadman 1
Willm Kent 1
Empty & vacant
Samll Wilson 1
Steven Tompson 1
Marke Scawby 1
Mr Canocke 3
Willm Sharper 1
James Leadall 1
Willm Tinsley 1
Edwd Reckitt 1
John Blyth 1
Empty
Willm Reekitt 1
Georg Gilbanke 1
Willm Hinchcliffe 1
Richard Bangforth 1
Edwd Ager 1
Robert Wilkinson 1
Willm Kent 1
Empty
Richd Shipton 2
Certd
Widd Chapman 1
Certd
John Chapman 1
Certd
George Gilburne 1
Certd
Thos Harness 1

f 360v c 1]

Robert Husband}
George Waineman} Collr
Willm Mealby Const

Akaster Selby (Acaster Selby)

Mr Cuthburd Harrisson 7
Richard Annison 2
Mrs Jefferson 1
Mr John Harrisson 1
Richard Masson 1
Simond Kirke 1
Thomas Browne 1
Thomas Mirfeild 1
Cuthbart Holmes 5
Robt Cowlin 1
Adam Tate 1
Thos Marchant 1
John Wilkinson 1
John Cawes 2
Timothy Thornton 1
John Kirke 2
John Lacocke 1
John Bartlby 1
Thos Foster 1
a distress
Oswald Moral 1
Widd Chadwell or Mr Harison 1
poor
Widd Mirfeild or Harison 1
poore

c 2]

Willm Cooke or Harisson 1
poore

Richard Pickard Collr
Simond Kirke Const

[46] The sheriff's copy of the Lady Day 1672 assessment, see 'The Documents Used in this Edition' above p. 83.

Askam Brian (Askham Bryan)

Willm Dunington	1
Mrs Flintt	1
Willm Gibbons	3
Widd Dunington	1
Willm Milns	1
Thomas Fearby	1
Wm Newark	2
Thos Cawood senr	1
Henry Blyth	2
John Firth	4
Richd Smeaton	2
Wm Dinis & Willm Wheatley	2
John Dunington	1
Richard Fox	1
Thomas Joy	1
Richard Milnes	1
Thom Traine	1
Thomas Shephard	1
John Dunington	1
Edwd Tomlinson	1
Ri Cooper	1

f 361r c 1]

George Cawood	1
John Fearby	4
Thomas Blackburne	1
Mr William Blyth	8
Mr Vincent	1
Mr John Geldart	12
Willm Wikeley	1
Thomas Barwicke	1
Thomas Richardson	1
Roger Daubyly	1
Willm Lightfoote	1
Thomas Robinson	1
George Catterton	1
John Smith	1
Henry Robinson	1
William Green	1
William Augustine	1
William Jawood	1
Robt Botterill	1
Mathew Cawood	1
Thomas Cawood junr	1
William Firth	1
Thomas Abbey	1
Francis Gib & Geo Day	2
Robert Cawood	1

George Waineman Colr
Richard Milnes Const

c 2]

Askam Richard (Askham Richard)

Mr John Swales	7
Mr Topham	2
Richard Cawood	1
John Flint	2
John Staineburne and Smithy	3
Thomas Cawood	2
Widdow Dixon	1
Willm Baines	1
Henry Dunington	1
Willm Poplewell	1
Thomas Nelson	3
Widd Allen	2
John Fox	3
Robt Nelson	1
Richard Cooper	1
John Nelson	1
Richard Bustard	1
Richard Grenes	1
Widdow Beane	1
Christopr Elisson	1
Willm Barker	1
Richard Ellitson	1
John Cooper	1
Mary Allen	1
Jo Nelson & Jo Gamble	1
Willm Halleley	1
Thos Cawood jun	1
Thomas Stainburne	1
	n. …[47]

Richard Pickard Collr
Thomas Nelson Const

f 361v c 1]

Akaster Maulbis (Acaster Malbis)

Francis Fox	1
Willm Marfeild	1
Edwd Faucitt	1
Willm Ryley	2
Thomas Tayler	1
John Vaux	1
Thomas Walker	1
Robert Darling	1
Thomas Taylor sen	1
Thomas Dinnarr	1
Ann Goodyeare	1
George Scarbrough	1
Thomas Tate	2
John Gibson	2
Ann Trewitt	1
Willm Metcalfe	1
Willm Woodworth	1
Thomas Teasdale	2
Willm Atkinson	2
John Teasdale	1
George Cawood	2
Willm Tanfeild	2
Ellis White	1
Dorcas Marshall	1
Thomas Brignall	1
Thomas Varley jun	2
Thomas Brignall	1
John Doubty	2
Willm Atkinson	1
Willm Wyrill	1
George Dinnar	1

[47] Possibly new build.

Thomas Doubty	1
Thomas Varley	2
John Whitehouse	1

c 2]

Willm Lesune	1
Edwd Vaux jun	1
Ann Waid	1
Mathew Darlinge	1
Mr James Moor	2
	Empty
Edmd Whitehead	1

George Waineman Collr
William Atkinson Const

Bickerton

Mr George Hemsworth	11
Anthony Jackson	2
Frances Wade widd	3
Thomas Brignall	1
Edward Tompson	1
Anthony Wardell	1
Arthur Hingston	1
Thomas Hallyley	3
George Rosse	1
John Becroft	1
Thomas Pickering	1
Phillip Adyson	1
John Coghill	1
Robert Halleley	2
Widdow Pettey	1
Willm Pullean	1
Christopr Dawson	1
	Ctd
John Dixon	1
	poore

f 362 c 1]

Robert Husband Collr
George Rose Const

Bilbrough

Dutches De Bucks	6
Chr Marsh	1
John Smith	1
Edward Morley	1
John Wyrill	1
Thomas March	2
Jane Talor	1
Chr Bawden	2
Chr Wright	3
Willm Smith	2
Mr Robert Anderson	1
Thomas Ketlewell	2
Willm Remyson & forge	2
Widdow Haslewood	1
Robert Moate	1
Thomas Fowler	1
Robert Andrew	1
Christopr Blyth	1
Henry Marshall	1
Franc Tompson	1
Thomas Butler	1
Robert Jewitt	2
Dorothy Tompson	1
Mrs Banks	2

c 2]

George Hall	1
	poore
Leonard Shawmand	1
	poore
Jane Taylor	1
	poore
John Chapman	1
	poore
Elizebeth Remington	1
	poore
Thomas Noble	3
	poore

Rich Pickard Collr
Edward Morley Const

Bilton

Thom Snawsdale Esqr	13
Willm Chambers	6
John Dickinson	1
John Peirson	1
Hugh Nodding	3
Widdow Hewley	1
Henry Ewdale	1
Widdow Staineburne	1
Mathew Peirson	1
John Thackerey	1
Phillip Pallister	1
Thomas Adamson	1
Widdow Hesletine	1
Thomas Netleton	1
John Adamson	1
Richard Burdsall	1
John Pallister	1
John Bedforth	1
Mr Richard Tate	5
John Adenell	1

f 362v c 1]

Mr George Hesletine	4
Christo or Widd Parker	1
Thomas Lilley	1
John Gray	1
Robert Remington	1
Robert Shore	2
Widdow Noding	2
Richard Marshall	1
George Parker	1
Willm Abbey	1
Thomas Longcaster	1
Thomas Hall	1
	Certd
George Moore	1
	Certd
John Dixon	1
	Certd

Geo Waineman Collr
Richd Burdsall Const

Bishop Thorp (Bishopthorpe)

The Ld Arch Bishopp	38
Mr Sooteworth	4[48]
Widd Clarke	2
Ann Bullock	1
Lancellott Watson	1
Willm Pullan	4
Thomas Barton	3
Jane Johnson	1
Edwd Boterill or Latham	4
George Hulley	1
Willm Jackson	1

c 2]

Thomas Hardisty	1
Christop Bewley	1
Willm Carter	2
Charles Pullen	1
George Bolton	1
Willm Clarke	1
Willm Knowles	1
Charles Story	3
James Skerrey	1
Thomas Earby	1
Thomas Pullen	1
Franc Leedes	1
James Dixon	1
Thomas Crosby	1
Henry Jackson	1
Emmett Botterill	1
John Pinder	1
Mr Francis Butler	3
John Ingleby	1
Richard Crosby	1
Mr Edwd Daniell	1
Francis Knowles	1
Edwd Botterill	3
Willm Shaw	1
Michaell Harrisson	1
Richard English	1
Richard Crosby	1
Edwd Shaw	1
Ann Holgate	1
	p
John Calvert	1
	p
Ann Boughton	1
	p
Mary Waide	1
	p

f 363 c 1]

Richard Pickard Collr
Francis Knowles Const

Bolton Peircy (Bolton Percy)

Mr Stevenson	2
Dr Tobias Weckam	12
Mr Willm Ingleby	10
Mr Christo Wharton	5
Robert or Cha Savidge	2[49]
Silvester Tompson	4
Mr Myers	1
John Houseman	3
Franc Sanderson	2
Henry Doughty	2
Henry Scott	1
George Richmond	1
George Spicer	1
Widd Waide	1
Richard Tompson	1
Widd Browne	1
Henry Tompson	1
Robt Denton	1
Willm Hawley	1
Ellin Hurst	1
Thomas Rodwell	2
Christopr Jarman	1
Henry Houseman	1
Henry Houseman sen	1
Hen Boulton	1

c 2]

Edwd Clayford	1
Thomas Vavisser	1
John Dinningley	1
Michaell Wilson	1
Christopr Batchlor	1
Widdow Pybus	1
Richard Savidge	2

Robt Husband }
George Waineman } Collr
Henry Houseman Const

Catterton

Robert Fostar sen	3
Robert Fostar jun	
	3
	1 Demol:
Willm Grainger	2
Dorothy Nicholson	1
Ralph Wood	1
Robert Grainger	1
Henry Fostar	1
Richard Powill	1
Richard Masson	1
Ellizebeth Nicholson	1
John Foster	1
Mary Grainger	1

Robt Husband }
Geo Waineman } Collr
William Grainger Const

f 363 c 1]

Coupman Thorp (Copmanthorpe)

Mr Walter Lacocke	1
more	3
Mr John Wood	5
Mr Wright	5

48 a distress.
49 1 Empty.

Thomas Swales 1
Henry Swales 2
Widdow Doubty 2
Richard Powill 3[50]
Widd Ellen Hunter 2
Widd Harland 1
Thomas Bateman 1
Thomas Marshall 1
Henry Carter 1
Leonard Nicholson jun 1
Thomas Clay 1
Edward Lund 1
James Watkinson 1
Thomas Kirby 1
Mr Robert Morley 1
Richard Hunter 2
Willm Lee 1
Dorothy Bateman Widd 1
Willm Hobson 2
Robt Hardin 2
Empty
Mr Roger Beckwith 2
George Waineman Collr
Willm Lee Const

c 2]

Coulton
(Colton)
Thomas Wise 3
John Dalton 1
John Rynneson 2
Robert Tompson 1
Willm Andrewes 3
Jno Caukeingam 1
Thomas Smith 1
Richard Rycroft 1
Robert Renyson 1
Robert Nicholson 2
John Rennisson 1
John Laprick 1
Allice Carrack 2
Richd Ableson 1
John Cross 1
Richd Marshall 2
Willm Nelson 1
Thomas Dalton 1
Willm Hopwood 1
Ri Latham 1
Willm Smith 2
Robert Manners 1
John Nicholson 1
Thomas Marshall 3
John Carrock 2
Thomas Fox 1

f 364 c 1]

Robt Husband }
Geo Waineman } Collrs
Willm Smith Constable

Dringhouses
Robt Brabner 1
Willm Bewley 1
Widd Richardson 1
George Browne 1
Symond Smith 1
Robinson Myers 2
Widd Parr 1
Widd Allen 1
Robt Cobb 2
John Thackeray 1
John Carter 3
Willm Hood 1
John Richmond 2
Willm Godson or Fenton 1
Robert Willaby 1
Thomas Smith 2
Willm Wyrill 2
Thomas Brigans 1
Widd Grayson 1
Widd Hudd 1
Richard Dockerey 1
John Carver 1
Robt Dockerey 3
John Richmond & smithy 2
John Caver & smithy 2

c 2]

John Richmond 13

Robt Husban}
Geo Waineman } Collr
Willm Smith Constable

Hutton & Angram
(Hutton Wandesley and Angram)
Willm Roundell Esqr 13
John Williamson 1
Henry Deighton 2
George Knowles 2
Willm Lambart 1
John Reeve sen 1
John Patterick 1
Guy Watterton now Ingram 1
Thomas Deighton 1
Bryan Tatman 1
Edward Jackson & smithy 3
new built
Edward Morley 1
Mr John Faucitt 1
John Hill 1
Ingram Alderson 1
Mary Abbey 1
John Cawood 1
John Reeve Junr 1
Willm Hill 1
Henry Allan 1
Edward Joy 1
Willm Burley 1
George Buckle 1
Willm Shaw 1
Thomas Allen 1

50 1 of these newly erected lyable the next time.

f 364v. c 1]

John Reeve 1
John Shaw 1
John Goodall 1
Edwd Jackson or Edm Wood 1
Ann Shaun 1
poore
John Wright junr 1
poore
John Wright senr 1
poore
Lawr Smith 1
Robt Husband Collr
John Williamson Const

Hessey (Hessay)
George Dixon 2
BryanMarshall 3
Bryan Tate 1
Thomas Gibson 1
Mr Fawcitt 1
Richard Pallister 1
Robert Calvart 1
Thomas Thackeray 1
John Taite 3
Thomas Calvert 3
Rowland Adisson 1
John Darwin 1

Richd Pickard Collr
John Darwent Const

c 2]

Houlegate (Holgate)
Richard Lepington 3
Mr Mewtas 2
George Thresh 1
Richard Shaw 2
Thomas Hollingworth 1
Widd Harp or Mary 1
Robt Husband Collr
Richd Shaw Const

Healaugh
The Lord Wharton 28
Mr Gunter 5
Mr Walker 3
Robert Shaw 1
Robert Fox 1
Richard Fowler sen 1
William Emerston 2
John Acombe jun 2
Thomas Fowler 2
William Mortimer 1
Robt White & Thos Maud 5
Richard Fowler 2
Robt Mounton 1

f 365r c 1

John Browne 3
Henry Dossie 3
Willm Jackson 1
Joseph Skunersley 2
Thomas Dixon 1
Peter Allen 2
Thoms Addinall 1
James Tomson 1
Willm Francke 1
George Robinson 1
Robt Darby & Smithy 2
Peter Stevenson 1
Richard Fowler jun 2
Widdow Allen 1
Widdow Johnson 1
George Duke 1
John Richinson 1
Henry Greene 1
James or Ma Robinson 1
Thomas Arthbell 3
Peter Abbey 1
Richard Grainger 1
John Dodgson 1
Richard Rycroft 1
Robert Mortimer 1
Thomas Dive 1
Thomas Francke 1
Michaell Darby 1
Widdow Stead 1
poore

Richard Pickard Collr
Peter Stevenson Const

c 2]

Knapton
Willm Shipton 2
Thomas Royston 2
Mr Prince or Peter Fowler 2
Elliz or Robt Gowland 2
Ann Loriman 2
Thomas Archer 1
Richard Deighton 1
George Marshall 1
John Gowland 2
Widdow Archer 1
John Robinson 1
Christopr Stevenson 1
William Shearburne 1
Willam Beasby 1
Richard Mulburne 1
Simond Bramstone 1
Joseph Shephard 1
Robert Topham 1
George Loriman 1

George Waineman Collr
John Robinson Const

f 365v c 1]

Midlethorpe (Middlethorpe)
Chr Brearey Alderm 10
Mr Beane 6
William Pretious 3
John Woodworth 1
Mr Henry Tompson 6

George Waineman Collr
John Woodworth Const

Marston
(Long Marston)

James Thwaite Esqr	11
Mr Micklethwate	9
Richard Ross	1
Marke Rhynolds	1
Robert Faucitt	1
Mr John Taylor	5
William Fowler	1
John Wheatley	1
Charles Gill	1
Thomas Hislopp	1
Robert Tompson	1
Edward Dixon	1
John Acombe	1
William Seller	1
William Idle	2
Thomas Reynold	1
Christopr Acombe	1
Willm Fletcher	1
Christopr Wheatley	1

c 2]

William Gold Gent	2
John Tompson	1
Henry Spence	1
Mary Mountaine	1
George Cartwright	2
Thomas Acombe	2
George Buckle	1
Widdow Faucitt	1
Margret Justice	1
George Shaun	1
Arthur Hall	1
John Baines	1
Henry Stringer	1
William Wardman	1
Ann Vary Widd	1
Thomas Wray	1
Richard Tompson	1
John Tuke	1
William Stubb	1
William Idle	1
Thomas Vary	1
	Ced
Robert Bootland	1
	Ced
Elliz Bentley	1
	Ced
Widdow Acomb	1
	Ced

Richard Pickard Collr[51]

f 366r c 1]

Moore Mountaine
(Moor Monkton)

Sir Thomas Slingsby Knt Bt	23
Richard Minings	1
Willm Deighton	1
Widdow Newham	1
James Dinis	1
Mr Hinckes	5
Richard Marshall Jun	1
Luke Barker	1
John Wigglesworth	1
John Gelthrope	1
Richard Smith	2
Willm Haire	1
Phillip Bullock	1
Seth Hoppes	1
Willm Harlington	1
John Marshall	2
John Barker	1
Miles Shephard	1
Thomas Crowdon	1
Christopr Dinis	1
Mr Richardson	1
Richard Lambart	2
Peter Johnson	1
Richard Marshall	1
Henry Haire	1
Richard Marshall	1
Mathew Calvert	1
John Shepherd	1
Margret Marshall	1
	Ced
Willm Shephard	1
	Ced
Ann Sanderson	1
	Ced
Bridgett Gray	1
	Ced
John Thackeray	1
	Ced
Thomas Marshall	1
	Ced

c 2]

Christopr Webster	1
Thomas Spenlive	1
Timothy Spenlove	1
	Ced

George Waineman Collr
Thos Marshall Const

Nunapleton
(Nun Appleton)

Ld Duke of Buckingham	40
Mr Willm Yarbrough	5
Henry Marshall	3
John Wright	1
John Carter	1
Michaell Ouseman	1
John Ryeley	1
Richard Redshaw	1
Willm Teasdall	1
John Watson	1
John Mollett	1
Robert Booth	2

[51] No constable recorded.

Gorge Tate	5
Christopr Batley	1
Phillop Bell	1
Marmaduke Hill	1
Widdow Levitt	1
Thomas Reynold	1
Thomas Spence	2
William Hill	1
Widdow Doughty	1

f 366v c 1]

John Carrocke	1
John Scott	1
Robert Stevenson	1
Richard Booth	1
Christopr Sanderson	1
Francis Beckwith	1
Henry Savidge	3
John Johnson	1
John Mollett junr	1
Robert Tate	1
Willm Hey	1
Franc Agar	1
Robt Doghty	1
Robert Halley	1
John Savidge	1
Robert Rhynold	1
Richard Bell	1
Matthew Hill	1
Richard Masson	1
James Alderson & forge	2
Willm Wass	1
Robert Greene	1
Robert Johnson	1
Thomas Foster	1
Michaell Cooper	2
Henry Bilbrough	1
Widdow Knowles	1
Joseph Leaper	1
Francis Campe	1
Thomas Gibbs	2
Robert Garbutt	2
Thomas Etherington	1
John Smith	1
Thomas Marshall	3
John Hawson	1
Richard Hill	1
Robt Bell	1
Francis Tate	1

c 2]

Robert Husband }
Geo Waineman } Collr
John Watson Const

Netherpoplton (Nether Poppleton)

Thomas Hutton Esqr	13
Mathew Prince	5
Edward Walker	1
Widdow Myers	1
Robt Deighton	1
Edmond Robotham	1
Willm Prince	2
Widdow Catterton	1
Thomas Lund	1
James Hardisty	1
Edward Gray	1
Mathew Tompson	1
John Wyrell	1
Henry Maugham	1
Richard Rubinson	1
Mr Roger Beckwith	4
Henry Spinke	1
Willm Nelson	1
Mr John Buckstone	3
Thomas Newman	1
Lawrant Hinchcliffe	1
Mathew Smith	1
Richard Cooper	1
Mr Hutton or Gunby	1

f 367 c 1]

Mr Hutton or Widd Webster	1

Richd Pickard Collr
William Hardisty Const

Oxton & Ouston

Thomas Birdsall	4
John Beane	3
Robert Harrisson	2
Robert Hill	2
Richard Atkinson	2
William Radley	1
Antony Yates	2
Christopher Colbeck	2
Jane Garbutt	1
John Hartley	1
Thomas Walker	3
Mr Beane senr	2
Chr Marsh or Yates	1

Richd Pickard Collr
Antony Yeates Const

Over Popleton (Upper Poppleton)

John Woodyard	1
Thomas Thorp	1
George Thorp	1

c 2]

William Smith	1
John Lindley	1
John or Geo Wyly	1
William Ridson	1
Thomas Blyth	1
George Cotterton	1
James Dutton	1
William Prince	1
	Empty
Widdow Gray	2
Robert Ager	1
John Fearby	1
Richard Watterson	1
Widdow Whitehouse	1
Mathew Blyth	2
Thomas Brogden	1
Thomas Prince	2
Widdow Bolland	2
Widdow Wright	1

John Blyth 1
Widdow Fearby 1
Robert Nelson 1
Thomas Carter 1
William Fearby 2
1 of these newly erected since Michs Last
William Marshall 1
Thomas Spinke 1
Mathew Blyth jun 1
Widdow Prince 2
Widdow Browne 1
Franc Tompson 1
William Silversides 1
Thomas Hey 2
Richard Heald 1
poore
William Cotterton 3
John Dutton 1
Empty
Mr Roger Beckwith owner 1
Empty
George Heslapp 2

f 367v c 1]

Widdow Adinell 1
Mr John Hill 3
Thomas Belton 1
Abraham Bridge 1
James Tomson 1
Widdow Marshall 1
poore

Robert Husband }
George Waineman } Collrs
Robt Nelson Const

Rufforth

Mr John Allon 7
Mr Calvart 5
Mr Gale 4

John Wilson 1
Thomas Hooper 1
John Gray 1
Willm Taylor 1
Thomas Bottrevill 1
Alice Leadom 1
Willm Carthwate 1
Mary Garbutt 1
John Cartwright 1
Mathew Hawkins 1
Mr Setterthwate 8
2 of these new built since Lady Day
John Knapton 1
John Norfolke 1
Thomas Cawood 1
Mary Hill 1
Willm Knapton sen 1
Henry Cartwright 1

c 2]

Thomas Chidson 1
George Hay 1
James Cartwright 1
Richard Gill 1
Mary Faucett 1
Thomas Cartwright 1
The Winde Milne 1
Thomas Fowler 1
Robt Hawkins 1
Willm Knapton 1
George Coupland 2
Ced
John Cotterton 1
Ced
Robert Smith 1
Ced
Ann Richinson 1
Ced
Christopr Johnson 1
Ced

Mrs Blackbeard 1
empty

Robert Husband Collr
John Hawkins Const

Steeton

Lord Fairfax 10
Willm Fairfax Esqr 5
John Wyrill 1
Willm Tessimond 3
John Wardmond 1
John Ryley Warran 1
John Fawlkingham 1
Margret Garbutt 1
Richard Wardman 1

f 368 c 1]

Richard Pickard Collr
Arthur Topham Const

Tadcaster
(East Tadcaster)

Mrs Stower 5
Mrs Morley 3 or 5[52]
Mr Wilkinson 3
John Parkinson 1
John Shearwood 2
Willm Loft & forge 2
Richd & Ann Boone 2
John Spencer 1
Ralph Beane 3
John Adcocke 4
Robt Goulthropp 1
Widd & Clement Webster 4
Thomas Jackson 1
Robt Barker 1
John Mawde 1
Robt Barker 2
Widdow Hopwood 1
Widd Beane 1
Robt Clinte 1

[52] 5 written over 3; or 3 written over 5.

Jane Harrisson 1
Mr John Lovell 2
Thomas Asquith 2
Willm Sidall 6
Thomas Pinder 2
Willm Liversidge 1

c 2]

Willm Hursley 1
John Dikes 1
Antony Wise 1
Ced
John Ouldam 1
poore
Widdow Laughton 1
Ced
Grace Warde 2
poore

George Waineman Coll
Robert Barker Const

Thorp Arch
Richard Brewerton 6
Widdow Smith 1
Mathew Elsworth 1
Thomas Jackson 5
Thomas Farrand 1
Robert Marshall 1
Christopher Fearne 2
Henry Hall 2
Ann Scott widd 1
George Marshall 1
John Wiseman 1
John Pickering 1
James Hopwood 1
John Hopwood 2
Thomas Bovill 1
John Foster 2
Toby Dickinson 2
Arthur Turton 1
Joseph Wardman 1
Christopr Foster 1

f 368v c 1]

Christopr Scott 1
Robrt Wilson 1
ThomasHill 1
Willm Hopwood 1
Mr George Procter 3
a distress
Robert Dobson 2
Widdow Marshall 1
Toby Dickinson 1
Thomas Farrand 1
Richard Tindall 1
Marke Younge 1
Christopr Nelson 1
Robert Williamson 1
Willm Plewes 1
Marke Wilson 1
Willm Selby 1
Thomas Bellases 1
Richard Nowill 1
Robert Elsworth 1
Elias Pickard 3
no distress
John Bell 1
Ced

Robt Husband }
George Waineman } Collrs
John Pickering Const

Tockwith
George Blyth 1
Willm Hopson 3
Robert Abbey 1
Henry Briggnall 1
Thomas Lazonby 1

c 2]

Henry Parker 1
John Tomlinson sen 3
John Tomlinson junr 3
John Foster 1
John Rose 1

John Sherwin 2
William Harper 2
Henry Rider 2
Henry Abbey 1
Henry Jennett 1
Robt Abbey 1
Thomas Merry 1
Thomas Snowden 1
John Burley 3
Oswald & John Fowler 2
Lancellot Wright 1
Bryan Abbey 1
Christop Shepherd 2
Willm Abbey 1
Richard Fowler 1
John Walkinton 1
Edward Fawcitt 1
Widdow Dryver 1
Christopher Houbeck 7
Miles Alderson 1
Mathew Carrock 2
Thomas Wilsthropp 1
John Abbey 1
Willm Carrett 1
Empty
Widdow Beelby 1
Henry Tompson 1
Francis Carter 1
Eliz or Wm Abbey 1
Thomas Well 1
John Lazonby 1

f 369r c 1]

Thomas Lolly 1
Robert Hunter 1
Thomas Shephard 1
poore

Robt Husband Collr
John Wilkinton Const

Wighill
The Lady Stapleton 15
Mr William Redman 2

Mathew Daniell 1
Empty
Robert Potter 2
Marke Wilson 3
James Stephenson 2
Adam Wiseman 1
Francis Potter 4
Robert Fish 1
a distress
Henry Wheelas 1
Willm Simpson 1
Robert Baldridge 2
a distress
Katherine Manners 1
Thomas Johnson 1
Thomas Carleton 1
Willm Potter 1
Willm Hunton 2
Mathew Starr 2
Charles Manners 2
pd one
Margret Chapman 1
Richd Simpson 1
Richard Halley 1
Richard Abbey 2

c 2]

Richard Hoggard 1
Antony Adinell Junr 1
Adam Wiseman 3
John Ilbeck 1
James Hartley 2
William Mannors 1
Antho Adinell senr 1
John Barker 1
Mr Wm Currer 6
Willm Potter 2
Mr Potter 2
Empty
Roger Stowings 8
John Adinell & forge 2
Marke Wilson 1

Robt Husband & }
George Waineman } Collr
Mr Redman Constable

Wibstropp (Wilstrop)
Richard Walmsley Esqr 7
Richard Fisher 1
Mr James Lightollers 2
Benieam Manings 2
Isabell Rooth 1
John Shaw 1
Oswald Gray 1
Plato Fisher 1
Gilbert Royston 1
George Applegarth 1
Thomas Holmes 2
Demolished

f 369v c 1]

Robt Husband Collr
Willm Apleyard Const

Walton
The Lady Fairfax 17
Widdow Turner 1
Robert Chambers 1
John White 2
Widdow Browne 3
John Apleyard 2
Thomas Graves 1
Christopher Tennant 1
Widdow Scott 1
Ralph Jackson 1
William Gamble 1
Peter Smith 2
Richard Graves 1
Joseph Lyth 1
Lawrance Noble 1
Robert Tompson 1
Widdow Chapman 1
Henry Hicks 2
William Layster 1
Christopher Daniell 1
Miles Potter 2
Peter Dobson 3
Henry Noble 1
John Smith 1
John Straw 1

c 2]

James Stead 2
James Scott 1
Richard Bramley 1
Robert Barker 1
Richard Gamble 1
Thomas Tomson 1
Thomas Hick 2
Marmad Tompson 1
Thomas Gamble 1
Widdow Wardman 1
Robert Farrey 1

Robt Husband &}
George Waineman} Collrs
Robt Farrey Const

Skyrack Wapentake

The National Archives, E179/210/417

m 1]

Skyracke Wapentake
(Skyrack Wapentake)

Ebberforth
(Aberford)

Mr Walter Hames	7
Maxi Tayler	1
Ri Cookeson	1
Geo Hicke	1
William Tasker	1
Leo Thirkill or Mr Roades	1
Laur Dunnill	3
Ri Collingworth	2
John Dickinson	1
Leo Thirkell	1
Robte Akid	3
William Makinder	2
Mr Waterhouse	3
John Hustler	1
Maxi Tayler	3
Mr Tho Plant	4
Ri Odman	1
Mr Ralph Tayler	3
Peter Slater	1
Widdow Slater	1
Lawrence Dunhill	1
John Carlin	1
Robert Spincke	3
Mr Rhoades	1
Sir Tho Gascoigne *pro* mill	2
Joseph Askwith	1
	50

These persons following are discharged by certificate

William Akester	1
George Robinson	1
Miles Akester	1

Robert Husband Collr
Peter Slater Const

Allerton Bywater

Jervas Jackson	2
George Webster	5
Alvery Spincke	3
Rich Middleton	3
John Bywater	3
John Greene	2
Widd Hoole	3
Willm Heaton	7
Edward Batty	3
John Duffan	1
Peter Wood	1
Edward Clough	2
John Holden	1
Henry Bramham	1
Tho Barritt	2
John Spinke	1
Tho Burrow	1
Edward Grave	1
Ri Johnson	1
Ri Hodgson	1
	44

Omitted by reason of poverty	1

Robert Husband Collr
John Duffan Const

Austrop
(Austhorpe)

Nicholas Moore Esq	8
Mr Gabriell Laton	6
Seth Loftus	4
Alveray Loftus	3
Rich Hutchinson	4
Willm Gibson	4
Edward Butterfeild	1
John Pye	2
Elizabeth Holland *pro* marito	1
Willm Scholefeild	2
Susan Wiggin	1

m 2]

John Levans	2
Robert Smith	1
William Shillitoe	1
John Hensworth	1
Robert Harry	1
	42

Omitted by reason of poverty	1

Robert Husband Collector
John Hemsworth Const

Allwoodley
(Alwoodley)

Richard Chambers	3
Robert Lake	1
Francis Lake	1
John Totty	1
Willm Atkinson	3
John Jennings	4
Robert Nunns	1
Francis Catherey	1
Samuel Midgley	2
Mr Tomlinson	8
Willm Smith	2
Benja Atkinson	2
John Cowper	2
Willm Cowtherey	3
	34

Empty
Mr Clifton 3
Rich Wiglesworth 2

Omitted by reason of poverty 1

Roger Hardcastle Collr
Benja Atkinson Const

Addle cum Eccopp
(Adel with Eccup)

Marke Cowper 1
Robert Richardson 1
Mr Samuell Midgley 5
John Allon 1
Widdow Atkinson 1
Widdow Atkinson 1
Chrofer Stead 1
Willm Barraclough 3
William Clough 1
Mr Booker 2
Randall Northouse 1
William Northouse 4
Ralph Allen 1
John Tompson 1
John Burnley 1
Mr Dawson 3
Thomas Bradbury 1
Francis Northouse 2
Rich Wright 1
John Wright 1
Wilfrey Harrison 1
Widd Harrison 1
Widd Midgley 2
Willm Bucktroute 1
Geo Carr 1
John Bentley 2
William Wetherell 2
John Wate 1
Tho Richardson 1
Will Walker 1
Mr Tho Kirke 4
John Oddye 1
Anthony Deane 1

Wid Horner 1
John Norcroft 1
John Collinson 2
Willm Wash 1
Chrofer Dale 2
Mr Wood 4
Abra Cloughton 1
Issa Waite 1
Robte Waite 2
Robte Nicholson 2
Mrs Kirke 11
Tho Inchcliffe 1
John Barrow 4
Chrofer Kirk 3
Tho Nicholson 1
John Rushforth 1
Mrs Kirk 1
Ri Hobson 2

m 3]

Mr Etherington 5
Ri Tidswell 2
Edward Midgley 1
Richard Nicholson 1
Tho Hudson 1
Tho Brooke 2
Geo Goothricke 1
Tho Tayler 1
Michaell Skelton 2
John Birkinshaw 1
Cuthbert Wilson 1
Marke Thresh 1
John Stead 1
Robte Dawson 2
John Thresh 1
John Tate 1
Henry Dishforth 1
Willm Midgley 3
Thomas Gill 1
John Blackburne 1
Widd Walker 1
Willm Jackson 1

125

Empty
Mr Wood 1
John Barraclough 1

These persons following are discharged by certificate

John Oglethorpe 1
Elizabeth Moss 1

Omitted by reason of poverty 2

Robert Husband Collr
John Thrush Const

Arthington

The Executors of
Henry Arthington Esq 19
Tho Fawkes 10
Robte Scratchard 1
Ri Jerman 1
Wid Buckle 1
Geo Carr 1
Samll Liversedge 1
William Brown 1
Willm Dawson 4
Michaell Waite 2
Robte Lawe 4
Hen Adingall 1
Widdow Illingworth 1
Tho Inchbard 1
Widd Henthorne 2
Widd Waddington 2
William Ingham 1
Francis Tomlinson 1
Widow Midgley 2
John Midgley 1
Edward Midgley 1
Ralph Midgley 2
Robert Whitehead 2
Willm Atkinson 7
Widd Atkinson 3
Peter Bland 2
Ralph Allen 1

John Ingham	1
John Allen	2
Widdow Winder sen	2
Ri Waite	1
William Waddington	1
WidWood	1
Wid Kitchin	1
John Wiggin	1
William Gill	1
Willm Hauke	3
Michaell Scatchard	1
William Lumley	1
Antho Rycroft	3

m 4]

William White	1
John White jun	1
Ri Denton	2
Robert Steele	1
Henry Pattison	2
Robert Hauckes	3
	104

These persons following are discharged by certificate

Leonard England	1
Widd Stainton	1
Ralph Hayes	1
Barba Lepton	2

Robert Husband Collector
Ralph Midgley Constable

Bardsey cum Rigton
(Bardsey with East Rigton)

Robert Waddington	8
John Fentiman viccar	4
Cuthbert Brearcliffe	4
Rich Doncaster	1
James Spurrill	1
Nicholas Gibson	1
Chropher Abbatt	1
Tho Stead	1
Tho Dabby	3
John Ellis	2
Tho Kilby	1
George Ottivell	2
Gilbert Kilby	1
Rich Ruskin	2
Rich Sharper	2
James Kay	2
William Stephenson	2
George Dinedale	2
Anne Waddington	3
Matthew Marsingale	1
Magda Chambers	2
Mr Lister	2
John Marshall	3
Mr Pearson	4
Tho Marshall	2
Willm Mawde	2
Tho Wright	2
Tho Marshall jun	3
Mr Lister	4
Tho Chambers	1
John Esh	1
Ephraim Batley	1
Robert Brearcliffe	2
	73

These persons following are discharged by certificate

Arthur Widdop	2
Willm Batley	2
John Winterburne	2

George Waineman Collr
Mr Nichas Lister Const

Bramhope

Chrofer Saxon	1
Willm Gawthropp	2
John Arthington	1
Tho Dauson	2
Mr Pickering	1
Widd Howden	1
Tho Dobson	2
Mr Waddington	5
John Dobson	1
John Waite	1
Willm Butterfeild	2
Widd Aldroide	1
John Holt	1
Henry Wood	1
Willm Peele	1
Joseph Welsh	1
Tho Savill	1
Joseph Crowther	1

m 5]

Major Waddington	1
Willm Richardson	1
Samuell Walker	1
Widd Waite	1
Willm Broadley	1
Mr Hopworth	2
Mr Dyneley	8
Robert Alroyde	1
Joseph Gill	3
Willm Gauthrey	1
James Ogden	1
James Appleyeard	1
Tho Cave	1
Robert Appleyeard	1
William Waddington	1
Willm Wherecer	1
Willm Appleyeard	1
Widdow Cowgill	1
Lawr Hawkroyd	1
Willm Lumley	1
Willm Cawthrey	1
Henry Atkinson	1
Christopher Walker	1
Willm Hall	1
Widd Atkinson	1
Benja Illingworth	1
John Illingworth	1
	63

George Waineman Collr
John Lambert Const

Baildon	
Mrs Janie Bailden	9
Jonathan Midgley	3
William Stead	4
Widd Metcalfe	3
Robte Parkinson & Schole	5
Abra Halliday	1
Thomas Lacocke	1
John Hudson	1
William Tayler	1
Alice Tayler	1
Rich Farrer	1
John Mann	2
Nicholas Bayley sen	2
Nicholas Bayley jun	2
Hannah Brooke	2
John Pighills	3
Jane Stead	2
William Bowling	1
Grace Johnson	1
Rich Butterfeild	1
Rich Pollard	1
John Fowler	2
John Butterfeild	1
Will Butler	1
Widd Butler	2
Robte Leach	1
William Exley	2
James Stead	1
John Stead	1
John Fowler	1
Thomas Milner	1
Stephen Hudson	2
William Hudson	2
Ri Ambler	1
John Mitton	2
Abra Waide	1
Widd Hardacree	2
Francis Mitton	1
William Birtwisle	1
Willm Hudson	1
John Hutchinson	1
Rich Atkinson	2
Robte Garnett sen	1

Will Ryley	1
Ellin Smith	1
John Baley	2
James Holmes	2
Antho Binns	1
Willm Hudson	1
John Clarke	1
Widd Fletcher	1
James Man	1
Tho Kirkman	1
m 6]	
Widow Lister	1
Leo Butterfeild	1
Robte Garnitt jun	1
Widd Hudson	1
Rich Batt	1
Widd Wilkinson	2
Matthew Coultas	1
Tho Poole	1
Jonas Baley for Martin house	1
Edmond Moore	1
Steph Hudson sen	2
Eliz Mann	1
Henry Mann	1
Laur Ambler sen	1
John Parrish	1
Geo Hutchinson	2
Willm Baley	1
	109

These persons following are discharged by certificate

Susann Farrey	1
John Halliday	1
Willm Cowgill	1
Willm Gill	1
Willm Harrison	2
Nicholas Stead	1

Roger Hardcastle Collr
Rich Butterfield Const

Bingley	
Tho Smith	1
Mary Smith	1
Thomas Keighley	2
William Scott	3
Robert Leach	3
James Keighley	2
Mr Bentley	3
Michaell Slater	1
Tho Scarrow	1
Tho Murgatroide	6
Rob Hardcastle *pro*	3
Tho Busworth	
Edward Skerrow	2
Abraham Sharpe	1
Jereme Greene	1
Arthur Pickles	1
James Keighley	1
Steph Hogg	1
Jonath Longbotham	1
Steph Hudson	1
Mr Mich Youngbotham	4
John Turner	1
Willm Hartley	1
Robte Emmitt	1
Widd Longbotham	1
William Crowther	2
Martin Lister	4
Rich Tompson	2
Ed Lupton sen	2
Widd Lupton	1
Willm Lupton	1
Willm Whiteacrees	1
Nathan Binns	1
Rich Garnitt	1
Jonas Mann	1
Edward Ambler	1
Jerom Tompson	2
Tho Dodson	1
James Booth	1
Tho Beane	1
Samuell Wood	1
Robte Tennant	2
Tho Tennant	2
Robte Denby	3

Widd Rawson	2
Widd Slater	1
Willm Rawson	2
Chrofer Garnett	1

[additional data taken from E179/368/8, part 9]

Jerom: Hillas	2
John Wilkinson	4
John Beane	2
Tho Inglethorpe	4
Widd Thornton	5
Robert Parrish	2
John Jewitt	1
Chrofer Mitchell	1
John Wright	1
John Walker	2
John Aldroyd	2
Matth: Midgley	1
Widd Whitley	3
Rich Remington	1
Francis Hide	2
Geo Whitley	1
Geo Farrand	2
Geo Gourner	1
Antho Whitley	2
John Tompson	2
Zachar: Harris	2
Chr: Gott	2
Nichol: Cowling	3
Geo Robinson	1
Widdow Skirrow	1
Michael Maude	1
Richard Walker	2
Willm Lister	2
Joseph Walker	2
Joseph Rawson	2
Mr Binns	8
Fran: Howgill	3
Galther Ingleworth	2
Michael Mawde	2
Thomas Wood	1
Willm Hide	1
Jerome Greene	1

Willm Holdsworth	1
Thomas Skerrah	2
Mr Fairbancke	6
Thomas Natter	1
Mr Currer & Warrenhouse & milne	18
John Rawson	1
Hen Buckworth	1
Tho Dobson	5
The Schoolhouse	3
Widd Whitley	4
John Whilley	1
Nicholas Cowling	1
William Hoyle	2
John Leach	2
Tho Lupton	2
Mr Farrand	6
More for Dan: Gleadall	1
John Tayler	4
Tho Smith	1
John Hudson	2
John Scott	5
Mr Stephen Farrand	4
Willm Mawde	2
Willm Farrand	2
Nicholas Whitacre	1
John Heaton	2
Chrofer Wilson	2
Francis Brush	2
Tho Murgatroide	3
John Murgatroide	1
Willm Herd	1
Thomas England	1
Ri: Waddington	2
Chr: Smith	1
Tho: Smith	1
Geo: Bland	1
John Whitecarr	2

[end of E179/368/8, part 9; continuation of E179/210/417, m 7]

John Briggs	1
Tho Haley	1

William Booth	1
John Ellison	2
Jonas Whitacrees	1
Will Waddington	1
Widd Wilkinson	1
John Ellison	1
John Hollingrave	1
John Leach	1
Geo Butler	1
John Moore	1
Rich Wright	1
Rich Driver	1
Edward Mercer	2
John Rhoades	1
Henry Shaw	1
Henry Midgley	1
Willm Midgley	1
Robert Midgley	1
Rich Midgley	1
James Holmes	1
Mr Ben Farrand	8
Sam Sunderland Esq	8
John Wright	2
John Longley	1
Mr Benja Farrand	4
Willm Dobson	5
Abra Parker	5
Tho Blakey	4
Willm Morley	1
Tho Blakey jun	2
	two
Will Hall	1
Robt Hall	1
Ri Wilkinson	2
James Whitakers	1
Charles Rogers	1
John Smith	1
William Bothomley	1
Char Waddington	1
Jacob Scott	2
John Smith	1
John Pickles	1
Widd Wilkinson	1
Rich Hargreaves	1
Rich Sugden	1

Willm Longfeild	1
Robte Oldfeild	1
Walter Waddington	1
Widd Smith	1
Constance Waddington	1
Willm Waddington	1
John Roades	1
Robte Wright	1
George Sugden	2

m 8]

James Holmes	1
Roger Shackleton	4
Joseph Waide	1
Robt Illingworth sen	1
Robt Illingworth jun	1
Willm Tayler	1
Rich Thackwray	1
Nicho Stead	3
Walter Midgley	1
Tho Milner	1
John Mitchell	3
Tho Booth	5
Widd Heaton	4
James Illingworth	2
Steph Waide	1
George Oldroyde	4
Abra Robinson	1
John Clayton	3
John Widdop	1
Joseph Dawson	3
Rich Francke	4
Isaac Leech	2
Grace Dickinson	1
Widd Farrer	1
Widd Hudson	1
James Robinson	1
Richard Walker	1
Tho Whitley	2
John Rawson	3
Thos Lister	4
Michaell Wade	2
Robte Lupton	2
Willm Marvill	4
James Woodhead	2
Robte Blakey	2
Jonas Appleyeard	4
Tho Rushworth	1
Geo Hudson	1
John Holdroyd	1
John Hodgson	1
Widd Holmes	3
Brian Lister	2
John Earthburne	1
Tho Swaine	2
John Lister	1
	434

These persons following are discharged by certificate

Nicholas Gleadall	1
William Clarke	1
John Hartley	1
John Kitchin	1
Benja Clarkhouse	1

m 9]

Omitted by reason of poverty 9

George Wainman Collr
Stephen Farran Const

Burley

Antho Field	2
Tho Squire	1
John Vitty	1
Willm Browne	1
Chrofer Whitehead	1
Hen Ryley	1
Edmond Hebden	2
Tho Pauson	1
Will Huddleston sen	1
Wm Huddleston jun	1
John Mawde	5
Leo Waddington	2
Sam Goodall	1
Will Tennant	1
Will Page	1
Will Kettlewell	1
Tho Beeston	2
Mr Ward *pro* Chappelhouse	3
Mr Fran Pullan	5
James Hainie	1
James Mawde	2
Mrs Clarkson	3
Mr Major Mawde	4
Mr Will Vavasor	7
Robert Twizleton	3
John Huddleston	1
John Mawde jun	1
George Smith	1
Tho Worse	2
Willm Jenkinson	3
Francis Walton	1
Jane Morley	1
Willm Moss	2
Willm Pickard	2
Antho Waddington	2
Tho Squire	1
Geo Knowles	1
Will Catton	1
Tho Dayhouse	1
James Stead	4
Willm Lister	2
Robte Wilson	2
Jonas Longbotham	3
Tho Hartley	2
Robert Butler	2
Chr Dobson jun	3
Paull Jewitt	2
Lawr Whitehead jun	1
Willm Jewitt	2
Willm Gill	2
John Tompson	1
Willm Walker	1

m 10]

Jerom Marshall	3
Andrew Moss	1

Chrofer Dobson	2
John Nicholson	2
Thomas Curtice	1
Thomas Rhoades	1
Nath Walker	1
Michaell Nicholson	1
Jo Stocks	1
Henry Nicholson	1
George Dobson	1
Jacob Elsworth	2
John Nicholson	2
	119

These persons following are discharged by certificate

John Walbanke	1
Janie Laty	1
James Walker	1
Faith Williamson	1
Willm Furnice	1
Willm Whitehead	1
Jonas Wright	1

Roger Hardcastle Collr
Samll Goodall Const

Barwicke in Elmet
(Barwick in Elmet)

Mr Jackson	2
John Hardcastle	3
Lawr Edmondson	3
John Nortas	1
Matth Ingle	1
Roger Gregson	2
Tho Bird	1
Tho Tayler	3
John Tayler	3
James Prince	2
Rich Greene	2
John Parker	1
Wid Tayler	2
John Moore	1
John Smith	2
John Tayler jun	1
Bartho Mamond	3
Robt Dyneley	2
Widd Knapton	4
Widd Seile	3
Joseph Strickland	2
Samuell Stowne	1
Leon Catton	1
James Orton	1
Mercy Hague	2

m 11]

Robte Collett	1
Tho Reaver	3
Geo Hayste	2
Ralph Collett	3
Richard Collett	1
John Ellis	2
Mr Postgate	2
John Burke	1
Will Briggs	3
Rich Burland	2
John Burland	1
Widdow Hague	1
Chr Smith	1
Joshua Turner	3
Geo Richmond	1
Geo Browne	1
Tho Knapton	1
Tho Stowing	5
Samuell Shenton	1
John Lee	2
Dr Dalton	10
Will Ellis Esq	9
John Dodgson	2
Tho Tate	2
Samuell Tate	1
Tho Lee	2
John Dodgson	1
Henry Hare	1
Mr Will Hodgson	3
Widd Settle	3
Eliza Settle	2
Rich Potter	1
John Hemsworth	1
Mr Ri Vivers	3
Henry Shaun	1
Robert Ball	1
Ri Ball	1
Mary Settle	1
Tho Potter	1
John Senior	1
Ri Daniell	2
Widd Settle	3
Rich Knapton	1
Will Settle	2
Will Tate	1
Roger Spincke	1
Willm Ingle	1
Willm Smith	1
Geo Spincke	3
Andrew Slater	1
Rich Jackson	1
Willm Bevers	3
Robt Oddy	1
Willm Tayler	2
Martin Cash	2
John Dunnill	1
Henry Bodill	1
Tho Barden	1
Rich Bevers	6
Rich Tate	1
John Stocker	1
Tho Hopwood	1
Willm Massy	2
Willm Oates	1
Widd Syham	1
Martin Clough	3
Willm Mounser	1
John Tayler	5
John Marston	1
Benja Place	1
Tho Hardwicke	3
Henry Wright	1
Geo Dickinson	1
Willm Constable	2
Rich Tompson	4
Tho Tompson	2
Mich Hill	2
Widd Hill	2

Robte Brooke	1
Robte Shore	1
Abra Rushworth	1

m 12]

George Clarkson	1
Tho Torrington	1
John Erington	3
Sr Tho Gascoigne	19
Francis Johnson	4
Willm Rushton	3
Tho Shippen	3
Rich Tayler	2
John Shippen	1
Widd Crompton	1
John Hardcastle	1
Will Breame jun	1
Will Breame	2
Widd Gibson	2
John Smith	1
Mr Devers	1
Tho Waumsley	1
Rich Shippen	1
Will Loftus	1
Rich Tate	1
Tho Tate	1
Will Vevers	2
Will Tate jun	1
Will Tayler	1
John Pitts	2
James Hunter	2
Robt Turner	1
Edward Inchcliffe	3
John Dyneley	3
Dorothy Oddy	1
Hen Haworth	1
Marke Brunton	1
John Dunnill	1
Peter Barker	1
Robert Greene	1
Willm Fawcitt	1
	276[53]

Empty and noe distress to be had	
Edward Potter	1
Steven Smith	2
Peter Wilson	2
Widdow Johnson	1
John Norten	1
Willm Jackson	1
	8

These persons following are discharged by certificate	
Willm Lamb	1
Tho Blackburne	1
Robt Briggs	1
Widd Bullocke	1
John Gibson	1
Rich Swales	2
Isaac Wood	1
Robert Saynor	2
Richard Farrah	2
John Tate sen	1
John Tate jun	1
Antho Wright	1
Oswald Harrison	1
Rich Ellis	1
Rich Styan	1
Rich Prince	1
	20

Omitted by reason of poverty	9

Robert Husband Collr
Robt Gregson Const

Chappel Allerton
(Chapel Allerton)

Mr Robert Ross	8
Tho Burley Esq	10
Mr Fearne	3

m 13]

Edward Rowden	4
Ralph Moore	2
James Brough	1
Tho Jackson	2
Samuell Totty	4
Hen Render	1
Joseph Thornton	1
John Barnard	1
Brian Wilson	2
John Cooke	1
Rich Parke	1
Matth Barnard	1
Fran Prince	1
John Walker	2
Willm Oldfeild	3
Marke Clarkson	2
Willm Briggs	4
Rich Preston	1
George Sparnitt	1
Will Metcalfe	2
Will Wade jun	1
Edward Tayler	3
Rich Oldfeild	2
John Rider	1
Mr Totty	1
Tho Naler	3
Will Slater	1
Robt Carritt sen	1
Chr Watson	2
Will Wade sen	2
John Bell	1
Geo Marshall	1
Mrs Killingbecke	6
Alderman Hicke	8
Mr Saxton	1
Rich Pickering	2
Robt Nunns	3
Mr Edward Marshall	8
Edward Backhouse	1
Willm Smith	1
Mr Henry Skelton *pro* Clapham	1

[53] There is a scribal error since the total is 278.

Tho Horberry 1
Mr Marshall mill 1
Tho Cutbert 1
Geo Pickering 1
Jo Midgley 1
Willm Woodman 1
Mrs Killingbecke *pro* Craven 1
Mr Thwaites 8
Matt Browne 1
Mr Tho Killingbecke 4
Mr Benja Totty 5
John Orton 1
Willm Hopton 2
Willm Bolton 1
Jane Robinson 1
Tho Bolton 2
Willm Kirkby 2
Samll Pickering 1
Edmond Whalley 2
Will Wallis 1
John Sowden 2
Widd Sowden 1
Edw Scruton 1
Widd Watson 3
James Blackburne 1
John Stancliffe 1
Will Bolton sen 1
Geo Goodricke 7
Fran Whitaker 1
Mr Foxcroft *pro* Tho Batty 2
John Matthew 1
John Horbury 2
169

m 14]

Empty & noe distress be had
Tho Wallis 1

The person following is discharged by certificate
William Robinson 1

Robert Husband Collr
Tho Bolton Const

Collingham

Mr Will Chambers of Compton 7
Robt Snawden 1
Michaell Tompson 1
Rich Fetherston 1
Willm Tompson 1
Will Croft 2
Miles Tompson 2
Francis Wilson 1
Tho Thompson 2
Robt Dalby 2
Anne Ingles 2
Robt Sharper 2
Willm Riddall 1
Joseph Croft 1
Will Hopwood 3
Clement Cryer 1
Willm Clifton 3
John Lobley 1
Willm Wildman 2
Hen Burnitt 1
Joseph Mountaine 1
John Foster 2
Tho Nettleton 1
41

Empty & noe distress to be had
Mr Gill *pro* vicciaridge 2

George Wainman Collr
Miles Tompson Const

Carlton

Timothy Dixon 4
Susann Bannister 3
Antho Hewicke 2
Tho Rawlinson 1
Joseph Barteram 1
James Keighley 1
Robert Dixon 1

Widdow Moore 1
William Booth 2
Tho Lambert 4
Robt Lambert 2
Edward Rhoades 1
23

George Waineman Collr
Benja Bannister Const

East Keswicke
(East Keswick)

Chrofer Hopwood 2
John Pullon 5
Matthew Stevenson 2
Anne Dawson 1
Geo Hopwood 1
Willm Inman 2
Willm Teale 1
Rich Dawson 1
Tho Hancocke 1
Henry Hodgson 3
Widd Laveron 2

m 15]

Joseph Turner 1
Robt Sutton or heires 2
Willm Pullan jun 3
John Laborne 2
Tho Cowper 1
Tho Mawde 2
Matthew Jackson 1
Tho Steele 4
Willm Ingle 1
William Retherey 1
Robt Sutton jun 1
Anne Thornhill 2
Brian Morris 1
Rich Allerton 1
James Gayton 1
James Harrison 1
Willm Clitherey 1
Tho Steele 1
Willm Hodgson 2

John Pullan	1
Will Hodgson sen	1
Matthew Teale	1
William Thornhill	1
Robert Ingle	1
Chr Brigland	1
	56[54]

Robert Husband Collr
Willm Pullan Const

Garforth

Cuthbert Barugh	3
Rich Warriner	1
Willm Joy	1
John England	1
Edward Hardy	1
Hen Smith	1
Mr Gilbert Witham	5
John Hunter	2
Widdow Shore	2
Will England	1
Cuth Bennett	2
John Barugh	1
Brian Tate	1
Cuth Smith	1
Rich Barley	1
William Johnson	1
Tho Barugh	1
Will Heslegrave	1
Will Peace	1
Randall Dalston	2
Tho Hunt	2
Mr Ri Brooke	7
Wid Varley	1
Tho Barugh	2
Ri Woodhouse	3
Cuth Hemsworth	1
William Hollins	1
John Fletcher	1
Tho Fletcher	1
John Marshall	1
Benja Johnson	1
John Wheelhouse	1
Sir Tho Gascoigne	1
Sir Will Lowther	9
James Brearcliff	2
George Bellasis	1
John Wetherill	2
Robte Ridgill	1
Geo Dawson	4
Michaell Wilson	1
Willm Prince	2
	75

Empty & noe distree to be had	
Mr Hall	1

Omitted by reason of poverty	1

Robert Husband Collr
Robert Ridgil Const

Guisley (Guiseley)

John Barber	2

m 16]

Samuell Myers	2
Chr Myers	2
Deane Hitch	6
Nicholas Poplewell	1
Hugh Browne	3
John Overend	2
Stephen Overend	1
John Marshall	1
Tho Hudson	2
George Bayley	2
George Smith	1
John Mawde	1
James Roades	1
George Hall	1
Mercy Overend	1
Willm Harrison	3
John Myers	2
Samuell Overend	2
Isaac Myers	1
Jonas Ine Jun	2
John Rhoades	1
Stephen Overend sen	1
Rich Rhoades	1
Timo Hog	1
Tho Lambert	2
John Overend	1
John Pickard	2
Issabell Popplewell	1
John Rhoades	2
Joseph Waite	1
Beatrix Rhoades	1
	53

Empty the free schoole & noe distress to be had	1

Roger Hardcastle Collr
Nicho Poplewell Consta

Harwood (Harewood)

Steven Harrison	3
Ri Cowert	2
Wid Walker	2
Matthew Vevers	1
Ri Bolton	1
Mrs Smith	1
Henry Rearton	3
Eliz Lee wid	2
Geo Harrison	5
Willm Hakes	1
John Covert	1
Mr Tho Nayler	3
Willm Slater	1
Ri Oxley	2
Willm Hall	2
Willm Jefferson	3
John Baitman	1
James Tompson	2

54 sic.

Willm Bolton	2
Willm Craven	2
John Bywater	1
John Gibson	1
Willm Cowper	2
Widd Dickinson	1
Robt Dickinson	2
Randall Batley	1
Joseph Jefferson	3
Willm Smith	2
Peter Wright	1
Robert Wiggin	1
Mary Hawke	1
Widd Benton	1
John Hopwood	2
Widd Harrison	1
Tho Jackson	2
Robt Ellis	2
Willm Siddall	1
Anthony Browne	1
Willm Brewerton	2
Willm Shutt	2
Willm Lee	1
Robte Dickinson	1
Antho Dickinson	1
James Stanley	3
Gregory Whitacres	1
Mr Hargreaves	18
Mr Gilbert Empson	5
John Coniston	2
Willm Stead	1
	12

Empty & noe distress to be had

Mr Ballance	1

These persons followeing are discharged by certificate

m 17]

Edward Poole	1
Widd Rennyson	2
Edward Robinson	2
William Kendall	2
Matthew Snowden	1
Wid Garforth	1
Rich Grafton	1
Gregory Clayton	1
Rich Balderston	1
	103

George Waineman Collr
William Shutt Const

Horsforth

John Stanhope Esq	2
Willm Wray	1
James Tennant	1
Robte Smith	1
William Pollard	3
Widd Walker	1
Tho Clarkson	2
Benja Swaine	2
John Clarkson	3
Thomas Fletcher	3
Will Cocke	2
Willm Deane	1
Abra Horne	1
Mr John Stanhop	10
Widd Deane	1
Antho Ibbotson	1
Stephen Holden	1
Willm Smith	1
Michaell Jackson	1
John Stables	1
Jerom Bradley	1
Ri Scobbard	1
John Williamson	1
Michaell Shaw	1
John Waite	1
Widd Driver	1
John Cowling	1
James Stables	2
Tho Ryley	1
Jonath Butterfeild	1
Willm Lupton	1
Jerom Butler	3
John Collison	1
Robert Craven	1
Chrofer Standidge	1
Robert Craven	1
John Craven	2
	two
Widd Lambert	1
Mr Edward Stanhope	7
Joseph Welsh	1
Geo Hunter	2
Chr Preston	1
Tho Lobley	1
Mr Ri Long	6
Widd Spence	1
Edward Relfe	1
Joseph Marshall	2
Widd Moore	1
Tho Collingworth	3
Edward Clarke	1
Brian Poe	2
Ri Lambert	2
Joseph Lambert	2
John Powell	1
John Gill	1
Rich Casson	2
Robert Thornton	2
Mr Morgan Watson	2
Chrofer Brotherhead	2
Mr John Masson	2
Mr Greenwood	5
Mr John Pollard	5
Willm Tompson	2
Willm Wood	1
John Clough	1
Abra Powell	1
George Thornton	2
Samuell Swaine	5
John Powell	1
Samuell Swaine jun	2
Robte Cawdrey	1
Chrofer Lupton	4
Ri Tompson	1
Abra Powell	1
Josias Gill	3
Bi Sikes	1
John Buckley	3

m 18]

Matthew Procter	1
Widd Totty	1
John Knubley	1
more a forge	1
Willm Longfellow	4
Willm Thornton	1
George Sikes	2
John Wright	2
James Gibson	2
Laur Smithies	2
Ri Powell	1
John Cloughton	1
John Smith	1
William Boyes	1
William Walker	2
Tho Longfellow	2
Isaac Longbotham	1
William Peace	1
Joseph Stables	1
Tho Butterfeild	1
	183

Empty & noe distress to be had

Mr Long	3

These persons followeing are discharged by certificate

Rich Snawden	1
Daniell Holdsworth	1
Ri Collingworth	2
Chr Burne	2
Ri Tompson	1
Jo Willy	2
Tho Batty	1
Will Hudson	2
Abra Collingson	1
Henry Nicholson	1
Tho Batty	1
Geo Wilkinson	1
John Graves sen	1
John Graves jun	1
Widd Craven	2
John Lister	1

Omitted by reason of poverty 8

Roger Hardcastle Collr
William Pollard Const

Headingley cum Burley
(Headingley with Burley)

Mr Antho Waide	13
Ri Wright	2
Mr Waide	4
Widd Beeston	3
John Kitchin	2
Tho Scruton	1
John Gill & forge	2
Tho Whitfeild	2
Mr Daniell Foxcroft	11
Widd Talliford & Oven	2
Willm Atkinson	2
Willm Dixon	1
John Browne	4
Ri Atkinson	3
Will Armitage	2
Tho Becke	2
Mr John Killingbecke	8
Willm Wriglesworth	1
Rich Spence	1
Widd Carritt	1
Mr Ross	2
Ri Newby	1
Will Dinison	2
Robte Horner	1
Robt Walker	1
John Bayley	3
James Greene	3
Tho Markindale	2
Miles Thislewood	1
Francis Topham	1
Rich Hague	3
Mr Baley	3
Mrs Anne Wood	3
Robert Morris	3
Francis Batty	1
Richard Hauge	1[55]

m 19]

Matthew Morris	3
Mr Hinchcliffe	2
John Wright	1
George Wilson	3
Mr Abra Hinchcliffe	9
Will Tompson	3
Mr Mayson	1
John Mowbray	2
Widd Wright	1
James Burnitt	1
Ri Haigh	1
Mr Jo Bayley	2
Mr Hinchcliffe	2
Tho Milnes	1
Tho Staveley	1
Widd Knight	1
Willm Beane	1
	133

Empty & noe distress to be had

Edward Kent	1

Roger Hardcastle Collr
John Gill Const

Hawkesworth
(Hawksworth)

Walter Hawkeworth Esq	17
Walter Calverley Esq	14
Nath Collier	3
Willm Marshall	3
Josias Collier	2
Samuell Marshall	1

[55] Entry added in a different hand on fold.

Joseph Marshall	1
John Halliday	1
Timothy Overend	1
Widdow Daniell	1
Will Bartle	1
Widdow Bake	1
Will Bolton	1
Tho Ward	1
Geo Nelson	2
Tho Pollard	1
Ri Rhoades	2
Will Hawksworth	1
Jo Nicholls sen	1
John Nicholls jun	2
Wid Pulland	1
Fran Pulland	1
Will Roades	1
Edm Watson	1
Widd Mitton	2
Chr Mitton	2
Wid Jenings	1
John Eastburne	1
Willm Jenings	1
Edm Jenings	1
Tho Jenings	1
Widd Holmes	2
Tho Ambler	2
Joseph Blades	2
John Milner	1
John Garnett	1
Fr Cowling	1
Tho Batt	1
John Padgett	2
John Hartley jun	3
Widd Cliffe	2
John Rhoades	2
John Hartley sen	3
Will Parrish	1
Tho Pawson	1
Willm Long	1
Ephraim Marshall	1
Samuell Longbotham	1
John Harrison	1
	98

These persons following are discharged by certificate

Wid Tomson	1
Widd Turner	1
Rich Wood	1

Omitted by reason of poverty	1

Roger Hardcastle Collr
Willm Holmes Const

m 20]

Ilkley

Mrs Eliz Harrison	8
Will Blake	3
Edmond Baldwin	2
John Walker	1
Will Oates	3
Mr Lawson	1
Will Blake	1
Will Ulley	2
Geo Scholefeild	2
John Lofthouse	3
Tho Squire	1
Mr Hastler	1
Widd Squire	2
Geo Rainford	3
Robt Falkoner	4
Lionell Lister	3
Mr Currer	2
Josias Lacocke	1
James Knipe	1
Wid Hudson	3
Willm Loftus	1
Mr Lawson	5
Will Schoafeild	1
Widd Hardwicke	2
Mr Currer	2
John Lister	1
Wid Bartlit	1
Joseph Blake	1
Ralph Falkoner	2
John Walker	4
Mrs Eliz Nowell	3
Geo Stead	3
Will Bullocke	1
Alex Squire	1
Will Bullocke *pro* Phillip	1
Mr Banckes	3
George Longfellow	1
Thomas Smith	1
Rich Crawshaw	3
John Hollings	1
Tho Wharton	1
Willm Lawson	2
James Stead	2
John Berry	2
Mr Tho Haber	5
Peter Longthorne	2
Willm Lister	1
John Dixon	1
Peter Lacocke	2
Tho Bartlit	1
John Yates	1
Rich Gibson	1
Robert Sugden	1
Willm Squire	3
John Beanland	2
James Ramsden	1
Peter Yates	1
	114

These persons following are discharged by Certificate

Tho Pollard	1
Mary Turner	2
Chr Hogg sen	1

Geo Waineman Collr
John Brearey Const

Kippax

The Lady Jane Bland	15
Mr Gray	4
Mr Joseph Feather	8
Mr Bickerdike	5

Mr James Babington	6
Laur Benson	3
Hen Browne	1
Willm Tayler	4
Rich Barker	2
Robert Tayler	4

m 21]

Mr Bargh	3
Willm Pearson	5
Gilbert Gray	2
Ri Brackley	2
Mary Freeman	2
Cuthbert Bramham	3
Tho Dodgson	1
Tho Gibson	1
Joseph Pollard farme	3
John Fewster	2
George Gibson	1
Willm Roydhouse	3
John Harrison	4
Barnard Croft	1
Lanc Flemming	5
Widd Jackson	1
John Lambert	2
Samuell Roydhouse	4
Willm Bramham	2
Lanc Cookson	1
Willm Rhoodes	2
John Wright	1
John Fisher	2
Joseph Scholes	1
Tho Vavasor	2
Rich Barker	1
Mr Robte Brooke	3
Arthur Westerman	1
Robte Grainger	1
John Benson	2

Abrah Dixon	1
Tho Tate sen	1
Tho Tate jun	1
Antho Wright	1
Mr Hunt	5
Mr Willm Atkins	2
Willm Bateman	1
Mr Freeman	2
Matth Pottage	1
Robte Walker	1
Mr Henry Slingsby ten[an]ts[56]	23
	155

These persons followeing are discharged by certificate

Robte Walton	1
Willm Bigland	2

Omitted by reason of poverty	1

Robert Husband Collr
Willm Barbar Const

Leedes East Parte
(Leeds, East Part)

Mr John Metcalfe	3
Mr Stables	9
Mr Cowper	7
Mrs Peace	9
Mr Baines	2
Willm Tatchwell	2
Tho Tayler	1
Francis Ward	1
Francis Breare	1
Widd Abbott	2
Edward Parker	2
Miles Ellerby	4
Francis Jagger	3
John Tindall	1
John Browne	2
Geo Hague	2
Chrofer Kendall	1
John Morton	1
James Blyth	4
Leonard Hodgson	1
Ri Smurthwaite	2
Willm Close	4
Willm Swillington	2
Thomas Fawcitt	1
John Wadsworth	1
Robte Lamberton	1
Tho Hodgson	1
Widd Conyers	1
John Thornton	1
Mr Ingram	4

m 22]

Willm Hargreave	1
John Harrison	1
Fra Bayley	2
Antho Crawmacke	2
Robte Martindale	1
Widd Cowill	3
John Saxon	1
Tho Turner	1
Tho King	1
Rich Ripley	1
Willm Bolland	2
John Oldfeild	2
Joseph Oldfeild	2
Robert Sarjeant	1
Mr Martin Iles	1
Math Lund	1
Rich Turner	2

[56] This entry has been interpreted as tenants occupying twenty-three houses each with one hearth. But, it should be noted that there were, at least by the early eighteenth century, and perhaps before, two large houses in Kippax, namely Kippax Park, occupied by the Bland family (in 1672 Lady Jane Bland was already there), and Kippax Hall. Yet there is no positive proof that the Hall belonged to the Slingsby family, nor even that it existed in 1672; see I. Hall, *Samuel Buck's Yorkshire Sketchbook* (Ilkley, 1979), 218, 222. Furthermore, the word tents abbreviated in this form in this period is generally used to refer to tenements.

Michaell Meeke 2
Marma Nelson 1
Willm Emetson 3
Rich Loftus 2
Mr John Kent 5
Tho Clough 2
Widd Becke 1
Edward Croft 1
Geo Binckes 2
Tho Barritt 1
Adam Clapham 1
Richard Barritt 1
one
Duke Servant 1
Adam Clapham 1
one
Tho Ellingworth 1
Joseph Borad 1
Willm Brooke 1
Willm Robinson 3
Tho Wilson 2
Widd Holmes 1
John Browne 1
Math Waite 1
Chr Orgrave 1
Robte Woodall 1
Tho Carr 3
George Jackson 1
Willm Peardon 1
Mrs Foster 3
James Atkinson 1
Martin Holmes 1
John Watson 1
Marma Burrough 1
Fra Fish 1
Willm Shore 3
John Power 1
Tho Bannister 2
Tho Cowper 1
Timo Lightfoote 1
Chr Thornton 1
Nicho Coblin 1
Edw Pauson 1
Chro Browne 2
Peter Twist 2

Tho Hunter 2
Tho Jackson 1
Widd Jackson 1
Geo Horner 2
Mary West 1
Jonath Scott 1
Mr Lanc Iveson 6
Willm Ingram 3
Hen Butterfeild 1
Tho Thompson 2
John Coates 1
Tho Snipe 1
John Grave 1
Geo Wray 2
Widd Glover 1
Robte Greene 1
Chr Coates 2
John Greene jun 1
John Greene sen 2
Antho Fetherston 1
Widd Guy 2
Henry Wainman 1
Widd Saule 2
Ralph Rawson 1
George Browne 1
206

Empty & noe distress to be had
Mr Chr Pawson 1
Seth Loftus 1
Mr Marma Hicke 2
Peter Smalpage 1

m 23]

Omitted by reason of poverty 7

Robert Husband Collr
Chr Coates Const

Leedes Milne Hill or Boares Lane (Leeds, Mill Hill or Boar Lane)

Henry Marshall 2
John Wilkinson 2
Alder Hicke 10
Alder Busfeild 12
Willm Coldcoll 2
Rich Greene 3
Mr Seth Pawson 5
Mr Willm Milner 7
Fran Stubbs 1
Willm Morris 3
Tho Angram 2
Samuell Williamson 1
Sam Williamson 2
Will Whitacre 1
Steven Hodgson 3
John Nicholson 1
John Wilson 2
Tho Smith 2
Garthres Youle 2
Marma Lotherington 1
Widd Whitley 3
Mr Marke Pickering 6
Widd Simpson 1
Brian Johnson 2
Chr Gibson 1
John Smith 2
Fr Hodgson 2
Robte Cherry 1
John Chapman 2
Robte Golding 3
Samuell Waide 1
Willm Milner 1
Chr Turner 2
Tho Phillip 2
Widd Walton 1
James Walton 1
John Dixon 1
Widd Gill 2
Bartho Horner 2
John Wailes 3
Samuell Ingram 1

Mr Sam Brogden	7
Robte Hunter	2
Mr Timo Harrison	5
Geo Ramforth	1
John Thoralston	2
Chrofer Brooke	2
John Witham	2
Daniell Phillipps	2
Ambrose Hargreaves	1
Tho Dickinson	1
Francis Holden	1
John Atkinson	2
Tho Dickinson	4
James Hudson	1
Samll Wriglesworth	1
John Falkener	1
Joseph Willans	1
Thomas White	1
Elkanah Wilson	1
Matthew Bolland	1
John Pearson	1
James Hopwood	2
Widd Mudd	1
Will Fotherby	1
Rich Thorpe	1
Ralph Olliver	1
Robte Blanden	2
Rich Sargison	1
Rich Close	1
Grace Nicholson	1
Jane Dawson	3
Rich Holmes	2
Anne Gilson	1
Tho Pinckney	1
Tho Smith	2
Alice Ward	1
Tho Tayler	2
Christo Topham	1
Will Blakeledge	3
Fran Wilson	1

m 24]

Tho Balmer	2
Robt Kendall	1

John Barkhouse	3
Francis Olliver	1
Stephen Ilbecke	2
Michaell Ward	1
Tho Falkiner	1
Edward Daniell	2
John Nicholson	2
Henry Forrest	1
George Woodall	1
Brian Farrah	1
Mr Nevills mill	1
Stephen Parkinson	3
Ralph Hicke	2
Ralph Thorpe	1
John Atkinson	1
James Parkin	2
Robert Medley	1
Willm Walton	1
John Smith	2
Robte Sawle	1
Chr Chamlett	1
Abra Baister	2
Tho Greathead	2
Math Bentley	2
Widd Matthew	1
Willm Headley	1
Tho Greathead	2
Edward Sarvant	1
Rich Tinckler	2
John Atkinson	2
Francis Oddye	1
Abra Matthew	3
Widd Matthew	5
Mr John Tayler	3
Widd Dilworth	2
Samuell Burnley	1
James Blackburne	1
Robte Wiglesworth	1
Joseph Dilworth	3
Mr Hen Wilkinson	6
Hen Barrowby	2
Widd Burnley	2
James Wilkinson	2
Geo Smith	2
Robte Kendall	1

Willm Hawden	2
George Smith	2
James Tillison	1
Robte Parkin	3
John Greene	3
Widd Barwicke	1
Roger Hawden	5
John Benson	3
Rowland Shaw	1
James Smith	2
Henry Cotton	1
Tho Barnard	1
Widd Harrison	1
Joseph Horner	1
John Servant	1
Tho Emmerson	1
Rowland Shaw	1
Henry Nordice	1
Matthew Whalley	2
Henry Adcocke	5
Peter Gillman	2
Widd Strickland	4
Fran Haber	2
Capt Baine	1
Widd Bernard	2
Henry Shann	1
John Fleeming	2
Widd Hardye	2
Ri Matthew	1
John Williamson	1
Tho Matthewes	1
Will Smith	1
Geo Lapis	5
Tho Parkinson	4
John Wadsworth	1
Arthur Roome	1
Hen Ellis	2
	327

Empty & noe distress to be had

Sarah West	1
Jonath Bradley	1
Tho Atkinson	2

m 25]

Mr Garnitt *pro* schoole	2

These persons followeing are discharged by certificate

Edward Lobley	1
Willm Dunn	1
Henry Metcalfe	1
Robert Burton	1
Will Metherricke	1
Widd Mudd	1
Roger Allen	1
Isaac Appleyeard	1
Widd Atkinson	1

George Waineman Collr
George Walker Const

Leedes Kirkgate (Leeds, Kirkgate)

John Ryder	4
Joseph Pullan	3
James Wildman	1
John Smith	3
Tho Pawson	2
Ald Dixon	1
Joseph Hill	6
Chr Pawson	4
Chr Pauson	4
James Holmes	1
Tho Smith	2
Richard Wright	1
Thomas French	3
Widd Tayler	2
Tho Potterton	2
John Hosh	3
Christopher Hudson	1
Joseph Collinson	1
Jonas Clarke	3
James Atherton	1
Isaac Blackburne	3
Widd Lake	1
Willm Burnitt	4
Willm Hargreaves	4
John Hargreaves	1
Tho Watson	2
Willm Swinden	1
Anne Britt	1
Bethell Brothericke	2
James Foster	4
Willm Cookeson	6
Tho Wadnall	4
Widd Lawrance	4
Arthur Burnam	2
Widd Greenwood	3
John Chilton	4
Samuell Catton	1
Robert Gayton	1
James Beilby	2
Tho Grainger	3
Robert Redshaw	1
John Walker	1
Robert Pickersgill	4
John Wiseman	1
Tho Walker	3
Tho Hardisty	2
Chrofer Harrison	3
Thomas Hopton	3
John Harrison	2
John Chevenger	2
Rich Mawde	3
Widd Jackson	2
Chrofer Ryder	2
Chrofer Wade	3
Chrofer Ryder	2
Chrofer Ryder	1
Richard Barras	2
Micha Idle	3
Robert Ellerson	3
Robert Tayler	2
John Goodricke	1
Mrs Burdett	1
Mr Varley	4
Mr Barley	1
Matthew Wilkinson	3
Samuell Barley	2
Willm Hogg	1
Widd Coward	3
Tho Price	1
Willm Hogg	4
John Waide	1

m 26]

John Settle	2
Tho Baxter	3
Tho Wright	2
John Cox	1
Robert Goodall	1
Tho Tayler	1
Richard Scholes	1
Willm Horne	2
John Clivinger	2
Widd Dixon	1
Willm Gornell	1
Mary Copperwhite	1
Edward Faile	2
John Butterfeild	1
Marmad Prockter	2
Willm Morris	1
Mr Paull Thearsby	6
Stephen Emmerson	2
Willm Cotton	2
Oswald Lamb	3
John Coning	2
Robert Chippin	5
Timo Anderson	2
Mary Mitchell	1
Willm Bramley	2
Widd Goodall	3
Robt Robinson	4
Willm Dodgson	3
Edw Robinson Esq	8
John Bowman	4
Samuell Mitchell	2
Mr Marm Cooke	7
Laur Moore	1
Rich Cotton	4
Leonard Wright	1
Matthew Kirkby	1
Mr John Thorsby	5
Mr Joseph Ibbison	7
Tho Bickerdike	5

Marke Broadley	7
Chrofer Toppin	1
Lawr Hall	2
Marma Gray	1
John King	1
Will Bacchus	3
John Tomison	6
Willm Atkinson	4
John Andrew	1
Rich Nelson	1
Ralph Tennant	1
Rich Walker	2
Mrs Mary Allertson	1
John Hunsley	1
Willm Lupton	1
James Ibbotson	6
Joshua Dixon	4
Widd Merrywether	1
Widd Hardisty	5
Roger Hillary	2
Mrs Whelpdale	4
Edmd Graves	2
Robert Richardson	1
Widd Dickinson	3
Luke Chamlett	1
John Metcalfe	1
Tho Robinson	5
Tho Atkinson	3
Robt Parkin	2
Widd Johnson	3
Widd Atkinson	6
Tho Thesby	1
Robt Lealand	3
Willm Walker	2
James Metcalfe	3
Ri Wood	1
Robte Slingsby	1
John Servant	1
Robte Reynolds	1
George Watson	2
John Hargreaves	1
James Dodson	1
Chr Cauder	4
John Pickersgill	4
Willm Clivenger	1

Ri Mawde	1
Ri Cooke	1
Seth Shepley	1
Tho Atkinson	1

m 27]

John Sarvent	1
Matth Meeke	3
Widd Greene	1
Abra Blakey	1
Ri Prett	1
Joseph Lightfoote	1
Geo Hawley	1
John Peace	2
	395

Empty & noe distress to be had

John Horner of Tadcaster	1
Mr Marshall	2
John Gray	1
Mr John Lodge	4
Mr John Lodge	10
John Sowden	1
Edward Billingham	1
John Chevenger	1
Widd Johnson	2
Willm Dickinson	1
John Nelthrop	1

The person following is discharged by certificate

Tho Raper	1

Omitted by reason of poverty	4

George Waineman Collr
John Butterfeild Const

Leedes Briggate
(Leeds, Briggate)

Joseph Scholefeild	5
Mr Conyers	3
Widd Scaife	4
John Todd	1
Tho Robinson	1
Widd Harwood	1
Michaell Bibby	1
Widd Lister	5
Charles Mann	9
Mrs Walker	9
John Borley	1
Alder Atkinson	8
Willm Dockray	1
Tho Howing	1
John Bray	5
Widd Edmondson	1
Jerom Thearsby	3
Willm Dawson	2
Francis Briggs	6
Willm Pickering	1
Thomas Tate	8
John Dawson	5
Joseph Stones	1
Rich Milner	2
James Nayler	3
James Nayler	6
Willm Johnson	5
John Meller	3
Jos Colsone	1
Tho Savile	2
Widd Reyner	1
Robert Townson	3
Willm Hodgson	3
Rich Farrer	8
Robert Butler	1
Tho Dawson	2
Mr John Brooke	3
Widd Brooke	5
John Jackson	1
Widd Hurst	14
Mr Towers	6
Willm Waugh	3
Mrs Mitley	2

Charles Gilbert	2
Michaell Turner	2
James Pinckney	4
James Pinckney jun	4
John Booth	2
Henry Stanhop	4
John Coletan	3

m 28]

Joseph Scholefeild	1
Timothy Smith	4
Tho Walker	2
Mr Neale	8
Alex Nelson	2
Mrs Bellord	1
Willm Woodhouse	1
William Baley	5
Ellin Grunhill	1
Tho Penington	1
Mr Boyes	4
Hen Atkinson	1
Matthew Hardwicke	5
Mr Hutchinson	6
Mr Crowle	10
Willm Fletcher	4
Rich Jackson	1
Willm Mitley	1
Hugh Whitfeild	2
Mr Rob Hickson	7
Samuell Boyes	6
Willm Ellis	2
Mr Webley	1
Mr Hasle	5
Mr Geo Jackson	7
John Whalley	3
Joseph Beale	4
Willm Atkinson	3
Willm Walker	1
George Crosgill	1
James Hopwood	4
John Hopkinson	4
Rich Hay	3
Willm Fenton	6
Geo Wombell	2
Mr Boyes	1
Richard Wilson	8
James Moxon jun	8
Will Parkinson sen	3
Isaac Blackburne	5
Geo Chambers	4
Willm Walker	2
John Lancaster	3
John Cloudesley	8
Edward Cady	7
Chr Clifton	4
Peter Parke	3
Mr Timo Brooke	6
Robert Towneson	1
John Hirst	2
Geo Nayler	1
Tho Forrest	1
Widd Goodall	1
Mr Rhoades	3
Tho Dyson	2
Widd Massy	3
Timothy Kent	6
James Heywood	3
John Milner	2
Humphrey Towldam	1
Jonathan Cloudesley	4
Thomas Belfeld	1
Mr Moxon sen	8
Rich Haddon	2
Timothy Stanley	3
Ri Farrand	1
Chrofer Raynford	6
Mr Ramford	2
Anne Jackson	1
Tho Atkinson	1
James Hudson	1
	423

Omitted by reason of poverty	1

Roger Hardcastle Collector
John Bray Constable

m 29]

Leedes Headrow
(Leeds, The Headrow)

Widd Greathead	2
Daniell Jackson	4
George Beckitt	3
Tho Snell	2
John Sawer	1
John Dawson	1
James Sumstor	1
Fran Potter	1
Robt Potter	3
Georg Beckett senr	1
Willm Wilkinson	4
Timothy Crabtree	5
Oliver Ballmer	8
Alderman Watkinson	11
Arthur Todd	8
John Garforth	2
John Wilkinson	3
Michaell Gunby	1
Widdow Gunby	1
Margrett Killingbecke	1
Thos Willie	3
John Maugham	2
Joseph Loftus	3
Thos Pickard	2
Simon Broderick	4
Francis Bowes	2
Widdow Crosfeild	1
John Longbotham	3
Abraham Row	1
Michaell Barwick	1
Edward Bland	1
William Kinge	1
Edward Mackerill	1
Richard Williamson	3
Edward Taylor	4
Alderman Armitage	7
John Wise	5
Willm Taylor Jun	4
Willm Taylor senr	2
Thos Stavley	5
Richard Graveson	3

Mark Taylor	1
Edward Phillips	1
Thos Smalepage	4
Edwd Humphr & Barth Ibittson	3
Robert Head	2
Thos Abbott	1
Joseph Scholefeild	4
Willm Brunton	2
William Pye	1
Willm Ouldrid	2
Widdow Layborne	3
Mrs Sikes	3
Mr Milnor	5
Mrs Hall	4
Ralph Kirton	2
Elezabeth Dixon	1
Mr George Banister	4
Robert Dixon	1
Mathew Preistley	1
Robert Cooper	4

m 30]

Stephen Savor	2
Richard Ingle	2
William Powell	7
Willm Topham	6
Edward Massey	2
Thomas Pannell	3
Richard Ibitson	1
John Walker	1
Widdow Jeffrey	2
George Stubline	1
Robert Gray	3
Widd Robinson	4
Robert Tanson	3
Rich Watson	2
John Wess	4
John Nettleton	1
Willm Rickinson	5
Tho Adworth	3
Miles Wrumsley	4
Joseph Milner	3
Marke Freeman	4
Widd Freeman	2
John Middleton sen	3
Tho Morton	2
Tho Cressy	3
Mr Thomas Yates	4
Alex Preistley	1
Alex Foster	4
Mrs Butler	2
Tho Stevenson	1
Willm Thelford	1
Widd Dinsdale	2
Widd Dinsdall	5
Willm Horner	1
Widd Dixon	3
Robert Hurst	3
Hen Blackburne	2
Gregory Freeman	2
Lanc Harrison	2
Henry Norton	4
James Esh	2
Jacob Hardwicke	2
Widd Smith	1
Robert Browne	1
Tho Wallis	4
Tho Tayler	1
Willm Wilson	1
Thomas Wilson	1[57]
Edward Rawdon	3
Ralph Dinsdall	3
Will Dinsdall	3
Widd Ibbotson	2
Jonath Luddington	2
James Sale	3
John Ordrian	1
John Phillips	3
Rowland Dodsworth	3
John Thackwray	4
Tho Burton	1
Tho Stevenson	2
Grace Deane	1
Easter Metcalfe	1
Charles Clarkson	3
Willm Dixon	1
Mr Gamble	2
Geo Broadley	2
John Hare	2
Abra Brookesbancke	5
Mr Joseph Ibbitson	2
Ri Story	5
Timothy Tayler	2
Willm Corvill	2
Robte Scott	2
Mrs Allan	2
Mr Hesle	3
John Dixon	1
John Barstow	3
Willm Woodhead	6

m 31]

Chrofer Stubbs	3
Jeffrey Simpson	2
Alex Smith	2
Thomas Hardike	2
Timo Hardike	3
Widd Skelton	1
Bartho Ibbotson	6
Willm Halliday	1
Jerom Barras	2
Willm Walton	1
Rich Wood	4
Rich Fawkiner	1
Willm Whalley	2
Phinney Lamb	2
Edward Bolton	2
Mrs Wiggins	1
Mr Lee	1
Benja Dyson	2
Tho Kawtry	2
Matth Cowper	1
Mr Odfeild	4
Samuell Greenwood	3
Willm Sturdy	2
Marke Coates	1

[57] Line inserted.

Mr Joseph Dixon	6
Mrs Smithson	7
Nath Jackson	1
Widd Falkiner	1
Robte Browne	1
John Midleton jun	3
Robte Atkinson	1
James Bradshaw	3
Edward Sawle	3
John Osburne	2
Henry Robinson	2
George Hawkesworth	1
Widd Walker	2
Tho Massan	3
Joseph Fountaines	4
Fran Sinnimond	4
John Walker	3
Rich Powell	4
Rich Hardy	1
Roger Wise	1
Thomas Sturdy	1
Anne Smith	1
Timothy Harwood	8
Tho Wilson	2
Robte Appleby	1
Geo Sigwicke	5
John Baines	3
Tho Powell	4
Mr Simpson	10
Robte Tompson	1
John Yates	4
John Hopwood	3
Samuell Simpson	3
John Cocker	2
Joseph Hillary	5
Chro Langdale	1
Mr Benson	8
Fran Wharton	1
Ellis Scholefeild	4
George Fewster	8
Simond Rotlidge	4
Geo Hargrave	5
Mr Geo Dixon	12
Daniell Fenton	6

Tho Richmond	2
	two
Mr Pollard	2
Peter Tompson	2
Daniell Parker	4
Willm Lumley	3
Willm Cocker	2
Mr Rich Bevitt	8
Edward Tayler	2
John Barnord	2
Mr Stevenson	7
Henry Gamble	1
James Hardisty	1
	610

Empty & noe distress to be had

Mr Sikes	2
Mr Metcalfe	3
George Dixon	1

m 32]

John Milner	1
Mr Watkinson	1
Widd Potter	1
James Foster	2
Willm Waide	1

These persons following are discharged by certificate

Anne Robinson	1
Elizabeth Tayler	1
Willm Holmshaw	1

Omitted by reason of poverty	7

Roger Hardcastle Collr
Edward Tayler Const

Leedes South Part
(Leeds, South Part)

Mr Peter Mason	6
Antho Story	4

Rich Harrison	4
Tho Metcalfe	2
Rich Dawtry	2
John Gilman	2
John Smith	2
Mr Hickson	1
Mr Robt Hickson & ten[an]ts	9
Chrofer Turton	2
Stephen Hansworth	1
Anne Fearnley	1
Stephen Hamsworth	1
Willm Eshall	2
Joseph Stead	1
Robt Bococke	1
Miles Douglas	3
Will Duglas	4
Widd Duglas	2
James Holmes	2
Widd Newill	4
Ri Hargreaves	2
Will Douglas	5
Laur Tattersall	3
Mr Streeton	4
Anth Dawson	2
Tho Pallister	2
Phill Ibbotson	2
Tho Kitchinman	6
Willm Tompson	2
Tho Cuins	2
John Kay	1
John Robinson	1
Roger Howden	1
John Shipley	3
Geo Kirton	3
Robte Anderson	1
Matthew Caley	3
Tho Hopkins	2
Mrs Kitchingman	5
John Haley	2
George Turton	5
Mr Sunderland	5
Mr John Kay Cler	4
Hen Atkinson	2
Tho Thornton	2

Willm Croft	1
Samll Howden	1
Tho Coulbecke	1
Robte Coulbecke	1
Mr Will Calverley	5
Henry Bramley	3
Tho Jackson	2
Robte Freeman	3
Mr Robte Ness	4
Will Coulbecke	3
John Messenger	1
Tho Robinson	3
Tho Robinson	4
Benja Gabbutt	1
Tho Graswicke	1
Jonath Downes	1
James Swift	2
Tho Cornforth	3
Widd Simpson	3
Chr Briggs	1

m 33]

Tho Moorehouse	2
Miles Cooke	3
Mr Will Carr	5
John Turner	2
Joseph Cowper	2
Antho Reame	1
George Hopperton	2
Mrs Armistead	1
Chrofer Bantam	1
Willm Greenwood	2
Tho Jackson	3
Chrofer Lindall	2
Ambrosse Ambler	2
Widd Cawood	3
Matth Lancaster	2
Roger Kilburne	1
George Morgan	3
Widd Pinckney	2
Marke Hutton	1
Willm Hurst	1
Willm Topham	3
Rich Dickinson	3
Ralph Grave	2
Tho Brethue	2
Rose Pye	2
Mr Massie	6
Mr Ness	1
Edward Turner	1
Rich Atkinson	2
Tho Teale	4
Ri Baitson	2
Willm Womersley	2
	241

Empty & noe distresse to be had	
Mr Hen Roundall	7
Mr Norfolke	3
Tho Clough	1

Omitted by reason of poverty	5

Robert Husband Collector
John Turner Const

m 34]

Leedes North Part
(Leeds, North Part)

Mr Godfrey Lawson	8
Mrs Margt Myers	4
Mrs Ursula Totty	3
Rich Lofthouse	2
Bartho Blaides	5
Chrofer Boyes	4
Matth Boyes sen	5
Mr Boyes jun	4
John Hirst	4
Willm Jackson	2
Ezekiell Wade	4
Mrs Redshaw	5
John Dyson	3
Robte Tayler	2
Chro Marsh	2
Grace Hoope	1
Alex Foster	5
Tho Foster	4
Mr Sam Sykes	6
Willm Beswicke	4
Thomas Vassie	2
Widd Boothman	1
Willm Snawden	5
John Carter	2
Willm Clarke	2
Mr Shadmore	5
Alex Foster jun	1
Mr Blacklocke	3
Joseph Blacklocke	2
Samuell Blacklocke	1
Willm Skurfeild	1
Widd Powell	2
Tho Prockter	1
John Rhoades	9
John Rhoades	5
Willm Batley	2
Mr Edward Hellewell	7
Tho Moseley	3
Mr John Garnett	6
Mary Farrand	1
Chr Banckhouse	2
Mr Greenwood	5
John Dyson	2
Isaack Wood	1
Robte Metcalfe	3
Robte Williamson	1
Widd Adingthwate	3
Edward Humphrey	2
Willm Dyson	2
Fran Wilson	2
Judeth Ware	3
Mr Geo Bannister	8
Austin Horsman sen	2
Edward Thornbury	1
John Leach	1
Mrs Collyer	8
Rich Lee	2
Rich Browne	1
Austin Horsman jun	2
Mr Tho Dixon	8
Geo Horsman	2
Ralph Horsman	2

Rich Pullen	1
John Walker	4
John Walker	1
John Overend	1
Antho Horsman	1
Mr Burniston Carter	1
James Marrow	1
John Smith	2
Leo Catley	2
Robte Jackson	1
Jaine Clarkson	1
Willm Shaw	2
Willm Smith	5
John Latham	2
John Willington	2
John Sheppeard	1
Willm Wilson	3
Edward Walker	1
Marma Goothricke	1
Willm Wilson	2
Rich Sikes	1
Mr Sikes	2
James Ripley	2

m 35]

John Cloudesley	4
Widd Lamb	1
Mr Willm Curtis	4
Mr Abra Akins	5
Tho Cowper	1
Tho Johnson	1
Tho Dockett	4
John Cooke	1
John Whitehead	1
Mich Spence	1
Mr Walker	2
Stephen Netherwood	3
Martin Browne	1
John Weddell	1
Tho Dowker	2
Nichol Netherwood	3
James Netherwood	4
Robte Holmes	1
James Netherwood	2
Rich Ferne	2

Tho Peckett sen	1
Hen Hutchinson	1
Antho Bollard	1
Willm Falkener	2
Antho Wade	1
Willm Snowden	1
Robte Spence	1
Antho Jackson	1
Chro Dodsworth	1
Willm Iles	1
Francis Sutton	1
Antho Ward	1
James Bolland	1
Geo Ryley jun	1
Willm Heven	2
Rich Richardson	1
Chro Harper	1
Rich Gill	2
Geo Ripley sen	2
Robte Ryder	1
Matthew Totty	1
Widd Netherwood	2
Tho Dinison	1
Nicho Freerson	1
Oswald Ryther	2
John Stables	1
Tho Leathley	1
Tho Dancer	1
Stephen Clough	1
Widd Jackson	1
Willm Knowles	1
Tho Jefferson	1
Willm Prockter	1
Leo Burnley	1
Tho Parkett	1
Bartho Watson	1
Hen Jackson	1
James Kendall	1
Tho Sandfeild	1
Peter Cloudesley	1
James Setterwood	2
John Romington	1
Daniell Wiston	2
Widd Newton	1
Jo Wheelehouse	1

Geo Dinison	2
Willm Dinson	1
Willm Dinson	1

m 36]

Tho Jefferson	2
Tho Jefferson	3
James Jefferson	1
Michaell Jefferson	1
Widd Bickerdike	1
Willm Jefferson	2
Tho Walker	1
Tho Linley sen	2
Willm Young	1
Mr Tho Rasin	2
Leo Wilkinson	1
Rich Clarke	2
Dorothy Jefferson	2
Matthew Oddy	1
Tho Jefferson	1
James Maugh	1
James Shewill	1
Christo Walker	1
John Wilkinson sen	1
Samuell Turner	1
Robert Freer	1
Tho Topham	2
John Kent	1
Robert Whitacre	1
James Oddye	1
John Tompson	1
Leonard Spence	2
Tho Baines	1
John Horne	1
Matthew Penniston	2
Tho Horne	1
James Mitchell	1
Ingram Holmes	1
Widd Jefferson	2
Mr John Walker	3
Mr Tho Faireburne	4
John Fairburne	3
James Ward	2
Rich Holmes	2
Geo Metcalfe	2

Robte Stockdall	3
John Jefferson	1
Willm Linsley	2
John Linsley	1
Geo Shewill	2
Jonath Kendall	2
Isaack Webster	2
John Dyson	2
John Dickinson	2
Rich Jefferson	2
John Dundall	2
John Smalpage	2
John Sikes	2
John Dunderdall	1
	one
Robert Longfellow	4
Mr Dixon	1
Tho Vassey	1
Peter Smalpage	4
Tho Walsington	1
Leonard Smalpage	3
James Tompson	1
Tho Atkinson	1
John Sewill	1
Mr Mich Gilbert	7
Henry Bolland	1

m 37]

Henry Bolland[58]	1
Tho Becke	2
Samuell Burray	3
Robert Satterthwaite	1
William Currand	2
John Atkinson	1
John Firne	2
John Collinson	1
Widd Boyes	2
Tho Atkinson	1
John Harrison	1
Ralph Horsman	1
Brian Mawde	6
	479

Empty & noe distress to be had	
Alex Foster	1
Mr Greenwood	2
Mr Sikes	1
Tho Dyson	1
Alex Horner	1
Tho Horne	1
Mr John Walker	3
Tho Foxcroft	1
Tho Smalpage	2
Joshua Hill	1
James Jefferson	1
Omitted by reason of poverty	4

Roger Hardcastle Coll
John Carter Const

Morton

m 38]

Mr Edmond Starke	16
Mrs Crooke	4
Tho Mawson	1
Willm Mitchell	3
Chr Beaneland	1
Mercy Berry	2
Abra Leech	1
Tho Fell	1
John Lister	1
Tho Lister	3
John Watters	2
John Smith	1
Widd Hainworth	1
Tho Lister sen	2
Mich Bradley	1
Mich Wood	3
Geo Turner	1
John Wood sen	1
Abr Longbotham	1

Henry Turner	2
Will Rufforth	1
Antho Inkeringall	1
Jer Phillipps	2
Chro Berry	1
Chr Smith	3
Tho Leach	2
Stephen Wilkinson	1
John Leach	2
Geo Beanland	2
Willm Emmott	1
Will Blakey	1
James Atkinson	1
Tho Amworth jun	1
Fran Smith	1
Willm Spence	1
John Rogers	1
John Clapham	1
John Coates	1
Tho Sharpe	2
Tho Wilkinson	3
Tho Smith	1
Robt Sugden	1
Samuell Coates	1
Tho Rogers	3

m 39]

Ri Hudson	1
Jona Shackleton	4
Tho Butterfeild	1
Chr Calverley	1
John Hall	1
Tho Butterfeild	1
Robte Wright	2
John Atkinson	1
John Maskew	1
James Widdopp	2
Margaret Wilkinson	1
Mr Tho Fell	9
John Catley	1
	109

[58] sic.

Omitted by reason of poverty 2

Roger Hardcastle Collector
Chrofer Calverley Consta

Menston

Charles Fairfax Esqr	13
Mr Richard Rhoads	4
Mr John Fairfax	5
Lawrence Curtasse	1
Willm Curtasse	1
John Pickard	1
Robt Oldfeild	1
Chro Pickard	1
Jerom Overend	1
John Wells	1
Widd Nelson	1
Miles Franckland	1
Mr Mawde	2
Charles Watson	1
Geo Roades	1
Lawr Curtice	1
Widd Marshall	1
Peter Spetch	1
Thomas Furnice	4
Ri Sowden	1
Geo Pollard	1
Robte Walker	2
Rich Walker	1
Willm Roades	1
Rich Ryley	1
Widd Wilson	1
John Rhoades	1
John Walker	1
Willm Tidewell	1
John Watson	1
Willm Ryley	1
John Tompson	1
Tho Surr	1
	57

Omitted by reason of poverty 2

Robert Husband Collr
George Pollard Const

Otley

Mrs Harrison	2
Eliz Cave	1
James Pickard	1
Chro Pickard	1
Mary Gibson	1
Peter Stead	3
John Butler	1
Guy Linsley	2
Mrs Prockter	1
James Rhoades sen	1
Willm Stead	1
Mary Wrayes	2
Widd Hogg	2
Hen Dixon	1
John Brearey	2
John Ryley	2
Peter Rhoades	5
Mrs Dawson	7
Tho West	4

m 40]

Mr Idle	5
Mr Pullan	5
James Appleyeard	3
Mr Edward Barker	7
Ri Hogg	5
John Thackwray	3
Chrofer Ward	3
Rich Cave	3
Rich Rhoades	3
Willm Mitchell	1
Henry Wyley	5
Tho Forrest	1
Robte Shaw	1
Rich Hogg	3
James Rhoades jun	4
Anne Hobson	6
Willm Javitt	3
Mr Steph Topham	12
Rich Clapham	3
Willm Waide	1
Willm Cave	3
Robte Hog	3
Seth Pullan	7
Tho Greene	1
Joan Burnitt	3
Tho Burnitt	2
Leonard Fletcher	2
Tho Ward	1
Geo Newsome	3
Chrofer Whitehead	3
Tho England	1
Chrofer Parker	3
John Neale	1
Chr Smith	1
Jerom Myers	1
Willm Browne	1
Widd Hobson	1
Tho Sedgwicke	1
Geo Parker	1
John Dade	2
John Mercer	4
Chr Bradley	3
Edward Fletcher	1
Tho Wilkinson	3
Tho Prockter	1
Widd Robinson	3
Widd West	3
Will Stead sen	2
Mr Barker	3
Mr Henry Wilkinson	10
Mary Dale widd	3
Tho Rowley	3
Mr Rich Rhoades	5
Willm Witham	2
Widd Braithwaite	5
Tho England	3
Tho England	2
Tho England	1
Chro Fletcher	1
Henry Neale jun	3
Chr Shaw	2
Willm Neale	2
Geo Burnitt	1
Tho Tayler	3

Thomas Driver	1
Widd Wilson	4
Anne Wood	2
Abra Hogg	3
Willm Clapham	1
Willm Tebbs	5
Robert Appleyeard	1
Antho Hall	5
Tho Cave	1
Tho Fletcher sen	1
Mr Miles Fletcher	4

m 41]

John Neale	2
Widd Tebbs	1
Laur Linley sen	1
Tho Cumge	1
Robte Preston	1
Tho Fletcher sen	2
Fra Hog	1
Mr Faukes	5
Widd Barker	1
Tho Wardman	1
Tho Cave	1
Tho Fletcher	4
Tho Stead	1
John Bolland	1
	278

Empty & noe distress to be had

The Courthouse	1
George Smith	1
The Freeschoole	1
Mr Waide	2

These persons following are discharged by Certificate

Eliz Cave	1
Widd Leedes	1
James Farnell	1
Rich Garnett	1
Omitted by reason of poverty	6

George Waineman Collr
John Bolland Const

Parlington

Sir Tho Gascoyne	12
Mr Hickersgill	4
Antho Fullthirst	2
Tho Horberry	2
Tho Simpson	3
Robte Thornes	1
Tho Bywater	1
Peter Addinell	1
Tho Howell	1
John Cryer	1
John Heptonstall	2
Franc Richinson	1
Robert Poplewell	1
Tho Lacy	1
Robte Harrison	1
Sir Tho Gascoyne mil	1
	35

Robert Husband Coll
Robert Harrison Const

Potter Newton

Mr Hardwicke	10
Edmond Cowper	3
Edward England	4
Richard Heigh	3
Willm Totty	4
Robert Tompson	2
Chrofer Robinson	3
Mr Quandam	5
Marke Kintchingman	2
Richard Hollins	2
Matthew Dawson	1
Geo Petch	1
Robert Sawkill	2
John Hey	4
Matthew Dauson	1
Robte Smith	1
Mr John Hargrave	4
Mr Henry Skelton	1
James Brough	1
Fran Sawkill	2
John Hemsworth	1

m 42]

Rich Bugshaw	1
Widd Atkinson	2
Tho Jackson	1
	61

Roger Hardcastle Collector
Edward Kent Const

Poole
(Pool)

George Laycocke	1
Tristram Tomlinson	4
Henry Moorehouse	1
Willm Hardcastle	1
Willm Dunnill	2
Major Earnshaw	2
Hen Rycroft	1
Francis Tomlinson	1
Hen Bake	2
Will Hobson	1
Widd Bell	2
Will Mirfeild	1
Will Bradford	1
Widd Mirfeild	1
Mich Coates	2
Tho Bell	2
Fran Riding	1
Samuell Binns	2
Widd Batty	2
John Shaw	1
Tho Dunill	1
Martin Coates	1
Willm Nicholson	7
Willm Mirfeild	4
Fran Tomlinson for the milne	1
Fran Tomlinson	1
	46

Empty & noe distress to be had
Walter Smith	3

Omitted by reason of poverty 2

George Waineman Collr
Francis Tomlinson Const

Roundhey (Roundhay)

Randolf Briggs	2
Willm Hewby	1
Willm Glover	2
Agnes Briggs	1
Chrofer Kirshaw	3
Mrs Posgate	2
Margarett Holmes	1
Eliz Clough	1
Francis West	2
Matthew Norton	2
John Holmes	2
Rich Aspinwall	2
Robte Holmes	1
John Rushworth	1
Rich Atkinson	1

m 43]

Tho Dodgson	1
Robte Smith	1
Martin West	1
Tho Walker	1
	28

Omitted by reason of poverty 1

Robte Husband Collr
Martin West Const

Rawden (Rawdon)

Abra Rhoades	1
Abra Marshall	3
Abra Grimshaw	2
John Hardacre	10
Jerom Cowper	2
John Marshall	4
Tho Marshall	3
Samuell Kellett & Oven	4
Tho Holden	1
Rich Gill	1
Willm Grimshaw	1
John Williamson	2
Henry Laton Esq	9
Fran Barwicke	1
Willm Walker	1
Tho Williamson	2
Samuell Foster	2
Widd Jackson	2
John Brooke	1
Leo Butterfeild	1
John Bleasdall	1
Roger Hardacree	2
Michaell Abbott	1
Widd Wilson	1
Willm Bayocke	1
Chrofer Rhoades	2
Francis Harper	1
Nathaniell Coates	3
Chro Ashley	1
John Holmes sen	1
Tho Rastricke	1
Edward Rastricke	1
Ri Linsley	1
Widd Butler	3
Widd Grimshaw	1
Jo Harrison	3
Samuell Exley	4
John Hird	3
Willm Browne	3
John Powell	2
Rich Cowper	2
Widd Hollings	1
Geo Williamson	1
Edward Grimshaw	1
Rich Chapman	1
Fran Knowles	1
Matth Brooke	2
Willm Watterson	1
John Harrison jun	1
Willm Clayton	1
Jonas Butterfeild	2
Abra Allon	1
Jonas Smith	2
Samuell Baitson	1
	107

The person under named in discharged by certificate
Ruben Rhoades	1

Roger Hardcastle Collr
Tho Saxton Const

m 44]

Shadwell

Sir John Savill	12
Fr Ingle	11
Robert Barker	1
James Clough	1
Chro Gibbons	1
Rich Thackwray	3
Tho Foxcroft	2
John Barrill	2
Geo Kitchin	1
Tho Law	2
Willm Turner	1
Willm Webster	1
Willm Gaile	1
Rich Gibban	1
Willm Stevenson	1
Randall Briggs	1
Willm Watson	2
Widd Turner	6
John Kitchingman	3
Widd Kitchingman	1
Will Willard	2
Will Cave	1
Will Tompson	2
Alex Daniell	1
Chro Grainge	2

Hen Stephenson	1
Ralph Walker	1
Peter Stephenson	1
Stephen Kitchinman	1
	66

The person following is discharged by certificate

Antho Gibbons	1

Robert Husband Collector
Henry Stevenson Const

Scarcroft

John Ryther Esq	6
Henry Crosley	2
Issabell Pattison	1
Robert Daniell	1
Robert Peate	1
Rich Daniell	1
Ri Ryther	2
Joseph Dixon	2
Tho Fisher	1
Tho Jewitt	1
Walter Robinson	1
John Betham	1
George Baitson	1
Willm Iveson	3
Mr Ryther	1
Robte Barker	2
Rich Savadge	1
	28

Empty & noe distress to be had

Tho Dawson	1

These p[er]sons following are discharged by certificate

Jennett Grainge	1
Tho Dixon	1

Roger Hardcastle Collr
Rich Daniell Const

Seacroft

James Nelstrop Esqr	9
Mr John Totty	4
James Emmerson	6
Tho Varley	3
John Murther	2
Gyles Beales	2
Willm Emanson	3

m 45]

Willm Wright	2
Willm Tompson	3
Willm Brooke	3
Alice Tompson	1
Willm Barnard	1
John Barther	4
Rich Walker	1
Humphr Reeditt	1
Mr Atkinson	3
Willm Vevars	1
Alice Carter	4
Henry Turton	1
Robert Walker	1
Fran Linley	2
Fran Ash	1
Clement Midgley	1
Eliz Haddocke	1
Tho Smith	1
Robert Skelton	2
Cuthbert Clayton	1
Ambros Burnley	1
George Mires	3
Robert Baley	5
Robert Lee	1
Tho Hatton	3
Ri Norton sen	1
Will Hiplin	2
Tho Hodgson	1
Robte Blackburne sen	1
Robt Blackburne jun	1
Jane Hutchinson	1
Rich Smith	2
Richard Strickland	2
Edward Ingle	4
Tho Jordan	2
Edward England	2
Edward Prince	5
Robt Dickinson	1
Willm Feild	1
John Beverley	2
John North	1
Fr Addyson	2
Peter Daniell	2
Susanna Milner	1
Willm Sharpas	2
Joseph Hanson	1
Clement Clayton	1
Tho Jordan	2
	117

Empty & noe distress to be had

Tho Wood	1
Peter Daniell	1
Ri Brooke	1

Omitted by reason of poverty	14

Robert Husband Collector
Tho Deardon Const

Swillington

Sir William Lowther	15
Phillip Rawley Esqr	19
Mr Hall	2
Mr Matth Hall	6
Willm Hilton	3
Robert Allon	4
John Chambers	3
Henry Atkinson	1
Willm Hilton	2
Rich Nicholson	6
Willm Harpam	4
Thomas Pullan	5
Willm Middleton	1
Edward Shackleton	1
Willm Townsend	1
John Schoales	3

m 46]

Willm Motley	1
Widd Trewitt	1
Walter Widdopp	2
Henry Morley	1
John Beale	1
Widd Harbotle	1
Robte Clough	5
Mary Webster	3
Robte Marsden	3
Willm Shippin	2
Will Rhoades	1
John Ballan	6
Tho Pease	1
Geo Tompson	2
Tho Schoales	1
John Reeder	1
Parsonage	5
Tho Prince	1
Geo Hall	1
Arthur Middleton	2
Bryan Adamson	2
Will Evers	1
Rich Prince	2
Widd Dawson	1
Willm Chambers	1
Robte Loft	1
John Moore jun	1
John Spincke jun	2
Tho Redman	1
Willm Backhouse	2
Mr Harpam farme	4
Willm Wetherell	2
Tho Wetherill	2
Henry Reeder	2
Willm Chambers	3
Willm Sissons	1
Will Grave	2
Henry Reeder	2
Henry Oates	2
Willm Shires	1
Willm Reeder	1
Willm Kitchin	1
Willm Cawood	1
Willm Ellis	4
Fran Chambers	3
Willm Shires	2
Widd Cundell	1
John Ledsome	1
Tho Burton	2
John Ellis	2
John Chappell	1
Mr Hall p[ro] Bullrthorpe	2
Benja Robinson	2
Tho Lockwood	1
Robt Dale	1
John Wright	1
John Moore sen	1
Widd Watson	1
Laur Townsend	2
	182

Empty & noe distress to be had	
Nicholas Redall	1
Willm Hemsworth	3
S[i]r Willm Lowther	1
Mr Savill	1
John Schoales	1

Omitted by reason of poverty	9

Robt Husband Collr
Will Kitching Const

Sturton Grainge (Sturton Grange)

Widd Burnam & ten[an]ts	7

Robert Husband Collr
Widd Burnam or tent Const

m 47]

Temple Newsam

Mr Ri Whright	4
Willm Dixon	4
Widd Duffeild	1
Will Latham	7
John Peele	4
Robt Reedon	4
Mr Luke Turner	4
The Lord Erwin	45
Mr Edward Thorpe	5
Henry Milner	4
Edward Turton	1
Willm Hodson	1
Fran Poole	1
John Hutton	1
Widd Bland	1
John Bland	1
Chro Phillipps	1
Charles Hutton	1
Rich Hardwicke	2
Mrs Dorothy Bolton	2
John Hardwicke	1
Brian Hardwicke sen	4
Willm Brooke	2
Ri Cunnill	1
John Squire	1
John Moore	1
Rich Fish	1
Rich Hardwicke jun	1
Willm Reeder	1
Henry Reeder	3
Brian Hardwicke	2
Mr James Dawson	6
Widd Austin	2
John Hutton	1
Rich Hardwicke	2
Rich Wilkes	4
Willm Beckitt	1
Rich Hardwicke	1
Widd Beckitt	1
Robert Milner	3
George Holmes	1
George Graves	1
Rich Wilkes	1
Tho Bywater	4
Mich Smith	1
Edward Cunnill	3
Richard Lister	1

John Gill	1
Stephen Tompson	1
Rich Wilkes	1
Lanc Lownsdale	3
Henry Skelton Esqr	10
Tho Myers	4
Michaell Bayley	2
Mr Rich Tompson	5
George Lofthouse	5
George Swinden	4
Rich Bland	1
Willm Gawler	1
Geor Pease	1
Tho Smith	1
Mr Robte Baines	3
John Rhoades	1
John Heald	2
Willm Jackson	1

m 48]

Willm Irish	1
Mich Graveller	2
Robte Gravellor	1
Chrofer Spincke	2
Willm Heild sen	2
Edward Holland	1
Hen Leacester	1
John Leacester	1
Roger Heild	1
Willm Barnley	1
Roger Heild sen	2
Ri Dawson	2
John Browne	1
John Judson	1
Tho Judson	1
Roger Heild jun	2
Mary Thorpe	2
Abr Brocklebancke	2
Henry Browne	1
Henry Burnley	1
Fr Cowper	2
John Wilke	2
Mr Lanc Iveson	3
Hen Brigham	2
John Greeberry	3
Rich Broadbelt	1
Rich Prince	4
Widd Cotterill	3
James Cooke	2
Widd Heald	2
Widd Leatham	1
Widdow Bywater	3
Widd Moxon	1
Mr Ri Booth	3
John Walker	2
Francis Birkdale	2
Edmond Clarke	2
Samuell Hart	2
Michaell Bagley	1
Cuthbert Gee	2
Tho Walker	1
Widd Harrison	1
James Swindon	1
Willm Atkinson	1
Mich Gravellor	1
John Walker	1
	270[59]

Empty & noe distress to be had

Mr Bywater	1
Mary Knipe	1
William Skelton	1
Michaell Wray	2
George Rogers	2
Henry Wilkinson	1
	8

These persons followeing are discharged by certificate

Margarett Whaley	1
Anne Walker	1
Tho Coleson	1
Discharged by reason of poverty	6
	9

Robert Husband Collr
Ri Prince Const

Thorpe Stapleton

Mr Antho Clarke	5

Robte Husband Collr
Mr Antho Clarke Const

m 49]

Thornouer (Thorner)

Jonas Smith gen	4
Mr Elias Chamberland	3
Tho Farvis	2
Mr Jackson	2
Willm Wilson	2
Henry Tarbottam	2
John Barker	1
John Burland	1
John Blackburne	3
Willm Richinson	1
Widd Batchler	1
Willm Batchler	2
Rich Hill	2
Rich Harrison	1
Edward Tompson	3
Willm Waddington	1
Widd Wetherhead	3
Widd Cowper	1
Tho Marritt	1
Joseph Spincke	4
Rich Robinson	1
Willm Wilson	3
David Tuke	4
Matth Pratt	1
Rich Tuke	3
Willm Prentice	1

[59] There is a scribal error since the total is 269.

Willm Oates	2
John Moore	1
John Baley	1
Robert Hopwood	2
John Richardson	1
John Fisher	1
Rich Tarbottam	1
Robert Prince	1
Thomas Jubb	3
Tho Heire	1
Vincent Nettleton	1
Robte Tayler	2
Alex Nettleton	1
John Wheelehouse	1
John Birkhead	2
Hen Brooke	2
Tho Burley	1
Robte Tayler	2
Rich Croft	1
Jhon Cowper	1
Rich Tompson	2
John Hague	2
Tho Atkinson	1
John Watson	3
John Sunderland	1
Gervas Lister	1
Rich Tuke	1
Will Robinson sen	1
Willm Shenton	1
Willm Robinson	1
John Stead	3
Rich Stead	1
Widd Hilton	1
Thomas Stead	1
Alex Watson	1
John Barnby	2
Samuell Walshaw	3
Willm Walshaw	1
Willm Richardson	1
John Pratt	1
John Atkinson	1
John Admergill	2

m 50]

David Setle	2
John Cooper	1
	116

Empty & noe distress to be had	
Mr Buell	2

Roger Hardcastle Collr
Willm Prentice Const

Wothersome

Richard Jackson & milne	5

Robert Husband Collr
Rich Jackson Const

Weardley

John Brooke	2
Robert Harrison	2
Stephen Harrison	2
Tho Gale	1
Alex Leadom	1
Edw Spence	2
John Watson	1
John Smith	1
Peter Scott	1
Stephen Collier	1
Willm Midgley	2
Ri Gaile	1
Thomas Browne	1
Widd Cowper	1
John Stephenson	1
Robte Waddington	1
Rich Smithson	1
Stephen Wright	1
Widd Judson	1
George Winde	1
Samuell Hall	1
Antho Hunter	1
Tho Harrops	1
Samuell Midgley	1
	29

George Wainman Collr
Tho Browne Const

Wike

Tho Pickard	3
Antho Stead	1
Willm Stead	1
John Stringer	1
Robert Twizleton	3
Ralph Holmes	3
William Walker	1
Widd Harrison	4
Chrofer Lawson	2
Antho Dinis	3
Willm Smith	2
	24

Robert Husband Collr
Chr Lawson Const

Wigton

Mr Littlewood	2
Henry Pullan	1
Will Matthewes	1
Samll Foxcroft	1
Matth Bingley	2
Matth Burdett	3
John Waide	1
Robte Wiggin	2
Tho Ambler	2
Rich Ambler	1
Widd Prince	1
John Batley	3
Rich Batley	1
Widd Kent	3
	24

Roger Hardcastle Collr
Matthew Bingley Const

m 51]

Yeadon

Tho Marhsall	1
John Jefferson	1

Chr Grimshaw	1
Ri Gibson	1
Dinison Lambert	1
Samuell Yeadon sen	1
John Overend	1
Rich Hobson	1
John Marshall	3
John Snowden	1
Edward Foster	1
Joseph Jenings	1
Willm Walker	1
Willm Rhoades	1
Willm Walker	1
Timothy Collier	4
Willm Dawson	2
Willm Pratt	1
Jerem Pratt	1
Samuell Cowper	2
Chrofer Bartle	1
Wilm Bailden	2
John Pratt	1
Willm Cowper	1
Widd Rangdale	1
Isaac Dawson	2
Rich Barwicke	1
Willm Ward	2
John Hird	3
Jonas Marshall	2
John Barugh	2
Willm Harper	1
Chr Rhoades sen	1
Jerom Marshall sen	1
Rich Heworth	1
Samuell Heworth	1
Issabell Ward	1
Chrofer Rhoades	1
Tho Pollard	1
Willm Denison	1
Steven Marshall	1
Widd Peele	1
John Smithson	1
Isaac Walker	2
Robert Askwith	1
Henry Pullan	1
Will Smith	4
John Broadley	2
John Umpleby	1
John Rowland	1
Mr John Marshall	1
Isaac Dawson	2
Charles Dunnill	3
Rich Wilson	1
Rich Bayley	2
Eliz Barber	1
Jerom Marshall	4
Samuell Walker	1
Willm Ward	1
Geo Padgitt	2
Giles Hamond	1
Mr Laton mill	1
Robte Marshall	1
Tho Robinson	2
	92
Omitted by reason of poverty	1

Roger Hardcastle Collector
Rich Haworth Const

The National Archives, 179/210/413

[cover]

Ebor Wap de Agbrigg et Morley
(Yorkshire Wapentakes of Agbrigg and Morley)

Subs Hearth Tax

m 1]

… Morley

Allerton cum Wilsden
(Allerton with Wilsden)

Peter Sunderland[60] Esq	6
Henry Robinson	2
Edward Casson	2
Martin Hodgson	1
Richard Blackburne	2
Jerem Oxley	2
John Hudson	3
John Barstow	1
Willm Topham	3
John Cockcroft	3
Widdow Lawe	1
Sarah Illingworth[61]	4
John Sagar	5
James Hill	3
Richard Baudwin	1
Thomas Sutcliffe	1
John Furnish	7
Abraham Roades	1
Willm Allerton	3
Isaak Rhoades[62]	1
Richard Stancliffe[63]	1
John Allerton	1
Thomas Rhoades	1
Edward Cooper	2
Jerem White	3
Jonas White	1
Joseph Lister	3
John Taylor	2
Nathaniell Jewitt	2
Mr Gakeroger	5
George Cockcroft	3
Willm Farrer	1
Mathew Hainworth	1
Christopr Wright	3
John Firth	3
John Hesletine[64]	1
John Sowden	1
James Greaues	1
John Lacock	1
Anthony Hurst	2
Jonathan Jewitt	4
John Drake	4
Willm Ellis	1
Abraham Baistow	2
Richard Staincliffe	1
Michaell Lumley	1
Jonas Wooler	1
Thomas Hill	3
Mary Hill	3
John Midgley	2
Robert Wood	2
Abraham Kitchin	1
Robert Leach	1
Thomas Wilman[65]	1
Toby Greenwood	1

m 2]

Edward Wood	1[66]
Jonas Bothamley	1[67]
Isaack Leach	3[68]
Willm Drake	1[69]
Thomas Midgley	2
Thomas Leach[70]	2
Willm Smith	1
Jane Wilkinson	1

60 The reading of this name is confirmed by the *Nomina Villarum*.
61 The reading of this name is confirmed by the *Nomina Villarum*.
62 The reading of the Christian name is confirmed by the *Nomina Villarum*.
63 The reading of the Christian name is confirmed by the *Nomina Villarum*.
64 The reading of the surname is confirmed by the *Nomina Villarum*.
65 The reading of the surname is confirmed by the *Nomina Villarum*.
66 The reading of the number of hearths is confirmed by the *Nomina Villarum*.
67 The reading of the name and the number of hearths is confirmed by the *Nomina Villarum*.
68 The reading of the Christian name and the number of hearths is confirmed by the *Nomina Villarum*.
69 The reading of the surname and the number of hearths is confirmed by the *Nomina Villarum*.
70 The reading of the surname and the number of hearths is confirmed by the *Nomina Villarum*.

Willm Robinson	1
Jerem Greenwood	1
Widdow Wilkinson	1
John Bevar	1
Isaac Denby	2
Thomas Smith	1
Thomas Rawson	1
Abraham Foster	1
Widdow Wood	1
Joseph Booth	3[71] three
John Wood	1
Jerem Walker	2
Jonas Wooler	1
Willm Booth	1
John Smith	1
Hugh Jawitt	2
Widdow Jawitt	2
Willm Wadington	1
John Wadington	1
Thomas Beaver	1
Robert Robinson	1
Abraham Denby	1
Willm Bearland	1
Moses Bower	1
Michaell Robinson	2
Willm Bins	1
Nathan Briggs	1
Nichollas Stead	4
	167

Omitted by reason of poverty	2

George Wainman Collr
John Hollings Const

Armley

John Robinson	2
John Sanders	2
Christopr More	2
Mathew Casson	1
Thomas More Jun	4
Richard Robinson	2
Edward Johnson	2
Mathew Pearson	1
Robert Murgett	1
Thomas Lazenby	1
John Wright	1
Mr Teasedall	2
James Speight	1
Jerem Langley	1
Willm Thornebeck	1
Robert Mathew	3
John Thornebeck	1
Mr Simpson	4
Thomas Robinson	2
Willm Pearson	2
Richard Aireton	2
Thomas Godfrey	1
Thomas Walker Jun	1
James Wyring	1
Edward Geldart	3
John Geldert	2
John Smith	2
Christopr Heblethwate	2
George More	1
Mr John Lund	5
Willm Thornebeck	1
John Horsman	1
John Beard	2
Widdow S...[72]	1
Michaell M...[73]	1
John Story[74]	1
Henry Tempest	1
Richard Kellit	3
Robert Cresdall	1
John More sen	2
Thomas Vevars	2
Widdow Barker	2

m 3]

Widdow Crosby	1
John Saxton	2
George Briggs	2
Richard ...[75]	2
Abraham Elsworth	1
John Armitage	2
Joseph Holdsworth	2
Christopr Weighton	2
John Holdsworth	1
Thomas Broadbelt	2
Thomas Walker sen	2
Willm Richinson	1
John Dawson	2
Christopr Watson	1
John Godfrey	1
Joseph Smeaton	1
Thomas Guy	1
Willm Geldart	4
	104

Omitted by reason of poverty	9

Robert Bennet Collr
Francis Story Const

Ardsley East (East Ardsley)

Willm Bowling	1
Thomas Dimond	4
Willm Richardson	2
Robert Denison	1
Willm Nayler	2
Grace Cassen	1
Henry Tate	1
Isaac Walton	2
Margret Naylor	1
Robert Shaw	8

71 3 written over 2.
72 Surname Spence in *Nomina Villarum.*
73 Surname Musgrave in *Nomina Villarum.*
74 The reading of the Christian and surnames are confirmed by the *Nomina Villarum.*
75 Surname Waite in *Nomina Villarum.*

Nichollas Beamond	2
Thomas Lee	1
John Smith	1
Henry Tate	1
Robert Simpson	1
John Parkins	3
Ellizabeth Hall	3
Thomas Bowman	1
Henry Cussen Sen	2
John Hargraues	2
Anthony Cooper Cler	8
Mathew Poole	2
John Gunby	1
Robert Fox	1
Willm Bywatter	1
Benjamin Deighton	5
Thomas Midleton	3
Robert Schoalay	2
Henry Foxcroft	7
Mathew Hull	1
John Hutchinson	2
Joseph Hurst	2
Edward Brooke	2
Giles Peckitt	1
Robert Westerman	2
John Nayler	1
John Penington	1
Mathew Casson	2
Anthony Casson	1
	85

Omitted by reason of poverty 4

Robt Husband Collr
Thomas Midleton Const

Ardsley West (West Ardsley)

Mr Robinson	7
Thomas Casson	3
John Casson	3
Joseph Briggs	2
Thomas Brooke	2
Rewbin Leighton	2

m 4]

Willm Bradforth	3
John Francke	2
Joseph Cryer	1
Willm Allerton	2
John Fox	1
Widdow Wilson	1
Widdow Foss	4
John Chippendall	10
Ralph Foss	1
Widd Spetch	3
Willm Westerman	1
Miles Attack	2
Mr John Pickering	7
Edward Pickard	1
Widdow Booth	1
John Newton	2
Timothy Ellis	2
James Wairing	1
James Askworth	1
Thomas Lee	1
Thomas Kidson	1
Widd Barras	3
John Burke	2
Jarvice Gomersall	2
Nicholas Dawson	2
John Adamson	2
John Allerton	2
Willm Robinson	3
Joseph Askwith	1
Thomas Kitson	2
Widdow Holmes	1
Widdow Sergant	2
Widdow Rhoades	2
Mr Christopr Marshall	7
Jarvas Gomersall	1
John Tyne	3
Alice Roades	3
John Horner	1
John Sharpe	1
James Pearson	1
Wilfrey Poole	1
John Harrison	2
Richard Harrison	1
Wilfrey Poole	1
John Jefferson	11
John Scurr	6
John Smith	2
Christopr Ardsley	2
Thomas Hewley	3
Thomas Hewley	1
John Bradley	2
Benjam Rhoades	3
George Haigh	2
Thomas Morton	2
Elliline Ellis	6
John Scurr	2
Widdow Netleton	1
Gregory Tomlinson	1
Nichollas Ayneyard	2
John Barras	1
Joseph Cryer	1
	161

Empty and noe distres to be had
James Horner 1

Robt Husband Collr
Joseph Cryer Con

Aketon (Ackton)

Mr Sunderland	10
Thomas Morley	5
John Holdsworth	4
Thomas Wilson	4
Willm Hutchinson	3
Jerem Wilson	4
John Marlin	2
Willm Wightman	2
Henry Austwick	3
Willm Skelton	2

m 5]

Willm Bentley	2
Willm Scoarer	1
George Allon	1
Michaell Bowling	1
	44

Omitted by reason of poverty	5
Thomas Midleton Collr	
Willm Skelton Const	

Altofts

Sir Francis Gotherick	9
Mr Favill	9
Willm Spinke	4
Edward Tinsley	5
George Cockell	4
Thomas Wawne	1
Willm Chapman	4
Widdow Dinison	2
Thomas Hewitson	2
Henry Furbisher	1
Willm Bloome	2
Henry Foxcroft	1
George Heptenstall	1
Richd Dinison Jun	1
John Pratt	1
Widdow Shillitoe	2
Edward Fether	2
James Shillitoe	1
John Ellis	2
George Wrightson	3
Widdow Nelson	1
Robert Nelson	1
Francis Salmon	1
Joseph Spinke	2
Widdow Frubisher	1
Robert Cooke	1
Robert Turner	1
Richard Tate	2
Widdow Martin	2
Richard More	1
Richard Dicyson	2
Richard Morton	1
Joseph Spinke	2
John Dixon	1
Francis Collitt	1
Widdow Shillitoe	1
Widdow Pratt	1
Robert Farrar	1
Widdow Hardisty	4
John Favill	3
Thomas Dobson	2
Jonathan Wawne	1
Willm Easton	1
Widdow Browne	2
John Parkins	2
Widdow Parkins	2
Richard Heptenstall	1
	98

Empty and noe distresse to be had	
Mr Wm Dinison	5
Omitted by reason of poverty	3
Thomas Middleton Collr	
Willm Eshton Const	

Almond Burry (Almondbury)

Willm Ramsden Esqr	25
Mr Ashton	10
Docter Johnson	6
Thomas Kay	6
John Wood	3
Thomas Liddall	1
Thomas Hall	2
Edmond Mellor	1
Richard Mellor	2

m 6]

Robert Rusby	2
John Harpin	1
Widd Bayley	5
Abraham Beamond	6
John Hurst	4
Thomas Bradley	1
Widdow Woodhead	3
Widdow Hurst	5
John Kay	4
John Dyson	2
Whatgodwill Crosland	4
Nichollas Graues	5
Thomas Gibson	10
Francis Horne	5
Mr Robert Ordsley	5
James Redfearne	4
Mr Robinson viccar	5
Edmond Hoyle	2
Whatgodwill Crosland Jun	4
Mr Farrand	2
Willm Horsfeild	2
Edward Walker	2
Mr Linley	4
George Watkinson	4
Thomas Whitacres	1
John Hemingway	4
Abraham Lockwood	2
Widdow Senyor	1
Thomas Berrey	1
John Hurst	2
James Beswick	1
John Marsden	1
John Horne	2
Mrs Ramsden	3
George Tweedall	1
George Brooke	1
Willm Brooke	1
Edmond Kay	1
Widdow Turton	1
Thomas Rallinson	1
Robert Twedall	1
Robert Bradley	1
Thomas Marsden	1
John Sikes	1
Widdow Blackburne	2
John Blackburne	2
John Armitage	2
John Beamont	1
George Sikes	1
Willm Oldfeild	1
George Feild	1
Willm Oldfeild	1
John Oldfeild	1
Joseph Armitage	2

Willm Withers	1
Richard Scholefeild	3
George Brooke	1
Widdow Blackburne	2
John Woodhead	1
Abraham Beamond	2
Edmond Field	2
John Kay	3
John Jepson	2
Samuell Whitehead	1
Widdow Roebuck	1
Joseph Winpeny	2
Willm Kay	1
Dorothy Gleadall	1
Richard Hatfeild	1
John Hoyle	2

m 7]

Joseph Winpeny	1
Widdow Megson	2
Mrs Ramsden	1
Georg Hinchcliffe	1
Thomas Kay	2
Robert Aineley	1
Widdow Parkins	1
Joseph Hurst	1
Joseph Armitage	2
Willm Hanson	1
James Milner	1
Abraham Horsfall	1
Thomas Wood	1
Richard Stringer	1
Whatgodwill Whitacrs	1
James Redfearne	1
Roger Dearneley	1
Joseph Lockwood	1
Widdow Firth	1
Willm Slayden	1
Widdow Orridge	2

John Crowcher	1
John Woodhead	1
Mr Ramsden	1
Widdow Blackburne	1
Mathew North	2
Robt Aineley	1
Thomas Broadley[76]	1
Thomas Gilbert	1
Thomas Brearley	1
Benj. Johnson[77]	2
Geo Senyor[78]	2
Jane Kay[79]	2
Joseph Whitehead[80]	1
Joseph Hague	2
Widdow Withers	1
	260

Empty & noe distress to be had	
Jon Elliston	3
Mr Apleyard	1
Richd Williamson	1
Omitted by reason of poverty	4

George Wainman Collr
Whatgodwill Crosland Const

Batley

Edward Copley Esq	13
John Wilby	3
Christopr Walshaw	1
Willm Wormold	2
John Timble	1
Widdow Hardcastle	3
John Armitage	1
Richard Mann	2
Nichollas Talbut	2

Joseph Brooke	3
Henry Crabtree	1
Thomas Mawburne	2
Robert Dixon	2
Roger Dixon	1
John Wood	2
Willm Broxup	2
Robert Turner	2
Thomas Tompson	4

m 8]

Willm Wormall	4
John Raynor	4
Richard Brigg	1
Robert Faucitt	2
Thomas Faucitt	1
Michaell Broadhead	3
John Smith	2
Jerem Shepley	2
Thomas Whaley	1
Widdow Thornman	1
Mr Heaton Cler	4
Joseph Beamond	3
Thomas Healey	2
Alverah Tingle	2
Joseph Oldroyd	1
Henry Earnshawe	2
Henry Earnshawe	1
Samuell Jackson	3
Widdow Hardwick	2
John Beamond	3
Samuell Hird	2
Daniell Swinden	2
Mrs Foxcroft	8
Aron Oldroyde	2
John Webster	3
Ralph Batty	3
John Chayster	2
Joseph Shepley	2

76 The reading of this surname is confirmed by the *Nomina Villarum*.
77 The reading of the Christian name and surname is confirmed by the *Nomina Villarum*.
78 The reading of the surname is confirmed by the *Nomina Villarum*.
79 The reading of the Christian name and surname is confirmed by the *Nomina Villarum*.
80 The reading of this surname is confirmed by the *Nomina Villarum*.

Godfrey Shepley	3
Robert Walker	3
Daniell Hird	2
James Hanson	1
Michaell Lee	3
Nathanll Booth	7
Widdow Franckland	1
John Briggs	1
Willm Tomlinson	2
Richard Watson	2
John Brooke	2
John Leadbeater	1
John Healey	3
Willm Lee	1
Willm Dixon	1
Richard Brigs	1
John Bowling	1
Richard Hardwick	3
James Booth	1
Edward Fearnsides	2
Richard Whitley	2
Widdow Strother	1
Mr Broadhead Cler	5
The Schoole	2
John Raynor	1
John Jenson	1
John Chester	1
Robert Turner	1
John Smith	2
Widdow Wilby	2
	174

These persons following are discharged by Certificates

Widdow Cooke	2
Widdow Hindley	1
John Smith or Conyrs	2
Alverah Armitage	1
John Faucitt	1
Steven Smith	1

m 9]

Widdow Tomlinson	1
Steven Wilson	1
Ralph Worsley	1
Willm Heavisides	1
Georg Gleadall	1
Abraham Watson	1
Widdow Rodwell	1
Christopr Smith	1
Christopr Newsam	1

Omitted by reason of poverty	1

Robert Corner Collr
Willm Beamon Const

Barkisland

John Ramsden	6
Gilbert Ramsden	2
Francis Wood	1
Thomas Shawhead	1
John Smith	1
Jeffrey Ramsden	2
Joseph Fox	2
George Houlroyd	4
Benjam Houlroyd	2
Luke Firth	1
Nathanll Carter	1
Anthony Thwaites sen	1
Widdow Firth	2
Anne Thwaites	1
Mr Thomas Horton	14
James Ryley	5
John Goodigon	3
Edward Denton	2
Joseph Whitley	4
Thomas Archer	1
Edward Denton	6
Isaac Houlroyd	4
John Hoyle	1
Willm Ramsden	1
Michaell Crosley	1
Mr Willm Horton	10
John Harrison	1
Robert Tattersall	1
Francis Nicholson	2 [81]
John Wormall	3
Widdow Deane	2
Nathanll Horton	1
James Cordley	1
Isaac Whitley	1
James Royd	1
Henry Feilding	2
John Wormall	1
James Lee	1

m 10]

Joseph Fish	1
Jerem Lang	1
Joseph Hoyle	1
Arthur Hurst	1
John Bothamley	1
Widdow Horsfeild	1
Simon Gleadall	2
Abraham Eastwood	1
Willm Poole	1
Widdow Battersby	7
George Smithies	2
Charles Turner	1
James Turner	1
John Firth	2
Joseph Brearley	2
Samuell Crowther	2
Widdow Whitley	1
Edward Marsden	1
Widdow Staincliff	3
Joseph Staincliff	2
John Smithyes	1
James Staincliff	2
Thomas Deane	1
Martin Bothamley	2
John Ramsden	2
Nathaniell Whitley	1

[81] 2 written over 1.

Samuell Woodhed	3
George Rawnsley	1
John Bothamley	3
James Whitley	2
Joseph Hoyroyd	2
John Whitley	1
Joseph Cocker	1
Henry Crosley	1
Thomas Mitton	1
Thomas Stansfeild	1
James Ashworth	1
Jacob Dewhurst	1
Michaell Firth	3
Michaell Lumb	1
Jonas Lumb	4
John Stead	5
Michaell Deane	2
John Bentley	4
Thomas Brooke	1
Richard Hardman	2
Edward Lathe	1
John Gleadall	4
John Ward	2
John Wormall	1
The Walke Milne	1
John Feilding	3
James Green	1
	192

Empty and noe distress to be had

John Gleadall	1
John Firth	1

Omitted by reason of poverty 4

Thomas Midleton Collr
Richard Ramsden Const

Bowling

Mr Linley	19
Richard Richardson	5
Willm Dixon	4
John Phillips	4
Willm Hodgson	2
Willm Swaine	2
Thomas Hodgson	2
Widdow Cardingley	1
Barnard Ellis	1
John Cordingley	1
John Sugden	2
Willm Crabtree	2
Abraham Wilson	1

m 11]

Richard Cordingley	1
Willm Nicholls	1
Thomas Cordingley	1
John Smithies	1
John Lidgert	1
Michaell Gargraue	4
Thomas Langcaster	3
Richard Jewit	1
John Jewitt	1
Richard Sugden	2
Willm Blackbrough	1
Robert Broadbent	1
Joseph Cawthrey	2
Daniell Ramsden	2
Willm Jewitt	2
Richard Pollard	3
Jerom Jawitt	2
Willm Gill	2
Joseph Bower	3
Anthony Hutchinson	2
Mathew Thornton	2
Richard Collinson	1
Willm Muff	1
Joseph Ramsden	2
Robert Dineson	1
Thomas Sharp	2
Isaac Nicholls	2
Richard Denison	1
Willm Wadsworth	1
James Allerton	1
Thomas Rauson	2
John Balme	2
John Balme sen	3
Christopr Thwaites	2
Jonas Graue	2
Francis Drake	1
John Apleyard	1
Michaell Pitts	4
Steven Jackson	1
Willm Marshall	1
Samuell Ba(r)stow	1
John Cordingley	2
Willm Rauson	2
Robt Greene	1
Willm Baxter	2

m 12]

Richard Cordingley	1
Jonathan Kendall	2
John Muffe	1
Jarvice Dickson	1
Widdow Pearson	1
Jonas Cordingley	1
John Kirke	1
Robert Wyrill	1
	132

Empty & noe distresse to be had

John Holmes	2
Jonathan Kendall	1

Those persons following are discharged by Certifts

Elizabeth Kellit	1
Richard Cordingley	1
Robert Booth	1

Omitted by reason of poverty 3

Robert More Collr
Wm Marshall Const

Boulton (Bolton)

Dorothy Lister	6
Mrs Stannop	5
Willm Hamond	1
John Powell	2
Joseph Lambert	1
John Lund	1
John Stead	1
John Lister	4
Mary Houldsworth	1
John Barber	4
David Hamer	1
Willm Lister	1
Richard Tompson	1

m 13]

John Midgley	2
Joseph Midgley	2
Thomas Ellingthorpe	1
Willm Rawson	2
Thomas Harper	1
	40

Robert More Collr
John Walker Const

Bradford Westgate

John Butler	3
Thomas Walker	7
Joseph Farran	5
John Illingworth	2
John Cooke	3
Timothy Lister	1
Willm Feild	4
Mr Thomas Wood	6
John Ellis	6
Francis Holmes	1
Thomas Tompson	1
Mr Thomas Wilkinson	4
Willm Hopkinson	8
John Halliday	3
Jerem Stead	2
Edward Tirrey	2
Willm Stead	2
Mrs Sturdy	7
Joseph Ryley	3
Richard Webster	2
Simon Nicholson	3
Jonas Holmes	1
Willm Norton	1
Daniell Knight	5
Abraham Wilkinson	2
Andrew Rewcastle	2
John Wilkinson	2
John Barker	2
Robert Jackson	5
Willm Lister	1
James Blackburne	1
Henry Burne	3
Willm Lister	1
Anne Rodley	2
John Greengate	2
Samuell Guy	4
Mr John Preston	5
Willm Younge	2
Richard Ward	1
James Phillops	5
Thomas Maude	1
Henry Sawley	4
John Worrell	1
Hugh Sawley	8
David Parkinson	5
Mr Willm Naylor	7
Christopr Ridlestone	3
Henry Atkinson	4
Willm Wilcock	2
James Naylor	6
Richard Naylor	3
John Walker	4
James Browden	1
Willm Oxley	2
John Dickinson	2
James Swaine	3
Willm Hopkinson	2
Mr Shutleworth Mill	1
Widdow Webster	5
Widdow Webster	5
Judeth Shires	2
John Dickinson	2
Abraham Swaine	2
Willm Swaine	3
Thomas Sharpe	4
John Murgetroyd	4
Jerem Watson	1
Willm Nicholls	2
Mathew Wright	3
Mr Brooksbanke	6

m 14]

John Ellis	1
John Clay	1
Joseph Booth	3
Widdow Vick	1
Cuthbert Rodgers	1
Abraham Sharpe	2
Widdow Roe	1
Samuell Hudson	1
John Kellitt	1
Widdow Thomas	1
Collonell Netherwood	2
Robert Smithson	4
Samuell Tetley	1
Mr Weddell	8
Henry Simpson	1
Daniell Jewitt	1
John Wadington	3
Toby West	2
Christopr Cocker	3
Mr John Richardson	8
Richard Cockcroft	5[82]
Alice Atkins	3
Susan Boardall	2
Willm Paley	2
Willm Cawcroft	1
Thomas Holmes	1
Mrs Ellin Robinson	3

82 3 over written by 5 and next to it written five.

Mr Thomas Sharpe	10
James Snawden	1
Hugh Andrew	5
Joseph Ryley	4
Willm Pinder	3
James Jubb	1
Jennet Curtice	1
Thomas Dodgson	1
Willm Crosdall	2
Hugh Snawden	1
Michaell Pitts	3
Robert Cocker	5
James Flaryburne	3
Robert Pearson	1
	324

Empty & noe distres to be had

Mr John Preston	3
Nathanll Holdsworth	1
Willm Swaine & forge	6

The p[er]son undernamed is discharged by Certifte

Richard Shaw	1

Omitted by reason of poverty	14

Robert More Collr
John Walker Const

Bradford Kirkgate

Willm Pollard	1
Thomas Bower	3
Lawrance Hunton	2
Widdow Blackburne	3
Thomas Rhoades	3
Charles Bland	2
James Denham	4
John Sharpe	5
Willm Acombe	1
Christopr Nicholls	1
Joseph Nicholls	4
George Turner	1
Mr Dixon	7
Widdow Lister	3
Richard Atkinson	2[83]
Annis Fletcher	1
James Beansley	3
Henry Law	2
John Hodgson	3

m 15]

Susan Swaine	1
John Kitchin	2
Robert Schoalay	4
Sarah Parkinson	3
Abraham Sutcliff	1
Widdow Hall	1
Willm Farrar	2
James Swaine	1
Toby West	1
Widdow West	1
Thomas Clarkson	1
John Boyes	1
Widdow Hindle	1
Mathew Drake	1
Willm Hodgson	1
Richard Eastwood	1
Richard Greene	2
Widdow Dawson	1
Mrs Musgraue	4
Mr Watterhouse	8
Widdow Rhoades	1
James Rhoades	8
Thomas Ledgart	6
Francis Rhoades	3
James Rhoades	1
Jonas Heape	2
Robert Bell	1
Nathanll Clegg	3
John Wilbecke	1
Widdow Wilkinson	1
Matthew Stead	2
John Stead	2
Willm Atkinson	3
Mr Henry Gill	1
Willm Feild	4
Willm Horton	3
Jonas Thornton	1
Rebecca Lonnsdale	1
Willm Taylor	2
Widdow Hird	1
Abraham Hodgson	2
Jerem Bankes	2
John Winn	1
Jonathan Turner	2
John Burnett	2
Mr Brighouse	4
Willm Green sen	2
Jerem Bower	6
Francis Dawson	2
John Kendall	1
John Turner	1
Jarvice Dixon	8
Widdow Hague	4
Edward Marshall	3
Martha Pulleine	3
Willm Dixon	2
Robert Taylor	2
James Scarr	2
Thomas Harrison	1
John Thornton	4
James Marshall	2
Christopr Pollard	1
Willm Dawson	4
Samuell Pollard	1
Christopr Gill	3
John Stead	1
Samuell Pollard	1
Thomas Jarmine	1
Isaac Kitchin	2[84]
Willm Kitchin	1
Timothy Netherwood	2

[83] 2 written over 1.
[84] 2 written over 1.

James Bond	2
Willm Cooke	1
	212

Empty and noe distresse to be had	
Collonll Shuttleworth Mill	1
Omitted by reason of poverty	2

Robert More Collr
Samll Lister Const

Bramley

Mr Michaell Midlebrooke	5
Christopr Snawden	5

m 16]

Richard Ellistone	2
Thomas Beane	2
Samuell Elistone	2
Daniell Parker	3
Christopr Atkinson	2
Samuell Goodall	5
George Stainforth	3
Samuell Wilkinson	1
Widdow Hall	1
Joseph Wood	4
Widdow Musgraue	3
Mr Martin Iles	5
Edward Tirry	2
Christopr Buckley	3
John Wood	3
Mary Yates	2
Mr John Green	4
Robert Baines & Tent	2
Widdow Cussen	2
Thomas Dickinson	1
Christopher Dutton	1
Widdow Vevars	1
Christopr Richardson	1
Widdow Westerman	2
John Westerman	1
Thomas Brotherick	2
Widdow Dawson	1
Mrs Morris or Tents	4
Lawrance Atkinson	2
Ellias Inchball	2
Willm Bankes	2
Peter Bankes	2
Ralph Walker	1
Joshua Wood	2
Robert Green	1
John Spurr	1
Willm Spurr	1
Marke Crosdale	1
Edward Smith	2
Thomas Bucktroote	1
Willm Naylor	1
Mr John Ross	2
John Tompson	3
Samuell Musgraue	1
Widdow Pawson	1
Henry Simpson	1
Mary Smith	1
John Hawe	1
Jonas Ross	2
Widdow Bins	2
John Musgraue	1
Thomas Brothorick	2
Thomas Harper	1
Henry Dickinson	2
George Flather	2
John Ross	2
Henry Cloas	1
Thomas Ellinson	2
Thomas Brooke	1
Willm Clarke	1
Willm Pease	1
Thomas Lawson	2
Deborah Hinchborne	1
Joshua Ross	1
	128

m 17]

Omitted by reason of poverty	1

Robert More Collr
George Gotherick Const

Beeston

Mr Jarvace Nevill	17
Mr Willm Pickering	7
Abraham Dixon	4
James Jubb	4
Willm Simpson	1
John Dobson	2
Robert Harper	4
Mr Hodgson	7
John Naylor	1
Widdow Denton	1
Thomas Ryley	1
Thomas Webster sen	2
Giles Pinckney	4
John Stones	2
Mr Josias Brooke	4
Richard Stockdale	2
Henry Catton	5
Richard Ward	1
Robert Leather	2
Mr Scurr	3
Robert Harper Jun	3
Henry Neatby	2
Mr Scurr	2
Miles Dawson	2
Docter Watkinson	3
John Neatby Jun	2
John Hitch	3
Mr Leonard Scurr	6
Brian Newby	2
Mr Scurr	2
Willm Gill	4
Richard Atkinson	3
Widdow Atkinson	1
Robert Harper	2
Thomas Thacker	1
Mr Willm Wickcliffe	3
Nathan Clarke	1
Richard Parke	2
Thomas Motley	2
Widdow Tompson	3
Thomas Moxon	2

Thomas Robinson	2
George Hewit	1
Widdow Grayson	1
Widdow Walker	1
John Wickliffe	2
Christopr Blackburne	2
Mr Willm Ellis	2
Richard Moxon	3
Adam Asherwood	2
Steven Emerson	3
John Webster	1
Miles Clarke	1
Ralph Blackburne	1
Richard Stockdale	1
Thomas Bywater	1
John Denton	2
Richard Atkinson	1
Adam Asherwood	1
Abraham Broadley	2
Willm Boulton	1
Widdow Hannsley	1
Anthony Whitley	1
John Neatby	1
Mr Scurr	1
Willm Procter	1
Widdow Leadman	1
James Hardcastle	1
Jane Jubb	1

m 18]

Willm Simpson	1
	165

Empty and noe distress to be had

Thomas Johnson	2

Omitted by reason of poverty	10

Robert More Collr
John Neatby Const

Crosland halfe
(Crosland Half)

Willm Brooksbanke	3
Robert Bins	3
George Mallinson	1
John Garside	2
Joseph Thorpe	1
John Dyson	2
James Dyson	6
Willm Dyson	2
Thomas Firth sen	1
Edward Hepworth	1
Robert Thornton	1
John Haigh	3
Widdow Kay	2
Edmond Kay	1
Willm Ellam	2
Willm Haigh	5
Willm Hart	2[85] two
John Crosland	1
Thomas Woodhead	1
Willm Marsden	1
Willm Hatfeild	1
Michaell Blackburn	2
John Apleyard	1
Joseph Hurst	1
John Armitage	1
Joseph Armitage	1
John Hart	1
Joshua Wilson	1
Robert Sikes	2
John Cryer	1
Thomas Beamond	1
Adam Beamond	1
Willm Haigh	1
Joseph Haigh	4
Joseph Haigh	1
Willm Lockwood	1
Thomas Haigh	1
Godfrey Haigh	1
Abraham Oldfeild	2
John Eastwood	1
Joseph Eastwood	1
Edward Birkhead	3
Widdow Eastwood	1
Widdow Haigh	2
Willm Haigh	1
John Harrison	2
Humphr Whitwham	2
Thomas Mellor	1
Thomas Mellor	1
James Beamond	1
James Dyson	2
Phillemon Dyson	1
Humphr Harrison	1
Lawrance Manknowles	2
John Dysonn	1
Widdow Beamond	1
Adam Beamond	1
Godfrey Beamond	2
Michaell Brooksbank	1
John Roberts	3
Widdow Oldfeild	1
Abraham Crosland	1
Jonathan Ayneley	1
Joseph Haigh	1
John Haigh	1

m 19]

George Haigh	1
	103

Empty and noe distres to be had

John Ratcliff	1

Omitted by reason of poverty	8

Thomas Midleton Collr
John Hart Const

Clayton

John Midgley	3
Isaac Hollings	5

85 2 written over 1

John Mortimer sen	2
John Mortimer Jun	2
John Sharpe	2
Mathew Rhoades	1
Deborah Milton	1
Widdow Booth	1
Michaell Hitchin	1
John Rhoades	2
Widdow Dawson	1
Francis Wilkinson	1
Willm Barstowe	1
Thomas Hollings	1
Widdow Milner	1
Widdow Jawitt	1
Willm Jackson	1
James Broadley	1
John Hurst	4
James Warberton	1
Joseph Armitage sen	1
Richard Mortimer	1
Abraham Nayler	2
John Smith	1
Willm Dawson	1
Jonas Hall	1
Thomas Brooke	1
Abraham More	1
Richard Ambler	1
Edward Aikeroyd	1
Widdow Hemingway	2
Richard Webster	3
Michaell Bentley	1
James Speight	2
Hirst Farme	1
John Snowden	1
Thomas Mortimer	1
Abraham Jackson	1
James Mortimer	2
Richard Milner	1
Edward Aikroyd	1
Mathew Hainworth	1
John Sutcliff	3
Richard Whitacrs	2
Willm Holmes	1

John Jawit	2
Widdow Sugden	1
John Rushworth	1
Michaell Ambler	1
Jonas Robinson	1
Anthony Smith	1
Robert Hainworth	1
Isaac Smith	2
Widdow Smith	1
Joshua Houlding	1
David Hainworth	1
Nathan Smith	1
Thomas Feild	1
James Cowgill	1
Widdow Preistley	1
Isaac Smith	1
Samuell Bateman	1
Jerem Holdsworth	3
Christophr Holdgate	1
Richard Mortimer	2
Richard Holdsworth	6
Widdow Milner	1
Jeremy Barlow Junr	1
Joseph Armitage	1
Thomas Broadley	1
John Smith	1
James Jewitt	1
Daniell Bateman	1
John Hurst	1
John Haineworth	1
John Hainworth	2

m 20]

Joseph Hamon	1
	110

Omitted by reason of poverty	7

Robert Husband Collr
Anthony Smith Const

Cleckheaton

Richard Brooke	3
John Taylor	2
James Taylor	1
Thomas Walker	2
John Blackburne	1
Jonas Bins	3
Willm Healey	2
Richard Whitley	1
John Charlesworth	3
Richard Chappell	1
Joshua Tayler	3
Joshua Tayler	3[86]
Willm Mortiman	1
Willm Langfeild	1
Edmond Marsh	2
John Charlesworth	1
Widdow Brooke	1
John Walker	1
John Smith	1
Abraham Smith	2
James Pearson	3
Willm Cordingley	2
Richard Rayner	2
Joseph Bawmforth	1
John Blackburne	2
John Pearson	3
John Shipley	2
Godfrey Fearnley	2
Willm Flather	1
Samuell Walker	3
John Pearson	1
John Smith	1
Samuell Bins	1
Henry Wadington	2
Isaac Firth	2
John Firth	1
Mr Thorndike	2
Henry Smith	1
John Mitchill	1
Willm Walker	1
Henry Pearson	1
Thomas Todd	1

[86] sic.

George Butler	3
Jonas Deighton	1
John Todd	1[87]
John Butterworth	3
Jerem Thornton	2
John Cutle	1
John Holdsworth	1
Richard Pollard	1
James Greaue	3
Willm Pearson	1
Robert Liversidge	2
Willm Healey	2
Willm Pinder	3
Edward Brooke	2
The Milne	1
Willm Walker	1
Joseph Pearson	1
	100

Empty and noe distres to be had

Thomas Oates	2

These p[er]sons following are discharged by Certificates

Richard Holdsworth	1
Willm Bankes	2

Omitted by reason of poverty	2

Roger Hardcastle Collr
Isaac Firth Const

m 21]

Calverley cum Fearsley (Calverley with Farsley)

Walter Calverley Esqr and Tennants	20
John Hollingworth	3
Joseph Rawson	1
Samuell Moss	1
Mr George Richardson	4
Richard Aikeroyde	1
Willm Tompson	2
Richard Gill	2
Francis Jackson	1
John Kitson	2
Samuell Kitchin	2
Willm Baites	1
Edward Kitchin	1
Willm Kitchin	1
Francis Knowles	4
Willm Coates	1
Willm Flather	1
Robert Haste	1
Nichollas Johnson	1
Widdow Williamson	1
John Robinson	1
Widdow Haire	2
Timothy Haire	1
Jerem Watterworth	2
Barnard Dawson	2
Thomas Browne	1
John Harper	3
Samuell Tennant	1
Willm Ward	1
Henry Haste	1
Thomas Fletcher	2
Andrew Haire	1
John Robson	1
Widdow Charlesworth	2
Mathew Myers	1
Mr Berrey	2
Widdow Allonbrigg	2
John Strickland	1
Richard Aske	3
James Brafitt	1
Mr Robert Ibison	1
James Milner	1
Jonas Smith	1
Hugh Watterworth	1
Samll Moss	3
Richard Ranson	1
Robert Snowden	6
Widdow Hainsworth	1
Willm Robinson	1
Widdow Brookesbanke	1
Samuell Smith	1
Widdow Stanley	3
Widdow Bins	1
Widdow Illingworth	4
Thomas Fairbanke	1
Willm Smith	2
Joseph Kitchin	1
Joseph Flather	4
Willm Nicholls	2
Daniell Thackeray	1
Widdow Thresh	1
Widdow Smith	2
Widdow Rhoades	1
Samuell Warde Jun	2
Brian Poe	1
Samuell Waid	1
John Carter	1
Willm Waid	1
Joseph Bradley	1
Willm Waid	1
Edmond Falshawe	1
Widdow Netleton	1
Joseph Waide	1
Richard Waide	1
Francis Walton	1
Willm Hainworth	1
	137

Empty and noe distrress to be had

Matthew Myers	1
The Free Schoole	1
Robert Houlegate	1

m 22]

These persons following are discharged by Certiftes

[87] Todd written twice, the first time corrected from Dodd.

Thomas Flather	2
Widdow Myers	1
Omitted by reason of poverty	4

Robert More Collr
Samuell Smith Const.

Churwell

Mr Robert Pickering sen	5
Mr Robert Pickering Jun	4
Willm Webster	1
Thomas Walker	2
Willm Brighton	1
John Crowther	2
James Haward	1
Thomas Kilborne	2
Mathew Jefferson	2
Thomas Best	5
Mathew Jefferson	2
Willm Burnley	4
Ralph Johnson	3
Christopher Bowes	1
Widdow Winter	2
Christopr Binkes	1
Willm Ellis	1
Thomas Kilburne sen	2
Willm Muster	1
Willm Walker	1
Francis Haigh	2
John Mattison	2
Willm Webster	1
John Richinson	2
Willm Lonnsdale	3
George Simond	1
Ralph Iveson	1
Thomas Askwith	1
	56
Omitted by reason of poverty	3

Robert More Collr
George Simond Const

Cumberworth halfe (Cumberworth Half)

Mathew Oxley	1
Willm Copley	1
John Bilcliff	2
Willm Brooke	2
Mr Wheatley	3
Widdow Oxley	3
Joseph Chld[88]	2
Willm Oxley	2
George Brooke	1
George Brooke Jun	2
Thomas Naylor	1
Robert Lockwood	2
Thomas Feild	1
Richard Turner	1
Edward Green sen	2
John Child	1
Thomas Horne	4
Henry Horne	2
John Ratcliff	1
Edward Gouldall	1
James Ellis	1
Thomas Firth	2
Daniell Dyson	1
Widdow Blackburne	1
Willm Morehouse	3
Henry Gillott	1
George Farrand	2
Willm Radley	1
Henry Gilliot	1
John Naylor	1
John Bradsbury	2
Willm Oxley	1
m 23]	
	52

Robert More Collr
John Lee Const

Criglestone (Crigglestone)

Andrew Steele	2
John Raynor	3
Widdow Hall	3
Thomas Parkinson	2
Francis Jepson	1
	one
Widdow Womersley	2
John Hurst	2
George Allot	5
John Kay	2
Richard Oxley	2
John Blacker	2
Esward Ardsley	2
Thomas Webster	2
John Bedforth	1
Thomas Bradfeild	1
John Clarkson	4
Willm Brooke	1
Thomas Garlicke	1
Thomas Milner	1
Widdow Milner	1
John Linley	2
Robert Cusworth	1
John Pollard	2
Widdow Cusworth	2
Francis Booth	4
Willm Brooke	1
Jonas Burnitt	5
Thomas Shillitoe	1
Bryan Clarkson	3
Jarvice Norton	5
Michaell Lee	1
Richard Mitchill & forg	2
Joseph Hutchinson	2
John Pearson	1
Thomas Almaine	1
Robert Rayner	3
Widdow Beavor	4
Edward Crawshawe	4
Willm Greenfeild	1
Anthony Tynne	2

[88] A dot above the name suggests the surname Child.

Francis Stringer	2
Widdow Parkins	3
Willm Baxter	2
Widdow Wood	1
Widdow Baine	5
Thomas Lee	1
Francis Pashley	2
John Challenger	3
Thomas Parkinson	2
Mr Joseph Poole	4
John Beamond	1
Michaell Mathowes	1
Thomas Booth	2
John Waid	1
Thomas Bedforth	2
John Bacon	3
John Clarke	2
Mr George Ellis	6
Robert Oxley	1
Joseph Dickson	3
Widdow Thornton	1
John Barke	1
Widdow Beck	2
Widdow Jackson	2
Willm Bacon	1
Christopher Gibson	1
Christopr Rhoades	4
Charles Winter	2
Thomas Sikes	1

m 24]

James Ellam	2
John Sparke	1
Richard Swallow	5
Joseph Morrell	4
Thomas Johnson	3
Widdow Johnson	2
Willm Norton	3
Mr Thomas Pilkinton	6
Richard Crosland	1
Willm Hawcroft	1
Anthony Tynn	1
Mrs Wood	2
John Hutchinson	1
	181

Empty & no distress to be had

Joseph Oxley	2

Omitted by reason of Poverty 15

Robt Bennit Collr
Jarvice Norton Const

Crofton

John Clayton Esqr	9
Edward Browne Cler	4
Thomas Watterson Esqr	5
Mr Wm Champney	11
Thomas Mason	5
Christopr Tucker	1
John Scholey	1
Widdow Wrayth	3
Willm Dodgson	3
John Dodgson	2
Samuell Haigh	2
Robert Bolland	2
Willm Hessam	2
Francis Field	1
Robert Hartley	1
Robert Mason	1
Edward Essam	1
Widdow Bingley	1
Francis Hepworth	3
Edward Nottingham	1
Edward Hearing	1
Robert Chadburne	2[89] two
Willm Duffin	2
Francis Hepworth	1
Lawrance Royston	1
Thomas Hargraues	2
Mathew Walker	1
Thomas Jubb	1
Joseph Ardsley	2
Robert Ratcliff	1
Thomas Quibell	1
John Firth	1
Richard Nottingham	1
Thomas More	2
	78

Omitted by reason of poverty 13

Thomas Midleton Collr
George Firth Const

Dewsberrey (Dewsbury)

John Peables Esqr	8
Mr Josias Broadhead	4
Thomas Netleton	6
Thomas Whitacrs	6
Edmond Copley	3
Edward Dawson	2
Christopr Dixon	4
Willm Shipley	2
Christopr Dixson	1
Willm Dawson	1
John Ashley	4
Thomas Fox	1
Martin Parker	2
Abraham Tilson	2
John Langfeild	2
John Graues	2
John Thornes	2
Nichollas Naylor	3
James Bradley	4
Widdow Bradley	4
Henry Ellis	1
Thomas Greenwood	3
Edward Whitley	4
Richard Savill	4[90] fower

[89] 2 written over 1
[90] 4 written over 2

Henry Ellis	2
Robert Wheatley	2
Edward Newshame	2
Widdow Auty	1
Simon Buckler	2
Thomas Carr	2
George Chestor	3
Michaell Wheatley	1
Henry Ellis sen	2
Jacob Earnshawe	1
Edward Ellis	1
Nichollas Ellis	1
Richard Jebson	4
Joseph Johnson	1
John Bedforth	7
John White	2
Henry Jebson	1
Widdow Hepworth	1
Sarah Williamson	3
Richard Tirrey	6
Richard Thackeray	2
James Fearley	3
Abraham Greenwood	1
John Greenwood	2
Israell Oldroyd	5
Richard Houldsworth	2
Willm Houldsworth	2
Edward Auty	3
Robert Linley	1
Tempest Wheatley	3
Henry Barber	3
Willm Wilson sen	1
Willm Wilson Jun	1
Timothy Kitchin	3
Robert Beckwith	2
Willm Whitley	1
Timothy Kidson	1
John Milnes sen	1
Richard Chester	1
John Crawshaw	1
John Morehouse	1
Willm Webster	4
John Barker	2
Joseph Oldroyde	10
James Williams	3
James Dawson	6
Robert Senyer	3
Esai Oldroyd	4
Richard Dawson	2
Willm Greene	1
Ayron Ellis	1
Willm Auty	3
Thomas Allon	1
John Jackson	1

m 26]

Willm Crosley	1
Nichollas West	1
Thomas Johnson	1
John Parker	1
Jonas Roberts	3
Robert Craven	1
John Graues	1
Willm Fostard	2
Thomas Brooke	2
Joseph Autey	1
Michaell Parker	2
Thomas Webster	5
	222

Empty and no distress to be had	
The parsonage house	2
Omitted by reason of poverty	13

Robert Corner Collr
Thomas Brooke Const

Dalton

Mr Richard Langley	3
Mr Arthur Langley	3
John Dyson	1
John Dyson	4
George Beamond	5
George Dyson	1
Arthur Brooke	1
Edmond Parkins	1
George Kilner	1
Arthur Brooke	1
Widdow Gleadall	1
Richard Dysonn	1
John Horsfall	2
John Brooke	4
Christopr Brooke	2
John Brooke	1
James Midleton	3
John North	3
Thomas Hurst	1
Willm Brooke	2
John Milns	2
Willm Haigh	2
Arthur Brooke	1
John Spivie	2
Abraham Lockwood	2
Richard North	1
Widdow Ledgert	1
Edward Brooke	1
John Thornton	2
Mr Ainely	2
John Lockwood	1
Adam Ledgert	2
Edward Hanson	2
Willm North	2
Abraham Kay	1
Richard Spivie	2
Mathew Hurst Jun	1
Edmond Spivie	1
George Hurst	1
Willm Wickerrman	4
Willm Kay	1
Richard Milnes	1
John Cooper	1
Joseph Walton	2
George Strafforth	1
Richard Thewliss	3
Joseph Dyson	2
Thomas Eastwood	2
John Dyson	1
Richard Horsfall	2
Walter Bradley	2
Thomas Kilner sen	1
Thomas Kilner Jun	1
John Horsfall	1

Richard Hepworth	2
Thomas North	1
John Hoyle	2
Joseph Senyer	1
Richard North	1
Mr Langley	1
Joseph Dyson	1
	104

Empty and no distress to be had

Willm North	1
Widdow Legard	1

m 27]

Omitted by reason of poverty	6

Robert Husband Collr
John Spivie Const

Drighlington cum Aldwalton (Drighlington with Adwalton)

John Rayner	3
Willm Darnbrooke	4
James Crabtree	2
James Whitehead	2
John Rayner	2
Willm Fawcett	2
Widdow Peele	5
Henry Brooke	1
Ellizabeth Brooke	4
Richard Brooke	3
Anne Scott	1
Willm Brooke	10
Mr George Usher	6
Richard Baine	5
Isaac Brooke	2
Steven Browne	1
Richard Hodgson	5
Isaac Smith	3
Joseph Wilson	2
George Stapleton	1
Willm Wary	3
Willm Browne	4
Thomas Wilson	2
John Scott	3
Joseph Scholefeild	1
Stephn Stainforth	1
Richard Margisson	2
James Sikes	2
Josias Ellingworth	4
Edmond Waide	3
Mr Willm Brooke	8
John Wood	6
Willm Scott	4
Willm Coward	1
John Holdsworth	1
Christopr Waide	1
Patient Margisson	1
Nichollas Dixon	1
Robert Bedforth	3
Francis Tompson	2
Robert Elstubb	1
Willm Batt	1
John Wilson	1
Richard Brooke	2
Willm Deacon	2
Robert Hargraues	2
Martin Barker	1
John Eltoft	1
Willm Robinson	1
	129

Empty and noe distress to be had

Mr Ballance Schoole	3
Omitted by reason of poverty	6

Robert Husband Collr
Henry Brooke Const

Ealland cum Greetland (Elland with Greetland)

Mr Willm Lambert	7
Willm Poole	2
Michell Illingworth	2
Ellizabeth Robinson	1
Rowland Parke	1
Daniell Maude	1
Rowland Parke Sen	1
Widdow Houldsworth	4
John Brooksbanke	3
Widdow Savill	5
Abraham Bentley	4
Gabriell Bentley	4
John Hoyle	3
Mary Bradley	1
Willm Harper	1
Joseph Crawther	1
Robert Langcaster	5
Isaac Baites	7
John Sharpe	2
Robert Lumbe	1
John Gillett	3
Mathew Baites	4
John Robinson[91]	…
Widdow Slator[92]	…
Michaell[93]	…
John[94]	…

m 28]

Willm Clayton	1
Richard Redihough	1
Willm Varley	1
Abraham Farrar	1
Robert Thomas	4
Abraham Baites	1
Caleb Cockcroft	1

91 Edge of membrane torn away. *Nomina Villarum* gives 2.
92 Edge of membrane torn away. *Nomina Villarum* gives 6.
93 The edge of the membrane is torn away, but the *Nomina Villarum* gives the surname as Crowther.
94 *Nomina Villarum* gives Sunderland and 1.

James Jashworth	2
Simeon Townend	2
Susan Thomas	1
Jonas Thomas	2
Abraham Farrar Jun	2
John Greenwood	1
Christopr Thomas	1
Widdow Lund	2
John Walker	2
Mr Daniell Towne	3
Ambros Wiggin	1
Richard Cockcroft	1
Gregory Boulton	1
	104

Omitted by reason of poverty 17

Robert Corner Collr
Luke Greenwood Const

Emley

Mr Edward Smith	11
Mrs Beatrice Allot	10
Thomas Robinson Cler	6
Mrs Mary Wheatley	5
Mr Robert Inman	4
Robert Page	4
Francis Taylor	4
Mathew Slack	1
Widdow Allot	8
Widdow Allot	4
James France	1
Mrs Wheatley	3
Mrs Wheatley	1
Mr Willm Wheatley	2
Richard Clayton	1
Adam Woffenden	4
Joseph Sikes	1
John Senyer	1
Joseph Marshall	1
John Taylor	1
John Auldfeild	1
Thomas Shaw	1
George Parker	1
Thomas Hawkesworth	1
Richard Mountaine	1
Christopr Allott	1
Widdow Blacker	1
Richard Smith	2[95] two
Daniell Ditch	1
John Denton	3
Thomas Archer	2
Simeon Vessoy	2
Parsevell Whitacres	1
John Sikes	2
Joseph Hepworth	2
Peter Warburton	3
Mary Kay	2
Widdow Marshall	1
Widdow Bedforth	1
Thomas Allot	1
John Hepworth	3
Willm Bedforth	2
John Lockwood	1
Nichollas Walshawe	4
John Gleadall	1
Martin Hepworth	1
Brice Allot	2
John Morehouse	1
Widdow Hague	2
Widdow Haire	3
James Wilkinson	1
John Booresouse	1
Grace Slack	1

m 29]

Thomas Bayldon	1
Willm Blacker	1
Richard Wilkinson	1
Willm Smith	2
Mr Richd Farington	1
	132

Omitted by reason of poverty 23

Robert Husband Collr
Nichollas Walshaw Const

Ecclesall
(Eccleshill)

Mr John Stanhop	8
John Raynor	3
Christopr Armistead	3
John Raynor	4
Widdow Aikeroyd	2
Jerem Sowden	2
John Hodgon	2
Widdow Browne	2
Willm Sowden	2
Richard Milnes	2
Widdow Keighley	1
John Nicholls	2
John Broadley	1
Lyonell Fletcher	1
Edward Thomas	1
Thomas Hill	1
James Milner	1
James Horton	1
Thomas Wilkinson	2
John Viccars	2
John Mathewes	1
John Brashawe	1
Robert Thornton	1
Willm Kitson	1
James Fletcher	1
Willm Robinson	1
Willm Farrer	1
James Fletcher	3
Willm Armitage	2
Cristopr Wilson	4
John Berrey	1
John Horsfeild	1
Widdow Beckwith	2
Abrah Barraclough & forg	2

[95] 2 written over 1

Abraham Nichols	1
Willm Norton	1
John Broadley	1
Martin Wilson	1
Widdow Iue	2[96]
	two
John Hurd	3
Lyonell Fletcher	1
John Viccars	1
James Viccars	2
Peter Cooper	1
Christopr Gill	1
Thomas Marton	1
Willm Swaine	2
Robert Armitage	2
Humphrey Kellitt	1
Jonas Deane	1
Willm Kidson Jun	2
John Whitehead	1
Willm Sowden	1
	91
m 30]	
Widdow Slater	4
Widdow Shaw	2
Richard Broadley	1
John Wilson	3
John Lawson	2
Widdow Horner	3
John Wilkinson	3
Widdow Robinson	1
Abraham Slater	4
Brian Thornhill	1
John Coates	3
Martin Crosley	2
Joseph Ackersley	1
Mr Teasedale	4
Widdow Wilson	3
Nathanll Carter	1
Martin Crosley	1

James Coates	2
Edward Saltenstall	3
John Armitage	1
Widdow Maywood	4
Toby Slator	2
Joseph Wrayth	3
Edmond Whitworth	1
Henry Sumerscales	3
John Milner	2
Mr Abraham Dyson	8
Michaell Wilson	2
James Coates	1
Lawrance Manknowles	6
John Clay	1
James Wells	1
Abraham Firth	4
Abraham Nicholls	1
John Slaytor	2
Henry Wilkinson	1
Toby Slator	2[97]
	two
Willm Wilson	1
Mr John Whittell	4
Robert Whittell	1
John Green	2
John Whittell	2
James Lumbe	1
Widdow Crowther	1
Willm Wells	2
James Burne	1
Mr Thurston	6
Henry Crosley	3
Benjam Hoyle	2
Gilbert Brooksbanke	3
Timothy Hoyle	1
Timothy Hoyle	1[98]
Michll Marwood	1
John Brooke	4
Edward Haigh	5
Michaell Haigh	2
Joseph Thornton	1

Willm Haigh	5
James Beamond	1
Jonas Pollard	1
Jonas Pollard Jun	2
John Horoby	2
Mrs Clay	1
Mr Clay	5
James Butterwood	5
John Sleeton	3
Nathanll Carter	2
John Garside	3
Henry Wilson	1
Ellingstone farme	1
Henry Ramsden	2
George Ramsden	1
Samuell Boyes	2
John Bentley	4
Mr Joseph Ramsden	6
James Raunsley	1
Edward Chadwick	1
Widdow Savill	1
John Maude	5
Michaell Gleadall	1
John Cradock	2
Widdow Bothamley	2
Mrs Dorathy Savill	6
Joseph Jagger	2
Widdow Ramsden	2
Edward Hague	2
Mathew Hill	1
Isaac Baites	2
m 31]	
Jerom Carter	3
Willm Denton	1
George Bothamley	1
James Gleadall	2
Joseph Smithson	3
David Preistley	1
Joseph Gleadell	1

[96] 2 written over 1.
[97] 2 written over 1.
[98] sic.

Mr Henry Ramsden	8
George Ramsden	5
John Preistley	1
John Hanson	2
	309
	1[99]
Total	310

Those persons following are discharged by Certificates

Widdow Langcaster	1
Willm Meadley	1
Nichollas Poole	1
Gilbert Crowther	1
John Sunderland	1
Ellizabeth Whitacrs	1
Nicholas Brooksbank	1
Abraham Haigh	1
Godfrey Crosland	1
Samuell Crosley	1
James Ashman	1
Thomas Shaw	1
Willm Hillam	1
John Wrigley	1
Anthony Hoyle	1
Michaell Robinson	1
Robert Hollingworth	1
Henry Preistley	1
John Whitworth	1

Omitted by reason of poverty	2

Thomas Midleton Collr
Henry Ramsden Const

Erringden

Robert Holshead	4
John Ulley	2[100]
	two
Joseph Wood	1
Daniell Holshead	1
John Thorpe	1
Abraham Heape	1
John Ashworth	2
Abraham Ashworth	2
John Ingham	1
John Chatburne	1
Isaac Ingham	1
Anthony Naylor	1
Thomas Witton	1
John Horne	1
Abraham Feilding	2
John Utley	1
Paull Greenwood	3
Mathew Sutcliffe	1
Willm Crabtree	2
Simeon Kershaw	2
John Briggs	2
Abraham Earnshaw	1
John Greenwood	2
Willm Barret	1
Henry Cockcroft	2
Henry Cockcroft sen	1
Robert Sutcliff	3
Nathanll Hellewell	1
Isaac Milton	2
John Hellewell	1
Robert Watmough	5
Simond Widdop	3
Willm Wriglesworth	1
Luke Greenwood	3
Willm Hanson	4
Richard Thomas	4
Robert Sutcliffe	5
Henry Clayton	1

m 32]

Robert More Collr
Jerem Sowden Const

Flockton Over (Flockton)

Sr John Kay	20
John Oates	8
John Pickup	2
Michaell Broadley	1
John Mason	1
Willm Stead	2
John Hamerton	1
Richard Armitage	1
Widdow Beamond	1
Richard Tyas	1
Widdow Fisher	1
John Armitage	3
Widdow Kay	2
John Ashton	2
Richard Deighton	3
Widdow Beamond	2
Thomas Lee	1
John Brooke	4
Thomas Hepworth	4
Richard Williamson	2
John Carter	1
Robert Carter	2[101]
	two
Joseph Greenald	2
Joseph Broadhead	1
Edward Day	1
John Kay	1
Edward Boothroyd	1
Christopr Sikes	1
John Littlewood	1
Joseph Lee	2
Edward Hanby	1
John Wood	1
Widdow Kay	1
	78

Omitted by reason of poverty	1

99 sic.
100 2 written over 1.
101 2 written over 1.

George Wainman Collr
Nichollas Broad Const

Flockton Nether (Flockton)

George Copley	2
Steven Eastwood & forge	3
Richard Procter	1
John Copley	3
Willm Mountaine	2
John Hardcastle	1
Mrs Farrington	3
Steven Walton	2
Richard Eastwood	1
Widdow Hardcastle	1
Widdow Watterhouse	2
Mathew Mitchell	2
Mathew Mitchell	1
Mathew Gawthrop	1
John Wriglesworth	6
John Blakey	1
John Archer	2
Willm Stringer	2
John Blakey	1
Katherine Shillitoe	1
Thomas Peace	2
Thomas Rhoades	2
Anthony Bedforth	1
Mathew Gawthrop	1
Richard Wilcock	3
George Bingley	1
John Bedforth	2
Robert Stox	1
George Kilner	1

m 33]

Robert Goulthrop	1
John Goulthrop	3
Robert Cropper	1
Thomas Bedforth	1
Toby Beamond	1
Widdow Beamond	1
John Coulthropp	1
	61

Omitted by reason of poverty	5

Geo Wainman Collr
Geo Bingley Const

Farnley Tyas

Sir John Kay	22
Richard Haire	4[102] fower
Ralph Horne	3
John Morehouse	1
Peter Kay	2
Willm Lodge	1
Robert Kay	1
Grace Dyson	1
Thomas Hepworth	1
John Lodge	1
Widdow Stansoll	2
Widdow Tyas	2
Robert Tweedall	1
George Harpin	1
John Scholefeild	2
Henry Longthwaite	1
Joseph Kay	2
Willm Wood	1
Richard Gill	2
John Eastwood	2
Widdow Harpin	2
Willm Kay Jun	2
George Thewlas	1
Francis Farrand	1
John Harpin	1
John Kay	1
Abraham Roberts	1
Widdow Sikes	1
Widdow Tyas	1
Thomas Mellor	2
Robert Wood	1
Willm Tweedlar	2
Miles Schoalefeild	1
Willm Sikes	1
Thomas Slayter	1
Joseph Hattersley	1
Widdow Farrand	1
John Kay	1
John Harpin	1
	76

Thomas Midleton Collr
John Harpin Const

Farnley by Leeds

Madam Danby	19
Widdow Musgraue	4
Widdow Bretherick	3
John Elwand	2
Edward Bickars	2
Thomas Pearson	2
Thomas Atkinson	2
Thomas Watson	2
John Webster	2
Richard Houldsworth	2
George Houldsworth	2
Willm Roberts	2
Widdow Hall	1
Allexandr Ross	1
Lancellot Mires	2
Willm Browne	2
Willm Atkinson	1
Widdow Wise	1
Thomas Chapman	1
Willm Chapman	2
Richard Atkinson	1
Mathew Wise	1
Robert Atkinson	1
George Armitage	1
James Bagthwaite	2

m 34]

Thomas Fearnley	1
Widdow Chapman	1

[102] 4 written over 2.

Richard Tayler	1
Anthony Harper	1
Christopr Swaine	1
John Briggs	1
John Harrison	1
Widdow Hurst	1
Christopr Robinson	1
Thomas Sikes	1
Richard Atkinson Jun	1
Thomas Roberts	1
Richard Mortiman	1
	74

Empty and noe distres to be had

Robert Harper	5

Omitted by reason of poverty	3

Robert More Collr
Thomas Watson Const

Fixby

Madam Thornhill	15
Edward Brooke	3
Robert Drake	4
Daniell Whitworth	3
Robert Crowther	3
Brian Stones	1
Joseph Deane	1
Robert Hague	1
Willm Marten	1
Andrew Heigh	1
George Houlroyd	1
Thomas Cooper	2
Willm Dyson	2
Widdow Brooke	1
John Lewcie	1
Thomas Marston	2
James Houldroyd	1
John Freeman	1
John Shepley	1
Willm Northend	1
	46

Omitted by reason of poverty	11

Robt Husband Collr
Robt Drake Const

Gomersall (Gomersal)

John Booth	8
John Man	1
John Raynor	2
Joseph Inchman	5
Robert Man	1
Widdow Hepworth	1
John Watson	1
Willm Brooke	2
Robert Dixon	4
Mr Thomas Thorndike	3
Richard Wilbeck	3
John Craven	1
John Dixon	3
Richard Green	4
Thomas Richardson	3
Robert Turner	1
Thomas Chidwick	2
Robert Brooke	2
George Anderton	1
John Stainthrop	2
Anthony Hopkinson	3
Robert Robinson	6
Edward Scoalfeild	1
John Smith	3
George Blackburne	2
Fluca Scholefeild	2
John Catsby	2
Willm Stead	4
Henry Jackson	1
Thomas Watson	1
Widdow Agland	1

m 35]

Mr Broadhead	5
John Hollins	3
John Stainthrop Jun	2
Jonathan Jagger	4
Willm Brooke	2
Thomas Walker	5
Joshua Porret	1
Thomas Craven	1
John Matson	1
James Brooke	1
John Wormall	1
John Porret	1
Samuell Scholefeild	2
John Rooke	2
James Lawe	3
Joseph Charlesworth	7
Cristopr Watson	5
Richard Liversidge	4
Richard Wilkinson	3
Ralph Musgraue	5
John Holdsworth	4
Francis Wainwright	1
Michell Slough	2
Willm Tetley	1
Richard Atkinson	1
Thomas Gomersall	1
John Hodgson	1
John Rookes	1
Robert Norton	1
George Tetley	1
Peter Hodgson	2
Richard Peacock	1
Roger Richmond	1
Thomas Richardson Jun	1
Willm Simpson	1
Robert Walshawe	1
The Milne	1
Richard Hopkinson	5
Willm Batt Esqr	13
Willm Webster	1
Richard Brooke	4
Willm Brooke	2
John Farnley	3
Edward Brooke	3
Richard Peele	10
Willm Tingle	1
John Crowther	1

Willm Rhoades	2
Willm Baule	1
Thomas Tayler	6
John Birkhead	2
James Farnley	1
Willm Kirshawe	1
John Kitson	3
John Cocker	1
Thomas Kitson	2
Robert Craven	1
Thomas Taylor	2
Tempest Pollard	9
Thomas Farnley	3
Willm Taylor	3
Willm Birkhead	4
John Walker	2
John Newby	3
John Craven	1
John Newby	3
Richard Archer	3
Mr Atkinson	6
Joshua Charlesworth	2
Thomas Gomersall	1
Willm Mitchill	2
Walter Speight	3
John Walker sen	1
Richard Chadwick	2
Widdow Wray	5
John Wray Jun	5
George Sikes	3
John Langfeild	3
Jennet Wright	2
Thomas Lee	2
Thomas Gomersall	4

m 36]

Widdow Baraclough	1
Edmond Brooke	3
Thomas Champton	1
Ezara Thornton	1
Richard Wilkinson	2
John Tetley	1
Robert Parret	1
	303

Empty and no distress to be had

Mr Timothy Brooke	3
Willm Batt Esqre	2

Omitted by reason of poverty 9

Robert Corner Collr
John Stainthrop Const

Gildersome

Mr John Smith	7
George Orrigg	1
Willm Thackeray	1
Thomas Benson	3
John Dickinson	3
Jerem Boulton	4
Jonathan Crowther	2
Willm Burnitt	2
Richard Crowther	2
Thomas Rowland	2
Willm Westerman	2
Richard Hardcastle	3
John Raynor	2
Jerem Atkinson	1
Henry Cooke Esqr	2
Mathew Midlebrooke	1
Widdow Whitacres	4
John Glover	2
Robert Atkinson	3
Gamalll Broadhead	3
Widdow Clough	1
Marke Ball	1
Joseph Westerman	1
Timothy Scott	2
Marmaduke Apleby	1
Mr John Grethead	6
Widdow Crowther	3
John Birkhead	3
Henry Scott	3
Thomas Crabtree	1
Samuell Oats	2
John Leathey	1
Richard Lepton	3

Francis Walker	1
Joseph Scott	3
Thomas Westerman	1
John Westerman	2
Widdow Westerman	1
Mr John Smith	3
Willm Dodgson	1
Elkana Brogden	1
Thomas Naylor	1
Christopr Ryley	3
Anthony Williamson	1
	96

Empty & no distres to be had

Widd Agland 1

Robt Husband Collr
Richard Hardcastle Const

Honley

Joseph Lockwood	2
John Winpeny	1
John Bayley	1
John Winpeny	2
Godfrey Whitehead	1
Anthony Dyson	1
Joshua Green	1
Edmond Eastwood	1
Arthur Jessop	1
Thomas Nicholls	2
Joseph Beamond	2
Abraham Beamond	1
Godfrey Oldfeild	1
Godfrey Berrey	1

m 37]

Edward Hoyle	1
Willm Dyson	1
Edward Hoyle	1
James Litlewood	1
Caleb Swallowe	1
Richard Litlewood	3
Abraham Swallow	1

Joseph Senyer	1
James Dyson	1
Richard Morton	5
John Armitage	3
Joseph Kay	2
Joseph Wilson	1
James Haigh	1
Thomas Lee	1
John Crosland	1
Dinis Heigh	1
Anthony Crosley	1
Willm Brooke	1
Richard Marsden	2
Richard Turton	1
Nichollas Grime	1
Joseph Sanderson	1
Francis Sanderson	4
Robert Aire	1
Henry Wilson	1
James Bawnford	1
Humphr Armitage	3
Mr Netleton	4
Henry France	1
Joseph Healey	1
Joshua Aynley	1
Thomas Crosley	1
Willm Morehouse	2
Widdow Healey	1
Joseph Healey	1
David Dixon	1
John Jessop	1
Willm France	1
John Ibbitson	2
John Crosley	2
Joseph Armitage	1
Edward Hepworth	2
James Taylor	1
Christopr Sanderson	1
Dinis Haigh	1
Richard Turton sen	2
Joseph Armitage	1
Thomas Turton	1
Joseph Tayler	1
Jeffrey Jagger	1
Roger Armitage	2

Robert Scholefeild	1
Widdow Armitage	1
	96
Empty and no distres to be had	
Nichols Hurst	2
Sr John Kay	1
John Cocken	1
Omitted by reason of poverty	3
Robt Bennit Collr	
Caleb Swallow Const	

Hallifax (Halifax)

Mr Richard Dolliffe	11
Thomas Jackman	7
Mr Mathew Widup	4
Mr John Wilson	7
John Hargraues	7
John Exley	2
Michaell Maude	4
Robert Gleadall	5
Richard Gascoyne	2
Alice Glover	4
John Whitley	3
Cristopr Ramsden	3
John Hayworth	2
Thomas Holmes	2
Willm Midgley	2
Isaac Clarke	2
Dr Maude	18
Nicholls Sugden	4
George Ashton	3
Francis Goodburne	2
Mr Mitchill	2
James Hodgson	5
m 38]	
John Hanson	4
Willm Pollard	4

Widdow Cawthrey	4
Marth Drake	3
John Jackson	4
Nichollas Armitage	4
John Taylor	2
James Starkey	3
Richard Viccars	3
Willm Ogden	3
John Lake	2
Thomas Bins	3
Rowland Holme	3
Mr Daniel Greenwood	9
Abraham Turner	2
John Viccars	6
Joseph Threapland	6
Mrs Anne Ramsden	9
Mrs Mitchill	8
Widdow Jepson	1
Nathanll Bins	1
Jonathan Ouldfeild	2
Mr Henry Gill	1
Samuell Royd	1
Mr Anthony Fox	6
Robert Smith	2
Thomas Sugden	3
Robert Hilton	1
John Roper	2
Christopr Hartley	3
Barnard Hartley	1
Dorothy Mitchill	1
Willm Davison	1
Willm Coape	3
Widdow Watson	3
Mr Edward Jackson	10
Thomas Hayworth	5
George Browne	2
Jonas Plamiers	3
Daniell Kershawe	2
John Wadsworth	1
Dr Hooke	8
Ellizabeth Robinson	2
Widdow Houghton	1
Widdow Robinson	4
Jerem Midgley	1
Sissilla Stox	1

Edward Marshall 1
Anne Briggs 1
John Broadley 4
Anthony Shepherd 4
Henry Hindle 5
Jonas Blamiers 3
Lawrance Hudson 1
Thomas Buterfeild 5
Sissilla Stox 1
Mr Thomas Gibson 10
Widdow Rideing 2
Thomas Jepson 4
Thomas Apleyard 2
John Firth 1
Margret Midgley 4
George Staineforth 3
Ashton Joanes 4
Luke Doson 3
John Browne 4
John Gill 3
Mr John Tompson 16
Widdow Lumbe 5
John Ashton 4
Michll Booth 6
Joseph Whitehead 2
Widdow Hartley 7
Thomas Dunn 3
Thomas Hartley 3
Robert Morris 2
Mr Richard Jackson 5
Mr James Scarbrough 4
Widdow Hind 4

m 39]

John Benson 5
Robert Cotton 1
Mary Broadley 1
John Gawbut 1
Willm Hollingworth 4
Widdow Lumbe 5
Richard Atkinson 3
Mr Joseph Dunn 6
John Goodburn 3
Widdow Lawson 2

Daniell Hemingway 3
Anne Croft 3
Thomas Gascoyne 1
Widdow Brooke 3
George Noble 4
John Windle 4
John Bentley 9
John Haggis 2
John Wadsworth 3
Samuell Hemingway 2
Widdow Watson 2
Edward Stox 3
Thomas Myers 2
Mr Thomas Carnill 13
Willm Barrot 7
John Nicholls & forge 3
Widdow Higgin 4
John Munkes 3
Ralph Crosby 2
James Whitairs 3
Jerem Boyes 1
Widdow Milner 2
John Bentley 2
Jerem Walton 5
Richard Barraclough 2
Thomas Dex 1
Thomas Wray 4
John Ingham 17
Edward Noble 1
Widdow Dickinson 1
Henry Green 8
Isabell Wharton 2
Thomas Mitchill 2
Mary Briggs Wid 4
Michll Hopwood 3
Mr Willm Antribus 9
James Mitchill 2
Samuell Bentley 6
Edward Stox 3
Christopr Mitchill 3
Mrs Smith 1
James Wilkinson 7
Sarah Pollard 1
Henry Harrison 3
Mrs Drake 2

Richard Cooke 3
Jerem Worrall 6
Willm Rylands 6
Mr John Leyroyd 4
John Blackburne 1
John Worrall 2
John Parker 3
Thomas Birch 4
Mr John Brearcliffe 5
Sarah Thomas 4
Tobias Maude 1
John Smith 4
Mr John Richardson 4
Willm Elbeck 1
John Ellam 6
Mary Tinsley 1
Mr John Leyroyd 7
Henry Jackson 2
John Hill 7
Jabbis Jagger 4
Mr Lister 4
Widdow Atkinson 5

m 40]

Lewis Brooksbanke 2
Mr Abrah Mitchill 6
Ingram Woodhead 6
Gabriell Leyroyd 4
James Sutcliff 4
John Clay 1
Sarah Midgley 1
Henry Gawthropp 2
Widdow Roberts 2
Martin Grimshaw 2
John Kempmet 2
James Wilson 2
John Tayler 2
Sarah Hepwood 2
Thomas Deane 2
Simon Horsfeild 3
John Briggs 1
James Hopkinson 5
Willm Bridge 3
Susan Parkinson 2

Mr Robert Barraclough	7	Thomas Story	1	Joseph Cadey	2
Edward Hanson	2	John Taylor	1	John Birch	1
Michaell Parkinson	2	Mr Samuell Newton	5	Joshua Suden	4
Abraham Brooksbanke	3	Willm Jackman	5	John Fairebanke	4
Abraham Wood	3	Mr John Boyes	5	James Butterwood	2
Martin Marshall	3	Mr Benjam Boyes	1	Widdow Briggs	2
George Roberts	3	Mr George Walker	2	John Harper	2
Willm Maskew	2	Feaby Duckworth	2	John Hodgson	4
Widdow Furnice	1	John Holdsworth	4	Joseph Firth	3
Joseph Ellingworth	3	Willm Jackman	1	John Thomas	2
Henry Stansfeild	2	John Batley	3	Willm Maude	8
Dorothy Roberts	1	Richard Duckworth	5	Joseph Wood	1
Christopr Tennant	5	Toby Maud	2	Richard Watkinson	2
John Cuncliffe	1	John Broadly	1	John Lacy	2
Easter Hoyle	4	James Wardle	3	Richard Blackburne	2
Henry Smith	3	Abraham Greene	2	Barbar Tompson	2
Arthur Milners	2	Abraham Sutcliff	4	John Hooker	2
Robert Hoult	1	John Maskew	10	Sarah Blackburne	1
Simon Sutcliff	3	John Sutcliff	1	Michaell Eastwood	1
Henry Lake	3	Abraham Shackleton	3	John Hodgson	3
more in Mount Pelin[103]	1	Michaell Healey	1	John Colbeck	6
Daniell Wadsworth	5	Mr Richard Barraclough	6	Hugh Glover	12
Joshua Firth	4	Henry Pellington	1	Widdow Deane	2
Joseph Dixon	1	Docter Samll Waide	4	Robert Halliday	2
Joseph Dixon	1[104]	John Tristrum	1	Widdow Ramsden	1
Nathanll Crowther	1	John Gaukoroyd	2	Widdow Booth	2
Mr John Smith	5	Richard Stansfeild	1	Edward Slator & tents	4
John Marser	7	Michaell Bentley	3	John Houldsworth	3
John Bollard	4	Mr Clough	5	Mathew Lumbe	8
Mr Jona Keighley	4	Thomas Horsfeild	3	James Briggs	4
Robert Smith	4	Mrs Walker	4	John Ramsden	1
Willm Ellis	2	Samuell Firth	3	Samuell Pauldin	2
Andrew Briggs	3	Thomas Oxley	2	Robert Knowles	2
Widdow Briggs	2	John Jaggor	2	George Tillotson	2
		Edward Scholefeild	1		
m 41]		Tobias Beverley	2	m 42]	
		Thomas Kitson	7		
Benjam Boyes	2	Joseph Rhoades	2	Anthony Holegate	2
Thomas Cockcroft	3	Thomas Ellison	2	John Briggs	1
Robert Hall	3	John Rookes	3	Sume	1047[105]
Mrs Law	3	Daniell Walshawe	1		

103 Mount Pellen.
104 sic.
105 There is a scribal error since the total is 1048.

Empty and noe distress to be had	
Mr Abr Wadsworth	2
Mr Abraham Mitchill	2
Samuel Hemingway	2
Edward Stockes	1
Mr Hodges	2
Ellinor Hartley	2
Thomas Myers	2
Robert Allonson	3
Robert Allonson	1
Mr Abraham Wood	1
Freeschoole	3
James Stead	2
Robert Jackson	4
Mrs Anne Brashawe	6
John Walton	3
Richard Duckworth	2
Mr Barraclough	1

These persons following are discharged by Certiftes

Thomas Walker	2
John Shaw	1
John Bewerley	2
Widdow Walker	1
Thomas Bairstow	2
Sarah Ryden	1
James Evens	1
Nichollas Scewby	1
Luke Horsfeild	1
John Firth	1
Widdow Maude	1
Mary Pearson	1
John Walker	1
Garrad Denton	1
Thomas Watson	1
Henry Cooe	1
Henry Watson	1
George Lister	1
Michaell Hodgson	1
Willm Dixon	1
Anthony Newton	1
Anthony Baistowe	1
John Hall	1
Willm Wray	1
Isaac Clarke	1
Thomas Gaston	1
George Story	1
John Whitley	1
Samuell Lister	1
George Leach	1
Sarah Midgley	1
Richard Wilkinson	1
James Wardell	1
John Whitley or Sam	1
Margret Pearson	1
Anthony Newton	1
Widdow Woodhead	1
Michll Greenwood	1
Richard Ramsden	1

Omitted by reason of poverty 111[106]

Richard Pickard Collr
John Tompson Const

Hiperholme cum Brighouse (Hipperholme with Brighouse)

John Rushworth	4

m 43]

John Hanson	3
James Phillip	2
John Hawroyd	3
Joseph Whitley	6
Jonathan Preistley	2
Michaell Empsall	1
Robert Heblethwate	3
Daniell Hening	1
Joseph Brooke	3
Leavie Crosley	2
Steven Hird	1
John Coates	4
Mr Steven Ellis	5
John Stox	3
John Wood	2
Richard Morley	4
Thomas Hanson	3
Richard Speight	2
Richard Hudson	1
Widdow Longbotham	1
Joseph Wright	4
John Hodgson	1
Samuell Smith	7
John Leyroyd	5
Michll Gibson	4
Joseph Hargraues	3
Widdow Brigg	2
Widdow Hoyle	2
John Womersley	1
Willm Brooke	3
John Clarke	2
Richard Longley	1
Willm Walker	4
Henry Hemingway	3
James Whitacres	4
Joseph Hoyle	4
Jerem Batley	3
John Snowden	3
John Turner	3
John Gill	1
Andrew Gill	4
Henry Birkhead	3
Richard Hargraues	3
Jonathan Wadington	1
John Snowden	1
James Mitchill	6
James Whitacre	1
Willm Walker	3
Thomas Coward	3
Nathanll Crosley	3
Widdow Wilson	1
Thomas Greenwood	1
Nathanll Shawwood	2

[106] The number is written as 'iii'.

John Thorpe	3
Joshua Exley	3
Willm Liversidge	2
Joseph Hopkinson	3
Nathanll Whittley	5
Nathanll Whitley	4
Richard Shewsmith	4
Henry Wadington	1
James Brooksbanke	1
Robert Wilson	2
Jerem Robinson	2
Andrew Marshall	2
John Kirshawe	3
Widdow Holdsworth	1
John Bland	2
Dinah Tetloue	3
Widdow Butler	1
James Brooksbanke	2[107]
	two
Richard Robinson	2
Samuell Wadington	2
Samuell Wadington	3
John Kirshaw	1
James Mitchill	3
Willm Ramsden	4
Thomas Oates	3
Willm Wilson	2

m 44]

Robert Smith	2
Widdow Preistley	4
Richard Langley	7
Jerem Field	4
Richard Apleyard	3
Samuell Apleyard	3
Mr Willm Horton	13
Willm Semord	3
Samuell Smith	1
Michll Empsall	3
Michll Watson	2
Willm Whitacre	2
Henry Brooke	1
Samuell Gill	2
Robert Hanson	2
John Lightooler	1
Willm Walker	1
Thomas Pawthrop	6
Widdow Methley	2
John Stox	3
Robert Gibson	4
John Gill	5
Jonath Shawe	4
James Stevenson	4
Francis Higinson	2
John Hanson	4
Abraham Crosley	1
Samuell Bentley	3
Daniell Methley	1
Michll Smith	1
John Barnes	1
John Baiwmforth	1
Robert Gibson	5
Willm Thorpe	3
Widdow Fletcher	4
John Scholefeild	8
Joseph Lister	3
Thomas Shewsmith	1
Henry Flather	1
Willm Wilton	3
Richard Iredale	4
Widdow Pellington	3
Widdow Richmond	1
John Wilton	3
Henry Brighouse	2
Thomas Taylor	6
Thomas Whitfeild	2
Judeth Hoyle	3
Henry Farrer	2
Willm Hanson	2
Henry Scholefeild	3
Samuell Clay	1
John Crabtree	3
Mr Taylor	1
Richard Whitfeild	2
Henry Brighouse	4
	378

Omitted by reason of poverty	7

Robert Husband &
George Wainman Collrs
Thomas Oates Const

Heptonstall

John Spinke	1
Henry Shackleton	1
Michaell Ulley	1
David Horsfall	1
Thomas Watson	1
Andrew Rigg	1
David Horsfall	1
John Mitchill	2
John Crabtree	1
Henry Cockcroft	2
Luke Townend	2
Thomas Greenwood	3
Mary Greenwood	1
Abraham Sunderland	2
Jonas Shackleton	1
Willm Shackleton	1
Widdow Crosley	2
Jonas Sugden	1
Elizabeth Eglin	2
Jonathan Booth	1

m 45]

John Greenwood	1
Michaell Eastwood	1
Thomas Sunderland	1
Paull Greenwood	1
Simeon Greenwood	1
Widdow Shackleton	1
Willm Greenwood	2
James Mitchill	1
Paull Townend	1
Thomas Greenwood	3
John Greenwood	2
John Wood	1

107 2 written over 1

John Sutcliffe	2
David Crosley	3
John Jagger	2
John Key	1
Judeth Greenwood	1
Willm Greenwood	1
John Heyworth	1
Willm Sunderland	1
Simeon Townend	1
Richard Maude	1
Richard Horsfall	1
David Dodgson	1
Christopr Carter	2
Abraham Sunderland	1
Hugh Lay	1
Richard Eastwood	1
John Hudson	1
Henry Draper	1
Richard Horsfall	1
Richard Horsfall	1[108]
John Greenwood	2
Widdow Shackleton	1
Thomas Foster	1
Joseph Hoyle	1
John Sunderland	1
Henry Horsfall	1
Henry Shackleton	1
Willm Sutcliffe	1
Joseph Sutcliffe	1
Willm Sutcliffe	1
John Foster	2
John Wadsworth	2
Robert Greenwood	1
Mathew Sutcliffe	1
Widdow Greenwood	1
David Smith	2
John Sutcliffe	1
Abraham Crabtree	1
Joseph Sutcliffe	2[109]
	two
John Sutcliffe	3

Jonas Thomas	3
John Bentley	2
Willm Draper	2[110]
	two
Richard Grimshaw	2
Roger Poole	1
Abraham Bentley	2
Willm Sutcliff	2
Joseph Sutcliff	2
Joseph Sutcliff	4
John Nowill	1
Thomas Brewer	5
Widdow Longley	2
John Wadsworth	8

m 46]

Jonas Grimshawe	3
John Ingham	1
Thomas Sutcliff	1
Barnard Cockshott	1
Willm Greenwood	2
John Grime forge	1
Henry Banister	3
Widdow Foster	6
John Chapman	2
James Earnshawe	1
James Kendall	2
Richard Thomas	4
John Kendall	2
Widdow Harwood	1
The Freeschoole	2
Jonathan Ingham	1
Widdow Grimshawe	4
	169

Robt Corner Collr
Jonas Thomas Const

Hartshead cum Clifton

Sir John Armitage	23
Robert Childe	2
Mathew Houldsworth	2
John Kitson	3
Mathew Naylor	2
Abrah Parker	1
Thomas Rounsley	2
Widdow Schofeild	1
Widdow Overend	1
Clement Clayton	1
Willm Ramsden	3
Thomas Fairburn	1
John Heap	3
Robt Tayler	1
James Raper	1
John Rayner	1
Thomas Hyley	5
Willm Mitchill	1
Abraham Rayner	2
Samuell Lumme	2
Francis Drake	1
John Ramsden	2
Michaell Greaves	1
Nathanll Drake	1
Samuell Drake	2
John Fairburne	2
Samuell Brooke	1
Miles Taylor	1
Willm Beelby	3
George Denham	1
Richard Mitchell	1
John Pilling	1
Widdow Shepherd	2
Richard Ramsden	1[111]
	one
John Briggs	1
Widdow Langcaster	1
Richard Walker	1
James Furnace	2
Thomas Naylor	8
John Rayner	3
Edward Rayner	1
Joseph Preistley	1

108 sic.
109 2 written over 1.
110 2 written over 1.
111 1 written over 2.

Widdow Drake	2
Thomas Cosson	1
Willm Blacker	1
Robert Whitehead	1
Samuell Farrer	1
Peter Bakes	1
Mathew Langley	2
Widdow Naylor	1
Richard Liversidge	2
Willm Taylor	2
Widdow Child	1
Christopr Emson	4
Willm Liversidge	4
Richard Liversidge	5
John Longley	1
Peter Sinkinson	2
Edward Ashton	1
John Raynor	3
Robert Mitchill	1
George Fearnley	2
Thomas Rayner	2
George Heald	1
John Rayner sen	3
John Fearnley	1
Jonas Drake	1
Robt Apleyard	2
Widdow Mitchill	1

m 47]

Henry Hanson sen	1
Henry Hanson Jun	1
Isaac Hemingway	1
Mathew Drake	1
John Ledgard	2
Richard Sheffeild	2
Willm Gleadall	1
Widdow Gleadall	1
John Jackson	1
Edmd Gibson	2
Thomas Hurst	1
Edmond Manering	1
John Walker	1
John Rayner	2
Widdow Hepworth	2
	165

Robt Bennit Collr
John Kidson Const

Hoothersfeild (Huddersfield)

Mr Mathew Wilkinson	8
Arthur Hurst	6
John Cooper	4
Richard Kidson	2
Widdow Woodhead	1
Willm Brooke	1
Edward Ainely	1
John Hanson	3
Robert More	2
James Hartcliffe	1
Edward Batty	1[112]
Widdow France	3
Jeffrey Ramsden	1
John Bankes	1
Samuell Haigh	1
Arthur Batley	1
John Cooper	2
George Sikes	1
Anthony Hurst sen	2
Richard Brooke	2
Willm Archer	1
Mrs Sarah Brooke	8
Edward Milner	5
John Woodhead	1
Samuell Smith	2
Walter Butler	1
Robert Green	2
Thomas Brooke	2
Widdow Hurst	5
Nichollas Cockin	2
Widdow Hurst	4
Thomas England	3
Arthur Hurst Jun	1
Robert Green	1
Edward Roulston	1
Isaac Goodyeare	1
Thomas Cooper	3
John Brooke	2
Isaac Goodyeare	1
Michaell Crosland	1
John Thornton	1
Joseph Brooke	1
Thomas Spivie	2
Ellias Roulston	3
Edward Wilson	1
Caleb Singleton	1
Robert Mitchill	2
John Marsden	3
Joseph Hepworth	1
Thomas Brooke	1
Robert Priscott	2
Mr Henry Hurst	3
Edward Brooke	1
John Stead	2
John Burges	1
Jonas Stead	1
John Firth	1
Thomas Bothamley	1
Thomas Marsdon	1
Mr Henry Hurst	5
Edward Shaw	4
Willm Broadley	3
Robert Staire	3
Widdow Shaw	1

m 48]

Richard Simpson	2
Edward Ingham	4
John Swallow Jun	2
Willm Bromall	3
Jarvas Kay	2
John Midwood	1
Thomas Breare	4
Widdow Walker	3
Willm Lockwood	2
Richard Shaw	1

[112] Line inserted.

Willm Mallinson	5
Edmond Shaw	3
Edward Brooke	2
Widdow Stacie	3
George Batley	3
Widdow Jepson	1
Abraham Woodhead	1
Anthony Hurst Jun	2
Joseph Sunderland	1
Willm Mallinson	2
Widdow Kay	2
Thomas Armitage	2
Willm Shaw	1
John Shaw	3
Robert Cliffe	1
Edmond Walker	5
Abraham Horsfeild	3
Richard Brooke	2
Thomas Gibson	2
James Mitchill	2
Thomas Mitchill	1
Thomas Gibson	1
Jerem Ambler	1
Widdow Rannsley	1
Michaell Hopper	1
Michaell Hopwood	1
Michaell Hopper	2
Michaell Hopwood	1
Widdow Mallinson	3
John Browne	2
Richd Senyer	1
James Hurst	1
Widdow Hurst	1
Widdow Netleton	2
John Gibson	1
Robert Ramsden	1[113] one
Willm Lilly	2
Samuell Armitage	1
Edmond Smithson	3
Willm Batty	1
John Hurst	1
Robert Reed	2
Michaell Hoyle	1
Henry Crowther	1
John Whitley	2
Robert Reed	1
Willm Dyson	1
Lyonll Browne	1
Arthur Brooke	1
John Starkey	4
Richard Armitage	1
Abraham Chappell	2
John Brooke	1
James Broadbent	1
	254

Omitted by reason of poverty	15

Richd Pickard Collr
Thomas Spivie Const

Holmeforth (Holmfirth)

Henry Jackson	3
Joseph Earnshawe	4
John Bearsall	1
James Roberts	1
James Earnshawe	1
Thomas Beardsall	1
James Hinchcliff	1

m 49]

Adam Green	1
James Haigh	2
Thomas Hinchcliffe	1
Timothy Eastwood	2
Oliver Hatfeild	1
Willm Hinchcliffe	1
John Mouldcliffe	1
Henry Marsh	1
Widdow Heyward	1
Ellizabeth Green	2
Isaac Heptenstall	1
Joseph Hinchcliff	1
Willm Earnshawe	1
Edmond Hinchcliffe	1
John Beavor	1
Godfrey Roberts	1
John Hirst	1
Widdow Litlewood	1
Nichollas Coudwell	1
Henry Taler	1
John Armitage	1
Godfrey Charlesworth	1
Robert France	1
George Shawe	1
Edmond Eastwood	1
Richard Hinchcliff	1
John Haigh	2
John Littlewood	1
James Hinchcliffe	1
James Konersley	1
Widdow Greene	2
John Hinchcliffe	1
Richard Marsh	1
Richard Hinchcliffe	1
Thomas Litlewood	1
Michaell Firth	1
Adam Mellor	1
Thomas Beamond	1
Richard Crosland	1
Widdow Thornton	1
John Hinchcliffe	1
Godfrey Littlewood	1
John Butterworth	1
John Marsden	1
Joshua Charlesworth	1
Richard Charlesworth	1
John Mellor	1
Henry Kay	1
Abraham Charlesworth	1
Abraham Rhoades	1
John Haigh	1
John Watterhouse	1
Thomas Haigh	1

113 1 written over 2.

James Haigh	1
Richard Blackburne	1
John Hinchcliffe	1
George Roberts	1
John Littlewood	1
John Oldam	1
Willm Goddart	1
George Hurst	2
Gilbert Roberts	3
John Hatfeild	1
Widdow Tayler	1
John Tayler	1
Godfrey Charlesworth	1
Richard Litlewood	2
Willm Almon	1
Willm Winpeny	1
Willm Gleadall	1
Emanuell Dewsnopp	1
David Dixon	2
Widdow Broadhead	1

m 50]

Ralph Williamson	2
Widdow Midgley	1
Henry Booth	5
James Batty	2
Whatgodwill Hurst	2
Richard Hinchcliffe	1
James Hurst	1
Richard Smith	1
Jennet Beaver	1
Thomas Batty	2
Luke Firth	1
John Tinker	1
Thomas Genn	2
Caleb Burrey	3
Willm Charlesworth	1
Joseph Batty	1
Abraham Berrey	1
Abraham Berrey	1[114]
Adam Lockwood	1
Samuell Bramall	1

Joseph Firth	2
Widdow Charlsworth	1
George Booth	1
John Charlsworth	2
Widdow Savill	2
John Haigh	1
Michll Wood	1
Robert Wagstaffe	2
Widdow Tinker	1
Abraham Beavor	1
George Greene	1
John Batty	1
Richard Walker	1
John Castle	1
Abraham Green	1
Ralph Williamson	1
Abraham Mellor	1
George Roberts	1
Joseph Charlesworth	1
John Hinchcliffe	1
Richard Hinchcliffe	1
Joseph Heape	1
Henry Marton	1
James Charlesworth	1
Gamal Roberts	1
James Bray	1
Widdow Bray	1
Arthur Morehouse	1
Gilbert Cartwright	1
Thomas Watterhouse	1
John Hinchcliffe	1
Widdow Beardsall	1
James Charlesworth	1
Alice Charlesworth	1
Jerem Kay	2
James Genn	1
John Hinchcliffe	1
Godfrey Crosland	2
Willm Hanson	1
Thomas Litlewood	1
John Hinchcliffe	1
Thomas Roberts	3
Richard Crosland	1

Christopr Wood	1
Thomas Firth	1
George Firth	2
David Graues	2
John Hollingworth	1
John Crosland	1
Joseph Cartwright	1
George Haward	1

m 51]

Robert Mellar	1
Abraham Beamond	1
James Turner	1
Godfrey Cartwright	1
Robert Hall	1
Joseph Hinchcliffe	1
John Dickson	1
Thomas Hinchcliffe	1
Richard Crosland	1
Thomas Crosland	2
Arthur Kay	1
Godfrey Cuttell	4
Bartholl Bray	1
Godfrey Booth	1
Joseph Booth	1
Humphr Brooke	1
Humphr Wilson	1
Francis Vessey	1
John Armitage	1
John Cattell	1
Widdow Bray	1
Abraham Dixon	2
Richard Walker	1
John Beavor	3
Dinis Haigh	1
Widdow Marsden	1
John Cartwright	1
Reynold Bower	1
Anthony Wilson	1
Henry Wilson	1
Robert Ellis	1
Anthony Wilson	2

[114] sic.

James Roberts	1
Thomas Roberts	1
Edmond Morehouse	2
Joseph Roberts	1
Widdow Broadhead	2
Judeth Thewlis	1
Richard Ellis	1
Thomas Ellis	1
John Broadhead	2
Robert Fox	1
Henry Gen	3
George Morehouse	4
Willm Brooke	1
Widdow Booth	1
Daniell Cartwright	1
John Morehouse	3
Godfrey Armitage	1
John Armitage	1
Thomas Morehouse	1
Anthony Wilson	2
Lawrance Hinchcliffe	1
John Castle	1
Ralph Robotham	1
Mr Jonas Kay	3
Joseph Kay	2
Robert Beavor	2
George Linley	2
Peter Harpin	2
George Tyas	3
George Linley	1
Henry Fretwell	1
Edward Beavor	1
Ralph Wadsworth	1
James Armitage	2
Willm Sharlsworth	1
Willm Beavor	2
Henry Eastwood	1
Cristian Bins	1
John Beavor	1
Richard Morton	1
John Marsh	1
Mathew Marsh	1
Edward Beavor	1
George Bray	1
Godfrey Beavor	1
John Charlesworth	1
Widdow Jackson	1
Abraham Beavor	1
m 52]	
Adam Kenyon	2
Christopr Kay sen	1
Robert Beavor	1
John Hattersley	1
George Castle	1
Joshua Tyas	2
Hugh Taylor	1
Christopr Kay	1
Christopr Kay	1[115]
John Armitage	1
Christopr Tinker	1
John Marsh	1
Thomas Morehouse	1
John Green	1
Joseph Berrey	2
Godfrey Hoult	1
Joseph Rhoade	1
James Taylor	1
Willm Tinker	1
Francis Beavor	1
Godfrey Linley	2
George Roebuck	2
John Crosland	1
Humphrey Bray	1
Humphrey Brooke	1
Godfrey Martin	3
Godfrey Martin	2
John Bray	1
Abraham Morehouse	1
Abraham Earnshawe	1
James Roberts	1
Jarvice Kay	1
John Rowley	2
Widdow Roebuck	2
Christopr Wood	2
Willm Thewlis	1
Joseph Thewlis	1
Widdow Martin	1
Jonathan Hobson	1
Godfrey Mathewman	1
Godfrey Mathewman	1[116]
Widdow Mathewman	2
Widdow Morehouse sen	1
Widdow Morehouse Jun	1
Willm Morehouse	2
Henry Morehouse	1
Mathew Morehouse	2
Mathew Morehouse	2[117]
Willm Newton	2
George Roebuck	1
Widdow Roebuck	1
John Roebuck	2
Joseph Archer	1
James Bray	1
Godfrey Morehouse	1
Willm Hurst	1
John Roebuck	1
Robt Hurst	2
Caleb Charlesworth	1
Willm Lockwood	1
Henry Wilby	1
Abraham Wilby	1
Michaell Haigh	1
Godfrey Beamond	2
Willm Rowles	1
Godfrey Berrey	1
Godfrey Crosland	1
Robert Kay	1
Richard Beavor	1
Thomas Cattell	2

115 sic.
116 sic.
117 sic.

Abrahaam Jagger	1
Robert Walshawe	1
James Broaadhead	1
John Brooke	1
Holmeforth milne	1
The New milne	1
Thomas Broadhead	1

m 53]

Willm Godart	1
Henry Hinchcliffe	1
Isaac Shaw	1
Edward Dearnley	1
Robert Cusworth	1
Godfrey Cattle	1
Daniell Bray	1
George Morehouse	1
George Tinker	1
Abraham Green	1
Adam Hurst	1
Richard Battey	1
George Hollingworth	1
	406

Empty and noe distres to be had

Josua Earnshawe	1
Thomas Ellis	1
James Roberts	1
Mr Allott	1

Omitted by reason of poverty 4

Roby Bennit Collr
Godfrey Morton Const

Horberry
(Horbury)

Mr Lake sen	12
Mr Lake Jun	6
Mr Thornton	8
Mr Longley	5
Mr Audsley	6
John Hurst Jun	2
Thomas Hunt	1
John Hunt	1
John Pollard	1
Christopr Coope	1
Robert Thornes sen	2
Widdow Thornes	2
	two
Michaell Goodall	1
John Brooksbanke	2
Willm Roberts	1
John Cawthorne	1
Edward Batty	1
Widdow Batty	2
John Copley	2
Richard Battey	1
Judeth Sunderland	3
John Hardishawe	1
Edmd Wood	2
Willm Briggs	3
Willm Wormall	3
John Issot	3
Robt Mansfeild	2
Robert Batty	1
Willm Stother	1
Francis Blacker	2
Francis Cater	2
Francis Stringer	2
Widdow Cawthorne	2
Richard Walker	2
Widdow Heald	2
Samuell Thorns	2
Tempest Pollard	2
John North	3
John Rhoades	3
Moses Issott	4
John Sunderland	1
Timothy Cawthorne	2
John Goodall	1
Richard Walker	2
Willm Wilson	3
Thomas Craven	2
Willm Castlehouse	1
Widdow Brooksbanke	1
Willm Batley	1
Willm Dawson	1

m 54]

Willm Hunt	2
John Armitage	1
Willm Burton	2
Thomas Totty	2
Mathew Stevenson	1
Mr Stapleton	7
Robert Gleadall	4
Robert Jagger	2
John Jagger	1
John Issot	1
Michaell Bins	1
John Eadson	1
Thomas Heigh	3
George Carr	2
Willm Wadsworth	2
John Issot	4
Robert Carr	1
Thomas Richardson	4
John Naylor	2
Widdow Fawitt	3
Widdow Langfeild	3
Mrs Ludington	2
Thomas Baitson	1
	170

Omitted by reason of poverty 5

Robt Benit Collr
John Pollard Const

Heaton cum Clayton
(Heaton with Clayton)

Mr Edward Bowling	6
Thomas Hill	1
Willm Greengate	1
John Greengate	1
Widdow Pickard	1
Willm Pollard	1
Jerem Both	2

Willm Furnish 1
Widdow Bell[118] 1
Thomas Leach 2
Thomas Greengate 1
Willm Furnish 1
Widdow Bell 0}[119]
Thomas Leach 0}[120]
Thomas Greengate 0}[121]
Willm Furnice 0}[122]
Edward Midgley 1
John Barstowe 1
Jerem Holmes 4
Robert Bens 2
Brian Roberts 1
Jonas Crabtree 3
Samuell Holmes Jun 2
John Jewitt 2
Edward Marshall 1
Willm Jewitt 1
Willm Crabtree 1
Henry Wilkinson 2
Christopr Frickleton 2
Margret Jewit 1
Samll Holmes sen 1
John Crabtree 1
Josias Craven sen 1
Josias Craven Jun 1
Richard Brooke 2
Robert Craven 3
Widdow Moss 1
Willm Shaw 1
Willm Bradshawe 4
Willm Capps 1

m 55]

Jonas Craven 1
Jonas Crabtree 1
James Lister 3
Thomas Exley 3
Willm Marshall 1
Willm Sharpe 2
John Stead 1
Richard Hopkinson 2
Ellias Booth 1
George Both 1
75

These persons following are discharged by Certiftes
John Craven 1
Ellizabeth Crabtree 1
Daniell Booth 1
Richard Hudson 1
Abraham Jewitt 1
Joseph Dixon 1
Michll Driver 1
Willm Pollard Jun 1
Widdow Spencer 1
Widdow Blackburn 1
Jerem Spencer 1
Richard Driver 1
Widdow Jewit 1
Samuell Swaine 1

Robt Husband Collr
Josias Craven Const

Haworth
Jonas Pickles 4
John Pickles 1
George Taylor sen 2
Widdow Tayler 1
John Taylor 1
Michll Pickles 1
Abraham Uttley 3
Widdow Dixon 1
Joseph Smith 3
Joseph Shackleton 1
John Pickles 1
John Greenwood 1
Willm Clayton sen 1
Willm Clayton Jun 1
Josias Smith 1
John Clayton sen 1
Widdow Pickles 1
Robert Godbert 2
Mary Holmes 1
Thomas Hudson 1
Thomas Redman 1
Richard Crabtree 1
John Redman 2
Michaell Driver 1
Widdow Greenwood 1
Michaell Shackleton 2
John Holmes 1
Joshua Heaton 2
Michaell Shackleton 2
John Cleyton 1
Paull Greenwood 1
John Bentley 1
Robert Clayton 1
Willm Oxnard 1
John Heaton 1
James Rawson 1
John Heaton 1
John Harrackes 1
John Clayton 1
Michaell Hanson 1
Jonas Smith 1
James Smith 1

m 56]

Mr John Ramsden 5
Timothy Gaukeroger 6
Willm Midgley 1
John Holmes 2
John Rushworth 1

118 There is a bracket linking Widdow Bell to Willm Furnice with the word 'mistake'.
119 0 written over 1.
120 0 written over 2.
121 0 written over 1.
122 0 written over 1.

Widdow Hartley 1
Ellizabet Smith 3
John Gaukeroger 3
Mr John Colyer 1
Edward Pickles 2[123]
two
Richard Mitchill 1
Joseph Pickles 2
Michall Harsley 1
Simon Sutcliffe 1
Thomas Pickles 2
Joseph Hall 1
Jonas Sutcliff 1
John Wright 1
Henry Baron 2
Thomas Pickles 2
Joseph Tothill 1
Jonas Wheelewright 2[124]
two
Joseph Midgley 1
Thomas Crosley 1
Willm Ickeringall 2
Thomas Mitchill 2
John Smith 1
John Baines 1
Willm Emott 1
Widdow Bins 1
John Holdsworth 1
Christopr Smith 1
John Boothman 1
Adam Wright 2
Nathanll Feather 2
Jonas Driver 1
Michaell Pickles 3
Willm Baines sen 1
Willm Midgley 1
Willm Baines Jun 1
Henry Aikeroyde 1
Henry Naylor 1
Willm Roberts 1
Richard Hanson 1

Michaell Pearson 2
Robert Pickles 1
John Briggs 1
John Binns 1
Thomas Feather 1
Michaell Rushworth 2
Henry Barron 1
Edward Widdupp 1
Barnard Heartley 1
Thomas Rushworth 2
Edward Feather 1
John Holmes 1
Josias Furnish 1
Lancellot Jackson 1
Jonas Briggs 1
John Ogden 1
Paull Kay 2
Richard Hanson 1
Grace Baines 1
John Baines 1
Michaell Pearson 1
Thomas Pearson 1
John Pearson 1
John Greenwood 1
John Widdup 2
Michaell Ogden 1
Buckley House 1
Willm Ogden sen 1

m 57]

Willm Ogden Jun 1
Widdow Bins 1
Jonas Fostar 1
Widdow Tillotson 2[125]
two
John Rushworth sen 1
Henry Craven 1
Jonas Tillotson 1
Willm Hay 1
Thomas Whitacres 2

Robert Smith 1
Grace Briggs 1
John Feather Jun 1
Willm Naylor 1
Thomas Baines 1
John Driver 2
Christopr Holmes 2
John Mitchill sen 1
John Mitchill Jun 1
Christopr Holmes 3
John Heartley 1
John Ramsden 1
John Garnet 1
Jonas Sutcliff 1
John Pickles 1
Jonas Pickles 1
Widdow Pickles 1
Sybell Horsfall 1
John Feather 3
Thomas Mitchill 1
Widdow Mitchill 1
Henry Mitchill 3
Peter Hartley 1
Hugh Sutcliffe 1
Thomas Horsfall 1
Willm Rushforth 1
James Rushforth 1
Robert Heaton 2
Ambros Hay 2
Willm Pickles 1
Abraham Pickles 1
John Sutccliffe 1
John Clayton 1
John Crabtree 1
Joseph Crabtree 1
Willm Rushforth 2
James Rushforth 1
Abraham Sutcliff 2
John Sutcliffe 1
Willm Hay 1
Steven Holmes 1

[123] 2 written over 3.
[124] 2 written over 1.
[125] 2 written over 1.

Mary Ogden 1
Henry Barron forge 1
Margret Bins 1
John Roades 1
Michaell Ogden 1
Joseph Sutcliffe 1
Freeschoole 1
Anne Feather 1
230

Empty and noe distres to be had
Mr John Colyer 1
Joseph Morrill 2

Omitted by reason of poverty 8

Robert Husband Collr
Jonas Crabtree Const

Hortons Ambo (Horton)
John Snipe 1
Thomas Hodgson 3
Martha Sutcliffe 1
John Smith 2
Mary Snowden 1

m 58]

David Fearnside 2
James Speight 1
Abraham Wilson 1
John Nevill 1
Nichollas Watson 1
Thomas Fox 1
Willm Jowitt 2
Jerem Haley 2
Edward Jackson 2
John Mortimer 2
James Firth 1
Isaac Longstaff 1
Thomas Gleadall 2
Robert Parkinson 2
Lyonell Fletcher 3

Jonas Briggs 1
George Westerman 2
Henry Langcaster 1
Thomas Kellet 1
Isaac Nicholls 1
Abraham Swaine 2
Willm Hollingrake 2
Willm Whitehead 3
Richard Parkinson 2
John Hodgson 1
Joseph Brooksbank 3
Thomas Kitching 2
Abraham Woodhead 1
Joseph Sugden 1
Gilbert Brooksbanke 2
Jerem Ashton 1
Abraham Kellit 2
Francis Morley 1
Mathew Green 1
Mary Mortimer 4
Thomas Hamond 3
Jerem Smith 1
Thomas Thornton 2
Jane Wadsworth 1
Henry Pollard 2
Willm Firth 1
Isaac Longbotham 3
John Duckworth 1
John Hillhouse 2
Widdow Fletcher 2
David Thornton 1
Thomas Ashton 2
Jerem Holdsworth 2
Joseph Shooesmith 3
Samuell Fearnside 1
Thomas Pickles 4
Richard Shepherd 1
Willm Swaine 2
Thomas Hamon 1
Abraham Darwin 1
Robert Sugden 1
Joseph Hopkinson 2
Mathew Milner 1
James Thornton 1
Christopr Lofthouse 3

Willm Sharpe 3
Richard Blackburne 1
John Whalley 1
Richard Hodgson 3
James Smith 1
James Sharpe 1
Robert Swaine 2
Willm Sharpe 3
Susan Thornton 3
Richard Thornton 1
Richard Wadsworth 2
Michaell Judson 1
Peter Clarke 1
Humphr Stead 1
Edward Fletcher 1
Mary Higson 1
John Judson 2
Thomas Swaine 2
John Hopkinson 3
Mary Thomas 2
Thomas Craven 1
Richard Casley 3
Jonas Rippon 2

m 59]

Mathew Oates 2
Thomas Mathewes 1
Abraham Thornton 2
Willm Baley 1
Richard Mortimer 3
Daniell Greenwood 2
Willm Clough 1
John Clough 1
Isaac Taylor 1
Mary Jewitt 1
Joseph Holdsworth 4
James Holmes 2
Richard Booth 2
John Higson 1
Thomas Swaine 3
Willm Sugden 1
Thomas Hopkinson 1
George Hoppey 2
Isaac Balme 2

Robert Wright	3
John Lister	7
Bridget White	1
John Sharpe	7
Michaell Kirshawe	1
Thomas Swaine	3
Jerem Rhoades	4
David Hamond	3
Joseph Wilkinson	1
John Taylor	2
John Thornton	1
	one
Anne Butterfeild	1
George Ward	2
John Firth	1
James Gleadall	2
Anne Stockdale	1
Richard Parkinson	1
	225

Omitted by reason of poverty 9

Robert More Collr
Joseph Shooesmith Const

Hunslett
(Hunslet)

Mr Willm Fenton	5
Mr John Fenton	5
John Brooke	2
John Casson	4
Mathew Broxup	2
Mrs Sarah Smithson	4
John Walker sen	4
John Walker Jun	2
Widdow Cooke	2
Charles Barker	3
Miles Barker	2
Willm Metcalfe	4
Henry Barlay	2
Widdow Beck	3
Richard Leathley	2
Mr Ness	5
Mr George Jackson	5
Willm Rushforth	4
Thomas Hutchinson	1
Richard Powell	3
John Colbeck	1
James Fowler	1
Thomas Midleton	2
John Dancer	1
Thomas Hopton	2
Mr Robert Brooke	6
Thomas Brice	1
Richard Coapland	2
Lawrance Sharpe	2

m 60]

Willm Hopton	2
Willm Lilly	5
Mr Mossey	3
David Richinson	2
John Tompson	3
John Tompson	2
John Tennant	4
Widdow Walker	3
James Walker	2
John Norfolke	2
Richard Childers	1
Willm Ellis	2
Thomas Glover	1
John Parker	3
Widdow Parker	2
Willm Parker	2
John Durance	2
Brian Wilkinson	1
John Buckley	2
Richard Turner	4
Willm Hutton	1
John Kilner	2
Willm Dobson	1
Andrew Mann	1
John Brafitt	2
Thomas Brafitt	3
Mr Thomas Fenton	4
Daniell Longstaff	5
Thomas Whitacrs	1
Widdow Burrowe	1
Thomas Fenton	3
Thomas Browne	2
Constant Thwaites	2
Daniell Langstaffe	1
John Tompson	1
Jane Smith	3
John Mann	1
John Hawman	2
Willm Hutchinson	1
Willm Dixon	1
Robert Jaques	1
Willm Falkiner	2
Daniell Langstaff	1
Willm Wriglesworth	3
Mr Willm Fenton	1
John Robinson	2
Willm Rawlin	1
Richard Cockeram	2
John Habor	4
Richard Thwaite	1
Widdow Laughton	2
John Capestock	2
John Carter	2
Thomas Chester	1
Samuell Fenton	5
Widdow Hutton	2
Richard Pickard	4
John Wilkinson	2
Mathew Silburne	2
Widdow Kilburne	3
George Silburne	3[126]
Henry Jolly	2
Mr Richard Sikes	7
Mr Timothy Dawson	1
Richard Roundthwaite	4
Mr Headley	9
John Waugh	3
Mr Ralph Dickson	11
Thomas Tennant	3

126 Line inserted.

Mr Willm Chapman	6
John Hobson	4
Mr Ralph Spencer	11
Marke Bradley	10
Willm Jackson	2
John Lighfoote	2

m 61]

Willm Netherwood	1
Willm Lambert	1
John Hodgson	1
Leonard Wood	1
James Barrowby	1
The Milns	2
Thomas Beckwith	1
Thomas Clough	1
Willm Chapman	2
Mr Idle	2
John Norfolke	1
Thomas Boynton	1
Jeffrey Beck	2
John Buckle	2
James Lindall	1
Danyell Kilburne	1
	310

Empty and noe distres to be had

Abraham Bradley	2
Thomas Walker	1

Omitted by reason of poverty	2

Robert More Collr
James Lindall Const

Houlbeck (Holbeck)

John Metcalfe	1
Widdow Lee	2
Robert Norris	1
Thomas Ryley	1
Toby Iles	2
James Asquith	1
Willm Ryley	1
James Ellis	1
Christopr Hodgson	2
Thomas Loftus	1
Anne Walker	1
Vincent Wilson	2
Christopr Walker	2
Thomas Lambert	3
Richard Barran	1
Willm Haworth	1
Michaell Barron	2
Mr Armitage	1
James Foster	1[127] one
Richard Jackson	2
Mr Robert Armitage	5
Thomas Jackson	4
Willm Dickinson	3
James Rawson	3
James Bratherick	1
Christopr Jackson	2
Christopr Jackson Jun	3
Adam Hargraues	7
Adam Hargraues	4
John Baines	2
Willm Linton	2
Mr John Musgraue	2
John Horner	2
Dinis Bradforth	2
Robert Holmes	2
Thomas Lupton	1
Willm Allotson	2
Ralph Wharton	2[128] two
Willm Arundall	3
John Wise	1
Widdow Darley	3
Henry Dickinson	2
James Wise	1
Thomas Marton	2
Israell Browne	3
John Wright	1
Anthony Smith	2
James Lambert	1
Lyonell Gibson	1
Thomas Wilkinson	1
Lawrance Sharpe	1
James Hinchcliffe	2

m 62]

Thomas Lee	2
Mathew Browne	2
Thomas Cliffton	2
John Cliffton	2
Nichollas Pollard	1
Thomas Idle	9
John Smith	1
Willm Dickinson	2
Willm Jackson	2
Thomas Atkinson	2
Widdow Windross	1
John Rhoades	2
Willm Hought	2
Mathew Mease	1
Thomas Launsdale	1
Thomas Lee	2
Henry Metcalfe	3
Edward Wildman	4
Henry Etherington	1
Thomas Loftus	2[129] two
Thomas Lambert	2[130] two
Widdow Theakstone	1
John Browne	2
Thomas Waite	1
Widdow Lee	2

127 1 written over 2.
128 2 written over 1.
129 2 written over 1.
130 2 written over 1.

Widdow Metcalfe	2
Thomas Marshall	1
Mr Michaell Benson	3
James Dawson	1
Ralph Pratt	1
Thomas Pratt	1
Michaell Dawson	1
Ralph Mawe	2
Willm Waide	1
James Kockeram	1
Thomas Stead	1
Oliver Wray	1
Const Gibson	1
Mr Etherington	3
Hugh Hamble	1
Mr Fallowfeild	9
Roger Oddy	3
Sampson Girstwith	2
Robert Brotherton	2
Robert Sanders	1
Robert Holmes	2[131] two
Brian Smith	1
Willm Dobson	2
Willm Burnley	1
Mr Toby Iles	4
Henry Story	1
Thomas Iles	2
Widdow Goodspeed	3
Humphr Mullinex	3
Thomas Lambert	2
Widdow Haigh	2
Jerem Kendall	1
Willm Bywatter	2
James Clint	2
Adam Storey	2
Willm Shaw	2
Mr Foster	4
Willm Lambert sen	1
Willm Stevens	1
Michaell Shawe	2
Mr Pickard Ministr	2

John Foss	1
George Tompson	2[132] two
John Colebeck	1
Anthony Cloudsley	1
John Smith	1
	240

Empty and noe distress to be had

Henry Naylor	2
Mr Winfeild	2
Mr Rasin	1

m 63]

John Rooth	1
Robt Ness	3
Willm Hodgson	2
Moses Jenkins	5
James Baraclough	2
James Lindall	2
Mr Rasin	2
James Lindall	1
Joseph Baines	1
Willm Jackson	2

Omitted by reason of poverty	22

Robert Bennet Collr
John Smith Const

Heckmondwike

Richard Rayner	5
Richard Atkinson	5
Richard Naylor	6
Abraham Naylor	4
Richard Armitage	2
John Whewell	1
Thomas Newsham	1
Thomas Wood Jun	1
Widdow Brooke	4
Joseph Wood	5
Willm Fox	1
Nicholls Poplewell	3
Thomas Wheatley	2
Marmaduke Richardson	3
Willm Blackbrough	1
Thomas Keighey	1
Abraham Beavor	4
Widdow Whewell	4
Abraham Whewell	1
Richard Oldroyd	2
Willm Poplewell	2
Edward Robinson	2
Mr Pickard	5
Richard Hemingway	2
John Stubley	2
John Ouldroyd	1
Widdow Raynor	5
John Hay	1
Thomas Dayle	1
Thomas Croft	1
Lyonell Fox	2
John Mann	1
Samuell Healey	1
Midleton Gosling	3
Jerem Peele	2
Michaell Mitchill	4
George Lee	2
Charles Sheafeild	1
Willm Walker	1
Joseph Swallow	1
Michaell Clarkson	1
Widdow Lee	2
Robert Linley	1
Willm Copley	2
Joseph Hepworth	1
John Furnice	2
Richard Sheafield	1
	106

Omitted by reason of poverty	3

[131] 2 written over 1.
[132] 2 written over 1.

Roger Hardcastle Collr
Marmad Richinson Const

Hunsworth

Mary Pearson	3
James Pearson	5
John Pearson	1
Thomas Stead	2
Henry Firth	5
Richard Netleton	1

m 64]

John Pearson sen	4
Paull Bankes	3
Jerem Fearnley	1
Willm Sharpe	3
James Murgerson	2
Willm Ramsden	2
John Robinson	2
Marth Woodhead	3
Mathew Smith	2
Willm Speight	1
Widdow Rhoades	1
John Barraclough	2
James Short	3
John Cordingley	1
Willm Firth	1
John Copley	2
John Cordingley	3
Richard Cordingley	1
Abraham Rhoades	1
	55

These persons following are discharged by Certifte

Edward Hall	2
Willm Denholme	1

Omitted by reason of poverty	6

Robert Corner Collr
Christopr Beamont Const

Idle

Humphrey Musgraue	1
Lawrance Buck	5[133] fiue
John Buck	2
Samuell Scawbert	2
Samuell Viccars	1
Joseph Viccars	3
Thomas Atkinson	2
Willm Swaine	1
Samuell Drake	2
Willm Scawberd	1
Willm Armitage	1
Thomas Tompson	2
Benjam Sandall	2
Samuell Marshall	2
Edward Kitson	1
Joseph Viccars	2
John Lobley	3
Alice Marshall	2
Widdow Dawson	1
John Sargisson	3
Willm Atkinson	2
Widdow Atkinson	3
Richard Simpson	3
John Simpson	3
Widdow Booth	2
James Booth	1
Thomas Stansfeild	3
Edward Clayton	1
Willm Buck	5
Robert Haire	2
Willm Jewitt	3
Willm Kellitt	2
Mr Pearson	3
Jane Harrison	1
Samuell Hobson	1
Willm Ogden	1
Abraham Cosson	1

Easter Bland	1
Willm Carlile	1
John Saltonstall	1
Edward Mackerith	2
Joseph Sandall	2
John Stead	3

m 65]

Samuell Hollins	1
Mr Sandall	3
John Sargisson	2
Willm Clarkeson	3
Robert Carrock	5
James Hobson	2
Nehemiah Sandall	3
John Dawson	1
Richard Sargisson	1
George Booth	1
Marmaduke Warwick	3
Marke Wheelehouse	3
John Pomfrett	2
Willm Pollard	1
Francis Drake	2
Willm Foster	1
James Berrey	1
Widdow Tonge	1
Richard Booth	1
Samuell Stables	2
Willm Walker	1
Thomas Ledgart	5
Widdow Farrar	1
Richard Crosedale	1
Willm Myers	1
Gilbert Steade	1
Jonath Goodall	2
John Booth	2
Mathew Foster	1
Jerem Wilfitt	6
Mary Dawson	1
John Watterhouse	2
Samuell Stables	2

[133] 5 written over 3.

George Skerroe sen	2
George Skerroe Jun	1
John Adcocke	2
Robert Craven	3
Thomas Rauson	1
John Slator	2
Jacob Ellison	2
Jonas Walker	1
Martin Dawson	1
John Midgley	1
Thomas Slaytor	2
Samuell Hogg	1
Edward Sands	1
Joseph Holmes	1
Widdow Scaife	2
Christopr Mitton	1
Thomas Baines	1
George Birch	1
Willm Denby	2
Willm Denby Jun	1
Thomas Armitage	1
Anthony Slator	1
James Booth	1
Willm Denby	1
Willm Collingworth	2
Christopr Wyrin	2
John Tasker	2
George Booth	1
Willm Deacon	1
Zachar Yeadall	1
Ephriam Sandall	1
John Sandall	1
Benjam Swaine	3
Widdow Graue	1
Robert Thornton	1
Willm Swaine	1
Widdow Hill	1
Widdow Crowther	1
Samuell Pollard	1
Marke Hillens	1
Robert Denby	1
	206

m 66]

Empty and noe distress to be had

Mrs Sharpe	1
James Keighley	1

Omitted by reason of poverty 4

Robert More Collr
Joseph Viccars Const

Kirkeheaton
(Kirkheaton)

The parsonage	6
Mrs Ashton	4
Thomas Pickles	5
Thomas Diccons	4
Samuell Jepson	3
Widdow Waller	1
Joseph Strafforth	1
John Sikes	2
Vallent Steele	2
Bartholl Stead	1
Willm Beamond	3
Robert Lyley sen	1
Robert Lyley Jun	2
	two
John Hopworth	2
Richard Copley	4
Arthur Lee	2
John Eastwood	2
Joseph Stocks	1
Widdow Castle	1
Henry Spivie	1
Thomas Crabtree	1
Richard Morton	2
Edward Morton	1
Thomas Ashton	1
Richard Senyer	2
Willm Ouldroyde	1
John Browne	1
Susan Hepworth	2[134]
	two
John Pickles	2
John Morton	1
Richard Peele	1
Richard Hepworth Jun	1
Isaac Blackburne	2
Abraham Charlsworth	1
John Jobson	1
Richard Hepworth	1
Widdow Armitage	4
John Hirst	3
Joshua Jackson	2
Christopr Casley	1
John Greenald	2
Thomas Chadwick	1
James Greenald	2
Willm Grime	1
Henry Brooke	1
Robert Stringer	1
Willm Hobson	3
Mathew Thomas	1
Thomas Morton	1
John Beamond	1
Michaell France	1
Edward Brooke	1
John Brooke	1
Jennit Lockwood	1
John Brooke	3
John Roebuck	4
Willm Hepworth	1
Joseph Strafforth	1
Judeth Castle	1
Samuell Mitchill	1
Abraham Dollive	1
James Greenald	1
Richard Dollive	1
Joseph Strafforth	1
Sarah Farrand	2
John Hamshire	1
Robert Wood	2

[134] 2 written over 1.

m 67]

Richard Heywood	1
Willm Strafforth	1
Richard Beamond	1
Thomas Hepworth	1
Mathew Thomas	1
Richard Oldroyd	1
John Oldroyd	1
Coll Stringer	1
John Tompson	1
	126

These persons following are discharged by Certfe

John Grime	1
Widdow Brooke	1
Widdow Crabtree	1

Omitted by reason of poverty 1

Robert Husband Collr
Samuell Mitchill Const

Kirke Burton (Kirkburton)

Joseph Briggs Cler	6
John Chappell	1
John Hurst	1
John Kay	1[135] one
John Kay	2
George Roebuck	2
Gilbert Winpeny	2
Samuell Wood	2
John Hutchinson	1
Richard Hutchinson	1
John Roebuck	2
Willm Booth	1
George Wood	1
Willm Senyer	1
John Cockill	2
Thomas Chappell	2
John Hardye	1
Thomas Walshawe	1
Thomas Hudson	3
John Moxon Sen	2
Henry Hill	1
John Fitton	1[136]
Joseph Booth	1
John Booth	1
John Fitton	3
Widdow Kay	1
Edward Senyer	1
Joseph Kay	1
John Smith	1
Edward Norcliff	2
John Chappell	1
George Haigh	1
Richard Horncliffe	1
Michaell Pitts	1
Richard Fitton	1
John Tinker	1
Mathew Broadhead	1
Joseph Haigh	2
George Haigh	2
Robert Dickinson	3
Willm Turner	2
Edward Noble	1
John Cockell	1
John Noble	1
George Haigh	1
Thomas Hudson	1
George Noble	1
Richard Mellor	2

m 68]

Richard Mellor	3
Willm Chappell	2
Richard Chappell	1
Humphr Hardy	2
Richard Smith	1
Thomas Hudson	1
Joseph Booth	1
John Mellor	2
Willm More	1
Mathew Booth	1
Henry Hill	1
John Armitage	1
Chr Booth	1
	90

Omitted by reason of poverty 8

Robert Husband Collr
George Haigh Const

Lepton

Edward Lee	2
Mr Richardson	7
Arthur Lee	5
Mr Beamond	6
Isaac Mallinson	1
Joseph Armitage	1
Allexandr Stoxs	1
John Crowther & mill	2
Joseph Senyor	1
Anne Schoafeild	1
John Watterhouse	1
Willm Hague	2
Jarvice Copley	1
Willm Whiall	1
John Mallinson	1
John Kilner	1
Joseph Wood	1
Thomas Beamond	1
John Beamond	1
Nichollas Armitage	2
Peter Stocks	3
Alverah Whitley	1
Robert Sikes	3
Christopr Sikes	1

[135] 1 written over 2.
[136] Line inserted.

John Brooke	4
Widdow Wood	1
George Mallinson	1
John Wood	1
Thomas Heald	1
John Greanald	1
Edmond Schofeild	1
John Sykes	1
Widdow Bingley	2
Joseph Kay	1
Joseph Wood Sen	1
Joseph Wood Jun	1
Thomas Wood	1
Willm Lodge	2
Thomas Hobson	1
Widdow Jessop	1
Arthur Brooke	1
Thomas Jessopp	1
John Sykes	1
John Hague	3
John Stead	2
Willm Jessop	1
John Parcevell	3
Anne Hopkins	3
Thomas Dransfeild	1
Willm Jessop	1
John Hurst	1
Widdow Jessop	1
Jarvice Drancefeild	2
Willm Pell	2

m 69]

Edmond Jessop	2
Willm Jessop	1
John France	2
Willm Turton	3
Widdow Kay	1
John Kay	1
Willm Pell	1
John Cooke	4
Richard Wilson	2
John Senyor	3
Widdow Hemingway	2
John Senyor	1
Willm Wilson	2
Widdow Dixon	1
John Morehouse	1
John Wood	1
Robert Chappell	1
Richard Burnit	1
David Mallinson	1
Willm Hanson	1
Willm Wood	1
	124

Empty and noe distress to be had	
Thomas Hopper	1

These persons following are discharged by Certificates	
Willm Grenald	2
Giles Kay	1
Willm Copley	1
Edmond Marsdon	1
Edward Hurst	1
John Dyson	1
Grace Swallow	1
Allexandr Whitley	1
Widdow Wood	1

Omitted by reason of poverty	1

Robert Husband Collr
John Sikes Const

Liversidge
(Liversedge)

John Green Gent	6
John Green Jun	7
Joseph Kitchin	1
Richard Kitchin	2
Robert Liversidge	2
John Kitson	4
Anthony Brooke	3
Lawrance Heyworth	1
Willm Newby	1
Edward Robinson	3
Robert Kirke	1
Willm Brooke	3
John Burne	1
Abraham Hollingrigg	2
Richard Thomas	1
Joseph Walker	2
Widdow Raynor	6
Wilfrey Armitage	2
Willm Walker	4
Robert Walker	3
James Boss	3
Widdow Rouss	2
Willm Rouss	2
Thomas Stead	1
John Child	2
Edward Beamond	5
John Cordingley	1
John Tompson	1

m 70]

Nichollas Tompson	1
Widdow Stapleton	2
Thomas Brooke	3
Jerem Poole	5
Widdow Stead	3
Mathew Dodgson	1
Willm Proctor	1
John Fletcher	1
Widdow Hewit	2
James Cordingley	1
Joseph Crawshaw	1
Joseph Longbotham	1
Widdow Barnitt	1
Robert Walker	2
Widdow Healey	1
Widdow Brooke	3
Edward Brooke	3
Giles Barran	1
Thomas Brooke sen	5
John Smith Jun	1
Willm Green	10
Willm Green	5
John Rhoades	3

Richard Raynard	3
Thomas Wood	1
Richard Raynor Jun	3
Robert Armitage	1
Willm Poplewell	1
Willm Wilby	1
Mathew Houldsworth	1
Richard Houldsworth	4
Abraham Haworth Jun	2
Thomas Rhoades	1
Widdow Beamont	1
Jerem Farrer	3
John Walker	1
Thomas Walker	3
Robert Walker Jun	5
John Walker	2
Robert Healey	1
Thomas Beamond	5
Richard Green	5
Richard Scholefeild	1
Thomas Exley	2
Edward Barraclough	1
Widdow Beamond	1
Abraham Hayworth	5
Edward Beamond	1
John Wise	1
Thomas Broadley	1
Widdow Rayner	1
James Walker	1
John Stapleton	2
Willm Walker Jun	4
John Hall	1
Joshua Healey	3
John Longs	1
Thomas Naylor	2
Abraham Rhoades	1
Widdow Raynor	1
Richard Greene	1
Jonas Deekes	2
Widdow Blackburn	1
Willm Watmough	1
Robert Greaues	2
Thomas Walker	1
Thomas Castlehouse	1
Thomas Hewitt	1
Widdow Castlehouse	1
John Davy	1
John Graue	1
Joseph Walker	1
Widdow Brooke	1

m 71]

Joseph Ingham	1
John Armitage	1
John Brooke	1
Willm Walker	1
	222

Omitted by reason of poverty	6

Roger Hardcastle Collr
John Green Const

Langsfeild
(Langfield)

Robert Horne	6
Willm Sutcliff	2
Edward Sutcliff	2
Abraham Taylor	1
John Farrar	1
Samuell Whitley	1
John Lawe	1
Paull Kershawe	1
Widdow Law	1
Abraham Baraclough	1
James Gibson	3
John Ingham sen	3
John Ingham	1
James Heworth	2
John Lawe	1
Samuell Lawe	2
Widdow Lawe	1
John Sutcliff	3
Jeram Ingham sen	1
Abraham Feilding	1
Jerem Heworth	1
Jerem Ingham Jun	1
Timothy Greenwood	1
Daniell Greenwood	1
Nathanll Utley	3
Abraham Crosley	1
Charles Greenhow	1
John Hodgson	1
Charles Hayworth sen	2
John Eastwood	1
Simeon Wilson	1
Henry Sutcliffe	1
Willm Lawe	1
Charles Hayworth Jun	2
John Whaley	1
Widdow Hayworth	3
Robert Farrer	2
Edmond Rideing	1
Robert Sutcliffe	2
Richard Sutcliffe	2
Widdow Greenwood	2
John Knowles	2
Anthony Crosley	1
Samuell Crosley	1
Roger Tetlowe	1
Simeon Lord	1
Abraham Feilding	1
Abraham Kershawe	1
Nichollas Ogden	2
Paull Kershawe	1
	77

Omitted by reason of poverty	9

Roger Hardcastle Collr
John Ingham Const

Maningham
(Manningham)

m 72]

Mr Thomas Lister	7
John Denton	5
Henry Bradshaw	5
Thomas Bramley	2
Samuell Waide	3

Isaac Boulton	2
John Bentley	3
Mr Thomas Wilkinson	4
Willm Waide	1
Robert Wilkinson	2
John Furnice	1
John Wilcock	2
John Cowson	1
Richard Laycock	1
Willm Dancer	2
Christopr Birtch	2
George Mortimer	2
Richard Wainwright	1
Willm Stead	1
John Hastler	1
Willm Kendall	1
John Lumb	1
Richard Wainwright	1
Richard Tempest	1
John Crosley	1
Jerem Drake	1
Willm Wilkinson	2
Christopr Smith	1
Barbara Apleyard	1
Widdow Hamond	1
John Jewitt	3
Mr Thomas Lister	1
Willm Northrop	1
Peter Smith	1
John Eastburne	1
John Gregson	6
John Drake	3
Jerem Booth	1
John Hardy	2
Samuell Crabtree	1
John Jewit sen	1
John Hoyle	1
Thomas Sugden	1
Nathan Hanson	3
Widd Laycock	1
Willm Jewitt	1
Willm Nawthrop	2
Abraham Crowther	1
George Nawthrop	4
Jonas Northrop	1
Jerem Northrop	3
Daniell Utley	1
Nathan Hanson	1
Henry Eastburne	1
Willm Shires	1
Willm Bawden	1
Abraham Crabtree	1
John Crabtree	1
John Parker	2
John Burnley	1
Willm Davie	2
John Jewit	2
John Crabtree	5
Samuell Crabtree	1
Willm Watterhouse	1
	119

Robert More Collr

John Jewit Const

Midleton cum Thorpe
(Middleton with Thorpe)

John Leigh Esq	8
The New Hall	9
John Cassan	2

m 73]

Thomas Robinson sen	1
John Roades	1
Robert Walker	2
Willm Mann	1
George Smith	2
Thomas Oakers	1
Thomas Cass	1
Thomas Robson	1
Widdow Glover	1
Daniell Dobson	1
Richard Cockeram	1
John Speight	2
Francis Backhouse	1
Widdow Wriglesworth	1
Michaell Dawson	2
Roger Cooper	1
Francis Smith	2
Willm Mann	1
John Holmes	1
Edward Morris	2
Edmond Tompson	2
Willm Mann	2
Gabriell Massey	3
Mr John Herber	4
Robert Burbeck	1
Christopr Watson	1
Thomas Howden	1
Thomas Mann	1
Thomas Walker sen	2
Robert Killingbeck	1
Thomas Roper	2
Charles Mann	1
Thomas Wildman	2
James Littlewood	1
John Wilkinson	1
Willm Walker	3
John Peakcock	1
Willm Ryley	2
Willm Askwith	1
John Walker	1
Ellizabeth Leigh	1
Mr Lee	1
Mrs Gascoyne	8
Richard Cromack	2
Nichollas Beamond	1
Henry Beamond	1
Richard Brewerton	3
John Netleton	2
John Scholes	1
Anne Holmes	1
Willm Parker	1
John Gleadall	1
Nichollas Westerman	2[137] two
Dorothy Dobson	1
	104

[137] 2 written over 1.

Empty and noe distress to be had
Mr Lee 1

Omitted by reason of poverty 1

Robert Husband Collr
Jerem Roades Const

Methley
John Savill Esqr 43

m 74]

Mr Conyers 6
Mr Ashton 9
Mr Calverley 9
Mr Shann 8
Mr Witham 8
John Farrer Sen 1
Thomas Smith 2
John Crowther 1
Richard Ward 2
John Nelson 4
Richard Laverack 3
Robert Milner 2
Anne Schoaley 6
Richard Wood 1
Bryan Maud 1
Mr Savill 8
John Cockell 3
Robert Hall 3
Robert Bradford 4
Edward Schoaley 3
Francis Stables 2
Widdow Webster 1
Robert Butterfeild 2
Edward Crosfeild 1
Willm Taylor 4
Robert Jagger 1
John Shann 1
Robert Norris 1
Thomas Heigham 2
Robert Hall 1
Richard Burton 2
John Burton 4
Ralph Wainwright 3
John Nunns 2
Mr Nunns 4
Robert Nuns 6
Willm Shipin 2
Willm Hutchinson 1
Willm Nuns 2
Joseph Barton 2
Mr Willm Smithson 3
Willm Elliot 2
Robert Webster 4
Mathew Ashton 2
Lancel Tompson 3
Willm Hutchinson 2
Jerem Shaw 1
Christopr Gaile 1
Thomas Hill 2
John Farrar Jun 2
Richard Ward 2
John Dinison 2
Henry Hollins 3
George Burton 3
Widdow Johnson 1
Mr Collins 8
Ralph Bradforth 1
John Hagger 1
Willm Wetherall 1
Gilbert Stringer 1

m 75]

John Lookes 2
Jonas Finch 4
Willm Shann 3
Willm Webster 4
Willm Ward 4
Samuell Clayton 1
Adam Lake 2
Robert Schoafeild 2
Abraham Hutchinson 1
Willm Heslegraue 1
Thomas Marshall 1
Willm Roebuck 2
Willm Rickitt 1
John Hartley 1
Mathew Emerson 1
Robert Looks 2
James Clough 2
Henry Tompson Jun 3
John Arnold 2
John Milner 2
Willm Waid 1
Christopr Snowden 3
Mathew Nunns 1
Thomas Crabtree 2
Willm Roberts 3
John Hollins sen 4
Willm Morrit 2
Henry Tompson sen 1
John Hollins Jun 2
Thomas Sharpe 1
Robert Peace 1
Willm Johnson 1
Willm Pickersgill 1
Robert Thornton 1
Mr Robinson 5
Mr Robinson 1
Willm Lund 1
John Shann 4
Richard Nelson 1
Brian Burnett 1
Everingham Constable 1
John Cockill 1
Anne Stevenson 1
Widdow Savill 3
Robert Milner 4
Willm Stanfeild 1
Gilbert Nunns 1
Martin Johnson 2
Willm Browne 1
Mary Clough 3
Ralph Lund 1
Thomas Heigham 1
Willm Shann 1
Willm Batty 1
Thomas Todd 1

317

m 76]

Empty and noe distres to be had

Robt Tate	1
Omitted by reason of poverty	11

Robert Husband Collr
Robert Bradsbury Const

Mirfeild
(Mirfield)

Castle Hall	9
Edward Hellewell	1
John Backhouse	3
Widdow Savill	1
Thomas Blackburn	3
Willm Hewbanke	5
Robert Stockes	2
Daniell Jepson	1
John Ledgart	1
Widdow Shepley	6
Thomas Crosland	2
Henry Walker	1
Towngate house	3
Thomas Crosland	5
Richard Lee	1
Willm Brooke forge	1
John Lee	1
John Crosland	1
Widdow Jepson	3
Willm Gantte	2
Willm Shepley	3
Gilbert Houldsworth	5
Richard Sheard	2
Thomas France	2
Mr Thomas Beamont	6
Robert Hurst	5
Thomas Jepson	2
Widdow Peele	6
Edward Jepson	2
Willm France	1
Anthony Hepworth	1
Richard Cossine	1
Thomas Houldsworth	1
Samuell Liversidge	2
George Brooke	3
Thomas Tompson	2
Robert Craven	2
John Hall	4
Willm Stockdall	1
Thomas Lee	2
James Ray	1
Jerem Oxley	1
Willm Hall	4
Thomas Sharpe	4
George Harpine	1
John Senior	1
Widdow Shepley	4
Widdow Lambert	3
Thomas Marshall	3
Thomas Senyor	1
Willm Linley	1
Richard Brooke	4
Steven Watson	3

m 77]

Widdow Shepley	2
John Oates	2
Thomas Sheard	1
Widdow Sheard	2
John Messenger	1
Gilbert Houldsworth	3
Thomas Houldsworth	1
John Woffenden	2
Thomas Jackson	1
Mr Allanson	2
Edward Hepworth	4
John Rooper	2
Thomas Goodale	2
Willm Thornton	2
Edward Barber	2
John Saile	1
Willm Barker	1
Isaac Barker	3
George Hurst	3
Richard Senyor	5
Robert Houldsworth	3
Widdow Sikes	1
Daniell Rhoades	1
Henry Rhoades	1
Joseph Johnson	1
Robert Ledgart	2
Joseph Ledgart	2
Thomas Owen	1
Widdow Twedles	1
Thomas Marriot	1
Widdow Ellis	1
John Hurst	1

m 78]

Willm Jepson	2
Mrs Beamont	8
Mr Thurgulant	11
Thomas Mann	2
Mr Thorpe	5
Thomas Blackburne	3
Daniell Thornton	2
Nathaniell Crosland	3
Mr Senyer	4
Joseph Hurst	5
John Ledgart	2
Jonath Heaton	1
Brian Wilde	1
Robert Ilburde	1
Richard Hepworth	2
Willm Bawmforth	2
Thomas Tweedles	1
Willm Blackburne	1
Joshua Hurst	3
Isaac Thornton	2
Richard Eshell	1
John Chappell	1
John Midworth	1
Mr Furnish	3
Thomas Stockes	1
George Wood	1
John Jepson	2
Willm Marshall	1
Thomas Hepworth	1
Widdow Roper	1

Michaell Shearde 2
Joseph Jessop 1
John Jepson 1
Peter Harey 1
Edward Brooke 3
Richard Walker 1
Martin Ledgart 1
278

Empty and noe distress to be had
The freeschoole 1

Omitted by reason of poverty 5

Roger Hardcastle Collr
Thomas Marriot Const

Morley
The Lord Brutenell 44
Edward Birtby 4
Samuell Birtby 5
Richard Askwith 1
Widdow Tingle 2
Robert Radcliff 2
Thomas Dawson 1
Willm Wood 1
Thomas Dawson 4
Miles Grant 1
Richard Hardcastle 1
Willm Cundell 2
Widdow Greaues 2
Willm Gaile 1
John Webster 2
Joseph Greathead 2
Ralph Webster 1
John Crowther 2
Mr Thos Crayler 5
John Crowther 3
James Webster 1
Joseph Greathead 1
Willm Clarke 2

John Clarke 2
John Greathead 2
Widdow Greathead 2
Mr Baley 4
Stephen Tompson 2

m 79]

John Ellis Sen 3
Richard Morley 3
John Barray 1
Widdow Clarke 2
Paull Ellis 2
Thomas Atkinson jun 2
Miles Towleson 1
Benjam Wilson 2
Widdow Askwith 1
John Meyard 1
Richard Turner 1
Ralph Harris 3
Joseph Dixon 3
Brian Poe 3[138]
three
Robert Hall 2
Jerem Oates 1
Timothy Richinson 1
Widdow Oates 1
Mercy Burnley 1
Widdow Burnell 2
Willm Roebuck 2
Samuell Ward 4
John Ward 2
Richard Audsley 2
Willm Westerman 1
John Westerman 1
Robert Morley 4
Widdow Morley 1
Joseph Armitage 2
Willm Ellis 2
Robert Ratcliff 2
Willm Askwith 1
Willm Tomlinson 2
John Slack 1

Widdow Askwith 1
Willm Hatley 2
Robert Ellis 1
John Dobson 1
Richard Askwith 1
Robert Halliday 1
Willm Revill 1
Paull Ellis 2
Edward Askwith 1
Willm Mathewes 1
Mathew Smurfitt 2
George Westorman 1
Henry Kippax 1
John Dixon 1
John Batley 1
Thomas Speight 1
John Walker 1
Widdow Blackburne 1
Willm Todd 1
Mathew Westaby 2
Isaac Rowland 1
John Bracebridge 2
John Ledgart 2
John Cundall 2
Richard Huntington 1
Chrisopr Atkinson 1
Widdow Thackeray 2
Mathew Midlebrooke 2
Abraham Harrison 2
Thomas Webster 1
Mathew Parker 1
Willm Midgley 1
Richard Turner? 1
Richard Askwith 1
Thomas Oakes 1
Widdow Speight 1

m 80]

Robert Blackburn 1
Widdow Sawle 1
Joseph Crowther 1
John Dickinson 1

[138] 3 written over 1.

John Warran	1
John Senyer	3
	222

Empty and noe distress to be had

Ralph Radcliffe	2
Willm Clarke & forge	1
John Sharpe	3[139] three
Willm Asquith	1

Omitted by reason of poverty 6

Robert Moore Collr
Ralph Webster Const

Meltham halfe (Meltham Half)

Mr James Taylor	4
Anthony Armitage	8
Anthony Oldfeild	2
James Watterhouse	1
Abraham Beamond sen	3[140] three
Thomas Beamond	2
Edward Watterhouse	2
Thomas Harrison	2
Isaac Watterhouse	2
Thomas Campinet	1
Widdow Woodhead	1
Godfrey Hurst	3
John Woodhead	3
John Wilson	1
Joseph Berrey	1
Godfrey Eastwood	1
Willm Campinet	2
James Taylor	1
Richard Feild	2
John Taylor	2
John Haigh	1
Godfrey Linley	1
George Taylor	1
Edmond Parkins	2
John Taylor	1
Michll Littlewood	1
Anne Dyson	1
John Armitage	1
James Taylor	1
Willm Parkins	1
Timothy Woodhead	1
Hugh Tayler	1
Abraham Beamond	1
John Littlewood	1
James Taylor	1
John Eastwood	1
Edward Hague	2
Abraham Hurst	1
Widdow Thorpe	1
John Berrey	2
Robert Shawe	2
Edward Mallinsall	1
Gilbert Firth	1
Widdow Smith	1
George Kay	1
Thomas Littlewood	1
Godfrey Littlewood	1
Thomas Hague	2
Widdow Kay	2
Willm Kay	2

m 81]

Abraham Beaver	1
Susan Wilson	1
Godfrey Booth	2
Humphr Woodhead	1
Thomas Woodhead	1
Michaell Woodhead	1
Richard Brooke	2
Willm Sanderson	1
John Wilson	1
Steven Mitchill	1
Willm Marsdon	1
Joseph Mathewman	1
Godfrey Littlewood	1
James Hague	2
Robert Wedall	1
Widdow Wilson	1
	100

Empty and no distres to be had

Christopr Garlick	2

Omitted by reason of poverty 2

Thomas Midleton Collr
James Taylor Const

Marsden

Henry Pogson	1
Michaell Carter	1
James Haigh	4
Henry Marsden	1
Edmond Haigh	1
Henry Firth	1
Joseph Campinet	1
John Aynley	1
John Hague	1
Richard Waterhouse	1
Thomas Hague	2
Widdow Marsden	2
John Kay sen	1
John Kay Jun	2
John Haigh	1
John Haigh	2
Thomas Gleadall	1
Thomas Marsden	2
John Gleadall	1
Henry Marsden	1

139 3 written over 6.
140 3 written over 6.

Thomas Haigh	2
Widdow Gleadall	1
John Marsden	1
Luke Marsden	1
John Senyor	2
Parsevell Marsden	1
John Marsden	1
Edmond Mellor	1
Widdow Marsden	1
Thomas Shawe	1
John Shawe	1
Giles Shawe	2
John Marsden	2
James Marsden	1
James Marsden	1[141]
Samuell Haigh	4
Willm Aineley	3
Thomas Haigh	3
Widdow Haigh	4
Luke Firth	2
John Mellor	1

m 82]

Thomas Mellor	1
Thomas Eastwood	1
John Hague	2
John Mellor	1
John Firth	1
John Shaw	1
John Shawe	1
Willm Shawe	1
Michaell Shawe	1
Andrew Shaw	1
Robert Wood	1
Widdow Shawe	1
John Woodhead	3
Widdow Shawe	2
John Shawe	2
Luke Shawe	1
Michaell Shawe	1
John Firth	1
John Marsden	1
Widdow Berrey	1
Edward Firth	1
John Woodhead	1
Willm Firth	1
John Mellor	1
James France	2
John Shawcross	1
James Carter	2
Sam Mellor	1
Jerem Haigh	1
Robert Mellor	1
John Haigh	1
John Mellor	1
John Haigh	2
Widdow Haigh	2
James France	1
Luke Firth	1
James Garside	1
John Woodhead	2
John Marsden	1
	113

Omitted by reason of poverty	2

Robert Bennit Collr
John Mellor Const

Midgley

Willm Farrer Esqr	11
John Hellewell	4
Jonas Bradley	3
Henry Hellewell	2
John Lockwood sen	2
John Lockwood Jun	4
Henry Lockwood	1
Abraham Tettler	1
James Hanson	1
Rubin Waide	1
James Murgetroyd	1
Jonas Bloomer	1
John Saltenstall	1
James Bridg	5
George Law	2
Robt Wetmough	2
Nathan Pickles	1
George Lund	1
Martin Longbotham	4
John Beamont	2

m 83]

Simon Hellewell	1
Mr Timothy Wadsworth	4
Israell Wild	4
Nicholls Brewer	3
Mr Thomas Murgetroyd	8
Christopr Shawe	1
Widdow Rideing	4
Henry Hellewell	4
Henry Shaw	4
John Core Jun	1
John Coare	1
Richard Midgley	1
John Cheatom	3
Daniell Bridge	2
James Ouldfeild	3
Samuell Milnes	2
Isaac Farrer	1
John Farrer	2[142] two
Thomas Bridge	1
John Wadsworth	2
John Cawthrey	1
James Briggs	1
James Oldfeild	1
Willm Midgley	5
John Fauthropp	3
James Ryley	1
Widdow Padget	3
Henry Murgetroyde	7
James Shawe	1
Robert Procter	4

141 sic.
142 2 written over 1.

Samuell Midgley 3
John Farrer 1
Jonath Shaw 1
Abraham Hellewell 1
Samuell Aikeroyd 1
Isaac Briggs 2
Thomas Ryley 1
Thomas Briggs 1
Nichollas Driver 1
Edmond Turner 2
James Greenwood 2
Christopr Hargraues 1
Isaac Slaiding 1
Willm Walker 1
Widdow Browne 1
Abell Ratcliffe 1
Mr Fairand 7
Henry Broadbelt 2
Willm Rawson 1
James Oldfeild 1
161

These persons following are discharged by Certificates
John Spencer 1
Grace Bay 1
Thomas Hellewell 1
John Wood 1
John Smith 1
James Farrer 1
Sarah Holdgate 1
Sarah Wormall 1
Simon Hill 1
Martin Jenkinson 1
Willm Aikeroyde 1
Abraham Milnes 1
Jonathan Crabtree 1
John Widdupp 1
Widdow Slaiding 1
Edward Shackleton 1
Samuell Smith 1
Martha Beamond 1

m 84]

Samuell Wood 1
Robert Colbeck 1

Roger Hardcastle Collr
John Lockwood Const

North Owram (Northowram)
Samuell Carnill 2
Daniell Gill 4
Daniell Bentley 6
Willm Jackson 1
Joseph Hodgson 2
Robert Hopwood 5
Francis Wilkinson 2
John Wilkinson 2
Jonathan Halleday 4
Samuell Barstow 2
Mathew Craven 3
John Ramsdell 2
John Staincliff 3
Joseph Sugden 4
John Lee 3
Thomas Whitley 1
Robert Crowther 2
Isaac Firth 1
Jonas Thomas 3
Isaac Firth 2
Daniell Mitchell 6
Timothy Hemingway 2
Robert Brearley 1
Abraham Swift 2
Simon Lord 2
John Taylor 2
Richard Hoyle 5
John Oates 1
Grace Northend 2
John Northend 1
John Garnett 2
Joseph Crowther 2
Daniell Pollington 2
Gilbert Sturdy 6
Jonathan Threapland 2
Richard Smith 2

Jerem Watson 1
Abraham Sowood 2
John Sharpe 1
Jerem Baxter 4
Samuell Midgley 2
Judeth Drake 3
Edward Hudson 2
Mr Olliver Hewood 3
Jonas Northend 2
Jonas Stevenson 4
Roger Stock 2
Willm Clay 4
Joseph Crowther 5
Henry Northend 4
Nathanll Crowther 5
John Wells 3
James Briggs 3
Giles Tennant 2
Thomas Tullan 1
Widdow Lee 1
The Occprs of Westcroft 6
Mr Dawson 4

m 85]

Isaac Longbotham 4
Richard Hepworth 3
Robert Harper 3
Robert Barstow 3
Anthony Wattorhouse 1
John Northend 1
Willm Shepherd 2
Robert Fearnside 2
John Hodgson 8
Willm Gill 2
John Houldsworth 4
Samuell Houldsworth 1
Thomas Rushworth 2
Abraham Sunderland 1
Edward Nicholls 2
Joseph Senyer 3
James Jagger 1
John Holdsworth 1
Jerem Holmes 1
John Holmes 2

Mathew Jagger	2
Susan Franckleton	1
	1[143]
Henry Wilson	1
Isaack Smith	3
Edward Gill	2
Mathew Elswicke	1
Joseph Thorpe	1
Willm Rhoades	2
John Whitley	2
Isaac Smith	1
Samuell Houldsworth	1
Jerem Barstowe	1
Samuell Rushworth	1
George Barstowe	1
Jerem Barstow	2
George Barstow	1
John Longbotham	3
Isaac Longbotham	1
Abraham Gill	2
Abrah Woodhead	3
James Smith	2
Thomas Oldfeild	3
Widdow Barraclough	2
Abraham Browne	1
Willm Hollingrake	1
Abraham Barraclough	1
Jonas Robshaw	1
James Dickinson	3
Richard Mitchill	1
James Taylor	2
Thomas Wood	1
Isaac Watterhouse	1
John Denton	1
Jonas Bawmforth	1
John Smith	3
Jerem Dickinson	3
John Ambler	1
Michall Robertshaw	1
Joseph Flather	3
Mathew Drake	1
John Smith	5

m 86]

John Hargraues	1
John Briggs	3
John Langley	1
Widdow Barstow	5
Willm Clarke	2
John Scott	1
John Whittley	2
Jonathan Crowther	1
Edward Northend	2
Robert Cowling	3
Mathew Croyser	1
Jonathan Crowther	1
Jonathan Crowther Jun	1
Andrew Watson	2
John Robertshaw	1
Thomas Flather	3
Thomas Firth	2
Willm Hodgson	2
Thomas Flather	1
Abraham Hargraues	2
Samuell Barstowe	1
Edward Hodgson	1
John Maud	1
John Pollard	3
John Phillops	3
John Wilson	1
John Wilson	1
Abraham Hall	6
Mathew Rideing	4
Mary Bentley	2
Mrs Briggs	9
Mr Jonath Hall	2
Willm Pearson	4
Mr Jonas Hall	7
Josias Wilson	3[144]
	three
Samuell Swift	3
John Medley	2
Joseph Hopkins	5
Thomas Kitson	7

Richard Townend	2
Samuell Barber	3
Samuell Lister	8
John Wilby	1
James Burrow	1
Henry Ford	4
Thomas Dawson	1
Thomas Carr	4
Michaell Woodhead	3
Richard Jebson	1
John Staincliff	7
John Nicholls	1
Joseph Saltenstalll	1
James Wallis	1
Widdow Midgley	1
Abraham Barraclough	1
Joseph Thorp	2
Nathanll Tilson	2
Willm Watkinson	2
Samuell Whitley	2
	426

Omitted by reason of poverty 13

Robert Corner Collr
Samuell Lister Const

m 87]

Norland

Michaell Wainhouse	5
Thomas Truemon	3
Francis Jagger	2
John Crowther	1
Joseph Jagger	2
John Murr	1
Jonathan Walton	3
Joseph Hoyldroyd	3
John Milner	4
Widdow Towne	5

[143] sic.
[144] 3 written over 1.

Nathanll Chadwick	3
John Walton	1
Widdow Towne	6
Nathanll Baites	3
Timothy Ramsden	5
Daniell Watterhouse	1
Robert Battersby	3
Daniell Hoyle	6
Samuell Wood	3
James Ratcliff	2
Joseph Taylor	3
Isaac Holmes	1
John Wainhouse	4
Henry Barrowe	3
Nathanll Hoylroyd	5
Widdow Towne sen	4
John Preistley	1
Daniell Baites	2
Isaac Hellewell	2
Widdow Woodhead	2
Widdow Gugeon	2
Joseph Houldroyd	2
Benjam Reyley	2
Thomas Atkins	1
John Firth	1
Isaac Clegg	2
Benjam Bates	5
John Watterhouse	2
Israell Wild	2
Benjam Howlroyd	3
Michaell Soothill	1
Edward Wainehouse	1
Timothy Stansfeild	2
Jonas Crowther	1
George Houldroyd	2
Samuell Thomas	1
John Brearley	4
Joshua Jagger	3
David Taylor	1
Timothy Chadwick	3
James Ratcliff	3
Widdow Ingham	1
John Collins	2
Widdow Eccles	2
John Durden	1
George Harrison	1
Willm Denton	2
Nathanll Houldroyd	1
	143

m 88]

Roger Hardcastle Collr
John Rayner Const

Norminton
(Normanton)

Mr Bunny	12
Mr Cooper	6
Mr Favell	6
Mr Hill Viccar	6
Mr Nicholls	5
Lyonell Spinke	3
Mr John Higgins	3
John Crawshaw	2
John Garlick	2
Willm Shillitoe	2
Willm Blewit	2
Thomas Pinder	2
Willm Redman	2
James Garlick	2
Robert Simpson	1
Robert Webster	1
Thomas Spinke	1
Widdow Watson	1
John Foulds	1
Widdow White	1
Peter Redman	2
Richard Newsam	1
Richard Denton	2
John Oakes	1
Richard Metcalfe	1
Thomas Broadley	1
Francis Hall	1
Widdow Lister	1
Willm Bedforth	1
Thomas Garlick	2
Richard Bulmer	1
Robert Pattrick	1
Thomas Ryley	1
John Jubbs	2
Robert Standish	1
	80
Omitted by reason of poverty	2

Thomas Midleton Collr
Lyonell Spinke Const

North Byerley
(North Bierley)

George RookesEsqr	10
Barbara Pearson	5
Widdow Hanson	2
John Ellis	2
Widdow Houldsworth	2
Willm Birkes	1
Widdow Walton	2
Widdow Walton	1
James Walton	2
John Robinson	1
Willm Booth	1
Willm Roades	1
Richard Pickles	1
Edward Wadington	1
Robert Birkeby	1
Joseph Threapland	2

m 89]

Thomas Faucett	1
Edward Wadington	1
Francis Barraclough	3
Abraham Pickles	2
Willm Whitley	1
Widdow Firth	2
Mathew Chippendale	2
Thomas Boore	1
Miles Smith	1
Thomas Viccars	4
Widdow Darwin	2
Richard Rowlinson	2
Abraham Barstowe	1
Nathanll Drake	1

John Fox 2
James Speight 1
John Smith 5
Randelph Wood 2
Willm Blamires 2
Lawrance Whitehead 1
Jonas Blamiers 1
Abraham Longbotham 1
Jonas Barraclough 1
John Sagar 2
Edward Hevit 1
Joseph Blamiers 2
Thomas Littlewood 2
Jerem Houldsworth 1
John Smith 3
Mr Samuell Crowther 4
Michaell Balme 3
Robert Booth 4
Samuell Swaine 2
John Crosland 1
Mary Robinson 1
Jonathan Faucit 1
Robert Wood 1
Willm Croft 1
Abraham Swaine 4
Abraham Baraclough 1
Willm Pollard 2
Edward Kellit 1
John Cordley 2
Mr John Wright 5
Jonas Rhoades 3
Luke Illingworth 2
John Sugden 1
Thomas Walker 3
Widdow Watterhouse 1
Willm Oddy 2
Mr Robert Watters 2
Susan Collinson 1
Jonas Booth 1
John Brooksbanke 3
James Sturdey 4
Thomas Netleton 1

Samuell Widdupp 3
Joseph Fearnley 2
George Tompson 3
Robert Robinson 1
Jerem Newby 1
Widdow Richardson 10
ten

Nichollas Pollard 4
James Sharpe 3

m 90]

Willm Pollard 4
Willm Gibson 2
Thomas Arundall 4
John Pollard 2
Widdow Pollard 1
Edward Threapland 1
Richard Stead 3
Willm Seed 1
James Pearson 2
John Royston 2
Abraham Rhoades 3
Mrs Richardson 6
George Franckland 2
Samuell Thornton 2
Mary Thornton 1
Willm Lawe 1
Richard Ashby 3
Robt Anderson 2
John Parish 1
Tobias Hopkinson 2[145]
two

Widdow Phillips 3
Richard Cordingley 3
Willm Ashton 1
Richard Veritye 2
Robert Womersley 1
Joseph Fearneley 1
Widdow Turner 3
Willm Illingworth 1
Widdow Hudson 1
Joseph Stancliffe 1

John Longbotham 1
Samuell Judson 1
234

Empty & no distress to be had
The heires of Thomas Ellison 1
Joseph Fearnley 1
Mr Rookes 1

Omitted by reason of poverty 13

Robert More Collr
Samll Widdup Const

Ossett

Willm Hopwood 4
John White 3
James Rider 1
Joseph Thornes 2
James Lee 1
James Maxfeild 1
Roger Hurst 2
Willm Pashley 1
John Townend 1
Willm Gill 2
Willm Parke 1
Henry Essot 3
Thomas Hepworth 2
John Lee 1
Richard Smith 3
Robert Netleton 1
James Ryder 2

m 91]

Widdow Peace 1
Widdow Cloughton 2
John Forrest 2
Robt Bradford 3[146]
two

145 2 written over 1.
146 3 written over 2.

Thomas Wormall	1
Joseph White	2
James Curtice	1
John Benshaw	2
John Lund	3
Edward Bradforth	3
Thomas Naylor	4
George Naylor	2
Mr Richard Netleton	1
Widdow Naylor	2
Christopr Brooke	1
Joseph Wilson	1
John Wardsall	2
George Otley	1
John Forrest	2
Anthony Armitage	1
John Bowland	2
Robert Pickard	3
James Wilson	2
Christopr Ardsley	2
Mr Kershaw	5
Robert Thorns sen	1
Widdow Peace	2
Robert Ardsley	1
Joseph Ardsley	3
George Glover	1
John Peace	2
Willm Sugden	1
John Ardsley	2
John Naylor	1
Joseph Jebson	2
Anthony Curtice	2
Joseph Midlebrooke	1
Edward Haigh	1
Robert Kidd	2
Willm Peace	2
Willm Ingham	1
Willm Milner	1
Robert Chipchase	1
Widdow Jagger	2
Willm Harrop	3
John Batty	2
Willm Hopwood	3
James Wilson sen	2
Willm Wilson	4
Edmond Speight	1
John Bould	1
James Grime	1
Thomas Terrey	1
Parcevell Terrey Jun	2}
and senior	2}[147]
George Netleton	2
Henry Schoalefeild[148]	1
Widdow Farnley	2
Richard Terrey Jun	4
Willm Kidson	2

m 92]

Joseph Nicholls	4
John Tirrey	1[149]
Richard Tirrey sen	1
Abraham Fletcher	1
Anne Shaw	1
James Grimes	1
Thomas Tirrey sen	1
Timothy Schoalfeild	3
Joseph Spurr	2
Maske Whitacrs	4
Anthony Whitley	1
John Spurr	2
John Ardsley	2
Thomas Pickard	1
Robert Barugh	1
John Armitage	1
Robert Moxon	1
Richard Foster	2
Willm Ingham	2
Richard Foster	1
Thomas Nelstropp	1
George Ellis	1
Samuell Walmsley	1
Thomas White	1
Willm Speight	1
John Batty Mill	1
Willm Pashley	1
Widdow Walshaw	1
Thomas Altwick	1
George Glover	1
Edmond Lord	1
Willm Carr	1
John Hawley	1
Samuell Pickard	2
	192

Empty and no distres to be had	
Major Reesby	1
Mr Hopkinson	1
Lord Brewtnell	2
Mr Mr Hopkinson	1

Omitted by reason of poverty	3

Robt Husband Collr
Anthony Whitley Const

Ovenden

Mr Joseph Furnice	7
Mr John Lister	10
John Bastow	2
Abraham Illingworth	2
Widdow Wood	4
John Ryall	3
John Illingworth	3
Samuell Deane	1
George Tillotson	3
Geo Firthe	3

m 93]

John Broadley	2
Widdow Eastwood	1

147 Line inserted.
148 Line inserted.
149 Line inserted.

John Ryall	1
Edward Doughty	3
Andrew Jackson	1
James Murgetroyd	5
Samuell Casson	3
Samuell Tasker	2
Timothy Mitchill	3
Joseph Watkinson	3
Thomas Preistley	5
Widdow Wilkinson	2
John More	1
John Feild	3
Widdow Garforth	3
Ambros Tetley	4
George Hesledin	3
John Denton	2
Alverah Bentley	1
Daniell Houldsworth	3
Joseph Tasker	1
Widdow Illingworth	2
John Illingworth	3
Isaac Hoyle	2
John Platt	2
John Wilson	3
Abraham Farrar	1
John Brathwaite	5
Mrs Wadington	10
Abraham Deane	2
Willm Kitchingman	3
Nichollas Kutcliff	4
Robert Doughty	3
Abraham Kirshaw	3
Isaac Wilson	2
John Barstow	1
Widdow Best	2
Widdow Best	3
John Keighley	1
Jonas Brigg	2
Abraham Houlegate	2
Willm Potterton	2
Abrahm Hemingway	2
John Starkey	4
Abraham Walton	1
John England	1
John Ryley	2

Henry Richardson	4
John Aikroyd	2
John Deane	1
John Ryley	4
Widdow Hodgson	1
James Wilson	3
Thomas Maukes	2
John Aigland	1
Samuell Tasker	1
John Wadsworth	3
Thomas Roper	2
Henry Taylor	2
Joshua Smith	1
Samuell Hoyle	2

m 94]

John Maude	1
Richard Northend	1
Abraham Jewitt	1
Miles Farnill	1
Christop Ramsden	1
Jacob Wilson	1
Titus Mitchill	1
Isaac Wilson	1
Michll Hawthrop	1
Willm Aikeroyd	1
Widdow Berrey	1
Abraham Bawmforth	1
John Teasedall	2
John Watterhouse	1
Abraham Briggs	3
Michaell Elswick	1
Daniell Lister	4
Nichollas Elbeck	4
Michll Wadington	3
John Illingworth	1
John Deane	4
Jona Scholefeild	3
Widdow Whitley	4
Jonathan Mitchill	2
Richard Crabtree	1
Thomas Shird	2
Michaell Murgetroyd	1
Mathew Crosor	2

George Ramsden	3
James Whitworth	2
Michaell Woodhead	1
Widdow John Eastwood	1
John Greenwood	1
Abraham Hindle	1
Willm Jenkinson	1
Edward Whitacre	1
James Butterfeild	1
Jonas Ingham	1
John Ainsworth	1
Willm Butler	1
Nichols Atkinson	1
Joseph Firth	1
John Mitchill	1
Robert Deane	2
Joseph Briggs	2
Mr Peele	4
Joseph Wilson	1
John Redihough	1
Joseph Crosley	1
Thomas Richinson	2
Abrah Blackburn	2
Joseph Rhoades	2
Michll Hesleden	4
John Sutcliff sen	1
Joseph More	1
Samuell Denton	2
James Whitehead	2
James Boulton	3
Martin Longbotham	3

m 95]

Robert Wright	1
Michaell Smith	2
Widdow Spencer	2
Jonas Ryley	4
Edmond Barstow	2
Abraham Deane	2
Christop Ramsden	1
John Bawmforth	1
Wilm Gott	1
Willm Deane	2
Willm Feild	1

Isaac Shawe	1
John Pickles	2
John Spencer	1
James Ingham	2
Henry More	2
Isaac Baites	1
Thomas Watterhouse	1
Henry Hanson	2
Widdow Crabtree	3
Abraham Earnshawe	1
James Baites	1
Willm Oates	1
Nicholls Rycroft	2
John Cockcroft	1
Jonath Cockcroft	2
Michll Whitwham	1
John Varley	2
Robert Hurst	1
Henry Horsfeild	1
John Craven	2
Widdow Crabtree	6
John Barstow	2

m 96]

Jonas Varley	1
Richard Bairstowe	1
Willm Rhoades	1
Anthony Scholefeild	3
Thomas Blakey	3
John Phillopp	1
Thomas Longbotham	3
John Pickles	1
John Brackburne	1
Dinis Illingworth	1
Anthony Croyer	2[150]
	two
John Ryley	1
John Illingworth	1
Samll Waite	2
John Lister	1
Anthony Driver	1

John Milner	2
Abraham Earnshawe	2
Widdow Briggs	1
John Robinson	1
Thomas Mercer	2
Abraham Tetloue	2
Thomas Spencer	2
Samuell Swift	2
James Harper	1
Joseph Watkinson	1
Illingworth farme	1
Willm Webster	1
Widdow Hanson	1
Thomas Sutcliff	1
John Whitley	1
	390

m 97]

Omitted by reason of poverty	9

Robt More Const
Joseph Rhoades Const

Pudsey

Mr Robert Milner	5
Mr James Sayles	7
Mr John Smith	4
Joseph Holdsworth	2
Thomas Hutchinson	2
Abraham Hutchinson	2
James Poole	1
Samuell Lumbley	4
Willm Child	1
Richard Lee	1
Widdow Whitacres	1
Gabriell Dodgson	1
John Deighton	1
Henry Belhouse	1
Thomas Lee	1
Richard Lumley	1
Willm Jenkinson	2

Samuell Stables	1
Willm Atkinson	3
Widdow Kitson	2
John Wilson	2
Timothy Calverley	1
Michaell Ryley	1
Thomas Butterfeild	1
Willm Child	1
John Lee	1
John Lee	1[151]
John Chapman	2
Michaell Ryley	1
Edward Hinchcliff	2
John Deighton	1
Mr Ingham	1
George Hudson	1
Jafet Atkinson	4
Edward Smith	2
Willm Lee	2
Joseph Linley	2
Thomas Wilden	2
Edward Wood	2
John Procter	1
John Haigh	2
Willm Rudd	1
Willm Lepton	3
Abraham Farrer	1
James Pearson	1
Thomas Taylor	1
Steven Harper	2
Thomas Mitchill	1
John Gaunt sen	2
Daniell Gaunt	1
Samuell Belhouse	2
Thomas Baines	1
Willm Hey	2
Jerem Crabtree	1

m 98]

John Galloway	2
Thomas Musgraue	1

[150] 2 written over 1.
[151] sic.

Samuell Lumby	2
Widdow Wise	1
Samuell Cawthrey	2
Willm Smith	1
Grace Milner	2
Richard Gaunt	2
Richard Lobley	4
Samuell Gaunt	1
Christopr Whitley	1
Willm Lumby	2
James Gaunt	1
Robert Burnell	1
Richard Farrar	1
Willm Hollingworth	1
John Wood	2
Willm Hall	2
Willm More	1
Widdow Hainworth	2
John Netleton	1
Henry Netleton	2
Dorothy Gaunt	1
Willm Moss	3
Willm Moss	2
Peter Pickersgill	1
Thomas Syser	3
Robert Sugden	2
Steven Stout	1
Richard Sugden	1
Timothy Elsworth	1
Willm Wainwright	1
Joseph Bower	1
Widdow Geldart	2
Tristrum Haire	1
Thomas Ellott	1
Willm Farray	1
Willm Sugden	1
Thomas Roborts	1
Willm Lee sen	1
Willm Lee Jun	1
Widdow Ditch	1
Willm Lee	1
Widdow Pawson	2
John Wilson	1
Edmond Boocock	1
James Crabtree	2
John Milner	1
Isaac Balme	2
Abraham Hainworth	1
Willm Kellit	1
	169

Empty and noe distres to be had

Humphrey Hutchinson	1

Omitted by reason of poverty	14

Robert More Collr
Samll Jenkinson Const

Quick

Thomas Wheele	1
James Schoafeild	1
Robert Walker	1
Ellexandr Schoafeild	1
James Bradbury	1
James Buckley	1

m 99]

Robert Harropp	1
Richard Bradsbury	1
Robert Platts	1
George Shaw	3
Lawrance Wood	1
Robert Tompson	1
Isaac Bothamley	1
John Bothamley	1
Willm Knight	1
Ralph Andrew	1
John Lawton	1
John Shaw	2
Widdow Schoafeild	1
John Schoafeild	1
Peter Bradbury	1
Willm Broadbent	2
John Whitehead	1
Edmond Buckley	1
George Winterbotham	1
James Greaue	1
John Whewell	1
John Rigley	1
Willm Ratcliffe	2
John Shaw	1
Willm Loes	1
Giles Shaw	2
James Whitehead sen	1
James Whitehead Jun	1
John Bradbury Jun	1
James Broadbent	2[152] two
Ellias Wrigley	1
Widdow Taylor	1
Widdow Wild	1
Mrs Lee	3
Peter Bradbury	4
Robert Taylor	1
James Taylor	1
Robert Broadbent	4
George Malledew	1
Edmond Ward	2
Edmond Farrand	1
John Schoafeild	1
John Taylor	1
Edmond Platts Jun	1
John Whewell	1
Ellias Wrigley	1
Thomas Malledew	1
John Foaley	1
Widdow Wrigley	1
Thomas Wild	1
Samuell Swift	1
John Farrand	1
Thomas Bradbury	1

m 100]

James Wrigley	1
James Broadbent	1

[152] 2 written over 1.

Thomas Bradbury	1
John Schoafeild	1
Henry Shawe	1
James Bradbury	1
Widdow Broadbent	1
Jane Broadbent	1
James Broadbent	1
George Hurst	1
George Broadbent sen	1
George Broadbent Jun	1
Edmond Schoafeild	1
Thomas Rhoades	2
Widdow Broadbent	1
John Whitehead	1
James Broadbent	1
Edmond Platts	1
Robert Tompson	1
Ambros Schoafeild	1
John Marshland	1
Widdow Platts	1
Edmond Platts	1
John Whitehead	1
Jarvas Walker executor	1
John Wood	1
John Shaw	1
Thomas Kenworthy	1
Widdow Whitehead	2
Richard Lawton	1
George Lauton	1
George Schoafeild	1
Edmond Schoafeild	1
Francis Schoafeild	1
Widdow Schoafeild	1
James Hall	1
Edmond Buckley	1
John Schoafeild	1
Edmond Schoafeild	1
George Garside	1
Robert Linthwaite	1
James Schoafeild	1
Thomas Milnes	1

Thomas Milnes	1[153]
Robert Whitehead	3
Daniell Whitehead	1
John Whitehead	1
John Wrigley	1
James Linthwaite	1
John Garside	1
Robert Schoafeild	1
Widdow Buckley	1
Isaac Lee	1
John Buckley	1
Edmond Buckley	1
Willm Buckley	1[154]
Henry Buckley	3
John Wood	1[155]
John Wrigley	1
Widdow Buckley	1
John Garside	2
Widdow Garside	1
John Garside	2
James Garside	1
John Garside	2

m 101]

Edmond Buckley	1[156]
John Garside	1
Francis Garside	1
Robert Garside	1
Henry Garside	1
Edmond Garside	1
Henry Buckley sen	1
Henry Buckley Jun	1
Robert Buckely Jun	1
John Buckley sen	1
Robert Buckely sen	1
John Buckley Jun	1
Ellizabeth Hill	1
Edmond Buckley	1
John Whitehead	1
James Kenworthy	1

Hugh Kenworthy	1
Willm Kenworthy	1
John Whitehead	1
James Kenworthy	3
John Bennyson	4
Enoch Andrew	2
Sallomon Hardy	1
Thomas Whitehead	3
Widdow Heworth	1
John Heworth	1
Thomas Shaw	1
John Barwick	1
John Shaw	1
John Winterbotham	2
Widdow Whitehead	1
Henry Shaw	2
Henry Whitehead	1
Willm Buckley	1
John Shaw	1
John Buckley	1
Jonathan Shawe	1
Widdow Taylor	1
John Lawton	1
Robert Winterbotham sen	1
Robert Winterbotham Jun	1
John Winterbotham sen	1
John Winterbotham Jun	1
John Winterbotham	1
James Clayton	1
James Lee sen	1
James Whitacrs	1
Joseph Taylor	1
Willm Schoafeild	1
James Buckley	1
Michaell Thorpe	3
Edmond Buckley	1
Samuell Haywood	2

153 sic.
154 Line inserted.
155 Line inserted.
156 Line inserted.

James Lee	1
Daniell Lee	1
James Lee Jun	1
George Thorpe	1
Samuell Lee	1
Edmond Lee	4
Widdow Dixon	1
Willm Garlick	1
Rowland Dixon	1
John Andrew	1
Richard Dransfeild	1
John Tweedall	1
Edmond Schoafeild	1
Abraham Lee	1
Willm Hardy	3
Edmond Buckley sen	1
Thomas Buckley	1

m 102]

Edmond Buckley jun	1
Phillp Buckley	1
Richard Ratcliffe	1
Joseph Whitehead	1
Ralph Howden	1
Willm Buckley	1
Willm Kenworthy	1
John Greaves	1
James Heslegraue	1
Henry Buckley	1
Edmond Buckley	1
Nichollas Booth	1
Ralph Hawksyard	1
Willm Lee	1
John Kenworthy	1
John Malledew	1
Allexandr Ratcliffe	2
James Shawe	1
Hugh Schoafeild	1
James Shaw	2
Widdow Shawe	1
Thomas Hawksyard	1
Isaac Whitehead	2
Henry Shaw	1
James Schoafeild	1
Robert Broadbent	1
John Platts	1
Robert Wheeley	1
Thomas Buckley	1
Edmond Ratcliffe	1
Willm Whewell	1
Ellexandr Ratcliffe	1
Abraham Wrigley	1
Thomas Winterbotham	1
Willm Taylor	1
John Schoafeild	1
Thomas Wood	1
John Whitehead	1
Thomas Hawksyard	1
James Lee	1
Edmond Bradbury	1
	281

Omitted by reason of poverty	12

Robt Bennit Collr
Michll Thorpe Const

Quarmby Linley Quarter (Quarmby Lindley Quarter)

Adam Armitage	2[157] two
Henry Hay Jun	1
John Yeadon	2
Willm Iberson	1
Edward Crosland	2
Anne Clay	2
Henry Hay Jun	1
George Crowther	1
Edward Hanson	1
Edward Brooke	1
Ellin Morehouse	2
Richard Hague	2[158] two
Edward Mellor	1
John Wilkinson sen	1
John Wilkinson Jun	1
Willm Royd	1

m 103]

Willm Morehouse	2
John Wilkinson	1
Willm Clay	1
John Hinchcliff	2
Widdow Clay	1
George Mallinson	2
George Clay	1
Edward Morton	2
Widdow Woffenden	3
Edward Harland	2
James Hague	2
Willm Clay	2
Widdow Morton	1
James Campinett	2
Edward Hoyle	1
Widdow Ogden	1
James Hague	3
John Marshland	1
Gilbert Crowther	1
George Brooke	1
Francis Copley	1
Michll Morton	1
Michll Walton	1
Edmond Watterhouse	1
Abraham Jagger	1
George Yeadon	1
Thomas Chapman	1
Abraham Morehouse	2
Willm Woffenden	3
Abraham Mallinson	1
Nicholas Coverdill	1
	68

[157] 2 written over 1.
[158] 2 written over 1.

Empty and noe distress to be had

Abraham Bentley	1
Thomas Jagger	1

The person undernamed is discharged by Certift

Thomas Crosland	1

Omitted by reason of poverty 4

Thomas Midleton Collr
Abra Morehouse Const

m 104]

Scamadine Quarter (Scammonden Quarter)

George Hay	3
George Hudson	3[159] three
Thomas Denton	4
Michll Hoyle	2
Richard Bothamley	2
George Hawksyard	1
Michll Goodley	1
George Hoyle	1
Michaell Jacker	1
John Stead	1
John Denton	1
John Gleadall	1
James Hoyle	2
Edward Hoyle	1
John Robinson	1
Michaell Hurst	2
Daniell Hoyle	1
Nathanll Hoyle	1
Willm Denton	2
John Bothamley	1
Edmond Cooper	1
Widdow Earnshaw	1
Michaell Staincliff	2
Thomas Baraclough	1
John Dyson	1
John Hoyle	2
John Hoy	2
James Haigh	1
John Hoyle	2
James Robinson	1
Isaac Wormall	1
George Taylor	1

m 105]

James Robinson	1
George Walker Jun	1
	50

Empty and noe distress to be had

Michaell Firth	1

Omitted by reason of poverty 3

Thomas Middleton Collr
Robt Malinson Const

Northcrosland Quartr (North Crosland Quarter)

Peter Kay	1
Thomas Lockwood	1
Michaell Blackburn	3[160] thre
Abraham Shaw	1
Robert Walker	1
Mary Walker	1
John Sikes	1
James Sikes	1
Thomas Mallinson	2
Edward Mallinson	1
James Baxter	1
Edward Armitage	1
George Parkins	1
Anne Dyson	1
George Dyson	1
Robert Garside	1
George Batley	1
John Sikes	1
John Hellewell	1
John Schoafeild	1
Edward Mallinson	1
George Sikes	1
John Parkins	1
James Bothamley	1
Willm Hellewell	3
John Butterworth	2
Willm Swallow	1
Widdow Haigh	1
John Walker	2
John Oxley	2
Willm Hurst	1
John Hurst	3
Nicholl Crowther	1
John Goodart	1
Henry Hague	3
George Shawe	1
Abraham Beamond	1
James Hurst	2
Widdow Shaw	1
John Apleyard	1
Robert Thornton	4
James Walker	8
John Thornton	1
Thomas Thornton	1
James Sikes	1
Robert Hirst	1
Francis Brooke	2
John France	1
Thomas Sikes Jun	2
Nichollas Beamond	1
Robt France	1
John Batty	1

159 3 written over 2.
160 3 written over 2.

m 106]

Willm Kay Jun	1
Widdow Armitage	1
Edward Beamond	1
Dorothy Turpin	2
John Collidge	1
Francis Knight	1
James Savill	1
Edmond Hellewell	1
James Mallinson	1
Andrew Hellewell	1
Richard Milns	1
	89

Empty and no distress to be had

Michael Hague	1

Omitted by reason of poverty	1

Cold Car Quartr (Golcar Quarter)

Nichollas Chadwick	2
John Hurst	1
Richard Lee	2
John Dyson	4
James Wilson	2
Hugh Ramsden	4
Jerem ~~Aineley~~	~~1~~
~~John Shaw~~	1[161]
Edward Lee	2
Thomas Foster	1
John Hurst	1
John Haigh	2
John Hurst	1
Willm Dyson	2
George Hurst	1
Edward Haigh	2
Anthony Bray	3
Joseph Whitwham	1
James Whitwham	1
John Hurst	1
James Hurst	3
James Rigley	2
Arthur Wilson	1
John Haigh	1
Widdow Walker	3
John Haigh	1
Willm Aineley	2
Widdow Eastwood	5
Joseph Apeleyard	1
John Eastwood	1
George Dyson	4
Nichollas Lockwood	2
James Dyson	5
Widdow Dyson	1
Widdow Hoyle	1
Toby Walker	1
George Ratcliffe	1
John Pogson	1
John Hague	1

m 107]

James Bray	1
John Bray	2
Hugh Ramsden	3
Widdow Broadbent	2
Edward Harlin	1
Willm Aineley	1
John Wilson	1
Edward Hurst	2
John Lockwood	3
Henry Pogson	1
James Grime	2
Robert Heywood	1
Joseph Dyson	1
James Goldthropp	1
Willm Dysonn	2
Richard Crosland	1
James Swinden	1
Widdow Brooke	1
John Taylor	1
John Haigh	1
John Hall	1
James Harrison	1
John Hinchcliffe	1
John Wilson sen	1
Robert Shaw	1[162] one
Edward Harlin	2
Widdow Dyson	1
Willm Dyson	1
	111[163]

Empty and noe distress to be had

James Whitley	1

Omitted by reason of poverty	4

Robt Bennit Collr
James Grimes Const

Longwood Quartr (Longwood Quarter)

Sarah Ramsden	1
Benjam Oldroyd	2
Willm Danton	1
John Denton	1
John Hinchcliffe	1
Michaell Dawson	1
Godfrey Hinchcliffe	1
Widdow Butterworth	1
John Denton	1
Thomas Oldfeild	1
Jarvas Ainley	1
Benjam Houldroyd	1
George Haigh	2
Joseph Nicholls	2

161 The hearth owned by John Shaw has not been struck through and it seems to have been included in the total for Golcar Quarter.

162 1 written over 3.

163 There is a scribal error since the total is 110.

John Owen	2
Henry Smith	2
Edward Hollingworth	3
Gilbert Ramsden	2
Joseph Ramsden	1
John Hanson	4
Mr John Taylor sen	1
Mr John Taylor Jun	5
Widdow Brayshay	2
Robert Thornton	1
Willm Crowther	1
James Sikes	1
John Hanson	2

m 108]

Edward Taylor	2
Willm Hurst	1
John Bawderston	1
Joseph Dawson	1
Edward Linley	2
Abraham Kay	1
Matthew Jagger	1
Edward Ainley	2
Willm Hague	1
Willm Sedgwick	2
John Hague	2
James Haigh	1
George Dawson	2
John Richardson	1
Henry Heigh	2
Widdow Gleadall	2
Edward Heigh	1
George Hurst	1
Widdow Hurst	1
John Hellewell	2[164] two
Robert Hanson	1
	74

Empty and noe distres to be had

George Ripley	1
Omitted by reason of poverty	1

Thomas Middleton Collr
Thomas Mallinson Const

Rothwell

Anthony More	4
Ralph Driver	1
Marmaduke Faucit	1
Abraham Pickard	1
Ellizab More	1
John Savill	2
Richard Willas	5
Willm More	4
Humphr More	2
Richard More	3
George Mathew	2
Mathew Powell	2
Willm Lightfoote	5
Robert Calverley	4
Thomas Walker	2
Willm Thornton	2
Willm Boyes	3
Henry Allerton	1
George Pearson	1
James Crosfeild	1
John Hall Sen	1
John Hall Jun	1
Thomas Gibson	1
John Glouer	3
Richard Faucit	5
Thomas Lupton	1
John More	1
Richard Bradforth	3
Mr Francis Laburne	8
Anne Milner wid	3

m 109]

Thomas Gibson	5
Widdow Feather	3
Widdow Dobson	3
Richard Lund	4
Mr Gravener	5
Steven Mathew	1
Edward Wolfolke	1
Dorothy Roberts	3
Willm Faucitt	3
Gabriell Brearcliffe	3
Mary Butterfeild	2
Griffin Stansfeild	2
John Clayreburn	4
Mr Stamper	5
Thomas Paine	3
Francis White	2
Willm Hall	1
Henry Clarebrough	2
Francis Croft	2
Martin Stansfeild	2
Robert More sen	3
Robert More Jun	3
Samuell Flockton	1
Mr Gravener	7
Thomas Midleham	1
John Wood	2
Marmaduke Milner	3
Martin Lupton	2
Gilbert Dobson	1
Robert Atkinson	5
John Stansfeild	1
Mr Robinson Mill	1
John More	2
John Dobson Jun	1
John Dobson sen	2
Mr Stamper	4
Henry Cockle	3
Ralph Brooke	2
Henry Johnson	2
Edward Hemingway	1
Willm Pearson	1
Steven Cockhill	3
Richard More	1
Willm Dobson	2
Mr Shaw	4
Samuell Croft	2

[164] 2 written over 1.

John Roberts	3
John Westerman	2
Steven Westerman	1
John Clough	2
Willm Atkinson	3
Thomas Flockton	3
Willm Mason	1
Mathew Dixon	1
Willm Lambert	2[165] two
John Layster	3
Widdow Layster	1
Richard Tate	1
Willm Pickard	1

m 110]

George Read	1
Francis Wood	1
Widdow Whitwood	1
Richard Earle	2
Vallentine Peckitt	2
Mr Gamble	3
James Westerman	2
Robert Heptenstall	1
Willm Webster	1
John Cheesbrough	1
Mr Booth	2
Mr Savill Jackson	7
Willm Carter	1
Christopr Roades	2
Robert Swift	2
Richard Dobson	1
John Dobson	1
Willm Poole	2
Edward Allon	3
Willm Stead sen	1
Willm Stead Jun	2
Robert Stead	1
Edward Schoales	1
Luke Liversidge	1
Robert Raynor	2
John Cockhill	2
Robert Raynor	1
George Liversidge	2
Marmad Milner	1
Willm Westerman	2
Willm Cockill	2
John Scott	1
Widdow Pickard	1
John Lee	2
Robert Rayner	1
Edward Parker	1
Richard Scott	1
Thomas Peckitt	2
Thomas Hudson	2
John Lightfoote	1
Thomas Parker	2
George Benson	2
Christopr Booth	2
more *pro* Greenfeilds	1
Roger Lake	1
Willm Wright	1
Henry Wriglesworth	1
Widdow Wriglesworth	2
John Lancaster	2

m 111]

John Hargraue	2
Christopr Dixon	1
John Westerman	2
John Vevars	1
Thomas Burton	1
Mr George Gamble	7
Robert Smith	1
Nichollas Westerman	2
James Burnell	2
Richard Woffenden	2
Edward Hickes	2
Mrs Hutchinson	4
Robert Hardisty	4
George Burnet	5
Samuell Watson	2
Henry Harrison	4
Widdow Wainwright	2
Henry Brashawe	1
John Harrison	2
John Ramsdin	1
John Lee	2
Robert White	2
Widdow Houldsworth	1
Henry Oades	1
Henry Armitage	2
John Netleton	1
Widdow Westerman	2
Robert Cowburne	1
John Westerman	2
Mr Hopkinson	8 Eight
Robert White	2
Robert Westerman	2
Edward Eshald	1
Willm Howson	2
Robert Bell	3
Willm Lilly	3
Willm Lilly	1
John Hudson	1
Thomas Flocton	2
Widdow Vevars	3
Henry Howson	1
Francis Terrington	1
Widdow Nutter	4
Anthony Parkins	3
Mrs Siddall	2
Simond Parker	1
Henry Gouldsbrough	2
Dinis Hodgson	1
Richard Flocton	3
Edward Langcaster	2
Willm Robinson	2
George Dobson	2

m 112]

John Freeman	2
Abraham Butterfeild	1
Edward Allon	1
Widdow Dobson	1

[165] 2 written over 1.

Richard Willy	1
Mrs Shaun	5
John Cryer	2
Humphr More	2
Widdow Dobson	2
Thomas Paire Mill	1
Roger Allon	2
Widdow Dobson	1
Robert Esh	2
Richard Wormall	1
John Wetherell	3
James Longley	2
Edward Langcaster	3
John Collinson	1
John Fawcitt	1
Steven Langcaster	3
Widdow Lambert	2
Widdow Hudson	1
John Shackleton	3
John Owin	1
Robert Carr	2
Thomas Britton	1
Christopr Carrter	2
Willm Harrison	3[166] three
Willm Arundell	1
Michaell Savill	1
John Everingham	1
Nathan Aikeroyd	2
Abraham Dobson	2
Richard Hurst	3
Lawrence Dobson sen	1
Mr Fairburne	5
Peter Flockton	2
Mr Willm Hill	7
Lawrence Dobson jun	1
John Gibson	1
Willm Atkinson	1
Thomas Flocton	2
John Walker	2
Joseph Rushworth	2
Joseph Lee	2
Widdow Martin	4
Robert Garlick	1
John Johnson sen	2
John Killam	5
John Killam	2
Widdow Moxon	1
James More	5
Willm Croft	2
George Johnson	1
Mr Thomas Dixson	7

m 113]

George Stones	1
Edward Scales Jun	1
John Liversidge	1
John Scailes	1
Willm Bowcock	1
Mathew Hetenscall	1
Ellizabeth Myre	1
Thomas Freeman	1
Leonard Pitt	1
John Hall	2
Mr Ralph Foster	8
Mr More	4
Ellias Ratcliffe	1
Mr Edward Canby	3
John Trelis	1
Willm Wriglesworth	2
John Roberts	2
Henry Allerton	1
Robert Bowling	1
George Falkiner	1
Thomas Barber	1
Edward Hick	1
Henry Heptenstall	1
Willm Wainwright	1
Edward Hemingway	1
Anne Brooke	2
Thomas Wriglesworth	2
Thomas Atkinson	1
Thomas Vevar	1
Widdow Whitwood	1
Francis Black	1
Thomas Cave	1
Michaell Hudson	2
Richard Wormall	2
	579

Empty and noe distress to be had

Widdow Lake	3
Willm Wormall	1
Mr Simpson	2
Richard Willy	1
Willm Dodgson	2
Willm Wormall	2
Phillip Hall	1
Edward Scoales	1

Omitted by reason of poverty 4

George Wainman Collr
Christopr Caarter Const

Rastrick

Mr Timothy Wadsworth	8
John Lumb	6

m 114]

John Hanson	4
Alice Ramsden	6
Anthony Bothamley	2
John Hurst	3
Widdow Ramsden	1
Samuell Hoyle	1
John Eccles	4
Thomas Apleyard	1
Jonas Preston	1
Robert Thornton	2
Samuell Brooke	2
John Bentley	2
Roger Hanson	3
John Pearson	4
Dorothy Cheatam	6

[166] E written over an erasure.

John Fox	1
John Stack	2
Mary Fox	2
Samuell Dyson	2
Nathanll Gleadell	3
Mr Rawnsley	5
Thomas Thornley	2
Abraham Milnes	1
John Smith	1
James Barber	1
John Leagerd	1
Thomas Mallinson	1
Isaac Baites	3
Edward Hanson	3
Ellizab. Mallinson	1
Samuell Armitage	2
Anne Garlick	1
Robert Ramsden	1
Edward Berrey	4
Richard Hanson	4
Thomas Whitehead	3
John Langcaster	2
Joseph Goodheire	1
Thomas Marsden	1
	104

Empty and noe distress to be had

Willm Knowles	2

Omitted by reason of poverty	4

Richd Pickard Collr
Isaac Baite Const

Rushworth (Rishworth)

George Firth	3
John Ryley	1
Simon Holdroyd	4
John Godley	2
James Shipp	2
Henry Dyson	2
John Godley	1

m 115]

Joseph Godley	1
Cuthbert Brearley	2
Joseph Ramsden	1
Widdow Whitley	2
John Brearley	2
Henry Schoalfeild	1
John Whitley	1
Jeffrey Fox	1
James Whitley	2
James Ryley	1
Michll Bothamley	4
John Whitley	1
Joseph Scott	1
Anthony Whitley	1
Anthony Whitley	1[167]
John Ramsden	1
John Godley	2
Samuell Ramsden	2
Adam Haigh	2
Samuell Whitley	2
Joseph Bothamley	2
Robert Hanson	1
James Heape	3
John Wormall	1
James Whitley	1
John Lee	2
John Whitley	2
John Dearding	3
Nichollas Barnes	2
Jerem. Whitley	2
Joseph Firth	1
John Holdroyd	4
John Bothamley	3
George Houlroyd	3
Joseph Houldroyd	2
Francis Green	1
Jerem Bothamley	2
Henry Farrar	2
John Cocker	2
Widdow Schoafeild	1
John Chadwick	1
John Norfolke	2
Abraham Farrer	1
Widdow Whitley	1
David Whitley	1
James Smith	2
John Lord	1
Widddow Bothamley	1
Nathanll Ryley	1
Henry Smith	1
George Bothamley	1
Arthur Whitley	1
James Crawshawe	1
George Rainforth	1
Abraham Firth	1
Arthur Hallas	1
Jonas Ainsworth	1

m 116]

Isaac Longbotham	1
Isaac Smith	1
Widdow Whitley	1
Thomas Dawson	1
	109

Empty and no distress to be had

Mathew Fox	2

Omitted by reason of poverty	1

Roger Hardcastle Collr
John Ripley Const

Shipley

Mr Willm Ramson	6
Joseph Drake	3
Nichollas Stead	3
John Lister	4

167 sic.

Willm Stead	2
Jerem Pickard	1
John Dixon	1
Edward Brooksbanke	1
John Pickard	2
Jonas Hargraues	1
Willm Naylor	5
Richard Tempest	2
John Hudson	2
John Feild	4
Jarvas Dixon	4
Jonas Briggs	3
Henry Grime	2
Jasper Pickard	1
John Mitchell	1
Francis Tayler	2[168] two
George Pickard	1
John Aldburgh	1
Willm Booth	3
Thomas Ellison	3
Willm Brooksbank	3
Willm Pickard	1
Miles Rushworth	2
Willm Feild	4
Mr Miles Rushworth	7
Joell Stead	1
	76

Empty and noe distress to be had

Peter Pickard	2

Omitted by reason of poverty	1

George Wainman Collr
George Pickard Const

Shittlington (Sitlington)[169]

Mr Robert Armitage	12
Mr Mathew Watterhouse	6
Widdow Shawe	1

m 117]

Richard Swallowe	4
Richard Wood	1
Willm Singleton	4
Christopr Rhoades	1
Gilbert Holdsworth	1
Richard Goodall	2
Robert Hall	1
Robert Clayton	3
Christopr Rhoades	1
Richard Clegg	1
Willm Wilkinson	1
Thomas Brooke	4
Widdow Newbold	3
John Crosland	1
Widdow Clegg	1
Steven Jepson	1
John Wilby	1
John More	2
Willm Clegg	1
John Jackson	1
John Walshawe	1
Thomas More	2
Richard Carter	1
John Fell	1
Willm Bayliffe	1
John Justice	1
John Walshawe Jun	3
George Stringer	1
Mr Faruins	3
Robert Hamshire	2
Nathanll Clegg	1
Robert Justice	1
Robert Lee	1
Widdow Cowart	1
Mr John Setterfeild	3
Thomas Baitson	3
Widdow Huntington	3
Richard Kimton	1
Widdow Lee	1
Widdow Wilcock	2
Thomas Bedforth	2
Thomas Walker	1
John Hutchinson	1
Joseph White	2
Thomas Hall	1
Thomas Armitage	1
John Armitage	1
George Goodall	1
Widdow Bington	2
James Greene	1
Robert Bedforth	1
John Nursey	2
Abraham Hutchinson	4
Andrew Donford	1
George Gowdall	2
Thomas Betson	2
Willm Jackson	1
Thomas Bedford	1

m 118]

Richard Carter	1
Thomas Walker	1
Robert Moulson	1
George White	1
John Schoalfeild	1
Robert Armitage	1
Thomas Hoult	1
Willm Armitage	1
Thomas Broadhead	2
Willm Allon	1
Edward Jackson	1
Toby Armitage	1
Richard Walker	1

168 2 written over 1.

169 The modern settlement of Sitlington is divided between the three settlements of Overton, Middlestown and Netherton.

Robert White	1
Thomas Baycliffe	1
Willm Tine	1
	131

Omitted by reason of poverty 5

Thomas Midleton Collr
Francis Clegg Const

Shepley

Thomas Firth	5
Edmond Morehouse	2
Richard Earnshawe	1
John Wortley	2
John Pogson	2
Willm Morehouse	3
Willm Hurst	3
Mathew Berrey	2
Willm Kay	1
John Booth	1
Joseph Hobson	1
Abraham Swallow	1
Willm Kay	3
Thomas Roebuck	2
Marke Burditt	2
John Beamond	1
John Archer	1
Willm Wortley	2
Widdow Hopkinson	1
Edward Walker	1
Ralph Goulthropp	3
Thomas Wood	1
Joseph Goulthropp	1
Thomas Firth	1
Thomas Bothamley	1
Abraham Hepworth	1
Joseph Marsden	1
Widdow Bray	2
John Bray	2
Edward Goulthropp	1
Willm Hobson	1
Thomas Archer	1

m 119]

Joseph Archer	1
Widdow Copley	3
Edward Armitage	3
	60

The person undernamed is discharged by Certifte

John Hobson 1

Richard Pickard Collr
Willm Hurst Const

Shelley

Edward Nicholls	5
Richard Mosley	3
Joseph Mosley	2
John Haigh	1
Giles Kay	1
Joseph Lockwood	2
Willm Booth	1
John Roebuck	2
James Hoyle	1
WIllm Tinker	3
Willm Hepworth	2
Mathew Nicholls	1
John Roebuck	1
Thomas Shaw	1
Joseph Hepworth	1
John Peace	2
Edward Senyer	3
Henry Mosley	1
Thomas Sikes	2
John Mosley	1
Christopr Tinker	1
Willm Cockin	1
John Wood	1
Richard Booth	2
Anthony Whitehead	1
John Wood	1
Joseph Batty	1
John Shaw	1
Robert Broadhead	1
Thomas Denton	1
John Hutchinson	1
Joseph Greene	1
Widdow Hoyle	1
Willm Hutchinson	1
Richard Thorpe	1
John Lee	1
John Tayler	1
John Armitage	1
Widdow Broadhead	1
Arthur Lee	1
John Roebuck	1
John Lockwood	1
Thomas Coudwell	2
John Taylor	1
Willm Hopkins	1
	63

George Wainman Collr
Joseph Hepworth Const

m 120]

Stanley

John Fenton	2
Robert Scott	3
Thomas Beckitt	2
John Naylor	2
Anne Naylor	1
Thomas Armitage	2
Thomas Lee & Com Oven	2
John Lund	1
John Browne	1
John Johnson	2
Willm Netleton	3
Willm Lee	2
Henry Darley	1
John Hey	2
Willm Brooke	1
Joseph Lee	1
Widdow Richardson	1
John Roper	2
John Wilkes	2
Mathew Smith	1
Robert Glover sen	2

WIllm Wormall	2
Thomas Smith	2
Michaell Wormall	2
Richard Preston	2
John Bowling	1
Ellin Bowling	1
John Browne	2
Richard Harrison	2
Thomas Crakill	1
Edward Brooke	1
Edward Lambe	3[170]
	three
Widdow Wormall	2
John Illingworth	2
Willm Longley	1
Thomas Longley	2
John Fossard	2
Portington Heaton	3
Widdow Lee	2
Willm Whalley	2
Richard Andrew	4
Willm Green	3
Portington Heaton	2
Robert Glover Jun	2
Anne Barker	2
John Glover	1
Edward Collett	2
Mr Brooke	2
James Wood	2
	two
Willm Hebden	1
Robert Benson Esq	12
John Siddall	3
Anthony Hobson Com Oven	1
John Maude	2
Mathew Glover	2
Jane Hall	1
Thomas Scott	2
Willm Stapleton	1
Robert Kirke	2
Christopr Kirke	1
George Scott	1

m 121]

Richard Dawson	1
Anne Clarke	1
Joseph Scott	3
John Kirke	2
John Ross	2
Jonas Ouldroyd	1
Richard Keighley	1
Widdow Fox	2
	two
Thomas Sharples	1
Robert Allon	1
Christopr Kirke	2
Richard Norfolke	1
John Glover	2
John Loxley	2
Joseph Ouldroyd	1
Thomas Clarke	1
John Ouldroyd	2
Willm Nowill	5
Mr Daniell Maude	6
Richard Loxley	2
George Illingworth	1
Mr Richard Hewitt	6
Lancellot Glover sen	3
Widdow Houldsworth	3
Christopr Houldsworth	6
Michaell Cooper	3
Robert Bedforth	1
Willm Smith	3
Willm Wadsworth	4
Henry Field	or
Mr Peables	2
Richard White	1
John Ouldroyde	1
Mr Roert Dyneley	8
Mr Dyneson	4
Abraham Clayton	2
Marmaduke Heigham	3
Thomas Smith	2
Willm Reed	1
Peter Smith	4

Lancellot Glover	3
George Gill	2
Katherine Stubbs	2
Widdow Clayton	1
Richard Marshall	3
Timothy Marshall	6
Thomas Savill Esqr	18
Willm Dixon	3
John Bedforth Jun	2
Widdow Frubisher	2
Widdow Batty	2
Thomas Baines	1
Robert Peaker	2
George Baines	1
John Baines	2
Willm Smith	2
Willm Hall	1

m 122]

Robert Craven	2
Richard Rauson	1
Willm Beamond	2
John Bedford sen	1
John Stables	1
Willm Colyer	2
Abraham Heigh	4
George Hebden	2
Abraham Peaker	3
Thomas Stables	1
Widdow Frubisher	1
John Clarkson	2
Randall Laysey	2
Fardinando Smith	2
Willm Wright	4
Mr Daniell Olley	4
Christopr Wright	2
Jerem Maude	3
Thomas Scatcherd	1
Willm Snowden	3
Willm Armitage	4
Widdow Smithson	1
Thomas Williams	2

170 3 written over 1

Willm Spinke	3
John Wood	3
Thomas Dodgson	3
Willm Robinson	3
Thomas Dodgson	4
Thomas Dodgson	3
Mathew Lawe	1
John Bateman	2
Francis Hatfeild	1
Mr Gedion Maude	3
John Mitchill	2
Widdow Roades	1
Mrs Winfeild	7
Willm Winfeild	2
Sir Lyonell Pilkington	14
Brian Mitchill	1
John Playster	1
Daniell Robinson	2
Edward Caue	1
Willm Moxon	2
Willm Carver	1
Lawrance Lumbe	1
Jarvice Harrison	1
Widdow Hanson	2
Robert Lawe	2
Widdow Hanson	2
Mr Jarvis Hatfeild	10
John Harrison	2
Thomas Kent	4
Willm Reynold	1
Mr Hill	1
Peter Moxon	2
Henry Beckitt	2
Thomas Waide	1
Joseph Cartnell	2
Widdow Balderston	1
John Birke	1
Robert Harrison	2
John Snyden	2

m 123]

Henry Burgon	3
Richard Harrison	1
John Roper	3
James Stockes	1
Marke Dewhurst	1
Godfrey Birkes	4
Robert Wood	3
John Roper	5
Joseph Hall	2
Joseph Pollard	2
Jerem Naylor	1
John Cromack	2
Robert Lawe	1
Jarvas Cassen	1
Allexand Robinson	2
Israell Waide	1
Widdow Lake	2
Widdow Thurton	2
Richard Smirfitt	4
Christopr Longbotham	2
Michaell Spinke	1
Barbara Smith	3
Henry Westerman	2
Thomas Fox	2
Brian Smith	1
Willm Ellis	1
John Smithson	1
Thomas Fox sen	1
John Sikes	2
Robert Smith	1
Martin Rodley	1
Mr John Bennet	4
James Child	2
John Illingworth	3
Mathias Pickersgill	2
Tempest Taylor	4
John Tompson	1
Widdow Townley	2
	496

Empty and noe distres to be had

Mr Gedion Maude	1
Thomas Hutchinson	3
Richard Norfolke	1
Thomas Smith	1
Thomas Grave	1
Thomas Murgetroyd	1
Mrs Jane Berry	1
Robert Beckitt	1
Willm Smith	2[171] two
John Blake	2
Robert Gelson	1
Robert Gelson	1[172]
John Thompson	1

Omitted by reason of poverty 29

Robert Bennet Collr
Willm Smith Const

Sharlstone
(Sharlston)

Thomas Stringer Esqr	14
Daniell Thorpe	4
Bartholl Broadley	1
Samuell Heather	4
Francis Clarke	3
Robert Masson	3

m 124]

Anthony Duffeild	3
Widdow Gascoyne	1
Widdow Mason	2
John Schoaley	1
Widdow Rowbuck	1
Widdow Jubb	1
Richard Smithson	1
John Coupland	2

171 2 written over 1
172 sic.

John Huntington	2
Thomas Smithson	1
Henry Nottingham	2
Francis Bloome	1
John Bloome	2
John Marshall	1
John Clarke	1
Widdow Duffeild	3
Henry Goodyeare	3
Grace Squire	6
Thomas Foster	1
Thomas Almond	1
Thomas Dautry	2
Francis Ardron	1
Willm Hudson	2
John Smithson	1
John Bowling	1
George Ramsden	1
Francis Oates	2
	75

Omitted by reason of poverty 11

Thomas Midleton Collr
Francis Blooome Const

Sandall Magna (Sandal Magna)

Mr Grice	8
Mr Stoppart	5
Mr Usher	5
Mr Ward	4
Edward Lawson	2
Christopr Firth	1
Joseph Hall	5
Amos Walshawe	4
Joab Cooper	4
John Lake	3
Thomas Pearson	4
Richard Hepworth	3
Willm Oxley	2
Thomas Bloome	1
Peter Caley	2
Thomas Kershaw	2
Mr Serrill Arthington	9
Mr Thomas Wray	7
Willm Lord	2
Josias Courd	3
George Lee	2
Mary Lee	2
Widdow Davison	2
Robert Hall	3
John Hall	5
Thomas Pollard	2
Widdow Medley	1
John Atkinson	1
Robert Hemsley	1
Willm Rhoades	3
Widdow Oxley	2

m 125]

Willm Carr	1
Richard Audsley	1
Widdow Kay[173]	2
Widdow Barker	2
Henry Bradley	5
Widdow Walker	1
Richard Healey	2
Anne Kershawe	1
Richard Hutchinson	4
Thomas Ramsden	1
Edmond Dyson	1
Robert Carter	2
James Roberts	2
Robert Dickinson	2
Anthony Crawshawe	1
Willm Whitmore	2
Joseph Lee	1
Samuell Ball	3
Abraham Roberts	2
Widdow Sidgsby	1
Joseph Simpson	3
Robert Wright	1
Robert Hepworth	1
John Hall	2
	144

Empty and no distres to be had

Mr Newill	3
George Firth	1
Sir Willm Dalton & Sir Geo	2

Omitted for reason of poverty 3

Robt Bennit Collr
Richd Hutchinson Const

Southill (Soothill)

Richard Netleton	7
John Hemingway	2
Thomas Aikeroyd	3
Simon Greenwood	3
John Greenwood	3
Henry Tilson	7
Willm Gill	1
Thomas Arthur	2
James Speight	2
Thomas Futhergill	2
Thomas Stapleton	1[174] one
Michaell Parker	1
Richard Wood	1
Anthony Lofthouse	1
John Carter	3
Willm Gill	1
Josias Clapham	1
Robert Speight	3
Willm Speight	1
Thomas Speight	1
Henry Speight	1

173 Carr added.
174 1 written over 2.

Anne Goodall	2
Richard Dixon	2
Robert Netleton	2
Marmad. Greenfeild	2

m 126]

Jonas Day	1
Thomas Graues	1
James Townend	2
Willm Speight	1
John Audsley	1
Thomas Stirke	1
Willm Jawitt	2
John Rhoades	2
Joseph Simpson	2
Joseph White	5
James Askwith	1
Anthony Goodall	2
Grace Bentley	1
Francis Cuningham	1
Thomas Cuningham	2
John Day	1
Richard Rhoades	2
Widdow Smith	4
Henry Musgraue	2
John Halleley	2
Thomas Carter	1
James Browne	2
John Robinson	2
Joseph Oates	4
Mary Fox	2
Daniell Hargraues	2
Gamiliell Brearey	1
John Brearey	1
Ellizab Westerman	1
Thomas Auty	1
Alice Fox	1
Thomas Dobson	1
Henry Robertshawe	4
John Hodgson	1
Sarah Netleton	1
Richard Chayster	1
Marke Whitacrs	1
Gamal Brearey	1
Alverah Goodall	1
John Mitchell	1
Widdow Naylor	2
Widdow Fostard	2
Willm Westerman	1
Willm Cawthorne	2
Samuell Tilson	2
	130

Empty and no distress to be had

Samuell Aikeroyd	1

Omitted by reason of poverty

Robert Husband Collr
Simon Greenwood Const

Snydall (Snydale)

Mr Thimbleby	12
Richard Procter	3
John Wager	3

m 127]

John Barugh	1
Alverah Cowthorne	1
Willm Barugh	1
Abraham Barugh	1
Henry Brooke	1
Willm Laycocke	1
Robert Fenton	1
Mrs Netleton	2
John Whitacrs	1
George Brooke	1
Widdow Issot	1
Widdow Peace	1
John Peace	1
Josias Mattison	1
Widdow Hembrough	2
Thomas Nowell	1
John Wright	1
Thomas Clarke	1
John Pordgett	1
	39

Omitted by reason of poverty	2

Thomas Middleton Collr
Abraham Barke Const

Sowerby

Michaell Barugh	2
John Cheatham	1
Samuell Lister	2
John Heape	1
Widdow Naylor	1
John Rylay	1
Abraham Ashworth	1
John Hoyle	1
John Heape	1
Joseph Holegate	4
Michaell Field	1
John Norminton	1
Mr Joseph Harton	9
Widdow Baites	1
John Burlay	1
Widdow Platts	2
James Ratcliff	3
Joseph Smith	3
John Ratcliff	5
Thomas Ratcliff	2
Samuell Hanson	3
John Farrer	1
Widdow Deplatoh	2
Samuell Smith	2
Joseph Maude	2
George Firth	2
John Hopkinson	3
Isaac Mitchill	2
John Lee sen	3
Samuell Wild Jun	4

m 128]

Samuell Wild sen	1
James Greenwood	2
Michaell Ogden	1
Mr Maude	4
Widdow Whitley	1

John Baites	3
Mr Deane	5
Mrs Robinson	2
Isaac Nicholls	3
Joseph Smith	1
John Houldroyd	7
John Firth	2
James Traviss	2
Michll Coardley	2
Henry Lord	1
Widdow Crosley	2
John Gaukeroger	2
Nathan Feilding	3
James Ogden	2
Simon Baites	1
John Hoyle	2
Daniell Whitlay	2
Richard Royde	2
John Firth	1
Nathanll Wood	3
George Clegg	1
Abraham Dyson	1
Charles Clegg	1
John Heape	1
Joseph Houldroyd	4
Michll Towne	1
Ambros Wilkinson	1
Simon Crosley	5
John Stock	2
Joseph Crabtree	1
Joseph Fox	2
John Ryley	1
Henry Ramsbotham	1
John Wilman	2
Abraham Hallewell	1
Jerem Ryley	1
John Rawson	1
Widdow Howroyd	2
Willm Wadsworth	1
George Firth	1
John Shepherd	1
Michaell Barret	3
Robert Preistley	3

John Taylor	1
John Currer	4
Richard Heworth	1
Abraham Hitchen	1
John Crosley	1
James Crosley	1
Henry Farrer	3
Jonathan Crowther	1
Abraham Nicholls	1
Susan Broadlay	1
George Houldgate	5

m 129]

John Dixon	7
Isaac Richmond	2
Mr Jospeh Briggs	2
Widdow Wheelewright	1
Widdow Hallewell	1
Michaell Thomas	1
Michaell Crowther	1
John Widdop	1
Thomas Murgetroyd	2
Richard Thomas	2
Isaac Fawcett	1
John Royde	1
Thomas Deane	2
Robert Ashworth	1
John Crowther	1
Robert Swaine	3
Mathew Wadsworth	1
Nathaniell Houlgate	1
John Jenus	1
Richard Ryley	1
James West	1
Theaphll Gleadell	3
John Platts	4
John Sutcliff	2
John Bothamley	1
Widdow Greenwood	1
Joseph Hallewell	1
Joseph Normonton	4
Henry Sutcliffe	3

Daniell Bentley	1
John Nicholls	1
Joseph Righills	2
John Lumb	1
Mathew Lumb	1
George Dickinson	1
John Midgley	1
Henry Haworth	2
John Smith	1
Jonas Gawkeroger	1
Henry Smith	1
Jonathan Hellewell	1
John Rawnsley	1
Michaell Earnshawe	1
Thomas Dodgson	1
Henry Hyley	3
Thomas Ibbitson	2
Isaac Crowther	1
Daniell Smith	1
John Hopkinson	4
Jonathan Illingworth	2
Jonas Platts	2
Henry Clay	4
Timothy Normon	3
John Hoyle	5[175] fiue
John Leah	3
Widdow Dobson	5
Abraham Ryley	4
Henry Ryley	1
James Halliwell	1
John Ryley	3
Pamph Hoyle	2

m 130]

Mary Ogden	1
Richard Midgley	3
John Wilson	1
Abraham Platts	5
Isaac Hopkinson	5
Samuell Siddall	1
John Clegg	1

175 5 written over 3. Even so, despite the annotation 'fiue', 3 was used in adding up the total.

Joseph Midgley	2
Joseph Stanfeild	4
Samuell Whitehead	1
Joseph Siddall	3
Timothy Bentley	8
Nichollas Stanfeild	3
Abraham Whitehead	1
John Chatburne	2
Izraell Tillotson	4
Thomas Ryley	1
John Ratcliff	3
John Wood	3
Thomas Parker	2
John Ridge	2
Nathanll Tillotson	4
John Fairbank	3
Jonas Haddock	1
Robert Tillotson	2
John Lee	3
Mr John Deardon	8
Abraham Naylor	1
Willm Bramley	2
Joseph Copper	1
John Baites	2
Widdow Crabtree	1
John Heape	2
Henry Bentley	4
Jonas Thomas	1
Isaac Farrar	9
Jonas Dixon	1
Jonas Earnshawe	1
Edward Bentley	4
Widdow Normonton	3
John Hoyle	2
John Leah	3
Richard Sutcliff	1
Simon Smith	1
Jonas Sugden	1
Willm Parker	1
Christopr Thomas	2[176]
	two
James Ratcliff	1
Henry Barrat	1

m 131]

Mr Bridges	5
Abraham Sutcliff	4
John Inglworth	1
Daniell Hellewell	3
John Whitacres	2
James Walker	2
Joseph Hanson	2
Abraham Hellewell	1
Jonathan Mitchill	1
Samuell Lowcocke	1
John Greenwood	4
Robert Scailes	1
Thomas Towne	1
John Holstead	1
Willm Normonton	2
John Sutcliff sen	1
John Sutcliff	1
Henry Sutcliff	1
Paull Houlstead	1
John Wilkinson	1
Henry Illingworth	5
Joseph Clay	4
James Ogden	1
John Marsden	1
John Dixon	1
Willm Sugden	1
James Barritt	1
Jonas Thomas	2
John Feilding	1
John Sharpe	2
Joseph Crosley	1
James Crosley	3
Mary Woodhead	1
John Redihough	1
Mrs Wakden	3
John Bins	1
Samuell Midgley	2
John Greenwood	4
James Baites	1
John Taylor	2
Henry Bothamley	1

Joseph Firth	1
George Ryley	1
James Crosley	3
Widdow Dyson	2
Michaell Ogden	2
Abraham Rawden	1
Nathanll Hoyle	2
John Ogden	1
Simon Gleadall	1
Joseph Green	1
John Egland	2
Thomas Blackburne	1
James Greene	1
Abraham Mitchill	1

m 132]

John Hollis	1
Thomas Blackburn	2
Jerem Hopkinson	5
Joseph Firth	2
Robert Exell	2
John Thorneber	2
John Heape	1
John Illingworth	1
Henry Heape	1
Joseph Preistley	4
Isaac Marsden	1
Henry Marsden	3
Jerem. Ramsden	1
Widdow Wood	1
Abraham Dyson	5
Michaell Jackson	1
Robert Crosley	1
Charles Farrer	1
James Lightowlers	2
Samuell Ramsden	1
John Bothamley	1
John Ryley	6
Joseph Whitley	1
John Turner	1
Henry Feilding	3
John Farrer	1

[176] 2 written over 1.

Michaell Crosley	2
John Farrer Jun	2
Samuell Dyson	5
Thomas Barber	3
Anthony Ginnus	1
John Oxley	1
John Crosley	3
James Carter	1
Jonas Whitley	2
John Hurst	1
Mr Wood	5
Thomas Rushton	1
John Crosley	3
Henry Wilson	4
Edward Hanson	1
Abraham Haworth	1
Jerem Lister	1
James Crosley	1
John Marsden	3
Joseph Gleadall	3
John Firth	1
Daniell Houlden	1
Widdow Hoyle	2
John Hoyldroyd	3
Widdow Firth	1
James Siddall	1
John Schoafeild	1
John Firth	1
Willm Sikes	1
James Dobson	4
John Rutcliffe	1
Henry Wilson	1

m 133]

Simond Bins	1
Widdow Lumb	1
John Gleadall	1
Henry Feilding	6
Nathanll Kershawe	3
Joseph Stanistone	2
Joseph Wilson	1
George Firth	2
Widdow Mitchill	1
Henry Shackleton	1
John Anlay	1
Simon Bennit	1
John Wilson	1
Robert Swaine	1
Abraham Nicholls	1
Widdow Feilding	4
John Hurst	1
Martin Butterworth	1
Henry Goodjon	1
Widdow Greenwood	1
Nathanll Houldroyd	1
John West	1
Anthony Shepard	1
John Houlroyd	2
Jerem Houlroyd	2
James Ratcliff	3
	668[177]

Empty and noe distress to be had	
Mr Barstow	2
Omitted by reason of poverty	12

Robert Corner Collr
James Stansfield Const

Shelfe
(Shelf)

John Best	6
Susan Brooksbank	5
John Appleyard	5
Jeremiah Brooksbank	5
Edward Slaytor	4
John Liversidge	4
David Brigg	4
Willm Hird	4
John Lumb	4
George Whitley	6
Anthony Lee	5
Thomas Soothill	4
Samuell Wardman	3
Samuell Briggs	2
John Brooke	3
Timothy Starkey	2
Abraham Hoult	3
James Jagger	3
John Lee	2

m 134]

Martin Croft	2
Ellizabeth Viccars	1
John Stockes	1
Robert Brewer	2
Samuell Wilson	1
Henry Wilson	1
James Schoafeild	1
John Aikeroyd Jun	1
John Woodhead	1
Joseph Knight	1
Nathanll Firth	2
Timothy Pickles	2
John Stocks	1
Mathew Houldsworth	1
Michaell Woodhead	2
John Sunderland	1
John Shooesmith	2
Peter Ambler	1
John Scott	1
John Watterhouse	2
Edmond Brocke	1
James Feilding	1
Joshua Rushworth	2
Jerem Thorpe	3
John Broadley	2
Willm Croft	2
Richard Bowcock	2
Widdow Benn	1
Joseph Croft	1
Martha Thorpe	3
John Lee	1
Nathanll Duckworth	3
Martha Thorpe	1
John Holmes	2
John Aikeroyd	2

177 There is a scribal error on the basis of n 172, since the total is 670.

Joseph Bentley 1
John Walker 1
135

Omitted by reason of poverty 6

Robt More Collr
Edwd Slator Const

Stansfeild (Stansfield)

Thomas Sutcliff 2
Willm Mitchill 1
Willm Eastwood 1
Abraham Marshall Jun 1
John Mitchill 2
John Stansfeild 1
Abraham Clegg 1
Abraham Armroyd 1
James Mitchill 1

m 135]

John Stansfeild 1
James Stansfeild 1
John Stansfeild 1
Henry Horsfall 1
James Greenwood 1
Abraham Marshall sen 1
George Mitchell 1
Edmond Stansfeild 1
Charles Stansfeild 1
Nichollas Feilding 1
John Feilding 3
Robert Armroyd 1
John Clegg 1
John Armroyd 1
Abraham Clegg 1
Ambros Greenwood 1
James Stansfeild 1
Timothy Crosby 1
Paull Greenwood 1
Christopr Howgate 1

Widdow Wilkinson 1
James Sootell 1
Richard Naylor 2
James Hellewell 1
Widdow Barker 1
Willm Crowther 1
John Stansfeild 1
John Woodhead 1
John Hellewell 1
Richard Crosley 1
Simon Crosley 1
Edmond Barker 4
Edmond Barker Jun 2
Thomas Barker 2
Simon Crosley 1
Thomas Hellewell 1
Richard Stansfeild 4
Thomas Stansfeild 2
John Pilling 6
Mrs Elliza Stansfeild 2
Henry Cawcroft 1
John Ogden 3
John Whitacres 1
John Earnshawe Jun 1
James Stansfeild 1
Widdow Midgley 1
Mrs James Stansfeild 1
John Roberts 1
John Widdop sen 3
John Widdop Jun 3
Simon Crabtree 2
Jonas Horsforth 1
Robert Sutcliffe 1
John Barker 1
Widdow Barker 1
John Earnshawe 1
Widdow Cockcroft 1
Widdow Barker 1

m 136]

Nathanll Sutcliffe 1
John Hudson 1

Richard Sutcliffe 2
James Greenwood 1
Daniell Sutcliffe 2
Abraham Earnshaw 1
Martin Wilkinson 1
Abraham Crabtree 1
John Eastwood 6
John Taylor sen 2
John Taylor Jun 2
John Hollingrake 1
Thomas Sutcliffe 2
John Clegg 1
John Eastwood 1
Widdow Hindle 2
Paull Bingley 1
John Gibson 1
Edward Sutcliffe sen 2
John Ogden 1
John Clay 1
John Eastwood 2
Jerem Ingham 1
John Haughton 1
Michaell Haughton 1
Abraham Stansfeild 2
Edward Sutcliff Jun 3
Willm Eastwood 2
Joseph Crosley 1
John Robertshaw 1
Henry Pickles 1
Paull Greenwood 1
Willm Eastwood 2
Nathanll Lee 1
Willm Crabtree 1
Jonas Robertshawe 3
John Halstead 4
John Ulley 1
Henry Wadsworth 1
Samuell Wadsworth 2
Michaell Utley 1
Samuell Briggs sen 1[178]
Samuell Briggs Jun 1
Michaell Eastwood 2[179]
two

178 Line inserted.
179 2 written over 1 with line inserted.

Jonathan Midgley	1
Jonas Wadsworth	1
Richard Sutcliffe	1
Henry Wadsworth	1
Paull Greenwood	1
Widdow Bentley	2
John Horsfeild	2
Jonas Greenwood	1
Widdow Greenwood	1
John Bentley	1
John Horsfall	1
Abraham Crosley	1

m 137]

Michaell Sutcliffe	1
Willm Shackleton	1
Henry Smith	1
Thomas Greenwood	2
Widdow Sutcliffe	1
John Kay	1
John Greenwood	3
Widdow Eastwood	1
Edmond Ashworth	1
Richard Wadsworth	2
Willm Varley	1
Lancellt Ashworth	2
Gilbert Hauton	1
John Thomas	1
John Horsfall	2
John Crabtree	1
Henry Sutcliff	2
John Speake	1
Thomas Greenwood	1
Paull Greenwood	2
Luke Greenwood	1
John Greenwood	1
Andrew Greenwood	1
Luke Greenwood	1
Hugh Lawson	1
Jerem Marshall	1
Thomas Crabtree	1
John Smith	1
Widdow Rigg	1
George Sutcliff	1
Richard Thomas	1
Simeon Crabtrree	1
Robert Suttill	1
Michaell Clegg	1
Simon Greenwood	1
Paull Greenwood	1
Abraham Clarke sen	1
Abraham Clarke Jun	1
Robert Armroyd	1
Jane Redshough	1
Robert Naylor	2
	227

Omitted by reason of poverty	16

Robert Corner Collr
Nicholls Sutcliffe Const

South Owram
(Southowram)

Mr Thomas Lister	8
John Staincliffe	8
Mr Lister	4
Mr Ellexand Baites	5
Daniell Whitehead	9
Robert Ramsden	6
Widdow Colbeck	4
Joseph Firth	4
Henry Grime	4
Thomas Ramsden	3
Samuell Hemingway	4
Daniell Hemingway	4
Widdow Platts	2
James Walker	4

m 138]

Daniell Sharpe	2
Thomas Geldart	1
John Wadington	4
Willm Wood	2
Jonas Ingham	2
Timothy Sutcliff	2
Willm Walker	6
Abraham Walker	5
Josua Scholfeild	2
Abraham Hemingway	2
Susans Lawe	2
John Nicholls	4
Thomas Wakefeild	5
John Wheeley	2
John Mitchell	1
George Stox	3
Joshua Ryley	1
John Whitley	1
John Charner	1
Richard Kendall	1
Edward Maude	3
John Firth	3
John Horeby	5
Edward Midgley	1
Thomas Hanson	3
James Schoalfeild	3
Edward Midgley jun	2
Abrah Ryley	2
Thomas Almeter	3
John Schoalefeild	1
Joseph Fenwick	2
Mrs Schoalefeild	4
Edward Midgley	4
Nathaniell Baxter	2
Samuell Craven	5[180] fiue.
Mrs Barraclough	3
Joseph Crowther	4
Richard Hall	2
Widdow Exley	3
Thomas Scott	1
Thomas Wilkinson	2
Thomas Hanson	4
Joseph Wood	4
George Pearson	2
Thomas Ramsden	3

[180] 5 written over 3.

Edward Jewitt	3
Isaac Illingworth	4
Richard Speight	3
John Ambler	2
Richard Nicholls	2
Willm Houldsworth	1
Joshua Nicholls	5
John Smith	5
John Hurst	2
Widdow Viccars	2
Thomas Greenhough	3
Robert Ramsden	3
Jerem Firth	2

m 139]

James Wadsworth	2
Abraham Illingworth	5
James Greenwood	2
John Lister	3
Grace Viccars	2
Mrs Cockman	2
John Crowther	6
John Fooler	2
John Wyley	2
Jonathan Bentley	2
Lewis Tate	2
Willm Pollard	1
Henry Heblethwate	1
John Bland	1
Willm Hutchinson	3
George Myres	1
John Bothamley	3
Thomas Kidson	2
Widdow Schoalefeild	3
Widdow Mitchill	1
John Robinson	1
Thomas Rawson	1
Widdow Houldsworth	1
Daniell Ducker	1
John Mitchell	3
Richard Walker	1
Samuell Poole	2
Daniell Duckworth	1
Joseph Hemingway	3
Samuell Poole	1
John Ramsden	2
Ellizab Ramsden	2
Samuell Poole	1
	292

Omitted by reason of poverty	11

Robert Corner Collr
George Stox Const

Slathwaite (Slaithwaite)

George Pyson	3
Willm Binns	3
Edward Parkins	3
Widdow Lockwood	2
Widdow Bothamley	2
John Sikes	1
Widdow Sikes	2
John Shawe	2
James Bothamley	2
Widdow Lockwood	2
George Lockwood	1[181] one.
James Sinden	1
John Poyson	1
Robert Parkins	1
Willm Sikes sen	1
Willm Sikes Jun	1
Thomas Parkins	2
Widdow Sikes	1

m 140]

Widdow Thorp	4
John Walker	1
John Hurst	2
Edward Marsden	1
John Heigh	1
Widdow Hoyle	1
John France	1
James Bawmforth	1
Widdow Tompson	1
James Broadbent	1
Joseph Bawmforth	1
John Armitage	2
Nichols Ainley	1
John Hoyle	1
John Crosland	2
John Shaw	1
James Wood	1
John Pogson	3
George Thorpp	1
George Shaw	1
John Sikes	2
John Armitage	1
Thomas Sikes	2
Edmond Sikes	1
Widdow Dalton	1
Widdow Hurst	1
John Haigh	1
John Dyson	1
Widdow Dyson	1
John Sikes	1
James Sikes	1
Willm Sikes	1
Edmond Sikes	1
Samuell France	1
Willm Hurst	1
George Hurst	1
John Shawe	1
Willm France	1
Willm Knight	1
Thomas Sikes	1
James Armitage	1
Nathanll Bothamley	1
John France	2
Jerem Wilkinson	3
Willm Sikes	2
John Ainley	2
Widdow Walker	1

181 1 written over 2.

James Pogson	2
Widdow Dyson	2
James Maye	1
James Carter	1
John Hurst	1
Mathew Walker	1
Thomas Haigh	1
Edmond Lee	1
John Calverley	1
James Sikes	1
Edmond Dyson	1
Humphr Kay	1
John Mellor	1

m 141]

Simon Dalton	1
Willm Sikes	1
James Mellor	1
James Bothamley	1
John Hurst	1
John Sikes	1
Widdow Swallow	1
John Bumforth	1
James Gleadall	1
Rebecca Lightoolers	1
Widdow Sikes	1
James France	1
Thomas Carter	1
John Charlesworth	1
Widdow Walker	1
John Sikes	1
Edmond Dyson	1
Thomas Pearson	1
Edmond Sikes	1
Joseph Shaw	1
Willm Buckley	1
Widdow Hurst	1
James Sikes	1
George Sikes	1
	133

Empty and noe distress to be had	
Edmond Lees forge	1
Thomas Midleton Collr	
Humphr Kay Const	

Stainland

Hugh Ramsden	2
Michaell Bentley	2
John Sutcliffe	1
Richard Whitley	4
Joseph Briggs	2
George Haigh	1
Brian Firth	2
Henry Gleadall	1
Widdow Gleadall	2[182] two
Willm Standinge	1
Edward Townend	2
John Crowther	1
Abraham Hellewell	2
Thomas Lockwood	2
Daniell Mellor	2
Thomas Preistley	2
Edward Preistley	2
Thomas Ryley	1
Henry Preistley	2
Willm Gleadall	2
Michaell Binns	2
John Garside	2
Thomas Hellewell	2
John Gleadall	2
Edward Hellewell	2

m 142]

George Smithies	2
John Gleadall	1
John Lumbe	1
George Preistley	1
George Gleadall	1
George Sikes	2
John Cordley	1
Timothy Higginson	1
John Howroyd	2
Henry Haigh	1
James Shawe	2
Edward Brooke	1
George Gleadall	1
George Sikes	1
Nathanll Bothamley	1
Jerem Bothamley	2[183] two
George Fairbanke	1
John Haigh	1
Widdow Bothamley	1
Widdow Hanson	1
John Sikes	1
John Hall	1
Ralph Bothamley	1
Joseph Wormall	2
John Bothamley	1
Isaac Whitley	1
Edmond Buckley	2
Benjam Wilson	1
Widdow Tompson	1
Henry Walton	1
Michaell Siddall	1
James Chadwick	1
James Scott	1
John Bawdwen	1
Anthony Bothamley	1
Simond Tennant	2
Joseph Shawe	1
Joseph Bothamley	1
Joseph Townend	1
Jonathan Nicholls	1
John Hanson	1
Jerem Watterhouse	1
Richard Denton	3
Widdow Denton	2
Thomas Hanson	1
Henry Haigh	1

182 2 written over 1.
183 2 written over 1.

Edward Dawson 1
Benjam Holeroyd 1
Godfrey Crosland 1
Widdow Thornton 3
John Barrand 1
John Hague 1
James Brooke 1
Gilbert Ramsden 1
John Ainley 1
Willm Milnes 1
Widdow Rigg 1

m 143]

John Jagger 2
Joseph Ramsden 1
Widdow Denton 1
120

These persons following are discharged by Certfs
Thomas Draper 1
Jarvace Wilkinson 2
John Wormall 1
Widdow Higinson 1
Richard Wood 2

Omitted by reason of Poverty 1

Robt Bennit Collr
Joseph Ramsden Collr

Scircoates (Skircoat)
Samuell King 5
Nathanll Hichine 2
Thomas Maukes 2
Joseph Whewell 3
James King 5
James Sutcliff Jun 2
Christopr Barker 2
Isaac Hooker 2
John Longbotham 3
John Crowther 1
Michaell Godley 4
Richard Hindley 1
Jonas Wood 2
Anthony Watterhouse 2
John Waide 4
James Stead 4
Isaac Watterhouse 4
Edward Whitacrs 2
James Sutcliff 3
Steven Milner 4
John Robinson 3
Michll Ryley 4
Willm Crowther 2
John Walton 4
Jonathan Laycock 1
Thomas Welsh 2
Mr Anthony Foxcroft 5
Mr Hodges 1
Henry Milner 5
John Wood 2
Samull Gill 3
Edmond Whitehead 1
Richard Robinson 4
John Hodgson 1
Benjam Baites 5
Abraham Hodgson 2
Mary Milner 4
Jonathan Laycock 2
Richard Blackett 5
Willm Thomas 4
James Kitson 2
Christopr Glossop 3
Richard Denby 3
Jerem Rossandell 4
Mr Richard Barraclough 8
Richard Barrand 1
Jonas Boardall 4

m 144]

Mr Richard Dolliffe 3
Willm Hornby 1
Robert Allonson 7
Mr George Towne 5
Isaac Bins 2
John Wainhouse 4
Isaac Suthill 2
Mr Robt Barraclough 1
George Wood 1
Benjam Felley 3
171

Empty and no distress to be had
Mr Hodges 1

Omitted by reason of Poverty 1

Roger Hardcastle Collr
Richd Hindle Const

Thornton
Widdow Hopkinson 3
James Hopkinson 2
Jacob Baites 1
Abrah Hainworth 2
Willm Ward 2
Michall Drake 1
Peter Jewitt 1
John Drake 1
Joseph Drake 10
Willm Baxter 5
Timothy Gibson 3
Henry Drake 1
Joseph Robinson 2
James Shirt Jun 2
Jonas Craven 1
Joseph Robertshaw 1
John Drake sen 1
John Hainworth sen 1
Jonas Robertshawe 1
John Hall 4
Willm Robertshaw 1
John Drake 1
Thomas Ambler 1
Jesper Drake 1
Jonas Dobson 1
Joseph Foster 1

John Robinson	1
John Greenhough	1
Jonas Jewitt	1
Jonas Booth	1
Robert Barstowe	1
Grace Pearson	1
Willm Pearson	2
Thomas Craven	1
James Hall	2
James Kighley	3
Sarah Craven	3
Jonas Jewitt	1

m 145]

John Ambler	1
Jerem Robertshawe	1
Michaell Bentley	1
Adam Bell	2
Nathan Hoyle	1
Margret Robinson	1
Mathew Foster	1
John Binke	1
Ellizabeth Pearson	2
Mathew Foster	2
James Thornton	2
John Nicholls	2
John Hainworth	1
Isaac Haley	5
Thomas Tullen	1
Mary Scott	1
Francis Lonnsdall	4
Willm Midgley	2
Michaell Fletcher	1
Little Hill	2
John Haineworth	3
Widdow Jowitt	1
Widdow Watkins	1
John Robertshaw	2
Mary Booth	3
Jerem Gleadall	4
Mr Josias Midgley	7
Joseph Robertshaw	1
Edward Robertshaw	1
Michaell Butterfeild	3

Jesper Haley	2
Abraham Butterfeild	1
Christopr Robinson	1
Abraham Haley	1
Abraham Whitacrs	1
Richard Whitacrs	2
Jonas Verley	1
Daniell Hopkinson	1
John Ashworth	1
James Bell	1
Jonas Rushworth	3
Bennet Briggs	2
John Foster	1
Richard Foster	1
Abraham Foster	1
Jane Foster	1
Thomas Horsfall	1
Jonas Craven	1
Michaell Craven	1
Samuell Driver	1
Michaell Horsfall	1
Richard Apleyeard	2
Robert Whitacrs	1
Robert Holmes	1
Willm Cordingley	1

m 146]

Jonas Horsfall	2
Jonas Pearson	2
Barnard Roe	2
Samuell Illingworth	1
Michaell Midgley	1
Mr Jonas Midgley	2
John Foster	1
Jonathan Foster	1
John Barstowe	1
George Fletcher	1
John Feather	1
Willm Rushworth	1

Empty and no distress to be had	
Thos Hainsworth	1

Omitted by reason of poverty	8

Robt Husband Collr
John Pearson Const

Tonge
(Tong)

Mr Robert Tempest	3
Tempest Cordingley	4
Mary Netleton	1
Richard Stead	2
James Stables	2
Richard Margorson	2
Willm Darnbrough	1
John Darnbrough	2
Richard Tempest	2
Willm Carr	1
John Cordingley	2
Richard Cordingley	1
Henry Shaw	1
Willm Procter	1
Jonathan Rayner	2
John Rayner	2
Widdow Lassy	2
Mathew Cordingley	3
Christopr Netleton	2
Richard Syser	3
John Hainworth	2
John Sharpe sen	2
Samuell Hollins	1
Richard Rayner	1
Thomas Stead	2
Richard Rayner	2
Thomas Copley	2
WIllm Stead	4
John Barker	1

m 147]

Joshua Stead	2
	two
Thomas Thackeray	1
Henry Cordinley	1
Christop Stead	2

Robert Sunderland	2
Nathll Rhoades	2
John Sharpe Jun	2
Willm Hepworth	1
Richard Naylor	1
Widdow Whitehead	3
Walter Cordingley	1
Willm Dawson	1
Sir John Tempest	8
Richard Pollard	5
Thomas Teale	2
Walter Hoole	1
Thomas Hargraves	1
Thomas Bromhead	3
Richard Bakes	2
Willm Fairebanke	1
Miles Webster	1
Ellizabeth Webster	1
Thomas Webster sen	2
Willm Butterfeild	2
Mr Henry Tempest	2
Thomas Goodall	1
Thomas Webster	1
Humphr Hutchinson	1
Willm Rawson	4
Mr Richard Coore	3
Jarvas Browne	4
Walter Hoole sen	1
Willm Crosley	1
Willm Stables	2
Richard Goodall	1
John Goodall	2
Jerem Wilkinson	1
Mary Benton	3
Joseph Greene	2
Josh Greene	3
Anne Benton	3
Willm Gomersall	1
James Brooke	1
Thomas Pollard	2
Richard Roe	1
Nichollas Browne	1
Thomas Webster	2
Christopr Lavorack	1
John Bloomers	1
Widdow Asby	1
John Kershawe	2
	152

m 148]

Empty and noe distres to be had	
Willm Speight	1
Omitted by reason of poverty	5

Robt More Collr
John Goodall Const

Thornhill

Mr Netleton	9
Mr Thomas Hobson	9
Mr Thomas Squire	7
Mr Savill	9
Mr Thomas Whitacrs	9
Thomas Newill	1
Thomas Walker	4
Henry Allon	3
Willm Elisall	5
Edward Crosbey	2
Willm Booth	4
Edward Slaydon	2
Richard White	2
Thomas Scargill	1
Thomas Walker	1
Thomas Crosley	1
Widdow Tayler	1
Robert Hepworth	2
Willm Sikes	1
Widdow Lee	1
Gamal Stevenson	2
John Woodhead	2
Willm Stevenson	2
Edward Briggs	1
John Hepworth	2
Mary Hepworth	3
Jarvice Child	2
John Tompson	1
John Spivey	2
Peter Geldart	3
Richard Clayton	1
Willm Stringer	2
Thomas Hall	1
John Inman	1
John Allon	1
George Wortley	1
George Haigh	1
Joseph Armitage	2
Robert Blackey	2
Edward Dixon	1
John Robinson	1
Thomas Pollard	2
Richard Sikes	1

m 149]

Thomas Brooke	1
Thomas Pulley	1
Christopr Cornwall	1
Willm Hey	1
Phillp Wilson	1
Thomas Smith	1
Widdow Hall	2
John Parkinson	1
James Lee	1
Thomas Walker	1
Mr Wilson	4
Willm Haigh	1
Willm Armitage	1
Joseph Padget	2
Mr Abraham Dyson	2
Richard Pollard	1
Sarah Steggs	1
Henry Watts	1
Widdow Lee	1
Robert Wood Mill	1
Robert Wood	1
	138

Omitted by reason of poverty	3

Thomas Middleton Collr
John Robinson Const

Thurstonland

Mr Willm Horsfeild	10
Abraham Lockwood	2
John Coundwell	4
Henry Gillion	2
Anthony Armitage	2
Henry Marsh	2
Widdow Gilliot	1
John Archer	2
Richard Earnshawe	1
Jarret Colyer	1
Michaell Rowley	1
Robert Pitts	2
John Wild	3
Thomas Day	1
Edward Rowley	3
Edward Ellis	2
Joseph Rushforth	1
Joseph Tinker	1
Robert More	1
Willm Brooke	1
John Lockwood	1
Willm Lockwood	1
John Hardy	1
John Roebotham	1
Abraham Bins	1

m 150]

John Noble	1
Thomas Lockwood	1
Alice Chappell	1
Jerem Batty	1
Anthony Armitage	1
Robert Ray	1
Thomas Morehouse	1
Willm Lockwood	1
Willm Moss	1
John Noble	1
John Jenkinson	1
Daniell Broadhead	2
John Taylor	1
Joseph Hepper	1
Phillp Bray	1
Thomas Morehouse	1
Abraham Lockwood	1
MR Horsfeild	1
Willm Brooke	1
	68

Robert Husband Collr
John Taylor Const

Wortley

Willm Oldroyd	10
John Spence	2
Ralph Richardson	2
Willm Shipton	2
John Baines	2
John Cliffton	2
Robert Clayton	2
Robert Clayton	1
John Smith	2
Willm Watterhouse	2
James Atkinson	2
Edward Pearson	2
Brian Sheafeild	2
Robert Gleadall	2
John Raynor	1
Thomas Barber	1
Richard Norton	1
James Pearson	2
John Hatcliff	1
John Spauton	1
James Browne	1
Richard Robinson	1
Benjam Hopton	2
Thomas Musgraue	1
John Ewbanke	5
Mary Croft	1
Roger More	1
Richard Craven	2
Edward Ullay	1
James Walker	1

m 151]

Willm Loughton	1
Richard Musgraue	1
John Flather	1
George Thackerey	2
James Robinson	1
Mathew Milner	2
Steven Wood	2
John Cliff	2
Peter Smith	1
Ralph Hodgson	2
Richard Gouldsbrough	2
Willm Pearson	1
Thomas Watson	3
Mr Mitchell	2
John Thackeray	1
Willm North	2
Thomas Snell	1
James Browne	2
James Browne Jun	1
Edward Roberts	2
John Harrison	1
	91

Empty and noe distress to be had

Christopr Jackson	1

Omitted by reason of poverty

Robt Bennit Collr
John Harison Const

Wike
(Wyke)

John Ridlestone	4
Willm Pollard	2
Richard Kershaw	1
Jonas Pearson	4
Richard Kirshawe	4
Richard Redlestone	3
Robert Birkby	4
Abraham Crosley	2
John Houldsworth	2
Jonath Wright	3
John Wright	4
Henry Higgins	1
Robert Ashworth	1

Willm Hemingway	2
Henry Crowther	2[184]
	two
Thomas Bins	1
Timothy Kirshaw	1
Henry Feild	2
Willm Liversidge	1
Ellizab Pollard	2
Edward Hague	3
John Saltonstall	1
Widdow Benson	1
Willm Benson	1
Joseph Midgley	1

m 152]

Willm Bentley	1
John Pearson	1
John Spencer	2
Richard Netleton	1
John Bolland	1
Daniell Houldsworth	1
Willm Pollard	2
Jonas Arnold	1
Willm Pearson	1
Edward Holdsworth	2
Widdow Bolland	2
James Bolland	1
John Senjor	1
Henry Robinson	2
Michaell Bentley	1
Francis Butterfeild	1
John Bolland	1
Willm Wright	1
John Ridlesdine	1
Willm Ridlesdine	1
Nathanll Sharpe	1
John Denbye	1
James Bolland	1
Joseph Ramsden	2
Widdow Birkby	1
John Bolland	1
Joshua Brooke	1
John Denby	1
John Graue	2
John Saltenstall	1
	90

Omitted by reason of poverty	1
	one

Georg Wainman Collr
Joshua Feild Const

Whittley (Whitley)

Sir Thomas Beamond	17
Thomas Walker	3
John Womersley	3
Willm Swinden	1
Widdow Wood	1
Francis Jubb	1
Joseph Stocks	1
Willm Swinden	1
Giles Hill	1
John Heape	1
Robert Hudlestone	1
Willm Chappell	1
Edmond Jessop	2
Joshua Crowther	1
Willm Hague	2
George Kay	2
Robert Lee	2
John Hague	3
Robert Thornton	2
	two
John Bingley	1
Willm Lee	2
Mathew Brooke	2
John Farrand	2

m 153]

John Blackburne	1
Mary Blackburne	1
Willm Hemingway	1
Richard Bingley	1
Edward North	2
Richard Dyson	1
Robert Hague	2
Francis Armitage	2
Richard North	1
Willm Langcaster	2
John Brooke	1
John Rawkestrawe	2
Thomas Jackson	1
Richard Jackson	2
John Hill	2
John Sheard	2
Widdow Faucitt	2
Willm Wilson	2
Ralph Blacker	2
Willm Pearson	2
Willm Hurst	1
George Armitage	2
John Kay	1
John Richardson	1
Richard Senyer	1
John Stead	2
Andrew Haigh	2
John Armitage	2
George Moulson	1
Willm Senyer	2
Thomas Fisher	1
Joseph Freckleton	1
Thomas Boothroyd	1
Willm Stead	2
Willm Lodge	1
Widdow Fisher	1
Willm Fisher	1
Joseph Fisher	1
Joseph Stocks	2
John Jessop	2
George Hudswell	1
George Moulson	1
	115

Empty and no distres to be had	
Willm Lodge	1

[184] 2 written over 1.

Omitted by reason of poverty 5

Thomas Midleton Collr
Mathew Brooke Const

Walton cum Britton
(Walton and West Bretton)

Widdow Wadsworth 6
Widdow West 4
Lawrance Coupland 3
Timothy Hurst 3
John Arrundell 2

m 154]

Mr Dutton 4
George Chapman 4
John Haigh 1
Richard Preston 3[185]
three
Widdow More 3
Nathan Arnold 2
Katherine Arnold 1
John Scott 3
Robert Goodyeare 4
John Goodyeare 2
Robert Hawksworth 3
John Turner 1
Samuell Goodyeare 1
Thomas Hurst 1
Widdow Browne 3
Joseph Booth 1
Richard Bramley 1
Widdow Goodyeare 2
Willm Weightman 5
John Conwigg 2
James Clayton Gent 4
Abram Robinson 1
Thomas Arundell 2
Henry Kershawe 1
Josias Kershawe 1
Jonathan Ball 2
Thomas Hammer 3
John Knulton 3
Joseph Wright 3
John Chappell 1
Ellizabeth Browne 3
Willm Townend 2
Anne Browne Vid 1
John Simpson 1
Ellizabeth Preston 1
Richard Bedforth 2
Susan Pearson 1
Thomas Copley 1
Willm Clayton 1
Willm Hurst 1
Ellizab Law Vid 2
Isabell Wright 1
Samuell Lockwood 3
Vallentine Watson 2
Mr Abrah Swallowe 6
Joseph Hinchcliff 4
Thomas Sikes 2
Nichollas Walshawe 2
two
George Sikes 2
John Longley 2
John Hall 1
Willm Sikes 2
Willm Robinson 1
Richard Wilton 1
Mathew Moake 1
Richard Sikes 1
Thomas Clarkson 1
Willm Brooke 1
Giles Kay 1
Widdow Sparke 1
John Brooke 1
Widdow Walker 1
George Newton 1
140

Omitted by reason of poverty 2

Thomas Midleton Collr
Thomas Arundall Const

m 155]

Warmfeild cum Heath
(Warmfield with Heath)

Sir George Dalston 20
Mrs Dorothy Armitage 13
Willm Mason 3
Paull Vevars 2
Joseph Oxley Jun 2
Robert Preston 3
Ellizabeth Preston 1
George Jubb 1
Willm Kay 4
WIllm Royston 1
Michaell Pearson 4
George Shillitoe 2
two
Ellizabeth Shillitoe 2
John Parkin 1
Thomas Pymott 2
John Robinson 2
James Burnby 1
Joseph Oxley sen 4
Rebecca Cley 2
Thomas Crowther 1
Willm Viccaridge 4
Thomas Barber 1
John Shillitoe 2
Willm Duffinden 1
Francis Shillitoe 3
Thomas Shepherd 4
James Foster 4
Willm Lilly 2
Willm Booth 1
John Lilly Jun 1
Hugh Shillitoe 2
John Sampson 1
Isabell Bell 1
Richard Williamson 1
John Scott 2

[185] 3 written over 1

Michaell Walker	2
John Milnthorpe	1
Steven Attough	1
Robert Simpson	1
Willm Hopwood	2
Joseph Simpson	1
Robert Halleday	1
Michaell Watson	1
Mathew Williamson	3
Thomas Browne	1
Roger Marshall	1
Mrs Windebanke	2[186] two
Robert Ward	1
Leonard Gauthrop	2
Thomas Chappell	1
Mathew Attough	1
Richard Austwick	2
Willm Booth	1
Widdow Hurst	7
	133

Empty and no distres to be had

Mathew Williamson	1

Omitted by reason of poverty	12

Thomas Midleton Collr
Willm Mason Const

Whittwood
(Whitwood)

Mr Robert Abbot	5
Arthur Chambers	3
Francis Shillitoe	7
Hugh Shillitoe	3

m 156]

Willm Shillitoe	2
John Bywatter	2
Widdow Bawgie	2
Edward Haigh	1
John Harrison	2
Willm Greenwood	1
John Todd	1
Gregory Briggs	1
Thomas Shillitoe	1
Robert Redman	1
Jarvice Green	1
Thomas Watson	1
John Thresh	1
	35

Empty and noe distress to be had

Richard Hepworth	1
Richard Hepworth	1[187]
Robert Denton forge	1

Omitted by reason of poverty	2

Thomas Middleton Collr
Willm Shillitoe Const

Wakefeild Westgate
(Wakefield, Westgate)

Willm Ward	4
James Stead	1
Harmond Taylor	6
Richard Ward	3
Nicholls Westerman	8
Widdow Gill	4
Thomas Harrison	5
John Robinson	10
John Hidd	4
Thomas Murgetroyd	6
Mr Olley	2
Francis Wheatley	4
Willm Lawson	4
John Marshall	1
George Blackburn	5
Edward Watkinson	8
Francis Bingham	4
Mr Sumerscales	6
John Clough	4
Widdow Beeston	7
Thomas Graues	8
Mr Menger	6
Widdow Stoxs	3
James Chadwick	3
Gen Harker	3
Mrs Maude	7
Willm Roades	4
James Aikeroyde[188]	2
Widdow Goodyson	2
Richard Wilson	8
Anne Hargraues	3
Mathew Forrest	1
Thomas Roades	1
James Robinson	1
Tunstall Robinson	3
James Birtch[189]	1
Joseph Kay	3
Tempest Brighton	3
Thomas Glover	1

m 157]

Barnard Tompson	3
John Croft	3
Widdow Buck	3
Marke Wild	2
Willm Beamond	6
Richard Moreby	2
Edward Walker	1

186 2 written over 1.
187 sic.
188 Alternative reading: Akeroyde.
189 The reading of this surname as Birtch rather than as Birlch is confirmed by the appearance of this name in the *Nomina Villarum*.

Thomas Roebuck	2
John Dinison	1
John Lenge	1
Nathanll Elsworth	4
John Fisher	1
Widdow Hewit	2
John Twisleton	2
Edward Schoaley	3
Willm Buckston	4
John Blackburn	4
Thomas Linley	3
John Harrison	4
George Bloome	1
Willm Wormall	4
Widdow Thackeray	1
John Cudworth	2
John Foxcroft	2
The house of Correction	6
Willm Ingle	2
Thomas Johnson	1
Robert Lister	2
Jerem Crosley	1
George Sandiforth	1
Willm Doughty	3
Widdow Cooke	2
James Chappell	2
James Hale	1
Richard Vawse	1
Willm Heward	5
Ralph Dawson	2
Marke Fawber	1
John Lee	1
John Lee	2
Samuell Graues	2
Willm Rhoades	1
Widdow Scruce	1
Walter Ward	1
Thomas Rose	1
Willm Bake	2
Thomas Tompson	1
Henry France	3
Elias Cuncliff	5
Willm Harrison	1
Thomas Wharton	4

Elias Cuncliff	1
John Scott	3
Richard Forrest	3
Richard Poole	3
Widdow Askeron	4
Thomas Mergerson	3
James Brathwaite	4
John Birch	3
Richard Harrison	5

m 158]

Thomas Hawkins	6
Samuell Hoyle	5
Richard Greathead	7
Widdow Dodgson	3
Mr Robert Rayner	11
James Watson	6
Willm Baines	3
Richard Norfolke	12
John Dixon	1
Anthony Foster	1
Mrs Naylor	4 fower
Robert Gelson	12
Robert Standeven	2
Mrs Musgraue	5
Francis Allon	1
John Healey	1
Phillp Lilly	5
Widdow Binns	3
Willm Wilson	3
Mr George Ratcliff	4
Thos Cherreyholme	4
Willm Pollard	3
Richard Cotton	1
John Poole	2
John Kirke	4
Willm Richardson	5
Mr Birkhead	2
Richard Smith	1
John Goodisson	3
Widdow Willy	3
Widdow Gimson	1
John Schoaley	2

Mrs Bromley	17
Mr Wrightson	2
Mr Robert Tompson	3
Mr Lee	7
Robert Bradley	3
Tempest Pollard	1
Richard Birkhead	6
John Longley	4
John Senyer	5
Thomas Benson	8
Lawrence Browne	4
John Stocks	7
Wilfrey Child	1
Robert Standeven	1
Richard Ellis	11
John Clough	2
Mr Francis Jenkinson	9
	530

Empty and no distres to be had

John Shilliton	2
Tunstall Robinson	2

m 159]

Mr Sikes	3
John Cromack	1

Omitted by reason of poverty	2

Richard Hardcastle Collr
Willm Lawson Const

Wakefeild Northgate
(Wakefield, Northgate)

Toby Sill	3
Mr Milner	2
Jonas Deane	1
George Walton	4
Richard Viccars	2
Willm Dawson	4
Israell Ouldroyd	1
Robert Allerton	1
Richard Pitt	1

Daniell Firth	3
Charles Nayler	7
	seaven
Thomas Healey	3
Thomas Bins	4
Richard Lambert	2
John Cuningham	3
Willm Hall	3
John Warner	6
John Linley	4
Robert Naylor	5
Thomas Bankes	5
Mrs Greenwood	2
Henry Nelson	2
George Elvidge	3
Widdow Flather	4
Willm Bywatter	2
John Carnill	2
Mr John Wilson	9
Mary Potter	4
Robert Milner	7
Thomas Barnard	4
John Hall	3
John Tanfeild	4
Willm Clarke	3
Willm Briggs	7
Willm Robinson	2
Edmond Fox	1
James Beswick	1
Edward Smith	1
Richard Allon	2
Mr John Yeoman	3
Willm Audsley	4
Willm Midlebrough	3
Richard Poole	5
Thomas Barugh	3
Reynold Tompson	2
Willm Shaun	4

m 160]

James Scrivener	2
Christopr Raper	2
John Hirst	5
Mr John Wetherill	15
John Hollingworth	2
Robert Rogers	1
Francis White Esqr	7
Abraham Hall	4
Francis Ward	2
Joseph Hoyle	10
Mr Clarke	4
Joseph Stocks	4
Willm Shaw	2
Mr Downer	4
Willm Sikes	2
Fardinando Waide	2
Leonard Winterburn	2
Robert Shepherd	2
Mr Scott	4
Willm Winn	6
Richard Senyer	2
Mr Daniell Robinson	2
Richard Ramsbotham	6
Mathew Robinson	3[190]
	three
Widdow Bailden	2
Willm Jackson	2
John Lewis	2
Margret Briggs	2
John Dawson	4
Widdow Blackburn	1
Henry Palister	2
James Dixon	9
Anne Lawson	4
Mrs Levitt	4
Robert Baurgh	1
John Watterhouse sen	2
Thomas Hurst	2
Willm Denison	7
Widdow Belnier	1
Henry Riddall	2
Timothy Lee	2
Willm Allon	3
John Bretner	1
John Jackson	2
Willm Oglethorp Esq	9
John Watterhouse	2
John Tempest	2
John Richardson	2
Willm Blyth	5
John Horsfall	9
James Marsden	1
Lawrance Horracks	2
Willm Clarebrough	3

m 161]

The Schoolehouse	2
John Briggs	1
John Naylor	4
	343

Empty and no distress to be had

Charles Naylor	2
George Waid	3
Willm Dixon	3
Omitted by reason of poverty	28

Robert Corner Collr
Thomas Hurst Const

Wakefeild Kirkegate (Wakefield, Kirkgate)

Thomas Woffenden	1
Francis Denton	7
Michaell Mathew	4
John Silvester	3
Richard Smith & Smithy	4
Willm Pinder	1
Richard Redley	5
John Nelson	2
Robert Shaw	3
Francis Browne	2
John Broadbanke	2
Francis Shore	2
Thomas Peace	6

[190] 3 written over 2.

Samuell Liversidge	8
Thomas Dickinson	1
Hugh Dewhurst	4
John Naylor	2
Widdow Broadley	2
Robert Broadley	2
Rebecca Bins	3
Richard Denton	2
John Snowden	2
Joseph Clayton	2
Mrs Bedford	1
Henry Kirby	1
Timothy Wheelewright	5
Willm Shutleworth	3
Mr Kirby	5
Thomas Pitt	4
Richard Denton	4
Giles Kirby	1
John Heather	2
Richard Clough	2
Widdow Brooke	2
John Brooksbanke	1
Willm Loxley	2
Richard Allon	2
John Bromhead	2
John Neale	3
Thomas Thorpe	3
Mr Olley	2
Christopr Wilson	5
Thomas Thorpe Jun	1

m 162]

John Clarke	3
Steven Oxley	4
Samuell Bins	3[191] three
Widdow Casson	1
Willm Crowther	2
Grace Prance	1
Anne Jackson	2
Edward Lee	3
Willm Robinson	5
Richard Morris	4
Mr Nevill milne	1
Thomas Hepworth	3
Willm Hoyle	3
James Hoyle	1
John Walker	4
Henry Holmes	2
Richard Feild	1
George Brooke	2
John Dixon	2
Robert Cooke	1
Richard Allon	1
Willm Parker	1
John Cooke	1
Willm Fletcher	2
Thomas Heward	1
Roger Shepard	2
Thomas Duffin	5
Robert Wood	2
James Oldroyd	2
Anthony Pratt	2
Willm Kay	1
Robert Fairbanke	4
Thomas Bethill	3
Widdow Taylor	4
James Holland	4
Robert Betson	2
John Wilman	4
Mr Willm Simpson	8
Mr James Lister	8
Mr Power	3
Mr Gelson	2
Peter Sarjant	2
John Thornton	4
Susan Browne	2
Mrs Watterhouse	2
Mr Richard Callis	2
Henry Williamson	2
Thomas Parkins	2
Willm Howle forge	1
Willm Howle	3
Willm Naylor	3
Peter Flocton	1
Robert Tompson	5
George Shepherd	1
John Nayler	3
Mr Morric Dun	4
Richard Birkitt	4
John Bateman	3
John Lee	1
Edward Netleton	2

m 163]

Robert Johnson	1
Widdow Mosley	2
Mr Buckwell	1
Willm Howle	1
	285[192]

Empty and no distres to be had

Mr John Wilson	6
John Longley	7
John Crowther	2
Mr Smith	3
Samuell Longbotham	1

These persons following are discharged by Certfs

Alice Crowther	1
Isaac Bankes	1
Thomas Allen	1
Widdow Burton	2
Widdow Silvester	1
Jane Atkinson	1
George Cavart	1
James Wilman	1
Willm Standerey	1
John Booth	1
John Ellis	1
Widdow Pratt	1

191 3 written over 2.

192 There is a scribal error since the total is 283.

Omitted by reason of poverty	15

Roger Hardcastle Collr
Willm Hoyle Const

Wadsworth

Widdow Shackleton	1
Joseph Shackleton	1
James Shackleton	1
Henry Wadsworth	1
Robert Rushton	1
John Kay	1
James Shackleton	1
Abrah Eastwood	1
Edmond Turner	1
Willm Hanson	2
Richard Wadsworth	1
John Shackleton	2
Abraham Hellewell	1
Henry Hellewell	1
Daniell Greenwood	1
John Shackleton	1
John Shakleton	1[193]
Willm Hellewell	2
Edmond Shackleton	1
Willm Greenwood	1
Edmond Shackleton	1
Aron Pickles	1
Edmond Wadsworth	1
James Greenwood	2
Thomas Cockcroft	1
Paull Greenwood	1
Ambros Greenwood	1
Abraham Wadsworth	1
Simon Redman	1
John Sutcliffe	1
Widdow Widdop	1

m 164]

Uriall Widdup	1
Christopr Thomas	1
Willm Redman	1
Willm Hellewell	1
James Harwood	1
Willm Clayton	3
John Redman	1
John Bankecroft	1
Jonas Pickells	1
Thomas Pickells	2
Jonas Barker	1
Simon Greenwood	1
James Greenwood	1
John Greenwood	2
John Greenwood	2[194]
Lideah Greenwood	1
Daniell Buckley	1
Widdow Hepworth	1
Ambros Widdop	1
Willm Wadsworth	1
Willm Thomas	1
John Eastwood	2
	two
John Widdop	2
Simon Buckley	1
John Horsfall	3
Widdow Wilkinson	1
Thomas Fountaine	1
John Greenwood	2
John Sutcliffe	1
Henry Loyd	1
Widdow Townend	1
Thomas Rushton	1
Abraham Hellewell	1
Josias Hoyle	2
Widdow Townend	1
Thomas Rushton	1
John Briggs	1
John Briggs	1
Willm Varley	1
Richard Wadsworth	2
Willm Ryles	6
Abraham Mitchill	1
James Whithwange	2
Edward Saltonstall	4
John Mitchill	2
Jonas Lister	2
Richard Tattersall	1
Edmond Rigg	4
Caleb Widdop	1
Richard Jackson	1
John Jawitt	1
John Dodgson	1
John Dilworth	1
John Jackson	1
Willm Walker	1
Henry Aikeroyde	1
Henry Spencer	1
Widdow Greenwood	3
Widdow Spencer	1
John Shaw	1

m 165]

John Gleadall	1
John Thomas	1
Henry Cockcroft	1
Widdow Sutcliffe	3
Widdow Stansfeild	1
Abraham Stansfeild	1
John Cockcroft	1
Timothy Wigen	1
Benjam Greenwood	3
John Mitchill	1
Steven Jackson	1
John Haworth	1
Willm Cockcroft	1
Willm Barcroft	1
Daniell Fauthropp	4
George Hargraues	3
Robert Hardman	2
Henry Cockcroft	2
John Parker	9
George Hargraues	2
Willm Cockcroft	6
Willm Sutcliff	4

[193] sic.
[194] sic.

Willm Thomas	3
Willm Sutcliff	3
Widdow Nayler	4
John Banister	3
Willm Cockcroft	2
Widdow Cockcroft	1
Widdow Nayler	1
Isaac Steding	1
Jonas Coates	2
Jasper Pilling	1
Richard Steding	1
James Greenwood	3
Henry Egland	1
Isaac Dewhurst	2
Richard Thomas	3
Willm Broadbelt	3
Robert Whitacres	1
Thomas Greenwood	3
Robt Thomas	4
Henry Lockwood	4
Edward Davie	3
Edward Saltonstall	1
Richard Cockcroft	2
	225

Roger Hardcastle Collr
James Shackleton Const

Warley

Jonathan Waide	1
John Murgetroyde	1
John Brear	1
John Crabtree	3
Anthony Shephard	1

m 166]

Mathew Crowther	1
Isaac Kitchin	1
Mathew Hesletine	2
John Murgatroyd	2
John Murgatroyd	2[195]
John Brear	2
Jonath Fairebanke	5
Mrs Murgetroyde	7
Richard Illingworth	1
John Hartley	2
Gregory Mitchell	1
John Sutcliffe	1
Michaell Frear	1
John Midgley	4
Willm Stainforth	1
Samll Midgley	1
Richard Thompson	2
John Ingham	1
Abraham Viccars	2
Isaac Child	1
Nathanll Colbeck	5
Henry Wadsworth	6
Isaac Kitchin sen	1
James Greenwood	1
John Smith	2
Widdow Deane	1
Thomas Farrer	1
Henry Skelton	1
Abrah Greenwood	2
John Hanson	1
John Viccars	1
John Hellewell	1
Abraham Sutcliffe	1
Daniell Skelton	1
John Harper	1
Richard Smith	1
Abraham Smith	1
Ambros Potchett	1
Abraham Sutcliff	1
Richard Smith	1
Widdow Wood	1
John Ryley	1
Nathanll Skelton	1
Edward Waite	1
Widdow Eastwood	1
Abraham Hellewell	1
Abraham Aikeroyd	2
John Shackleton	1
Thomas Deane	1
Abraham Apleyard	1
Widdow Wadsworth	1
Abraham Skelton	1
Abraham Aikeroyd	1
Thomas Waide	1
Widdow Walton	1
John Clay	1
Jerem Clay sen	1
Humphr Waide	1
Michaell Wood	1

m 167]

Edward Hurst	1
Jerem Clay Jun	1
Henry Wadsworth	1
Willm Slayden	1
Willm Apleyard	1
Timothy Greenwood	2
Jonas Thomas	1
Jon Aikeroyd	1
John Waide	1
Jonas Wood	1
Edward Denton	1
John Ryley	1
Abraham Wheelwright	1
Richard Oxnopp	1
Willm Calvert	2
Willm Clay	1
Timothy Breare	1
John Briggs	2
John Crabtree	1
Joseph Hargraues	1
Samuell Hargraues	1
Willm Ingham	1
John Greenwood	1
John Wadsworth	4
Timothy Wadsworth	1
John Pighills	1
Widdow Waide	5
Robert Farrer	1
Anthony Coldcall	1
Widdow Murgetroyd	2

[195] sic.

Ellias Whitacre	1
Thomas Atkinson	1
Richard Baxendall	4
Rydeing head	2
James Richardson	2
John Murgetroyde	6
Widdow Blakey	2
Mathew Mitchell	3
James Smith	1
James Ingham	2
Thomas Crosley	2
Timothy Towne	5
Henry Walker	2
Willm Murgetroyd	2
Timothy Marsden	1
Widdow Wouenden	1
Edmond Starkey	6
Michaell Smith	1
Michaell Bentley	2
John Bentley	1
Gate sloopes	1
Willm Ingham	2
Edmond Tattersall	5
Widdow Nicholson	5
	fiue
John Chapman	2
Willm Greenwood	2

m 168]

Robert Spencer	5
Jonas Crowther	3
Timothy Tattersall	6
James Ingham	2[196]
	two.
Henry Hague	3
Thomas Emott	4
George Lunn	5
Robert Thomas	4
Edward Tattersall	2
Edmond Tattersall	6
Abraham Heworth	1
Richard Foster	1
John Roades	1
John Bankcroft	1
George Fairbanke	1
Jon? Crowther	2
Henry Halstead	4
James Boulton	2
Widdow Lacy	1
Thomas Tewman[197]	3
Nathan Murgetroyd	2
Daniell Baites	5
Jonathan Tattersall	5
John Steele	2
Arthur Maude	1
James Green Jun	1
James Green sen	2
Michaell Colbeck	2
John Butterworth	2
Jonas[198] Crowther	1
John Bancroft Jun	1
Robert Royde	1
George Fairbanke	6
James Chadwick	5
Samuell Robertshaw	2
Henry Storke	2
Thomas Schoalefeild	1
John Wilkinson	1
James Whitacre	4
Edward Robertshawe	1
Willm Wood	2
John Watterhouse	1
Michaell Colbeck	4
Willm Colbeck	5
Samuell King	1
Jacob Farrow	3
Joseph Hoyle	2
Sarah Cooke	1
Willm Wadsworth	1
Joseph Boulton	4
Joseph Cockcroft	3
Edward Denton	2
Edward Wood	2

m 169]

Nathaniell More	1
James Marsden	4
Thomas Smith	3
James Wodington	3
Thomas Turnor	2
Richard Wood	2
James Oldfeild	4
Thomas Bentley	2
Widdow Brrow[199]	3
Widdow Marsden	1
James Tayler	1
Widdow Leach	1
James Murgetroyd	3
Thomas Broadbelt	1
James Murgetroyde	1
	370

Roger Hardcastle Collr
Thomas Turner Const

[196] 2 written over 1.
[197] Trewman in *Nomina Villarum.*
[198] James in *Nomina Villarum.*
[199] Barrow in *Nomina Villarum.*

Barkston Ash Wapentake

The National Archives, E179/262/14

m 1]

Barkston Ash Wapentake

Abberforth (Aberford)

Mr George Rhoades	6
Mr Marke Plant	6
Wid Dauson	5
Leonard Howdall	3
Chrofer Dodgson	6
William Akitt	4
Robert Hicke	4
more a forge	1
John Marshall	2
John Smith	2
Willim Akitt	2
Mrs Ickeringall	4
John Popleton	1
Richard Browne	1
Thomas Slater	1
Robert Bucktroute	2
Fr Silverwood	1
John Dawson	3
	2
	56

Empty & no distres to be had

Mr Rhoades	1

Omitted by reason of Extreame Poverty	2

Robert Husband Collr
Leonard Houdall Const

Bramham

Nichollas Lake	10
Oglethorp hall	10
Bramham Biggin	7
Edward Beale gen	9
Hope Hall	5
Willm Smith	1
Tho Senior	3
John Dickinson sen sen	1
Christopher Powell	3
Willm Clough	1
more a forge	1
Willm Powell	1
Widd Powell	1
Henry Shippen	1
Wid Senior	1
Willm Denton	1
John Hopwood	2
John Fawcitt	1
Willm Middleton	1
Ri Smith	1
Rich Smith	1
John Powell	2
Ri Bustard	1
Rob Fairburne	1
Henry Fewler	1
Chr Witton	1
Willm Brighton	1
Rich Stables	2
Chr Hill	1
Willm Snaw	1
Edward Knapton	1
William Atkinson	1
William Harpam	3
Rich Starverley	1
Tho Tate	2
Tho Lee	1
John Baitson	1
Chr Bustard	2
John Petty	1
George Burley	1
James Dalloby	1
John Smith	3
Tho Senior jun	1
Willm Fairburne sen	1
John Jackson	1
John Farrer	4
New Milne	1
Slate Milne	1
Chr Bowman	2

m 2]

Willm Armstrong	1
Willm Willan	1
Willm Fairburne	1
Tho Houseman	1
Widd Richardson	1
John Smith jun	4
Willm Clough	1
Tho Thompson	1
Tho Dodgson	1
Tho Hill Cler	4
Marma Shepheard	1
John Clough	3
James Powell	3
Tho Darley	1
Tho Sanior	1
John Richinson	1
Rob Knapton sen	4
Rich Stables	1
	133

These persons following are discharged by certificate

Matthew Gibson	1
Tho Richardson	1

Omitted by reason of poverty	3

Robert Husband Collr
Robert Fairburne Const

Brayton

John Walker	1
Fr Kershaw	1
Henry Smith	1

Willm Kershaw	1
Willm Richardson	1
John Arnold	1
Tho Beale	3
Robert Spincke	1
Willm Loftus	1
Henry Beale & forge	2
Tho Robinson	1
Tho Collitt	1
Tho Walker	2
Peter Lamb	2
Edward Collitt	1
Rob Wood	1
Rob Boyes	1
Fard Hornby	1
John Longthropp	1
Jonas Arnold	1
George Fish *pro* Milne	1
Steven Horsman	3
Christopher Lamb	1
John Walker	1
Edmond Lawson	1
Mr Robert Shereburne	4
Ri Foster	5
Tho Spincke	1
Robert Walker	2
John Walker	2
Mr Peter Tomlinson	4
Tho Morritt	2
Willm Sweeting	1
Thomas Graves	3
Geo Fish	1
John Morritt	6
Willm Tomlinson	1
Tho Morritt jun	2
Widd Faireland	2
Issabell Walker & Robinson	1
Willm Thush	1
Geo Rogers	2
Phil Wood	1
Rob Robinson	1
Willm Robinson de p[ar]ke	2
	76

Empty & noe distress to be had

Willm Woodhouse	1

The person undernamed is discharged by certificate

m 3]

Geo Fallis	1

Roger Hardcastle Collr
Tho Spincke Const

Barley
(Barlow)

Robert Tod	4
Mary Clay	1
Edward Watson	1
Willm Wood	1
Mrs Sawer	17
Barthol Wilson	1
Willm Bramham	1
Paul Palmer	1
Thomas Jewison	1
John Hall	2
Roger Sanders	1
Robert Bennett	2
John Smith	1
Geo Remington	5
Wid Blyth	1
James Beale	1
Tho Lee	1
Tho Robinson	1
Tho Lamb	1
Henry Richardson	1
Joseph Inchboard	2
Edward Willowby	1
William Whitley	1
John Saunders	1
John Harrison	1
Thomas Grub	1
Peter Watson	1
Mrs Milnes	2

Rich Ibbotson & forge	2
Robert Vallance	1
Widdow Watson	1
Willm Tomlinson	2
Willm Etty	1
Thomas Halliday	1
Robert Baley	1
Tho Tomlinson	2
Tho Stringer	1
	67

Omitted by reason of poverty	2

Ri Pickard Collr
Bartho Watson Const

Barston Towne
(Barkston)

Ri Buckland	1
Ri Turpin	1
Marke Varley	1
Ri Richardson	1
Laur Skelton	1
Mr Simpson	5
George Gibson	3
Willm Heigh	1
George Skelton	1
Joseph Turpin	1
Willm Heigh jun	1
Willm Heigh sen	3
John Shipton	1
Tho Wade	1
John Bolland	1
Gabriell Browne	3
Mary Nicholson	3
Robert Lister	1
John Tod	1
Alex Tutle	1
Wid Wade	1
Chr Lawson	1
Edward Surfitt	1
Wid Sissons	1
John Sissons	1
John Bell	1

John Heigh	1
John Mitchell	1
	40

Omitted by reason of poverty	7

Ri Pickard Collr
Ri Sissons Const

m 4]

Byronn cum Poole
(Byram with Pool)

William Burland	1
John Cockill	1
John Fairburne	1
John Bramham	2
John Musgrave	2
Mr Ramsden *pro* Milne	1
John Ramsden Esq	26
John Chapman	1
John Richardson	3
Tho Busby	1
Marg Berridge widd	3
	42

George Waineman Collr
James Chapman Const

Burne
(Burn)

Mr John Ashton	8
Mr Peter Tomlinson	5
Sr Tho Longdevile	6
Mr Ashton	1
John Tomlinson	2
Willm Morrett	2
Ri Poole	4
Willm Robinson	1
John Lamb	1
John Wood	1
Willm Speight	1
John Tayler	1
John Goodyeare	1
Daniell Arnold	2
Robert Greene	1
Richard Lamb	1
Alice Arnold	2
Richard Arnold	2
Jane Jubb	2
Abr Collitt	1
Matthew Fox	2
Sr Tho Longdevile	1
Willim Crosland	1
Anne Tompson	1
Willm Rogers	1
Willm Kirtison	1
Michaell Goodyeare	1
Mary Wood	1
John Wood *pro* Simpson	1
Willm Sampson	1
	56

Georg Waineman Collr
Matthew Fox Const

Birkin

Mr Everingham Cressy	14
John Possgate sen	4
Willm Lake	1
Willm Batman	1
Richard Possgate	1
George Woodhouse	1
Willm Wright	2
Tho Tortill	2
Henry Ellis	2
George Fewster	1
Mary Cobcroft	1
Stephen Ellis	1
Widdow Hinsley	1
Wid Tompson	1
Chr Batman	1
Tho Cobcroft	1
Tho Tutall jun	4
Willm Holland	2
Mr Thornton	11
Willm Richardson	1
James Robinson	1
John Temperton forge	1
	55

Robert Husband Collr
Thomas Tootill Const

Burton Salmond
(Burton Salmon)

Mary Rhoades	1
Marmad Hodgson	1
Mrs Grace Sikes	3

m 5]

Mr Norman	9
George Akinson	1
Richard Hall	1
William Gilson	1
Matthew Birkinshaw	1
Marg Rawson wid	4
Benja Spincke	2
John Wilkinson	6
William Burland	3
Widd Boulton	1
James Butler	1
Michaell Cowling	3
Mrs Norman	1
Willm Story	1
John Thorner	2
James Bramham & forge	3
	45

Richard Pickard Collr
Mich Cowling Const

Brotherton

Brotherton Tindall Esq	19
Robert Dyneley	5
William Walker	2
Jerem Walker	4
John Bramham	1
Geo Stringer	2
Tho Bywater	1

Samuell Scott	1
George Browne	1
Abraham Ryley	1
John Greene	4
Matthew Coates	5
John Wheatcroft	2
Mr Bell viccar	3
Robert Halliday	1
William Burton	2
William Illingworth	2
Edward Rhoades	3
Ro Turton & James Barker	2
Mr Bolton	3
Mr Badley	4
Michaell Tully	2
Marke Burland	4
Ro Bence	1
Elizabeth Stringer and Tho Chapman	2
Willm Wilkes	3
Mrs Rayner	2
William Newby	1
Widdow Ducker	3
Richard Walker	1
Barthol Ibotson	3
Robert Nelson	3
William Craggs	1
Doroth Bloone	3
James Gilson	1
Mr Twizleton	4
Willm Burland	3
John Barker	1
Robert Wright	4
William Scott	1
Thomas Hamond	1
Roger Wilson	5
Alex Stileman	7
Mr Fothergill	7
Henry Elson	2
Tho Bardin	1
Mr Ingram	1
Edward Britlebancke	1
Edward Briggs	1
John Hancocke	1
Willm Hamlocke	1
Antho Carr	1
Matthew Stringer	1
more a forge	1
John Cockroft	1
Wid Illingworth	1
	144

Empty & noe distress to be found

Edward Rhoades	1
William Graveley	1

Roger Hardcastle Collector
John Bloome Constable

m 6]

Cawood

Widd & James Smith	7
Willm Leadom	3
John Roebucke	2
Willm Tompson	1
Wid Watson	4
Mr Ri Smith	2
Rob Wilson	5
John Wheatley	2
Tho Fetherston	2
Edward Cundill	2
Tho Sissons	1
Willm Hill	1
Widd Nainburne	4
Willm Stevens	5
Robert Turner	3
Widdow Tompson	1
Tho Wilkinson	4
Mr Needome	8
Mr James Beverley	3
Elizabeth Greene	1
Mrs Lowd	8
Wid Bland	1
John Ryles	1
John Rossindale	1
Robert Stainton	1
Phillip Rossinden	1
Jane Spincke	1
Chrofer Empson	1
Tho Tod	2
Willm Tomlinson	2
Robte Furrington	1
William Roote	1
Nicholas Doughty	1
Nicholas Flawith	1
Mr Wilbore	6
Mr Walker	5
Tho Roebucke	1
John Roebucke	2
Widd Pape	1
Ri Bell	1
Robt Cowper	2
Tho Rossendale	1
Tho Tod	2
Geo Howell	6
Marmad Mare	3
Robert Akister	4
Tho Plewes	1
Christor Jackson	1
Tho Skelton	1
Henry Bilbrough	1
Hen Skyles	2
Widdow Parcivell	4
Willm Matheray	3
Chrofer Knapton	2
Math Wells	4
Ro Walker}	
Matr Tuke}	
Joshua Rawlin}	
Tho Goodyeare	1
Tho Bucke	2
Willm Nicholson	2
John Drax	2
Mrs Richardson	7
Henry Oddy	2
Willm Emmott	1
John Wilson	5
Willm Burley	5
Mrs Ashton	4
Mr James Smith mill	1
John Batter	2

William Halliley	3
Anthony Scholey	4
William Robinson	4
Michaell Tayler	1
Widdow Duffin	5
Matthew Walker	3
Widd Stothard	4
John Richardson	4
Tho Potter	2
Widdow Buckle	4
Widdow Neudicke	4
more a forge	1
Rich Browne	3
Widdow Matheray	4
Tho Doughty	3
Willm Wilson	2
Robt Temperton	3

m 7]

Willm Smith	4
Rich Easingwold	4
Vincent Halliday	1
Mr Ashton or Smith	5
John Brathwaite	5
Mr Morritt	3
John Wilson	2
Tho Braidhorne	1
William Stothard	2
James Brindholme	3
William Fentiman	1
Widdow Needham	1
John Thorpe	1
Cawood Castle	24
James Brindleholme	2
Willm Maderey jun	4
George Ellis	2
Tho Simpson	2
Ri Parnam	1
John Carnaby	4
John Hall & corn [*recte* com(mon)] Oven	2
Willm Watson	1
Robert Fisher	1
Thomas Baxter	1
John Johnson	2
Antho Middleton or Humph Rippon	1
	305

Empty

Tho Fox	1
Martha Parcivall	3
Mary Johnson	2
Tho Mann	1
	7

These persons following are discharged by certificate

John Robinson	1
Roger Deighton	1
William Ellis	1
Anne Appleby	1
Fr Greene	1
Arthur Lund	1
Edward Barran	1
John Edlin	1
Ri Westerman	1
Alice Hunter	1
Robert Akister	1
William Laikland	1
Brian Law	1
Lawr Fletcher	1
Willm Nicholson	1
	15

Omitted by reason of poverty 34

Robt Husband Collector
Tho Baxter Const

Chappell Hadlesey (Chapel Haddlesey)

Willm Tomlinson	1
John Jackson	1
Willm Chapman	1
Tho Elcocke	1
John Roades	1
Eliz Copland	1
Willm Stones	1
John Davison	2
Edward Hine sen	1
Robert Graves	1
Abra Westerman	1
Ri Possgate	2
Thomas Davison	2
Wid Walker	4
John Bramley	1
Edward Hine jun	2
Edward Morris	1
Thomas Morris	2
Wid Barker	1
Peter Tomlinson	2
Joseph Bramley	4
	33

Robert Husband Collr
Alexander Hollins Const

m 8]

Camplesforth (Camblesforth)

Mr Christopher Adams	7
Tho Elland	2
Willm Pickard	2
Charles Farum	1
Edward Atkinson	2
Christopher Bawne	1
John Ryley	1
Richard Palner	2
Tho Fryer	1
Samuell Jinson	1
Richard Underwood	1
Timothy Oakes or Ellison	1
John Bell	1
Widd Ellison	1
John Lonnsdale	1
Michaell Nessey	2
Tho Rodwell	1
Steven Hollins	1
Robert Wilson	1
William Tindall	1

Robert Kirkby 1
John Cliffe 2
Wid Hedley 1
Robert Spencer 2
Charles Rickall 1
Tho Fish 1
Will Audas 2
John Robinson 1
Brexhouse 1
John Darham 2
Mr Scaife 1
Francis Walker 1
Widd Bramham 1
Widd Dickinson 1
9

George Waineman Collr
John Ryley Const

Clifforth (Clifford)

John Beilby Esq 10
Mr Pullan 4
James Stead 3
Ri Nicholson 1
Fran Kilner 1
Tho Tompson or Jo 1
Ri Notson 1
Abra Wright 1
Robte Morley 1
Geo Reighton 1
Will Previlley 1
Will Richardson 2
Jane Busterd 1
Ellin Calverley 1
Tho Procter 3
Tho Knapton 1
Willm Scott 1
Ri Knapton 1
Geo Hopwood & forge 4
James Cooper 1
John Cundall 1
Willm Hopwood *pro* plewland 2
Margt Knapton widdow 1
Matthew Lee 1
Peter Selby 1
John Faireburne 1
Sr Tho Gascoigne 1
Rich Nicholson 1
Rich Powell 2
Willm Knapton 1
Anne Scott 1
John Atkinson 1
Sr Tho Gascoigne 2
Tho Rigton 1
Willm Abbey 1
George Gurley 1
59

These persons followeing are discharged by certificate
Widd Duffeild 1
John Bell 1

Omitted by reason of poverty 2

Robt Husband Collector
John Fairburne Const

Carelton (Carlton)

George Scoley sen 2
George Scoley jun 1
Tho Stevenson 3

m 9]

Richard Hutton 2
Tho Marvell 2
Elizab Pearcy 1
Geo Pearcy 1
Tho Collon 1
Willm Baumforth 3
Mary Arnold 1
John Ingram 2
Willm Gibson 1
Matth Horsman 1
Robert Kellington 2
John Elland 2
Willm Ballance 2
Mary Hacker 2
Maxim Sainter 1
Joseph Rogers 3
Parcivall Ellis 3
John Sothaby for Mr Bolton 3
Mrs Bolton 1
Widd Wentworth 1
Antho Ward 1
John Cowgill 2
Tho Ward 2
Tho Jubb 1
John Pearcy 1
Mr Tayler 3
John Etherington 2
John Grundall 2
Robte Hood & forge 2
John Halliwell 1
John Cockwell 1
Willm Steele 1
Hen Redforth and Motherby 3
Christopher Hutchinson 1
John Browne 2
Rose Lantley 2
Margarett Girdler 1
Jacob Langtropp 1
John Watson 2
Antho Wilson 2
Wid Rogers 1
Robert Stringer 1
Robert Peircy 1
Thomas Aucocke 2
Dorothy Hinsley 1
Ri Kirkby 2
James Vallance 1
Leonard Tranfeild 1
Tho Pearcy 1
Tho Rickard 2
Tho Ward 2
Richard Dickinson 3
John Heaton 2

William Peeres	2
John Wilbore	1
Luce Aucocke	2
Simond Hembrough	1
Rich Boyes	1
Willm Ine sen	1
Willm Ine jun	1
Willm Colcole	1
Robert Laughty	1
Nichols Farrer	1
Joseph Shilven	1
John Swift	1
William Pearcy	1
John Pearcy	3
Thomas Whitley	2
Willm Cuninworth	2
Robert Walker	1
Trn Ballance	2
Tho Shillinns	1
Robte Littlewood	1
Tho Cockhill	2
John Richardson	3
Geo Jubb	1
John Yorson	1
Sr Miles Stapleton	23
more for Cusquo	10
Mr Hugh Tayler	10
Thomas Barugh	3
Tho Buck	3
Willm Kendall	1
Abra Arnold	1

m 10]

Tho French	1
George Johnson	1
	181

Omitted by reason of poverty 7

Robert Husband and George Waineman Collrs
William Balance Const

Drax cum Newland (Drax with Newland)

Tho Akers	3
Tho Andrew	3
Brockholes	3
Michaell Nesse	2
Widdow Rusholme	2
Widdow Padgitt	2
Willm Tayler	1
Robert Lee	1
Rich Richinson	1
John Berridge	1
Wm Jaques	1
Ri Tayler	2
Willm Tomisin	2
Gabriell Brooke	2
Mr John Little	5
Willm Mitchell	5
Robert Ellis	2
Geo Kirkby	1
Bartho Coates	1
Tho Clayton	2
John Rayby	1
Edward Binns *pro* Hembrough	2
Tho Jackson	2
Mrs Mawde	1
Mr Taylor	7
Willm Turner	2
Ro Hill or Turner	1
Ri Markham	2
John Stubs	2
Willm Browne	4
Willm Tompson	1
Tho Turner	2
Widdow Banne	2
Robert Spencer	1
Tho Whitehead	1
Willm Clayton	2
John Hogley	2
Willm Knowles	1
Henry Hill	1
Ri Andrew	1
Abra Barrill	2
Peter Smake	2
John Tayler	1
Peter Weddell	1
Robert Bayle	2
Mr Lewans	7
James Hogley	1
Robert Bayley	2
Widd Padgitt	5
Widd Hembrough	7
Ri Hembrough	2
Mary Walker	1
John Cooling	1
Chrofer Hembrough	1
Phillip Twizleton Esq	21
Mrs Beale	1
Chrofer Barker jun	1
Robte Powles & forge	3
Edward Durham	2
Widdow Mitchell	2
Tho Ryley	1
John Wilson jun	1
Widd Steare	2
Tristram Preston	2
John Revell	1
Christopher Barker sen	1
Widd Remington	1
John Hare	2
Willm Hembrough	2
Willm Rouklidge	1
Edward Cutforth & John Hall	3
John Durham	2
Thomas Hembrough	3
Widd Grevons	1
Wid Hembrough	1
Watkinson house	1
Widdow Godfey	1

m 11]

Ellias Hembrough	1
Edward Atkinson	2
John Walker	1
Mr Gower	5
Abra Decon	5
Mary Thackray	1

George Hembrough	2
Widd Freare	2
William Rickard	3
Widd Harrison	2
Edward Hembrough	1
Michaell Thackwray	2
Willm Widehouse	2
John Widdowes	2
Chrofer Fairewether	3
Willm Rickard	1
Robte Frear	1
Mr Tayler of Coates	7
Ri Fairland	6
William Durham	2
Tho Thackwray	2
Tho Dent	2
Mr Wm Batt *pro* Mr Poole	5
Willm Bolton	1
John Wilson	1
Joseph Wilkinson	1
	234

Empty	
Coll Twizleton	1

Robt Husband Collr
Ri Hembrough Const

Fenton cum Biggin (Little Fenton with Biggin)

Mr Matterham	6
Tho Emerson	1
John Bewley	2
Widd Knowles	3
John Tosh	1
Tho Parr	4
John Bolton	1
Henry Squire	1
Robert Greenwood	1
Tho Wilson	2
Rich Daniell	3
Brian Tasker	1
Willm Johnson	1
John Bullocke	1
Mr Toby Birdsall	1
Robert Middleton	1
John Squire	1
Fr Wind	2
Ri Daniell	1
Matthew Nelstrop	1
Ri Olliver	1
Anne Tosh	1
Vincent Stainton	1
John Wilkinson	1
Widd Brigham	1
Tho Smith	1
Ambrose Lee	1
Willm Halleley	1
Geo Hope	1
Robte Stainton	1
Mr Fran Thirkill	3
John Staker	1
Willm Nelstropp	1
Widd Tone	1
Tho Harrison	1
Willm Hawton	1
Tho Knowles	1
Geo Cawood	1
	55

Omitted by reason of poverty	1

Robte Husband Collr
Willm Johnson Const

Faireburne (Fairburn)

Mr Jerome Spincke	8
John Searby	2
John Pearcy or Bearcliff	8
Widdow Brearcliffe	4
Robert Askam	3
Widdow Askam	4
William Rhoades & forge	3
Cuthbert Twizleton	3
Anne Bolton	5
Tho Hall	3
Willm Oldfeild	1

m 12]

John Johnson	1
Ri Oldfeild	3
John Story	2
John Jackson	1
William Wilkinson	4
Tho Webster	1
Willm Backhouse	2
John Banister	1
Rich Tompson	1
Tho Lee	1
Tho Hewitt & forge	2
Tho Barton	1
John Dawson	1
Tho Norden	1
John Holden	2
John Sangton	1
Tho Lee	2
Tho Williamson	1
Tho Key	1
Ri Turner	1
Antho Raper	1
William Carrier	1
William Rowley	1
Geo Barton	1
Brian Barton	1
	79

Omitted by reason of poverty	1

Robte Husband Collr
John Johnson Const

Gateforth

William Bolton	1
Willm Wray	1
James Atkinson	1
Ri Gilliam	1
Margarett Bilbrough	1

Willm Tomlin 1
Willm Deane 1
Chr Thompson of Spofforth 1
Willm Wilson 2
Robte Long 1
Gervas Cressy 8
John Levans or Mr George Crowle 5
Willm Remington 8
Arthur Bell & forge 3
Willm Sainter 1
John Tompson 1
Tho Bolton 1
Willm Mitchell 1
Edward Bolton 4
John Levans *pro* Cobcroft 2
Ri. Long 1
Fr Bell 1
Anne Bolton 2
Anne Ashforth 1
Rich Waddington 1
George Appleton 1
John Wood 1
Rob Walker 2
Rob Wood 1
Rob Wood 1
Rob Bennett 1
Mrs Brooke 1
Willm Coates 1
Tho Thomlinson 1
Gabriell Brooke 1
John Spofforth 1
John Crosland 1
Gabriell Brooke 4
George Remington 1
Tristrum Peake 1
John Burnby 1
Paul Waller 1
Geo Houlden Milner 1
Willm Remington 7
Roger Burdax 1
81

Empty
John Leavans 1

Robt Husband Collr
Ri Waddington Const

Grimstone
(Grimston)
Tho Hall 24
Eliz Barterd 1
John Millett 5

m 13]

Willm Lancaster 1
John Fentiman 1
Christopher Daniell 2
Widdow Irish 1
Stephen Welburne 1
Stephen Brearey 1
Rich Parrison 1
Brian Lancaster 1
Robte Willowby 1
Willm Hutton 2
Willm Sweeke 1
43

Omitted by reason of poverty 1

Roger Hardcastle Collr
Steven Welburne Const

Huddlestone cum Lumby
(Huddleston with Lumby)
Ri Ward 1
Ri Beale 1
Luke Daniell 1
Willm Shearcroft 2
Anne Batman 1
John Shearcroft 1
John Shearcroft 1
Sr Francis Hungate 13
Ri Halliday 5
Henry Morton 1
27

George Wainman Collr
John Shearcroft Const

Hurst Courtney
(Hirst Courtney)
George Nayler 1
Amerill Baxter 2
Tho Barfe 4
Robte Smith 2
Amerill Lengthropp 1
Ri Sainter 1
Geo Heanley 1
Geo Arnitt 1
Amerill Peeres 1
John Lund 1
Rich Jeffrey 1
Willm Knowles 1
William Harram 2
Robte Heanley 2
Andrew Northin 1
John Baxter 3
Willm Chapman 1
Robte Lound 1
Widd Pemrose 1
John Scarr 1
John Copley 1
Tho Healey 2
32

Empty
Robte Sainter of Hamleton 1

Robte Husband Collr
Tho Barfe Const

Hillam
Mercy Hemingway 1
Rich Harrison 1
Widd Dickins 1
Tho Richardson for Harpham 4
Lanc Bew 4
John Halleley 4
Samuell Mackerill 4

Willm Richardson 3
John Barker 1
George Wells 1
Charles Smith 1
George Illingworth 1
Robte Spincke 1
George Bewe sen 1
John Tayler 1
Widdow Spincke 4
Andrew Armstrong 1
Willm Bramham gen 1
Edward Walker 1

m 14]

Widdow Harrison 1
Benja Spincke 1
John Barker 1
Peter Bell 1
Robte Spincke 2
John Musgrave 1
Widd Bowcocke 1
Posthumus Spincke 2
George Illingworth 1
Henry Playforth 2
Abra Tayler 1
John Laveracke 1
Matthew Spincke 3
Widdow Nelson 2
Geo Bew jun 3
Anne Pearson 5
Alice Cockell 4
Tho Harrison & mill 2
Willm Johnson 1
Willm Wells 1
John Tayler 1
John Altoft 1
Geo Wells & 1
West

75

Empty
Tho Jenkinson 3

Roger Hardcastle Collr
Peter Bell Const

Haddlesey West
(West Haddlesey)

John Cooke 1
Willm Posgate 2
Willm Cowper 1
Edward Smith 1
John Lake 2
Hen Hobman 3
John Rhoades 3
Reynold Bromley 1
Tho Morrett 2
Willm Matthewes 1
James Bromley 1
Wid Stockhill 1
John Morrett 2
William Pagett 3
Anne Cooper 1
John Holmes 2
Widd Spofforth 1
John Davison 2
Tho Cooke 1
one
Widdow Midlam 1
Edward Davison 2
Robert Davison 1
Willm Hodgson 2
Tho Bell 1
John Steele 2
Willm Spofforth 2
Willm Miles 1

43

Robt Husband Collr
Henry Hobman Constal

Hambleton

Eliza Lund 2
Urias Turner 1
Anne Hembrough 1
Bartho Middleton 2
Mr Ra Wood *pro* Gell 1
Mr Thomlinson or 2
Mr Bracebridge
Thomas Barnby 1
Matthew Crookdyke 2
William Bracebridge 2
William Leadson 1
Edward Richardson 2
Elizabeth Marshall 1
Widdow Bracebridge 2
Willm Houghton 1
James Dunderdill 1
Willm Heptenstall 1
Willim Wood 1
Anne Gaggs 1
John Graves 1
Widdow Prodfoote 1
Tho Medley 1
Tho Rickall 2
Willm Randerson 1
Willm Bradshaw 1
Robte Spincke 1
Chrofer Durham 1
Robte Leadson or 1
George Motherby
Nephtaly Bracebridg 1
Francis Morley 3

m 15]

Tho Johnson 1
Michaell Tomlinson 1
Tho Steere 2
Willm Knowles jun 1
Willm Shaw 1
James Wyrill 1
John Bradshaw 1
Willm Spight 2
George Wilson 2
Jerom Morley 3
Ri Procter 1
Wid Knowles 2
Tho Bentley 1
Willm Shaw 1
Tho Marshall 1
George Richardson 1
Ri Gregson 1
Geo Bewe 2
Mr Tho Weddell 7
Michaell Tomlinson 3

Geo Motherby	2
Widd Sharpe	1
Chrofer Hill	1
Tho Thomlinson	1
George Arnold	2
Willm Smith	2
Edward Knowles	1
Geo Pattericke	1
Jo Hamers or	1
Jane Wyrell	
Robte Lund	2
Robte Leadshaw	2
Anne Smith	1
Thomas Welburne	1
Robte Sentor	1
Robte Tomlinson	1
Mr Willm Tomlinson	2
Willm Tompson	1
	97

Omitted by reason of poverty	12

Roger Hardcastle Collr
Gabriell Knowles Const

Kirk Fenton
(Church Fenton)

The Parsonage	6
Joseph Birdsall	3
Mr Bowcocke	2
Mr Tho Birdsall	5
Theoph Brogden	3
Robte Browne	4
Tho Bucke	6
Joseph Hudson	3
Rich Beare	2
Henry Cass	2
Tho Birdsall	3
Widd Birdsall	2
Eliz Harrison	1
Willm Brigham	1
Geo Taleforth	1
Willm Middleton	1
Henry Button	1
Ri Braithwaite	1
Willm Lacocke	1
John Leeming	1
Robert Maud	1
Adam Harrison	1
Geo Collins	1
John Anderson	1
Widd Jackson	1
Widd Denton	1
Widd Lee	1
Stephen Cooke	1
Tho Whiteing	1
Mary Wrightson	1
John Clarkson	2
James Goodyeare	1
Richard Lovell	1
Wid Tod	1
Wid Turpin	1
Edward Fish	1
Robte Holmes	1
Francis Atkinson	1
Chrofer Waterhouse	2
Geo Harrison	2
Tho Browne	3

m 16]

Geo Dobson	1
Tho Procter	1
Mr Tho Widd	1
Robte Clayton	1
	79

The person under named is discharged by certificate

Thomas Preston	1

Robert Husband Collector
Joseph Hudson Constable

Kirkby Wharfe

Mr Geo Stanhop	2
Mr Rob Sands	5
Willm Settle	1
Willm Greenwood	1
James Nodder	1
James Gawthrop & forge	2
Sarah Greenwood	1
Mr Ray for Mr Tompson	4
& forge & forge	2
Willm Nodder	2
Geo Bucke	2
Robte Bradley	1
Mr Harper	1
Mr Leedes	7
Mr Clapham	4
Mr George Stanhop	5
	41

Empty	
Barnett Holme	1

Omitted by reason of poverty	1

Roger Hardcastle Collr
Robert Bradley Constal

Leadston
(Ledston)

Sr John Lewis	25
Edward Crosley	4
Thomas Tayler	1
John Revill	1
Widd Carter	1
Ri Lake	1
Geo Fryer	1
James Cassall	2
Henry Bywater	2
William Middleton	2
James Lupoe	3
Eliza Lake	2
Widd Gilson	1
Jacob Peace	2
Sarah Burman	1
William Foster	1
James Brishawe	1

Matthew Bramham and forge	2
William Askam	1
John Bellaby	1
Wid Cuming	1
James Baker	1
Rich Marshall	1
Willm Hansey	2
Miles Lake	1
Willm Marshall	1
Widd Killingbecke	1
George Ward	1
	64

Omitted by reason of poverty	2

Robte Husband Collector[200]
Will Lake Constable[201]

Ledsham

Sr John Lewis	3
Mr Hamond	5

m 17]

Mr John Shires	9
Widd Lake	3
Robert Lake	1
Mr John Belton	6
Hen Stilling	5
Ri Askam	1
Hen Johnson	2
James Belton	3
Thomas Brearcliffe	1
Henry Dutton	1
Tho Johnson	1
Willm Coopland	2
John Duffan	1
Henry Barker	2
Tho Langdale	1
Henry Marsh	1
Geo Dawson	1
Leonard Standish	1
Marke Fearnley	3
John Robinson	1
John Lawson forge	1
Tho Redman	1
Will Standidge	1
	57

Robert Husband Collector[202]
George Scott Constable[203]

Micklefeild (Micklefield)

Mr Tho Twizleton	4
John Gibson	4
Marke Hopwood	4
John Hopwood	2
James Lupoe	2
Robert Fountaines	2
Tho Simpson	2
John Ellis	1
William Harley	2
Susann Marsh	1
Hen Browne	1
Chrofer Batman	1
Willm Greenwood	1
Willm Fenton	1
Cuthbert Harling	1
Tho Dent	1
Bridgett Ellis	1
Matthew Hodgson	1
	32

Omitted by reason of poverty	2

Robert Husband Collr
Tho Jackson Const

Munck Fryston (Monk Fryston)

Abra Sturdy	2
Jude Clarkson	1
Robte Wells	1
John Bustard	3
Jo Bingley or Clifford	2
Hugh Revill	2
Doctor Troutbecke	4
Mr Math Hall	8
Tho Hall	5
Willm Jelson	1
Richard Hemingway	1
Tho Muse	2
Ri Turner	1
Will Jelson	1
Marke Anderson	2
Marke Anderton	4
Antho Heptonstall	1
Will Wilson	2
Tho Hodgson	1
James Powell	2
James Bramham	1
Wid Middleton	1
Wid Hamond	2
James Webster	1
Geo Wells for Ri Taylor	1
Ri Hentenstall	1
John Jelson	1
Tho West	1
John Bustard	1
Tho Bradshaw	1
Henry Edmonds Esq	8
Matth Hall	2
Francis Woade	2
Mr Chris Hamond	6
Francis Woad	2
Ralph Tayler	1
Robert Berridge	1
Ri Heptonstall	1

[200] sic.
[201] sic.
[202] sic.
[203] sic.

Tho Robinson 1
Willm Gilliam 4[204]

m 18]

Joseph Melson 1
Ralph Tayler 1
87

Roger Hardcastle Collr
Tho West Const

Newthropp
(Newthorpe)
Will Coopland 3
Widd Barker 1
Wid Dickinson 1
Robte Gilliam 1
Thomas Hemsworth 1
Abr Caley or
Ro Heires 1
John Johnson 1
9

George Waineman Collr
Wm Coopland Constable

Newton cum Touwston
(Newton Kyme with
Toulston)
Mr Henry Pearcy 6
Willm Fairfax Esq 5
Geo Scott 2
Willm Marshall gen 3
Phillip Cawood 1
Chr Wyley 1
John Hewes 1
Ri Stead 1
Tho Richardson 1
Joseph Warden 2
Tho Morley & forge 2
Robte Daniell 1
Tho Frere 1
Tho Browne 1
Matth Lake 1
Ri or Henry Stead 2
Ri Morley 1
Willm Harrison 1
Matthew Daniell 1
George Wise 1
Edw Siddall 3
The Lady Barwicke 15
Tho Wilson sen 1
Ri Fuller 1
Tho Scott 2
Marke Appleyeard 2
Fr Knapton 3
Peter Tayler 1
Tho Wilson jun 1
64

Robert Husband Collector
Peter Tayler Constable

Ryther cum Osendike
(Ryther with Ozendyke)
John Robinson Esq 14
Robert Morrett Cler 5
Mr Tompson 1
Widd Knowles 2
Willm Pickering 2
Tho Cawood 1
Widd Shann 1
Robert Slater 1
Edmond Bewley 1
Susann Collins 5
George Shann 1
Tho Lobley 1
Willm Spincke 1
John Hall 1
Susann Lepton 3
Robert Heigh 3
Elizab Nelstrop 2
Tho Hutchinson 1
George Raby 1
Mr Laton 4

m 19]

Thomas Wilson 2
Robert Hay 1
Laur Middleton 2
Ri Godfrey 1
Ri Sanderson 2
Tho Wilson 1
Jaine Wilkinson 2
William Gill 1
John Beane 2
John Massey jun 1
John Cutt 1
Chr Ardall 1
William Lake 2
Francis Faucitt 1
Edward Leafe 2
Matthew Well 5
John Spincke 1
Mr Walter Vavasor *pro*
Ledhill 5
Tho Siddall 1
James Speight & forge 4
Tho Howley 2
91

George Waineman Collr
John Beane Const

Saxton cum Sardingwells
(Saxton with Scarthingwell)
Sr Francis Hungate 20
Wm Hamond Esq 17
Thomas Bywater 3
John Holdsworth 3
Willm Ingle 1
Henry Bickerdike 1
Will Allonson & forge 2
Richard Gilliam jun 1
Richard Gilliam sen 1
Rob Doubty 1
Anne Storks 1
Willmus Smith 2

[204] Line added in another hand.

Widd Dawson	1
Tho Robinson	1
Robte Burley	1
Marmad Barker	1
Robte Armistead	1
Mr Bower	1
John Johnson	1
Mary Fletcher	1
Anne Allinson wid	1
Fr Gillam	1
Tho Tayler	1
John Howden	1
Leonard Barker	1
Henry Clarkson	1
Ri Gibson	1
Robte Heslegrave	1
Ri Bellerby	1
Hen Bickerdike	1
Willm Dawson	1
Willm Hudson	1
Tho Coates	1
Ri Standidge	1
John Powell	1
Brian Bell	1
	77

Omitted by reason of poverty	9

George Wainman Collr
Tho Cooke Const

Sutton

John Wright	2
Widd Stabbs	1
Tho Thompson	1
Willm Greene	1
Widdow Cowper	1
Chrofer Halliley	1
Mr Willm Goldsbrough	4
Willm Goodricke	1
Godfrey Turner	2
John Dyson	1
Robte Bramham	2
Fr Wilkes	1
Michaell Cattison	1
Willm Tompson	1
Willm Wright	1
Tho Howdell	1
John Gootherícke	1
Widdow Wright	1
Will Bramham	1
	25

m 20]

Richard Pickard Collr
Ri Stevenson Constable

Stuton cum Heslewood (Stutton with Hazlewood)

Sr Walter Vavasor	20
Mr John Cowlam	2
Willm Wright	2
Willm Abbey	1
Marke Brashaw	1
Francis Challenor	1
Thomas Hopwood	1
George Parker	1
Tho Loft	1
Tobias Cox	1
Willm Swales	1
Wid Tayler	2
John Jilson	3
John Daniell	1
William Hudson	2
Matthew Fletcher	1
Robert Jackson	1
Stephen Collier	1
Alice Crooke	1
Robert Hutchinson	1
William Turpin	1
Robert Hudson	1
Fredricke Tayler	2
Michaell Coulton & forge	2
Ri Atkinson	1
Lewis Tompson	2
John Horner	1
John Daniell sen	2
The milne	1
Anne Nicholson	1
Robert Dilworth	1
	60

George Wainman Collr
Frether Tayler Const

South Milford

Francis Foljamb Esq	12
William Wilburne	1
Thomas Batter	1
John Gawtrey	1
John Nurser	1
Willm Halliley jun	4
Tho Prince	4
Robte Duffan	3
John Richardson	3
John Turpin	1
James Smith	1
Widdow Welburne	1
Thomas Hague	1
Antho Ashton	1
Thomas England	3
William Johnson	1
Rich Paver	1
Francis Wales	1
William Halliley	3
Hen Snawden	1
Ri Ingle	1
Will Fletcher	1
Widdow Wainewright	3
Tho Bolton	1
Math Spincke	4
Will Halliley	1
Tho Halliley	2
Wid Cass	2
Godfrey Roebucke	1
Godfrey Richardson	1
Willm Tompson	1
Richard Ryley	1
John Abbott	2
Widdow Hollingworth	1
Willm Blackburne	1
Willm Myres	1

Ri Hollingworth 1
Widdow Chappell 1
John Lancaster 4
Robt Sampson 1
Henry Stead 1
James Calverley 4
Ri Norden 1
Henry Johnson 1
Ri Johnson for 3
Mr Stapleton
Robert Hamond 6

m 21]

Robert Burnam 5
William Halliley 2
Robte Smith 1
Ri Duffin 1
Ro Smith *pro* Wid
Bramham 1
John Latham 1
Willm Hewitt 3
Ri Auckland 1
Ri Backhouse 3
Willm Daniell 1
Widd Eliz Johnson 1
Chr Robinson 1
John Flint 1
William Shearcroft 1
John Dawson 1
116

These persons following are discharged by certificate
James Dawson & forge 2
Elizabeth Siddall 1
Thomas Leadom 1
Tho Hasle 1
Ralph Pheaton 1
Stephen Carlin 1
7

Omitted by reason of poverty 1

Robte Husband Collr
Robte Sampson Const

Selby

Widdow Jones 4
Wid Tarbotham 2
Matthew Tompson 1
Richard Marshall 4
John Hobson 3
Tho Palmer jun 4
John Dickinson 1
Robte Waite 3
Richard Hamerton 3
Matthew Webster 2
Joseph Poole 3
Thomas Nutt 3
John Godbehere 3
John Atkinson 1
Ri Leatham 2
Henry Watson 2
Willm Hutt 2
George Brough 1
Tho Plaxton 1
Widd Blaxton 2
Ri Woodham 2
Tho Woodham 1
Mr John Waite 4
Tho Wade 2
Ri Plaxton 2
Willm Waite jun 2
John Whitwell 3
John Nutt 1
Tho Atkinson 1
David Morritt 1
John Blaxton 1
John Huggitt 2
Tho Tayler 3
Will Cuningham 4
Willm Spincke 2
Willm Reane 1
Mrs Reynord 5
Willm Wass 2
Mary Flemin 1
Mrs Armstrong 4
Mr Walmsley 2

Nath Thomas 4
Willm Palmer 3
Thomas Westaby 4
Simon Spofforth 3
John Tompson 2
Anthony Collier 1
George Caudy 4
Widd Ubancke 2
Hen Woodhouse 1
Mr Rasin 5
Ri Swan 2
Rob Carter 3
John Midleton 3
George Carlton 5

m 22]

John Settle 4
Mr Robte Cressy 1
more in Bondgate 2
Benja Maude 4
Widdow Wright 3
Tho Wright 3
John Becke 2
Willm Becke 4
Thomas Collas 1
Robte Godbehere 2
Robte Rusholme 1
James Edmonds 3
Brian Wilburne 1
Mr Squire 3
The Townehall 2
Robte Ibbotson 3
Tho Pearson 4
Stephen Shepheard 2
Willm Meadley 1
John Lake 3
Willm Porrett 3
Mrs Bransby 3
Gilbert Atkinson 1
Edward Overing 1
John Perrott 2
Chr Highley *pro*
Thompson 1
Willm Lewis 2

Mr Chr Bacon 4
Tho Shepheard 2
Mr Willm Firth 3
Mary Anley widd 3
Kettlewell Mawde 2
Henry Wisdome 1
John Royston 2
Mrs Cheatom 4
Mrs Kirlew 4
Mr Dawtry 5
Willm Mawde 4
Widdow Palme 3
Widdow Stany 2
Ri Hopkinson 3
Willm Barrett 4
Mr John Firth 5
Mr Bealby 4
Tho Rheame 2
Tho Ibbotson 3
Ri Linley 4
Jos Robinson or 2
Wm Hide
Marke Walden 1
William Middleton 3
Ri Baines 5
Mr Long 6
Willm Armstrong 2
Mr Calvert 4
Mr Moorewood 6
Robert Watson 6
John Chambers 3
Mr John Hodgson 7
Leo Wilkinson 3
Ri Abbott 3
Mr Jam Barmingham 4
John Potter 1
Robte Hodgson 2
Adam Tomlinson 3
Rich Ewbancke 3
John Day 5
Mr Malleverer 4
Tho Chambers 2
Tho Barton 2
Tho Greaves 1
Tho Long 2

Tho Knight 2
Mr Roothes 2
Ellin Sawer 1
Willm Moore 2
Ellin Waide 2
Ri Sayner 5
Marke Range 1
Georg Loftus & forge 3
Antho Carter 4
Tho Darnbrough & forge 3
Mr Metcalfe *pro* Hutchison 2
Mr Baine of Wistow 5
Barth Bramham & forge 3
John Giles 2
Mr Willm Beilby 2
Mr Long 2
Francis Aske 4
Willm Barrett 2
Nicholas Spence 1
Tho Carrier 1
Will Millington 1

m 23]

Tho Crabtree 1
Michaell Barker 1
Willm West 2
Willm Moxon 2
Tho Meerebecke 3
John Wood ten 3
Tho Gibson 4
Ri Lamb 2
John Whitacrees 1
Willm Gibson 2
John Curtas 1
Willlm Firth 2
Wid Nottingham 2
Geo Peele 2
Willm Lund 1
Willm Day 4
Willm Wiseman 2
Ri or John Todd 1

Geo Anderson 1
Daniell Hutton 1
Tho Tayler 4
Widd Trevis 4
Jo Wiseman & workehay 4
Elizabeth Verdin 3
Mr Bossall 5
Tho Tayler 4
John Cross 3
Wm Smith *pro* Lofsomehouse 3
Robt Watson 2
Tho Walker 3
Mary Liddall 3
Mr Walmsley mill 1
Widd Shepheard 3
Dinnis Clough 1
Ri Cutler 3
Stephen With 2
Ri Wade 3
Widdow Tompson 2
Ralph Wilson 1
John Walker 2
Thomas Sugden 1
Robte Aske 1
Robte Beilby 4
Willm Waterhouse 3
Adam Tomlinson 3
Isaack Shepheard 1
Edmond Clough 1
Jeremy Waller 1
Mr Dealtry *pro* Walker 3
John Dickinson 1
Willm Beilby sen 3
John Cutler 4
Tho Lund 1
Samuell Hague 4
Widdow Barkinshaw 3
Michaell Haddlesay 1
John Wright Carpinter 1
Mrs Andleton 2
Robert Barnitt 2
Michaell Tayler 1
Andrew Bilbrough 3

Mrs Pollard 1
Jos Johnson for Browne 4
John Grainger 2
Willm Cowling 2
Edmond Shepheard 3
William Gurton 2
Robt Dockeray 2
Peter Acomb 1
Thomas Walker 1
James Barton 3
Thomas Fothergill 2
Willm Waite 4
Thomas Hembrough 2
Ri Wade 3
Widdow Webster 2
John Slater 4
John Day 2
John Addaman 1
Antho Colyer *pro* Carter 5
John Cross 4
Charles Walmsley Esq 13
Mr Pockley 8
Mr Firth *pro* Wid Coopland 1
Widd Owston 1
Henry Mercer 1

m 24]

Willm Goodall 1
Margarett Leathom 1
Willm Mercer 1
Tho Morton 1
Hen Wess 2
Hen Thornton 2
Paull Fletcher 3
614

Empty & noe distress to be had
Mrs Lodge & Mrs Marshall 5
Joseph Wood or Harrison 1
Ri Wrigley or Mr Dautry 2
Widd Wilson 1
John Bawne 2
Michaell Brewster 1
12

Omitted by reason of poverty 35

Rich Pickard Const
Benjamine Mawde & Robert Ake Const

Sheareburne (Sherburn in Elmet)

The heires of Mr Odingsell 14
Robert Hewes 5
Thomas Gamble 1
Ri Mitchell 1
William Parke 1
William Lee 1
John Turpin 1
Tho Hardisty 4
John Walker 2
Mr Baine Viccar 4
William Howdell 2
Francis Burton 2
Ri Rycroft 1
John Hutton 2
James Robinson 2
Wid Hamond 1
Mr Howden 4
Tho Turpin 2
John Turpin 2
Hugh Cressy 1
John Hemsworth 3
Willm Parke 1
John Marshall 3
Chr Browne 1
Francis Burton 3
Tho Sowden 1
Willm Baker 1
Samuell Hamond 1
Peter Hamond 3
Tho Brooke 1
Michaell Gillan jun 1
Willm Hemsworth 2
John Brearcliffe and Tho Roper 2
John Hutton 4
Ri Tayler 1
George Picke 1
Edward Massey 4
Willm Calvert 4
Willm Knapton 3
Robte Gilliam 1
Robert Knapton 2
Widd Gayton 1
Widd Bilton 1
Tho Burland 1
Willm Tutell 4
Willm Bilton 1
John Bernard 1
David Rodwell 1
John Thirkell 5
Tho Little 3
John Fewler 1

m 25]

Mary Mann 1
Simon Barnby 4
Robte Hewes jun 5
Hewon Duffeild 3
Robte Nicholson 1
John Wardropp 4
James Stuttard 1
Anne Stephenson widd 1
Ri Baker 1
Willm Halliley 1
Robte Durdan 1
Widd Bell 1
John Mayboy 1
Jerome Roe 1
Peter Hemsworth 1
Ri Tate 1
Jo Mansfeild 1

Mrs Baley	3
Robte Durdon a Tanhouse	1
John Hutton	4
Willm Bywater	2
William Somers	1
Margarett Gilliam widd	1
Rich Tate	2
Edward Empson	2
Widdow Coopland	1
William Stoker	2
Robert Halliley	1
Ri Tompson	1
Robte Bywater	4
Sarah Latham wid	1
Issabell Gayton widd	4
Wid Halliley	7
Rob Hewes jun & Tho Tasker	5
Thomas Tasker	1
Willm Crosland	3
Roger Smith	1
John Wheeledale	1
Willm Bennett	1
Tho Tayller	1
Geo Hartley	2
Widd Peacocke	1
James Robinson	1
Willm Hope	1
Alice Powell	1
William Steadman	1
Tho Slater	1
Jerem Rawe	1
Willm Burland	1
John Shaw	1
	205

Empty & noe distress to be had

Tho Mitton	1
Sr Fr Hungate for Courthouse	1
John Bycroft	1

These persons followeing are discharged by certificate

Ri Wheeldrake	1
John Pickering	1
Robert Carter	1
Marke Duffeild	1
Richard Wheeldrake	1
Widd Brooke	1
Stephen Barber	1
John Mercer	1
Jonath Enneax	1
Andrew Weddell	2
	11

Omitted by reason of poverty 2

Richard Pickard Collr
Willm Howdill Const

Tadcaster

Mr Tayller	9
Widd Mercer	11
Stephen Tayller	2
Robert Hay	3
Willm Watson	4
Edward Marshall	6
John Hartley	7
Edward Bustard	4
Ellex Turpin	2
Michaell Horner	1
Peter Hayton	1
Willm Appleyard	2
Widdow White	3
Widdow Johnson or Mercer	1
Ri Richardson	1
Thomas Burton	2
John Hodgson	2
Wm Cowgill	2

m 26]

John Daniell	1
Willm Fowler	1
Richard Young	1
Andrew Turner	2
John Horner	3
Steven Wilson or Gilson	1
Widdow Bilbrough	4
Geo Barker	6
Robert Morley	8
Mrs Lamb	2
Edward Holmes *pro* Young	2
Mr Jackson	8
William Marshall	4
Thomas Petty	1
Willm Bowman	4
Tho Goodburne sen	2
Tho Goodburne jun	2
Nicholas Penniston	4
John Barker	1
Tho Cockshott	1
Ri Appleyeard	2
Tho Camy	1
John Ryther	1
Robert Smithies	1
Robert Cooke	2
William Wilkinson	3
Rich Abby	2
Widdow Mirfeild	2
John Inman	3
William Watkinson	4
Widd Mitchell	7
Tho Goodburne	1
Antho Saxton	3
Mr Benington	4
Nicholas Horner	1
Robert Westwood	1
Robert Cooke	3
Francis Sainter	1
John Loft	3
Alex Cadell	1
John Hartley	2
William Gurnell	1
John Fawcitt	1
Tho Horner	1
John Parker Carier	1

James Burniston 1
James Wiggins 1
175 175[205]

Omitted by reason of poverty 5

Robt Husband Collector
Tho Burton Const

Thorpe Willoby (Thorpe Willoughby)

Robert Shearburne 1
William Arnold 2
Geo Howdall 1
Valen Arnold 1
John Smith 1
Willm Graves 1
Thomas Booth 1
Alice Lowrence 1
Robt Fawcitt 2
Widdow Grubb 2
Tho Smith 1
John Barnsby 4
Widd Godsey 1
William Richardson 2

m 27]

George Tayler 1
Edward Hopkinson 2
William Graves 2
Robert Lamb 2
John Savage 1
John Jackson 1
30

Omitted by reason of poverty 2

Roger Hardcastle Collr
Tho Booth Const

Towton

Mr Fletcher 10
John Wilkinson sen 1
John Staimston 1
Dorothy Beane 2
John Beane 2
John Clarkson 1
John Wilkinson sen[206] 1
Fran Fletcher 1
John Tompson 2
Christopher Beane 1
Thomas Gibson 1
John Foster 1
Ellen Wright 1
Willm Beane 1
John Wilkinson jun 1
Tho Coupland 1
Jeffrey Beane 1
29

Omitted by reason of poverty 1

Ri Pickard Collr
Fran Fletcher Const

Temple Hurst (Temple Hirst)

Mr Tayler 5
Robt Skelton 1
John Lund jun 1
John Leeck 2
John Iveson 1
Anne Davison 3
Mr Metcalfe 8
Tho Northend 1
John Lund sen 3
Christopher Baites 1
Rich Sainter 3
Willm Harrison 2
Christo Eyonson 1
Ri Gryme 1

Tho Lake 1
Joan Smith or George Lowther 1
Roger Lund 1
Arthur Jonson 1
37

Rich Pickard Collect
Tho Lake Const

Uskelfe (Ulleskelf)

Tho Newhill 1
Tho Oliver 1
John Sissons 3 three

m 28]

Georg Nicholson 2
Stephen Brearey 1
Tho Scott 1
Ri Stother 2
George Reynoldson sen 5
Willm Graves 1
George Turpin 1
Rich Bell 1
Widd Pickard 1
Chrofer Ellis 1
William Brearey 1
Widd Cooke 2
Willm Boyes 1
Antho Cooke 3
Willm Duce 3
John Browne 2
Tho Stother 4
John Dennis 1
John Langfeild 2
John Judson 1
Tho Nicholson 2
Alex Loft 1

[205] sic.
[206] sic.

Ephraim Stead	1
Nicholas Daniell	1
George Nicholson	1
Ri Webster	1
Chr Daniell	1
Hen Stainbrough	1
Tho Mannaver	1
Willm Duke	1
Anne Siddall	1
Leonard Lazenby	1
Willm Wharldale	1
Ri Tayler	2
John Beane	1
Willm Pickering	4
Francis Stoker	1
Ri Turpin	1
Edward Dennis	1
Robte Bramham	1
Widd Turpin	1
Ambrose Lee	1
Sr John Lewis	13
Mary Johnson	1
Thomas Olliver	1
Geo Richardson	1
Robert Bramham	1
Mr Newark	2
Jacob Atkinson	1
Mary Nother	3
	91

George Waineman Collr
John Browne Const

Wistow

Willm Barras	1
Joseph Otley	1
Mr Tho Baites or Smith	3
Henry Biard Cler	11
Richard Carter	2
Thomas Woodall	2
Jaine Rowden	2
Tho Rawson jun	1
Joan Wilson	1
Francis Hewley	4
Humphrey Rawson	3
John Chelwell Cler	3
Geo Heighome	4
Mr Jo Hargreaves	4

m 29]

Rich Cleaveing	2
Mrs Ann Hewley	4
Mr George Hewley	5
William Hodgson	2
Mr John Beverley	4
Dorothy Story	3
Matth Hewitt	1
Mr Tho Obye	1
Ri Hunter	2
Roger Ellis	3
Willm Dunn	5
Willm Harrison	2
Mr Geo Crowle	7
Charles Backhouse	1
Widd Metcalfe	2
Jeffrey Metcalfe	3
John Marshall	6
Margarett Hill	1
Beatrix Roome	1
John Dobb	1
Willm Jackson	2
Mr Tomlinson of Yorke	3
Leonard Woodall	1
Chrofer Bramingham	1
George Nelson	1
Ralph Woodall	1
John Wilson	4
Elizabeth Metcalfe	2
Mr John Baines	8
Brian Dalby	1
Tho Pearse	3
Brian Amger	2
Jarome Morley	3
William Shaw	3
Isaack Brungee	1
Leonard Metcalfe	2
Simond Wright	3
John Dove	3
Doctor Tho Hewley	9
John Hargreaves	4
John Cumberland	2
Sr John Hewley	2
John Dinnis	1
Tho Simpson	1
Henry Simpson	1
John Easingwold	2
Tho Lake	2
Tho Askew	1
John Hornshaw	1[207]
George Reynold	1
Anne Quarry	1
Christopr Rowden	1
Richard Wright	2
John Swaine	1
Ursulac Jackson	1
John Woodell	3
Mr Matteran	3
Edward Wise	1
Thomas Haire	1
Elizabeth Chamberlaine	3
Margret Reynold	1
Thomas Winteringham	3
Willm Sumerton	2
Thomas Pearce	3
Willm Rumond	5
Mr John Gomersall	7
Christopr Woodall	1

m 30]

Robert Stringfeild	1
Anne Rumans	5
George Walkinton	2
Mr Milner	4
Richard Gelson	1

[207] Inserted in a different hand.

Robert Todd	1
Thomas Johnson	2
Richard Wright	2
	226

Empty and no distres to be had

Robert Wilson	1

Omitted by reason of poverty 12

Richd Pickard Collr
Willm Jackson Const

Wee three of the Justices of the peace for the west Ryding of the County of yorke who haue herevnto subscribed doe approve of this certificate

Edward Copley
Ro Benson
Henry Marsden
Joh Peabless
Clk pac

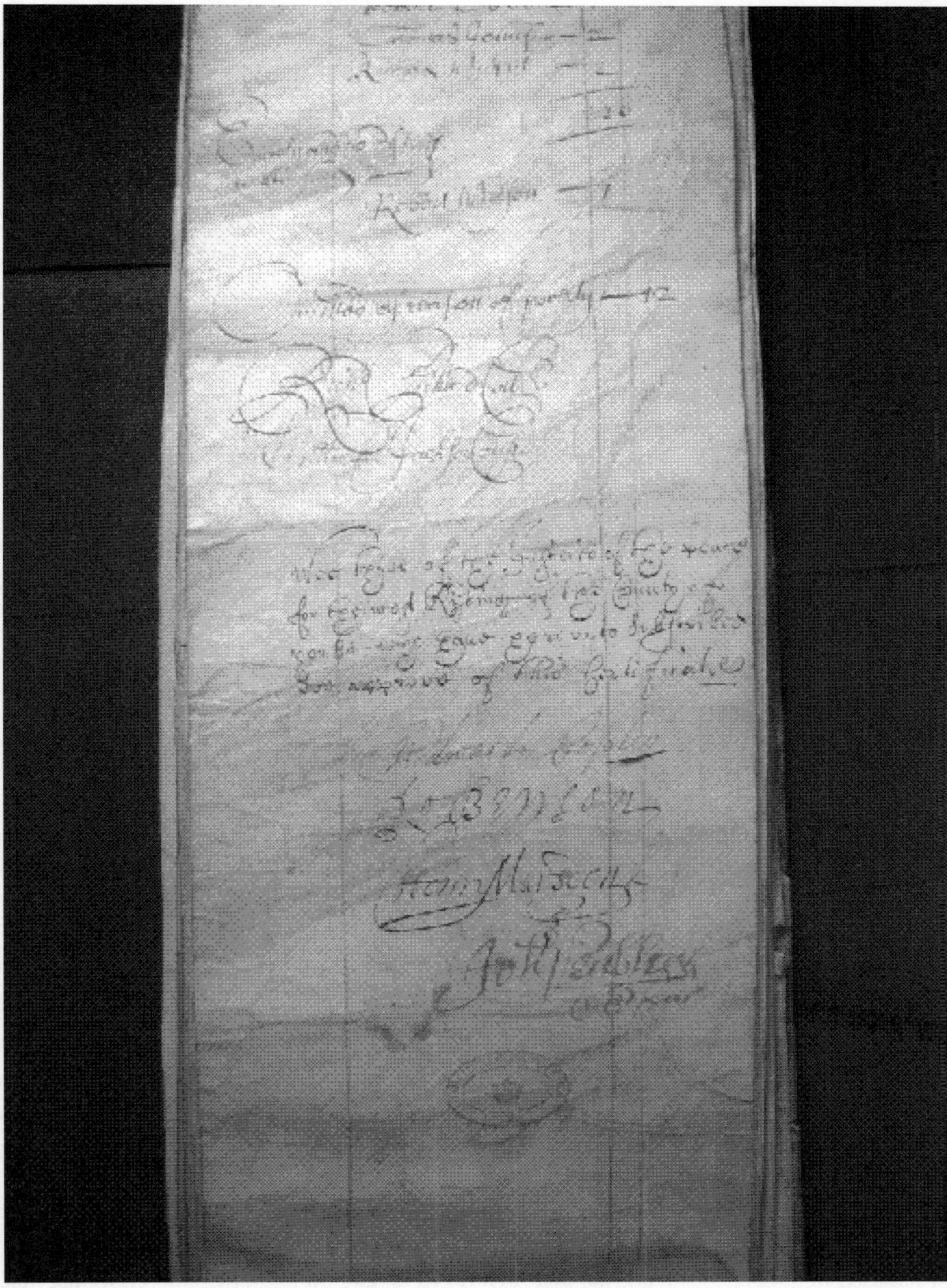

Plate 17 The original end of the Lady Day 1672 assessment roll for the West Riding, with the signatures of three justices and the clerk of the peace. It is now the last membrane of the Barkston Ash Wapentake assessment. The end of the assessment for Womersley is visible at the top. National Archives E179/262/14 m.30. See transcript opposite, and comment p. 81

Plate 18 The beginning of the assessment for Osgoldcross Wapentake. This is taken from the Lady Day 1673 assessment. The listing of the names in three columns is different from the single column format used in the previous year. National Archives E179/262/13 m.89. See transcript opposite, and comment p. 83

LADY DAY ASSESSMENT 1673

Osgoldcross Wapentake[208]

The National Archives, E179/262/13

m 89, c 1]

Osgoldcross Wapentake

Armine (Airmyn)

Thomas Clarke	1
Robert Keadall	1
Peter Mathewes	1
Willm Markham	3
Samuell Markham	2
Cuthbert Hoope	1
Richard Robinson	1
Widdow Mergisson	5
Joshua Lee	2
Mr John Storr	4
Willm Newmarsh	3
Martin Wood	1
Thomas Baites	1
Ellizabeth Horsall	1
Samuell Markham	3
Thomas Roothoram	1
Edward Clough	1
John Burrowe	1
John Trimingham	1
Robert Beckitt	1
Edward Feilding	1
Brian Nelthrop	1
Richard Scott	1
John Snowe	1
Willm Jackson	1
Robert Tindall	1
George Wilson	1
Willm Easby	1
Elizabeth Stafforth	1
Widdow Wilde	1
Robert Randall	1
Widdow Horsall	1
Richard Pattrick	1
Richard Stafford	1
John Waid	4
Willm Wilfitt	1
Anthony Brewit	1
John Knipe	1
Nichollas Scales	1
Thomas Baites	1
Tristram Rooth	2
	60
Omitted by reason of poverty	11

Richd Nicholson Collr
Joshua Lee Const

c 2]

Ackworth

Willm Rookeby Esqr	14
Jerem Boulton	5
Willm Lambe Esqr	7
Mr Abott	7
James Ash	2
Richard Pickering	4}
more	1}
Robert Hewitt	6
Thomas Slator	1
Widdow Austwick	3
John Ash	3
John Rushforth	1
Willm Butterworth	1
Widdow Styreing	1
Paull Simpson	1
Leonard Pinder	1
Thomas Childe	1
Willm Horncastle	2
Francis Wilson	1
John Aspiner	1
Willm Snary	1
John Burton	1
Anthony Crawshawe	1
Willm Wright	2
Thomas Cawood	3
Willm Sanderson	2
John Ellis	2
Steven Cawood	2
John Wright	1
Willm Stead	1
John Ward	1
Robert Bushill	1
Thomas Austwicke	2
Richard Cliffe	1
Richard Knutton	2
Thomas Cawood	5
Henry Austwicke	2
Richard Mason	3
Mathew Hanscombe	2
Henry Walker	1

208 Because of the poor condition of the relevant section of the Lady Day 1672 roll, see above 13–14, 83–4 and below 561–2, the assessment for this wapentake has been taken from that for Lady Day 1673, which was also used for the Michaelmas 1673 and Lady Day 1674 collections.

John Sharpe 1
Willm Hewitt 1
Mathew Wright 1
Thomas Scholey 2

c 3]

Francis Burgesse 4
John Rushforth 1
John Scholey 1
Mary Beate 1
Willm Ash 2
Thomas Wood 4
Rowland Jagger 1
Thomas Clarke 2
Widdow Morley 2
John Birkes 2
John Walker 3
Ralph Foothead 1
Mary Morton 1
John Greenfeild 3
Samuell Cawood 4
Robert Hewitt 2
Widdow Astwick 3
John Parkinson 2
John Greenfeild 2
Thomas Hewitt 4
Edward Brownbridge 1
Edward Wright 3
Willm Austwick 3
Willm Austwick 2
Robert Hewitt 2
Henry Hoope 1
George Heptenstall 1
James Croft 3
Thomas Calverley 5
Henry Ledgerd 1
Willm Chaple 1
Marke Casle 2
James Norton 1
Willm Parkinson 1
Mathew Lambe 2
Thomas Whittenstall 1
Thomas Baylye 2
Willm Nelthrope 1
John Johnson 1
John Pickering 4
Widdow Croft 3
Thomas Hewitt 2
Willm Walker 4
John Walker 1
John Lambert 2

m 89v, c 1]

James Croft 4
Nichollas Rudd 1
George Allen 2
Henry Tayler 1
George Parkins 1
Mr Lambe 1
Thomas Tayler 1
Daniell Ellis 1
Jonas Barker 1
Willm Wilson 1
Thomas Hellewell 1
John Lambert 6
Widdow Roydhouse 3
Thomas Birkes 1
224

Omitted by reason of poverty 20

Robert More Collr
Steven Cawood Const

Adlingfleete (Adlingfleet)

Willm Jarvas 1
Robert Rookall 2
Roger Drewrey 3
Henry Stainforth 2
Christopr Wilson 2
Edmond Morley 3
Mr Warsop 2
John Morley 2
Robert Parrott 2
Robert Godfrey 2
Robert Heather 1
John Mattison 1
Heward Gardum 1
John Peper 1
Richard Drinkill 1
Willm Atkinson 1
Jarmin Milner 2
Joseph Jaques 4
Thomas Fletcher 1
John Knowles 1
Charles Maskill 1
James Moxen 1
Francis Anderson 1
Simon Clayton 2
Christopr Colison 1
Michaell Emerson 1
John Gardum 1
Willm Milner 1
Thomas Gibbons 1
Thomas Muskill 1
Christopr Adams 1

c 2]

Anthony Manners 1
James Hinde 1
Richard Ellison 1
Robert Pickhaver 1
51

Omitted by reason of poverty 8

Robt More Collr
John Pepper Const

Beghall (Beal)

Mr James Creswicke 9
Jarvas Scholay 4
Richard Dicons 2
Thomas Ellis 2
John Padgett 2
Charles West 2
Thomas Duckett 2
Thomas Schoaley 1
John Hall 1

Michaell Calverley	1
Peter Verdin	2
Willm Verdein	1
Henry Edmondson	2
Mathew Whittwood	5
Willm Felds	1
Michaell Calverley	2
Mrs Bradford	2
Thomas Grime	1
Willm Thorpe	1
Richard Stones	1
John Elliot	2
Willm Dickons	1
Henry Dickons	1
Richard Stones	3
Willm Hall	2
Widdow Schoalay	3
Widdow Harrison	1
Widdow Kay	1
Widdow Rosse	1
Henry Dickons	2
Widdow Monkton	1
Jarvas Marshall	2
Thomas Johnson	1
Richard Hall	1
Henry Cavill	1
Theophls Brooke	1
Willm Rosse	1
Francis Burne	1
Mr John Rayner	4
Steven Richinson	2
Theophis Brooke	3

c 3]

Richard Rodwell	3
John Taylor	1
Robert Hall	2
Robert Swifte	3
Willm Kellingley	3
John Mitchill	4
Willm Walker	1
Willm Tomlin	1
Elizabeth Gamble	1
	98

Empty & no distres to be had

Roger Clarke	1

Omitted by reason of poverty	4

Richd Nicholson Collr
Peter Verdin Const

Balne

Mr Thomas Rooth	8
Christopr Towtill	3
Roger Hawkes	2
James Knipe	1
John Dilcocke	1
John Hudson	1
Richard Wheene	1
Thomas Rawson	2
Nichollas Smith	3
John Midleton	1
John Baldiston	1
John Letham	2
Widdow Mayer	1
John Sutton	1
Thomas Letham	3
Widdow Smith	1
Robert Webster	1
John Hanson	1
Willm Doughty	5
Willm Jenkinson	1
Edward Huthersall	3
Willm Gamble	1
Joseph Burnley	1
Robert Richardson	1
John Winn	2
Robert Wilkinson	1
Richard Batty	1
John More	2
James Birtwisle	1
Willm Carter	1
John Spinke	1
Robert Buttrey	3
Willm Bateman	4
Richard Greene	1
	63

m 90, c 1]

Empty & no distres to be had

Ann Hutton	1

Omitted by reason of poverty	2

Richard Nicholson Collr
John Bilcliffe Const

Burghwallis

Michaell Anne Esqr	11
Mr Gleadall	5
Samuell Cawthorne	2
Richard Pretious	1
John Winn	3
Thomas Turner	1
Robert Jubb	2
Edmond Ackland	1
Willm England	2
John Turner	2
Thomas Gibson	1
Thomas Pettey	1
Leonard Turner	1
John Jackson	1
Robert Pickhaver	1
Widdow Porter	1
Widdow Viccars	2
John Harrison	1
Edmd Heather	1
John Robinson	2
James Heather	1
Mr Anne	1
	44

Empty & no distres to be had

Willm Jenings	1

Omitted by reason of poverty	2

Thomas Midleton Collr
John Winn Const

Badsworth
Sir John Bright 20
Mr Edward Dodsworth 4
Mr Rowland Stewart 5
Mr Thomas Chapman 4
Thomas Pearson 2
James Hewit 2
James Blakelock 2
Richard Clarke 1
Thomas Clayton 1
Thomas Cockett 1
Francis Whittenstall 1
Thomas Wright 2
Thomas Jackson 1
James Heaton 3

c 2]

Edward Houghland 1
Mrs Anne Sidgwick 3
John Ostcliffe 1
Willm Wintworth 1
Thomas Whittonstall 1
56

Empty & no distres to be had
Sir John Bright 1

Omitted by reason of poverty 2

Richard Nicholson Collr
James Hewitt Const

Bramwith
Mr Cooke 4
Mr George Rasin 2
Willm Cooling 2
John Wright 1
Mr Lyonell Copley 3
Willm Gamble 1
Willm Reynold 2
Thomas Parkin 1
Francis Dickinson 3
Thomas West 1
John Scott 3
Willm Gamble 1
Willm Gamble 3
Nathanll Golton 1
Willm Wright 1
Thomas Slayden 2
Thomas Watson 2
Willm Broghill 2
Widdow Deareman 3
Thomas Stones 3
Willm Sharpas 2
Richard Milwood 1
Margret Reynold 2
John Midleton 1
John Watson 2
Richard Milford 1
Thomas Elton 1
John Scott 1
Richard Jenings 1
Thomas Kelsay 1
Mr George Rasin 3
Thomas Jenings 1
Willm Watson 1
Thomas Rayney 1
60

Empty & no distres to be had
Dorothy Duckitt 2

Omitted by reason of poverty 1

Thomas Midleton Collr
John Wilson Const

c 3]

Castleford
Docter Berbeck 5
John Pease 2
John Lake 3
Thomas Webster 1
Edmond Akester 1
Willm Bloome 1
John Shillitoe 2
Thomas Ashton 1
Elizabeth Pinder 3
John Norton 1
Thomas Machen 1
Willm Ashton 1
John Gibson 1
Richard Duffeild 1
John Duffin 1
John Walsh 1
Widdow Burton 1
John Brough 2
Richard Dawson 1
Edward Batty 2
Robert Warren 1
Ralph Watson 2
George Ledgerd 2
Jennet Duffeild 1
Thomas Gibson 9
Willm Gawthrop 1
James Wilson 1
Richard Dixon 2
Jarvas Shillitoe 1
Widdow Shillitoe 1
Richard Machin 2
Willm Sisson 1
56

Omitted by reason poverty 4

Robt Bennitt Collr
John Pease Const

Cowicke (Cowick)
Sir John Dawney 26
Mr Cuthbert Richardson 4
Henry Pickering 4
Thomas Hogley 1
Henry Redman 1
Paull Lambert 1
John Sikes 2
Richard Norton 1

Oswald Wilson 1
Brian Law 2
Richard Gleadowe 5
Mary Pitt 1

m 90v, c 1]

John Redman 1
Mathew Smeaton 1
John Hessey 4
John Lambert 2
James Yeadon 3
Thomas Bogg 2
Mathew Smith 1
Nichollas Prince 1
Widdow Rooth 3
Ellizabeth Bradley 2
Thomas Langerake 1
Richard Markham 2
Willm Prance 1
Thomas Barnby 2
John Hicks 1
Richard Towler 3
Mr Tompson 2
Henry Sikes 1
Thomas Motherby 1
Thomas Sikes 3
John Gibson 3
Nichollas Lumley 2
Willm Cooke 1
John Arthington 1
Brian Ossett 1
Willm Motherby 3
James Gleadowe 2
John Laydstocke 1
Mathew Marshall 1
George Prince 1
John Rooth 4
Willm Stevenson 4
Christopr Hick 2
John Pearse 2
Thomas Smeaton 1
Willm Dilcock 1
Thomas Heaton 2
Willm Stables 3

Francis Arthington 1
Richard Padgett 2
Widdow Dawson 3
Paull Rudd 1
Willm Pearson 1
Widdow Motherby 1
Francis Hudlestone 2
Robert Hall 2
Thomas England 2
Widdow Gleadowe 1
Willm Murfitt 2
Thomas Jackson 1
Richard Smith 1
George Booth 3
Francis Browne 1
Thomas Midleton 2

c 2]

Christopr Walker 1
Thomas Sikes 1
Samuell Halliday 4
Thomas Gleadowe 3
Mary Booth 1
Mrs Rickard 3
Paull Watterlane 1
Edward Markham 1
Charles Fisher 1
Widdow Winteringham 1
Edward Hudson 1
Thomas Lawe 1
Widdow Freeman 1
John Scowthropp 1
Robert Hall 1
Christopr Glew 1
Roger Richinson 1
George Robinson 1
Willm Armestronge 2
John Stones 1
Isabell Bradley 1
Francis Peirson 1
Willm Hall 2
Henry Arthington 1
Robert Rudd 1
181

Empty & no distres
to be had
Mr Headley 1
Mr Mountice 1

These persons following
are discharged by
Certifts
Thomas Morris 1
Samuell Wanne 1
John Denby 1

Robt More Collr
Charles Fisher Const

Campsall
Sir Thomas Yarbrough 10
Mr Midleton 8
Mr Horncastle 4
Mr Sutcliffe 4
Robert Beamond 1
Sir Thomas Yarbrough 1
John Maplebeck 1
John Maplebeck 1
John Maplebeck 2
John Sayle 3
Willm Briggs 2
Laurence Smithies 1

c 3]

Gilbert Broghill 1
George Elliot 1
Robert Wintergham 1
Thomas Fletcher 1
Bartholl Hogly 1
Barthol Swainson 1
Thomas Lee 4
Willm Conway 1
John Burrey 1
John Towtill 1
Alvera Whitacre 1
James Watkin 1
Christopr Walker 3
John Hopkinson 1

Thomas Fletcher	2
George Scholey	1
Robert Winteringham	2
Thomas Watkin	1
Richard Watkin	1
John Ellam	3
Thomas Usher	1
John Pearmar	1
Francis Fayram	1
James Wood	1
Widdow Guest	1
Widdow Arlington	2
Widdow Winteringham	1
Willm Wilson	1
	76

Omitted by reason of poverty 3

Thomas Midleton Collr
Thomas Ushay Const

Credling Stubbs (Cridling Stubbs)

Mr Francis Ward	10
Mr John Turner	5
Mr George Booth	9
Mr Crosland	4
John Bedford	2
Thomas Eadon	1
Willm Bedford	2
Willm Battle	1
John Smith	1
Willm Briggs	1
Henry Mitton	2
	38

Empty & no distres to be had
Widdow Everingham 4

Robert More Collr
Willm Briggs Const

m 91, c 1]

Darrington

John Cookeson	1
Richard Cookeson	6
Thomas Farnhill	3
Edward Crosland	3
Mr Batty	1
Hugh Shillitoe	1
Mr Procter	4
Joseph Walker	5
Thomas Steele	3
Robert Heaton	2
Michaell Heaton	1
Willm Hall	1
Mrs Elizab Beale	8
Thomas Hall	1
Robert Silvester	2
Thomas Howden	2
John Roadhouse	2
Willm Banks	2
John Greene	1
Richard Simpson	1
Anne Hurst	1
Thomas Wareing	1
John Jackson	1
Richard Speight	2
Henry Nayler	1
Samuell Jackson	6
John Adams	2
Thomas Sayle	3
Marmaduke Wilson	5
Robert Cooper	1
John Bramham	1
Barthol Brayshaw	1
Jane Wilkinson	1
Water Milne	1
Nichollas Greene	1
Widdow Whitley	1
Thomas Jackson	1
	80

Empty & no distres to be had
Thomas Jackson 1

Peter Swift	2
Mrs Beale	1

Omitted by reason of poverty 2

Thomas Midleton Collr
Nichollas Greene Const

Egbroughs Ambo (Eggboroughs, High and Low)

Mr Auby	9
Mr Oglethorp	6
Willm Wilson	1
Willm Midleton	1
John Grime	1

c 2]

Barthol Barker	1
Thomas Jackson	2
Richard Ellis	1
Willm Towtill	1
John Browne	1
Henry Browne	1
Henry Moston	1
Anne Webster	1
Willm Bateman	2
Thomas Beale	2
Thomas Green	3
Henry Midleton	1
Willm Everingham	1
George Bateman	3
Willm Furis	3
Robert Towfall	1
John Lintall	2
Robert Bellard	1
Francis Moverley	2
Nichollas Walker	1
Widdow Lund	1
Mr John Horsall	5
Thomas Coates	1
Willm Wilson	1

Widdow Coates	1
Widdow Sikes	1
	59

Omitted by reason of poverty 2

Richd Nicholson Collr
Willm Wilson Const

Fenwick

Madam Swift	1
John Simons	3
Hannah Crawshawe	4
Richard Simonds	2
Thomas Hobson	2
Anne Yates	2
John Marr	1
Robert Hobson	2
Thomas Hobson	2
Mr John Noble	4
John Ridley	1
Mr Richard Nicholson	4
Godfrey Crawshey	3
Robert Askeron	3
Widdow Gibbon	3
John Marr	1
Christopr Cooke	1
John Arlington	1
Wentworth Balderson	1
Darcy Earle	1
Mary Cooke	1

c 3]

Daniell Boyes	1
Willm Stead	2
Willm Pell	1
	47

Omitted by reason of poverty 1

Thomas Midleton Collr
Richard Simond Const

Fetherstone (Featherstone)

Mr Thomas Hippon	9
Mr Edward Hippon	6
Thomas Fleeming	3
Thomas Dixon	4
Mr Beale	5
Peter Harrison	1
Thomas Milner	1
Willm Weightman	2
John Smalepage	2
James Atkinson	5
Mr Scholay	3
Mrs Usher	2
Mathew Glover	2
Nichollas Jubb	2
George England	1
Joshua Woodhead	2
Willm Child	2
John Darley	2
Margret Feather	1
Willm Oldfeild	1
John Sharpe	1
James Arnold	1
Willm Bloome	1
Willm Pettey	1
Willm Simpson	4
Willm Mallinson	1
John Collet	1
Robert Shepherd	2
Widdow Hall	1
Thomas Brighton	1
Willm Weightman	1
Willm Usher	1
Allen Clarkson	1
	73

Empty & no distres to be had

The Vickeridge	3
Mr John Hamerton	1

Omitted by reason of poverty 10

Robt More Collr
Robt Webster Const

Folkerby (Fockerby)

Mr Dauy	5
Robert Cooke	2
John Barnard	2

m 91v, c 1]

Robert Wright	1
Walter Mattison	2
James Drewry	2
Robert Bradley	1
Christopr Scoales	1
Christopr Drewrey	1
Thomas Crowther	1
John Foster	1
Robert Bell	1
Mr Parrot	1
Willm Clarke	1
Willm Drinkall	1
	23

Omitted by reason of poverty 1

Robert More Collr
John Barnard Const

Firrybridg als Ferry Fryston (Ferrybridge alias Ferry Fryston)

George Apleyard	4
Richard Greene	1
Widdow Shillitoe	4
Peter Hollings	3
John Linsdall	1
Gabriell Tootell	2
Widdow Coopland	2
Widdow Shillitoe	1
Widdow Burton	1
Thomas Dickons	1
Peter Bywater	1
John Norton	2

John Meareing	3
Willm Linsdall	1
John Burton	2
Jarvas Green	1
Mr Robert Simond	2
Willm Walls	1
John Cross	1
Thomas Hollings	1
Nichollas Bywatter	2
Thomas Turton	1
Peter Burton	5
Widdow Goodyeare	1
Mrs Hayford	15
Willm Shillitoe	1
Richard Ward	3
Michaell Iles	3
John Gibson	4
Anne Burton	4
Peter Chambers	1
Widdow Wareing	1
George Mawson	3
John Towneson	1
John Tompson	1
Willm Smith	3

c 2]

Widdow Senas	2
John Watkins	1
Richard Docker	2
Mr Gleadowe	1
Mr Gleadowe	8
Francis Dodgson	2
Widdow Docker	1
Willm Shillitoe	3
John Wheelwright	1
Steven Cutt	2
Robert Clarkson	1
Lawrence Tompson	6
John Moreby	2
Jane Shaw	4
John Ingland	3
John Tompson	1
John Hedlam	2
	126

Empty & no distres to be had	
Mr Crowle	2
Widdow Woodyeare	1
Mrs Meareing	3
Mr John Firth	2
Omitted by reason of poverty	8

Robt More Collr
John Townson Const

Gowdall

John Everingham	1
Charles Johnson	1
Marke Croft	1
John Stowage	1
Anthony Browne	2
John Cooper	2
Charles Rickard Esqr	4
Robert Pickhaver	2
James Bawne	2
Barnard Harwood	1
John Bird	1
Hannah Bawne	1
Michaell Fisher	2
John Lambert	1
John Fisher	1
Widdow Pattison	1
Widdow Dods	1
Thomas Ellis	2
John Whitwham	2
Thomas Marriot	1
Samuell Ashton	1
George Bell	1
George Bell	1

c 3]

Sir John Dawney	2
Widdow Jackson	1
Willm Cornewell	1
James Ellison	2
Michaell Harrison	1

Roger Scadlock	1
Moses Walker	1
Mathew Walker	1
John Buck	1
Richard Grime	6
Roger Scadlock	1
Thomas Grime	1
John Charner	1
	53

These persons following are dischargd by Certfts

Dorothy Fisher	1
Widdow Norton	1
Epham Jackson	1
Margret Jackson	1
John Midleton	1

Richard Nicholson Collr
George Bell Const

Gowle
(Goole)

Mr John Empson	5
John Tompson	1
Thomas Tompson	1
Robert Willowby	3
Willm Anderson	1
Richard Ryley	3
Jarvas Cornwall	3
Henry Parker	1
John Cornewall	5
Willm Iveson	1
Widdow Abbot	2
Thomas Richardson	1
John Emson	1
Charles Stainforth	1
Robert Wilbore	1
John Lusby	1
Robert Stevenson	4
Anthony Empson	4
Willm Upleby	2
Richard Empson	5
Thomas Nelson	2

Willm Adsett 4
Widdow Freeman 2
John Stevenson 2

m 92, c 1]

Simon Stevenson 2
Willm Emson 1
John Greeve 4
Willm Johnson 2
Francis Gibson 2
Willm Lockwood 2
Mr Johnson 4
Thomas Gibson 1
Thomas Swann 1
Willm Uppleby 4
John Coultherd 1
Willm Stevenson 1
James Wrigleworth 1
Joseph Cornwall 3
85

Empty & no distres
to be had
Richard Godfrey 1

Omitted by reason of
poverty 6

Robt More Collr
John Greeve Const

Heck
Charles Rickard Esqr 13
Thomas English 2
Willm Walker 1
Francis Walker 1
Arthur Kay 2
Richard Sissons 2
Humphr Brewer 1
John Wheene 1
Thomas Apleby 1
Robert Pitt 1
Robert Wilfleete 1
Joseph Freare 1
Joseph Moxon 1
Thomas Aineley 1
George Parker 2
Willm Carter 2
Richard Parker 1
George Shackleton 3
Mr Buck 3
William Carter 1
Charles Wheene 1
Willm Graues 2
Widdow Naylor 1
Widdow Wilfleete 1
Charles Wood 2
Willm Broadbent 1
Ralph Rysome 2
Widdow Elliot 2
John Usher 2
John Harrand 1
56

Omitted by reason of
poverty 1

c 2]

Richd Nicholson Collr
John Wheene Const

Hensall
George Rawden 3
Richard Makeing 2
Henry Bedford 4
Richard Barber 1
Widdow Mann 1
Richard Huthersall 5
George Makeing 2
John Smith 2
Charles Tompson 4
Richard Hewitson 1
Richard Herbin 2
Joseph Brooke 1
Robert Sidburry 1
Willm Makeing 4
Roger Clarke 1
Roger Laveracke 1
Thomas Harram 5
Willm Smith 3
Widdow Birkes 2
Richard Erbin 2
James Reynold 1
Thomas Bramley 2
Widdow Hewitson 1
Phillip Dewhurst 1
John Makeing 2
Mrs Kent 1
55

Empty & no distress
to be had
John Grime 1

Omitted by reason of
poverty 1

Richd Nicholson Collr
George Machen Const

Hooke
(Hook)
Robert Newmarsh 1
Richard Bayley 2
Peter Jefferson 1
Benjam Snowe 1
Widdow Stevenson 1
Robert Mitchill 2
John Mitchill 1
Thomas Jackson 1
James Bayley 1
John Firth 1
John Mitchill 1
Robert Jefferson 2

c 3]

Thomas Jefferson 1
Timothy Thackrey 1
Willm Firth 1
John Roberts 1
Willm Scales 1
Thomas Jefferson 2

Richard Godfrey 1
Thomas Lightfoote 2
Robert Viccars 1
Willm Roote 1
Willm Gibson 2
Richard Bedford 1
Mary Birkeby 1
Thomas Marshall 1
Willm Bilbrough 1
Robert West 1
Margret Spinke 1
Willm Smith 3
Timothy Thackrey 1
Willm Markam 2
Edward Hesletine 2
Richard Rimington 1
Allen Hick 2
Henry Rogers 2
James Bagby 2
Jacob Beckitt 1
Richard Spinke 1
John Jefferson 5
Willm Dugdale 1
Willm Jackson 1
Peter Smith 1
Denis Pattrick 1
David Bayley 1
Franc Lightfoote 1
Thomas Emson 1
Edward Bayley 2
Francis Addison 1
Katherine Spinke 1
Simon Geldergale 2
Thomas Brigham 1
Henry Stocks 1
Luke Farr 1
73

Richd Nicholson Collr
Richd Godfrey Const

Haldanby cum Eastoft
(Haldenby with Eastoft)
John Houldenby Esq 4
John Smith 3
Thomas Copley 1
John Bretton 1
Robert Houldenby 1
Nichollas Bradley 1
Jarvas Bull 1

m 92v, c 1]

Willm Bonell 1
Anthony Buckley 1
Willm Hutchinson 1
Richard Cooke 1
Thomas Bradley 1
John Eastoft Esqr 9
Christopr Green 2
Jerem Tompson 2
Edward More 2
Robert Gathorne 1
John Selar 1
Edward Theaker 1
Willm Osburne 2
Henry Gilliot 2
Willm Gludham 1
Mathew Glew 1
Richard Errat 1
John Gathorne 1
Robert Watts 2
George Barnes 1
Thomas Finingley 1
Robert Gathorne 1
Richard Markindale 1
Robert Rakestrawe 1
Christopr Harrison 1
Willm Mattison 2
John Hall 1
Widdow Barbor 1
Robert Osburne 1
Mathew Collins 1
Thomas Shearewood 1
Thomas Flower 1
Thomas Goodworth 1
60

Omitted by reason of poverty 4

Robt More Collr
Robt Cooke Const

Houghton
John Shillitoe 8
John Rawson 4
John Nunns 4
Richard Linley 2
Peter Mirfin 1
Thomas Bilcliffe 4
Anne Fleeming 3
Mr Sissons 1
Thomas Prince 2
Willm Shillitoe 4
Robert Bradshawe 1
John Huntris 1
Marke Shackleton 2

c 2]

George Shillitoe 1
Willm Nelson 1
Willm Sissons 4
John Scott 2
Luke Wilkinson 2
John Brockton 1
Francis Bankes 1
Thomas Watkin 1
Richard Townley 1
Leonard Townley 1
John Linley 1
Henry Morley 1
Richard Bilcliffe 2
Richard Poplewell 2
John Fletcher 1
Thomas Sugberrey 1
Theophll Pettey 1
Willm Brearey 1
Thomas Prince 1
63

Empty & no distres to be had
Robert Hepworth 1

Omitted by reason of poverty	4
Robert More Collr	
Richd Linley Const	

Knottingley

Arthur Ingram Esqr	9
Mr Samuell Powle	8
Mr George Booth	5
Mrs Ellizabeth Francke	3
Thomas Towtill	3
Rowland Buttler	3
Willm Atkinson	3
Willm Denby	1
Henry Rigill	3
Jonas Allon	2
Samuell Allon	2
Richard Hodgson	1
Henry Smith	7
John Smith	1
Robert Hewitt	1
Arthur Allonson	1
Thomas Simpson	4
Widdow Burton	3
Willm Smith	5
Willm Hodgson	1
Thomas Clarke	1
Mr Daniell Sikes	7
Widdow Browne	2
Widdow Whitacrs	2

c 3]

Richard Smith	1
Robert Lawrence	3
Thomas Longwood	2
Willm Clarke	1
Willm Thackrey	2
Mary Prince	1
Thomas Nell	2
Willm Green	1
Michaell Gaggs	2
John Roebuck	3
Willm Medley	1
Samuell Tompson	1
John Simpson	2
Willm Atkinson	3
John Barker	3
Mr Usher	4
John Soffton	1
John Pocklington	2
Christor Longwood	2
Robert Clarkson	2
Widdow Spencer	3
Widdow Swinden	4
George Preston	1
Mrs Withers	6
George Bowling	1
Thomas Boulton	3
Charles West	2
Richard Hudson	1
John Chainbridge	1
Willm Chainbridge	1
John Tompson	4
Willm Simpson	2
Widdow Allon	2
John Tompson	3
John Tayler	1
Willm Atkinson	2
Willm Stones	5
Widdow Nott	2
Thomas Softon	1
James Wilkinson	1
Willm Adams	4
Widdow Nell	3
Roger Jessop	1
John Stones	3
Thomas Gags	5
Robert Medley	1
John Medley	1
Willm Browne	5
Marke Andrew	3
Willm Redings	2
Mr Guy Taler	2
Michaell Iles	2

m 93, c 1]

Anthony Wilson	1
	196
Empty & no distres to be had	
Steven Cutt	4
John England	3
Lawrence Tompson	1
Willm Atkinson	1
Mrs Iles	1
Omitted by reason of poverty	19
Robert More Collr	
Charles West Const	

Kellington

Mrs Bradford	5
Thomas Horne	1
Steven Sharphouse	2
Thomas Pearson	3
John Skelton	1
Peter Cutt	5
Steven Sharpas	2
John Richardson	1
Mr Wood	3
Marke Ward	1
John Skelton	2
Willm Horsall	1
Peter Cutt	2
Peter Cutt	3
James Cooke	1
Michaell Calverley	1
Willm Webster	1
Thomas Horne	1
Willm Bewley	1
Thomas Barton	1
John Brumley	4
John Wareing	1
Willm Harrison	3
Willm Hewitt	2
Thomas Barton	1
John Brogden	2
Willm Hewit	2
John Tompson	1
Thomas Jelson	1
Richard Tompson	1

Willm Thorpe 2
John Bird 1
Nichollas Bateman 4
Willm Whiteside 2
Willm Shireson 2
George Dewhurst 2
Willm Pickhaver 1

70

Empty & no distres to be had
Willm Cassen 1

c 2]

Omited by reason of poverty 3

Robert More Collr
James Cooke Const

Kirke Smeaton
(Kirk Smeaton)

Mr Oates 5
Mr Rasby 7
Mr Walker 4
Mr Harpam 4
Widdow Elliot 1
George Allen 1
Mr Rasby 2
Willm Norton 2
Willm Pinder 1
John Wright 2
Widdow Finney 1
Mr Sikes 2
George Scholey 1
George Grinder 3
Thomas Arlington 1
Thomas Grainger 2
Thomas Allen 1
Willm Grinder 1
John Walker 1
Willm Byard 1
Thomas Clough 2
Thomas Johnson 1
John Walker 1
Robert Clayburne 1
Henry Fosterd 1
Richard Mawson 1
Richard Allen 1
George Walker 1
Mr Holegate 7
Willm Askeron 2
Widdow Armroyde 1
John Hunscroft 2

64

Empty & no distres to be had
Sir Thomas Yarbrough 1
John Rushworth 5

Omitted by reason of poverty 5

Thomas Midleton Collr
John Shawe Const

Mosse
(Moss)

Willm Watson 2
Widdow Cooke 2
Francis Furth 1

c 3]

Richard Nutt 1
Willm Jenings 1
Widdow Haworth 2
Widdow Wilson 1
Widdow Robinson 3
Willm Nutt 1
John Smith 1
Willm Good 1
John Sharples 2
Mr Henry Saxton 3
John Scott 1
Phillip Sayle 1
Ralph Usher 1
Thomas Crabtree 1
Edward Doughty 2
Robert Creakill 2
Richard Doughty 2
John Doughty 1
Thomas Birks 1
Thomas Cawthorne 1
Robert Crawshawe 1
Widdow Viccars 1
Mr Fauge 4
Richard Winteringham 2
Leonard Tuniham[209] 1
Robert Clough 2
Willm Birkes 2
Edward Mirfin 4
Francis Machin 2
Leonard Dickering 1
James Sharples 1
Edward Bowser 1
Thomas Hudson 1
John Lawe 3
John Duckett 2
Willm Nutt 2
Richard Bradley 1

65

Empty & no distres to be had
Willm Fauge

Omitted by reason of poverty 4

Thomas Midleton Collr
Richard Bradley Const

Norton

Toby Humphrey Esqr 12
Mr Willm Roe 4
Willm Hudson 1

[209] Alternatively 'Tumham'.

Thomas Cawood 1
Robert Pinder 2
Henry Hudson 1
Thomas Hall 3
Thomas Fletcher 2

m 93v, c 1]

Willm Newby 1
Mathew Dixon 1
Willm Woodhouse 1
Richard Tompson 2
Edmund Hanson 2
Edmund Carter 1
Willm Barker 1
Willm Woodhouse 1
John Woodhouse 2
Willm Draper 3
John Pinder 3
Robert Woodhouse 3
Bartholl Longfellow 3
Nichollas Wood 1
James Pitt 1
Robert Holmes 3
Willm Towtill 1
Willm France 3
Willm Pinder 3
Willm Roebuck 1
Samuell Sivers 2
Willm Roebuck 2
Thomas Goodridg 1
Roger Frankish 1
Henry Moore 1
John Dawson 1
Widdow Nevison 7
John Towtill 1
Christopr Watkin 1
James Watkin 2
John Briggs 1
Margret Woodhouse 1
John Woodhouse 1
John Briggs 1
John Bramley 1
Thomas Burman 1
Thomas Crosley 1
Willm Walker 2
Widdow Hornecastle 1
Willm Hudson 1
93

Empty & no distres to be had
Willm Draper 1

Omitted by reason of poverty 3

Thomas Midleton Collr
Edmund Hanson Const

North Elmesall (North Elmsall)
Thomas Wentworth Esqr 22
Ellizabeth Day 5
Barbara Day 4
Francis Conway 3
Thomas Jarvice 1
Paull Tune 1
Francis Reynold 1

c 2]

John Aykeroyde 1
Richard Lawe 3
Christopr Emerson 2
Thomas Turton 1
Willm Pickering 2
John Turman 1
Richard Parkins 1
Edward Misdall 3
Michaell Knutton 1
James Pickering 1
James Turton 1
Willm Ellison 1
55

Empty & no distres to be had
Cuthbert Pennington 1

Omitted by reason of poverty 3

Thomas Midleton Collr
Willm Pickering Const

Ouston (Owston)
The Lady Adams 11
Mr Pygott 6
Mr Twist 2
Thomas Parkins 1
Joseph Hudson 3
Willm Wilson 1
Barnaby Firth 3
Thomas Lambert 1
Richard Pagdin 2
Steven Hurst 1
Thomas Atkinson 3
Richard Crabtree 3
Steven Cutler 1
Jonas Marlin 2
John Gillin 3
James Mangill 1
Willm Sayle 1
Widdow Hurst 1
Widdow Longbotham 2
Widdow Marlin 2
Francis Clarke 2
Robert Jackson 2
Richard Viccars 1
Robert Cooke 1
George Bowser 1
John Hudson 2
John Burley 1
James Birks 1
Henry Bower 1
Willm Viccars 2
Widdow Greene 1
John Harrison 5
Richard Mangell 1

c 3]

Widdow Cowart 1
Joseph Burton 1

Willm Lee 1
Tristram Smeaton 1
Widdow Norton 1
John Freare 1
Edward Bradford 1
78

Empty & no distres to be had
Phillip Astwick heires 1

Thomas Midleton Collr
Richard Bagden Const

Ousefleete (Ousefleet)
Willm Wilde 2
Robert North 3
Robert Bishop 1
Robert Milner 1
John Milner 4
Richard Graues 3
John Freeman 2
Thomas Freeman 1
John Godfrey 2
George Forrest 1
Thomas Maude 1
Anne Harrison 1
Thomas Leavens 1
Marke Edward 1
Robert Milner 1
Alexandr Milner 2
Thomas Pepper 1
Willm Wells 2
Robert Mosley 1
Willm Collins 1
Thomas Bower 1
Thomas Wells 1
Richard Wells 1
James Longbones 1
Francis Ayre 1
Thomas Goodworth 1
John Watson 1
Thomas Tempest 1
Robert Hotham 1
Robert Lister 1
Bridget Brearcliffe 1
Willm Wells 7
Elizabeth Bancroft 2
Willm Mell 1
James Cooper 1
John Beck 1
Willm Smith 1

m 94, c 1]

Thomas Hallalay 1
Robert Hill 1
Robert Procter 1
Willm Pepper 1
John Bradley 1
John Tinker 1
Robert Bishop 1
Thomas Ralson 1
64

Omitted by reason of poverty 8

Robert More Collr
Robert Milner Const

Pollington
Willm Chester 3
Thomas Manson 1
Thomas Moxson 2
Willm Topcliffe 2
Michaell Dunn 1
Richard Brooke 1
Anne Curtious 1
Willm Slayden 1
John Salmon 1
John Slack 1
John Heptenstall 1
Mr John Gathorne 3
Robert Curtees 1
Richard Hodgson 1
Thomas Mann 1
Willm Pygott 2
John Durham 1
John Swainson 1
Willm Calverley 1
Griffin Scowthrop 2
Thomas Wilson 1
John Calverley 1
Thomas Mann 2
Willm Cowler 1
Thomas Letham 2
Thomas Smith 1
Richard Parker 2
Thomas Boner 3
Thomas Dilcocke 1
Robert Wood 1
Samuell Salmond 2
Widdow Rooth 2
George Ward 1
John Watson 1
Richard Breers 1
John Slayden 2
John Midleton 2

c 2]

Widdow Arnold 1
Willm Slayden 1
John Midleton 2
Thomas Foster 1
John Eccles 1
Thomas Midleton 3
Christopr Jenison 1
John Lawe 2
Widdow Dawney 1
George Parker 1
Mathew Tayler 1
Thomas Dilcocke 1
John Jenison 1
John Midleton 3
Mr Richard Rooth 9
Edward Beverley 1
John Scawthrop 2
Willm Birkes 1
Roger Hodgson 2
Willm Wood 1
90

Omitted by reason of poverty 2

Richard Nicholson Collr
John Calverley Const

Pontefract Micklegate

John Watson	3
Edmond Marshall	1
Alderman Wilkinson	7
Widdow Beardshawe	5
John Beardshawe	1
Peter Scaife	2
John Savill	3
Mr John Dixon	6
John Browne	4
John Browne	5
Mr Fox	2
John Burrell	1
Willm Mawthropp	1
Richard Smith	3
Willm Mawthropp	1
Willm Farrer	5
Francis Lee	3
Widdow Lund	5
Alderman Rushby	6
Mrs Tankerd	5
Richard Turner	2
Mr Francis Farrer	6
Martin Reynold	2
Robert Sutton	4

c 3]

Thomas Reedar	5
Willm Barme	5
Thomas Cooke	1
John Blacker	3
Dinah Winfeild	1
Henry Cattle	1
Richard Headley	4
Robert Calverley	4
John Boyes	2
Widdow Spence	3
Willm Williamson	2
Richard England	2
Henry Calfe	3
Robert Wilson	3
Henry Parker	1
Robert Byron	1
Gilbert Hough	3
Anthony Medley	3
Mathias Burnit	2
Rachel Lund	1
John Daniell	1
Mrs Wilkinson	2
Mrs Wilkinson	6
Willm Pollard	3
Mr Ayscough	7
Leonard Johnson	1
Mr Lee	4
Thomas More	1
Willm Cressey	3
George Ogden	1
James Hurst	1
Willm Cromack	2
Aldm Rushby	2
Thomas Burnill	1
Robert Hornecastle	1
George Carter	1
	170

Omitted by reason of poverty 13

Robt Bennit Collr
John Browne Const

Pontefract Neate Market

Mathew Howdall	2
George Ogden	2
John Walton	2
John Inchborne	3
Mrs Oates	1
Robert Revill	5
Thomas Usher	1
Willm Bracebridge	4
Mr Christor Longe	7

m 94v, c 1]

Robert Lee	5
Willm Simpson	2
Mr John Cooper	4
Widdow Gaskin	3
Widdow Shillitoe	1
Widdow Clitheroe	1
James Hewitt	3
Mr Willm Oates	7
Willm Briggs	2
John Lee	3
Willm Coates	2
Robert Curtious	1
George Chambers	3
Thomas Burton	2
Widdow Redhead	1
Widdow Jackson	2
Richard Hatton	4
Richard Rawson	3
Thomas Weightman	5
Francis Howden	2
Robert Sutton	5
George Shillitoe	2
James Hurst	4
Mr Edward Holecoate	5
Samuell Bradley	4
John Gilliam	1
Thomas Schoalfeild	6
Thomas Schoalfeild	1
Leonard Lumbe	1
Richard Austwick Alderm	11
Francis Howden	6
Henry Towne	2
Mr John Lambe	5
Anthony Rowden	5
Barbara Roydhouse	4
Alderm Francke	9
Robert Stables	10
Steven Standeven	4
George Methley	4
Thomas Methley	2
Willm Ellam	1
Michaell Heptenstall	2

Richard Viccars	4
Brian Lund	5
John Webster	3
John Oxley	2
James Harrison	3
Willm Nodder	3
Mr Edwd Booth	5
Abraham Berrey	3
Docter Johnson	11
Thomas Hawksworth	3

c 2]

John Colbeck	2
Willm Starkey	3
Thomas Sayle	2
William Baxter	2
John Scholfeild	4
Willm Scholfeild	1
Georg Shillitoe Alderm	5
John Lapidge	3
Thomas Hawksworth	2
Richard Wheelas	2
Francis Pinder	3
Michaell France	1
	249

Empty & no distress to be had	
Mr Allot	1
Omitted by reason of poverty	20

Robert Bennit Collr
Robert Stables Const

Pontefract New Markett
(Pontefract, New Market)

Willm Houlegate	6
Willm Simpson	4
Mr Robert Tatham	7
Willm Hanley	6
Mr Richard Lyle	6
Docter Drake	2
Richard Lobley	1
Mr Kellam	6
Leonard Hartley	5
Thomas Hathorne	6
Thomas Feild	2
Thomas Hall	4
Robert Clarkson	4
Christopr Hafford Alder	5
Joseph Wilson	4
Henry Ellison	6
Mr Trevis	4
Peter Swift	8
John Chambers	2
Mr Leonard Ward	4
Willm Feild	3
Francis West	2
Willm Knutton	1
Widdow Boulton	3
Thomas Tompson	2
Widdow Cliffe	3
John Nelson	3
Thomas Bolmer	7
John Fox	4
John Pell	1
John Varley	2
Mr Richard Smith	7

c 3]

Thomas Lapidge	8
Mr John Cooper	6
Mr Steven Pearson	4
John Johnson Alderm	6
George Harrison	4
Samuell Tayler Alderm	4
Thomas Shillitoe	2
Thomas English	1
Mr Boniface	5
Thomas English	4
Thomas English	6
Timothy Feild	6
Mrs Withers	8
Jonathan Knowles	2
George Daniell	5
Mary Morrit	4
Thomas English	1
John Bracebridge	1
Willm Stables	3
	210

Empty & no distres to be had	
Comon Hall	1
Omitted by reason of poverty	5

Robert More Collr
Willm Simpson Const

Pontefract Roppergate
(Pontefract, Roper Gate)

Widdow Oxley	4
John Outibridge	1
Mr Trickitt	6
Richard Slack	3
John Beardshaw	1
Henry Allon	1
Willm Farr	1
Widdow Pearson	2
Henry Shackleton	2
Robert Smithies	1
Willm Fall	1
Mr Steven Cooper	6
Mr Clarke	4
Widdow Donkin	1
John Hancocke	1
Mrs Ramsden	5
Thomas Reynard	4
Thomas Reynard	1
Widdow Brooke	2
Widdow Moore	3
Ellin Thwaites	4
Richard Taylor	5
Thomas Bromhead	4

m 95, c 1]

Willm Coates	5
Mr Hill	1
	69

Empty & no distres to be had
Mrs Cooper 2

Omitted by reason of poverty 2

Robert Bennit Collr
John Outibridg Const

Pontefract Castle & Parke (Pontefract Castle and Park)
Mr Ayre 7
Mr Booth 5
Mr Booth 4
John Greenwood 2
18

Omitted by reason of poverty 3

Robt More Collr
Willm Booth Const

Pontefract Bayligate (Pontefract, Bailey Gate)
Willm Hawton 1
Elizabeth Foster 3
Abraham Wilson 4
Mrs Tankerd 6
Thomas Adamson 2
Mr Nayler 3
John Inchboard 2
Abraham Gilliam 1
Richard Taylor 1
Richard Turner 1
Thomas English 1
George Rigley 1
George Rigley 4
John Wright 2
John Townend 1
James Hurst 2
Thomas Knowles 1
Samuell Willan 1
Mr John Drake 4
Samuell Willan 1
Joseph Walker 2
John Hopkinson 2
John Skipton 2
Mathew Cliffe 2
Mr Nicholls Stables 6
Samuell Fentiman 1
John Savill 2
Willm Green 1
Richard Cattell 2

c 2]

John Hodgson 3
Francis Farrer 3
Zachar Stables 4
Thomas Burman 4
Mr Askinden 1
Widdow Secker 1
Docter Drake 9
Widdow Deane 2
John Cressey 4
John Howard 2
Christopr Smith 4
Willm Moxon 2
Thomas Jackson Alderm 5
Gabriell Howden 1
Christopr Stones 1
Widdow Moulton 2
Widdow Westerby 1
John Pettey 2
The New Hall 34
Peter Watson 1
John Wright 1
Bondgate Milne 1
John Crosse 1
Willm Turner 1
Francis Langfeild 1
Thomas Cockill 2
Willm Browne 1
Hayford Browne 2
Steven Duffeild 1
Willm Ellerby 1
Docter Johnson 3
163

Empty & no distres to be had
Thomas Feilding 5
Mr Swift 2
George Chambers 1
John Stables 2
Nichollas Tupman 5

Omitted by reason of poverty 22

Robt Bennit Collr
John Haward Const

Purston Jaglin
Sir Edmund Winn 14
Phillip Hamerton Esqr 5
Mr John Hamerten 8
Mr Lockwood 7
Mrs Anne Nott 4
Mr Rhoades 4
John Ouldroyd 2

c 3]

John Walker 2
Elizabeth Procter 2
Mary Gilliam 2
Richard Knowles 3
Robert Outibridge 2
Anne Shillitoe 2
Marke Roe 1
John Potter 3
Nichollas Pye 1
Timothy Rhoades 2
Thomas Green 2
James Schoaley 4
Michaell Shillitoe 2
Willm Crawshawe 3
Willm Procter 1
Thomas Wilson 3
Willm Atkinson 2
Robert Royd 2
Peter Wright 1
John Wilson 4

Willm Crawshawe	2
Elizabeth Freeman	1
Widdow Browne	1
Peter Wilson	1
George Dixon	1
Thomas Freeman	1
Elizabeth Wilson	2
Thomas Browne	1
Willm Freeman	1
Robert Walker	3
John Roydhouse	2
Elizab Tompson	3
Thomas Tellowe	1
Thomas Roebucke	3
Jane Wrightson	1
Richard Jenkinson	1
Thomas Daltrie	1
Jonas Wilson	1
George Maning	1
Elizabeth Shillitoe	1
	117

Empty & no distres to be had

Mr Lockwood	2

Omitted by reason of poverty	11

Robt Bennit Collr
Richd Procter Const

Rawcliffe

John Boynton Esq	13
Mr Adams	9
Susan Gathorne	6
Sampson Mangell	2

m 95v, c 1]

George Midleham	1
John Bue	2
Ralph Scott	7
Anthony Coventry	2
Robert West	2
John Nicholson	4
George Lightfoote	3
George Thorpe	5
Thomas Girdler	2
Willm Beverley	1
Edward Pears	1
Willm Martindall	2
Robert Smith	1
Thomas Hembrough	1
Mr Hayworth	6
Edward Errat	1
Willm Maples	1
Thomas Tayler	1
James Wriglesworth	1
Robert Crabtree	1
Edward Hembrough	1
John Hart	1
John Cocke	1
Joan Birkes	3
Widdow Pashley	3
Sarah Tayler	2
Richard Pattrick	2
John Bigley	1
George Heptenstall	1
Thomas Whiteside	2
Willm Whiteside	4
John Pattrick	2
Willm Knipe	4
Thomas Stevenson	1
John Totherington	6
	six
Thomas Hutchinson	2
Willm Hutch	2
John Cornewall	5
Thomas Brighton	5
John Fox	1
Thomas Winder	2
Anthony Freeman	1
Anthony Ambler	1
Barthol Topc1iffe	1
Anthony Ambler	1
Willm Morley	2
John Briggs	4
John Hembrough	1
John Meggot	3
Thomas Fleeming	1
John Lister	2
Thomas Hollings	3
Joseph Barker	1

c 2]

Widdow Leavens	2
Henry Leavens	2
Robert Stones	4
Lancellot Fox	3
Willm Taylor	2
Hugh Hogg	1
Edward Bins	2
Anthony Bowland	1
John Totterington	3
Widdow Robinson	1
John Totterington	2
John Fingley	1
Richard Hopper	1
Willm Cutforth	1
Anne Taylor	2
Phillp Vanderwert	1
John Bowland	2
Steven Eagermond	1
Thomas Spencer	1
Edward Romley	3
Mr Birkes	5
Roger Pickhaver	1
George Tayler	3
Anthony Bastowe	2
John Stones	2
John Hancocke	4
George Walker	1
Thomas Bilbrough	1
Willm Hoyle	1
Robert Bowland	1
Thomas Topcliffe	2
Joseph Hollings	1
Joseph Sutton	1
	208

These persons following are discharged by Certifts

Anthony Hall	1
Ellizabeth Harte	1

Hannah Harte 1
Widdow Hall 1
Widdow White 1
Widdow Browne 1
Henry Pinder 1
Willm Cocke 1
Thomas Beamond 1
John Hayles 2
Joseph Webster 1
Widdow Coventrie 1
Widdow Hoppin 1
Widdow Fingley 1
Willm Sutton 1
Hannah Atkinson 1

c 3]

Widdow Margeson 1
Jarvas Grainger 1
Willm Fairley 1
Willm Cooper 1
Francis Hollins 1
Francis Bawmforth 1
Willm Speight 1
Robert Meggot 1
Willm Fearne 1
George Jackson 1
Willm Rusholme 1
Willm Atkinson 1
Willm Hodgson 1
Widdow Wilson 1
Robert Stevenson 1
Edward Taylor 1
Widdow Hembrough 1
Widdow Towton 1
John Willis 1
Thomas Maples 1
Thomas Acklam 1
John Fleeman 1
Thomas Rednes 1

Omitted by reason of poverty 18

Richd Nicholson Collr
Hugh Hogg Const

Reedness
John Stevenson 1
John Leavens 1
John Jackson 1
John Wilson 4
Robert Holdenby 2
John Whitehead 2
John Harrison 2
John Setterington 1
Toby Smith 3
Robert Wilson 1
Thomas Tyson 2
John Dudeing 3
Robert Atkinson 1
Anne Stevenson 2
Steven Holdenby 3
Willm Tompson 3
Thomas Freeman 1
Jonas Mann 1
Thomas Reynold 2
John Laverack 1

m 96, c 1]

Mr Warton 2
John Staneley 1
Simon Richardson 1
Jonas Jackson 1
Richard Arnold 1
George Nicholson 4
Thomas Cooke 3
Robert Browne 1
John Lyhman 1
Willm Drinkall 1
Robert Whitehead 1
Robert Robinson 1
Willm Mann 2
Thomas Whitehead 1
James Emson 4
Thomas Harrison 4
Thomas Tindall 1
Willm Tindall 1
Willm Taylor 2
John Hayworth 5
John Midleton 1
Thomas Turry 1
John Tompson 3
Henry Neskall 1
Willm Taylor 1
Joseph Stevenson 1
Henry Wressell 1
Thomas Wressell 3
Mathew Birkinshawe 1
Joseph Stevenson 1
John Burrel 2
John Walker 4
Joseph Reynold 2
Roger Parret 1
Robert Beamsley 1
Willm Ramsley 1
Thomas Dunne 1
Anne Deane 1
John Houlden 1
James Gathorne 1
George Hewit 1
Thomas Sellay 1
John Gunby 1
John Burkill 1
Joseph Whitehead 3
3

Omitted by reason of poverty 9

Robt More Collr
Thomas Tyson Const

Snaith
Sir Thomas Yarbrough 18
Docter Talbutt 3

c 2]

Widdow Barraclough 1
Willm Motherby 2
Mrs Robinson 6
Thomas Rickard 2
Mrs Burgon 7
John Clarkson 1
John Bateman 3

Michaell Ellam	4
Willm Noble	4
George Allenson	5
Edward Clarke	3
Thomas Gibson	2
Jerem Vause	1
Widdow Hill	1
Willm Morris	2
Edward Jackson	5
Thomas Cuniworth	1
George Haukes	2
Richard Smith	1
John Lawson	1
Widdow Reyner	2
Margery Jenyson	6
Robert Todd Cler	5
Willm Cattison	2
George Burliston	1
Willm Hawkins	5
Hercules Buck	2
Peter Wrath	3
James Midleton	2
Christopr Bayley	3
John Wrath	3
John Morris	1
Nichollas Motherby	2
Henry Cooper	2
Henry Motherby	1
Thomas Hawton	2
Mr Robert Ballance	5
Oswald Motherby	2
Charles Fisher	1
Willm Headley	1
John Whitley	1
Thomas Walker	3
Robert Laverack	5
Brian Dawson	2
Hugh Chester	2
Docter Talbut	5
Joseph Frickley	4
George Denby	3
Peter Midleton	1
Edward Wilkin	1
George Musgraue	1
Thomas Bogg	1
Thomas Windle	1
John Stables	1
Thomas Conyworth	1

c 3]

Edmond Bradley	1
Widdow Hargill	2
Thomas Fish	1
James Atkinson	1
Cornill Barker	1
Thomas Fish	1
Mathew Walker	1
Hemy Bell	2
Richard Motherby	1
John Stones	1
Robert Midleton	3
Thomas Headley	6
Willm Mountrie	4
Robert Scothrop	4
	187

Empty & no distress to be had

Anthony Atkinson	3
Robert Smithson	4
Robert Smithson	1
Anne Mespah	1
Mathew Walker	1

These persons following are discharged by Certiftes

Thomas Denby	2
Ellizabeth Fish	1
Jane Yorke	2
Hemy Pickering	1

Omitted by reason of poverty 18

Robert More Collr
James Atkinson Const

Sutton cum Askeran (Sutton with Askern)

Widdow Crawshawe	5
Leonard Simpson	2
George Ward	1
Thomas Midleton	2
Widdow Washington	2
Richard Dilcocke	3
Willm Weightman	2
John Holmes	2
Mr Carter	6
Alice Harrison	3
Willm Foores	2
Widdow Hurst	1
Robert Midleton	4
Willm Hanson	2
Thomas Holmes	2
Willm Bushell	1
Richard Maplebeck	1
John Maplebeck	1
Mr Humphrey	11
Willm Cooke	5
Mrs Jane Cooke	2

m 96v, c 1]

Hastings Aukland	1
Henry Smith	2
Richard France	1
William Wild	1
John Maplebeck	1
Willm Jackson	1
Richard Browne	3
James Hudson	1
Robert Aukland	2
	73

Empty & no distress to be had

Mr Humphrey 1

Omitted by reason of poverty 3

Thomas Midleton Collr
Richd Browne Const

Smeaton Perva (Little Smeaton)

Mrs Copley	5
Willm Burges	1
Willm Wickham	1
Robert Wordropp	1
Richard Finney	4
Richard Marton	1
Widdow Wentworth	2
John Hudson	1
Anne Scholey	1
George Saile	4
Mary Clarburne	2
Henry Steele	1
Hugh Pinder	3
Edward Brewster	1
John Hurst	1
John Pease	1
Phillp Heptenstall	1
Robert Strainger	1
John Boyne	2
John Barker	1
Mrs Copley	2
	37

Empty & no distres to be had

John Adams	2

Thomas Midleton Collr
Willm Burgas Const

Stubs Walding (Walden Stubbs)

Mr Pearcy	13
Michaell Woadhause	4
Willm Askeron	2
John Huscroft	2
Thomas Pollard	2
Lawrence Slater	1
Francis Day	1

c 2]

Willm Rogers	1
Widdow White	1
John Foores	1
Thomas Martin	1
John Robotham	1
Willm Singleton	1
John Cary	1
Willm Wheeldrake	1
Thomas Conway	1
Willm Mitton	1
	35

Richd Nicholson Collr
Willm Singleton Const

Skellow

Willm Rookeby Esqr	8
John Harrison	4
Willm Harrison	5
Robert Brooke	3
Widdow Wilson	1
John Jennings	2
Robert Cawthorne	1
James Martin	1
Robert Wilson	1
Thomas Schoales	1
Francis Wilson	1
John Baley	1
Richard Drable	1
Robert Bayley	1
Mathew Cawthorne	2
George Dickinson	2
John Gilling	1
James Cawthorne	2
Thurston Smeaton	1
James Blake	1
Widdow Pinder	1
	41

Robt Bennit Collr
Francis Wilson Const

Swinfleete (Swinefleet)

Mr Thomas Stevenson	7
Jerem Simpson	3
Willm Simpson	1
Willm Stevenson	2
Mountame Morton	2
Joseph Hutton	1
Robert Deane	1
Thomas Shilton	1
Thomas Harrison	2
John Gleadall	1
Willm Waid	1
Grace Gilliott	1

c 3]

Thomas Pearson	1
John Bateman	1
Thomas Hesle	1
Thomas Ludington	1
Robert Harrison	2
Thomas Althropp	2
Robert Houghton	1
Robert Foxe	1
John Davis	2
Sarah Shirlock	2
Christopr Watkin	2
Leonard Viccars	1
Willm Hide	1
Thomas Houghton	1
John Hogg	3
Thomas Batman	2
John Freeman	2
Richard Johnson	3
Robert Sellay	2
Willm Hewson	2
John Stevenson	2
George Dunn	2
John Watkinson	3
Thomas Adwick	2
Widdow Batman	1
Hemy Scott	1
Thomas Adwick	1
Richard Hide	2
Robert Raper	1
Samuell Spinke	2
Thomas Arlush	1
Thomas Harrison	2
Christopr Tompson	1

Mathew Hewson	1
Christopr Tompson	2
John Stevenson	1
Widdow Shirlock	1
Robert Gilliot	1
Widdow Sedgby	1
Thomas Hart	1
	85

Omitted by reason of poverty 6

Robert More Collr
Thomas Harison Const

Skelbrooke

John Copley Esqr	2
Mr Parker	18
Roger Wilson	3
Widdow Horncastle	2
Elizabeth Brears	2
Thomas Tumon	1
Thomas England	1

m 97, c 1]

Joseph Machin	1
Thomas Horncastle	1
Willm Scholey	2
Robert Wilson	2
Thomas Martin	2
Barnaby Frear	2
	39

Thomas Midleton Collr
Thomas England Const

South Kirby
(South Kirkby)

Mr Francis Armitage	5
Mr Edward Watson	10
Mrs Anne Thornhill	6
Mr Peighing Cler	4
Richard Armroyd	1
John Houlegate	3
Willm Saile	1
Thomas Nodder	3
Willm Wilkinson	3
Michaell Lake	5
Alverah Bingley	2
Barnard Sayle	2
John Wilkinson	2
Henry Abbotson	2
John Merriot	1
Dorothy Hewit	2
George Wood	3
George Hogley	3
Francis Machin	2
Richard Smith	2
Robert Allon	2
Thomas Bingley	4
Ellin Wareing	2
Jane Swallowe	1
Thomas Armroyde	1
Thomas Ibetson	1
Robert Wilson	3
Robert White	1
Richard Buttrey	3
Willm Hogley	3
Richard Conway	1
Edward Norton	1
Willm Fish	1
Richard Copley	1
Samuell Bullas	1
Edward Crosley	1
John Machin	3
Thomas Loft	2
John Morret	1
James Wareing	2
Mrs Ellizab Horncastle	3
Thomas Sale	1
Mrs Horncastle	1
Thomas Ibbetson	2
Elizabeth Clarkson	2

c 2]

Robert Crosley	2
Luke Scott	1
Widdow Goodyson	1
Robert Hinde	1
Robert Shillitoe	3
Robert Otley	1
Mrs Wentworth	1
Elizabeth Wilkinson	2
Elias Shillitoe	1
Willm Allom	1
Widdow Marryon	1
Richard Ibbitson	1
Daniell Nodder	1
Robert Hanley	1
Wentworth Machon	2
Richard Watterton	1
Anne Conway	1
John Brotherton	1
Thomas Bloome	1
George Gee	1
Willm Bloome	1
Robert Singleton	1
Richard Wilkinson	2
	135

Omitted by reason of poverty 5

Thomas Midleton Collr
Edward Crosland Const

South Elmesall
(South Elmsall)

Mr Jonas Buckley	6
Mr Hugh Wentworth	3
Widow Day	4
Robert Crosley	2
Richard Holme	3
Richard Kendall	1
Mr Wrightson	4
Francis Tayler	3
Thomas Day	2
George Fletcher	1
Edward Boswell	1
John Day	2
Nichollas Morris	2
Wilfrey Issott	2
Edward Horncastle	2

Thomas Cawthorne	4
Robert Armroyde	2
John England	1
Mr Ackersley	6
Widdow Slack	2
John England	1
Willm Rogers	3
Willm Shirt	1
Robert Thornton	1
John Ledgerd	1

c 3]

Brian Flower	1
Thomas Brewster	2
Robert Brewster	3
Richard Rogers	1
Richard Day	1
Thomas Norton	3
Mary Day	1
Willm Ledgerd	1
Robert Watkins	1
Willm Horncastle	1
Willm Faber	1
	76

Empty & no distres to be had

Mr Day	2

Omitted by reason of poverty	2

Thomas Midleton Collr
Willm Horncastle Const

Stappleton (Stapleton)

Mr Greenwood	10
Michaell Shackleton	2
Mr James Carter	4
Richard Shackleton	4
Willm Green	1
Willm Tomkinson	2
John Shawe	1
George Littleboyes	1
Willm Jackson	1
Richard Sutton	1
Thomas Carter	1
	28

Thomas Midleton Collr
Richard Sutton Const

Thorp Audlin (Thorpe Audlin)

Mr Samuell Saltenstall	10
The Earle of Winchelsey	8
Mr Wood	6
Henry Bedford	4
John Jackson	3
John Rushworth	3
Willm Jackson	4
Richard Arnold	1
Richard Bond	1
Richard Pinder	1
Thomas Dixon	1
John Horncastle	4
Jane Towtill	1
Widow Watkin	1
Thomas Pinder	1

m 97v, c 1]

Francis Blackbume	1
Hemy Fewler	1
Willm Dixon	1
Richard Wood	1
Leonard Wilkinson	1
James Wood	1
Robert Wright	1
Thomas Bretton	1
Robert Wilkinson	1
Edward Wright	1
Abigall Milner	3
John Smith	1
John Adron	1
Mrs Grace Wilcocke	1
	65

Richd Nicholson Collr
Leonard Wilkinson Const

Tanshelfe (Tanshelf)

Elizabeth Akester	1
Mr Ward	10
Robert Williamson	3
Mr Leonard Stables	6
Nicholas Hodgson	2
Willm Shillitoe	2
Edward Makin	4
Widdow Green	2
George Walker	1
Robert Lund	3
John Lapidge	3
George Crosland	2
Henry Slack	3
Samuell Collet	1
Thomas Glover	2
Mr Shillitoe	3
Thomas Jenkinson	1
Thomas Robinson	1
John Butler	2
John Rusby	4
John Barton	1
Mr Mitchill	6
Mr Stannop	3
Willm Fentiman	1
Richard Slack	1
Marmad North	2
Mr Willm Ramsdon	7
John Hitching Esqr	5
Mr Fairfax	4
John Hanley	4
James Williams	2
James Williams	2
Widdow Pattrick	1
Willm Webster	1

c 2]

Leonard Bramham	3
Thomas Bramham	1

Willm Sharpe	2
John Crowther	1
John Pattrick	1
Thomas Towtill	2
Richard Outbridge	1
Willm Green	2
John Towtill	1
Elizab Stables	1
Mr Lambe	7
Thomas Crosland	5
Mr Burges	2
Mr Heptenstall	3
Widdow Ash	3
Thomas Bolge	2
John Chadburne	1
Mr Shillitoe	6
Mr Adams	6
	146 146[210]

Empty & no distres to be had

Sir Thomas Wentworth	6

Omitted by reason of poverty	6

Robt More Collr
John Burton Const

Upton

Mrs Sarah Ward	9
Thomas Watkins	2
Thomas Cooke	2
James Norton	1
Richard Wood	2
Anne Bingley	2
Richard Watkins	1
David Marshall	1
Robert Falkener	2
Richard Whitacre	1
Susan Watkins	2
Robert Watkins	1
John Hudson	1
John Slack	1
Leonard Whittenstall	1
James Brooke	1
Alice Whitacrs	1
Robert Calverley	1
James Walker	1
	33

c 3]

Empty & noe distres to be had

Mrs Ward	1

Robt Bennit Collr
John Hudson Const

Whitgift

Mr Thomas Ballance	4
Mr John Worsley	3
Willm Clarke	1
Ellis Wright	1
Willm Hutchinson	1
Richard Hall	2
Thomas Kirby	1
Charles Roberts	2
Edward Williamson	1
Edward Holdenby	1
John Hall	2
Marke Watson	1
John Martingdale	1
Mr Robert Stevenson	4
Willm Kirby	1
Francis Parke	1
Andrew Kitchin	2
Thomas Wright	1
Steven Wright	1
John Freeman	1
John Wright	1
Willm Clarke	1
Willm Ayre	1
Mathew Wright	1
Robert Wiles	1
John Osburne	1
Willm Nowill	1
Edward Williamson	2
Anne Smith	1
Richard Hall	1
Robert West	2
Willm Petch	1
Robert Watson	1
	47

Empty & no distres to be had

John Pinder	1

Omitted by reason of poverty	2

Robt More Collr
Willm Kirby Constable
Constable

m 98, c 1]

Whitley

Thomas Walton	1
Robert Rhoades	1
John Scholey	1
George Siddall	1
James Marshall	1
Steven Shipman	1
George Walton	1
James Marshall	1
Susan Netleton	1
Robert Jaques	4
Peter Marshall	1
Willm Green	1
Dorothy Wilson	1
Willm Scholey	1
John Gascoyne	1
Charles Midleton	1
Edward Padget	1

[210] sic.

Thomas Healey	1
Thomas Howdall	3
Jarvas Vause	1
Zachar Jaques	3
Thomas Nelson	1
Widdow Wright	1
John Woodhouse	1
Elizab Rushworth	1
Henry Fletcher	1
James Hudson	1
Phillp Bustard	1
George Ley	1
Mary Tompson	1
Willm Rawden	2
Willm White	1
	40

Omitted by reason of poverty 5

Robt More Collr
James Marshall Const

Womersley

Mr Slater Cler	2
Mr Willm Turner	11
Mr Foster	6
George Midleton	3
Willm Chorrey	1
George Midleton	1

c 2]

Henry Midleton	2
Robert Morton	1
Thomas Singleton	1
Steven Kent	1
Robert Jepson	2
Jarvas Cooke	2
Widdow Webster	1
Henry Hanley	1
John Fox	2
Widdow More	1
John Boyne	2
John Midleton	2
Widdow Hudson	1
George Jeffcocke	3
James Arlington	1
Zachariah Bradford	1
Thomas Shackleton	2
Willm Speight	1
Willm Brogden	2
Widdow Smith	1
Widdow Cooper	1
Robert Jackson	1
Mr Willm Ellin	4
Widdow Steele	1
Robert Wykeham	1
Henry Medley	1
Henry Midleton	1
Arthur Heptenstall	1
John Ellin	2
Thomas Clarke	1
John White	1
Thomas Midleton	1
John Moody	1
Widdow Jackson	1
Willm Saynor	1
Robert Brogdin	2
John Beale	1
Richard Stones	1
Thomas Dransfeild	1
Mrs Everingham	3
James Mitchill	1
Thomas Midleton	2
George Pearson	1
Henry Hopkins	1
John Thurland	2
Willm Jenings	1
	89

c 3]

Empty & no distres to be had
Peter Walton 1

Omitted by reason of poverty 2

Thomas Midleton Collr
John Boyne Const

LADY DAY ASSESSMENT 1672

Staincross Wapentake

The National Archives, E179/210/412

m 1]

Ardsley

William Beardshaw 2
Thomas Brooksbanke Jun 1
John Kay 2
Henry Overam 1
Richard Oxley 2
Thomas Wall 1
George Milner 3
Robert Woodall 1
John Oddy 1
Willm Scoar 2
Willm Micklethwaite 2
Thomas Roberts 1
Willm Oddy 1
Mr Richard Maywood 8
Richard Naylor *pro* Chapman 1
Edward Sleshaw 1
Richard Oddy 1
Widdow Bayley 1
Robert Fox 2
Elias Wood 3
James Fowleo 1
John Aineley 2
Richard Key 2
Thomas Seyner 1
Willm Kay 2
Richard Wood 2
John Osburne 1
Jonathan White 1
Edward Oldfeild 5
Henry Ellis 2
Willm Broadhead 1
John Prince 6
George Broadhead 1
John Aineley 1
Richard Senyer 69

The p[er]son following is discharged by Certificate
Thomas Brooksbanke 2

Omitted by reason of Extreame poverty 7

Robert Corner Collr
Thomas Roberts Const

Bretton (Bretton, West Bretton)

Sir Thomas Wentworth 13
Edward Monstone 2
Robert Firth 1
John Mountaine 1
Mathew Bearshawe 1
Thomas Newton 1
Michaell Smith 1
Nichollas Casson 1
Edward Berrey 1
James Hardcastle 1
Matthew Hardcastle 1
24

Robert More Collr
Michll Smith Const

Barnsley

Joseph Priestley 4
Richard Atkinson 2

m 2]

Mary Shepherd 1
James Watterhouse 3
John Hutchinson 1
Dorothy Barber 5
Thomas Spavin 3
Lancellt Dickinson 3
Robert Hurst 3
Josias Jessop 3
James Heath 4
Willm Crawshaw 6
Willm Atkinson or} 2
John Smith}
Daniell Parker 2
Robert Letham 4
James Mosse 2
James Mosse 1
Mr Stephen Ludlam 7
Widd Thrift 2
Wm Robinson 5
William Cooke 9
George Wilkinson 7
John Simpson 2
Jonathan Linley 4
Toby Bings 4
Mr Robert Daniell 10
Widdow Hainsworth 6
William Bagaley Junr 4
Francis Langley 9
Mr Francis Usher 5
Mr Robert Wood 5
Thomas Wood 6
Widdow Hobson 3
Nathaniell Olley 4
William Oxley 1

Thomas Parkins	3
Widdow Brighouse	4
Edward Heath	3
William Oxley Jnr	4
Widd Lambert	2
Geo Trueloue	1
more a com oven	2
William Staynforth de Houghton	1
Johathan Briggs	2
John Graues	2
Thomas Osgathorp	3
Mathew Wood	1
Widdow Swallow	4
Richard Hudson & Forge & forge	6[211]
Widdow Hinchcliff	5
Tho Addy	3
John Dawson	1
John Abbot	2
John Foster	3
John Rooke	3
Geo Moore	2
Richard Codd	1
Jarvas Ellison	1
Jonathan Clark & Forge	2
John Clark & Forge	2
Jonas Clarke	1
John Dranfeild	6
James Allen	2
William Headen	4
John Clarke	5
Widdow Hewerd	4
Mr Wood	6
Thomas Heyley	4
Thomas Ellis	3
Mr Green	6
Thomas Browneley	5
Stephen Ludlam	1
Christopher Haslam	8
Thomas Oxley & John	6
Richard Leak	4
Thomas Osgathorpe	6

m 3]

William Pattison	4
Widdow Fayrham	4
Richard Addy	1
Samuell Sherreshaw	4
Edward Norton	4
Mr Francis or John Drainfeild	1
John Ditch	3
Richard Woodcock	2
Joseph Anderton	4
Willm Holegate and} Michael Dines}	4
Dorothy Crawfoote	2
John Smith house & shop	7
Thomas Stacy	3
Widdow Scamarill	2
Willm Roe	2
Geo Gill Jun	2
Deborah Crawforth	1
Pretious Barber	6
James Ashforth	2
Mr Daniell	5
Willm Crosland *pro* Oven	4
Mrs Martha Crosland	3
Mr Edward Armitage	6
Jane Wood	3
Oliver Bagshawe	1
Thomas Rhoades	4
James Cornfeild	2
John Woodcock	1
Jennet Bothamley	2
Robert Chappell	5
George Hopton	2
Thomas Woodcock	2
Joseph Woodcock	1
Willm Rooke	4
Willm Anderton	1
Richard Ellison	3
John Ardington	1

Robert Leadhain *pro* Walker	
Thomas Linely	1
Francis Oxley	3
Widdow White	1
Margret Crawshawe	1
Mr John Robinson	2
Henry Denton	1
Thomas Frudd	2
	395

Empty and noe distres to be had

Thomas Waide	2
John Beckitt	2
Willm Daniell	5
John Smith	1
John Bayley	3

These persons following are discharged by Certificates

James Bird	1
Robert Shipherd	1
Jane Hall	1
Richard Shepherd	1
Willm Fostard	2
John Seyner	1

Omitted by reason of Poverty 13

Robert More Collr
James Allen Const

Barugh

m 4]

George Hague	1
Arthur Clarkson	4
Widdow Hawley	1
Widdow Cudworth	1

211 sic.

Thomas Rhoades	4
Widdow Webster	3
Thomas Orcliff	2
Mr Marsh	1
Richard Lee	1
George Stevenson	2
Thomas White	1
Widdow Ellison	1
Willm Feild	1
Joseph Bingley	1
Richard South	1
Richard Ellison	2
Richard Nightingale	2
Robert Drewrey sen	1
Thomas Woodcocke	1
John Barber	5
Henry Cox	3
Robert Wilkinson & forges	3
Thomas Williamson	1
Mathew Woodcocke	1
Widdow Lake	1
John Woodcocke	1
Thomas Littlewood	4
Edward Lee	1
Widdow Traviss	1
Francis Ellison	1
Henry Theaker	1
Thomas Woodcocke	1
Francis South	1
Willm Drury & forge	2
	58

Robert Corner Collr
Ri Nigthingale Const

Brearley (Brierley)

The Honrble the Lord Halifax	13
more for Mathew Setle house	5
Joseph Dymond	3
John Halleley	2
George Holcot	3
Widdow Shutcliffe	1
Joseph Armitage	1
Widdow Shutcliffe	1
Richard Stead	1
Willm Whitwell	3
Mr Nightingale	2
John Marshall	4
Richard Richardson	2
John Hoyland	3
Thomas Green	2
Thomas Cawthorne	4
Jonathan Roe	3
Matthew Fidling	2
Widdow Milner	3
Joseph Gill	3
Thomas Shaw	3
Widdow Greene	1

m 5]

John Hoyland	3
Willm Speight	3
Jonathan Halliley	2
Giles Battyson	1
Willm Speight	2
James Berrey	1
Thomas Watterworth	2
Anthony Hill	1
John Bell	1
Allexander Berrey	1
Richard Hewitt	1
George Holegate	1
Willm Gill	1
Richard Berrey	2
Richard Bedforth & forg	2
	89

Omitted by reason of poverty	4

Thomas Middleton Collr
Thomas Watterworth Const

Cudworth

Thomas Walker	2
Willm Simpson	2
Nathaniell Lister	4
Thomas Townend	2
Caleb Tompson & forge	2
Henry Popleton	3
Richard Sugdall	1
Robert Wadsworth	2
Mary Cooper	1
Robert Downend	1
George Beavers	1
Henry Midleton	1
John Oddy	6
Thomas Charlesworth	1
Richard White	2
John Carrington	3
Math Addy or Broadhead	2
Francis Scamaden	1
Willm Broadhead sen	3
James Green	2
Henry Anderton	1
Willm Pyne	1
Robert Sikes	2
George Addy	2
Stanley Shaw	2
John More	1
James Green	1
Henry Green	1
Thomas Beckitt	1
Thomas Dodgson	1
John Smith	1
Robert Boulton	1
James Simond	1
John Lyell	2
Henry Boulton	1

m 6]

Widdow Jagger	1
Nichollas Shillitoe	1
Widdow Bradley	1
	64

These persons following are discharged by Certificate

Widdow Bloome	1
Widdow Greene	1
Joseph Sikes	1

Omitted by reason of Poverty	1

Thomas Midleton Collr
James Green Const

Carleton (Carlton)

Stanhope Dixon	14
Mr Blythman	7
Mr Blythman	4
Robert Pitt	2
John Rimington	3
Saml Senyer	1
Francis Crosse	2
Hannah Pitt	2
Joseph Bailden	1
John Thwaites	2
John Firth	2
John Hinchcliffe	2
James Townenedd	3
Widdow Firth	2
Willm Simpson	1
Henry Ellis	2
Willm Beckwith	2
Richard Crookes	2
Richard Johnson	2
George Bramham	1
Robert Bray	1
Thomas Simpson	1
Robert Hodgson	1
Arthur Sutcliff	1
Willm Wainwright	1
Peter Dunn	1
Joseph Woffenden	3
Abraham Haigh	1
Peter Dunn	1
Thomas Lockwood	1
Robert West	2
	71

The person following is discharged by Certificate

Widdow Broadhead	1

Robert Corner Collr
Robert West Const

Cawthorne

Mrs Allott	9
Mr Green	6
Mr Spencer	5
Mr Maylin	6
Mr Green de Ellmhurst	5
Mr Walbanke	3
Mr Spencer in Cawthorne	4
Godfrey Thornton	4
Henry Sikes	1
Thomas Smith	5
Mathew Swallowe	2
George Shirt	1
Thomas Wainwright	3
Mathew Walker & forge	2
Robert Taylor	1
Robert Dyson	1
Henry Turton	2

m 7]

Willm Tayler	3
Timothy Streete	2
John Moxon	3
Robert Baxter	4
Richard Micklethwate	4
Thomas Cawthrope & forge	3
Willm Cawthrope	1
Thomas Dixon	1
Widdow Fawley	1
John Fawley	1
Mr Ritchingman	3
Thomas Downing	2
Timothy Shirt	4
John Roebuck	1
John Hargraues	2
Thomas Farnley	3
Edward Firth	2
Mathew Crosland	2
Thomas Morton	1
John Firth	2
Robert Bower	1
Thomas Woffenden	1
John Bower	1
John Butterwood	2
John Lynley	2
Willm Littlewood	6
John Shirt	4
John Turton and} Henry Hall}	3
Lyonell Hawkesworth	2
Willm Pashley	3
Rihd Moakson	1
Robert Archdale	3
John Wainwright	1
Jonathan Bower	2
Robert Morton	1
Lyonell Micklethwate	1
Joseph Micklethwate	2
Willm Sherritt	4
Robert Woffenden	2
John Woffenden	1
Joseph Armitage	4
John Dixon	1
Mary Scamadine	2
Mathew Bothamley	5
Richard Thackerey	2
Jonathan Morton	1
Willm Stevenson	1
John Tayler	1
	165

Robert Bennit Collr
John Roebuck Const

Cumberworth

John Firth	3
Marke Shaw	3
Abraham Hepworth	2
James Holkins	1
George Pollard	1
Edward Wood	1
Abraham Wood	1
Henry Hoyle	2
John Wayneshawe	2
James Firth	3
Edward Bilcliffe	1
Josias Arnald	1
Henry Gillet	1
Richard Littlewood	3

m 8]

Widdow Wadsworth	5
James Batty	2
John Hepworth	1
Willm Oxley	2
John Hurst	1
Robert Oxley	1
Thomas Green	1
Thomas Jubb	2
Robert Signior	2
John Lockwood	2
Widdow Copley	2
John Lee	3
John Lockwood sen	2
John Wainwright	1
Christoph Hepworth	3
Andrew Streete	1
Josias Massay	4
Thomas Walker	2
George Starr and forge	1
	63

Empty and no distres to be had

Robert Allenson	2

Robert More Collr
Thomas Littlewood Const

Chevitt (Chevet)

Mr Sanford Nevill	33
	33

Robert More Collr
Mr Nevill Const

Clayton (Clayton West)

Sir George Cooke	9
Mr Richard Allott	11
Richard Bothamley	5
John Oxley	4
Francis Oxley	2
Willm Deighton	3
Francis Ellis	2
Amor Lockwood	1
John Moore	2
Widdow Ellis	2
Richard Ellis	2
John Sluther	3
John Nichols	2
John Copley	1
Robert Charlesworth	1
Mathew Feild	2
John Inman Cler	3
Thomas Turner	1
James Feild	1
Widdow Hawkesworth	5
Sarah Clayton	1
Daniell Knight	3
Alice Naylor	1
Richard Nutt	1
Ralph Thurnally	1
Mary Waller	1
Henry Sikes	1
Samll Cawther	1
Willm Thornhill	1
	73

m 9]

Omitted by reason of poverty	9

Robert Alore Collr
Richd Hunt Const

Dodworth

Mr Willm Brooke & Sonne	9
Mr Thomas Sayner	8
John Atkinson	3
John Brooke	5
Ralph Foster	9
Mr John Wadsworth	6
John Kay	2
James Linley	2
Jarvas Shaw	2
George or John Hurst	6
Mary Armitage	3
Susan Hobson	2
George Houghland	1
Richard Hattersley	1
John Armitage sen	1
Christoph Smith	1
Ralph Kershawe	2
Willm Watterhouse	1
Richard Dobson	2
Robert Hudson	1
John Linley	1
Widdow Linley	1
Timothy Shaw	1
John Hurst	1
Richard Crawshaw Jun	2
John Rawson	6
Edmond Brooke	2
Ellias Naylor	3
Nichollas Andrew	2
Thomas Crawshaw of Dodsworth Bottom	1
Peter Sample	1
Mathew Hurst	1
Joseph Booth	2
Abraham Denton	2
George Lee	1
Richard Crawshawe	1
John Hobson	6
Edmond Brooke	1

Mr Thomas Brooke *pro* Turton	1
Willm Hudson forge	1
Willm Harrison	1
	105
Omitted by reason of Poverty	1
Thomas Middleton Collr	
Ri Crawshawe Const	

Darton

Richd Smithhurst Cler	5
Willm Beamont	4
John Hutchinson	2
John Denton	3
Robert Webster & forge	2
David Haigh	1
Widdow Lister	1
Richard Eastwood	1

m 10]

Thomas Rogers	1
John Webster and forges	4
George Stafforth and forg	2
Thomas Webster & forg	3
Thomas Horsfeild	1
Frances Sparke	1
Robert Gibson & forg	2
George Jubb	1
Richard Deplidge	1
Willm Lister and forge	3
Henry Charlesworth	3
John Haigh	1
Widdow Haigh	1
John Mabson	1
Thomas Lockwood	1
James Haigh	1
Widdow Kay	1
Jarvas Newton	1
John Hurst	2
Willm Thornley	1
John Newton	1
Thomas Webster	2
Widdow Morehouse	1
Edward Turner	1
Richard Carr	3
Steven Haslard	1
George Walker	1
Nathaniell Denton	3
Richard Gill	2
Robert Slater	2
John Slayter	1
George Polland	3
John Denton	1
Richard Denton	1
Nathaniell Carr	2
John Silvester	1}
Widdow Mabson	2}
Thomas Hague	1
Thomas Thornley	2
George Carr	7
	seaven
Peter Baites	3
Widdow Barber	1
Edward Barber	1
John Browne	2
John Browne sen	1
John Silvester	3
Mr Amor Bradford	5
John Shaw	2
John Phillips	1
	108
Empty and no distres to be had	
Henry Popleton	2
Omitted by reason of poverty	5
Thomas Midleton Collr	
Thomas Webster Const	

Denby

Mr Barnby	5
Thomas Clayton	6
Widdow Burdett	1
Tobias Burdett	4
John Clayton	3
Mr Cotton	7
John Linley	1
Thomas Burditt	5
Richard Hawksworth	5
John Rowbuck	3
Thomas Burditt	1

m 11]

George Burditt	2
Thomas Hayes	5
Joseph Hinchcliffe	1
Thomas Shillitoe	1
Widdow Moorehouse	1
Willm Moore	1
Walter Poe	1
John Maister	1
Emor Burdett	3
Thomas Jessop	1
Thomas Crowther	1
Godfrey Charlesworth	1
John Gawber	1
Widdow Robinson	3
Ellin Ward	3
Joseph Masley	3
Thomas Marshall jun	3
Richard Prest	1
John Shaw	1
John Dawson	1
Richard Marshall sen	2
John Wood	1
John Dickinson	5
Joseph Baley	2
Edward Goodall	2
Joseph Shaw	1
Ralph Swift	2
Abraham Crosley	3
Richard Micklethwaite	2
Francis West	1
Ralph Horne	2
Richard Hanwell	3
Thomas Haigh	4

Timothy Booth	1
Lawrance Hicke	1
Jennet Hatfeild	1
Willm Gaunt	1
Joseph Pollard	1
Samuell Gawber	1
Roger Rhoades	1
Thomas Gaunt	2
	115

The person undernamed is discharged by Certificate

Willm Hamshire	1

Robt More Collr
Math Burdett Const

Gunthwaite

The Hall	12
John Swift	2
Arthur Brooksbanke	1
Richard Shaw	2
Anne Hawksworth	2
Mary Hawksworth	3
	22

Robert More Collr
Richd Shaw Const

Havercrft (Havercroft)

John Gill Gent	7
Willm Horne or} John Mabson }	3
Anne Schoaley	3
John Clarkson	2
John Crosley	2
Robert Green	1
John Swainson	1
Ellis Ratcliffe	1
Thomas Ellis	1
	21

Robert More Collr
Wm Duffan Const

m 12]

High Hoyland

Mr Hearing	5
Mr Bowleth	4
Joseph Waritt	5
Robert Moore	4
Robert Smith	1
Willm Dyson	1
George Houlden	1
Joseph Houlden	1
Widdow Houlden	1
Widdow Pollard	1
John Apleyard	4
Francis Pollard	1
Willm Pollard	2
Edw Nichols or John Hill	2
John Clayton	1
Thomas Earnshawe	1
John Ellis	3
Christopr Woffenden	3
Thomas Sikes	5
John Sikes	1
Willm Oxley	2
Widdow Oxley	1
Thomas Hardcastle	2
Thomas Sikes	2
Peter Warberton	1
Francis Corner	1
Robert Woodsworth	1
Joshua Haigh	1
	58

Robert More Collr
Mathew Pollard Const

Hymsworth (Hemsworth)

Widdow Huscroft	5
Mr Mason Cler	7
Mrs Charman	6
Mr Wood *pro* Schoolehouse	2
Mr Wreightson	6
Mr Ramsden	4
Mrs Wood de Land	6
Willm Heaton	8
John Rushworth	3
Thomas Wood sen	3
John Beamond	5
Widdow Hurst	3
John Wood More Top	6
Thomas Crowley	4
Thomas Bradshaw	2
Willm Child	1
John Rawson	2
Widdow Secker & Grainger	2
The [*recte* Tho] Rhoadehouse	1
Robert Heslegraue	1
Robert Emerson	1
The Hospitall	4
John Matson	2
Thomas Oweram	4
Thomas Lister	2
Thomas Wood Jun	3
Thomas Hepworth	2
Widd Townend sen	2
Joshua Collett	1
Thomas Carbridge	1
Thomas Collett Jun	1
Michaell Lake	3
Richard Shepherd and forge	3

m 13]

John Heaton	4
James Wareing Jun	3
Mathew Lake	1
Joseph Brooke	1
William Schoaley	1
John Clayton	2
John Green Jnr	1
William Beckitt	4
James Wareing Snr	2
Geo Arrundall	2
John More	2
James Townend	2

William Bayes	1
William Shooer	1
John Abson	2
Richard Crossland	1
Henry Liversidge	2
Mathew Prince	1
John Beatham	1
John Gilliat	1
Widdow Towne Jun	2
John Green sen	2
Richard Atcliffe	2
Mathew Beckitt	1
John Crosland	2
James Crosby	1
Peter Allen	1
Thomas Kay	3
Thomas Paine	2
Ri Firth and corn [*recte* com(mon)] Oven	2
Coward Rhoades	1
	160

Omitted by reason of Poverty 8

Robert Corner Collr
John Wood Const

Hunshelf

William Shelton	7
Joseph Shelton	2
William Denghouse	2
Jarvas Mason	2
Geo Walker	4
	fower
John Heward	3
Mr Alsopp	4
	fower
Tho Linley	3
Stephen West	5
William Wadsworth	2
Tho Arnfeild	2
John Sampson	2
John Preist	3
Jonas Rich	1
Thomas Hobson	2
Jonas Broadhead and forge	2
George Dyson	2
Willm Sanderson	2
Thomas Crosley	1
Thomas Dyson	1
Willm Marsden	2
Joseph Morton	2
Willm Bagshaw	1
Francis Wadsworth	1
Christopr Sanderson	1
George Hellewell	6
John Senyer	1
Francis Armitage	1
Richard Greaues	1
Edmond Stockes	1
Ralph Parkin	1
Thomas Armfeild	1
Willm Sanderson	1

m 14]

Edward Bramam	1
John Hoyland	1
Francis South	1
John Marsden	1
Edward Pitt	1
	77

Empty and no distress to be had
The Executor of Sir Francis Wortley 1

Omitted by reason of Poverty 1

Robert Bennet Collr
John West Const

Hoyland Swaine

Mr John Setwell	8
Willm Hinchcliffe	3
Thomas Walshawe	3
John Claudwell	4
John Holmes	3
Willm Saunderson	2
Richard Holmes	3
Robert Hudson	3
Francis Moxon	2
Christophr Green	2
Emor Moxon	3[212]
John Wallom	3
	three
Mary Carleton	1
Thomas Beete	1
Robert Chadwell	1
John Mitchill	1
Richard Chappell	1
Willm Ibbetson Jun	1
Willm Ibbetson sen	1
John Green	1
Joseph Lister	1
Nehemiah Harghland	1
Joseph Lister	1
John Broadhead	2
Jacob Moxon	1
Widdow Disberres	1
Joshua Linley	1
John Fell	1
John Broadhead	1
John Wadsworth	1
Reynold Burden	2
Richard Ellis	1
John Moxon	1
John Moxon mason	1
Marke Goodare	1
John Cawdall	1
Francis Moxon jun	1
Thomas Walshawe	1
	65[213]

212 sic.
213 There is a scribal error since the total is 67.

The person undernamed is discharged by Certificate

Widdow Hawksworth	1

Robertm Bennet Collr
Daniell Moxon Const

Ingbirtesworth (Ingbirchworth)

Mr John Micklethwaite	5
John Micklethwaite sonne of Richard	4
John Micklethwaite sonne of Anthony	4
John Blakey	4
Willm Barker & forge	3
Mrs Ellizabeth Shirt	4

m 15]

George Shaw senr	1
George Shaw Jun	2
George Firth	2
John Ellis	2
John Roebuck	1
John Haigh	2
	34

Robert More Collr
John Haigh Const

Kexbrough

Sr Francis Burditt	8
Joseph Quinby	1
Widdow Wildsmith	2
John Poplewell	4
Mr Willm Cotton	5
John White	1
John Bedford	1
Francis White	2
Thomas Walker	1
James Charlesworth	3
Robert Mason	1
John White	3
Willm Childe	3
Richard Machen	2
John Addy	4
Widdow Addy	2
John Browne	1
John Browne	2
Abraham Hinchcilffe	2
Widdow Addy	1
James Hall	1
Christopr Wainwright	1
Robert Ball	1
Matthew Ellis	7
Christopr Graues	3
John Walker	2
Thomas Gibson	1
Francis Watton	1
John Poplewell	1
Francis Poplewell	2
John Wilcocke	1
Willm Drancefeild	1
Anthony Drancefeild	1
John Scoaray	1
	73

Omitted by reason of Poverty	2

Robert More Collr
Wm Drancefeild Const

Langsett

Robert Blackburne	4
Henry Dickinson	3
John Birkes	1
John Coudwell Smith	1
Thomas Swinden	1
Henry Marsden	2
John Waston	1
Francis Woodhead	1
George Trant	1
Widdow Haigh	3
Willm Couldwell	2
Samuell Cackle	4

m 16]

John Hinchcliffe	3
Pheynold Preist	1
Widdow Trent	1
Richard Streete	3
Joshua Green	1
Robert Walker	1
Richard Marsden	1
Danniell Marsden	1
Willm Marsden	1
James Bolnehouse	1
John Mitchill	1
Richard Mitchill	1
Widdow Earnshawe	1
Edward Man	1
Edward Kay Sen	1
Edward Kay Jun	1
Isaac Wadsworth	2
Christopr Marsden	1
Richard Green	3
John West	1
John Charlesworth	1
James Ashworth	1
Abraham Shaw	1
John Crosley	1
Ralph Hanley	1
John Rawley	1
Jon Swaile} Richard Broadhead or Ri Smith	1
Joseph Hinchcliffe	1
Henry Hinchcliffe	1
	60

Robert More Collr
Wm Marsden Const

m 16 cont]

Munck Britton (Monk Bretton)

Richard Hutchinson	2
Richard Wood	8

Gamaliell Milner	3
Willm Milner Sen	9
Willm Milner Jun	3
John Johnson	3
Thomas Johnson	1
Willm Crookes	1
Bartholl Cowper	3
	three
Thomas Johnson	5
Mary Broadhead	3
Thomas Lister	1
Widdow Crookes	5
George Illis	3
John Steele	5
Jonath Broadhead	3
Jude Clarkson	7
Richard Tyas	1
Willm Wood	5
Willm Silvester	2
Richard Eagebrooke	3
Widdow Pashley	1
Widdow Turton	1
John Foster	1
Willm Hall	1
Thomas Houlegate	1
Thomas Parker	2
Thomas Jubb	2
Edward Pitt or} Widd Foster}	3
John Scamadon	1
Bartholl Sooke	1

m 17]

John White	1
Widd Hargraues	3
Wreaburn Wildman	1
Joseph Richardson	1
Jonathan Rhoades	2
Thomas Lister Jun	1
Robert Dobson	2
James Turton	1
	102

Omitted by reason of Poverty	4

Robert Corner Collr
John Foster Const

Nostall

The Hall	24
The Walke Milne	1
Thomas Topham	3
	28

Robert Corner Collr
Samuell Oxley Const

Notton

George Senyer	1
Thomas Turton	1
George Schoaley	1
John Rhoades & forge	3
Wm Totty	2
Elias Kay	1
Thomas Ellis	3
John Denton	1
Robert Foster	2
John Totty	2
John Gill	3
Thomas Heaton	1
Widdow Shawe	1
John Shawe	2
Widdow Hogley	1
Widdow Remington	4
Willm Green	1
Widd Milner	2
Richard Tottey	1
Widdow Elliot	2
Willm Dyson	1
Luke Winter	1
Nathanll Dyson	1
Robert Elliot	3
Henry Ellis	1
John Hutchinson	1
Joshua Milner	1
Henry Moore	1
Willm Heaton	4
Thomas Turner	2
	51

Thomas Midleton Collr
Nathanll Dodgson Const

Oxspringe (Oxspring)

Francis Morton	4
Francis Marsden	2
Jonathan Cocke	3
Jonas Cocke	1
Thomas Pashley	1
John Earnshaw	1
Christopr Green Milnr	1
Robert Ellis	1
Willm Burgan	1
John Earnshaw	1
Willm Wyley	1
Jon Michill	1
Edmond Rodwell	1
John Hall	2
Richard Wyley	1

m 18]

John Watson	1
Robert Thornley	1
Widdow Streete	1
Ham Cartwright	1
Francis Bugan	3
Ralph Cock	2
Samll Ridgley	2
Robert Marsden	1
	34

Robt More Collr
Hamnet Cartwright Const

Penistone

Henry Swift Cler	5
Josias Wadsworth	7
Ambros Wadsworth	4
Thomas Greaues	5
Mary Rawbuck	3
John Bever	2
Ralph Mathewman	2
Jonathan Wadsworth	3

Widdow Wadsworth	2
John West	1
Robert Marsden	1
John Thirkill	1
John Watson	1
John Thirkill	1
Robert Marsden	1
Willm Shaw	2
Mr Shaw	2
Abraham Beaver	2
Widdow Cooke	1
Thomas Mitchill	1
John Bawmforth	1
John Mitchill	2
Richard Rhoades	1
John Jessopp	2
John Morton	1
John Wadsworth	2
Thomas Graues	1
Mathew Rawbuck	1
	58

Robert Bennet Collr
John West Const

Ryall
(Ryhill)

John Gill	2
Anthony Shepherd	1
Jerem Waring	2
Widdow Robinson	2
Samuell Scholey	2
Edward Booth	
John Winter or}	2
James Rhoads}	
Widdow Carr	1
Willm Heath	4
Widdow Rawson	4
Thomas Owram	3
George Senyer	4
Thomas Calverley & forg	3
George North	1
John Hurst	1
John Tomlinson	1
Widdow Dautrey	1
George Hunte	1
Mr Kent	6
John Brownley	3
Thomas Broadley	1
Edward Lambert	2
The Hall	1
Benjamin Arnold	1

m 19]

James Abbot and forg	2
Willm Scholey & forg	3
Thomas Wainewright	1
	56

The person undernamed is discharged by Certificate

Isabell Story Widd	2

Robert Corner Collr
Thomas Bradley Const

Royston

Mr John Dutton Cler	4
Mr John Wood	6
Isaac Hepworth	4
Widdow Marsh	2
Robert Speed	3
Thomas Barkinshawe	1
George Bramhall	2
Jarvas Bramhall	2
John Feather	2
Francis Woodhouse	2
John Senyer	3
John Scruce	1
Jonas Tompson	1
Thomas Wainwright	2
Willm Feares	1
Richard Mackin	1
John Senjor	1
Henry Burnley	1
Jarvas Hurst	1
Thomas Crosley	1
Thomas Massey	1
Francis More	2
John Denton	1
John Moore	1
Robert More	1
Richard Rowley	1
Robert Broadhead	1
John Higham	2
Lancellot Stublin	1
Richard Rowley	1
Thomas Simpson	1
	54

These persons following are discharged by Certificates

John Broadhead	1
Widd Birkhead	1
Mary Gill	2

Robert Corner Collr
Henry Burnley Const

Silkstone
(Silkstone)

Mr Shearman	7
Mr Winwood	6
Mr Francis Burdet	3
Mr Francis Burdet	6
Noble Thorpp	5
Mr Scot pro John Pilmay	4
Henry Lee	3
John Coudwell	4
John Lee	4
John Hurst and Timothy	4
Richard Wood	4
John Hawkesworth	2
John Burditt	4
Abraham Hawksworth	2
John Hawksworth	1
Robert Downeing	3

m 20]

Widdow Tennand	4
John Horsfeild	2

Hugh Walker	3 three
Willm Turton	1
Hugh Burgon	1
Willm Lawson	1
Leonard Burgas	3
Thomas Didsbury	2
Widdow Hurst More Topp	1
Edmond Dolliffe	1
Nichollas Slack	1
Francis Hinchcliff	1
Richard Laycocke	1
John Streete	1
Francis Lawson	1
Widdow More	1
Henry Robinson	1
Richd Burdett	3
Francis Bockey	1
Richd Charlesworth	2
Richd Ottey	1
Joseph Broadhead	1
Robert Burgon	2
James Downing	1
Abraham Lockwood	1
Joseph Hawksworth	1
Thomas Pimperton	1
	102

Omitted by reason of Poverty	1

Robert More Collr
Robert Burgan Const

South Enley (South Hiendley)

Mr Burrey	12
Michaell Lambe	4
Edward Binington	3
Mathias Oxley	1
Mathew Clarke	3
Willm Beadome	1
Nicholas Tensley	1
Willm Horncastle	1
Richard Dewhurst	1
Alice Wager	1
Thomas Hudlestone	1
John Shepherd	1
John Beetham	1
John Matson	1
Willm Batison	1
Jonas Shepherd	1
Mr Jerem Milner	2
Robert Wright	1
John Swift	2
Richard Crosley	3
Jonas Downes	1
Ralph Downes	1
Thomas Dodgson	2
James Green	2
Thomas Firth	1
Michaell Battison	1
Phillp Shillitoe	1
Edward Barker	2
Michaell Hall	1
Edward Green	2
Steven Cuttell	2
Richard Senyer	1
Thomas Greene	1
Willm Downes	1
Willm Allon	1

m 21]

Empty and noe distress to be had

Mr Goodson	1
Wm Allon	1

Thomas Midleton Collr
James Green Const

Shafton

Widdow Marshall	1
John Marshall	5
Joseph Swift	3
Brian Medley	1
Thomas Gibson	3
Doctor Bury	3
Joseph Hodgson	2
Henry Pitt	1
Lancellot Jubb	1
John Beavers	1
Henry Wroe	2
Willm Horne	3
John Twigg	2
John Walker	2
Thomas Coldwell	2
Widow Dunwell	1
Judeth Clarkson	2
John Child	2
Richard Gill	5
Thomas Twigg	1
Peter Armroyd	1
Thomas Hardman	1
	45

Thomas Midleton Collr
Joseph Hodgson Const

Stainbrough (Stainborough)

Sir Jarvas Cutler	6
Mr Morton	4
Mrs West	5
Richard Walker	7
Willm Creswick	4
John Birkhead	3
Henry Hawksworth	1
John Moxon	1
Adam Ward	1
Adam Wadsworth	2
John Tompson	1
John Birkhead	2
Willm Hawkesworth	1
Anne Hawkesworth	1
Richard Beardsall and forge	2
Henry Trickett	1
George Moxon	1
Willm Woodcocke	1
John Norcliffe	1
Daniell Silverwood	1
Richard Wood	1
	47

The person undernamed is discharged by Certificate

John Bargas	2

Robert Corner Collr
Richard Beardsell Const

Tankersley

The Earle Strafford	25
Mr Nicholas Graues	5
Jarvas Woodhead	3
John Hill	3

m 22]

Willm Clarke	4
John Beale	1
Thomas Blackamore	1
John Dobson	1
Willm Parkins	1
Willm Greene	1
John Nicholson	2
Wm Milner	1
Richd Beamond	2
John Firth	2
Willm Woodhead	1
Thomas Smith	2
Robert Parkins	3
George Archdale	4
Daniell Patrick	1
Robert Aunt	2
Richard Smith	2
Nichollas Richardson	1
Widdow Ellmhurst	1
Christopr Wood	1
Thomas Savill	3
Thomas Linley	1
Willm Langley	3
Nicholas Rhoades	2
Robert Wilson	1
John Harrison	1
Widdow Smith	1
Daniell Pattrick	3
Willm Green	2
Richard Woodhead	1
John Atkinson	2
	90

Robert Corner Collr
Willm Green Const

Thurguland (Thurgoland)

Mr Thomas Reareforth	9
Mr Samll Savill	8
Francis Buckley	1
Mr Morton	2
John Kay	2
Edward Hudson	1
John Hawksworth	5
John Woodcock	1
Willm Rich	1
Samuell Streete	3
John Lee	2
John Ellis	1
John Slacke	2
Steven Greene	3
Widdow Chappell	1
John Wilson	2
George Swift	1
Widdow Lee	2
Widdow Flather & forge	4
Henry Parkinshaw	2
Willm Sowerby	1
John Wadsworth	2
	two
Widdow Flather	1
James Browne or Bower	1
Richd Milnethorp or}	2
George Moxson}	
Edward Walton	2
Widdow Moxon	1

m 23]

Adam Dickson	1
John Webster	1
Henry Walker	1
Robert Askue	2
Richard Milnthorpe	1
Widdow Walker	1
Widdow Clayton	1
Henry Walker	1
Ellias Morton	1
Robert Ambler	1
Willm Coldwell	1
Thomas Grayforth	1
James Burland	1
George Viccars	1
John Hargraues	1
James Hurst	1
Thomas Swaine	1
Thomas Machin	1
	82

Empty and noe distres to be had

Edward Smith	3

Omitted by reason of Poverty	2

Robert Bennet Collr
Samuell Streete Const

Thurlston (Thurlstone)

Mr Salvanus Rich	6
Willm Rich	3
John Cordwell	2
Edward Rich Jun	1
Reynold Apleyard	2
Thomas Bray	3
Willm Apleyard	2
Richard Greene	1
John Wainwright	1
John Milnes	1
Ralph Milns	1
James Mitchill	1
John Moorehouse	1
Rheynold Rich	1
Willm Wadsworth	2
Francis Haigh	3
Willm Haigh	2

Ralph Marsden 1
Thomas Ellis 2
James Marsden 1
Joseph Lambert 1
Willm Horsell 1
John Haigh 1
James Cropper 1
Joseph Tayler 1
Edmond Wallis 5
five
Willm Beaver 5
George Morton 3
John Haigh sen 2
Willm Haigh 2
David Graues 1
Edward Hellewell 1
Edward Rich sen 1
Richard Marshall 1
Nichollas Sanderson 1
Joseph Otheram 1
Edward Benyson 1
John Shaw 1
Edward Francke 1
John Senyer 3

m 24]

Widdow Swallow 1
John Batty 1
Robert Hobson 1
Edmond Tayler 1
Thomas Hinchcliffe 3
Sarah Saunderson 1
Thomas Haigh 4
Richard Marsden 3
John Rich 1
John Marsden 1
Daniell Rich 3
Paull Graves 2
Widdow Smith 1
Widdow Milnes 1
George Laughton or Laugton 1
Joseph Linley 1
Widdow Outheram 1
Richard Henry 1
Widdow Henry 1
Thomas Walker 1
John Smith 1
Francis Batty 1
Daniell Rich 1
Richard Hemingley 1
Joseph Hooley 1
106

Robt More Collr
James Marsden Const

Wooley (Woolley)

John Wentworth Esqr 13
James Coates 1
Anne Headon 2
Joseph Cranshaw 8
Richard Burnley 1
Anthony Crawshaw 2
Thomas Hawcroft 2
Richard Webb 2
Richard Scaife 1
Thomas Ellis 4
Samuell Greenwood 2
John Fretwell 1
Samuell Burley 1
John Oddy 1
Mathew Webster 1
Anthony Crawshaw Jun 1
Joseph Olleyes 1
Thomas Preistley 1
Willm Hilton 3
Richard Clarke Jun 2
John Totty 2
John Hawcroft 1
Widdow Breare 4
Thomas Wood 2
Richard Haigh 2
Edmond Bace or Race 1
Thomas Hutchinson 1
Widdow Penington 1
John Cusworth 1
Richard Lambe 6
Anthony Lacocke 3
Mr George Wheatley 7
Edward Howden 3
Mary Brownley 4
Francis Ball 1
George Hutchinson 3
Thomas Scaife 1
Henry Longley 1
Robert Arnold 4
Samuell Willey 1
Robert Olley 1
Emanuell Foster 2
Henry Dyson 1

m 25]

Willm Lee 1
Sir Thomas Wentworth 6
Mathew Prince 5
Richard Langley 2
117

These persons following are discharged by Certificates
Willm Tayler 1
Francis Midleton 1
Thomas Bingley 2
Willm Longley 2
Widdow Hinchcliffe 2

Robert More Collr
Thomas English Const

Worsbrough

Henry Edmonds Esqr 13
Mr Woodworth 9
Ellias Oxley 1
Widdow Bradley 4
Joseph Linley 1
Robert Oxley 1
Francis Hall 2
John Allott 8
Jarvis Parkins 3
Willm Tattersall 1

Widdow Watson 1
John Secker 2
Edward Rocke 2
Richard Parkins 2
Thomas Cawthoran 4
Richard Ellis 1
Robert Tayler 8
John Ellis 3
John Robinson 1
John Hall 1
Jonath Rayner 3
Thomas Oxley 3
Mr Richard Ellmhurst 2
James Wilcock 4
Robert Linley 1
Richard Todington 2
Gilbert Irish 2
Widdow Wilcock 1
John Wilson 2
Joseph Shaw 1
Widdow Heesom 3
Anthony Robinson 1
Widdow Woodhead 1
Richard Tottington Jun 1
Jonathan Rheynold Jun 1
Thomas Smith 1
Christopr Foster 1
John Butteroyd 1
Robert Ellison 2
Daniell Ellis 4
Willm Beckit 3
Thomas Catling 1
Fancis Smith 1
Willm Beckit 3
Robert Parkins 1
John Bingley 4
John Cudworth 1
George Wood 1
Willm Eastwood 2
Widdow Hall 2
Robert Copley 4
John Cawood 2
Roger Willey 2
Joseph Crosland 1
Widdow Carr sen 3
Leonard Sissons 4
John Carrington 4

m 26]

John South 2
John Sterman 2
James Usherworth 1
Thomas Hinch 3
Edward Crawshaw 3
Mr Jarvas Rockley 6
Widdow Bingley 4
Roger Cowood 3
Richard Tattington 3
James Barnley 4
Francis Savill 2
Widdow Hesletine 3
Widdow Pogson 1
James Wildsmith 2
Thomas Revill 1
John Baxter 1
Willm Skyers 4
Mr Richard Rockley 3
Willm Pogson Jun 1
Worsbrough Milne 1
Mr Hayforth and others 2
John Robinson 1
Thomas Wildsmith 1
Joseph Shaw 2
John Pashley 1
Thomas Wood 2
Robert Wood 1
Jona Guest 1
Widdow Rockley 1
Thomas Smith 1
Willm Ashmore 2
Patrick Gibson 2
Francis Bedford 2
Abraham Rock 1
George Woodhead 1
233

Certified for
John Turton 1
John Woodhead 1
John Tottington 1
Wllm Mellord 1
Thomas Shaw 1
5

Thomas Middleton Collr
George Wood Const

Wintersett

Mr Willm Champney 4
Edmond Scoalrey 1
Mathew Beamond 1
Abraham Aspiner 1
George Brownell and}
Willm Champney} 4
George Schoaley 2
James Woffenden 1
Thomas Barber Jun 1
John Blackburne 4
Margret Schoalemekr 1
Thomas Barber Jun 3
Robert Fish 1
Edward Jenkinson Jun 2
Edward Jenkinson sen 1
John Huntington 2
Richard Olley 1
John Topham 1
31

m 27]

Empty and no distress to be had
John Dinis or Mr Jo Barber 3

Thomas Midleton Collr
Mathew Beamont Const

Wortley

John Berrey 2
Willm Parkins 3
Godfrey Berrey 1
Widdow Berrey 2
Willm Fletcher and} 6

Samuell Hague}
Edward Fairburne 1
Thomas Dickinson 1
Willm Birkinshaw 2
Thomas and George Stones 2
John Hurst 2
John Parkins 1
John Turner 1
Robert Tayler 2
two
Willm Turner sen 1
Thomas Turner Jun 1
John Winterbotthom 2
Francis Walker 2
Thomas Turner 1
John Smith 2
Willm Gleadall 2
John Hodgson 4
Mr John Wilson 2
Willm Turner 2
John Turner 1
Francis Berrey 1
Widdow Ward 2
Richard Smith 2
Widdow Wood 3
Richard Green 4
Robert Green 1
Thomas Whittells 1
Widdow Laycocke 3
Ambros Wood 1
Richard Swindin 1
Henry Hurst 2
Willm Booth 1
Willm Greene 2
John Hinchcliffe 1
John Laypage 2
Edward Bramall 2
Mrs Wortley 2
John Smith 5
Nichollas Ludham 2
Widdow Wainwright 1
Thomas Wainwright 1
Wortley Hall 18
John Neverson 4
John Eatam 1
Richard Bingley 1
Willm Smith 1
Thomas Bingley 2
Francis Broadbent 1
Thomas Hall 1
John Walker 2
Nichollas Cocke 1
Samuell Moxon 2
John Harrison 2
Widd Walker 1
Willm Baumforth 1
Richard Walker 3
Thomas Walker 4
Sparling Birkinshaw 1
John Stainland 4
Thomas Windle 2
Robert Cundy 5
James Topham 2
Richard Stead 2
Widdow Bland 4
Widdow Hagnet forg 2
Thomas Gershame 2
Edward Gillot 1
Willm Birkinshawe 2
John Sharpe 1
Willm Eaton 3
Edward Windle 1
Widdow Eaton 1
Thomas Archdale 1
The Milne 1
John Broadbent 1
Arthur Sutcliff 1
Martin Hattersley 3
Richard Turner in ye parke 1
Willm Wood 3
Richard Hurst 1
176

Empty and no distress to be had
Sir Francis Wortley heires 1

These persons following are discharged by Certificates
Thomas Sharpe 1
Richard Turner 1

Thomas Midleton Collr
John Ayreton Const

Strafforth and Tickhill Wapentake

The National Archives, E179/262/15

m 1]

Strafford and Tickill Weapontacke (Strafforth and Tickhill Wapentake)

Adwick upon Dearne

Widdow Revill	2
Widdow Begley	2
Richard Trippit	1
Willm Wharram	1
John Bingley	2
Margret Revill	1
John Hawitt	1
Widdow Hogley	2
Widdow Axe	1
Godfrey Hogley	1
Widdow Bingley	1
Widdow Mellory	1
Thomas Lambert	1
Widdow Wharram	1
Widdow Liversidge	1
Willm Whittacris	1
Thomas Whittacris	2
John Cooke	3
Thomas Golland	1
Major Rearbey	2
	28

Omitted by reason of poverty 1

Thomas Midleton Collr
Thomas Golland Const

Aldwark (Aldwarke)

Francis Faljambe Esqr	17
Robert Moore Collr	
Sqire Foljambe Const	

Armthorp (Armthorpe)

Thomas Winter	1
John Baggeley	1
Sir Thomas Daniell	1
Mr Holmes	5
Richard Fostard	1
John Sharpe	2
George Scholey	3[214] three
Robert Newshome	1
Richard Plumley	1
Widdow Watson	5
Martha Winter	1
George Scholey	2
John Scholefeild	1
Thomas Adams	1
Francis Stabbs	1
Richard Hudson & forge	2
George Newshome	1
Sir Thomas Daniell	1
George Scholey	1
Richard Stabbs	3
Elizabeth Stabbs	1

m 2]

Francis Silvester	2
John Cartis	1
George Newshome	1
Richard Newsham	1
John Wilson	1
Widdow Ovtbridge	2
Phillip Newshome	1
Henry Stainton	1
Robert Newsom	3
Thomas Law	2
	51

Empty & noe distress to be had 1[215]
Sir Thomas Danielle 1

Omitted by reason of poverty 7

Thomas Midleton Collr
John Schoalfeild Const

Aukley (Auckley)

Mr Levens	2
Widdow Tuke	1
Richard Shemeld	1
Thomas Taylor	1
Willm Thompson	1
Thomas Tuke	2
Mr John Killam	3
Henry Barton	2
Robert Ledgart	2
Willm Wright	2
Willm Woodhead	1
John Robinson	1
Willm Killam	1
Francis Shemeld	3
Thomas Loynd	1
Robert Sedday	1
	25

Robert Bennet Collr
Robert Ledgart Const

[214] 3 written over 5.
[215] sic.

Austerfeild (Austerfield)

Thomas Hides	1
Widdow Revill	2
John Weston	1
Francis Coulson	1
Francis Whittacris	1
Willm Ellis	1
Thomas Vessey	2
Ann Moore	1
Willm Baines	1
Widdow Hall	2
John Blegate	2
Willm Holegate	1
Willm Batterick	2
Mr Robert Wigglesworth	2
George Smith	1
Willm Chapman	1
George Skinner	2
John Smith	1

m 3]

Judith Hall	3
Bryan Moore	2
Bryan Drewry	2
Willm Briggs	3
Thomas Hoyland	5
Willm Vessey	1
George Vessey	2
Thomas Barton	1
Willm Grindall	1
Willm Ellis	2
John Whittacre	1
	48

Empty and noe distress to be had

Eliz Drewry	1
Mr Lister	1
Willm Holegate forge	1

Omitted by reason of poverty 4

Robert Bennet Collr
Robert Drewrey Const

Ashton cum Aughton (Aston with Aughton)

The Honrble Coniers Darcy Esqr	27
Mr West	8
John Hill	3
Mrs Fletcher	8
Mr Willowby	6
Richard Kelke	2
Widdow Chapman	2
Nicholas Keney	3
Henry Wood	2
John Liddall	1
Willm Petty	2
Richard Roulston	4
George Inkersall	4
Elizabeth Grime	1
John Simmes	1
John Ball	2
John Morton	1
Thomas Kenney	1
Jarvas Kippax	1
Francis Petty	2
George Morehouse	3
Robert Ellis	1
Edward Morton	1
Anthony Davy	1
Phillip Challoner	6
Arthur Air	3
Nichollas Schoaley Senr	3
Robert Micach	1
Nicholas Scoaley	2
Godfray Schoaley	1
George Wilkinson	1
Thomas Jenkinson	1
Thomas Hemingway	1
John Abdy	7
Gilbert Dudsbury	2

m 4]

Francis Duckinfeild	1
James Hobson	2
Willm Rushby	1
Richard Baley	1
Thomas Schoaley	2
Robert Schoaley	1
Nicholas Linley	1
Mr Spencer	1
James Simonett	2
Francis Simonett	2
Edmond Chamney Junr	1
Widdow Morton	1
Willm Youle	1
Richard Schoaley	3
Edward Kestin	2
	137

Empty and noe distress to be had

Thomas Herring	1

Omitted by reason of poverty 11

Robert Benit Collr
James Hobson Const

Attercliffe cum Darnell (Attercliffe and Darnall)

Sir John Bright	17
Willm Spencer Esqr	11
John Fretwell	7
Richard Nicholson	6
George Carr	3
Godfrey Smith	1
Richard Laughton	2
Widdow Smith	2
Thomas Marsh	2
Widdow Marsh	2[216] two
Thomas Morton	1

[216] 2 written over 1.

John Sparke 1
Thomas Booth 2
Thomas Hunt 3
Widdow Walker 4
John Rogers 1
George Challoner 2
Hugh Challoner 1
Allexandr Jarvis 2
George Ludlam 4
Thomas Horobin 1
Widdow Cooper 1
Joseph Beldom 1
George Parkin 1
Joseph Kent 1
John Stainforth 7
Robert Booth 2
Richard Newburne 1

m 5]

John Shepherd 1
Willm Bawmforth 3
Robert Bawmforth 1
Richard Revill 1
George Hibbard 2
Robert Horner 3
George Bullas 1
Edward Swift 2
Willm Newburne 2
Willm Stainforth 2
John Rose 2
Thomas Kickson 1
John Ramskor 2
Joseph Beighton 1
John Barbor 1
John Holland 1
George Holland 1
George Bradbury 1
Thomas Pearson 2
Robert Parkin 1
John Pogmore 1
John Newbald 1
Widdow Sawerby 1

Widdow Knot 1
George Hibbard 1
Widdow Nicholson 3
Joseph Nicholson 3
Mr Anthony Berrey 11
James Smith 4
Humphrey Almond 1
Willm Levick 1
James Newbald 1
John Green 3
Thomas Scargill 1
John Baite 3
Willm Dungworth 1
John Willy 1
John Bramhall 3
Stephen Carr 4
Thomas Challoner 1
Willm Marshland 3
Willm Stainforth 4
David Lee 3
Nichollas Swift 1
John Bullas 2
Ellias Carr 2
Samuell Barker 1
Robert Shaw 3
John Urin 2

m 6]

Willm Sellick 3
Willm Dungworth 3
Widdow Highley 1
Samuell Stainforth 4
George Brewell 1
Jos Walton 1
John Twigg 1
Mr Bloome 6
James Wilson 3
Joseph Topliffe 1
Thomas Purd 1
Mathew Oakes 2
Robert Turner 2
Thomas Wood 2

Widdow Rhoades 2
Widdow Rhoades 2[217]
Robert Beighton 1
Samuell Chadwick 1
Willm Smith 3
James Holmes 2
229

Empty and noe distres to be had
Mr Chappell 1
Thomas Newbald 1
Mr Willm Spencer 4
John Boyes 1

These persons following are discharged by Certifts
Willm Woodhouse 1
John Stainforth 1
Widdow Stainforth 1
Widdow Longley 2
Nicholas Smith and forge 2
Willm Penistone 1
John Staycie 3
John Gotherd 1
Thomas Stacie 1
Widdow Beighton 1
James Newbald & forge 3
Widdow Stainforth 1
Richard Austick 2
Johnson & 3
Godfrey Bright 2
Roger Ausburne 1
Thomas Sowerby 1
Robert Steele 2

Omitted by reason of poverty 5

Robert Moore Collr
Willm Dungworth Const

217 sic.

These persons following are the Cutlers belonging to Shefeild who deposited the duty for their Forges but refused to pay the Money without a Tryall at Law

m 7]

Widdow Knott	1
John Fretwell	1
George Carr	1
Richard Laughton	1
Widdow Smith	2
Thomas Marsh	1
John Sparke	1
Thomas Hunt	1
Thomas Horobin	1
Joseph Beldom	1
George Parkin	1
Joseph Kent	1
Richard Newburne	1
Willm Bawmforth	1
George Hibbard	2
George Bullas	1
Joseph Beighton	1
John Barber	1
John Holland	1
George Holland	1
Robert Parkin	1
John Newbald	1
John Green	2
Thomas Scargill	2
John Bate	1
Thomas Challoner	2[218] two
John Bullas	1
Elias Carr	1
Robert Shay	1
John Urin	1
Willm Dungworth	1
John Twigg	1
Joseph Topcliff	2
Thomas Purd	2
Robert Beighton	1
Samuell Chadwick	1
Willm Smith	2
James Newbald	1
	46

Adwicke de Streete (Adwick le Street)

Mr Washington	16
Richard Sayle	1
John Harrison	1
Anne Sayle	1
Godfrey Clarke	1
The Lady Adams	2
Thomas Clarke	2
Robert Stones	4
George Jenings	2
Widdow France	1
George Maud	3
Richard Slack	2
Francis Grant	1
Paul Inkalsall	2
Thomas France	1
John Lewin	1
Robert Dey	1
Thomas Sayle	2
Thomas Shirtclyffe	4
Darcey Clarke	3

m 8]

Thomas Bradforth	1
Willm Furnish	3
James Best	1
Willm Atkinson	1
Thomas Moody	1
Thomas Mangold	1
Mr Weshington	3
Mr Harrison Cler	3
Willm Sayle	1
Joseph Marshall	1
Richard Rymer	1
Jane France	2
John Clarke	1
Mathew Hurst	1
Walter Thackeray	1
Christopr Harrison	2
George Maude	1
James Butterwood	1
Thomas Foster	1
Thomas Clarke	1
John Whitacrs	1
	80

The person vndernamed is discharged by Certfte

Dary Atkinson	1

Omitted by reason of poverty	3

Robt More Collr
John Whitacres Const

Anston cum Membris (Anston with members)

Widdow Roewood	1
Widdow Kippax	1
John Bland	2
Robert Kitchin	3
George Johnson	1
John Watkinson	1
Isaac Sculthrop	2
Robert Clarke	2
Widdow Kirshawe	1[219] one
Edward Pagden	1
John Sampson	1
Arthur Pearson	3

[218] 2 written over 1.
[219] 1 written over 2.

Michaell Hesle	1
Thomas Fox	1
George Johnson	2
Willm Ellis	4
Humphrey Bins	1
Willm Wright	2
Oliver Heptenstall	1
John Clarke	1
Thomas Baites	1
George Norlidge	2
Willm Roebuck	3
Thomas Newbald	1
Robert Wright	4
John Booth	1
Thomas Fox	2
Robert Kitchin	2
Thomas Johnson	1
Richard Walker	1
Richard Johnson	1
John Revill	1
Nicholas Linley	1
Captaine Kirke	5
Willm Linley	1
John Kirke	2
Richard Jepson	3
Thomas Linley	1

m 9]

Richard Booth	1
Willm Rogers	1
Isabell Garland	1
John Sikes	1
Martin Parr	1
John Wild	2
Mrs Hutton	7
Robert Rogers	1
Joseph Sculthorp	2
Thomas Parkins	2
Jarvice Wareing	1
Willm Whitehead	1
Willm Wood	1
Jarvice Battersby	1
Ann Kirke	1
Jarvice Battersby	1
Mrs Millenex	8
Roger Holland	1
Mr Burdin	11
Robert Lister	1
	111

Empty and noe distress to be had

John Ramsden	2
in ye Church	1

Omitted by reason of poverty 10

Robert Bennet Collr
Robert Lister Const

Brampton Bierlow

Nicholas Pearson	3
Willm Beckitt	1
Widdow Pate	1
Thomas Goodall	1
John Lissan	2
Robert Lyle	1
Widdow Cornelley	1
Richard Walker	3
Willm Pearson	1
Richard Hill	2
Jane Ward	4
John Beckitt	1
Willm Ellam	1
Nicholas Goodarr	1
John Wormley	4
Willm Heward	2
Thomas Waide	1
John Shipherd	2
Jonas Maud	1
Widdow Bloome	1
John Firth	1
Jarvice Parkin	1
Willm Roebucke	3
George Chappell	2
Widdow Hudson	1
Brampton Hall	7
Thomas Baxter	1
Christopher Foulston	1

m 10]

John Schoaley	2
John Carr	2
Richard Ellison	1
Hugh Allen	1
Joseph Hawinshaw	1
Robert Pitts	1
John Taylor	2
Willm Wadsworth	1
Widdow Hattersley	2
Willm Skyars	4
Robert Stanistreet	3
Richard Marshall	4
Phillip Flint	1
John Tinsley	1
Ann Shaw	1
Mr Baxter	5
Willm Slack	4
Thomas Hutchinson	1
Widdow Hudson	1
Thomas Hewitt	1
Robert Hudson	1
Thomas Cawthorne	1
Thomas Tyas	1
Edward Forth Jnr	1
John Ellam	4
Willm Coss	1
George Fowston	3
Richard Karr	2
Richard Gawrill	2
Richard Coss	1
Humphrey Jackson	2
	109

Empty and noe distress to be had

the Ld Strafford	3
Robert Hudson	1
John Ellam Mill	1

Omitted by reason of poverty 8

Thomas Midleton Collr
Robert Lyle Constable

Brightside Byerley (Brightside Bierlow)

Robert Hoole	4
Robert Hoole	3
Edward Hill	2
Nathanll Robinson	2
John Marshland	5
Widdow Hart	1
Widdow Wilkinson	3
Nichollas Taylor	2
John Shemeld	4
Edward Hill	3
George Wilkinson	3
James Adames	1
Edmond Barker	2
Edward Hill	2
Edmond Barker	1
Willm Denton	1
Ellias Loyd	2
Henry Nott Sen	2
Henry Nott Jun	1
John Archdale	1
Robert Robinson	1
Henry Smith	1
Widdow Barnsley	6

m 10]

Widdow Hall	1
Joshua Barnsley	2
Robert Stacy	3
John Brownill	1
Willm Brownill	2
John Bright	3
Widdow Barnsley	2
John Gray	1
John Hill	2
John Burgon	1
John Robinson	2
Ralph Hides	2
John Pearson	2
Widdow Pearson	1
John Pearson	2
Widdow Fox	1
Robert Bownes	5
Josua Shaw	4
Robert Downes	1
George Machin	3
Mr Haudcock	7
Edward Lambe	1
Francis Baley	1
John Graves	2
Widdow Thompson	2
John Havdcock	3
John Marsden	1
Josep Capper	5
Joseph Capper	1
Robert Swift	1
John Ashforth	1
Edward Thompson	1
Georg Hobson	2
Francis Woolhous	1
Widdow Hill	1
John Wildsmith	6
Widdow Wilkinson	2
Ralph Carr	1
Willm Ronkesley	1
Willm Shirtcliff	1
Robert Allon	5
Willm Mason	3
Richard Shirtcliff	2
Ralph Wildsmith	3
Obadiah Treeton	2
Thomas Broadbelt	1
James Dawson	1
Timothy Stacie	3
Hugh Webster	1
Willm Penley	1
Jonathan Webster	1
Mr George Wild	4
Henry Cawton	3
Widdow Rhoades	5
Mr Copley	1
Robert Allon	1
	172

Empty and noe distress to be had

Francis Barley	4
Malin Sowerby	1
Joseph Caper	2

m 12]

These persons following are discharged by Certificates

Thomas Dowfin	1
James Hinch	1
Widdow Hobson	1
George Crux	1
John Sands	1

Omitted by reason of Poverty 24

Robert Moore Collr
George Wild Const

These persons following are the Cutlers belonging to Sheffeild who deposited for their forges but refused to pay ye money without a Tryall at law

Robert Hole	1
Nathanll Robinson	1
Widdow Hart	1
Widdow Wilkinson	2
Willm Denton	1
Elias Loyd	1
Robert Robinson	1
Henry Smith	1
Widdow Barnsley	1
Joshua Barnsley	1
John Burgon	1
John Robinson	1
George Machin	3
Edward Lambe	1
John Graues	2
Widdow Tompson	1
Joseph Capper or Jon Tomson	1
Edward Tompson	1
Robert Allen	1
Willm Mason	1

Richd Shyrtcliffe 1
Timothy Stacy 1
26

m 13]

Robert Moore Collr
George Wild Const

Bradfeild Parish
(Bradfield Parish)

Richard Brunshead 3
John Smalfeild 1
Thomas Stead 2
Willm Hobson 1
Mr Fox 5
Robert Ward 5
John Gold 1
Willm Hudson 4
Robert Stones 1
Widdow Brunshead 2
John Corbidge 1
Thomas Lockwood 1
Willm Bagshey 1
Thomas Oxley 1
Henry Brumchead 1
Georg Dungworth 1
Widdow Sanderson 1
Edward Hudson 1
Willm Wadsworth 3
Widdow Hinchcliffe 3
John Parkins 3
Nicholas Ibbotson 2
Abram Slack 3
Rowland Midleton 2
Willm Crossley 1
John Dodworth 1
Thomas Bilcliff 1
Reynold Hawkworth 2
Willm Matley 2
Richard Burley 1
Mathew Hill 1
Edward Adamson 3
Edward Adamson Junr 1
Widdow Whitley 1
John Hey 1
Richard Watterhouse 1
Robert Hague 1
George Thompson 1
Ralph Hoyle 1
Willm Harrison 2
Walter Hirst 1
Nicholas Fearnley 1
John Ibbitson 3
Anthony Warrall 1
Robert Ayre 2
Adam Hawkesworth 2
Willm Hawkesworth 1
Richard Mellor 1
Mr Greaves 6
Robert Haukesworth 2
Thomas Loxley Junr 1

m 14]

Richard Ibberson 3
Thomas Marsden 1
James Rongsley 3
Widdow Revill 2
Edward Swinden 2
Joseph Marriot 2
Widdow Graves 1
John Hudson 1
Christopher Yellot 3
Richard Hancocke 1
Willm Swickitt 1
John Beighton 3
Ralph Brunchead 2
Robert Shaw Jun 1
John Whitehead 1
Thomas Ibberson 1
Thomas Rigg 1
Francis Hawksworth 2
Francis Hellewell 1
Anthony Worrall Sen 2
Thomas Worrall 1
Richard Bacon 3
George Lee 1
John Fanshawe 1
Thomas Bocken 1
Ralph Foster sen 1
Ralph Foster Jun 1
Ralph Graues 1
John Newton 1
John Hattersley 1
Henry Hawksworth 1
John Shaw 1
George Wilcock 1
Thomas Taylor 1
John Bradshaw 1
Willm Marsh 1
Robert Bilcliff 2
John Mariot sen 2
John Mariot Jun 1
Henry Worrall 2
Steven Barbor 1
Robert Botham 1
Adam Morton 1
Willm Earnshawe 1
Mr Morewood 5
Mr Morewood 2
Thomas Potter 1
Godfrey Rowley 2
Ralph Graues 2
Robert Wainwright 1
Henry Hoyle 1
George Shawe 3
Richard Woolen 3
Richard Morehouse 1
Jonathan Shawe 2
Widdow Shawe 1
Edward Revill 3
John Revill 3
Richard Hudson 1
John Hoyland 2
John Hancock 1
Jonathan Wilson 1

m 15]

George Gilliot 2
Robert Ayre 3
Willm Woolen 1
Francis Taylor 5
Willm Bacon 1

Edward Ayre 1
Thomas Shaw sen 1
Thomas Shaw Jun 1
Willm Hoyland 2
John Revill 1
Edward Revill 1
George Hoyland 2
Widdow Rawson 2
John Bacon 2
Robert Shaw 1
Thomas Cutbert 1
Robert Shaw 1
Abraham Sendus 1
Widdow Burdikin 1
Henry Shaw 1
Willm Hoyland 1
George Shawe 3
John Hoyland 1
John Hoyland Jun 1
John Bacon 4
Edward Bramall 3
Willm Shaw 2

Staveington (Stannington)

Thomas Webster 3
Widdow Lord 3
Francis Fenton 1
Francis Barbar 2
Hugh Lockwood 1
John Oates 1
George Marriot 1
Joseph Dungworth 1
Nichollas Bower 1
Humphr Marshall 1
John Wheatby 1
Richard Hawksworth 1
George Greaues 2
George Steven 1
Willm Dungworth 2
Thomas Dungworth 2
Hugh Webster 1
Richard Hoyland 2
Francis Hoyland 1
Willm Crapper 1

Francis Dungworth 1
Willm Bockin 2
John Drabb 1
Henry Booth 1
Willm Hawksworth 2
Mr Revill 6
Thomas Hill 1
Widdow Revill 1
John Wainewright 1
Willm Creswick 1

m 16]

Hellin Scargill 1
Richard Greaues 1
John Hall 1
Rowland Bramall 2
John Wildsmith 2
John Britlebanke 1
Thomas Hague 1
Willm Littlewood 1
Willm Ibberson 1
Willm Grey 1
Thomas Creswick 5
Widdow Swinden 1
Francis Creswicke 1
Richard Greaues 2
Christopr Hawkesworth 1
Edward Brumby 2
Mr Millar 1
John Marsden 1
Willm Marsh 1
Nichollas Morton 1
John Marriott 3
Rowland Bramald 1
George Smith 1
Willm Shaw 4
Ralph Greaues 2
Edwd Hinchcliffe 1
Edwd Bramald 2
Richd Revill 1
John Ibbittson 1
Edward Wainewright 1
Henry Trickitt 2
Francis Roughsby 1

John Smith 1
Edward Hall 1
Thomas Darwent 1
Robert Hartley 1
Francis Drable 1
Willm Greaues 3
John Sikes 2
Henry Marsden 1
Christopr Greaues 2
John Brunshead 1

Waldeshelfe (Waldershelf)

Daniell Rich 4
Willm Cooke 2
Widdow Cooke 1
Martin Jepson 1
Ralph Saunderson 4
Thomas Hattersby 3
John Wainwright 5
Joseph Charlsworth 1
John Downing 6
Thomas Ellis 2
John Woodhouse 1
Henry Woodhouse 1
John Swallow 1

m 17]

Robert Sanderson 3
Nichollas Hawley 1
Francis Hawley 1
George Wood 1
Thomas Roper 1
John Hide 1
Nichollas Walker 3
John Broadhead 1
James Marsden 1
George Coldwell 1
Willm Hellewell 1
Mr Hawksworth 7
George Ibberson 2
John Pott 1
Thomas Ward 1
John Smith 1

Thomas Ward	4
George Mellor	1
Edward Bramald Jun	2
Nichollas Morton	1
Mr Foster	1
Mr Foster	4
Widdow Woodson	1
George Woodson	1[220]
John Wilkinson	1
Willm Wodson	2[221]
Georg Jillot	1
Godfrey Jillot	1
Mr South	3
Richard Morton	1
John Hill	1
Richard Mathewman	1
Edward Bramald	1
John Dransfeild	1
Thomas Broadhead	1
Henry Woodcocke	1
Christopr Page	1
John Senyer	2
Richard Woodhead Jun	1
Reynold Ayre	1[222]
George Hoyland	1
Richard Marton	2
Ralph Hague	1
John Brunchead	2
Reynald Robinson	1
Widdow Hawksworth	2
George Wood	1
Richard Woodhead	3
Widdow Lee	1
Willm Carr	1
John Ibberson	1
Willm Swickitt	1
Martin Stanley	1
Widdow Whitley	1
Thomas Elliot	1
Willm Tingle	1

Reynold Woodson	1
Edward Greaues	4
Arthur Fearest	2
Abraham Ibberson	2
John Stanley	1
Richard Wheelden	1
Thomas Greyson	1
Ralph Greyson	1

m 18]

Giles Shaw	1
John Marsden	1
Thomas Garlike	1
John Graves	1
Willm Croswick	1
John Creswick	1
Edmond Cocker	1
Luke Horsfeild	1
George Page	3
John Marsden	3
Abraham Ibberson	1
John Hellewell	2
John Broadhead	1
George Broadhead	1
Widdow Mathewman	1
Lord Hallifax Manr	2
Christopr Turner	1
Willm Wheeldin	1

Westnall

Mr Wilson	8
Mr Fox	4
George Woodhead	1
Willm Ibberson	1
John Hall	2
Thomas Gilliot	2
Willm Ibberson sen	1
Richard Morton	2[223] two
Henry Hawksworth	1

Thomas Marsden	2
John Marsden	1
Ambros Marsden	1
Benjam Shaw	2
John Downing	1
John Yellot	1
Jonathan Bagshawe	1
George Crawshaw	2
John Downing Jun	1
Thomas Crawshaw	1
Edward Bramall	2
Jonathan Sanderson	1
Nichollas Burley	1
Thomas Morton	1
Thomas Whitley	1
Thomas Hudson	1
Christopr Whitley	1
Mr Morton	6[224] six
John Beighton	3
Widdow Hague	1
Ralph Hudson	1
Edmond Hobson	1
Francis Watterhouse	2
Jonathan Saunderson	2
Thomas Stead	4
John Morton	3
Willm Watterhouse	3
Thomas Hudson	1
Nichollas Shaw	1
George Hall	3
Widdow Hurt	2
Thomas Hall	3
George Hall	1
Rowland Tompson	4

m 19]

Ralph Watterhouse	3
George Tompson	1

220 Line inserted.
221 Line inserted.
222 Line inserted.
223 2 written over 1.
224 6 written over 5.

Nichollas Tompson	1
Ralph Mathewman	2
Lyonell Smilter	1
Widdow Hague	1
John Hoyland	1
Joseph Rawley	1
John Darnald	1
Edmond Watterhouse	2
John Rawley	1
Reynold Tompson	1
Thomas Gregory	2
Henry Hudson	1
James Street	1
Mr Stead	6
Edmond Watterhouse	1
Richard Stones	1
Thomas Ibbotson	3
Nichollas Sampson	2
Thomas Broadhead	1
Jonas Taylor	2
Henry Watterhouse	1
Henry Hobson	1
Edmond Ayre	2
Abraham Bayley	1
Robert Saunderson	1
George Yellot	1
John Saunderson	1
Widdow Hobson	1
John Ibbotson	3
Christopr Taylor	1
George Ellor	4
Joseph Bayley	1
Robert Shaw	1
Jonathan Drable	2
George Shaw	2
Thomas Silvester	3
Christopr Taylor	2
	643

Empty and no distress to be had

John Downing	1
George Hall	1
John Stead	3
Richard Bayley	1

These persons following are discharged by Certificates

Willm Barlow	1
Widdow Bincliffe	1
Gilbert Morton	1
Robert Wilson	1
Richard Hobson	1
Francis Mathewman	1

Omitted by reason of poverty 2

Thomas Midleton Collr
George Worrell Const

Bentley cum Arksey (Bentley with Arksey)

Mr Samuell Hall 7

m 20]

Jonathan Smith	1
John Huscroft	1
Thomas Stringer	1
Richard Hall	1
Willm Birkes	1
John Read	4
Willm Turwhite	3
Ralph Clay	1
Mr Adwick	8
Nathanll Speight	1
Richard Foster	1
Godfrey Gilling	1
Richard Hoole	1
Robert Crawshawe	1
Willm White	2
Richard Jackson	2
George Smith	1
Willm Crawshaw	3
Richard Ademan	1
Widdow Bradford	4
Mr Harvie	3
Widdow Walles	2
Mr John Bradford	8
John Dawson	1
Richard Dunworth	4
Samuell Viccars	1
Brian Clarkson	1
Andrew Scott	1
John Flower	1
John Smith	1
Martin Green	1
John Adwick	5
Thomas Turtwhite	3
Willm Hall	1
Mr Samuell Jenings	7
Thomas Balderson	1
Daniell Broughton	1
Richard Adwick	2
John Elton	1
Widdow Smith	1
John Cocking	3
Widdow Hall	3
Willm Peace	7
Robert Cotton	2
The parsonage	6
Ellizabeth Plumer	1
Mr Wilbore	9
George Showre	4
Willm Rogers	1
Widdow Foster	1
Timothy Aire	1
Roger Foster Jun	3
George Simpson	2
Widdow Pickering	4
Willm Arthington	2
Willm Hanley	2
Lewis Smeaton	1
Richard Harriot	2
Thomas Hill	4
Robert Hall	1
John Tiffin	4
	fower
Willm Huscroft	1
Humphrey Robson	1
Godfrey Foster	2
Willm Graues	3

m 21]

Robert Petty	1
Mathew Jackson	2
John Foster	1
Willm Oakes	1
James Guest	3
Widdow Tiffin	1
Willm Hanley	3
Mrs Beamond	4
Samuell Broughton	3
John Hill	1
Ralph Broughton	3
Samuell Broughton	3
Mr Ralph Walker	5
Richard Hall	3
John Broughton	4
Thomas Pearson	4
Richard Jenings	2
Thomas Pearson	2
George Goodison	1
Willm Bussey	1
Willm Addinett	1
Mr Longley	2
Ralph Broughton	4
Thomas Crosby	7
Widdow Pickering	2
Roger Foster	2
Mrs Linlay	3
Robert Bradford	1
Ellizabeth Hall	1
James Addison	3
John Carver	1
John Ledgett	1
Robert Viccars	5
Edward Shirtcliffe	1
	244

Empty and no distress to be had

Francis Silvester	2
The heires of viccars	2
Mr Hall	2
Samuell Broughton	3

These persons following are discharged by Certftes

Anne Suth	1
Widdow Butler	1
Rowland Beamond	1
Robert Carver	1
Thomas Nicholson	1
George Nicholson	1
Thomas Windle	1
Robert Hill	1
Thomas Hall	1
Willm Pigburne	2
Willm Otley	2
Widdow Lee	1
Widdow Burton	1
Widdow Coe	1
Ellzabeth Thornton	1
John Lee	1
Widdow Winn	1
Widdow Milner	1

Omitted by reason of poverty	2

Robert Bennit Collr
Robert Bradford Const

m 22]

Boulton upon Dearne (Bolton upon Dearne)

Mr Riginald Watson	4
Willm Bingley	4
John Butterworth	1
James Rawood	1
John Pygott	3
Robert Gotherd	2
Henry Ottley	2
Henry Ellis	1
John Longbotham	1
Willm Ramsden	1
Thomas Adamson	1
Richard Webster	1
Willm Shepherd	3
Godfrey Bingley	1
Richard Tyas	3
John Burks	2
Widdow Hall	1
Martin Shaw	1
Mr Wikam	3
Widdow Burks	1
John Wiggin	1
Willm Wotherd	2
Richard Shepherd	3
Willm Kempe	1
George Wotherd	1
Thomas Roberts	1
Godfrey Bingley	3
Richard Tompson	1
Emanuell Watson	4
Widdow Ward	2
John Milburne	1
Willm Tyas	3
Richard Pygott	1
Robert Armroyd	2
Anne Wright	4
Thomas Wright	1
Richard Wilcock	1
Nathanll Denton	1
John Turton	1
Widdow Dey	2
Widdow Greaues	2
Nichollas Brumit	2
John Morley	1
John Wainwright	1
Willm Kirby	1
Robert Wilson	1
Widdow Burke	1
Thomas Armroyd	2
John Waid	3
Widdow Ward	3
Richard Sharpe	4
Thomas Pygott	3
Willm Robinson	2
Robert Sharpe	1
Francis Cottan	1
Thomas Pygott	2
Widdow Cottam	1
	104

These persons following are discharged by Certificates

John Balderston	1
Widdow Pattrick	2
Marke More	2

Omitted by reason of poverty 4

Thomas Midleton Collr
Nichollas Bronshead Const

m 23]

Barnbrough (Barnburgh)

Mr Vincent	16
Mr Kay	8
Mrs Viccars	6
John Whitacrs	1
Francis Morton	2
Widdow Roberts	1
Mrs Alice Luling	1
John Roberts sen	1
Joshua Burley	2
Willm Tyas	1
Willm Bingley	3
Thomas Preistley	1
Richard Bowser	4
Ralph Preistley	1
Edward Swallow	2
Widdow Whitacre	3
Samuell Box	1
John Denton	1
John Roberts Jun	4
Widdow Roberts	2
John Swallow	1
Thomas Denton	1
Richard Swindin	1
Mr Box	3
Richard Swallow	1
Edward Box	3
John Wharam	1
Thomas Jissup	1
George Hall	1
George Frear	2
Richard Box	1
Willm Crook	1
Widdow Sharpe	3
John Machin	1
Edward Tompson	1
John Machin	1
Widdow Lewis	1
Lenard Bows	1
	86

Empty and no distress to be had

Mr Vincent	1

Omitted by reason of poverty 4

Thomas Midleton Collr
Lewis Viccars Const

Brodsworth cum Pigburne (Brodsworth with Pickburn)

Mrs Wentworth	12
Mr Brooke	5
Thomas Holme	2
Willm Wood	1
Willm Clarkson	1
Richard Beaman	1
Widdow Ellis	1
Willm Blake	2
George Dyson	1
Thomas Heaton	1
Thomas Heslewood	1
Francis Elam	1
John Fostard	1
Peter Maud	1
Elizabeth Bark	2
Widdow Maud	3
Ann Hall	1
Widdow Midleton	1

m 24]

Marke Wood	1
John Beale	2
Hugh Smith	1
Widdow Shirtcliffe	1
Barnaby Hurst	2
Mrs Wentworth	2
Thomas Flower	1
Willm Robert	1
Widdow Midleton	1
Robert Hurst	1
Mr Ranson	6
Mr Viccars	5
Thomas Downing	1
John Whitacrs	2
George Hartley	1
Richard Pygott	1
Robert Waide	1
Widdow Major	1
Widdow Shirtcliffe	1
Willm Hall	1
Katherine Viccars	4
Mathew Beale	1
Willm Sykers	1
Robert Jackson	1
Mathew Beale	1
	79

Empty and no distress to be had

Robert Hurst	1
Robert Firth	2

Omitted by reason of poverty 7

Thomas Midleton Collr
Peter Maude Const

Bilam (Bilham)

Mr Turner	6
Thomas Hoole	2
Mrs Langsdale	2

Henry Roebuck 1
George Preistley 3
Widdow Bingley 1
Thomas Anstan 2
Henry Hurst 1
Thomas Fletcher 1
Thomas Ellam 1
James England 1
21

Empty & no distress to be had
The Lady Hooten 2

Omitted by reason of poverty 1

Thomas Midleton Collr
Henry Hurst Const

Billingley
Widdow Hearin 1
Widdow Elliot 2
Mr Smith 2
Willm Bayley 1
Edward Naylor 1
Willm Robinson 2
Leonard Byard 2
Mr Winfeild 6
Hugh Bennill 2
Jonas Roberts 1
John Fox 1
Willm Rome 1
Francis Bennill 1
John Pigott 1
Willm Pigott 1
Thomas Andrew 1
Richard Townend 1

m 25]

John Hill 1
Willm Peaker 1
Peter Pygott 1
30

Omitted by reason of poverty 1

Thomas Midleton Collr
Willm Robinson Const

Brampton
(Brampton en le Morthen)
John Bowles Esqr 9
Mr George Lord 6
John Fisher 1
Edward Smithies 1
Thomas Mallinson 3
Richard Jarvice sen 1
Henry Walker 1
Richard Jarvice Jun 1
Henry Hall 1
Willm Heywood 1
Willm Peper 1
Robert Hurst 1
Mr Nathanll Revill 8
Nichols Swallow 1
Robert Syberry 2
John Wild 1
Widdow Wood 2
Thomas Marshall 1
Nichollas Steele 1
43

Omitted by reason of poverty 3

Robert Bennit Collr
Henry Walker Const

Brimsforth
(Brinsworth)
Mr Laughton 11
Robert Oxley 1
Widdow Green 2
Mr Laughton 1
Edmond Swift 2
Willm Wood 1
Nichollas Waddy 2
Thomas Stephenson 2

Willm Vessey 2
James Wood 3
Thomas Thompson 1
James Holland 1
George Shepherd 1
Edward Gyles 1
Willm Stringer 3
Robert Green 3
Vallentine Hart 9
46

Omitted by reason of poverty 5

Robert More Collr
Edmond Swift Const

Bramley
Docter Ayre 11
Mathew Watterhouse 1
John Yates 2
Samuell Roper 3
Thomas Spencer 1
Dorothy Simpson 2
Thomas Hartley 1
Mr Willm Spencer 9
Willm Hill 3

m 26]

Nichollas Dawson 1
Henry Revell 1
Thomas Wilson 1
John Heptenstall 1
Thomas Oxspring 2
George Oxspring 1
Robert Wharam 1
Willm Ward 2
Thomas Shepley 1
Christopr Revell 2
Willm Ward 3
Nathanll Ellistone 1
Willm Stead 2
Widdow Marshall 1
53

Empty and noe distress to be had
Franc Wastindge 3

Robert More Collr
John Heptonstall Const

Bawtrey
(Bawtry)
Mr Thomas Lister 12[225]
more *pro* Partridge house 10
Thomas Clapham 2
James Gabitas 4
Mr Watton 4
Mr Partridge 4
John Buney 5
Mr Langley 4
Widdow Roebotham 4
Robert Wells 2
Willm Shaw 2
Mr Phillips 3
Richard Pipes 3
Widdow Jenings 2
Thomas Hellefeild 1
Jonathan Roe 1
Willm Morton 1
George Scarbrough 2
Mr Pitchforke 2
Thomas Lund 6
Mr Daniell Soolie 7
Mr Lambe 4
Robert Broughton 2
Richard Donwell 2
James Morris 1
Mr Yowle 3
Mrs Bradley 3
Edward Fairfoote 1
Richard Chatterton 3
John Noble 4
Widdow Brooke 2
Widdow Smout 3
Christopr Hoyle 3
Francis Geldart 1
Ralph Spencer 2
Widdow Sumerviell 3
Thomas Brewton 4
Lutlay Walker 2
Mr Partridge 14
John Smith 4

m 27]

Thomas Mirfin 2
Mr Trubshawe 6
John Robinson 3
Thomas Watterhouse 5
Mr Samuell Smith 6
Mr Bower 5
Richard Cartmell 1
Widdow Walton 3
Robert Spauald 3
Samuell Mawe 2
Mr Wharton 9
Mr John Lee 3
Widdow Walton 4
194

Empty & no distress to be had
Mr Clarke 3

Robert Bennit Collr
Robert Spavald

Blaxton
John Parkinson 1
Widdow Bradbury 1
Edward Mott 1
Willm Chester 1
Richard Metcalfe 4
John Tuke 1
John Makeing 1
Widdow Metcalfe 1
John Dixon 2
John Barton 1
Willm Capper 1
Thomas Morris 1
Widdow Lambert 1
Mrs Withers 1
Peter Pecuday 1
19

Empty & no distress to be had
Mr Harey 1

Omitted by reason of poverty 3

Robert Bennit Collr
Robert Northew Const

Brathwell
(Braithwell)
John Shephard 4
John Amrey 1
John Gleadall 2
Thomas Boswell Cler 5
Thomas Gray 1
Mr Watterhouse 8
Jane Wilson 1
Mr Boswell 4
James Lee 2
John Tompson 4
Thomas Amerey 3
Robert Ash 1
Jonas Chapell 1
Robert Steele 1
George Poole 1
Robert Gleadall 1
Francis Langwith 1
Widdow Allen 1
Richard Oxspring 1
Widdow Lawson 1
Thomas Simpson 1
Thomas Wass 1
Dinis Base 1
Charles Mare 1

[225] 12 written over 10; next to which is written 'twelue'

m 28]

Mary Dickinson	1
Widdow More	2
Richard Simpson	1
Mrs Watterhouse	8
Thomas Amry	2
Thomas Ward	1
Richard Ward	1
Thomas Hill	2
Richard Ward	1
Thomas Bowles	2
Thomas French	1
John Tompson	2
David Arnold	1
John Needom	1
Nichollas Hunt	3
George Longwith	1
George Nell	1
Widdow Shepherd	2
James Hewitt	2
Thomas Amrey	2
Isaac Ingall	2
Thomas Dickinson	1
Ralph Hunt	1
John Roebuck	1
George Hudson	1
Edward Parkin	1
Robert Steele	1
Ralph Fretwell	4
Nichols Roades	1
Willm Sikes	1
	99

Empty & no distress to be had

Robert Farbanks	3
Thomas Amry	2
Richard Ward	1

Omitted by reason of poverty 1

Robert Moore Collr
John Amerey Const

Barmby super Dunn (Barnby Dun)

Roger Portington Esqr	5
Mr Ward	10
Mrs Gregory	13
Mr Pownall	5
Mr Kay Viccaridge	3
Mr Portington	2
Robert Crosley	1
Mrs Gregory	1
Widdow Ellive	1
John Hopton	2

m 28]

Godfrey Bingley	2
Willm Hill	2
Widdow Hawksworth	2
Richard Beeforth	2
Richard Bingley	2
Henry Hill	2
Widdow Jenings	2
Robert Seaton	5
John Balderston	1
Ralph Carter	3
Thomas Stocks	1
Richard Abbot	1
Richard Hallas	1
Allexand Hunt	2
John Foster	1
John Jenings	3
Mrs Jones	1
John Foster	2
Tristram Wilbore	1
Willm Hunt	2
Allan Cockin	1
Willm Crabtree	1
David Saunderson	1
Richard Jenings	2
Robert Hunt sen	3
Robert Jenings	1
Widdow Robinson	1
Widdow Bawmforth	1
Widdow Ward	1
Robert Hunt Jun	1
John Kershay	1
Humphr Spooner	1
Widdow Handley	2
Richard Sugden	2
Willm Shillitoe	1
Willm Rooth	2
Willm Lee	1
Mr Winteringham	4
Christopr Robinson	1
Mathew Bingley	3
Thomas Martin	2
Jonathan Parish	2
John Waite	4
Thomas Bolderston	1
Willm Kettle	1
Thomas Hawksworth	2
Robert Jenings	2
Leonard Wrayth	2
Robert Marshall	1
Earle of Lynsey	2
Willm Harrison	1
Willm Robinson	1
	133

Empty & no distres to be had

Ralph Cartan	1
John Hunt	1
Widdow Jenings	1
Edward Murfin	1
Willowby Rookby Esqr	2

m 30]

Omitted by reason of poverty 6

Thomas Midleton Collr
Thomas Hopton Const

Clayton cum Frickley (Clayton with Frickley)

Anne Norcroft	3
Thomas Turner	1
Christopr Hurst	1

John Sayle	1
Riben Tompson	4
Ruben Norcroft	2
Toby Swinden	1
Barnard Raynford	1
Thomas Fletcher	1
Roger Swan	1
Phillp Sunderland	2
John Sunderland	2
Mr Champney	4
Phillip Baite	1
Robert Ushay	1
Phillp Norcroft	2
Thomas Norcroft	2
Mr Page	1
Henry Smith	1
John Robchester	1
Edward Tompson	2
John Lister	1
Jarvas Harrison	2
Nichollas Pyper	1
John Wharam	3
Richard Gascoyne	1
Godfrey Lister	1
Martin Beckitt	1
Widdow Jackson	10
Christopr Hurst	1
	56

Empty & no distress to be had

Thos Wharam	1

Omitted by reason of poverty	2

Thomas Midleton Collr
Christohr Hurst Const

Cadeby

Edward Whitley	2
Willm Viccars	2
Richard Foster	3
Thomas Foster	3
Henry Tonge	3
Henry Hatfeild	2
Edward Gleadall	1
Willm Rushforth	1
Willm Fostard	2
Phillip Viccars	2
Thomas Sikes	1
George Wainwright	1
Widdow Sikes	1
George Wainwright	1

m 31]

Richard Johnson	1
Thomas Tyas	1
Henry Worrell	2
John Hepworth	1
Ellizabeth Youle	1
	31

Omitted by reason of poverty	2

Robert More Collr
Thomas Foster Const

Cantley

Willm Rodwell	2
Mr George Rasine	2
Simon Litlewood	1
John Fenton	1
Sir Thos Wolstenholme	2
Nichollas Hickson	2
John Richardson	1
Thomas Lawe	2
Mrs Childers	4
	fower
Robert Chester	1
John Tayler	1
Thomas Foster	1
Willm Ashley	1
Willm Milner	1
Widdow Ledger	2
Robert Mouldson	1
Robert Foster	1
Richard Cansby	1
Mr Levill	1
John Smith	4
John Freeman	2[226]
	two
Richard Pigburne	1
Charles Gibson	1
Henry Robinson	1
Widdow Pygott	2
Thomas Ingle	1
Widdow Smith	2
Francis Chester	2
James Smith	2
Henry Chester	1
Willm Glouer	1
George Littlewood	2
Edward Newsam	1
Willm Sayles	1
Godfrey Treeton	1
Anthony Fryer	1
Henry Mosley	4
Francis Firth	3
John Milner	3
Alverah Chester	2
James Winder	1
George Nell	2
Willm Tompson	1
Thomas Mouldson	1
Samuell Mouldson	1

m 32]

John Leetham	1
Robert Tattersall	4
Hastins Wood	4
Thomas Rodwell	2
Thomas Smith	2
John Rawson	1
Mrs Jackson	2
	88

[226] 2 written over 1.

Robert Bennit Collr	
Willm Bird Const	

Conisbrough

Mr Gill Jun	4
Mr Saxton	2
Thomas Wasse	5
Mathew Pursland	8
Mr Gill sen	5[227]
	five
Mr Shirtcliffe	3
Thomas Bingley	2
Willm Rutton	2
Richard Broadhead	1
Francis Wardley	2
Widdow Wood	2
Richard Nicholson	1
Richard Ellam	5
John Harley Jun	1
George Wood	2
Allexander Hallam	1
Henry Flower	3
Robert Curtice	1
John Taylor	1
Widdow Drable	2
Edward Leadbeater	1
John Bayley	2
Edward Dickinson	2
Widdow Nicholson	1
John Butterwood	1
John Guest	2
Richard Taylor	1
John Darling	2
Richard Wood	2
Henry Norburne	1
Willm Blackburne	2
Thomas Rogers	2
Leanard Pearson	2
Thomas Boswile	3
Widdow Pogson	1
Willm Broadhead	1
Mr Lee	2
John Pearson	1
John Curtice	1
Nichollas Crumbeck	1

m 33]

John Nevill	4
John Heward	2
George Burks	4
Richard Mastin	4
John Hawksworth	3
Henry Robinson	3
Willm Hoyle	2
George Booth	1
Richard Dey	2
Willm Swallowe	2
Anne Harrison	2
John Harley	1
John Hewitt	2
Henry Robinson	1
Richard Hallam	1
Richard Rawood	1
Richard Amerey sen	2
Richard Amerey Jun	1
Willm Copley	1
Robert Nicholson	3
Christopr Fayram	4
Michaell Chapman	1
Jarvas Bosvile	4
Richard Amerey	2
Richard Rawood	1
Willm Fostard	3
Robert Fairbanke	4
John Ellam	4
Willm South	1
Mr Adams	7
John Shepherd	1
Martin Tattersall	2
Richard Tompson	3
Willm Carter	2
John Levill	1
	166

Empty and no distress to be had

John Taylor	1
Mr Stockham	1
Samuell Womersley	1
Susan Champney	1
Mr Woodyeare	1
Omitted by reason of poverty	6
Thomas Midleton Collr	
John Levill Const	

Darefeild (Darfield)

Docter Dixon	9
Mr Hemingway	7
Timothy Shaddock	4
Henry Reyney	4
John Slack	4
Thomas Bawmforth	3
Francis Wadsworth	1
John Johnson	1
Thomas Senyard	1
Thomas Townend	10

m 34]

Willm Rouse	3
Mr Wainwright	9
Thomas Senyard	1
Willm Birks	2
Joseph Swinden	3
Widdow Bloome	2
Widdow Cawthorne	1
Mathew Hargraue	1
Robert Marr	1
Willm Warbleton	1
Thomas Horsfeild	1
Widdow Cawthorne	3
Mr Eaton	8

227 5 written over 3.

Mrs Loueday	3
Henry Hargitt	2
Mrs Stones	1
Willm Day	2
Richard Freeman	3
Thomas Holdsworth	1
John Chadwick	1
George Shearman	2
Thomas Bradley	2
Thomas Audsley	4
Mary Lockwood	1
Thomas Bradley	1
John Kelshay	4
John Ellis	1
Nichollas Marshall	2
Sarah Clarke	2
	112

Empty and no distres to be had

Mr Angell	1
Mr Wood	2
Mr Wainewright	3

Omitted by reason of poverty 5

Thomas Midleton Collr
Willm Waireing Const

Dinington (Dinnington)

John Tagg	4
Willm Procter	1
Thomas Tagg	3
Willm Apleby	2
John Morton	1
John Cottingham	1
Francis Newbolt	2
John Procter	2
Willm Gleadall	2
John Bayles	1
Widdow Spencer	2
Charles Bales	2
Richard Gilberd	1
Thomas Spencer Cler	3
John Hopkinson	2
Henry Pashley	3
Simon Gilbert	1

m 35]

John Bales	2
Jarvas Kippax	2
Thomas Cowdall	1
Charles Bales	1
Robert Procter	3
Willm Burras	1
Christopr Smith	1[228]
	44

Empty & no distres to be had

Thomas Holland	1

Omitted by reason of poverty 4

Robert More Collr
Willm Greadhill Const

Dalton

James Brownend	2
Mr Thomas Hurst	6
Widdow Woodall	1
Thomas Jackson	1
Richard Dawson	1
Thomas Hewit	1
Michaell Attie	2
Thomas Whittles	1
George Machon	2
Johnath Hurst	3
John Syberrie	2
Widdow Hurst	4
Thomas Booth	1
Richard Westerman	1
Samuell Wilson	1
Willm Cutt	1
Thomas Shouslock	2
John Yealand	1
Robert Apleby	2
Robert Woodall	2
Edward Shepard	1
Thomas Winke	1
Christopr Radlay	4
	43

Omitted by reason of poverty 4

Robert Bennit Collr
Thomas Hurst Const

Doncaster Marketplace

Willm Bird	2
Willm Midleton	2
James Barke	1
Mr Carlile	3
Widdow Firth	4
Thomas Mann	4
Mr Wilbore	3
Mary Kitson	3
Mr Thwaites	1
Mr Braiksford	3
Mary Asbon	1
Mathew Bingley	3
John Ward	3
Robert Hudson	4
Willm Green	6
Thomas Glensover Jun	3
Alderman Webster	10
Mr Walker	8
John Blyth	3
Alderman Martin	7

m 36]

Willm Broughton	3
Willm Barwick	3

[228] Entry inserted.

John Squire	6
Anthony Beckitt	4
Widdow Wright	4
Thomas Glensover sen	2
Mr Jefferson	4
Widdow Mann	4
Jeffrey Whitacres	5
Willm Moody	5
Andrew Martin	4
Willm Heaton	3
Robert Parill	3
Mr Henry Wadsworth	5
Mr Bradford	6
Widdow Rhoades	2
Widdow Crawshawe	1
Phillip Basset	5
Mrs Copley	13
	156

The person vndernamed is discharged by Certifte

Ann Massy vid	1

Robert More Collr
Wm Bird Const Const

Doncaster St Georgegate (Doncaster, St George Gate)

Mr Vincent	3
Mr Jackson	5
Mr Thomas Squire	10
Samuell Blyth	3
John Wainman	1
Ellizab Tomlinson	1
Willm Wilkinson	1
Anthony Birkes	1
Robert Parsisson	3
John Peacock	3
Richard Shepherd	3
George Ward	2
Robert Browne	2
Mrs Chatterton	2
Thomas Smith	2
Mary Tyas	1
Mr Webster	9
John Bellamy	2
	54

Omitted by reason of poverty	2

Robert More Collr
John Wainman Const

Marshgate (Doncaster, Marsh Gate)

Thomas Smith	2
Anne Roebotham	2
Edward Halliday	3
Ellin Craggs	2
Willm Hall	2
Widdow Hall	2
John Newsham	3
Robert Oxley	2
Paull Johnson	6
Thomas Tyas	1
Henry Wadsworth	3
John Tymin	4
Robert Butterwood	2
Willm Adwick	2
Mr Boswell	10
Robert Wilson	2
John Graue	2
	50

Empty & no distres to be had

Mr Wande	1

These persons following are discharged by Certifts

William Raisn Esq	2
John Booth	1
James Swift	1
Widdow Ridgway	1

m 37]

Omitted by reason of poverty	4

Robert Bennit Collr
Thomas Tyas Const

Frenchgate Doncaster (Doncaster, French Gate)

Richard Treue	2
Widdow White	4
Thomas Kippax	1
Robert Tross	1
Widdow Hall	3
Willm Cossen	4
Mr Justice	12
Mr Richard Clay	16
Robert Wells	4
John Tross	3
John Aire	4
Widdow Harris	1
Daniell Allon	3
Willm Cooke	1
Mrs Mellis	14
Mr Clarke	8
Widdow Wilson	2
Mr Gross	2
John Webstor	2
Mrs Hunt	18
John Adinell	4
Mr Willm Shepherd	1
Alderm Shepherd	8
John Marshall	3
Mr Gilliam	5
Richard Drakes	1
Willm Bailden	3
	130

Empty & no distress to be had

Anne Brumley	1
John Broughton	3

Robert More Collr
Joseph Bell Const

Fishergate
(Doncaster, Fisher Gate)
Jane Pearson 1
Abraham Wilson 1
Francis Cutts 1
Thomas Bonehouse 1
Mrs Wilbore 1
John Green 3
Mr Baldwin 6
Phillip Kirke 6
Mr Armitage 7
Mathew Walker 2
John Johnson 4
Richard Steele 2[229] two
Thomas Dixon 5
Mathew Cooper 4
Robert Dixon 3
Mr Schoray 9
Thomas Wright 1
Alderman Lee 6
John Lee 3
Widdow Creekill 5
Henry Abbey 2
73

Empty & no distress to be had
Mr Shepherd 1

Omitted by reason of poverty 1

Robt More Collr
Richard Spencer Const

Baxtergate
(Doncaster, Baxter Gate)
Robert Ibitson 1
Mr Robert Auby 4

m 38]

Mr Ralph Hesle 1
John France 4
Andrew Oglethorpe 1
Mrs Oglethorpe 1
Thomas Hurst 1
Andrew Oglethorpe 1
John Marrew 1
Mr George Rasin 5
Mr Finch 2
Mrs Finch 6
Mr John Elliker 6
Alderman Burton 3
Mr Maud 1
Thomas Raynor 1
Mr Marrow 5
Widdow Doughty 4
Mr George Holmes 8
Mr Henry Shaw 7
Mr Hall 5
John Peacock 4
Mr Wm Arthur 3
John Marshall 1
76

Empty and no distress to be had
Widdow Gray 1
Mr Brigham 1

Omitted by reason of poverty 1

Robert Bennit Collr
Robert Ibetson Const

Frenchgate
(Doncaster, French Gate)
Willm Marples 3
Willm Dickinson 2
John Burton 2
John Burton 3
James Richinson 3
Anne Firth 5
Mr Thomas Waite 3
Christopr Justice 3
Mrs Marshall 18
Willm Wood 7
Richard Speight 3
Willm Wells 4
Widdow Allon 3
Phillp Barton 4
Anne Justice 1
Willm Howson 5
Anne Ball 1
Mr Willm Croft 4
Ottelwell Roebotham 4
Thomas Cooke 5
Willm Tippin 1
Mrs Burnill 3
Widdow Headinglay 8
Thomas Speight 2
Mr Ayre 5
Mrs Eastoft 4
Abraham Pilling 4
Robert Ridgill 1
Widdow Shelton 1
Willm Butterwood 1
Leonard Crooks 1
Thomas Taylor 1
Richard Smith 1[230] one
Mr Richard Whitacres 4
John Britlebanke 3
Francis Holmes 1
Willm Allon 1
George Tyas 3
Roger Elwick 2
Mr Curtious 2
132

Empty & no distress to be had
Mr Rasin 4
Mr Walker 3

Omitted by reason of poverty 4

[229] 2 written over 1.
[230] 1 written over 2.

Robt Benit Collr
Jacob Bell Const

m 39]

Halgate
(Doncaster, Hall Gate)

Susan Martin	4
John Oxinge	1
Gilbert Croft	3
Dorothy Blyth	3
Willm Marsh	1
Willm Yates	1
Richard Wilbore	1
Thomas Radley	1
Thomas Smith	1
Robert Beckitt	2
Vincent Bininglay	5
Mr Thwaites	8
Mr George Parke	7
Mr Willm Patterson	11
Robert Shearewood	1
Mr Patterson	2
Willm Kewerden	1
Francis Marsh	1
Mr Read	6
John Mathewes	1
Willm Hampton	1
Mr Anthony Wright	2
Edward Barras	2
	66

Empty & no distress to be had

Antho Revil	5
Mr Levitt	1
Mr Anthony Wright	1
Mr Clarke	1
Charles Cooke	1

Omitted by reason of poverty 15

Robert Bennit Collr
Anthony Beckitt Const

Highstreete & Scots Lane
(Doncaster, High Street and Scot Lane)

John Winn	1
James Ogdin	2
Thomas Taylor	4
Robert Hampton	3
Mrs Thorp	2
Ellizabeth Briggs	3
John Jackson	2
Edward Dowler	4
Mary Oxley	5
Thomas Schoray	5
Captin Webster	2
Widdow Cussen	1
Patrick Vaughan	1
Robert Hall	1
Mary Bonas	1
Thomas Howden	1
Robert Fixby	1
Widdow Barrick	2
Widdow Lettice	1
Willm Forge	1
John Holmes	1
Thomas Walker	1
Thomas Graunt	1
Vollont Moxon	2
Martin Grant	2
Robert Lambe	1
Docter Yarbrough	6
Docter Danby	4
James Dyson	1
Obediah Martin Aldr	2
Mr Radish	1
Widdow Shawe	3
Robert Murfitt	3
Christopr Shaw	3
Mr Wortley	5
Mr Dinis Ward	4
Anne Kinson	3

m 40]

Mr Curtious	6
Mr Brigham	4
John Noble	3
Mr Crawshawe	6
Willm Beamond	5
The Honble the Lord Carlinford	17
George Cowling	1
Richard Bradforth	5
Francis Barnes	2
Edward Martin	3
Mr Gibson	6
Mary Oxley	4
John Killam	8
	156

Empty & no distress to be had

Mr Carlile	6

These persons following are discharged by Certifte

Widdow Hill	1
Widdow West	1
Thomas Fenton	1
Richard Drable	1
Thomas Gunter &c	3

Omitted by reason of poverty 7

Robert More Collr
Thomas Raynor Const

St Pulch Within Barr
(Doncaster, St Sepulchre Gate within the Bar)

Mr John Maddox	5
John Hickson	1
Willm Foster	2
Mr Richard Killam	5
Mr Baites	6
Widdow Aire	3
John Broughton	1
Robert Speight	4
Jar Bell	5

Andrew Martin	5
Reynold Spofford	5
Widdow Ashley	5
Thomas Pickering	1
Alice Wilkinson	1
Widdow Wombell	3
Thomas Parkin	1
Richard Wright Aldrm	9
John Broughton	1
Anne Levitt	2
Willm Ramsgill	3
Alderman Rasin	6
	74

Empty & no distres to be had

Mr Ftzwin	4
John Broughton	1

These persons following are discharged by Certificates

Alice Dickinson	1
John Marsh	1
Alice Wilkinson	1
Dorothy Parkin	1

Omited by reason of poverty 4

Robt More Collr
John Hickton Const

Doncaster Markit Place (Doncaster, Market Place)

Mr Jarvice Holmes	2
Anne Farham	1

m 41]

Mrs Lee	3
Mr Peter Hudson	4
Mr John Burton	5
Willm Bassit	3
John Briggs	3
Robert Saye	3
Mr Godfrey Inman	6
Willm Beard	2
Thomas Ward	2
Robert Martin	2
Martin Dawson	2
John Winn	3
Anne Sugden	4
Mr Catterill	3
John Waid	5
Widdow Nicholson	1
Rebecca Howden	1
Thomas Fletcher	1
Mary Martin	1
Mathew Kitchin	4
Mr Rasin	1
John Jennings	2
Willm Hunt	4
Willm Barke	2
Richard Wilson	2
Nichollas Saule	4
John Harper	2
Mr Richard Loue	1
Richard Sharpe	3
Robert Walker	3
Mr Thwates	5
Mrs Lawe	1
Ellizabeth Smeaton	3
Mr Robert Squire	6
Emmot Strafford	1
Mrs Whitacrs	2
Thomas Barnes	2
Ellin Roades	2
Mrs Cooper	3
	110

Empty and no distress to be had

Jonathan Roe	2

Omited by reason of poverty 3

Robert Bennit Collr
Willm Bird Const

St Pulchers Without Barr (Doncaster, St Sepulchre Gate without Barr)

Mr Pell	5
John Atkinson	2
Willm Wilson	1
Bartholl Lamb[231]	1
Willm Pearson	2
Thomas Parret	3
John Lacy	1
Mr Kellam	1
Willm Latham	1
Ralph Maycock	4
John Jarrett	5
Widdow Jarrett	2
John Hemsley	2
	30

Empty & no distress to be had

Alderm Rasin	1
Anthony Martin	1

These persons following are discharged by Certificates

Alice Dent	1
John Dickinson	1
Widdow Gamble	1
Francis Watson	1

m 42]

Jane Rawson	1
Robert Haworth	1
Widdow Greaues	1
Widdow Fleeming	1
Mary Longe	1
George Dickinson	1
John Stowe	1

[231] Clamb written above Lamb.

Dinis West	1
Luce Mason	1
Edward Milner	1
Richard Shillitoe	1
Robert Littlewood	1
Widdow Anderson	1
Richard Wharam	1
Hanna Box	2
Robert Garnit	1
Omitted by reason of poverty	6

Robert Bennit Collr
John Atkinson Const

Denaby

Mr Killingbeck	11
George Roberts	2
John Tyas	1
Daniell Roebuck	2
Willm Tyas	2
Henry Roberts jun	2
Robert Jarvas	2
Michaell Davis	1
Richard Sheepshanke	1
Samuell Roberts	1
Henry Roberts sen	4
Nichollas Booker	1
Edward Lambert	2
James Roberts	2
John Roberts Jun	1
Clodeus Reyney	3
	38
Empty & noe distres to be had	
Sir John Rearsby	1
Omitted by reason of poverty	3

Thomas Midleton Collr
John Killingbecke Const

Ecclesfeild
(Ecclesfield)

Mr Robert Green	6
Mr Wright	6
Robert Cooke	5
John Clarke	5
Widdow Ibbotson	1
Nichollas Ibotson	5
Widdow Birks	7
Widdow Bayley	3
John Jepson	2
Widdow Rose	2
Henry Ibetson	2
Lyon Ludlam	3
Willm Carr	3
Thomas Robinson	1
Charles Clarke	1
Henry Marsden	1
Richard Webster	1
Nichollas Twibell	3
Nichollas Twibell	4
Thomas Birkes	1

m 43]

Hugh Millar	2
Rowland Jepson	1
Charles Beard	1
Willm Jepson	1
John Hilton	1
Thomas Tompson	1
John Ragg	2
Peter Dey	1
Widdow Burks	2
John Shaw	1
Willm Jepson sen	2
Christopher Woodhead	3
Willm Dey	2
Willm Hawley	3
Widdow Linley	2
Nichollas Basforth	1
Richard Wood	2
John Kay	2
Willm Hunter	2
Willm Frickley	1
Jerem Lord	2
Daniell Fayram	1
Robert Sutton	3
Widdow Holmes	2
Jonas Basforth	1
Widdow Wigfeild	1
Nichollas Hoyland	1
Nichollas Wood	3
Widdow Cawood	1
Christopr Woodhead	4
John Lockwood	3
John Hartley	2
Thomas Machin	2
Ralph Millar	3
Ralph Carr	1
Hugh Millar	1
Anthony Combe	1
Mathew Combe	2[232] two
Abraham Booth	2
Robert Carr	3
Richard Lord	1
Willm Mason	1
Widdow Carr	3
Jonathan Hargraues	2
Thomas Setterfett	1
Francis Marshall	1
Jonathan Hardwicke	1
John Bullas	1
Thomas Bullas	1
Widdow Tompson	2
Ralph Bower	2
George Hines	1
Willm Barber	4
Thomas Pearson	3
John Smith	5
Willm Tompson	2
Thomas Ayre	3
Thomas Wilson	3
Willm Hides	3
John Parker	4

[232] 2 written over 1.

John Walker	1
Robert Carr	2
Leonard Hawksworth	1
Thomas Walker	1

m 44]

Willm Smith	1
Thomas Beard	1
Richard Parkin	1
Henry Oxley	1
Zachar Beard	1
George Stones	1
Widdow Smith	2
Widdow Cowper	2[233] two
Widdow Parkin	1
Thomas Smith	2
George Phipps	4
Thomas Stone	2
Widdow Parkin	1
Thomas Smith	1
Thomas Parkin	2
Willm Smith	3
Thomas Cutt	1
George Guest	2
Richard Gibson	1
Widdow Parkin	1
Thomas Houghton	1
Henry Broadley	2
Thomas Parkin	1
John Booth	1
Mr Freeman	6
Thomas Hague	1
Mr Worrall	4
Thomas Booth	1
John Bayley	2
Richard Best Jun	2
Willm Walker	1
Thomas Hobson	1
Nichollas Bullas	2
Samuell Stanley	3

George Allan	4
Thomas Silvester	3
Widdow Booth	3
Thomas Chappell	1
Widdow Gill	3
Thomas Smith	1
Gerad Guest	1
Robert Smith	2
Mrs Northall	4
Richard Ellam	3
Mr Green	9
Edward Machin	2
Jonathan Winfeild	2
John Wood	2
Robert Bincliff	2
John Bradley	1
Joseph Shaw	2
Nichollas Fostard	1
Widdow Bury	2
Mr Watts	10
John Hurt	2
Edward Hague	1
Steven Daniell	1
Nichollas Hague	1
Thomas Wilkinson	2
Willm Wilson	1
Willm Hague	1
John Whitacer	2
Mathew Eaton	1

m 45]

Mr Shirtcliff	9
James Garnall	2
John Whitacres	2
John Brownall	1
Willm Howdin	1
Henry Brownell	1
Widdow Roberts	2
Edward Hall	1
Willm Fletcher	1
Richard Beet	1

Robert Bullas	2
John Burnit	1
Anthony Revill	1
Richard Carr	3
George Scoales	3
Nichollas Samson	3
Ralph Carr	3
Richard Carr	3
Nichollas Mathewman	4
Abraham Roberts	2
Richard Mathewman	2
Nichollas Sampson	3
Nichollas Turbell	2
Widdow Sadler	1
Henry Sadler	1
Willm Carr	6
John Heward	3
Lawrance Stainforth	4
Widdow Rawson	2
John Hawksley	1
Widdow Collins	1
Joseph Nutt	1
Richard Milner	2
Widdow Rawson	5
James Stainforth	2[234] two
Henry Crapper	1
Henry Wilkinson	2
Ralph Butterworth	2
John Machin	2
John Oddy	1
Richard Oddy	1
Widdow Wilkinson	1
John Ealand	1
Abraham Roberts	3
Willm Stainforth	2
George Oxspring	3
Mr Hopkins	4
Thomas Carr	2
Willm Colley	1
Mathew Parker	1
Willm Wood	4

[233] 2 written over 1.
[234] 2 written over 1.

Nichollas Milner	1
Thomas Milner	2
Robt Wilkinson	2
Thomas Bayley	2
Richard Jolley	2
John Burks	2
Willm Burks	1
John Hawksley Jun	1
Nichollas Broadbent	2
Willm Rawson	2
George Carr	3
James Twibell	3
Richard Roebuck	1
Richard Tompson	1
John Brooke	1
Nichollas Slayter	1
Nichollas Fearnley	1

m 46]

Mrs Preist	6
Willm Osburne	3[235] three
Allice Wright	1
George Bowser	1
Ralph Smith	1
Thomas Hall	1
Willm Rimington	1
Willm Scoales	1
George Parker	1
George Parkin	2
John Parkins	1
John Woffenden	1
James Oxspring	2
John Blyth	2
Widdow Lockwood	1
Robert Carr	3
John Ealand	5
Thomas Morton	3
Lancel Bradbury	1
Mr Burras	4
Richard Tompson	2
Willm Smith	1
Hugh Lakwood	1
Thomas Milner	1
Thomas Beardshay	3
James Adams	1
John Cartey	1
Alice Law	1
Thomas Creswick	1
Robert Wainwright	1
Widdow Howden	1
Roger Hellifeild	3
Henry Swift	1
Willm Fenton	1
Henry Hall	1
George Parkin	1
Robert Mathewman	2
George Hobson	2
Willm Hobson	1 one
Thomas Hobson	1
Hugh Fenton	1
Benjam Taylor	4
Widdow Creswick	2
Widdow Creswicke	3
George Ellar	1
Edmon Hall	1
Gregory Revill	1
Willm Cuthbert	2
George Hobson	3
Widdow Barber	3
Michaell Woodhouse	2
Widdow Tayler	3
	548[236]

Empty & no distress to be had

John Hill	3
John Dyson	1
Mr Benjam Clarke	5
John Ealand	1
Widdow Hartley	1

Omitted by reason of poverty 38

Thomas Midleton Collr
James Oxspring Const

These persons following are Cutlers belonging to Sheffield who deposited the duty for their Forges but Refused to pay the Money without a Tryall at Law

Smithies

Charles Clarke	1
Hugh Millar	1
Charles Beard	1
Willm Jepson	1
Willm Hawley	1
Ralph Carr	1
Hugh Millor	1

m 47]

Anthony Combe	1
Abraham Booth	1
Richard Lord	1
Willm Mason	1
John Bullas	1
Ralph Bower	1
Thomas Walker	1
Richard Parkin	1
Zachar Beard	1
Thomas Parkin	1
George Guest	1
Thomas Houghton	1
John Booth	1
Willm Walker	1
Thomas Silvester	1
Widdow Gill	1
Edward Hague	1
Nichollas Hague	1

235 3 written over 2.
236 There is a scribal error since the total is 547.

Richard Beet	1
John Burnit	1
Joseph Nutt	1
Richard Milnar	1
Thomas Carr	1
Willm Colley	1
Nichollas Milner	1
Thomas Milner	1
Willm Osburne	1
George Parker	1
Thomas Morton	1
Willm Smith	1
Hugh Lockwood	1
Henry Swift	1
Willm Hobson	1
George Hobson	1
	[41][237]

Extrop & Balby (Hexthorpe and Balby)

John Poole	3
Richard Hargraue	1
George Gresson	2
Thomas Fisher	1
Thomas Watson	1
Thomas Dawson	1
John Mason	3
John Roebuck	2
Thomas Horobin	1
Richard Hill	1
Samuell Best	1
Richard Roebuck	1
Mrs Wass	2
Thomas Pickhaver	1
Paull Hanson	1
Willm Fearnley	2
John Broughton	3
Edward Box	3
John Broughton	1
Thomas Broughton	3
John Walker	3
Widdow Johnson	1
Willm Broughton	3
John Killam	3
Widdow Broughton	4
Thomas Killam	2
	50

Empty & no distress to be had

Mr Dins	1
Mr Shepherd	1

m 48]

Thomas Broughton	1

These persons following are discharged by Certifs

Ellizabeth Hill	1
Robert Ellis	1
John Barugh	1
George Revill	1

Robert More Collr
John Broughton Const

Edlington

Sir Thomas Wharton	21
Mr Watkinson	6
George Spooner	4
Thomas Winter	2
Widdow Armitage	5
George Nell	2
Ralph Hill	1
John Nicholson	1
Thomas Roebotham	3
John Nell	1
George Wharton	1
John Simpson	1
Widdow Nicholson	1
Willm Travise	1
	50

Empty & no distress to be had

Joseph Armroyd	12

Omitted by reason of Poverty	5

Thomas Midleton Collr
George Nell Const

Ecclesall

Richard Bacon	2
Thomas Fisher	1
John Allott	4
Willm Machon	1
Richard Longden	1
Thomas Hoyland	1
Robert Machon	1
Mr Henry Bright sen	3
Mr Henry Bright Jun	7
James Mitchill	2
Willm Stones	1
Thomas Brooke	1
George Bougham	1
John Burlay	4
John Overton	1
Michaell Ryles	5
John Oates	1
Thomas Overton	1
Francis Whitacrs	1
Edward Biggin	2
Willm Hall	1
Robert Redfearne	2
Thomas Storke	2[238]
	two
Thomas Lee sen	2
Robert Union	2
Widdow Union	1
John Webster	4
John Stones	4
Robert Jeffcock	1
Willm Webster	4

237 No total given; see above Hey, 'West Riding in the Late Seventeenth Century', pp. 52–4.
238 2 written over 1.

Willm Phillips	1
Mr Allexand Ashton	6
Widdow Downes	1
Thomas Harrop	1

m 49]

John Stones	3
Richard Jeffcock	2
Richard Jeffcock	1
George Meales	1
Henry Watson	3
Widdow Watson	1
Willm Badger	1
Samuell Pickford	1
Mr Bright	2
John Dale	1
Mr Thomas Bright	1
Richard Taylor	1
Clement Parke	2[239] two
Mr Thomas Bright	6
Thomas Dale	4
Willm Oates	1
Richard Woodroofe	1
Mr John Bright	3
Mrs Bright	3
John Jeffcock	1
Thomas Rhoades	1
Edward Barnes	1
Thomas Oates	2
Richard Starke	1
John Firth	3
Thomas Newbald	3
Joseph Lee	4
Thomas Watson	3
John Barton	1
Edward Graues	1
Thomas Dent	4
Steven Sutton	1
Thomas Stainroyd	2
Willm Thornelly	1
Anthony Fox	2
Christopr Barker	1
Mr Willm Tayler	3
Robert Firth	1
Thomas Firth	2
Steven Fox	4
Roger Leadbeater	1
Mr Baxter	5
Thomas Parr	2
Mr John Pearson	4
John Pearson	2
Thomas Pearson	2
Steven Bright	4
George Ludlam	3
Gilbert Tompson	1
Widdow Wainewright	3
John Savidge	3
Richard Gascoyne	1
Richard Batty	3
Thomas Machon	3
Robert Spencer	2
Mary Union	2
Mr John Stones	5
Roger Lee	5
Steven Green	3
Leonard Roberts	3
John Platts	2
Willm Creswick	2[240] two
George Creswick	3
Thomas Smeadley	3
George Pearson	4
Mr Schoarah	2
Steven Newton	2
Edward Webster	1

m 50]

Willm Oates	7
Willm Spooner	4
Mr Jessopp	11
George Hoyland	3
Widdow Shemeld	2
Samuell Wild	3
Willm Wild	2
Willm Hayles	1
Willm Woodroofe	4
John Hoyle	4
Anthony Bartin	1
Adam Fox	1
John Pinder	1
	273

Empty and noe distress to be had

Willm Harrison	3
Willm Rawson	1
Joseph Shemeld	1

These persons following are discharged by Certificates

Joseph Machon	1
Phillp Pitchforke	1
Widdow Hoole	2
Robert Newbald	1
Ellizab Mounkson	1
Willm Mounkson	1
Lawrance Savidge	1
Willm Osburn	2
Widdow Hancocke	1
Anthony Chapman	1
Robert Walker	1
Widdow Wright	1
Widdow Turner	1
	15

Robert Bennit Collr
Richd Bacon Const

These persons following are the Cutlers belonging to Sheffeild whoe deposited their

[239] 2 written over 1.
[240] 2 written over 1.

duty for their Forges but refused to pay the money without a Tryall at Law

John Barlay	1
Henry Watson	1
Willm Oates	1
John Jeffcock	1
Thomas Oates	1
John Firth	1
John Barton	1
Anthony Fox	1
Christopr Barker	1
Roger Leadbeater	1
John Pearson	1
Thomas Machon	1
Steven Fox	1
George Creswick	1
Thomas Smeadley	1
George Pearson	1
Thomas Mooake	1
Willm Oates	2
Samuell Wild	1
Totall	20

Firbeck

Sir Francis Faine	15
Mr Samuell Sanderson	4
Willm Hunt	2
Robert Hunt	2
Katherine Yates	2
Mr Chadwick	2
Mr Robert Sanderson	8

m 51]

Jarvice Boulton	1
Nichollas Mayer	1
Willm Jenkinson	1
Sir Francis Faine	2
Willm Talbutt	2
John Showler	1
Widdow Boulton	2
Simon Abbot	1
Sir Franis Faine	2
Edward Shephard	1
John Gaunt	2
George Hunt	1
Willm Fox	2
	54

Omitted by reason of poverty	2

Robert More Collr
Willm Stringfellow Const

Fishlack (Fishlake)

John Carter	2
Thomas Padley	2
Thomas Padley	1
Thomas Fairburne	4
Willm Clarke	1
Nichollas Crabtree	1
Robert Dickinson	2[241] two
Widdow Beamon	1
Richard Whitacrs	1
Henry Wright	2
Thomas Doughty	1
John Pettey	3
Mr Malum	2
Richard Crabtrey	4
Willm Parkin	1
Thomas Bilsbury	1
Thomas Wood	1
Willm Clarke	2
John Brogdin	1
Willm Doughty	4
Steven Milnes	3
Willm Smith	1
Thomas Waite	2
Richard Goodridge	2
James Clarke	3
Mr Parkin	10
Anne Clarke	2
Richard Dawson	2
Thomas Parkin	4
John Dawson	1
Willm Allon	1
John Taylor	1
John Brewster	1
John Whitacre	3
John Bunkin	1
Richard Jackson	1
Thomas Crowdson	1
Willm Pease	2
John Pettey sen	2
Widdow Hill	1
Widdow Saule	1
Robert Stochard	4
Steven Wharam	1
Robert Sikes	1
Willm Byfeild	1
John Waite	2
John Waitte	2

m 52]

Willm Gootheridge	1
Thomas Aikin	2
John Doughty	1
Widdow Jurdy	1
John Doughty	4
Willm Wright	1
Thomas Goodridge	1
Thomas Chancey	1
Thomas Reyney	2
Anne Allon	1
John Parkin	1
Robert Barker	1
John Padley	3
Robert Wright	1
Robert Bladworth	2
George Wright	2
Widdow Atkinson	2
Willm Doughty	1
Willm Chantrey	2

[241] 2 written over 1

Richard Swindall	1
Henry Doughty	2
Thomas Womersley	2
Willm Brears	2
Mr Wormley	7
Willm Crabtree	1
Robert Hill	3
Widdow Hill	1
Robert Womersley	4
Widdow West	1
Thomas Bladworth	1
Thomas Wright	1
Thomas Milns	4
John Mitchill	3
John Doughty	1
Willm Parkin	2
Samuell Pitchin	2
Robert Beamon	1}
Richard Goodridge	2}
Richard Doughty	2
Thomas Goodridg	2
Richard Sayle	1
Peter Wright	2
Mary Doughty	1
John Wilson	1
David Tebb	1[242]
Ellizabeth Moakes	2
Willm Goodridge	1
Thomas Waite	1
Sarah Goodridge	2
Ellizabeth Goodridge	1
Willm Bladworth	1
Mary Parkin	1
John Bladworth	2
Thomas Parkin	2
Robert Wayte	2
Willm Trimingham	2
Richard Gamble	2
John Crabtrey	1
Widdow Crabtrey	1
Willm Leavons	1
Willm Trimingham	1
	197

Empty and no distress to be had	
Thomas Denton	1
Mr Simpson	1
Jane Leatham	1
Joseph Walker	2

m 53]

These persons following are discharged by Certifts	
Widdow Crabtree	1
Rebecca Bridge	1
Widdow Atkinson	1
Richard Steele	1
Mary Williams	1
Omitted by reason of Poverty	11

Thomas Midleton Collr
Robert Sikes Const

Greasbrook (Greasbrough)

Thomas Armitage	4
Robert Hurst	2
Henry Wainwright	3
Willm Liversidge	1
Samuell Younge	1
Thomas Walker	2
Thomas Roberts	3
Joseph Hurst	3
Robert Oxspringe	3
Daniell Simpson	1
John Medlay	1
Brian Hinchcliff	5
Richard Armitage	1
Thomas Foulster	2
Widdow Armitage	1
Edward Hanson	2
Willm Hinchcliff	2
Willm Foster	1
Widdow Steares	3
Widdow Nevisson	1
Thomas Ransday	2
Samuell Harrison	4
Thomas Hurst	2
Francis Holmes	3
Anthony Wild	2
Robert Fulliloue	2
Willm Shepherd	2
Mr Thomas Setterthwate	5
Willm Guest	1
Nichollas Willie	1
John Firth	2
Henry Fullieloue	2
Abraham Munck	2
George Knott	1
Thomas Firth	2
James Firth	1
Steven Hinchcliffe	3
John Hibbird	2
Edward Hanson	1
Willm Rhoades	1
Thomas Howill	3
Robert Rose	4
Edward Briggs	2
George Whitley	1
Widdow Newbald	5
Edward Gill Esqr	19
Anthony Fulliloue	2
Robert Greenwood	1
Willm Dyson	1
Willm Yates	1
Luke Stafford	1
Willm Walker	1
John Beate	1
John Strafford	3
Thomas Liversidge	2
Roger Murgetroyd	3
Anne Dyson	1

242 1written over 2.

m 54]

Widdow Hurst	2
Willm Guest	3
John Secker	2
Willm Ward	1
Richard Hurst	1
Blythman Swallowe	3
Thomas Whitley	1
Mr Robert Heward	3
	150

Empty & no distres to be had

The Chappell house	2
Roger Murgetroyd	1

Omitted by reason of poverty 20

Robert Bennet Collr
John Firth Const

Hooton Pannell (Hooton Pagnell)

The Lady Hooton	23
Mr Marsh	4
Willm Ingland	2
Willm Greaues Jun	3
John Sykes	2
Widdow Johnson	1
Willm Greaues sen	1
Thomas Shippin	2
Luke Roberts	1
John Tyas	1
George Shaw	2
Willm England	2
Widdow Wikam	1
Richard Tyas	2
Henry Morley	1
Mr Stanhope	3
Richard Traves	2
Widdow Arley	1
Anthony Mitchill	1
Willm Luland	2
Willm Burton sen	1
Willm Mitchill	2
Henry Robinson	1
John Burges	4
George Jubb	3
John Baxter	1
Willm Burton Jun	2
Thomas Mariot	1
Widdow Fletcher	3
Francis Conway	1
John Smith	1
Mrs Copley	3
Thomas Shelley	3
Francis Heaton	6
Richard Blake	2
Henry England	1
Widdow Taylor	1
	93

Omitted by reason of poverty 3

Thomas Midleton Collr
John Burges Const

Houghton Magna (Great Houghton)

The Lady Rhoads	13
Mr Box	6
Willm Saunderson	3
Daniell Ranson	2
Willm Barrand	1
Lewis Crawshaw	1
Willm Stainforth	2
Henry Shepherd	1
Thomas Hinde	1
Thomas Fox	1
Thomas Liversidge	1

m 55]

Henry Abbot	1
Godfrey Greene	1
Willm Mathew	2
Willm Smith	1
Henry Bingley	2
Francis Kilkragge	1
Mr Wikam	4
George Jenkinson	1
Jarvas Abbot	1
Henry Shepherd	1
Robert Hague	1
Thomas Abott	1
Thomas More	1
John More	1
	51

Thomas Midleton Collr
Thomas Liversidg Const

Houghton parva (Little Houghton)

Darcy Shepherd	1
Willm Robinson	1
Willm Jackson	1
Sarah Watson	1
Joseph Houldsworth	1
John Shay	2
Thomas Saunderson	2
Mr Cooper	2
Mathew Oxley	1
Robert Hewitt	1
Willm Roulston	1
Widdow Harison	1
John Slacke	2
Willm Parkin	2
John Pruston	1
Richard Wilson	1
Willm Pruston	1
Thomas Watson	1
Ellizab Pruston	1
	24

Thomas Midleton Collr
Mathew Oxley Const

Hoyland

Sir Willm Rookeby	16
John Harrison	1
Robert Singleton	3
Mr Townend	8
Willm Coe	2
Joseph Naylor	1

Thomas Dobson	1
John Stansall	1
Mr Thomas Townend	7
George Durdam	1
John Woodhead	1
Willm Wigfeild	2
Widdow Hattersley	2
Willm Adamson	1
Robert Tompson	1
Willm Saunderson	3
Thomas Swift	1
Francis Swift	1
Thomas Wilson	1
John Rogers	1
Richard Butteroyd	1
Willm Webster	2
John Sayle	1
Thomas Robinson	1
Thomas Bateman	1
Willm Armitage	1
Richard Sleaton	1
Nichollas Tinley	5
Jane Carr	1

m 56]

Robert Beamon	1
Willm Wood	3
Widdow Otley	1
Willm Hoyland	2
John Freeman	3
John Colyer	1
John Hill	3
Thomas Hoyle	1
Robert Watson	2
Francis Clapham	1
Willm Pashley	1
George Hattersley	1
Trymon Armfeild	1
	90

Empty & no distress to be had	
Thomas Adamson	2
Thomas Adamson	1
Omited by reason of Poverty	11

Thomas Midleton Collr
Willm Coe Const

Hutton Roberts
(Hooton Roberts)

Thomas Roebuck	3
Edward Nicholson	1
Willm Woodson	1
Widdow Wainwright	2
The Countess of Strafford	14
Mr Barras	4
George Wainwright	2
Willm Nicholson	3
George GoodLad	1
John Johnson	1
Widdow Green	2
James Wheatcroft	2
Edward Pearson Jun	2
Richard Robinson	1
Thomas Nicholson	2
Roger Dauies	1
	42
Omitted by reason of poverty	10

Robert Bennit Collr
Willm Nelson Const

Harthill & Woodall

Sir Thomas Osburne Knt & Baront	26
Edward Barnby	1
Widdow Barnby	1
Christopr Shells	1
Thomas Stainland	2
Humphr Mullin	2
John Topham	2
Christopr Shells	1
George Whitehead	2
Robert Whitehead	1
Robert Marsh	1
Widdow Kitching	1
Henry Whitehead	1
Robert Marsh	2
John Ellis	1
Thomas Needan	1
Roger Belke	1
Robert Whitehead	1
Willm Hartley	1
Widdow Farnesworth	1
George Howkin	1
George Whitehead	2
Henry Wright	1
Widdow Barley	1
Richard Whitehead	1
Willm Bettony	1

m 57]

Robert White	1
Willm Smith	1
Willm Cheshire	1
Widdow Rutherford	3
John Taylor	1
Maxem White	4
Thomas Taylor	2
Widdow Marsh	3
John Barke	1
Thomas Shirtcliffe	1
Peter Dawes	2
Richard Wilkinson	1
Widdow Whitley	2
Joseph Drew	3
Thomas White	1
Thomas Shells	2
Thomas Choole	2
John Trevers	2
Willm More	2
Richard Barke	1
Roger Barley	1
John Westerne	1
Anthony Simons	2
George Mullen	2
Mr Carver	8
Sibell Bullevant	3

Marke Wareing	2
Widdow Belke	1
Richard Hallam	2
Thomas Harny	2
Mr Willm Kitching	9
George White	2
Widdow Stacy	1
Maxem Jenings	1
Nichollas Hirst	1
Richard Belck	1
Willm Wilson	2
John Keny	1
Robert Taylor	1
John Barnby	1
Robert Milner	2
	139

Empty & no distress to be had

Antho Simonet	1
John Treveis	1

These persons following are discharged by Certifts

Francis Greaues & Wilkinson	3
Widdow Spencer	1
Francis Winkes	1
George Martin	1
Thomas Barley	1
George Rogers	1
Thomas Kippas	1
Anne Brewhouse	1
Thomas Abty	1
George Story	1
John Fishburne	1
Omitted by reason of poverty	2

Robert More Collr
Thomas Barnby Const

Hallam uper part (Upper Hallam)

John Dale	2
Widdow Beighton	1
George Barnsley	3
Mr Robert Hall	8
Mathew Archdale	1
Widdow Dale	1

m 58]

Thomas Machin	1
Mr Hall	4
Godfrey Arsdale	1
Robert Farnclough	1
John Machin	1
Robert Ashton	1
Willm Bawmforth	2
Phillp Hawxtworth	3
John Bawmeforth	4
Adam Haxworth	1
Fullwood Hall	7
Jerem Smalfeild	2
Widdow Handcock	1
John Union	1
Thomas Union	1
Thomas Lord	1
Willm Carnell	1
John Gregory	2
Richard Greaues	1
Richard Bridge	1
John Hind	1
Robert Greaues	2
Joseph Tysan	1
Willm Wogden	1
Robert Hawksworth	1
John Marriot	1
John Bramham	1
John Hall	2
George Ronkersley	1
John Morton	1
John Marriot	3
Willm Tingle	1
Steven Fox	2

John Bromhead	3
Henry Bromhead	2
Henry Bromhead	3
Edward Dale	1
Thomas Corbridge	3
Anthony Broadhead	1
Thomas Blackburn	2
Richard Dale	1
Henry Stones	1
Anthony Green	1
Thomas Tyson	1
Edward Webster	1
Willm Fox	2
Willm Fox	1
Widdow Fox	1
John Barnsley	1
Willm Milnes	1
Widdow Beighton	1
Willm Wester Jun	3
Steven Heyland	3
Henry Scargill	2
Steven Heyland	2
John Smith	1
Thomas Marston	2
Walter Hurt	1
Robert Hind	2
Thomas Hind	2
Henry Darwin	4
Willm Webster Jun	2
Widdow Sheldon	1
Thomas Taylor	1
George Lord	1
Willm Ashforth	2
Peter Hewland	1
John Morehouse	1
Robert Union	1
George Barnsley	1
Richard Stones	1
Robert Ridge	1
	131[243]
Omitted by reason of Poverty	6

[243] There is a scribal error since the total is 133.

m 59]

Robert More Collr
John Dale Const

Hallam Lower part (Nether Hallam)

Joseph Wild	1
John Foster	1
Francis Spooner	2
Willm Jellot	1
Richard Webster	1
Willm Spooner	1
Richard Loyd	1
Willm Webster	4
Robert Goodale	1
Thomas Cutt	1
Thomas Walker	2
Thomas Webster	1
Thomas Walker	1
Joseph Smith	1
Thomas Smith	2
Robert Hoyland	1
Martin Lassells	2
Thomas Newton	1
Robert Tayler	2
Richard Broadbent	1
Robert Stevenson	1
Willm Stones	5
John Fearnley	2
John Fearnley	2[244]
Thomas Oxspring	1
Widdow Swift	6
Christopr Chapman	1
Nathanll Garlick	1
George Hollingworth	2
John Ashforth	1
Thomas Brownell	1
Edward Hague	2
Thomas Bower	1
John Bradshawe	2
Henry Taler	1
Willm Reyney	3
Hugh Hides	1
Robert Cooke	2
John Haile	1
Widdow Haile	1
Joseph Hides	1
John Hides	1
Edward Ranson	3
John Ranson vid	4
Thomas Wilson	1
Widdow Hill	1
Richard Woolhouse	1
Thomas Wainwright	1
Willm Wainwright	2
Phillp Ashbury	1
John Wainwright	1
Widdow Slack	4
John Brough	4
Robert Stacy	7
Willm Bower	1
James Mycock	1
John Swift	5
Willm Aldam	2
John Ranson	4
George Baumforth	5
	115

Empty & no distress to be had

Richard Woodroofe	1
John Webster	1

Omitted by reason of poverty 10

Robt More Collr
Francis Spoonr Const

m 60]

These Persons following are the Cutlers belonging to Sheffeild who deposited the duty for theire forges but refused to pay the Money wthout a Tryall at Law

Phillip Hawksworth	1
Robert Hinde[245]	1
Thomas Webster	1
Thomas Smith	1
Robert Stevenson	1
Nathan Garlick	1
George Hollingworth	1
Thomas Brownell	1
Willm Rayney	1
Hugh Hides	1
John Wainwright	1
Widdow Slack	1
George Bawmforth	3
	15

Hampall cum Stubbs (Hamphall & Hampall Stubbs)

Mr Rowlston	8
Mr Stanhope	9
Richard Sikes	6
John Wharam	2
Capt Washington	3
Widdow Rusby	2
	30

Thomas Midleton Collr
George Machon Const

Hansworth (Handsworth)

Samuell Drake Dr of Divinity	8
Allexand Newbald	3
John Savidge	4
Phillop Challoner	3

244 sic.
245 Robert Hinde and 1 are linked by a bracket marked upper part.

Robert Hartley	2
Thomas Hartley	1
Willm Stacy	1
Joseph Cowley	3
Robert Firth	4
Willm Fenton	4
Robert Firth	2
Joseph Firth	2
Robert Bradburry	5
Richard Wood	1
Thomas Oudale	1
John Oudale	1
Ralph Cartwright	1
Willm Green	1
Jonathan Holland	1
Widdow Simond	3
Willm Fox	1
John Turner	1
John Jenkinson	3
Francis Fenton	3
John Clarke	1
Mr Woodroofe	5
George Martin	1
Widdow Tompson	1
George Jackson	2
Widdow Hartley	1
John Allen	2
Francis Wastinnd	2
Mr Trippet	6

m 61]

George Harrison	5
John Austwick	1
John Vaines	1
John Parker	2
Edmond Jeffcock	1
Willm Martin	1
Widdow Martin	1
Joseph Whitacres	1
John Sowerby	3
Robert Jarvice	1
Mallin Jarvice	1
Edward Taylor	1
Jonathan Beighton	4
~~Mallin~~ Stacy[246]	4
Thomas Stacy	7
Mary Stacy	6
Anne Osgathorp	1
Widdow Fenton	1
Godfrey Hancocke	5
Thomas Stacy	2
Thomas Pursloue	1
Willm Ellis	3
Hugh Challoner	1
John Parr	1
Willm Tayler	1
Robert Wild	1
Edward Brookfeild	1
John Roger	1
Widdow Revill	2
Francis Bunting	2
Widdow Birkes Jun	2[247]
John Ratcliffe	2
John Shepley	2
John Gatecliffe	2
Willm Turner	2
John Kay	1
Phillp Allen	1
Robert Harrison	2
Robert Turner	5
John Lee	1
Willm Osgathorp	2
Thomas Marriot	2
Robert Stacy	3
Jo Inkersall	1
Willm Lemon	1
Willm Bullas	1
Robert Stacy	2
Willm Rogers	1
John Firth	3
Robert Jarvice	1
Mary Rowland	1
George Warter	2
Widdow Birkes	1
John Parker	2
John Nodder	6
Willm Allen	1
Mathew Rogers	1
Thomas Lambert	3
Godfrey Newbald	3
Robert Shawe	1
Edward Newbald	3
Roger Beldon	1
	205

Empty and no distres to be had

Lord Haward	1
Sanderson Watson	2
John Aikins	3
Edward Newbard	1
Joseph Newbard	4

These persons following are discharged by Certifs

Robert Simond	1
John Swinterton	1
Ellin Cartwright	1
Widdow North	1

m 62]

Omited by reason of Poverty 1

Robert More Collr
Roger Baildon Const

Hickleton

Sir John Jackson	32
Christopr Stead	2
Robert Stead	1
Willm Pygot	3
Samuell Roberts	3

[246] Christian name Mallin struck through.
[247] 2 written over 1.

Jane Haworth	1
Jerem Oates	1
Thomas Atkinson	1
Thomas Smith	2
Samuel Linsey	2
Richard Wainwright	3
Widdow Browne	1
John Taylor	1
Nichollas Smith	1
Katherin Syminit	3
Willm Smith	1
Robert Drable	1
	59

Omitted by reason of poverty	1

Thomas Midleton Collr
Thomas Atkinson Const

Hatfeild
(Hatfield)

Mr Lee	15
Richard More	2
John Dickinson	2
Richard More	2
Willm More	2
Mrs Hanson	2
Thomas More	2
Mr Dawtrey	2
Mr Hatfeild	11
Thomas Woodcocke	6
John Robinson	2
Thomas Hill	1
Richard Stones	4
Miles Sutcliff	2
John Crosley	3
John West	2
John Moulson	2
Copley Tomlinson	1
Henry More	1
John Fall	1
Mr Simpson	4
Mathew Saunderson	2
Mr Bradbury	13
Mathew Whitehead	1
Widdow Fisher	2
Willm Parkin	3
Willm Broadley	4
Robert Brooke	6
John West	3
Joseph Mitchill	2
Mary Farrar	3
Mr White	6
Mr Rawles	4
Mrs Drewrey	4
Willm Woodcocke	3
Lawrance Fox	3
Robert Killam	1

m 62]

Thomas White	3
Widdow Robinson	2
Thomas Box	1
John Preistley	2
Willm Mosley	1
Willm Fox	1
Willm Viccars	2
Richard Godson	1
Widdow Bursall	1
John Cooke	4
Robert Sutcliffe	1
Mrs Beamond	4
Widdow Udin	1
Edward Fox	3
Charles Cooke	3
Michaell Hanley	2
Thomas Shepherd	1
Thomas Coupland	1
Emanuell Say	2
Mr Clewith	1
John Fox	3
Thomas Deareman	2
Bartholl Newsom	2
John Roberts	2
Mary Chamery	1
Widdow Green	2
Barthol Newsome	3
Anthony Champley	1
Emanll Say	1
Thomas Woodcocke	1
Richard Stones	2
Richard Man	1
Earle of Devnshire	9
Mr Simpson	7
Robert Hawksworth	2
Richard Rigill	2
Willm Simpson	1
Widdow Hallas	2
Willm Darling	1
Willm Whitehead	2
Widdow Esh	1
Robert Ellis	1
Willm Poole	1
Richard Tirrey	1
Robert Tebb	1
Richard Houlegate	1
John Batley	1
Thomas Fox	1
Willm Boulton	2
Widdow Smith	2
Richard Barton	1
John Drewboy	1
Widdow Barge	1
Mathew Prim	2
Thomas Harison	1
Abraham Amory	2
James Stevenson	1
Isaac Amory	1
John Dumoulin	1
James Joglar	1
James Ramerey	1
James Hauer	1
Thomas Awkland	1
Francis Oxley	1
Peter Lelow	2[248]
	two
Isaac Vomplew	1

[248] 2 writtenover 1.

Mrs Keighley 7
Widdow Anchor 2
John Teese 1
Mr Vallenbergh 10
Willm Foster 2

m 63]

John Milman 2
John Leckin 2
Widdow Watkin 1
John Veny 1
Francis Wood 1
Benjam Guy 1
273

Empty & no distress to be had
Mr Simpson 3
Willm Sillaby 1
Francis Scawsby 2
John Veny 1

These persons following are discharged by Ceertfs
Henry Johnson 1
Richard Denby 1

Omitted by reason of Poverty 17

Thomas Midleton Collr
Willm Broadley Const

Hatfeild Woodhouse (Hatfield Woodhouse)
Henry Holegate 1
Nichodemus Tompson 2
Thomas Nowill 3
John Elliot 1
Richard Hudson 2
Isaac Dearman 2
John Stables 1
John Tompson 1
Mr White 1
Willm Jackson 1
John Stones 1
Thomas Chester 1
Richard Nowill 1
Anne Wright 1
Richard Hudson 1
Mathew White 3
Thomas Sutcliff 1
Robert Smithy 1
Charles Ellis 1
Edward Houlgate 1
Thomas Scholey 1
John Rawson 2
George Armfeild 2
Richard Stones 1
John Lund 1
John Lund Jun 1
Widdow Downing 1
Henry Casson 1
Robert Coulson 1
Widdow Shepherd 1
Francis Coulson 1
Richard Shepherd 1
Thomas Woodcock 3
Edmond Bower 3
Godfrey Chester 1
Mr Wintringham 4
Richard Moulson 2
Francis Newsom 2
Thomas Batley 1
Robert Crooks 1
Willm Linley 1
Widdow Hudson 2
Willm Marshall 1
Widdow Atkinson 1
Robert White 1
Zachar Burton 2
Thomas Winder 2
Isaac Vormale 2
John Judworth 2
Richard Troughton 2
John Aikeroyd 2
Robert Stones 2
Willm Hurt 2
Thomas Standing 1

m 64]

Charles Dickinson 1
Thomas Ellis 1
Isaac Decow 2
Charles Womacke 2
Robert Amory 1
Edward Fostard 2
Thomas Maw 2
Widdow Batley 1
Willm Winter 2
Mrs Maw 4
Widdow Malinson 2
Widdow Woodcocke 4
Thomas Outbridge 2
Samuell Firth 1
John Base 1
John Machin 2
111[249]

Empty & no distress to be had
Willm Ryley 1
Ann Cassan 2
Ellizabeth Hudson 2
John Judworth 1
Thomas White 3
Willm Heaton 1

Omitted by reason of Poverty 8

Thomas Midleton Collr
Thomas Newill Const

Kimberworth
Nathanll Darwin 1
Thomas Richinson 2

[249] The number 111 has been written over 110.

Mr Copley	1
Robert Robinson	1
John Barnsley	1
Simon Greenwood	1
Henry Pulleine	1
Simon Greenwood	2
George Cooke	2
John Foulston	1
Widdow Wass	1
Samuell Birks	1
Thomas Birks	2
Robert Lavorack	3
Robert Rawlins	1
Joseph Swallow	2
John Birkes	1
Edmond Wainwright	1
John Hartley	2
Edward Wainwright	1
Edwd Wainwright	1
Nichollas Silvester	1
Thomas Stacy	1
Nicholls Robinson	1
Peter Holmes	2
Widdow Tupman	3
Widdow Dyson	1
Thomas Hill	3
Mr Barnsley	5
Richard Ellam	2
Widdow Darwin	1
George Browne	2
Richard Eardley	2
Roger Cutloue	2
Richard Walker	2
Frances Nerburne	2
John Mitchill	1
Willm Mitchill	2
Robert Carr	3
Robert Kirke	1
George Swallow	1
Richard Swallow	1
Richard Nutt	2
John Wadsworth	2[250]
George Marsh	2
Richard Nutt Jun	1[251]
Joseph Milner	1
Nathaniell Robinson	2[252]
Willm Willy	2
Richard Muscroft	2

m 65]

Thomas Machon	2
Hugh Wilkinson	1
Robert Steele	3
Willm Kent	3
John Cutler	1
Robert Cutler	1
Ralph Haigh	3
Thomas Webster	2
George Holegate	3
Robert Kent	3
Robert Kent	2
Edmond Greenwood	2
Robert Bankes	3
Widdow Cross	3
Willm Cutler	1
Willm Hellefeild	4
Willm Ridley	4
Widdow Garret	2
Mr Firth	4
Mathew Didsbury	1
Thomas White	3
Humphr Emison	1
Roger Murgotroyd	3
Richard White	1
Francis Waite	2
Widdow Smith	3
Mr Thomas Kay	5
George Burgon	2
Thomas Bradbury	2
Roger Murgotroyd	2
John Murgetroyd	2
Willm Jarvas	1
Anne Emley	4
Thomas Burgon	3
Anne Dawes	2
Mr Copley	5
Richard Kent	1
Willm Kent	1
Thomas Crofton	1
Henry Hall	1
Thomas Greenwood	1
George Jenkinson	2
Thomas Hugall	1
John Newbald	1
	180

These persons following are discharged by Certificates

Robert Dawes	1
John Harrison	1
Joseph Smith	1
Robert Walker	1
John Taler	1
Joseph Darwin	2
George Axe	1

Omitted by reason of Poverty 16

Robert More Collr
Nathanll Darwin Const

Kirksandall
(Kirk Sandall)

Willm Fawkingham	1
Willm Taylor	3
Samuell Sayle	2
Willm Hague	4
Joshua Parish	2
Thomas Bayles	3
Ralph Akeland	1

250 Line inserted.
251 Line inserted.
252 2 written over 1.

Willm Wilson	3
Thomas Bayles	2
Thomas Fawkingham	1

m 66]

John Rusby	2
Thomas Hoyland	11
Willm Graues	1
Robert Serjent	1
Daniell Graues	2
Mrs Rookeby	12
Willm Watson	2
Jarvice Watson	2
Mr Bosvile	4
Mr Rookeby	1
John Pigburne	1
Nichollas Greaues	2
John Colley	1
Richard Greaues	2
	66

Empty & no distress to be had

Mr Ward	1
Mrs Rookeby	2

Thomas Midleton Collr
Thomas Bayles Const

Letwell

Sir Ralph Knight	14
Mr Joseph Baine	2
Mr Chadwick	7
Lawrance Pagden	2
Mrs Margret Chadwick	3
Richard Chambers	2
John Hunt	2
Francis Baxter	1
Mr Marsh	5
Francis Bailden	2
Godfrey Watkinson	1
Mr Chadwick	2
Robert Walley	2
Stafford Savidge	2
Widdow Browne	1
	48

Empty & no distress to be had

Sir Ralph Knight	1

Omitted by reason of Poverty	5

Robt More Collr
Godfrey Watkinson Const

Langfitt cum Tilts
(Langthwaite with Tilts)

Willm Child	1
	[1][253]

Robert More Collr
Wm Child Const

Lovversall
(Loversall)

Mrs Wheatley	9
Willm Oldfeild	1
Robert Pashley	1
Richard Nicholson	1
John Ellison	1
Robert Scailes	1
Robert Hawksworth	2
Willm Carver	1
John Pagden	1
John Boulton	1
Willm Pagden	1
Lawrance Champney	1
Daniell Keale	1
John Ellison	1
Francis Crawshaw	2
Thomas Amory	1
Francis Crawshaw	3
Richard Chappell	1
Richard Oldfeild	2
Peter Roebuck	1

m 67]

John Crawshawe	1
Robert Blacksmith	2
Thomas Slyrein	1
John Carr	3
	40

Robert More Collr
Lawrance Champney Const

Laughton Le Morthing
(Laughton en le Morthen)

Edward Roberts	1
Thomas Right	1
Robert Robinson	1
Jarvas Rhoades	1
Mary Shay	1
John Roebuck	1
Widdow Sayle	3
John Sayle	4
George Aire	1
John Mirfin	1
Marmaduke Justice	1
Robert Seaton	4
Robert Seaton Tanner	3
John Mirfin	1
Francis Ward	3
Mr Willm Beckwith	12
Mr John Bromhead	5
The Schoole	2
John Ashmore	2
Thomas Leadbeater	1
Thomas Boler	1
Thomas Dauy	1
John Turner	2
Thomas Leadbeater	1
Mr Henry Adams	5
Willm Mirfin	1
Mr Hatfeild	10

[253] No total given.

John Mirfin	1
Thomas Spencer	1
Willm Mirfin	1
Robert Chesshire	1
Thomas Skinner	1
Francis Rogers	1
Thomas Turner	1
John Fewston	1
Robert Steele	1
Thomas Chapman	1
John Spencer	5
George Ellis	1
John Tompson	1
Willm Morley	1
Willm Holmes	1
John Johnson	2
Willm Stacy	2
Daniell Hall	2
James Sikes	1
John Gleadall	1
Richard South	1
Daniell Hall	1
Robert Yates	1
Widdow Exley	1
Thomas Sharpe	1
Timothy Northrope	1
Isaac Watson	1
Willm Sayles	6
Nichollas Pearson	14
George Stacy	4
Robert Rushby	2
Epiphan Richinson	3
George Hall	1
Mr Whitehurst	3
Anthony Ellis	1
Willm Adroron	1
Nicholls Hutchinson	1
Widdow Wood	1

m 68]

John Misterton	6
Widdow Mirfin	1
Mr Beckwith	1
John Whalley	1
Mr Bareley	1
Robert Mirfin Gent	3
Robert Winter	1
Thomas Halliday	1
James Pashley	4
Jarvas Rushby	2
Willm Shaw	2
Nathanll Clayton	4[254]
	four
John Jawitt	2
Widdow Holland	1
Willm Booth	1
Richard Leadbeater	3
Robert Seaton	4
George Spencer	5
Nichollas Pearson	4
Robert Steele	3
Mr George Laughton	6
Mr Willm Laughton	6
Samuell Pearson	3
George Strawe	1
Nichollas Yates	4
	211

Empty & no distres to be had

Nathanll Clayton	1
Ralph Spencer	5

These persons following are discharged by Certificates

Willm Penistone	2
Widdow Foulstone	1
Widdow Smith	1
Willm Greene	1
Anthony Sissons	1
Edward Mirfin	1
Willm Hudson	1

Omitted by reason of Poverty 3

Robt More Collr
John Jewit Const

Marr

Edward Lewis Esqr	14
Mr Bentlay	1
George Greenbrough	1
Richard Gilling	1
Michaell Varley	1
Willm Healey	2
Robert Headley	1
John Viccars	1
James Headley	1
Willm Wainewright	1
Mary Scholey	1
Widdow Tyas	1
John Apleyard	1
Dinis Mason	1
John Berrey	1
Richard Hauley	2
Barnard Roswell	3
	34

Empty & no distres to be had

Richard Machon	1
Thomas Viccars	1

These persons following are discharged by Certifts

Widdow Smeaton	1
Richard Raynor	1
Jane Wilkinson	1
Anne Ashley	1
Margret Jenings	1

Omitted by reason of Poverty 1

Robt Bennit Collr
Richard Hanley Const

[254] 4 written over 2.

Melton super Monton (High Melton)

Richard Beckitt 1
Richard Holmes 1

m 69]

Henry Mathewman 1
Willm Scorney 2
George Batt 1
Willm Atkinson 1
Edmond Heward 2
Thomas Child 2
Widdow Shepherd 2
Mr Langley 8
Thomas Whitacrs 4
Henry Skelton 2
John Richardson 2
Willm Birkes 3
John Fountaine Esqr 12
John Wood 1
Willm Healey 1
Francis Traviss 1
George Hoyley 2
Thomas Foster 2
Thomas Lee 1
Richard Smith 1
53

Empty & no distres to be had
Mr Binns 4
John Fountaine Esqr 6

The person vndernamed is discharged by Certfte
Thomas Dawson 1

Omitted by reason of Poverty 3
Robt More Collr
Emonll Haworth Const

Mexbrough (Mexborough)

Captin Savill 8
Mr Horne 8
Michaell Harrop 1
Robert Watson 1
Richard Moody 1
John Hanson 2
Willm Cox 2
John Wood 1
Willm Pearson 2
Roger Watson 2[255] two
Margret Stanley 1
Robert Viccars 1
Roger Watson 1
John Ax 3
John Fayrburn 2
Willm Pinin 2
John Laughton 5
John Hinch 1
Robert Stanley 1
Thomas Wood 1
Samuell Cooke 1
Richard Winter 1
John Watson 3
John Pearson 2
Henry Royds 1
John Oldum 2
John Blacksmith 2
John Akeley 1
Thomas Hepworth 2[256] two
Robert Jisupp 1
Widdow Fostard 1
James Cox 2
Mary Roberts 2
67

Empty & no distres to be had
Mr Horne 3
Mr Horne 1
Mr Wortley 1

Omitted by reason of Poverty 6

Thomas Midleton Collr
Richd Moody Const

Maultby (Maltby)

m 70]

Mr John Revill 3
Mr Roger Fretwell 5
Thomas Lister 2
Willm Spencer 3
John Wright 2
Mr Thomas Wright 2
Robert Strangwidge 1
Thomas Shepherd 1
John Robinett 1
John Daniell 1
Thomas Shelton 1
Thomas Wild 3
Nichollas Sanderson 4
Richard Fretwell 3
James Fretwell 1
Gilbert Didsbury 1
Thomas Chaister 1
John Beard 1
Mr Wright 8
John Pashley 3
John Shephard 2
Gabriell Normavile 3
James Pashley 2
Susan Heinley 1
Thomas Yates 1
Thomas Wild 3
Robert Pye 1
Thomas Scales 1

[255] 2 written over 1.
[256] 2 written over 1.

Widdow Clayton	1
John Shacklock	1
Richard Jenkinson	1
Thomas Taylor	3
John Strangwidge	2
Willm Dale	1
Willm Jackson	1
James Chaystor	2
Willm Fretwell	5
John Topham	4
Ralph Spencer	4
Willm Richinson	1
Willm Fisher	1
Thomas Robinson	1
Michaell Pashley	2
Nichollas Yates	3
John Best	3
Thomas Herring	3
Henry Champney	1
Richard Goodison	1
Lord Vicount Castleton	30
Mr Barnes	5
Robert Roobotham	3
Willm Langwith	1
James Hunt	3
Widdow Yates	1
Godfrey Dewhurst	3
Humphr Parkin	2
Mr Nichols Saunderson	8
Thomas Lawrance	3
Richard Union	2
John Richinson	1
	164

Empty & noe distres to be had

John Parkin	1
Lord Castleton	2

Omitted by reason of Poverty	4

Robert More Collr
John Straingewayes Const

Rawmarsh

Mr Samuell Wainwright	7
Robert Fretwell	1
James Hanley	2
Robert Rhoades	1
John Rhoades	2

m 71]

Humphr Jackson	3
George Nicholls	1
Willm Nightscales	3
Willm Wainwright	2
Edward Goodwin Gent	7
Willm Dawe	2
Richard Foster	1
Robert Ellam	3
John Wadsworth	1
Willm Blacksmith	2
Jane Ward	1
Robert Torr	3
Richard Tinker	1
Francis Hilton	1
Willm Hauley	1
John Mann	1
Widdow Badeley	2
Willm Dodgson	1
John Dodgson	1
John Sharpe	1
Joseph Wagstaffe	2[257]
	two
Widdow Inman	1
Mr Blakeman	3
Mr Barnesley	1
Mr Barnesley	2
Godfrey Brooke	3
John Hall	2
Mr Christopr Adams Rector	4
Joseph Clarke	1
Thomas Clarke	1
Thomas Seaton	1
Mary Hurst vid	2

Thomas Marriot	2
Willm Hauley	1
Willm Ramsden	1
George Silcock	4
Anthony Jackson	1
Widdow Shepland	1
Robert Clarke	1
John Sharpe	1
Widdow Cheese	1
Thomas Ellis	1
Robert Sharpe	1
Thomas Ellis Jun	1
Thomas Wright	1
Nichollas Machin	2
Henry Wright	1
Thomas Tyas	1
Thomas Jessup	2
Thomas Bushforth	1
John Hebden	2
John Moxon	1
John Hatfeild Gener	9
Richard Viccars	1
	3

Empty & no distress to be had

Widd Aunt	1
Thomas Firth	1
Willm Goodwin	1

There persons following are discharged by Certificates

Widd Rhoades	1
Robert Amory	1
Willm Cutler	1
John Rhoades sen	1
John Cartwright	1
Anthony Goodwin	1
Richard Simond	1
Henry Wright	1
John Rushforth	1
Anthony Crowther	1
Mary Dodgson	2

[257] 2 written over 1.

m 72]

Omitted by reason of Poverty 2

Robert More Collr
Thomas Rushworth Const

Ranfeild (Ravenfield)

George Westby Esqr 12
Thomas Marriot 1
Richard Jarvice 1
John Tinker 1
Francis Mirfin 1
George Brooke 4
Thomas Bowor 1
Thomas Smeaton 2
Richard Goss 1
Oliver Robuck 1
John Bilam 3
Humphr Jackson 2
Jarvas Goodlad 2
Widdow Goodlad 1
Richard Gillifor 3
Widdow Rhoades 1
Widdow Parkins 1
Joseph Bower 1
Widdow Champney 3
Willm Holdsworth 2
Thomas Gamble 2
Willm Machon 1
Robert Watson 2[258] two
Robert Tyas 1
Anthony Smeaton 1
Mathew Brooke 1

52

Empty and no distres to be had
Mr Westby 1

Robert Benit Collr
Thomas Mariot Const

Rossington

Richard Firth 2
Widdow Firth 1
Edward Hall 4
Thomas Best 3
George Hall 2
John Gresson 3
Thomas Cambe 2
Richard Hurst 1
John Scolay 1
Joseph Strawe 2[259] two
John Nicholson 1
Willm Nicholson 2
John Marfin 2
Thomas Butterill 3
John Cambe 2
George Judd 2
Edward Hall 5
Steven Lambe 1
Nathanll Carter 1
John Bodwell 2
John Bridon 3
John Hall 3
Henry Flower 1
Willm Killam 2
Thomas Camp 3

54

These persons following are discharged by Certifts
Thomas Newton 1
Edmond Walker 1
Dorothy Flagitt 1

m 73]

Omitted by reason of poverty 4

Robert Bennit Collr
Thomas Kenney Const

Rotheram (Rotherham)

Francis Mountney Esqr 9
Nicholls Clarker 2
Thomas Stevenson 4
John Holmeshaw 2
Thomas Rusby 2
Alice Doffin 1
Mr Thomas Turner 6
Robert Kirby 1
John Birkhead 1
Jonathan Gee 3
Mr Jonath Staineford 9
Mrs Linlay 5
John Hollis &c 6
Robert Bromley 6
Mr Mirfin 6
Mr Saxton 10
Willm Oxley 2
Widdow Richmond 2
John Broughton 3
John Drewe 6
Mr Elie 7
Willm Hen 1
Robert Stones Jun 2
Willm Carr 1
Widdow Emott 3
Richard Hunt 3
Widdow Taylor 4
John Huscroft 2
Mrs Hargraues 1
John Wharton 1
Henry Ayre 2
Widdow Townend 3
James Ward 1
Widdow Tindall 5
Widdow Spandman 4
Richard Winter 1
Richard Johnson 1

[258] 2 written over 1.
[259] 2 writtenover 1.

Thomas Johnson	2
Joseph Platts	3
Thomas Gyles	1
Anthony Bright	1
John Platts	2
Thomas Spooner	3
Thomas Wild	2
John Gregs	1
Ralph Wollen	2
James Hugill	9
Ralph Wollen	3
Ralph Wollen	3[260]
John Henfray	2
Richard Henfray	1
Henry Greggs	1
Samuell Knapton	1
Godfrey Wainwright	3
George Hall	2
Robert Graues	1
Widdow Rich	2
Henry Gascoyne	2
James Fell Jun	3
John Gascoyne	1
Joseph Greenwood	3
Willm Stanley	2
Thomas Dolfin	1
Widdow Simms	3
Francis Black	1
George Carr	3
Henry Earnshawe	3
John Feild	1
Robert Stones	1

m 74]

Easter Wollen	3
Willm Lee	5
Mr Stireing	3
Ellizab Revill	1
John Winter	4
Gilbert Catterton	1
Godfrey Fowler	3
Henry Lillye	4
John Tim	3
Richard Carr	2
Widdow Shaw	4
Peter Brook	2
Mr Charles Darwent	6
Willm Kay	5
John Benlay	5
Robert Broadbent	5
John Tower	2
Mr James Malin	9
Widdow Birch	1
Richard Milner	3
John Heaton	3
Mr Mandevile	5
Ralph Barlawe	4
Mr John Paule	3
John Huscroft	5
John Cawthorne	3
John Holmes	3
Richard Schoalay	3
Widdow Roberts	2
Widdow Baylie	2
Thomas Shent	2
Mrs Willm Longley	9
Thomas Kent	4
Mrs Shawe	6
Mr Mandivile	4
Thomas Hallam	1
Edward Leadbeater	2
Willm Tompson	2
Mr Mandivile	1
Mr Thomas Blake	5
Edward Midlam	2
Mr Worrall	4
Widdow Cossins	2
John Steele	2
Willm Pattrick	1
Willm Baines	3
Robert Cooper	1
John Mossey	2
David Mossey	2
Robert Hancock	3
Richard Lee	1
John Tirry	5
Joseph Storrs	2
Mr Willm Smith	4
Widdow Silvester	1
George Dawson	2
Willm Foe	2
Willm Parkins	1
Mrs Wilkinson	8}
more	2}
Mrs Jarret	2
Mr Turner	2
Widdow Hancock	3
Nichollas Hobson	3
Mr Willm Stevenson	3
John Lee	2
George Murgetroyd	6
Willm Hellewell	1
Widdow Browne	7
Thomas Whittles	2
John Chadwick	5
Henry Hinch	2
Lyonell Ebson	2

m 75]

Lyonell Copley Esqr	14
John Hustey	2
Sarah Dickinson	5
George Murgetroyd	5
Mr Cayton	5
Willm Broadhead	3
John Kay	4
Mr Turner	6
Richard Bell	3
Christopr Cutler	2
James Hugill	4
Henry Yates	5
Benjam Barshawe	2
Thomas Westgate	2
Mr James Bromhead	5
Thomas Greenwood	2
Nichollas Ayre	1
Willm Hall	3
Simon Cundall	3
John Hamerton	3

[260] sic.

Thomas Roebotham	3
Mr Turner	3
John Binie	1
Richard Tinker	3
Thomas Leadbeater	1
Thomas Wharton	2[261] two
James Hague	1
Mr Mountney	1
John Hamshaw	1
Mr Mountney	2
Thomas Houlegate	1
Willm Hellefeild	4
Francis Tompson	1
Widdow Wilkinson	4
Mrs Wood	3
Richard Morton	2
Mr Tinker	3
Mr Tinker	2
Roger Hellefeild	4
Mr Staineford	5
Paull Tompson	2
Richard Cauthorne	2
Mr Mirfin	5
	562
Empty & no distress to be had	
West	3
Mr Jonat Stamford	1
Edward Graues	5
Mr Elie	2
Edmond Stocks	2
Widdow Rawlinson	2
Aldrm Webster of Doncastr	3
Earle of Arundale	10
These persons following are discharged by Certificates	
George Hague	1
Willm Beighton	1

Nichollas Swift	1
Widdow Lee	1
James Wilson	2
Omitted by reason of Poverty	35
Robert Bennit Collr	
John Maylin Const	
Scawsby	
The Lady Adams	15
	15
Robert Bennit Collr	
Samll Swinden Const	
m 76]	
Stotfeild (Stotfold)	
Mr Stannop	6
	6
Robt Bennit Collr	
Mr Stannop tent Const	
Sprotbrough	
Sir Godfrey Copley Bart	21
Nichollas Hawksworth	2
Joseph Hawksworth	5
Francis Weshington Cler	8
Thomas Fowler	1
Edward Watson	1
Francis Clay	2
John Lee	1
Thomas Hewit	1
Henry Dickinson	1
Richard Simpson	2
Thomas Houlegate	3
Thomas Wainwright	3

Jarvice Slack	1
Willm Clarke	4
Edward Mastin	1
Mr Wrightson	7
Margret Hepworth	2
Francis Boulton	1
Richard Corbridge	3
Thomas Towler	2
Nichols Keniley	1
Edward Hall	3
Thomas Barwick	1
Thomas Haword	3
	80
Robert More Collr	
John Lee Const	
Swinton	
Richard Barber	2
John Fayrburne	1
Humphr Addy	1
Martin Elam	6
Mr Blythman	8
Richard Bowser	1
Thomas Wilcocke	1
Allexand Thackerey	1
John Bramwith	2
Nathanll Naylor	1
Lancell Bridge	2
Willm Bingley	2
Widdow Fostard	2
John Addy	1
Thomas Ward	1
Darcy Stones	4
Willm Fairburne	1
Richard Watson	1
Godfrey Shells	1
Widdow Dawes	2
Samuell Burton	1
Henry Wilcocke	1
James Asop	2
John Parkin	2
Willm Addy	1

[261] 2 written over 1.

Richard Addy	2
Richard Dickinson	1
George Wilkinson	2
Thomas Broadhead	1
John Lambert	1
Henry Firth	1
Thomas Webster	2
Thomas Cutts	1
Thomas Bandison	1
Mathew Cross	1

m 77]

John Cross	1
Willm Wood	1
Charles Hill	1
	64

Omitted by reason of Poverty 1

Robert Bennit Collr
John Lee Const

Stansell cum Willingley
(Stancill with Wellingley)

Edward Smith	1
Willm Wright	2
Mr Battey	1
Anne Walker	1
Anne Wilston	1
Peter Bradforth	1
John Smith	1
Mr Wharton	5
Willm Hinch	3
Mr Withers	4
Thomas Ellam	4
	24

Omitted by reason of Poverty 1

Robt More Collr
John Smith Const

Stainton cum Hillaby
(Stainton with Hellaby)

Mr Hunt	8
John Armitage	3
Willm Fosterd	1
Richard Shephard	2
Widdow Pashley	2
Widdow Pashley	2
John Sanderson	2
Richard Pearson	1
Godfrey Shircliffe	1
Willm Holland	1
Willm Fretwell Cler	4
John Bevor	1
Joan Dunke	1
Robert Ward	3
Mr Barnes	4
Mr Fretwell	8
Willm Woodall	3
Richard Richinson	1
George Box	8
Steven Radley	1
Isaac Heigholme	1
	58

Robert Bennit Collr
John Bevor Const

Sikehouse
(Sykehouse)

Anthony Frankish	1
Robert Beamon	1
Richard Lacock	5
Richard Haworth	4
John Petty	2
John Wilkinson	2
Thomas Hawton	2
Nicholls Ayre	1
Alice Howson	2
Thomas Lockwood	1
Robert Cooke	2
Henry Cooke	2
Robert Smith	1
Mrs Byard	8
Edward Cooke	4
Thomas Pattrick	1
Willm Pease	1
Richard Naylor	3
Robert Denton	1
Henry Wood	1

m 78]

Mr Waller	5
Isabell Watt	3
Richard Jackson	2
Willm Wilman	1
Edward Wright Jun	2
Thomas Gleadow	2
Robert Denton	1
Edward Wilson	2
Richard Huscroft	1
Thomas Dinis	1
Thomas Crabtree	2
Henry Cooke	6
Jane Jackson	2
Nicholls Watson	1[262] one
Edward Wright sen	1
Nichollas Pearson	3
John Huscroft	2
John Hall	6
John Cooke	1
Anne Smith	1
Richard Denton	1
Robert Smith	1
Thomas Fish	1
Edward Wilson	1
Joshua Laverack	3
Willm Dale	1
Martin Smith	1
Barbar Crosley	1
George Beamond	2
George Pease	2
Mr Bridges	4
Henry Wood	1

262 1 written over 2.

Thomas Wood	1
Jane Fish	1
Samuell Cooke	6
Jacob Cooke	1
Robert Thorpe	9
Willm Benson	2
Sarah Maplebeck	1
Richard Cooke sen	2[263] two
Robert Burnley	1
Richard Lawson	1
John Reyney	1
Richard Cooke Jun	3
Richard Browne	1
Edmond Howson	1
Nichollas Pease	3
Edward Cooke	1
Ellizab Reynald	2
Robert Wright	1
Edmond Howson	1
Alice Howson	1
John Cooke	1
John Simon	1
Willm Crudd	1
	152

Empty & no distress to be had

Mr Edward Canby	2
Roger Cutler	1
Edward Wilson	1
Mr Bridges	1
Mary Grim	1
Willm Howson	2
Mr Poole	1

Those persons following are discharged by Certifts

Thomas Grene	1

m 79]

Thomas Clarke	1
John Hanson	1
Richd Hobson	1
Widdow Hill	2
Mary Heathy	1
John Walker	2
Mary Howson	1
Henry Pickard	1
Willm Steward	1
Thomas Peace	1

Omitted by reason of poverty	4

Thomas Midleton Collr
Robert Denton Const

Sheffeild (Sheffield)

Edward Sanderson	3
Thomas Newbald	2
Roger Trickitt	2
Widdow Lee	2
Godfrey Walter	1
John Hawley	2
Willm Burgon	1[264]
Willm Speight	2
John Stainford	4
Widdow Hobson	2
Lyonell Shacklock	2
Joseph Shemeld	4
Edward Barlowe	4
Mr Pruce	5
John Showor	4
Willm Stones	4
George Metcalfe	2
Samuell Sanderson	4
Widdow Wright	5
Joseph Clayton	1
Thomas Wright	3
Willm Freeman	1
Jarvace Fleeming	3
John Broughton	3
Nicholls Stainforth	3
Widdow Ellis	4
Mr Simpson	7
Henry Hancocke	2
George Thompson	10
Steven Bright	2
Willm Fox	3
Thomas Mason	5 1[265]
Richard Bower	3
George Hutchinson	2
Thomas Cooke	2
Christopr Burlay	2
Joseph Downes	6
Mr Watterhouse	5
Robert Bullas	2
Samuell Roberts	3
John Dalton	5
Robert Howsley	4
Joseph Taylor	2
Mallin Sowerby	15
Richard Downes	2
Willm Swinney	3
Samuell Hancock	3
Thomas Marriot	6
Lyonoll Revell	5
John Parker	1

m 80]

George Pearson	3
Richard Roberts	6
Richard Woodroue	8
Castle Shemeld	4
Widdow Taylor	2
Willm Turner	1
John Whitley	5 2[266]
Robert Nicholls	3

[263] 2 written over 1.
[264] 1 written over 2.
[265] It seems that the second number is a scribal query.
[266] It seems that the second number is a scribal query.

Widdow Kirkham	2
Mathew Clegg	1
Edmond Grubb	2
Edward Rawson	2
John Downes	5
Nichollas Oates	4
George Scargill	3
Widdow Crooke	3
Thomas Scargill	2
Mr Chappell	10
Robert Pinder	5
Robert Ellis	5
Widdow Barton	2
John Stacy	6
Widdow Steven	2
Edward Hellefeild	2
Thomas Johnson	2
Anthony Sims	3
Robert Rippon	1
Henry Gillot	2
John Swift	3
Robert Collie	2
Willm Hawke	1
John Clayton	1
Joseph Hobson	3
Thomas Monke	1
James Spencer	4
Robert Fisher	4
John Steven	2
Nichols Stainforth	1
Willm Ratcliffe	1
Joseph Smith	1
Francis Brownell	4
Edward Steven	3 3[267]
John Winter	2
James Carr	2
John Firth	2
Thomas Monke sen	4
Robert Brealsforth	3
Joseph Bradbury	2
Thomas Tricket	2
Robert Cutforthhaugh	1
Willm Webster	4

Thomas Mathewman	3
Widdow Sutton	4
Joseph Brockfeild	1
James Tupman	1
James Barber	1
Robert Machon	1
Robert Turner	1
Mallin Gillot	1
Richard Webster	1
Widdow Lockwood	2
John Sutton	2
John Barber	4
Nathanll Hall	1
John Pearson	1
Widdow Siminet	1
Henry Gillit	1
George Scargill	2

m 81]

Ralph Hide	2
Thomas Platts	2
Robert Turner	1
Widdow Ellis	2
Thomas Jeffcocke	2
Thomas Spooner	4
George Tricket	1
Richard Sims	7
Joseph Hauley	3
Samuell Barlay	3
Humphr Swinden	2
Thomas Creswick	1
Mathew Arnall	2
Mathew Arnall	8
John Swallowe	5
John Stireing	4
Cutlers Hall	1
Willm Burlay	4
Thomas Burlay	2
Godfrey Creswick	4
Willm Creswick	2
Robert Hudson	8
John Brelsforth	3

James Webster	3
Widdow Creswick	4
Thomas Creswick	2
Willm Fox	2
Ralph Shore	1
Henry Stringfellow	2
Widdow Sands	2
Willm Sands	2
Christop Stewardson	2
Robert Hancock	1
Richard Barber	5
John Carr	4
Willm Twibell	2
Edward Britlebank	2
Willm Shirtcliff	3
Robert Shirtcliff	1
Thomas Rose	4
Willm Thorpe	1
Ellin Lee	1
Thomas Redford	2
Gilbert Roberts	4
Willm Scargill	3
John Shower	5
John Wigfeild	2
Robert Broadbent	1
Robert Pearson	1
Widdow Mason	1
John Woodhouse	1
Willm Nuns	1
Thomas Pearson	2
Nichollas Roewood	3
John Graues	2
Richard Webster	3
George Fox	4
Widdow Pell	4
Joseph Arnold	2
Mr Lobley	6
2d part Mr Thomas Burbeck	6
Steven Fox	4
Mr Ranson	10
John Senior	3
John Pearson	2

267 It seems that the second number is a scribal query.

Willm Harvie 2
Willm Bullas 4

m 82]

John Trippit 6
Robert Trippit 2
Edward Roberts 8
Mr Godart 5
Mr Samuell Savidge 2
Widdow Stacy 3
John Bower 4
Mr Francis Barlowe 12
Abigall Rawlinson 5
James Goody 5
Joseph Mower 4
Mr Thomas Britland 4
Mr Cooke 5
Widdow Wood 5
Widdow Walton 3
Mr James Bright 3
Anthony Hall 7
The Freeschoole 3
Willm Rawlin 3
Mr Dewrant 3
Mr Richard Taylor 2
Thomas Webster 2
Richard Bullas 3
Willm Collie 2
John Hick 4
Robert Allon 4
John Wilkinson 1
Anthony Woodhouse 1
Obediah Barlay 2
John Townes 2
Joseph Smith 1
Robert Crookes 2
John Bright 1
James Newton 5
Francis Hobson 1
Thomas Robinson 1
Robert Nichols sen 1
Robert Tibbott 3

Steven Ludlam 2
Richard Roberts 2
Willm Mathewes 4
Mr Bolton 4
Mr Bolton 6
Thomas Jenings Jun 4
Widdow Savidge 4
Thomas Parkins 3
Steven Allon 2
Thomas James 1
Mr Wadsworth 6
Mr Andrew Bacon 3
Richard Meales 2
Thomas Jenings sen 4
Robert Howsley 1
Joshua Scargill 5
Willm Ellis 2
Thomas Ellis 2
Widdow Elliot 3
Joseph Thorpe 1
Willm Ward 1
George Chowe 6
& Nicholl[268]
Willm Turner 3
Joseph Hancock 5
Mr Richard Paramore 4
Thomas Badger Jun 2
Robert Thwates 2
John Hancock 3

m 83]

Thomas France 1
Willm Dawson 1
Ralph Clayton 2
Anthony Beate 1
Mr Browne 3
Mr Gardiner 4
Willm Webster 3
George More 2
John Stainforth 2
John Curr 1
Widdow Rogers 1

John Rogers 1
Willm Twigg 1
Thomas Pearson 2
John Watkin 3
Willm Green 3
Charles Hancock 4
Thomas Revill 2
Widdow Fox 1
Widdow Waid 1
Mathew Youle 3
Andrew Foster 1
Richard Yates 1
Robert Twigg 1
Eusebus Hancocke 1
Thomas White 3
John Thwaites 1
James Hoole 2
Robert Spooner 2
Willm Marshall 1
Thomas Hudson 1
Steven Stacye 3
Widdow Steven 1
George Spooner 1
Widdow Rogers 4
James Rockley 2
Rebecca Mathewman 2
John Stevenson 1
John Webster 5
Willm Rogers 1
Robert Kirby 4
Ellexander Watson 1
Robert Fisher 1
James Creswick 4
John Ranson 3
Joseph Butler 2
John Hawley sen 3
Willm Cattrill 1
Michaell Wright 2
Willm Elland 3
Widdow Peck 3
Robert Nuns 3
George Harison 1
Edward Ellis 3

[268] inserted in another hand.

Thomas Barber	5
Mr James Curtious	4
Widdow Stones	2
George Stones	2
Thomas Poynton	2
Willm Allon	1
Thomas Cowley	1
Willm Crawshay	5
Charles Clayton	5
Mr Poole	4
Thomas Heward	3
Daniell Bacon	3
John Ayre	11[269]
John Hick	3
Widdow Hancocke	3
John France	1
Joshua White	6
Thomas Scargill	1
Samuell Nicholls	2
Isaac Vaines	2
Thomas Badger sen	1
Rowland Bramhald	2
Willm Busfeild	1
Willm Ellis	2
George Bullas	2
Richard Abdies	1

m 84]

Thomas Godart	2
Mallin Stacie	1
Joseph Stacie	3
George Shore	2
Mallin Pye	2
James Rose	3
Joshua Baites	5
Mr Fisher	6
Edmond Laythwood	3
Willm Leach	1
Francis Cawton	3
Thomas Berrey	1
Ellias Trickitt	1

Thomas Creswick sen	3
Henry Longson	2
Thomas Revill	2
Thomas Bullas	2
Edward Badger	2
Widdow Stacy	3
Edward Robinson	2
Willm Scargill	7
Robert Inman	3
Thomas Oxley	1
John Stevenson	2
George Jeffcock	1
John Adamson	1
Abell Yates	3
Jonathan Webster	3
Thomas France	3
Joseph Hauley	3
Joseph Nutt	2
Margret Arsdale	4
Jonas Taylor	2
Thomas Lemons	3
George Roger	1
Charles Simond	1
Richard Mathewman	1
John Jeffcock	2
John Twigg	1
Napthan Chapman	7
Thomas Twigg	6
Willm Quicksall	1
Robert Nutt	6
Joshua Wilkinson	2
Robert Shawe	3
Robert Stainforth	2
Widdow Windle	1
Willm Hartley	2
Edward Crosley	1
John Spencer	1
Edward Croswick	3
James Stainforth	7
Mr Boulton	5
	fiue
Boas Warrin	2

Thomas Dodsworth	3
John Clayton	3
Daniell Meares	1
Thomas Tucker	4
Samuell Tayler	3
Godfrey Wild	3
George Turner	1
The Bathhouse &c	3
Mr Nevill	21
Mr Ratcliffe	36
Mr Mirfin	5
Nichollas Lumax	1
Nichollas Ashmore	1
Michll Newbald	3
Samuell Saineford	5
Mr Gamble	1
John Barker	3
John Barker	2
George Chapman	1
Anthony Morton	1
	1190[270]

m 85]

These persons following are the Cutlers belonging to Sheffeild who deposited the Duty for their forges but refused to pay ye money without A Tryall at Law

Willm Burgon	2
John Stainford	2
Edward Barlowe	1
Willm Stones	1
Joseph Clayton	2
Willm Rich	1
Christopr Burlay	3
Joseph Downes	1
Mallin Sowerby	1
Samuell Hancock	1
George Pearson	1

[269] 'elewen' is written next to 11.
[270] There is a scribal error since the total is 1196.

Castle Shemeld	1[271]
Willm Turner	1
John Whitley	1
John Downes	1
Nichollas Oates	1
Robert Ellis	1
Widdow Barton	1
Widdow Steven	1
Edward Hellefeild	2
Thomas Johnson	1
Anthony Sims	2
Robert Rippon	1
Henry Gillot	2
Robert Colley	2
Thomas Colley	1
Willm Hawke	2
John Clayton	2
Thomas Monke	1
John Steven	1
Nichollas Stainforth	1
Willm Ratcliffe	1
Joseph Smith	2
Francis Browne Jun	1
Edward Stevens	2
John Winter	1
John Firth	1
Thomas Monke sen	1
Robert Bralesforth	1
Thomas Tricket	1
Willm Webster	1
Thomas Mathewman	1
Thomas Twigg	2
James Tupman	2
Robert Macon	2
Richard Webster	2
Widdow Lockwood	1

m 86]

John Sutton	1
John Barber	3
Thomas Melton	1
Ralph Hide	2
Thomas Platts	1
Widdow Ellis	1
Thomas Jeffcock	2
George Tricket	2
Richard Sims	2
Joseph Hauley	1
Mathew Arnoll	1
Mathew Arnoll	1[272]
Willm Barlay	3
Thomas Barlay	1
Godfrey Creswick	1
Willm Creswick	1
John Brelsforth	1
James Webster	1
Widdow Creswick	1
Thomas Creswick	1
Ralph Shore	2
Henry Stringfellow	1
Widdow Sands	2
Willm Sands	2
John Carr	1
Willm Twibell	1
Edward Britlebanke	1
Willm Shirtcliffe	1
Thomas Redford	1
Gilbert Roberts	1
John Wigfeild	1
Robert Broadbent	2
Widdow Mason	1
John Woodhouse	1
Willm Nunns	1
Thomas Pearson	1
Nichollas Rowood	2
Richard Webster	2
George Fox	1
Widdow Pell	1
James Steven	1
Joseph Arnold	2
Thomas Mawer	2
2d pt Willm Harvie	1
John Tripit	1
Robert Tripit	1
John Bower	1
Joseph Mower	1
Richard Bullas	1
Anthony Woodhouse	2
Thomas Jenings Jun	1
Thomas Jenings sen	1

m 87]

Robert Hewsley	1
Willm Ellis	1
Thomas Ellis	2
George Chowe	1
Nichollas Chowe	1
Mr Richard Paramore	1
Thomas Badger Jun	2
Robert Thwaites	1
Willm Webster	1
John Staineforth	2
Thomas Pearson	2
Thomas Revell	1
Widdow Fox	1
Widdow Waid	1
Andrew Foster	1
Thomas Howsley	1
George Spooner	1
Rebecca Mathewman	1
John Stephenson	1
John Webster	1
John Hawley sen	1
Robert Nuns	1
George Harrison	1
Edward Ellis	1
Thomas Barber	1
George Stones	2
Thomas Cowley	1
Willm Crawshawe	1
Isaac Vaines	1
Thomas Badger sen	2
Rowland Bramhoyld	2
Willm Ellis	1

[271] 1 written over 2.
[272] sic.

Richard Abdies	1
Joseph Stacy	1
George Shore	1
Willm Leach	2
Ellas Trickitt	2
Thomas Creswick sen	1
Thomas Revill	1
Thomas Bullas	1
Edward Badger	2
Thomas Oxley	1
George Jeffcocke	2
Abell Yates	1
Jonath Webster	1
Joseph Hauley	1
Joseph Nutt	2
Jonas Taylor	1
George Roger	2
Richard Mathewman	1
John Jeffcocke	2
John Twigge	2
Napthal Chapman	1
Thomas Twigg	4
Robert Nutt	1
Robert Stainforth	1
Willm Hartley	1
Edward Crosley	1
Thomas Dodsworth	1
	210

m 88]

Empty & no distres

Widdow Wright	1
Thomas Creswick	2
John Marshall	1
Thomas Stone Jun	2[273]
John Ayre	2
Robert Rawlin	1
Widdow Midleton	2
Robert Stainforth	2
Isaac Parke	1
George Smeadly	2
John Bright	2
Joseph Wawton	3
Thomas Melton	1

Those persons following are discharged by Certificates

Thomas Grubb	1
Thomas Whittington	1
Thomas Melton	1
John Cartreit	1
Richard Jackson	2
Godfrey Creswick	1
Anthony Milnes	1
Thomas Bright	2
Thomas Willie	1
Henry Bingham	1
John Webster	2
Thomas Heward	1
Edward Roberts	1
Benjam Thwaites	1
Widdow Ashton	1
Richard Rich	1
George Baite	1
Thomas Peck	2
Livian Bingley	1
Francis Sikes	2
Robert Stainland	1
Widdow Atkinson	2
Nichollas Shirtclifte	1

Omitted by reason of poverty 54

Robert Bennit Collr

Thomas Badger Const

Staineforth cum Bramwith (Stainforth with Bramwith)

Robert West	1
Richard Naylor	2
Richard Ross	3
Charles Heathy	2
Thomas Walton	1
Mrs Cowling	1
Thomas Laverack	2
John Lauerack	3
Robert Mallison	2
Christopr Barker	3
Mr Stapleton	4
Willm Mallison	3
Humphr Tonge	2
Widdow Barker	4
John Stadder	1
Mrs Portington	7
Richard Youle	1
Robert Reader	3
Edward Turner	2
Thomas Killam	2
Thomas Standwith	3
John Lund	3

m 89]

Willm Naylor	1
John Jackson	1
Henry Yates	1
John Malison	3
Widdow Oughton	4
Willm Malison sen	1
Samuell Simpson	2
Widdow Chantrey	2
Thomas Smith	2
Mrs Portington	1
Robert Emson	2
John Law	1
Widdow Emson	1
Nichollas Clough	1
Widdow Simpson	2
John Simpson	1
Thomas Mearbecke	1
Widdow Killam	2
Willm Haworth	2
Robert Reeder	1
John Benson	4
Widdow Simpson	1
Thomas Waite	1

[273] 2 written over 1.

Mr Hatfeild 1
Mr Rasine 12
John Jillot 2
Zachar Downing 1
Thomas Downing 1
Thomas Balderston 1
John West 1
Thomas Golton 2
Robert Smith 1
Edward Murfin 2
Willm Crabtreey 2
Richard Swash 1
120

Empty & no distres to be had
Edward West 1
Thomas Walton 1
Mr Firz William 6
Thomas Smith 1

The person vndernamed is discharged by Certificate
Francis Birdsall 1

Omitted by reason of poverty 3

Thomas Midleton Collr
Thomas Waite Const

Sunderland (Tickhill Sunderland)
Willm Lambert 4
Lawrance Horner 2
Ann Ingall 1
Robert Smith 1
Thomas Hudson 2
George Poole 2
Willm Robinson 1
Joseph Addyson 3
Richard Copley 2
Robert Hall 3
Mr Vessey 3
Willm Marshall 1
Willm Nicholson 1
Mr Willm Loughton 3
Robert Simpson 2
John Snydall 2
Peter Hoyle 1
Thomas Bower 3
Willm Lee 1
Nichollas Spencer 1
Richard Boswell 1
Thomas Fox 1
Thomas Roebuck 2
Richard Broadbent 4
The Paper Milne 2
Willm Madson 2
Edward Ridge 1
Mr Orray 1
John Bradforth 1
Ralph Smith 2

m 90]

Willm Moody 1
George Roebuck 1
Willm Lee 2
John Parsisson 1
Thomas Smith 1
Robert Gaunt 2
John Marr 2
Thomas White 2
Thomas Marr 1
Thomas Jurdan 1
Henry Burne 1
Thomas Fairnworth 3
Daniell Ogden 1
John Lambert 3
JAnne Ingall[274] 1
Willm Langcaster 1
Francis Smith 4
John Skinner 2
Thomas Watson 1
Thomas Robuck 1
Willm Turwin 1
Thomas Haire 1
Sarah Nicholson 1
Thomas Goodjeare 3
George Booker 4
George Holmes 3
Willm Booker 1
Robert Johnson 3
105

Empty & no distres to be had
Willm Cooke 1
Willm Hudson 1

Omitted by reason of Poverty 1

Robert More Collr
George Holmes Const

Tickill Towne (Tickhill Town)
Ralph Hansby Esqr 24
Godfrey Ward 1
John Broadbent 2
Robert Swift 4
Richard Hole 2
Nichollas Padley 2
Robert Hanson 1
Willm Shepherd 3
Thomas Sybery 2
John Turner 2
Mr Nicholas Wilson 8
Mr John Slyman 7
Thomas Smith 1
Nichollas Hurst 1
Willm Bentle 1
Willm Askome 1
Henry Schoray 1
George Carr 4

274 sic.

John Smith	1
Willm White	1
Widdow Roberts	3
George Hole	2
Marke Oakes	1
Thomas Hole	3
George Booker	3
Richard Lane	1
John Simpson	4
Henry Tompson	1
John White	2
Widdow Clegg	1
John Hole	2
Widdow Ingle	2
Willm Netleship	2
John Oxenford	2
Edward Pattrick	1

m 91]

Willm Pell	2
John More	1
Edward Revell	1
Willm Reeder	2
John Towler	1
Willm Randall	1
Willm Hole sen	4
Thomas Thornton	2
John Hole	3
Robert Dunn	2
Willm Ramsgill	2
Willm Towler	1
Thomas Roberts	2
Francis Pashley	1
John Wombell	4
	128

Empty & no distress to be had

The Milne	1
The West Milne	1
Mr Batty	6
Leonard Berrey	1
The Freeschoole	1

These persons following are discharged by Certfts

Christopr Boulton	2
John Martin	1

Omitted by reason of Poverty 2

Robert More Collr
Willm Reeder Const

Tickill Northgate (Tickhill, Northgate)

Mr John Laughton	11
Mary Wicam	1
Humphr Holmes	1
Edward Simpson	6
Widdow Oughbridg	1
Willm Gaunt	1
John Whipwhang	1
Thomas Hickson sen	2
Thomas Ingland	1
John Ingland	1
Nichols Hacket	3
John Robinson	1
Widdow Charles	5
Miles Stockes	2
Thomas Aukland	4
Robert Copley	1
Thomas Towfeild	2
Willm Amerey	1
John Shepherd	1
Marmad Newmarsh	1
Robert Carr	1
Thomas Hickson	2
Henry Stockes	2
George Ingland	1
James Howson	1
Richard Greaues	3
Mrs Horton	5
Widdow Dawson	3
James Howson	2
Thomas Howson	1
Widdow Charles	1
Willm Troughton	1
Mr Wharton	2
Willm Nicholls	4
George Carington	1
Thomas Woodall	3
Edmond Woodall	2
Henry Booth	2
Willm Troughton	3
Edward Hickson	3
Mr Turnill	4
Mr Laughton	3
Widdow Hamerton	5
John Roebuck	2

m 92]

Widdow Clegg	2
John Towler	4
Anthony Addy	5
Widdow Hudson	2
Martin Lee	1
Mr Wharton	1
Widdow Hodgson	1
Robert Hole	2
Widdow Swift	1
John Hole	2
John Brewit	2
Widdow Oddy	3
James Ridor	1
Thomas Hickson Jun	2
Mr Burtinshaw	3
	136

Empty & no distres to be had

Mr Towfeild	1

Omitted by reason of Poverty 1

Robert More Collr
Thomas Hickson Const

Thribergh (Thrybergh)

Sir John Rearsby Bart	22
John Cross	1

The Milnes	2
Sir John Rearsby	2
Abrah Aineley	1
Ralph Clarke	1
Gregory Bower	1
Widdow Leach	1
Godfrey Wigfeild	2
Willm Watterhouse	3
James Haworth	1
Edward Robuck	2
Thomas Robuck	1
Robert Chappell	1
John Smith	2
Thomas Holmes	1
Joseph Nantcliffe	1
Willm Smith	4
Thomas Lister	1
Steven Liversidge	1
Robert Yates	1
Widdow Tyas	1
Edward Ratcliffe	2
Willm Carr	2
Thomas Nicholson	1
S[i]r John Rearsby	1
Francis Fowler	3
The parsonage	7[275]
	69

Omitted by reason of Poverty 3

Robert Bennit Collr
Thomas Chappell Const

Thurnscoe

Doctor Spencer	5
Mr Grant	5
Mr Traggit	5
Mr Benton	3
Roger Jissup	2
George Mounks	1
Willm Allon	1
John Robinson	1

m 93]

Roger Robinson	1
Thomas Dale	1
Darcy Otley	1
Adam Rayner	1
Thomas Rayner	1
John Stead	1
Michaell Mastin	1
Roger Twotill	1
Mr Beestin	4
James Mortimer	2
James Otley	1
Willm Allan	1
Willm Roebuck	1
Mr Beestin	2
Widdow Varmun	1
	43

Omitted by reason of Poverty 1

Thomas Midleton Collr
James Mortimer Const

Todwicke (Todwick)

Richard Belke	4
Mr John Hexem	6
Francis Hopkinson	1
Robert Getlay	2
Thomas Linlay	2
Simon Gill	3
Timothy Farrer	2
John Johnson	2
George Fox	2
John Fox	1[276]
	one
Roger Belke	2
Willm Belke	1
Anthony Newbolt	1
Thomas Wastindge	1

Mr John Gorland	7
John Nicholson	2
Gilbert Poplewell	1
Edward Newbolt	2
Martin Parkin	1
Mr Franc Rearsby	1
Jarvice Fox	1
	45

Robert Bennit Collr
Robert Getley Const

Tinsley

Henry Ashforth	1
John Owtram	1
Willm Austwick	1
Widdow Cliffton	1
John Rogers	1
Edmond Downes	1
Henry Greaues	1
Oniciforus Austwick	2
John Challoner	1
Seth Shepley	2
Thomas Jarvice	2
Thomas Brooke	2
George Beardsall	3
Seth Shepley Jun	1
Willm Shepley	4
George Oakes	1
George Shippard	1
John Nicholson	1
John Parr	1
Willm Harrison Jun	3

m 94]

John Orrobin	3
Willm Harrison sen	6
George Rich	1
Richard Wood	1
Widdow Jenkinson	1
Willm Shepherd	1

275 7 writen over 6; 'seaven' is written after 7.
276 1 written over 2.

James Hattersley 1
Richard Wood 1
Thomas Cock 3
Mr Richard Burrass 6
Parker Bennit 2
Joseph Sturtevant 2
Willm Hoole 5
Widdow Setterthwaite 1
Willm Booth 3
Nichollas Jellot 1
Thomas Fowler 1
Thomas Starkey 3
Alphonsus Morton 1
Widdow Hatfeild 2
Richard Harwood 2
Ann Ludlam 2
Thomas Pye 2
82

Empty & no distress to be had
Mr Staineforth 4
Nichollas Hobson 2

Omitted by reason of Poverty 3

Robert More Collr
Seth Shepley Const

Thorpe Solvin (Thorpe Salvin)
Sir Thomas Robinson Bart 20
Mr Rogers 8
John Dinglay 1
Thomas Nemes 1
George Chantrie 1
Thomas Wilson 3
John Thornillie 1
John Wild 1
Widdow Emerson 1
Widdow Cuthbert 1
Widdow Antley 1
John Rogers 1
John Martin 2
Francis Parr 1
Roger Shipton 3
Widdow Wright 1
Edward Rayles 2
Edmond Price 2
Jarvas Stawell 2
Widdow Binnie 2
John Langwith 1
George Burlay 1
Willm Allon 1
Widdow Wright 1
S[i]r Thomas Osburne 2

George Martin 1
John Westerman 1
63

Empty & no distress to be had
Robert Benney 1

The person vndernamed is discharged by Certificate

John Milner 1

Omitted by reason of Poverty 2

m 95]

Robert Bennit Collr
Willm Ellin Const

Treeton
Mr Michll Adams 8
Willm Turner 2
Thomas Towles 4
Mr Westby 1
Widdow French 3
Willm Hilton 3
Willm Goodall 1
Willlm Potter 5
John Anderon 1
John Anderon Cler 1
Jarvas Fox 1
Henry Earnshawe 1
Willm Sedgfeild 1
John Anderon 5
Thomas Adamson 3
Thomas Adamson 1
Richard Shepherd 2
Francis Wortley 2
Thomas Jawit 3
Thomas Caworth 2
Richard Shepherd 1
Edward Fox 1
Ralph Smalepage 1
Richard Charles 1
Nichollas Beighton 1
Thomas Herring 1
Willm Archer 2
Henry Yaule 3
John Antley 1
John Pashley 1
Mrs Place 1
Thomas Pashley 1
Thomas Robinit 4
Francis Calvert 3
Godfrey Turner 1
Edward Wilson 1
Willm Watterhouse 1
75

Empty & no distress to be had
Willm Sissons 1
Robert Pashley 2

Omitted by reason of poverty 8

Robert More Collr
Willm Goodall Const

Thorne
Edward Stear 7
John More 2

Thomas Kirby 1
Richard Clayton 2
John Herbert 2
Joseph Womersley 2
Anthony Atkinson 3
Thomas Goodare 6
George Wayte 1
Lancellt Sullaby 1
Widdow Pears 1
Thomas Litlewood 1
John Taylor 1
John Spencer 1
Mary Ferraby 1
Peter Jackson 4
Robert Karlile 3
Samuell Malison 2
Mr Holmes 5
Widdow Margraue 3
Henry Watts 3

m 96]

Mr Naylor 4
George Littlewood 1
Bartholl Allinson 2
Godfrey Petty 4
Thomas Candy 7
Willm Hall 1
John Bond 1
Francis Alsop 1
Widdow Alsop 1
Isaac Blackburne 2
Richard Megit 1
John Haggit 1
John Driver 1
Widdow Oram 2
Francis Bond 3
John Howard 3
Thomas Hall 1
Mathew Gresham 1
Edward Ferraby 2
Peter Reeder 3
Willm Brooke 2
Thomas Kirby 2

Edward Starkey 3
Alice Parkins 3
Henry Gleadhill 2
Willm Chambers 1
Thomas Brockhoole 1
John Grayburne 1
Henry Paylor 2
Willm Shillitoe 1
Jennet Wharldall 1
George Beckitt 1
Willm Moverley 2
Willm Coleman 3
Edward Graues 1
Jane Bovill 1
Mathew Sutton 1
Richard Blaylocke 1
Mary Steare 3
James Chansey 1
Willm Darling 4
Abraham Dawson 1
John Shillitoe 2
Robert Pruston 2
Clare Burton 1
Robert Burton 1
James Oram 1
Thomas Killam 2
John Watson 1
Mrs Hanson 4
Thomas Coleman 2
Richard Bramham 1
Ellizabeth Oram 2
Thomas Burr 2
Francis Burr 1
Robert Standeland 4
Thomas Cutts 3
Marmaduke Auby 3
John Richardson 2
George Ellis 1
Anne Hill 2
Robert Airton 1
Christopr Bell 1
Edward Wright 2[277]
two

Thomas Cooke 1
George Cutler 1
George Sawnderson 3

m 97]

Henry Hepworth 3
John Turner 2
Vallentine Martin 3
Richard Doughty 1
Mr Howard 3
Mr Canby 6
Mrs Prole 4
Willm Gray 1
John Wright 1
Robert Ferraby 3
John Darling 3
Roger Stear 1
Mr Southwell 2
Thomas Moulson 1
Edmond Cole 4
Henry Russells 1
Christopr Midlebrooke 3
Absolom Legrand 2
Margret Wells 2
Richard Nicholson 1
Rebecca Cooke 2
Thomas Midlebrooke 4
Christopr Browne 4
Thomas Crabtrey 2
Willm Briggs 2
Mrs Starkey 6
Thomas Breedy 2
John Drewry 3
Joseph Turner 2
Widdow Margisson 2
Mr Cor Prole 3
John Trotter 2
Thomas Boynton 1
Thomas Burr 1
Mr Foster 10
Mr Spurgan 2
Mr Myers 5

[277] 2 written over 1.

Willm Dawson	1
Willm Midlebrooke	2
Henry Crooke	2
Thomas Taylor	1
Mr Southwell	2
John West	2
Willm Burtwizle	1
Mr Willm Fostard	5
Widdow Bradford	1
Isaac Chapman	4
George Stear	2
James Chansey	1
Mr Robert Starkey	2
Mr Richard Starkey	4
John Tasker	2
George Hatfeild	2
Joseph Lockwood	1
Widdow Smith	1
Joseph Stear	1
Thomas Margison	1
Nathanll Gurrey	1
Willm Skirlew	2
Mr Benjam Canby	4
Thomas Rhoades	1
Anne Wells	1
Henry Cosse	1
Thomas Ellis	1
John Conyers	1
Roger Jackson	1
John Bond	1
Robert Hallifax	1
	331

m 98]

Dikesmarsh
(Dikes Marsh)

Mr Canby	4
Widdow Leanard	2
Peter Teese	2
John Veny	9
James Nodam	2
Widdow Rooks	2
Isaac Deebee	3
Benjam Guy	3
Robert Margesson	2
John Teese	3
David Mamillion	2
Andrew Watterloue	2
Robert Barker	2
Widdow Prim	3
Thomas Martison	1
Thomas Hartley	2
David Tall	2
Isaac Decon	5
Richard Stones	3
Mr Southwell	2
John Palmer	1
Willm Scholey	1
Leonard Harrison	4
Willm Huscroft	1
Henry Harman	1
Hugh White	1
S[i]r Thomas Abdy	1
Willm Heaton	1
Thomas Denton	1
John Lyster	1
John Sayle	1
Thomas Hynesley	1
	~~402~~
	71

Empty & no distress to be had

Thomas Cooke	2
Willm Hall	1
Mr Darling	4
Phillp Hepworth	1
Mr Hewey	4
Mr Corn Prole	1
Roger Nicholson	1

These persons following are discharged by Certificates

John Heaton	1
Edward Hanson	1
Christopr Cade	1
Willm Graues	1
Thomas Burgas	1
John Sutton	1
Edward Rodwell	1
Richard Cooke	1
Willm Watson	1
Willm Bilton	1
Willm Bladworth	1
Thomas Wilburne	1
John Eccles	1
Widdow Midlebrook	1
Richard Benson	1
Thomas Pooles	1
Edward Rodwell	1
John Tangate	1
John Sikes	2
Edward Casling	1

m 99]

George Midlebrooke	1
Willm Chancey	2
Robert Tongate	1
Willm Watson	1
John Heaton	1
Widdow Blackburne	1
Willm Wilburne	1
John Loft	1
Nichollas Clarke	1
John Hall	1
Anne West	1
Willm Jackson	1
Thomas Bell	1
Simon Green	1
Thomas Green	1
George Batty	1
Willm Spinke	1
Widdow Britton	1

Omitted by reason of Poverty 6

Thomas Midleton Collr
Benjam Canby Const

Ullay
(Ulley)

Mr Nichols Stones	2
Mr Robert Bogg	5

John Clarke	1
Mrs Shirtcliff	2
John Schoalay	2
Ralph Goodall	1
John Coes	1
John Schoaley	1
Willm Coe	1
Willm Tyas	1
Richard Heywood	1
Nicholls Rogers	2
Thomas Rogers	4
Godfrey Scholey	2
Edward Wriglesworth	1
Willm Champney	1
Willm Binnie	2
Willm Ollerton	1
Willm Ollerton	2
Joseph Shepherd	1
	34

Empty & no distres to be had

Willm Ollerton	3

Robt Bennit Collr
Thomas Rodgers Const

Wath upon Dearne

Thomas Hepworth	1
Nichollas Morton	1
Thomas Fessan	2
Richard Nicholls	2
John Gawthrey	3
Ralph Forge	2
Thomas Barraclough	1
Widdow Shay	1
John Jackson	3
Widdow Smith	2
Widdow Yates	2
Robert Skargill	1
Willm Cushworth	1
Richard Barraclough	2
George Hoyland	4
John Smith	2
Nichollas Carr	1
Francis Tottington	1
Francis Carr	2
John Kay	3
Nichollas Wright	1
Henry Wright	1
John Carr	2
Willm Addy	1
John Turner	1

m 100]

Henry Fayram	3
John Kay	2
Mr Coates	7
Richard Walker	2
Widdow Gantrey	1
James Clayton	4
Mastin House	1
Willm Carr	5
Mr Ludlam	3
Thomas Tynley	3
Richard Tynley	4
Thomas Burks	1
Nichollas Machin	1
Widdow Earle	1
John Kempe	2
John Amerey	1
Widdow Kitchingman	1
Richard Robinson	1
Widdow Tompson	1
	87

Empty & no distres to be had

Widdow Howgate	1
James Clayton	1

Thomas Midleton Collr
Ralph Forge Const

Wombell (Wombwell)

Mrs Wombell	10
Richard Brooksbanke	1
Widdow Johnson	1
Thomas Winter	1
Widdow Hoyland	1
Roger Bryndgmade	1
Francis Lynley	1
John Davis	3
John Ellam	2
Robert Linley	1
Martin Jubb	1
Willm Hicke	1
Thomas Wilton	1
Willm Moulson	2
Samuell Swyndin	1
Widdow Ardron	1
Thomas Cowper	2
Edward Greene	1
Willm Brooke	1
Thomas Wilson	1
Josias Holdsworth	2
John Armitage	1
John Johnson	3
Widdow Allan	2
John Oates	2
Mathew Rhoades	2
George Wilson	1
Thomas Clarkson	2
George Bradley	3
John Scholefeild	4
Willm Tompson	2
George Greene	1
Francis Stead	1
Richard Burks	1
Widdow Hoyland	1
Widdow Reynald	1
Henry Tayler	3
Willm Roe	2
Winfrid Smith	2
Widdow Smith	2
Willm Grey	2
Widdow Viccars	3

m 101]

John Athey	1
Willm Mount	1
Willm Reynald	3

Thomas Allon 1
John Hoyland 2
Steven Smith 1
Widdow Wombell 2
John Wright 2
Richard Scales 2
Robert Gustrey 2
Thomas Gawthrop 1
Willm Armitage 3
Willm Sayle 1
Nichollas Baraclough 2
Widdow Carr 1
Robert Seckar 1
Willm Clarkson 1
Robert Thorsby 2
Thomas Ellis 2
Willm Stacy 3
Widdow Viccars 2
John Twigg 2
Widdow Swindin 6
Thomas Smith 2
Willm Marsden 1
Widdow Bradley 3
Richard Cooper 6
Lawrance Colley 1
Robert Singleton 2
Richard Mathewman 3
Mr Taylor 3
Aldum Milne 1
143

Empty & no distress to be had
Mrs Wombell 1

Omitted by reason of Poverty 4

Thomas Midleton Collr
Richard Linley Const

Wentworth
The Honble Willm
Earle of Strafford 43
Nichollas Strafford 3
Thomas Foulston 1
Henry Hodgkinson 4
Marke Burkes 1
Robert Fleetwood 3
John Charleton 3
Michaell Ellis 2
The Freare house 10
Widdow Frankis 2
Willm Bradbury 1
Robert Rawlin 4
Francis Hodgkinson 2
Ellin Hodgkinson 1
Willm Bower 1
Willm Oldfeild 1
Widdow Jessop 2
John Scargill 1
Richard Cooke 1
Francis Milnthorp 3
George Peverill 6
Willm Slack 2

m 102]

Mr Hodgkinson 6
Mrs Wilson 4
Mrs Pickles 2
Willm Martin 2
Nichollas Smith 1
Edward Watterhouse 1
George Smith 1
Willm Hoole 2
Mary Goodison 2
Ellizabeth Goodison 1
Nicholas Jepson 1
Willm Butterworth 1
John Butterworth 1
Mary Guest 1
John Trickett 2
John Strafforth 1
Roger Bradley 2
Richard Green 1
Willm Green 1
Mr Boswell Vessey 3
Henry Wilkinson 2
John Scoaray 1

Willm Hill 2
Widdow Smith 1
Henry Darwin 1
Widdow Crawshawe 3
Richard Lee 1
Widdow Issot 2
Thomas Pillie 3
Nichollas Parkins 2
Ellexandr Hill 2
Richard Bullas 1
Widdow Bullas 1
John Tompson 1
Willm Smith 1
Willm Frankis 4
Thomas Hatterslay 1
Daniell Casson 1
Jerem Fullieloue 2
Willm Swallow 2
John Dysan 1
Edward Fairewether 1
Earle of Strafford 3
172

Empty & no distress to be had
Earle of Strafford 1
Mr Hodgkinson 1

Omitted by reason of poverty 5

Robt Bennit Collr
Nicholls Smith Const

Wheatley & Sandall
Sir George Cooke 11
Mr Gamble 2
Thomas Heaton 1
Mr Waid 1
Mr Waid 2
Widdow Conway 3
Thomas Winn 1
Willm Heaton 2
Thomas Brinster 2
Widdow Cockin 2

Mr Gamble	8
Mary Missin	2
	37

Empty & no distres to be had

Sir Geo Cooke	1

Omitted by reason of Poverty 2

Thomas Midleton Collr
James Cockill Const

m 103]

Wickerslay (Wickersley)

Edward Raine Cler	6
Widdow Sherle	4
Willm Wild	3
George Carr	3
Widdow Murfin	1
John Ratcliff	2
Thomas Syberrey	2
George Downes	1
Robert Lund	1
Robert Woodall	3
Joseph Lord	4
Thomas Ibberson	2
Edward Giberthorp	3
John Shirle	4
Anthony Yates	2
John Shepherd	1
Robert Tomlinson	1
Edward Brewitt	1
Francis Lambert	2
Thomas Warbleton	1
Willm Snydall	3
John Rockley	1
Thomas Watson	1
Thomas Bradley	2
Widdow Grime	1
John Hall	1
Mary Bradlay	4
	60

Omitted by reason of poverty 1

Robert More Collr
Francis Lambert Const

Warmsworth

Mr Childers	12
Christopr Poole	1
Henry Whitacres	1
Ellizabeth Radley	1
Thomas Newitt	3
Peter Parsison	1
Robert Brumhead	1
Richard Bawtrey	2
Widdow Hurt	2
John Burgan	2
Thomas Farray	3
Mr Roksby	5
Richard Killam	4
Mr Batty	12
Mr Batty	2
Widdow Ellis	1
Joseph Shaw	1
John Killam	5
James Steele	1
Willm Amory	1
Richard Shaw	1
Thomas Oldum	3
Richard Amory	1
Thomas Walker	1
John Swales	5
Widdow Ward	3
James Barlow	1
Edward Barlow	1
	77

Thomas Midleton Collr
Willm Ellis Const

Woodsetts cum Gilderingwells (Woodsetts with Gildingwells)

Thomas Garland	4
Widdow Cooke	2
Richard Nelson	1
Widdow Morton	1

m 104]

John Goodson	1
Widdow Booth	2
Roger Benshaw	5
John Nelson	2
Brian Naylor	1
George Newton	2
Sir Ralph Knight	1
John Twibell	4
Nicholas Twibell	2
Alice Wright	3
Widdow Swift	1
Mr Phillips	3
Widdow Armfeild	2
	37

Empty & no distres to be had

Samuell Cutcliff	3

These persons following are discharged by Certificates

Willm Revill	1
James Sawood	1
Thomas Revill	1

Omitted by reason of poverty 3

Robert Bennit Collr
George Norton Const

Wailes (Wales)

Walgraue Turner	2
John Turner	1
Edward Hill	5
John Watson	1
Willm Fisher	2
Robert Shorter	1

Widdow Smith	2
George Bentley	1
Robert Pearson	3
Thomas Pashley	1
John Clarke	2
James Ingle	3
Willm Linlay	1
Mr Francis Humphrey	4
John Clarke	2
Henry Walker	1
Francis Billam	2
Henry Cawton	1
Robert Harris	6
Henry Bentley	2
Anthony Poole	1
George Watson	2
Widdow Watson	2
Mary Belke	1
Willm Rogers	2
Widdow Rogers	1
Anthony Billam	1
Francis Calvert	2
Thomas Billam	2
John Whitehead	1
Nichollas Clarke	1
Widdow Robinit	1
Widdow Stacy	1
Willm Rogers	1
Francis Clarke	3
Edward Clarke	1
Widdow Jarvice	4
	70

These persons following are discharged by Certificates

m 105]

Alice Stacy	1
John Hudson	1
Robert Smith	2
Robert Fox	1

Omitted by Reason of poverty	3

Robert Bennet Collr
Edward Hill Const

Wiston alias Whiston (Whiston)

Mr George Stringer	11
James Tompson	4
George Rich	2
Robert Tompson	3
John Cooper	1
Thomas Jarvice	2
Joseph Sheppard	1
Charles Warbleton	1
Richard Tompson	1
Willm Hilton	1
Thomas Ludlam	2
John Turner	1
Widdow Cossins	1
John Abtie	3
Henry Champnie	6
Willm Billam	2
Mr Thomas Rawson	8[278] eight
Mr Nathanll Revill	4
Willm Tompson	1
John Hall	1
Edward Butler	1
John Jenkinson	1
Willm Wastnidge	1
Willm Storke	2
Mary Storke	2[279] two
Robert Wright	1
Willm Coe	2
James Hamond	1
George Robinson	2
Willm Inman	1
Anne Starke	7
John Burnley	3
Francis Hanby	1
Thomas Hall	1
George Neale	1
Widdow Bentham	6
Luke Stafforth	2
Nicholls Whittles	2
Mr Copley	5
Willm Lee	3
Thomas Syberrey	3
Charles Storkes	2
Charles Smith	2
Thomas Shepherd	2
George Coe	7
James Harrison	1
Mrs Westby	9
Widdow Mercer	1
Mr Rawson	1
Edward Ranby	3
Mrs Briggs	3
Francis Ellis	1
James Howin	1
John Dowfin	1
George Johnson	1
Samuell Roper	3
James Lee	1
Willm Radley senr	1
Willm Radley	3
Robert Wild	4
Robert Spencer	1
Nichollas Wriglesworth	2
Richard Poulton	1
Christopr Lee	1
	156

m 106]

Omitted by reason of poverty	3

Robert Bennit Collr
Willm Hilton Const

278 8 written over 7.
279 2 written over 1.

Wadworth

Lyonell Copley Esqr	18
Mr Batt	8
Thomas Maxfeild	1
James Elliot	1
George Ward	2
Widdow Parsonson	1
Lyonell Parsonson	1
Richard Parsison	1
Dorothy Ward	1
John Rowlin	1
The Viccardge	4
Edward Samson	1
Abram Naylor	1
Anthony Needom	1
Willm Hurst	1
Nicholls Shepherd	1
James Booth	1
Robt Woodrofe	1
Robert Waide	1
John Parsonson	4
Willm Waid	2
Robert Swift	1
Willm Lawe	1
George Hodgson	1
Thomas Barke	1
John Hodgson	1
Thomas Varnam	1
Thomas Martin	1
Richard Oakes	2
Willm Jubb	1
Richard Maxfeild	1
Edward Varnam	3
Abraham Pegg Cler	3
John Murfin	1
Widdow Marshall	1
Widdow Blackburne	1
Widdow Ranfeild	1
Thomas Wilson	1
John Makin	1
Lawrance Elvidge	1
Francis Booth	2
Jonathan Brownill	1
Robert Elvidge	2
George Elvidge	3
Robert Yates	2
Widdow Parsonson	1
Mr Towfeild	6
John Firth	1
Willm Parsonson	1
Willm Kidson	1
Thomas Minskipp	1
Anthony Birkinshawe	1
	99

Empty & no distres to be had

The Lady Mounkson	1
Nether Hall	8

The persons following are discharged by Certifts

Thomas Sarbut	1
Jennet Amre	1
Mary Hewit	1
Thomas Saile	1
Richard Law	1
John Smith	1
Richard Wright	2
Robert Waide	1
Lawrance Kirby	1

Omitted by Reason of Poverty	1

Robert More Collr
Willm Parsonson Const

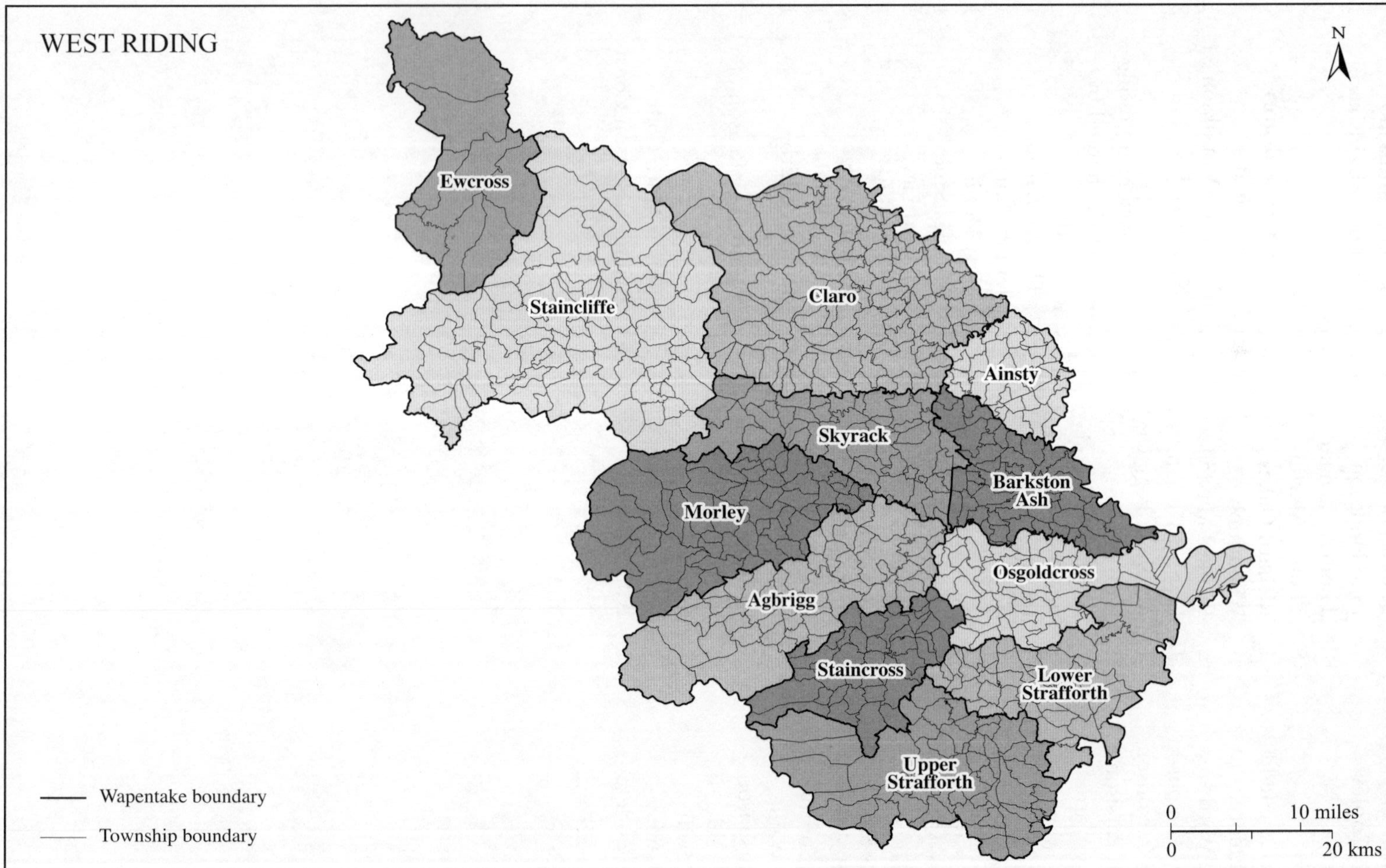

Map 18 The wapentakes of the West Riding of Yorkshire

Totals of Households and Hearths At Lady Day 1672

This table is arranged by townships within wapentakes. In this table the wapentakes are arranged alphabetically, rather than geographically as they were in the transcript of the assessment. For convenience of reference the wapentake map from the front end-paper is repeated opposite. As in the transcript, the data for Osgoldcross wapentake is taken from the Lady Day 1673 assessment. All of the data from the these assessments is also displayed in the form of maps 3 to 13 within David Hey's 'The West Riding in the Late Seventeenth Century', pp. 11–60.

Explanatory Note

Whereas the figures in the columns of hearths 1 to 9 record the number of households, the figures in the 10+ column show the hearth numbers in individual houses in square brackets.

	Number of hearths										List of 10+	Total house-holds	Total hearths
	1	2	3	4	5	6	7	8	9	10+			
Agbrigg Wapentake													
Ackton													
Paying	3	4	2	3	1					1	[10]	14	44
Non-paying *No data*													
Poor	5											5	5
Empty *No data*													
Total Ackton	8	4	2	3	1					1		19	49
Almondbury													
Paying	60	30	5	8	6	3				3	[10, 10, 25]	115	260
Non-paying *No data*													
Poor	4											4	4
Empty	2		1									3	5
Total Almondbury	66	30	6	8	6	3				3		122	269
Altofts													
Paying	23	15	2	4	1				2			47	98
Non-paying *No data*													
Poor	3											3	3
Empty					1							1	5
Total Altofts	26	15	2	4	2				2			51	106

	Number of hearths										List of 10+	Total house-holds	Total hearths
	1	2	3	4	5	6	7	8	9	10+			
Batley													
Paying	25	29	14	4	1		1	1		1	[13]	76	174
Non-paying	13	2										15	17
Poor	1											1	1
Empty *No data*													
Total Batley	39	31	14	4	1		1	1		1		92	192
Crigglestone													
Paying	30	28	10	7	5	2						82	181
Non-paying *No data*													
Poor	15											15	15
Empty		1										1	2
Total Crigglestone	45	29	10	7	5	2						98	198
Crofton													
Paying	17	9	3	1	2				1	1	[11]	34	78
Non-paying *No data*													
Poor	13											13	13
Empty *No data*													
Total Crofton	30	9	3	1	2				1	1		47	91
Crosland halfe													
Paying	43	15	5	1	1	1						66	103
Non-paying *No data*													
Poor	8											8	8
Empty	1											1	1
Total Crosland halfe	52	15	5	1	1	1						75	112
Cumberworth halfe													
Paying	17	11	3	1								32	52
Non-paying *No data*													
Poor *No data*													
Empty *No data*													
Total Cumberworth	17	11	3	1								32	52
Dalton													
Paying	32	20	5	3	1							61	104
Non-paying *No data*													
Poor	6											6	6
Empty	2											2	2
Total Dalton	40	20	5	3	1							69	112
Dewsbury													
Paying	33	24	14	10	2	4	1	1		1	[10]	90	222
Non-paying *No data*													
Poor	13											13	13
Empty		1										1	2
Total Dewsbury	46	25	14	10	2	4	1	1		1		104	237

	Number of hearths										List of 10+	Total house-holds	Total hearths
	1	2	3	4	5	6	7	8	9	10+			
East Ardsley													
Paying	18	13	3	1	1		1	2				39	85
Non-paying *No data*													
Poor	4											4	4
Empty *No data*													
Total East Ardsley	22	13	3	1	1		1	2				43	89
Emley													
Paying	31	11	5	6	1	1		1		2	[10, 11]	58	132
Non-paying *No data*													
Poor	23											23	23
Empty *No data*													
Total Emley	54	11	5	6	1	1		1		2		81	155
Farnley Tyas													
Paying	25	11	1	1						1	[22]	39	76
Non-paying *No data*													
Poor *No data*													
Empty *No data*													
Total Farnley Tyas	25	11	1	1						1		39	76
Flockton Nether													
Paying	20	10	5			1						36	61
Non-paying *No data*													
Poor	5											5	5
Empty *No data*													
Total Flockton Nether	25	10	5			1						41	66
Flockton Over													
Paying	18	9	2	2				1		1	[20]	33	78
Non-paying *No data*													
Poor	1											1	1
Empty *No data*													
Total Flockton Over	19	9	2	2				1		1		34	79
Golcar													
Paying	41	16	5	3	2							67	110
Non-paying *No data*													
Poor	4											4	4
Empty	1											1	1
Total Golcar	46	16	5	3	2							72	115
Holme													
Paying	255	52	10	3	1							321	406
Non-paying *No data*													
Poor	4											4	4
Empty	4											4	4
Total Holme	263	52	10	3	1							329	414

	Number of hearths										List of 10+	Total house-holds	Total hearths
	1	2	3	4	5	6	7	8	9	10+			
Honley													
Paying	50	12	3	2	1							68	96
Non-paying *No data*													
Poor	3											3	3
Empty	2	1										3	4
Total Honley	55	13	3	2	1							74	103
Horbury													
Paying	26	27	10	4	1	2	1	1		1	[12]	73	170
Non-paying *No data*													
Poor	5											5	5
Empty *No data*													
Total Horbury	31	27	10	4	1	2	1	1		1		78	175
Huddersfield													
Paying	63	33	18	6	5	1		2				128	254
Non-paying *No data*													
Poor	15											15	15
Empty *No data*													
Total Huddersfield	78	33	18	6	5	1		2				143	269
Kirkburton													
Paying	40	16	4			1						61	90
Non-paying *No data*													
Poor	8											8	8
Empty *No data*													
Total Kirkburton	48	16	4			1						69	98
Kirkheaton													
Paying	48	16	5	5	1	1						76	126
Non-paying	3											3	3
Poor	1											1	1
Empty *No data*													
Total Kirkheaton	52	16	5	5	1	1						80	130
Lepton													
Paying	49	14	7	2	1	1	1					75	124
Non-paying	8	1										9	10
Poor	1											1	1
Empty	1											1	1
Total Lepton	59	15	7	2	1	1	1					86	136
Lindley													
Paying	13	4								1	[15]	18	36
Non-paying *No data*													
Poor *No data*													
Empty *No data*													
Total Lindley	13	4								1		18	36

	Number of hearths										List of 10+	Total house-holds	Total hearths
	1	2	3	4	5	6	7	8	9	10+			
Lindley cum Quarmby													
Paying	29	15	3									47	63
Non-paying	1											1	1
Poor	4											4	4
Empty	2											2	2
Total Lindley cum Quarmby	36	15	3									54	75
Longwood Quarter													
Paying	28	17	1	1	1							48	74
Non-paying *No data*													
Poor	1											1	1
Empty	1											1	1
Total Longwood Quarter	30	17	1	1	1							50	76
Marsden													
Paying	56	18	3	3								80	113
Non-paying *No data*													
Poor	2											2	2
Empty *No data*													
Total Marsden	58	18	3	3								82	115
Meltham													
Paying	43	18	3	1				1				66	100
Non-paying *No data*													
Poor	2											2	2
Empty		1										1	2
Total Meltham	45	19	3	1				1				69	104
Methley													
Paying	48	30	15	12	1	3		4	2	1	[43]	116	317
Non-paying *No data*													
Poor	11											11	11
Empty	1											1	1
Total Methley	60	30	15	12	1	3		4	2	1		128	329
Middleton and Thorpe on the Hill													
Paying	34	16	3	1				2	1			57	104
Non-paying *No data*													
Poor	1											1	1
Empty	1											1	1
Total Middleton and Thorpe on the Hill	36	16	3	1				2	1			59	106

	Number of hearths										List of 10+	Total house-holds	Total hearths
	1	2	3	4	5	6	7	8	9	10+			
Mirfeild													
Paying	53	31	18	7	7	3		1	1	1	[11]	122	278
Non-paying *No data*													
Poor	5											5	5
Empty	1											1	1
Total Mirfeild	59	31	18	7	7	3		1	1	1		128	284
Morley													
Paying	53	35	7	6	2					1	[44]	104	222
Non-paying *No data*													
Poor	6											6	6
Empty	2	1	1									4	7
Total Morley	61	36	8	6	2					1		114	235
Normanton													
Paying	17	11	2		1	3				1	[12]	35	80
Non-paying *No data*													
Poor	2											2	2
Empty *No data*													
Total Normanton	19	11	2		1	3				1		37	82
North Crosland													
Paying	49	8	4	1				1				63	89
Non-paying *No data*													
Poor	1											1	1
Empty	1											1	1
Total North Crosland	51	8	4	1				1				65	91
Ossett													
Paying	56	37	11	6	1							111	192
Non-paying *No data*													
Poor	3											3	3
Empty	3	1										4	5
Total Ossett	62	38	11	6	1							118	200
Quick													
Paying	205	18	8	4								235	281
Non-paying *No data*													
Poor	12											12	12
Empty *No data*													
Total Quick	217	18	8	4								247	293
Rothwell													
Paying	118	94	34	13	12		5	3				279	579
Non-paying *No data*													
Poor	4											4	4
Empty	4	3	1									8	13
Total Rothwell		126	97	35	13	12		5	3			291	596

	Number of hearths 1	2	3	4	5	6	7	8	9	10+	List of 10+	Total house-holds	Total hearths
Sandall Magna													
Paying	16	19	7	5	5		1	1	1			55	144
Non-paying *No data*													
Poor	3											3	3
Empty	1	1	1									3	6
Total Sandall Magna	20	20	8	5	5		1	1	1			61	153
Scammonden													
Paying	22	9	2	1								34	50
Non-paying *No data*													
Poor	3											3	3
Empty	1											1	1
Total Scammonden	26	9	2	1								38	54
Sharlstone													
Paying	16	8	5	2		1				1	[14]	33	75
Non-paying *No data*													
Poor	11											11	11
Empty *No data*													
Total Sharlstone	27	8	5	2		1				1		44	86
Shelley													
Paying	33	8	3		1							45	63
Non-paying *No data*													
Poor *No data*													
Empty *No data*													
Total Shelley	33	8	3		1							45	63
Shepley													
Paying	19	9	6		1							35	60
Non-paying	1											1	1
Poor *No data*													
Empty *No data*													
Total Shepley	20	9	6		1							36	61
Sitlington													
Paying	52	12	7	4		1				1	[12]	77	131
Non-paying *No data*													
Poor	5											5	5
Empty *No data*													
Total Sitlington	57	12	7	4		1				1		82	136
Slaithwaite													
Paying	80	17	5	1								103	133
Non-paying *No data*													
Poor *No data*													
Empty	1											1	1
Total Slaithwaite	81	17	5	1								104	134

	Number of hearths										List of 10+	Total house-holds	Total hearths
	1	2	3	4	5	6	7	8	9	10+			
Snydale													
Paying	17	2	2							1	[12]	22	39
Non-paying *No data*													
Poor	2											2	2
Empty *No data*													
Total Snydale	19	2	2							1		24	41
Soothill													
Paying	34	25	5	3	1		2					70	130
Non-paying *No data*													
Poor	1											1	1
Empty	1											1	1
Total Soothill	36	25	5	3	1		2					72	132
Stanley													
Paying	74	88	29	14	2	4	1	1		4	[10, 12, 14, 18]	217	496
Non-paying *No data*													
Poor	29											29	29
Empty	10	2	1									13	17
Total Stanley	113	90	30	14	2	4	1	1		4		259	542
Thornhill													
Paying	35	17	3	3	1		1		4			64	138
Non-paying *No data*													
Poor	3											3	3
Empty *No data*													
Total Thornhill	38	17	3	3	1		1		4			67	141
Thurstonland													
Paying	32	8	2	1						1	[10]	44	68
Non-paying *No data*													
Poor *No data*													
Empty *No data*													
Total Thurstonland	32	8	2	1						1		44	68
Wakefield, Kirkgate													
Paying	26	37	17	15	7	1	1	3				107	283
Non-paying	11	1										12	13
Poor	15											15	15
Empty	1	1	1			1	1					5	19
Total Wakefield, Kirkgate	53	39	18	15	7	2	2	3				139	330
Wakefield, Northgate													
Paying	14	36	14	19	5	3	5		4	2	[10, 15]	102	343
Non-paying *No data*													
Poor	28											28	28
Empty		1	2									3	8
Total Wakefield, Northgate	42	37	16	19	5	3	5		4	2		133	379

	Number of hearths										List of 10+	Total house-holds	Total hearths
	1	2	3	4	5	6	7	8	9	10+			
Wakefield, Westgate													
Paying	37	23	29	22	10	9	5	5	1	7	[10, 11, 11, 11, 12, 12, 17]	148	530
Non-paying *No data*													
Poor	2											2	2
Empty	1	2	1									4	8
Total Wakefield, Westgate	40	25	30	22	10	9	5	5	1	7		154	540
Walton and West Bretton													
Paying	31	16	12	6	1	2						68	140
Non-paying *No data*													
Poor	2											2	2
Empty *No data*													
Total Walton and West Bretton	33	16	12	6	1	2						70	142
Warmfield cum Heath													
Paying	25	16	4	6			1			2	[13, 20]	54	133
Non-paying *No data*													
Poor	12											12	12
Empty	1											1	1
Total Warmfield cum Heath	38	16	4	6			1			2		67	146
West Ardsley													
Paying	25	24	10	1		2	3			2	[10, 11]	67	161
Non-paying *No data*													
Poor *No data*													
Empty	1											1	1
Total West Ardsley	26	24	10	1		2	3			2		68	162
Whitley													
Paying	33	28	3							1	[17]	65	115
Non-paying *No data*													
Poor	5											5	5
Empty	1											1	1
Total Whitley	39	28	3							1		71	121
Whitwood													
Paying	9	4	2		1		1					17	35
Non-paying *No data*													
Poor	2											2	2
Empty	3											3	3
Total Whitwood	14	4	2		1		1					22	40
Total Agbrigg	**2806**	**1203**	**429**	**235**	**95**	**51**	**32**	**31**	**17**	**39**		**4938**	**9416**

	Number of hearths										List of 10+	Total house-holds	Total hearths
	1	2	3	4	5	6	7	8	9	10+			
Ainsty Wapentake													
Acaster Malbis													
Paying	29	10										39	49
Non-paying *No data*													
Poor *No data*													
Empty		1										1	2
Total Acaster Malbis	29	11										40	51
Acaster Selby													
Paying	14	3			1		1					19	32
Non-paying *No data*													
Poor	3											3	3
Empty	1											1	1
Total Acaster Selby	18	3			1		1					23	36
Acomb													
Paying	27	10	1				1		1			40	66
Non-paying	3	1										4	5
Poor *No data*													
Empty	3	1										4	5
Total Acomb	33	12	1				1		1			48	76
Askham Bryan													
Paying	36	5	1	2				1		1	[12]	46	77
Non-paying *No data*													
Poor *No data*													
Empty *No data*													
Total Askham Bryan	36	5	1	2				1		1		46	77
Askham Richard													
Paying	20	4	3				1					28	44
Non-paying *No data*													
Poor *No data*													
Empty *No data*													
Total Askham Richard	20	4	3				1					28	44
Bickerton													
Paying	11	2	2							1	[11]	16	32
Non-paying	1											1	1
Poor	1											1	1
Empty *No data*													
Total Bickerton	13	2	2							1		18	34

	Number of hearths										List of 10+	Total house-holds	Total hearths
	1	2	3	4	5	6	7	8	9	10+			
Bilbrough													
Paying	15	7	1			1						24	38
Non-paying *No data*													
Poor	5		1									6	8
Empty *No data*													
Total Bilbrough	20	7	2			1						30	46
Bilton													
Paying	24	2	1	1	1	1				1	[13]	31	59
Non-paying	3											3	3
Poor *No data*													
Empty *No data*													
Total Bilton	27	2	1	1	1	1				1		34	62
Bishopthorpe													
Paying	29	2	4	2						1	[38]	38	91
Non-paying *No data*													
Poor	4											4	4
Empty				1								1	4
Total Bishopthorpe	33	2	4	3						1		43	99
Bolton Percy													
Paying	21	5	1	1	1					2	[10, 12]	31	65
Non-paying *No data*													
Poor *No data*													
Empty		1										1	2
Total Bolton Percy	21	6	1	1	1					2		32	67
Catterton													
Paying	9	1	2									12	17
Non-paying *No data*													
Poor *No data*													
Empty *No data*													
Total Catterton	9	1	2									12	17
Colton													
Paying	17	6	3									26	38
Non-paying *No data*													
Poor *No data*													
Empty *No data*													
Total Colton	17	6	3									26	38
Copmanthorpe													
Paying	14	6	2	2	24	42							
Non-paying *No data*													
Poor *No data*													
Empty		1										1	2
Total Copmanthorpe	14	7	2		2							25	44

	Number of hearths										List of 10+	Total house-holds	Total hearths
	1	2	3	4	5	6	7	8	9	10+			
Dringhouses													
Paying	16	7	2							1	[13]	26	49
Non-paying *No data*													
Poor *No data*													
Empty *No data*													
Total Dringhouses	16	7	2							1		26	49
East Tadcaster													
Paying	13	7	2	2	2	1						27	57
Non-paying	2											2	2
Poor	1	1										2	3
Empty *No data*													
Total East Tadcaster	16	8	2	2	2	1						31	62
Healaugh													
Paying	26	8	4		2					1	[28]	41	92
Non-paying *No data*													
Poor	1											1	1
Empty *No data*													
Total Healaugh	27	8	4		2					1		42	93
Hessay													
Paying	8	1	3									12	19
Non-paying *No data*													
Poor *No data*													
Empty *No data*													
Total Hessay	8	1	3									12	19
Holgate													
Paying	3	2	1									6	10
Non-paying *No data*													
Poor *No data*													
Empty *No data*													
Total Holgate	3	2	1									6	10
Hutton Wandesley and Angram													
Paying	26	2	1							1	[13]	30	46
Non-paying *No data*													
Poor	3											3	3
Empty *No data*													
Total Hutton Wandesley and Angram	29	2	1							1		33	49

	Number of hearths										List of 10+	Total house-holds	Total hearths
	1	2	3	4	5	6	7	8	9	10+			
Knapton													
Paying	13	6										19	25
Non-paying *No data*													
Poor *No data*													
Empty *No data*													
Total Knapton	13	6										19	25
Long Marston													
Paying	32	4			1				1	1	[11]	39	65
Non-paying	4											4	4
Poor *No data*													
Empty *No data*													
Total Long Marston	36	4			1				1	1		43	69
Middlethorpe													
Paying	1		1			2				1	[10]	5	26
Non-paying *No data*													
Poor *No data*													
Empty *No data*													
Total Middlethorpe	1		1			2				1		5	26
Moor Monkton													
Paying	25	3			1					1	[23]	30	59
Non-paying	7											7	7
Poor *No data*													
Empty *No data*													
Total Moor Monkton	32	3			1					1		37	66
Nether Poppleton													
Paying	20	1	1	1	1					1	[13]	25	47
Non-paying *No data*													
Poor *No data*													
Empty *No data*													
Total Nether Poppleton	20	1	1	1	1					1		25	47
Nun Appleton													
Paying	47	6	3		2					1	[40]	59	118
Non-paying *No data*													
Poor *No data*													
Empty *No data*													
Total Nun Appleton	47	6	3		2					1		59	118

	Number of hearths										List of 10+	Total house-holds	Total hearths
	1	2	3	4	5	6	7	8	9	10+			
Oxton & Ouston													
Paying	4	6	2	1								13	26
Non-paying *No data*													
Poor *No data*													
Empty *No data*													
Total Oxton & Ouston	4	6	2	1								13	26
Rufforth													
Paying	26			1	1		1	1				30	50
Non-paying	4	1										5	6
Poor *No data*													
Empty	1											1	1
Total Rufforth	31	1		1	1		1	1				36	57
Steeton													
Paying	6		1		1					1	[10]	9	24
Non-paying *No data*													
Poor *No data*													
Empty *No data*													
Total Steeton	6		1		1					1		9	24
Thorp Arch													
Paying	30	6			1	1						38	53
Non-paying	1											1	1
Poor *No data*													
Empty			2									2	6
Total Thorp Arch	31	6	2		1	1						41	60
Tockwith													
Paying	30	6	4				1					41	61
Non-paying *No data*													
Poor	1											1	1
Empty	1											1	1
Total Tockwith	32	6	4				1					43	63
Upper Poppleton													
Paying	30	8	2									40	52
Non-paying *No data*													
Poor	2											2	2
Empty	3											3	3
Total Upper Poppleton	35	8	2									45	57
Walton													
Paying	26	7	2							1	[17]	36	63
Non-paying *No data*													
Poor *No data*													
Empty *No data*													
Total Walton	26	7	2							1		36	63

	Number of hearths										List of 10+	Total house-holds	Total hearths
	1	2	3	4	5	6	7	8	9	10+			
Wighill													
Paying	17	10	2	1		1		1		1	[15]	33	76
Non-paying *No data*													
Poor *No data*													
Empty	2	2										4	6
Total Wighill	19	12	2	1		1		1		1		37	82
Wilstrop													
Paying	7	3					1					11	20
Non-paying *No data*													
Poor *No data*													
Empty *No data*													
Total Wilstrop	7	3					1					11	20
Total Ainsty	**729**	**165**	**55**	**13**	**17**	**7**	**6**	**3**	**2**	**17**		**1014**	**1776**
Barkston Ash Wapentake													
Aberford													
Paying	5	5	2	3	1	3						19	56
Non-paying *No data*													
Poor	2											2	2
Empty	1											1	1
Total Aberford	8	5	2	3	1	3						22	59
Barkston													
Paying	23		4		1							28	40
Non-paying *No data*													
Poor	7											7	7
Empty *No data*													
Total Barkston	30		4		1							35	47
Barlow													
Paying	27	7		1	1					1	[17]	37	67
Non-paying *No data*													
Poor	2											2	2
Empty *No data*													
Total Barlow	29	7	1		1					1		39	69
Birkin													
Paying	14	4		2						2	[11, 14]	22	55
Non-paying *No data*													
Poor *No data*													
Empty *No data*													
Total Birkin	14	4		2						2		22	55

	Number of hearths										List of 10+	Total house-holds	Total hearths
	1	2	3	4	5	6	7	8	9	10+			
Bramham													
Paying	46	6	6	4	1		1		1	2	[10, 10]	67	133
Non-paying	2											2	2
Poor	3											3	3
Empty *No data*													
Total Bramham	51	6	6	4	1		1		1	2		72	138
Brayton													
Paying	28	10	3	2	1	1						45	76
Non-paying	1											1	1
Poor *No data*													
Empty	1											1	1
Total Brayton	30	10	3	2	1	1						47	78
Brotherton													
Paying	25	10	9	6	3		2			1	[19]	56	144
Non-paying *No data*													
Poor *No data*													
Empty	2											2	2
Total Brotherton	27	10	9	6	3		2			1		58	146
Burn													
Paying	19	7		1	1	1		1				30	56
Non-paying *No data*													
Poor *No data*													
Empty *No data*													
Total Burn	19	7		1	1	1		1				30	56
Burton Salmon													
Paying	10	2	4	1		1			1			19	45
Non-paying *No data*													
Poor *No data*													
Empty *No data*													
Total Burton Salmon	10	2	4	1		1			1			19	45
Byram cum Sutton													
Paying	6	2	2							1	[26]	11	42
Non-paying *No data*													
Poor *No data*													
Empty *No data*													
Total Byram cum Sutton	6	2	2							1		11	42
Camblesforth													
Paying	24	9					1					34	49
Non-paying *No data*													
Poor *No data*													
Empty *No data*													
Total Camblesforth	24	9					1					34	49

	Number of hearths										List of 10+	Total house-holds	Total hearths
	1	2	3	4	5	6	7	8	9	10+			
Carlton													
Paying	46	28	12							3	[10, 10, 23]	89	181
Non-paying *No data*													
Poor	7											7	7
Empty *No data*													
Total Carlton	53	28	12							3		96	188
Cawood													
Paying	39	26	12	18	8	2	2	2		1	[24]	110	305
Non-paying	15											15	15
Poor	34											34	34
Empty	2	1	1									4	7
Total Cawood	90	27	13	18	8	2	2	2		1		163	361
Chapel Haddlesey													
Paying	13	6		2								21	33
Non-paying *No data*													
Poor *No data*													
Empty *No data*													
Total Chapel Haddlesey	13	6		2								21	33
Church Fenton													
Paying	29	7	5	1	1	2						45	79
Non-paying	1											1	1
Poor *No data*													
Empty *No data*													
Total Church Fenton	30	7	5	1	1	2						46	80
Clifford													
Paying	27	4	2	2						1	[10]	36	59
Non-paying	2											2	2
Poor	2											2	2
Empty *No data*													
Total Clifford	31	4	2	2						1		40	63
Drax and Newland													
Paying	43	39	8	1	6	1	4			1	[21]	103	234
Non-paying *No data*													
Poor *No data*													
Empty	1											1	1
Total Drax and Newland	44	39	8	1	6	1	4			1		104	235

	Number of hearths										List of 10+	Total house-holds	Total hearths
	1	2	3	4	5	6	7	8	9	10+			
Fairburn													
Paying	19	6	5	3	1			2				36	79
Non-paying *No data*													
Poor	1											1	1
Empty *No data*													
Total Fairburn	20	6	5	3	1			2				37	80
Gateforth													
Paying	34	4	1	2	1		1	2				45	81
Non-paying *No data*													
Poor *No data*													
Empty	1											1	1
Total Gateforth	35	4	1	2	1		1	2				46	82
Grimston													
Paying	10	2			1					1	[24]	14	43
Non-paying *No data*													
Poor	1											1	1
Empty *No data*													
Total Grimston	11	2			1					1		15	44
Hambleton													
Paying	43	19	3				1					66	97
Non-paying *No data*													
Poor	12											12	12
Empty *No data*													
Total Hambleton	55	19	3				1					78	109
Hillam													
Paying	27	5	3	6	1							42	75
Non-paying *No data*													
Poor *No data*													
Empty			1									1	3
Total Hillam	27	5	4	6	1							43	78
Hirst Courtney													
Paying	15	5	1	1								22	32
Non-paying *No data*													
Poor *No data*													
Empty	1											1	1
Total Hirst Courtney	16	5	1	1								23	33
Huddleston cum Lumby													
Paying	7	1			1					1	[13]	10	27
Non-paying *No data*													
Poor *No data*													
Empty *No data*													
Total Huddleston cum Lumby	7	1			1					1		10	27

	Number of hearths										List of 10+	Total house-holds	Total hearths
	1	2	3	4	5	6	7	8	9	10+			
Kirkby Wharfe													
Paying	6	5		2	2		1					16	41
Non-paying *No data*													
Poor	1											1	1
Empty	1											1	1
Total Kirkby Wharfe	8	5		2	2		1					18	43
Ledsham													
Paying	14	3	4		2	1			1			25	57
Non-paying *No data*													
Poor *No data*													
Empty *No data*													
Total Ledsham	14	3	4		2	1			1			25	57
Ledston													
Paying	18	7	1	1						1	[25]	28	64
Non-paying *No data*													
Poor	2											2	2
Empty *No data*													
Total Ledston	20	7	1	1						1		30	66
Little Fenton													
Paying	30	3	3	1		1						38	55
Non-paying *No data*													
Poor	1											1	1
Empty *No data*													
Total Little Fenton	31	3	3	1		1						39	56
Micklefield													
Paying	10	5		3								18	32
Non-paying *No data*													
Poor	2											2	2
Empty *No data*													
Total Micklefield	12	5		3								20	34
Monk Fryston													
Paying	23	11	1	3	1	1		2				42	87
Non-paying *No data*													
Poor *No data*													
Empty *No data*													
Total Monk Fryston	23	11	1	3	1	1		2				42	87
Newthorpe													
Paying	6		1									7	9
Non-paying *No data*													
Poor *No data*													
Empty *No data*													
Total Newthorpe	6		1									7	9

	Number of hearths										List of 10+	Total house-holds	Total hearths
	1	2	3	4	5	6	7	8	9	10+			
Newton Kyme cum Toulston													
Paying	17	6	3		1	1				1	[15]	29	64
Non-paying *No data*													
Poor *No data*													
Empty *No data*													
Total Newton Kyme cum Toulston	17	6	3		1	1				1		29	64
Ryther cum Ossendyke/ Ozendyke													
Paying	21	11	2	2	4					1	[14]	41	91
Non-paying *No data*													
Poor *No data*													
Empty *No data*													
Total Ryther cum Ossendyke/Ozendyke	21	11	2	2	4					1		41	91
Saxton with Scarthingwell													
Paying	30	2	2							2	[17, 20]	36	77
Non-paying *No data*													
Poor	9											9	9
Empty *No data*													
Total Saxton with Scarthingwell	39	2	2							2		45	86
Selby													
Paying	63	68	54	38	11	3	1	1		1	[13]	240	614
Non-paying *No data*													
Poor	35											35	35
Empty	3	2			1							6	12
Total Selby	101	70	54	38	12	3	1	1		1		281	661
Sherburn in Elmet													
Paying	59	15	9	12	4		1			1	[14]	101	205
Non-paying	9	1										10	11
Poor	2											2	2
Empty	3											3	3
Total Sherburn in Elmet	73	16	9	12	4		1			1		116	221
South Milford													
Paying	41	4	8	5	1	1				1	[12]	61	116
Non-paying	5	1										6	7
Poor	1											1	1
Empty *No data*													
Total South Milford	47	5	8	5	1	1				1		68	124

	Number of hearths										List of 10+	Total house-holds	Total hearths
	1	2	3	4	5	6	7	8	9	10+			
Stutton with Hazlewood													
Paying	21	8	1							1	[20]	31	60
Non-paying *No data*													
Poor *No data*													
Empty *No data*													
Total Stutton with Hazlewood	21	8	1							1		31	60
Sutton													
Paying	15	3		1								19	25
Non-paying *No data*													
Poor *No data*													
Empty *No data*													
Total Sutton	15	3		1								19	25
Tadcaster													
Paying	25	16	8	8		2	2	2	1	1	[11]	65	175
Non-paying *No data*													
Poor	5											5	5
Empty *No data*													
Total Tadcaster	30	16	8	8		2	2	2	1	1		70	180
Temple Hirst													
Paying	11	2	3		1			1				18	37
Non-paying *No data*													
Poor *No data*													
Empty *No data*													
Total Temple Hirst	11	2	3		1			1				18	37
Thorpe Willoughby													
Paying	12	7		1								20	30
Non-paying *No data*													
Poor	2											2	2
Empty *No data*													
Total Thorpe Willoughby	14	7		1								22	32
Towton													
Paying	13	3								1	[10]	17	29
Non-paying *No data*													
Poor	1											1	1
Empty *No data*													
Total Towton	14	3								1		18	30

	Number of hearths										List of 10+	Total house-holds	Total hearths
	1	2	3	4	5	6	7	8	9	10+			
Ulleskelf													
Paying	37	8	4	2	1					1	[13]	53	91
Non-paying *No data*													
Poor *No data*													
Empty *No data*													
Total Ulleskelf	37	8	4	2	1					1		53	91
West Haddlesey													
Paying	14	10	3									27	43
Non-paying *No data*													
Poor *No data*													
Empty *No data*													
Total West Haddlesey	14	10	3									27	43
Wistow													
Paying	33	21	17	8	4	1	2	1	1	1	[11]	89	226
Non-paying *No data*													
Poor	12											12	12
Empty	1											1	1
Total Wistow	46	21	17	8	4	1	2	1	1	1		102	239
Total Barkston Ash	**1294**	**437**	**208**	**143**	**62**	**22**	**19**	**14**	**5**	**28**		**2232**	**4533**
Claro Wapentake													
Aismunderby with Bondgate													
Paying	13	6	2		1	1	2			1	[16]	26	72
Non-paying *No data*													
Poor *No data*													
Empty	3											3	3
Total Aismunderby with Bondgate	16	6	2		1	1	2			1		29	75
Aldborough													
Paying	51	10	1		1				1			64	88
Non-paying	2	1										3	4
Poor	8											8	8
Empty *No data*													
Total Aldborough	61	11	1		1				1			75	100
Aldfield													
Paying	17	3	2	1		1				1	[15]	25	54
Non-paying *No data*													
Poor	3											3	3
Empty *No data*													
Total Aldfield	20	3	2	1		1				1		28	57

	Number of hearths										List of 10+	Total house-holds	Total hearths
	1	2	3	4	5	6	7	8	9	10+			
Allerton and Flaxby													
Paying	17	9	2				1			1	[24]	30	72
Non-paying *No data*													
Poor	5											5	5
Empty *No data*													
Total Allerton and Flaxby	22	9	2				1			1		35	77
Arkendale													
Paying	39	8	4									51	67
Non-paying	4											4	4
Poor	6											6	6
Empty *No data*													
Total Arkendale	49	8	4									61	77
Askwith													
Paying	31	19	2	2								54	83
Non-paying	3											3	3
Poor *No data*													
Empty *No data*													
Total Askwith	34	19	2	2								57	86
Azerley													
Paying	40	22	1						2			65	105
Non-paying *No data*													
Poor	7											7	7
Empty *No data*													
Total Azerley	47	22	1						2			72	112
Beamsley													
Paying	43	14	6	1						1	[14]	65	107
Non-paying *No data*													
Poor *No data*													
Empty *No data*													
Total Beamsley	43	14	6	1						1		65	107
Bewerley													
Paying	35	15	4	3								57	89
Non-paying *No data*													
Poor *No data*													
Empty *No data*													
Total Bewerley	35	15	4	3								57	89
Birstwith													
Paying	40	11	4	2								57	82
Non-paying *No data*													
Poor *No data*													
Empty *No data*													
Total Birstwith	40	11	4	2								57	82

	Number of hearths										List of 10+	Total house-holds	Total hearths
	1	2	3	4	5	6	7	8	9	10+			
Bishop Monkton													
Paying	38	10	3									51	67
Non-paying *No data*													
Poor	7											7	7
Empty *No data*													
Total Bishop Monkton	45	10	3									58	74
Bishop Thornton													
Paying	30	11	3	1			1	3				49	96
Non-paying *No data*													
Poor *No data*													
Empty	1											1	1
Total Bishop Thornton	31	11	3	1			1	3				50	97
Bishopside													
Paying	46	25	12	5	1	2						91	169
Non-paying *No data*													
Poor	6											6	6
Empty	1	1										2	3
Total Bishopside	53	26	12	5	1	2						99	178
Bishopton and Clotherholme													
Paying	12	7	3		2	1						25	51
Non-paying	1	1										2	3
Poor	5											5	5
Empty		1										1	2
Total Bishopton and Clotherholme	18	9	3		2	1						33	61
Blubberhouses													
Paying	16	3										19	22
Non-paying *No data*													
Poor *No data*													
Empty *No data*													
Total Blubberhouses	16	3										19	22
Boroughbridge													
Paying	9	8	9	3		2		3	2	1	[10]	37	128
Non-paying *No data*													
Poor	10											10	10
Empty	1											1	1
Total Boroughbridge	20	8	9	3		2		3	2	1		48	139

	Number of hearths										List of 10+	Total house-holds	Total hearths
	1	2	3	4	5	6	7	8	9	10+			
Brearton													
Paying	15	7	1	1								24	35
Non-paying *No data*													
Poor *No data*													
Empty *No data*													
Total Brearton	15	7	1	1								24	35
Bridge Hewick													
Paying	8	3	3									14	23
Non-paying	3											3	3
Poor *No data*													
Empty *No data*													
Total Bridge Hewick	11	3	3									17	26
Burton Leonard													
Paying	32	8	1	1	2							44	65
Non-paying		2										2	4
Poor	4											4	4
Empty *No data*													
Total Burton Leonard	36	10	1	1	2							50	73
Castley													
Paying	10	3		1	1							15	26
Non-paying *No data*													
Poor	2											2	2
Empty *No data*													
Total Castley	12	3		1	1							17	28
Cattal													
Paying	24	7										31	38
Non-paying *No data*													
Poor	4											4	4
Empty *No data*													
Total Cattal	28	7										35	42
Clifton with Norwood													
Paying	50	18	1									69	89
Non-paying *No data*													
Poor	6											6	6
Empty *No data*													
Total Clifton with Norwood	56	18	1									75	95

	Number of hearths										List of 10+	Total house-holds	Total hearths
	1	2	3	4	5	6	7	8	9	10+			
Clint													
Paying	31	20	1	3								55	86
Non-paying *No data*													
Poor	7											7	7
Empty *No data*													
Total Clint	38	20	1	3								62	93
Coneythorpe													
Paying	16	2	1									19	23
Non-paying *No data*													
Poor	4											4	4
Empty *No data*													
Total Coneythorpe	20	2	1									23	27
Copgrove													
Paying	11	6	1	1			1					20	37
Non-paying *No data*													
Poor *No data*													
Empty *No data*													
Total Copgrove	11	6	1	1			1					20	37
Copt Hewick													
Paying	13	3		1								17	23
Non-paying *No data*													
Poor	6											6	6
Empty *No data*													
Total Copt Hewick	19	3		1								23	29
Cowthorpe													
Paying	9	3	2							1	[12]	15	33
Non-paying	2											2	2
Poor	4											4	4
Empty *No data*													
Total Cowthorpe	15	3	2							1		21	39
Dacre													
Paying	39	23	6		1		1		1			71	124
Non-paying *No data*													
Poor *No data*													
Empty *No data*													
Total Dacre	39	23	6		1		1		1			71	124
Denton													
Paying	12	11		2						1	[19]	26	61
Non-paying *No data*													
Poor *No data*													
Empty *No data*													
Total Denton	12	11		2						1		26	61

	Number of hearths										List of 10+	Total house-holds	Total hearths
	1	2	3	4	5	6	7	8	9	10+			
Dunkeswick													
Paying	20		2		1		1					24	38
Non-paying *No data*													
Poor	13											13	13
Empty *No data*													
Total Dunkeswick	33		2		1		1					37	51
Dunsforth													
Paying	17	6	1	1		1						26	42
Non-paying *No data*													
Poor *No data*													
Empty	1											1	1
Total Dunsforth	18	6	1	1		1						27	43
Farnham													
Paying	10	7	5	1		1						24	49
Non-paying *No data*													
Poor	1											1	1
Empty *No data*													
Total Farnham	11	7	5	1		1						25	50
Farnley													
Paying	40	7	1							1	[15]	49	72
Non-paying *No data*													
Poor *No data*													
Empty *No data*													
Total Farnley	40	7	1							1		49	72
Felliscliffe													
Paying	56	11	2									69	84
Non-paying *No data*													
Poor *No data*													
Empty *No data*													
Total Felliscliffe	56	11	2									69	84
Ferrensby													
Paying	9	2	3	1								15	26
Non-paying *No data*													
Poor	3											3	3
Empty *No data*													
Total Ferrensby	12	2	3	1								18	29
Follifoot													
Paying	34	12	3	2								51	75
Non-paying	6											6	6
Poor *No data*													
Empty *No data*													
Total Follifoot	40	12	3	2								57	81

	Number of hearths									List of 10+	Total house-holds	Total hearths
	1	2	3	4	5	6	7	8	9	10+			
Fountains Abbey													
Paying	2	3	1	1	1					1	[11]	9	31
Non-paying *No data*													
Poor *No data*													
Empty *No data*													
Total Fountains Abbey	2	3	1	1	1					1		9	31
Fountains Earth													
Paying	21	13	4	2	1							41	72
Non-paying *No data*													
Poor *No data*													
Empty *No data*													
Total Fountains Earth	21	13	4	2	1							41	72
Givendale													
Paying		2										2	4
Non-paying *No data*													
Poor *No data*													
Empty *No data*													
Total Givendale		2										2	4
Goldsborough													
Paying	25	3	1	1						1	[29]	31	67
Non-paying *No data*													
Poor *No data*													
Empty *No data*													
Total Goldsborough	25	3	1	1						1		31	67
Grantley and Eavestone													
Paying	37	5	4	2								48	67
Non-paying *No data*													
Poor	2											2	2
Empty *No data*													
Total Grantley and Eavestone	39	5	4	2								50	69
Great Ouseburn													
Paying	29	12	3	2								46	70
Non-paying	9	1										10	11
Poor *No data*													
Empty *No data*													
Total Great Ouseburn	38	13	3	2								56	81

	Number of hearths										List of 10+	Total house-holds	Total hearths
	1	2	3	4	5	6	7	8	9	10+			
Great Ribston with Walshford													
Paying	7	2	1						1			11	23
Non-paying			1									1	3
Poor	1											1	1
Empty			1									1	3
Total Great Ribston with Walshford	8	2	3						1			14	30
Great Timble and Fewston													
Paying	55	16	3		1	1						76	107
Non-paying *No data*													
Poor	3											3	3
Empty	1											1	1
Total Great Timble and Fewston	59	16	3		1	1						80	111
Green Hammerton													
Paying	23	4	1		1	1			1			31	54
Non-paying *No data*													
Poor	3											3	3
Empty			1									1	3
Total Green Hammerton	26	4	2		1	1			1			35	60
Grewelthorpe													
Paying	54	22	3	2	1	1		1				84	134
Non-paying *No data*													
Poor	6											6	6
Empty *No data*													
Total Grewelthorpe	60	22	3	2	1	1		1				90	140
Hampsthwaite													
Paying	21	9	2	4								36	61
Non-paying *No data*													
Poor *No data*													
Empty		1										1	2
Total Hampsthwaite	21	10	2	4								37	63
Harrogate													
Paying	37	18	5		1	1	2			2	[10, 22]	66	145
Non-paying *No data*													
Poor	7											7	7
Empty	1	1										2	3
Total Harrogate	45	19	5		1	1	2			2		75	155

	Number of hearths										List of 10+	Total house-holds	Total hearths
	1	2	3	4	5	6	7	8	9	10+	10+		
Hartwith cum Winsley													
Paying	25	18	10	2	2							57	109
Non-paying *No data*													
Poor	11											11	11
Empty *No data*													
Total Hartwith cum Winsley	36	18	10	2	2							68	120
Haverah Park													
Paying	7	3		1								11	17
Non-paying *No data*													
Poor	1											1	1
Empty *No data*													
Total Haverah Park	8	3		1								12	18
Humburton and Milby													
Paying	3	3	1									7	12
Non-paying *No data*													
Poor *No data*													
Empty *No data*													
Total Humburton and Milby	3	3	1									7	12
Hunsingore													
Paying	22	7	3	1								33	49
Non-paying	2									1	[10]	3	12
Poor	3											3	3
Empty *No data*													
Total Hunsingore	27	7	3	1						1		39	64
Ingerthorpe													
Paying	12	2							1			15	25
Non-paying *No data*													
Poor	6											6	6
Empty *No data*													
Total Ingerthorpe	18	2							1			21	31
Kearby with Netherby													
Paying	15	2	3					2				22	44
Non-paying *No data*													
Poor	4											4	4
Empty			1									1	3
Total Kearby with Netherby	19	2	4					2				27	51

	Number of hearths										List of 10+	Total house-holds	Total hearths
	1	2	3	4	5	6	7	8	9	10+			
Killinghall													
Paying	31	10	3	2	2		1					49	85
Non-paying *No data*													
Poor	2											2	2
Empty	1		1	1								3	8
Total Killinghall	34	10	4	3	2		1					54	95
Kirby Hall													
Paying	1		1	1		1				1	[15]	5	29
Non-paying *No data*													
Poor	1											1	1
Empty *No data*													
Total Kirby Hall	2		1	1		1				1		6	30
Kirk Deighton													
Paying	20	4		1			2					27	46
Non-paying *No data*													
Poor	1											1	1
Empty		1										1	2
Total Kirk Deighton	21	5		1			2					29	49
Kirk Hammerton													
Paying	26	5	2					1				34	50
Non-paying	2											2	2
Poor	6											6	6
Empty *No data*													
Total Kirk Hammerton	34	5	2					1				42	58
Kirkby Malzeard													
Paying	36	13	3	4			1	1				58	102
Non-paying *No data*													
Poor	9											9	9
Empty *No data*													
Total Kirkby Malzeard	45	13	3	4			1	1				67	111
Kirkby Overblow													
Paying	26	3	1	1			1		2			34	64
Non-paying *No data*													
Poor	11											11	11
Empty *No data*													
Total Kirkby Overblow	37	3	1	1			1		2			45	75

	Number of hearths										List of 10+	Total house-holds	Total hearths
	1	2	3	4	5	6	7	8	9	10+			
Knaresborough													
Paying	74	40	27	14	4	5	2					166	355
Non-paying *No data*													
Poor	15											15	15
Empty	1	2	1									4	8
Total Knaresborough	90	42	28	14	4	5	2					185	378
Knaresborough, Tentergate													
Paying	22	17	1	1	1		1					43	75
Non-paying *No data*													
Poor	2											2	2
Empty *No data*													
Total Knaresborough, Tentergate	24	17	1	1	1		1					45	77
Laverton													
Paying	50	11	1	1		1						64	85
Non-paying *No data*													
Poor	13											13	13
Empty *No data*													
Total Laverton	63	11	1	1		1						77	98
Leathley													
Paying	38	8	3			1				1	[11]	51	80
Non-paying	2											2	2
Poor *No data*													
Empty *No data*													
Total Leathley	40	8	3			1				1		53	82
Linton													
Paying	6	5	2		1							14	27
Non-paying *No data*													
Poor	2											2	2
Empty *No data*													
Total Linton	8	5	2		1							16	29
Little Cattall													
Paying										1	[19]	1	19
Non-paying *No data*													
Poor *No data*													
Empty *No data*													
Total Little Cattall										1		1	19
Little Ouseburn													
Paying	16	7	1									24	33
Non-paying *No data*													
Poor	4											4	4
Empty *No data*													
Total Little Ouseburn	20	7	1									28	37

	Number of hearths										List of 10+	Total house-holds	Total hearths
	1	2	3	4	5	6	7	8	9	10+			
Little Ribston													
Paying	20	4	1									25	31
Non-paying	5											5	5
Poor *No data*													
Empty *No data*													
Total Little Ribston	25	4	1									30	36
Little Timble													
Paying	6				1		1					8	19
Non-paying *No data*													
Poor *No data*													
Empty *No data*													
Total Little Timble	6				1		1					8	19
Markington with Wallathwate													
Paying	22	12	1	2	1		1					39	70
Non-paying		1										1	2
Poor	5											5	5
Empty *No data*													
Total Markington with Wallathwate	27	13	1	2	1		1					45	77
Marton cum Grafton													
Paying	35	10		2								47	63
Non-paying *No data*													
Poor	6											6	6
Empty	1											1	1
Total Marton cum Grafton	42	10		2								54	70
Menwith cum Darley													
Paying	39	19	4	1	1							64	98
Non-paying *No data*													
Poor	7											7	7
Empty *No data*													
Total Menwith cum Darley	46	19	4	1	1							71	105
Middleton and Stockeld													
Paying	17	6	2							1	[41]	26	76
Non-paying *No data*													
Poor	3											3	3
Empty *No data*													
Total Middleton and Stockeld	20	6	2							1		29	79

	Number of hearths										List of 10+	Total house-holds	Total hearths
	1	2	3	4	5	6	7	8	9	10+			
Minskip													
Paying	30	6										36	42
Non-paying *No data*													
Poor	4											4	4
Empty *No data*													
Total Minskip	34	6										40	46
Nesfield													
Paying	28	5	1	1	2							37	55
Non-paying *No data*													
Poor	1											1	1
Empty *No data*													
Total Nesfield	29	5	1	1	2							38	56
Newby with Mulwith													
Paying	1	1	1							1	[12]	4	18
Non-paying *No data*													
Poor	1											1	1
Empty *No data*													
Total Newby with Mulwith	2	1	1							1		5	19
Newell with Clifton													
Paying	20	9	2	1	2					1	[16]	35	74
Non-paying *No data*													
Poor *No data*													
Empty *No data*													
Total Newell with Clifton	20	9	2	1	2					1		35	74
Nidd													
Paying	12	6	1	1			1			1	[10]	22	48
Non-paying *No data*													
Poor	2											2	2
Empty *No data*													
Total Nidd	14	6	1	1			1			1		24	50
North Deighton													
Paying	10	4	2				1			1	[10]	18	41
Non-paying *No data*													
Poor *No data*													
Empty	2											2	2
Total North Deighton	12	4	2				1			1		20	43

	Number of hearths										List of 10+	Total house-holds	Total hearths
	1	2	3	4	5	6	7	8	9	10+			
North Stainley with Sleningford													
Paying	29	4	3		2		1			2	[11, 13]	41	87
Non-paying *No data*													
Poor	5											5	5
Empty		1										1	2
Total North Stainley with Sleningford	34	5	3		2		1			2		47	94
Nun Monkton													
Paying	34	9	3	2						1	[21]	49	90
Non-paying *No data*													
Poor	6											6	6
Empty *No data*													
Total Nun Monkton	40	9	3	2						1		55	96
Nunwick cum Howgrave													
Paying	4	1		1								6	10
Non-paying	1											1	1
Poor	1											1	1
Empty	1											1	1
Total Nunwick cum Howgrave	7	1		1								9	13
Pannal													
Paying	58	24	5	4			1	1	2			95	170
Non-paying	6											6	6
Poor	7											7	7
Empty *No data*													
Total Pannal	71	24	5	4			1	1	2			108	183
Plompton													
Paying	27	4	1		1					1	[11]	34	54
Non-paying	2											2	2
Poor	1											1	1
Empty	1											1	1
Total Plompton	31	4	1		1					1		38	58
Rigton													
Paying	41	8	1	1								51	64
Non-paying *No data*													
Poor	3											3	3
Empty *No data*													
Total Rigton	44	8	1	1								54	67

	Number of hearths										List of 10+	Total households	Total hearths
	1	2	3	4	5	6	7	8	9	10+			
Ripley													
Paying	14	14	3	3	2	1				1	[24]	38	103
Non-paying *No data*													
Poor	9											9	9
Empty *No data*													
Total Ripley	23	14	3	3	2	1				1		47	112
Ripon Allhallowgate													
Paying	35	15	8	6	2	3		1		5	[11, 11, 12, 12, 14]	75	209
Non-paying	6	1										7	8
Poor	13											13	13
Empty	1		1									2	4
Total Ripon Allhallowgate	55	16	9	6	2	3		1		5		97	234
Ripon Crossgate													
Paying	40	24	20	17	12	12	3	4	1			133	410
Non-paying	10	1										11	12
Poor	12											12	12
Empty	1	3		2	1							7	20
Total Ripon Crossgate	63	28	20	19	13	12	3	4	1			163	454
Ripon Skellgate													
Paying	12	17	6	3	1	1	2					42	101
Non-paying		1										1	2
Poor *No data*													
Empty *No data*													
Total Ripon Skellgate	12	18	6	3	1	1	2					43	103
Ripon Westgate													
Paying	19	3	10	4	1	1						38	82
Non-paying *No data*													
Poor	6											6	6
Empty	1	2					1					4	12
Total Ripon Westgate	26	5	10	4	1	1	1					48	100
Roecliffe													
Paying	23	11	2									36	51
Non-paying *No data*													
Poor	3											3	3
Empty *No data*													
Total Roecliffe	26	11	2									39	54

	Number of hearths										List of 10+	Total house-holds	Total hearths
	1	2	3	4	5	6	7	8	9	10+			
Sawley													
Paying	53	9	3	1	1		2					69	103
Non-paying *No data*													
Poor	7											7	7
Empty *No data*													
Total Sawley	60	9	3	1	1		2					76	110
Scotton													
Paying	21	4	2	1				1				29	47
Non-paying *No data*													
Poor	7											7	7
Empty	2											2	2
Total Scotton	30	4	2	1				1				38	56
Scriven													
Paying	12	7					1					20	33
Non-paying *No data*													
Poor *No data*													
Empty *No data*													
Total Scriven	12	7					1					20	33
Sharow													
Paying	6	7	1		1							15	28
Non-paying *No data*													
Poor	8											8	8
Empty *No data*													
Total Sharow	14	7	1		1							23	36
Sicklinghall													
Paying	26	3	2						1			32	47
Non-paying	1											1	1
Poor	8											8	8
Empty *No data*													
Total Sicklinghall	35	3	2						1			41	56
Skelton													
Paying	26	6	1	1								34	45
Non-paying *No data*													
Poor	6											6	6
Empty *No data*													
Total Skelton	32	6	1	1								40	51
South Stainley with Cayton													
Paying	1	4	2	2		1		1		1	[18]	12	55
Non-paying *No data*													
Poor	2											2	2
Empty *No data*													
Total South Stainley with Cayton	3	4	2	2		1		1		1		14	57

	Number of hearths										List of 10+	Total house-holds	Total hearths
	1	2	3	4	5	6	7	8	9	10+			
Spofforth													
Paying	55	17	6	2					1	2	[10, 12]	83	146
Non-paying *No data*													
Poor	2											2	2
Empty *No data*													
Total Spofforth	57	17	6	2					1	2		85	148
Stainburne													
Paying	26	6	1									33	41
Non-paying *No data*													
Poor *No data*													
Empty			1									1	3
Total Stainburne	26	6	2									34	44
Staveley													
Paying	18	11		2		1						32	54
Non-paying *No data*													
Poor *No data*													
Empty *No data*													
Total Staveley	18	11		2		1						32	54
Stonebeck Down													
Paying	51	16	4					1				72	103
Non-paying *No data*													
Poor	2											2	2
Empty	2											2	2
Total Stonebeck Down	55	16	4					1				76	107
Stonebeck Up													
Paying	25	18	2	1								46	71
Non-paying *No data*													
Poor *No data*													
Empty *No data*													
Total Stonebeck Up	25	18	2	1								46	71
Studley Roger													
Paying	10	5	1	3								19	35
Non-paying *No data*													
Poor	1											1	1
Empty *No data*													
Total Studley Roger	11	5	1	3								20	36
Thruscross													
Paying	55	26	3									84	116
Non-paying *No data*													
Poor *No data*													
Empty *No data*													
Total Thruscross	55	26	3									84	116

	Number of hearths										List of 10+	Total house-holds	Total hearths
	1	2	3	4	5	6	7	8	9	10+			
Weeton and Huby													
Paying	23	7	5									35	52
Non-paying	4											4	4
Poor *No data*													
Empty	1	1										2	3
Total Weeton and Huby	28	8	5									41	59
Weston													
Paying	16	8		1	1					1	[24]	27	65
Non-paying *No data*													
Poor *No data*													
Empty *No data*													
Total Weston	16	8		1	1					1		27	65
Westwick													
Paying	1						1					2	8
Non-paying *No data*													
Poor *No data*													
Empty *No data*													
Total Westwick	1						1					2	8
Wetherby													
Paying	9	22	14	9	1			2				57	152
Non-paying *No data*													
Poor	12											12	12
Empty *No data*													
Total Wetherby	21	22	14	9	1			2				69	164
Whitcliffe with Thorpe, later Littlethorpe													
Paying	11	8	1	1		1			1			23	49
Non-paying *No data*													
Poor	4											4	4
Empty *No data*													
Total Whitcliffe with Thorpe, later Littlethorpe	15	8	1	1		1			1			27	53
Whixley													
Paying	42	14	4	2	2		1	1		1	[11]	67	126
Non-paying *No data*													
Poor	8											8	8
Empty *No data*													
Total Whixley	50	14	4	2	2		1	1		1		75	134
Total Claro	**3218**	**1044**	**319**	**154**	**60**	**43**	**32**	**25**	**17**	**36**		**4948**	**8570**

	Number of hearths										List of 10+	Total house-holds	Total hearths
	1	2	3	4	5	6	7	8	9	10+			
Ewcross Wapentake													
Austwick													
Paying	99	48	4	3	2		2			1	[11]	159	254
Non-paying *No data*													
Poor	9											9	9
Empty	3											3	3
Total Austwick	111	48	4	3	2		2			1		171	266
Bentham													
Paying	90	29	6	3	1	2						131	195
Non-paying *No data*													
Poor *No data*													
Empty *No data*													
Total Bentham	90	29	6	3	1	2						131	195
Burton													
Paying	19	10	3	1								33	52
Non-paying *No data*													
Poor	10											10	10
Empty	1											1	1
Total Burton	30	10	3	1								44	63
Clapham													
Paying	40	17	5	3		1						66	107
Non-paying *No data*													
Poor	8											8	8
Empty *No data*													
Total Clapham	48	17	5	3		1						74	115
Dent													
Paying	258	80	20	7	3							368	521
Non-paying	1	1										2	3
Poor	3											3	3
Empty	1	1										2	3
Total Dent	263	82	20	7	3							375	530
Horton in Ribblesdale													
Paying	63	37	6	5								111	175
Non-paying	1											1	1
Poor	2											2	2
Empty *No data*													
Total Horton in Ribblesdale	66	37	6	5								114	178

	Number of hearths										List of 10+	Total house-holds	Total hearths
	1	2	3	4	5	6	7	8	9	10+			
Ingleton													
Paying	31	18	5	1						1	[14]	56	100
Non-paying *No data*													
Poor	19											19	19
Empty	1											1	1
Total Ingleton	51	18	5	1						1		76	120
Ingleton Fells													
Paying	25	7	2	2								36	53
Non-paying *No data*													
Poor *No data*													
Empty *No data*													
Total Ingleton Fells	25	7	2	2								36	53
Newby													
Paying	31	13	5									49	72
Non-paying *No data*													
Poor	2											2	2
Empty *No data*													
Total Newby	33	13	5									51	74
Sedbergh													
Paying	44	14	5									63	87
Non-paying *No data*													
Poor *No data*													
Empty *No data*													
Total Sedbergh	44	14	5									63	87
Sedbergh Scoolebancke													
Paying	39	18	10	2	1	1	1					72	131
Non-paying *No data*													
Poor	7											7	7
Empty *No data*													
Total Sedbergh Scoolebancke	46	18	10	2	1	1	1					79	138
Sedbergh, Howgill													
Paying	24	7		4	1		1					37	66
Non-paying *No data*													
Poor *No data*													
Empty *No data*													
Total Sedbergh, Howgill	24	7		4	1		1					37	66

	Number of hearths										List of 10+	Total house-holds	Total hearths
	1	2	3	4	5	6	7	8	9	10+			
Sedburgh, Marthwaite													
Paying	35	18	2	3						1	[11]	59	100
Non-paying *No data*													
Poor	2											2	2
Empty *No data*													
Total Sedburgh, Marthwaite	37	18	2	3						1		61	102
Thornton in Lonsdale													
Paying	32	10	6	2	1			1				52	91
Non-paying *No data*													
Poor	2											2	2
Empty	1											1	1
Total Thornton in Lonsdale	35	10	6	2	1			1				55	94
Twisleton and Cold Cotes													
Paying	12	13		1		2						28	54
Non-paying *No data*													
Poor *No data*													
Empty *No data*													
Total Twisleton and Cold Cotes	12	13		1		2						28	54
Total Ewcross	**915**	**341**	**79**	**37**	**9**	**6**	**4**	**1**		**3**		**1395**	**2135**
Morley Wapentake													
Allerton and Wilsden													
Paying	51	18	14	4	2	1	1					91	168
Non-paying *No data*													
Poor	2											2	2
Empty *No data*													
Total Allerton and Wilsden	53	18	14	4	2	1	1					93	170
Armley													
Paying	28	25	3	3	1							60	104
Non-paying *No data*													
Poor	9											9	9
Empty *No data*													
Total Armley	37	25	3	3	1							69	113

	Number of hearths										List of 10+	Total house-holds	Total hearths
	1	2	3	4	5	6	7	8	9	10+			
Barkisland													
Paying	48	23	7	6	2	2	1			2	[10, 14]	91	192
Non-paying *No data*													
Poor	4											4	4
Empty	2											2	2
Total Barkisland	54	23	7	6	2	2	1			2		97	198
Beeston													
Paying	28	22	9	6	1	1	2			1	[17]	70	165
Non-paying *No data*													
Poor	10											10	10
Empty		1										1	2
Total Beeston	38	23	9	6	1	1	2			1		81	177
Bolton													
Paying	10	4		2	1	1						18	37
Non-paying *No data*													
Poor *No data*													
Empty *No data*													
Total Bolton	10	4		2	1	1						18	37
Bowling													
Paying	32	24	4	4	1					1	[19]	66	132
Non-paying	3											3	3
Poor	3											3	3
Empty	1	1										2	3
Total Bowling	39	25	4	4	1					1		74	141
Bradford Kirkgate													
Paying	38	24	14	9	1	2	1	3				92	212
Non-paying *No data*													
Poor	2											2	2
Empty	1											1	1
Total Bradford Kirkgate	41	24	14	9	1	2	1	3				95	215
Bradford Westgate													
Paying	33	26	19	10	11	4	3	4		1	[10]	111	324
Non-paying	1											1	1
Poor	14											14	14
Empty	1		1			1						3	10
Total Bradford Westgate	49	26	20	10	11	5	3	4		1		129	349
Bramley													
Paying	28	25	6	3	4							66	128
Non-paying *No data*													
Poor	1											1	1
Empty *No data*													
Total Bramley	29	25	6	3	4							67	129

	Number of hearths										List of 10+	Total house-holds	Total hearths
	1	2	3	4	5	6	7	8	9	10+			
Calverley with Farsley													
Paying	50	15	5	4		1				1	[20]	76	137
Non-paying	1	1										2	3
Poor	4											4	4
Empty	3											3	3
Total Calverley with Farsley	58	16	5	4		1				1		85	147
Churwell													
Paying	12	10	2	2	2							28	56
Non-paying *No data*													
Poor	3											3	3
Empty *No data*													
Total Churwell	15	10	2	2	2							31	59
Clayton													
Paying	57	13	4	1	1	1						77	110
Non-paying *No data*													
Poor	7											7	7
Empty *No data*													
Total Clayton	64	13	4	1	1	1						84	117
Cleckheaton													
Paying	30	17	12									59	100
Non-paying	1	1										2	3
Poor	2											2	2
Empty		1										1	2
Total Cleckheaton	33	19	12									64	107
Drighlington and Adwalton													
Paying	17	13	7	5	3	2		1		1	[10]	49	129
Non-paying *No data*													
Poor	6											6	6
Empty			1									1	3
Total Drighlington and Adwalton	23	13	8	5	3	2		1		1		56	138
Eccleshill													
Paying	67	44	18	10	6	4		3				152	327
Non-paying	19											19	19
Poor	2											2	2
Empty *No data*													
Total Eccleshill	88	44	18	10	6	4		3				173	348

	Number of hearths										List of 10+	Total households	Total hearths
	1	2	3	4	5	6	7	8	9	10+			
Elland with Greetland													
Paying	22	10	4	5	2	1	2					46	104
Non-paying *No data*													
Poor	17											17	17
Empty *No data*													
Total Elland with Greetland	39	10	4	5	2	1	2					63	121
Erringden													
Paying	19	10	4	3	2							38	73
Non-paying *No data*													
Poor *No data*													
Empty *No data*													
Total Erringden	19	10	4	3	2							38	73
Farnley													
Paying	22	13	1	1						1	[19]	38	74
Non-paying *No data*													
Poor	3											3	3
Empty					1							1	5
Total Farnley	25	13	1	1	1					1		42	82
Fixby													
Paying	12	3	3	1						1	[15]	20	46
Non-paying *No data*													
Poor	11											11	11
Empty *No data*													
Total Fixby	23	3	3	1						1		31	57
Gildersome													
Paying	17	11	12	2		1	1					44	96
Non-paying *No data*													
Poor *No data*													
Empty	1											1	1
Total Gildersome	18	11	12	2		1	1					45	97
Gomersall													
Paying	47	26	21	9	8	3	1	1	1	2	[10, 13]	119	303
Non-paying *No data*													
Poor	9											9	9
Empty		1	1									2	5
Total Gomersall	56	27	22	9	8	3	1	1	1	2		130	317

	Number of hearths										List of 10+	Total house-holds	Total hearths
	1	2	3	4	5	6	7	8	9	10+			
Halifax													
Paying	61	81	60	48	21	13	11	5	4	9	[10, 10, 10, 11, 12, 13, 16, 17, 18]	313	1048
Non-paying	36	3										39	42
Poor	111											111	111
Empty	4	8	3	1		1						17	39
Total Halifax	212	92	63	49	21	14	11	5	4	9		480	1240
Hartshead cum Clifton													
Paying	47	24	7	2	2			1		1	[23]	84	165
Non-paying *No data*													
Poor *No data*													
Empty *No data*													
Total Hartshead cumClifton	47	24	7	2	2			1		1		84	165
Haworth													
Paying	131	30	8	1	1	1						172	230
Non-paying *No data*													
Poor	8											8	8
Empty	1	1										2	3
Total Haworth	140	31	8	1	1	1						182	241
Heaton and Clayton													
Paying	29	10	4	2		1						46	75
Non-paying	14											14	14
Poor *No data*													
Empty *No data*													
Total Heaton and Clayton	43	10	4	2		1						60	89
Heckmondwike													
Paying	20	13	3	5	5	1						47	106
Non-paying *No data*													
Poor	3											3	3
Empty *No data*													
Total Heckmondwike	23	13	3	5	5	1						50	109
Heptonstall													
Paying	61	28	7	3	1	1		1				102	169
Non-paying *No data*													
Poor *No data*													
Empty *No data*													
Total Heptonstall	61	28	7	3	1	1		1				102	169

	Number of hearths										List of 10+	Total house-holds	Total hearths
	1	2	3	4	5	6	7	8	9	10+			
Hipperholme with Brighouse													
Paying	33	30	39	21	5	4	2	1		1	[13]	136	378
Non-paying *No data*													
Poor	7											7	7
Empty *No data*													
Total Hipperholme with Brighouse	40	30	39	21	5	4	2	1		1		143	385
Holbeck													
Paying	51	50	13	5	1		1		2			123	240
Non-paying *No data*													
Poor	22											22	22
Empty	4	7	1		1							13	26
Total Holbeck	77	57	14	5	2		1		2			158	288
Hortons Ambo													
Paying	60	39	19	4			2					124	225
Non-paying *No data*													
Poor	9											9	9
Empty *No data*													
Total Hortons Ambo	69	39	19	4			2					133	234
Hunslet													
Paying	36	43	15	12	7	2	1	1		3	[10, 11, 11]	120	310
Non-paying *No data*													
Poor	2											2	2
Empty	1	1										2	3
Total Hunslet	39	44	15	12	7	2	1		1	3		124	315
Hunsworth													
Paying	9	7	6	1	2							25	55
Non-paying	1	1										2	3
Poor	6											6	6
Empty *No data*													
Total Hunsworth	16	8	6	1	2							33	64
Idle													
Paying	61	34	17		4	1						117	206
Non-paying *No data*													
Poor	4											4	4
Empty	2											2	2
Total Idle	67	34	17		4	1						123	212

	Number of hearths										List of 10+	Total house-holds	Total hearths
	1	2	3	4	5	6	7	8	9	10+			
Langfield													
Paying	32	12	5			1						50	77
Non-paying *No data*													
Poor	9											9	9
Empty *No data*													
Total Langfield	41	12	5			1						59	86
Liversedge													
Paying	56	18	15	4	8	2	1			1	[10]	105	222
Non-paying *No data*													
Poor	6											6	6
Empty *No data*													
Total Liversedge	62	18	15	4	8	2	1			1		111	228
Manningham													
Paying	39	13	6	2	3	1	1					65	119
Non-paying *No data*													
Poor *No data*													
Empty *No data*													
Total Manningham	39	13	6	2	3	1	1					65	119
Midgley													
Paying	35	13	7	9	2		2	1		1	[11]	70	161
Non-paying	20											20	20
Poor *No data*													
Empty *No data*													
Total Midgley	55	13	7	9	2		2	1		1		90	181
Norland													
Paying	17	17	13	4	5	2						58	143
Non-paying *No data*													
Poor *No data*													
Empty *No data*													
Total Norland	17	17	13	4	5	2	58	143					
North Bierley													
Paying	50	33	15	8	3	1				2	[10, 10]	112	234
Non-paying *No data*													
Poor	13											13	13
Empty	3											3	3
Total North Bierley	66	33	15	8	3	1				2		128	250
Northowram													
Paying	64	54	29	14	7	5	3	2	1			179	426
Non-paying *No data*													
Poor	13											13	13
Empty *No data*													
Total Northowram	77	54	29	14	7	5	3	2	1			192	439

	Number of hearths										List of 10+	Total house-holds	Total hearths
	1	2	3	4	5	6	7	8	9	10+			
Ovenden													
Paying	88	56	30	13	3	1	1			2	[10, 10]	194	390
Non-paying *No data*													
Poor	9											9	9
Empty *No data*													
Total Ovenden	97	56	30	13	3	1	1			2		203	399
Pudsey													
Paying	61	34	4	4	1		1					105	169
Non-paying *No data*													
Poor	14											14	14
Empty	1											1	1
Total Pudsey	76	34	4	4	1		1					120	184
Rastrick													
Paying	15	10	6	5	1	3		1				41	104
Non-paying *No data*													
Poor	4											4	4
Empty		1										1	2
Total Rastrick	19	11	6	5	1	3		1				46	110
Rishworth													
Paying	38	22	5	3								68	109
Non-paying *No data*													
Poor	1											1	1
Empty		1										1	2
Total Rishworth	39	23	5	3								70	112
Shelf													
Paying	21	16	7	6	5	2						57	135
Non-paying *No data*													
Poor	6											6	6
Empty *No data*													
Total Shelf	27	16	7	6	5	2						63	141
Shipley													
Paying	10	7	6	4	1	1	1					30	76
Non-paying *No data*													
Poor	1											1	1
Empty		1										1	2
Total Shipley	11	8	6	4	1	1	1					32	79
Skircoat													
Paying	10	16	9	13	7		1	1				57	171
Non-paying *No data*													
Poor	1											1	1
Empty	1											1	1
Total Skircoat	12	16	9	13	7		1	1				59	173

	Number of hearths										List of 10+	Total house-holds	Total hearths
	1	2	3	4	5	6	7	8	9	10+			
Southowram													
Paying	23	33	20	15	8	3		2	1			105	292
Non-paying *No data*													
Poor	11											11	11
Empty *No data*													
Total Southowram	34	33	20	15	8	3		2	1			116	303
Sowerby													
Paying	180	71	42	23	14	2	2	2	2			338	670
Non-paying *No data*													
Poor	12											12	12
Empty		1										1	2
Total Sowerby	192	72	42	23	14	2	2	2	2			351	684
Stainland													
Paying	54	28	2	1								85	120
Non-paying	3	2										5	7
Poor	1											1	1
Empty *No data*													
Total Stainland	58	30	2	1								91	128
Stansfield													
Paying	122	30	7	3		2						164	227
Non-paying *No data*													
Poor	16											16	16
Empty *No data*													
Total Stansfield	138	30	7	3		2						180	243
Thornton													
Paying	67	23	8	3	2		1			1	[10]	105	176
Non-paying *No data*													
Poor	8											8	8
Empty	1											1	1
Total Thornton	76	23	8	3	2		1			1		114	185
Tonge													
Paying	34	31	9	4	1			1				80	152
Non-paying *No data*													
Poor	5											5	5
Empty	1											1	1
Total Tonge	40	31	9	4	1			1				86	158
Wadsworth													
Paying	90	22	14	7		2			1			136	225
Non-paying *No data*													
Poor *No data*													
Empty *No data*													
Total Wadsworth	90	22	14	7		2			1			136	225

	Number of hearths										List of 10+	Total house-holds	Total hearths
	1	2	3	4	5	6	7	8	9	10+			
Warley													
Paying	104	43	11	11	12	6	1					188	370
Non-paying *No data*													
Poor *No data*													
Empty *No data*													
Total Warley	104	43	11	11	12	6	1					188	370
Wortley													
Paying	23	25	1		1					1	[10]	51	91
Non-paying *No data*													
Poor	5											5	5
Empty	1											1	1
Total Wortley	29	25	1		1					1		57	97
Wyke													
Paying	33	14	3	5								55	90
Non-paying *No data*													
Poor	1											1	1
Empty *No data*													
Total Wyke	34	14	3	5								56	91
Total Morley	**3078**	**1439**	**648**	**356**	**183**	**84**	**44**	**30**	**13**	**33**		**5908**	**11831**
Osgoldcross Wapentake													
Ackworth													
Paying	49	26	12	8	3	2	2			1	[14]	103	224
Non-paying *No data*													
Poor	20											20	20
Empty *No data*													
Total Ackworth	69	26	12	8	3	2	2			1		123	244
Adlingfleet													
Paying	23	9	2	1								35	51
Non-paying *No data*													
Poor	8											8	8
Empty *No data*													
Total Adlingfleet	31	9	2	1								43	59
Airmyn													
Paying	32	3	3	2	1							41	60
Non-paying *No data*													
Poor	11											11	11
Empty *No data*													
Total Airmyn	43	3	3	2	1							52	71

	Number of hearths										List of 10+	Total house-holds	Total hearths
	1	2	3	4	5	6	7	8	9	10+			
Badsworth													
Paying	9	4	2	2	1					1	[20]	19	56
Non-paying *No data*													
Poor	2											2	2
Empty	1											1	1
Total Badsworth	12	4	2	2	1					1		22	59
Balne													
Paying	21	5	5	1	1			1				34	63
Non-paying *No data*													
Poor	2											2	2
Empty	1											1	1
Total Balne	24	5	5	1	1			1				37	66
Beal													
Paying	24	15	6	3	1				1			50	98
Non-paying *No data*													
Poor	4											4	4
Empty	1											1	1
Total Beal	29	15	6	3	1				1			55	103
Burghwallis													
Paying	13	6	1		1					1	[11]	22	44
Non-paying *No data*													
Poor	2											2	2
Empty	1											1	1
Total Burghwallis	16	6	1		1					1		25	47
Campsall													
Paying	27	5	3	3			1			1	[10]	40	76
Non-paying *No data*													
Poor	3											3	3
Empty *No data*													
Total Campsall	30	5	3	3			1			1		43	79
Castleford													
Paying	20	8	2		1				1			32	56
Non-paying *No data*													
Poor	4											4	4
Empty *No data*													
Total Castleford	24	8	2		1				1			36	60
Cridling Stubbs													
Paying	4	3		1	1				1	1	[10]	11	38
Non-paying *No data*													
Poor *No data*													
Empty				1								1	4
Total Cridling Stubbs	4	3		2	1				1	1		12	42

	Number of hearths										List of 10+	Total house-holds	Total hearths
	1	2	3	4	5	6	7	8	9	10+			
Darrington													
Paying	20	7	4	1	2	2		1				37	80
Non-paying *No data*													
Poor	2											2	2
Empty	2	1										3	4
Total Darrington	24	8	4	1	2	2		1				42	86
East & West Cowick													
Paying	51	21	11	6	1					1	[26]	91	181
Non-paying	3											3	3
Poor *No data*													
Empty	2											2	2
Total East & West Cowick	56	21	11	6	1					1		96	186
Featherstone													
Paying	16	9	2	2	2	1			1			33	73
Non-paying *No data*													
Poor	10											10	10
Empty	1		1									2	4
Total Featherstone	27	9	3	2	2	1			1			45	87
Fenwick													
Paying	11	6	4	3								24	47
Non-paying *No data*													
Poor	1											1	1
Empty *No data*													
Total Fenwick	12	6	4	3								25	48
Ferrybridge													
Paying	24	12	8	5	1	1		1		1	[15]	53	126
Non-paying *No data*													
Poor	8											8	8
Empty	1	2	1									4	8
Total Ferrybridge	33	14	9	5	1	1		1		1		65	142
Fockerby													
Paying	10	4			1							15	23
Non-paying *No data*													
Poor	1											1	1
Empty *No data*													
Total Fockerby	11	4			1							16	24
Glass Houghton													
Paying	18	7	1	5				1				32	63
Non-paying *No data*													
Poor	4											4	4
Empty	1											1	1
Total Glass Houghton	23	7	1	5				1				37	68

	Number of hearths									List of 10+	Total house-holds	Total hearths
	1	2	3	4	5	6	7	8	9	10+			
Goole													
Paying	16	9	4	6	3							38	85
Non-paying *No data*													
Poor	6											6	6
Empty	1											1	1
Total Goole	23	9	4	6	3							45	92
Gowdall													
Paying	25	9		1		1						36	53
Non-paying	5											5	5
Poor *No data*													
Empty *No data*													
Total Gowdall	30	9		1		1						41	58
Great Heck													
Paying	17	10	2							1	[13]	30	56
Non-paying *No data*													
Poor	1											1	1
Empty *No data*													
Total Great Heck	18	10	2							1		31	57
Haldenby and Eastoft													
Paying	30	7	1	1					1			40	60
Non-paying *No data*													
Poor	4											4	4
Empty *No data*													
Total Haldenby and Eastoft	34	7	1	1					1			44	64
Hensall													
Paying	11	8	2	3	2							26	55
Non-paying *No data*													
Poor	1											1	1
Empty	1											1	1
Total Hensall	13	8	2	3	2							28	57
High & Low Eggborough													
Paying	20	5	3		1	1			1			31	59
Non-paying *No data*													
Poor	2											2	2
Empty *No data*													
Total High & Low Eggborough	22	5	3		1	1			1			33	61

	Number of hearths										List of 10+	Total households	Total hearths
	1	2	3	4	5	6	7	8	9	10+			
Hook													
Paying	39	13	1		1							54	73
Non-paying *No data*													
Poor *No data*													
Empty *No data*													
Total Hook	39	13	1		1							54	73
Kellington													
Paying	18	11	4	2	2							37	70
Non-paying *No data*													
Poor	3											3	3
Empty	1											1	1
Total Kellington	22	11	4	2	2							41	74
Kirk Bramwith													
Paying	17	9	7	1								34	60
Non-paying *No data*													
Poor	1											1	1
Empty	1											1	2
Total Kirk Bramwith	18	10	7	1								36	63
Kirk Smeaton													
Paying	18	8	1	2	1		2					32	64
Non-paying *No data*													
Poor	5											5	5
Empty	1				1							2	6
Total Kirk Smeaton	24	8	1	2	2		2					39	75
Knottingley													
Paying	26	20	16	5	5	1	2	1	1			77	195
Non-paying *No data*													
Poor	19											19	19
Empty	3		1	1								5	10
Total Knottingley	48	20	17	6	5	1	2	1	1			101	225
Little Smeaton													
Paying	13	4	1	2	1							21	37
Non-paying *No data*													
Poor *No data*													
Empty		1										1	2
Total Little Smeaton	13	5	1	2	1							22	39
Moss													
Paying	22	13	3	2								40	65
Non-paying *No data*													
Poor	4											4	4
Empty *No data*	0												
Total Moss	26	13	3	2								44	69

	Number of hearths										List of 10+	Total house-holds	Total hearths
	1	2	3	4	5	6	7	8	9	10+			
North Elmsall													
Paying	11	2	3	1	1					1	[22]	19	55
Non-paying *No data*													
Poor	3											3	3
Empty	1											1	1
Total North Elmsall	15	2	3	1	1					1		23	59
Norton													
Paying	28	9	8	1			1			1	[12]	48	93
Non-paying *No data*													
Poor	3											3	3
Empty	1											1	1
Total Norton	32	9	8	1			1			1		52	97
Ousefleet													
Paying	35	6	2	1			1					45	64
Non-paying *No data*													
Poor	8											8	8
Empty *No data*													
Total Ousefleet	43	6	2	1			1					53	72
Owston													
Paying	23	9	5		1	1				1	[11]	40	78
Non-paying *No data*													
Poor *No data*													
Empty	1											1	1
Total Owston	24	9	5		1	1				1		41	79
Pollington													
Paying	36	15	5						1			57	90
Non-paying *No data*													
Poor	2											2	2
Empty *No data*													
Total Pollington	38	15	5						1			59	92
Pontefract Castle & Parke													
Paying		1		1	1		1					4	18
Non-paying *No data*													
Poor	3											3	3
Empty *No data*													
Total Pontefract Castle & Parke	3	1		1	1		1					7	21

	Number of hearths										List of 10+	Total house-holds	Total hearths
	1	2	3	4	5	6	7	8	9	10+			
Pontefract Neate Market													
Paying	12	19	14	10	10	2	2		1	3	[10, 11, 11]	73	249
Non-paying *No data*													
Poor	20											20	20
Empty	1											1	1
Total Pontefract Neate Market	33	19	14	10	10	2	2		1	3		94	270
Pontefract New Markett													
Paying	6	8	5	12	4	10	3	3				51	210
Non-paying *No data*													
Poor	5											5	5
Empty	1											1	1
Total Pontefract New Markett	12	8	5	12	4	10	3	3				57	216
Pontefract, Bailey Gate													
Paying	26	17	5	7	1	2			1	1	[34]	60	163
Non-paying *No data*													
Poor	22											22	22
Empty	1	2			2							5	15
Total Pontefract, Bailey Gate	49	19	5	7	3	2			1	1		87	200
Pontefract, Micklegate													
Paying	19	11	12	5	7	4	2					60	170
Non-paying *No data*													
Poor	13											13	13
Empty *No data*													
Total Pontefract, Micklegate	32	11	12	5	7	4	2					73	183
Pontefract, Roper Gate													
Paying	10	3	2	5	3	2						25	69
Non-paying *No data*													
Poor	2											2	2
Empty		1										1	2
Total Pontefract, Roper Gate	12	4	2	5	3	2						28	73

	Number of hearths										List of 10+	Total house-holds	Total hearths
	1	2	3	4	5	6	7	8	9	10+			
Purston Jaglin													
Paying	18	14	7	4	1		1	1		1	[14]	47	117
Non-paying *No data*													
Poor	11											11	11
Empty		1										1	2
Total Purston Jaglin	29	15	7	4	1		1	1		1		59	130
Rawcliffe													
Paying	40	25	9	6	4	3	1		1	1	[13]	90	208
Non-paying	38	1										39	40
Poor	18											18	18
Empty *No data*													
Total Rawcliffe	96	26	9	6	4	3	1		1	1		147	266
Reedness													
Paying	40	11	9	5	1							66	114
Non-paying *No data*													
Poor	9											9	9
Empty *No data*													
Total Reedness	49	11	9	5	1							75	123
Skelbrooke													
Paying	4	7	1							1	[18]	13	39
Non-paying *No data*													
Poor *No data*													
Empty *No data*													
Total Skelbrooke	4	7	1							1		13	39
Skellow													
Paying	13	4	1	1	1			1				21	41
Non-paying *No data*													
Poor *No data*													
Empty *No data*													
Total Skellow	13	4	1	1	1			1				21	41
Snaith													
Paying	28	17	9	5	7	3	1			1	[18]	71	187
Non-paying	2	2										4	6
Poor	18											18	18
Empty	3		1	1								5	10
Total Snaith	51	19	10	6	7	3	1			1		98	221
South Elmsall													
Paying	16	9	6	3		2						36	76
Non-paying *No data*													
Poor	2											2	2
Empty		1										1	2
Total South Elmsall	18	10	6	3		2						39	80

	Number of hearths										List of 10+	Total house-holds	Total hearths
	1	2	3	4	5	6	7	8	9	10+			
South Kirkby													
Paying	34	17	11	2	2	1				1	[10]	68	135
Non-paying *No data*													
Poor	5											5	5
Empty *No data*													
Total South Kirkby	39	17	11	2	2	1				1		73	140
Stapleton													
Paying	6	2		2						1	[10]	11	28
Non-paying *No data*													
Poor *No data*													
Empty *No data*													
Total Stapleton	6	2		2						1		11	28
Sutton and Askern													
Paying	11	11	3	1	2	1				1	[11]	30	73
Non-paying *No data*													
Poor	3											3	3
Empty	1											1	1
Total Sutton and Askern	15	11	3	1	2	1				1		34	77
Swinefleet													
Paying	28	19	4				1					52	85
Non-paying *No data*													
Poor	6											6	6
Empty *No data*													
Total Swinefleet	34	19	4				1					58	91
Tanshelf													
Paying	17	14	9	4	2	4	2			1	[10]	53	146
Non-paying *No data*													
Poor	6											6	6
Empty						1						1	6
Total Tanshelf	23	14	9	4	2	5	2			1		60	158
Thorpe Audlin													
Paying	20		3	3		1		1		1	[10]	29	65
Non-paying *No data*													
Poor *No data*													
Empty *No data*													
Total Thorpe Audlin	20		3	3		1		1		1		29	65
Upton													
Paying	12	6							1			19	33
Non-paying *No data*													
Poor *No data*													
Empty	1											1	1
Total Upton	13	6							1			20	34

	Number of hearths										List of 10+	Total house-holds	Total hearths
	1	2	3	4	5	6	7	8	9	10+			
Walden Stubbs													
Paying	12	3		1						1	[13]	17	35
Non-paying *No data*													
Poor *No data*													
Empty *No data*													
Total Walden Stubbs	12	3		1						1		17	35
Whitgift													
Paying	24	6	1	2								33	47
Non-paying *No data*													
Poor	2											2	2
Empty	1											1	1
Total Whitgift	27	6	1	2								36	50
Whitley													
Paying	28	1	2	1								32	40
Non-paying *No data*													
Poor	5											5	5
Empty *No data*													
Total Whitley	33	1	2	1								37	45
Womersley													
Paying	33	13	3	1		1				1	[11]	52	89
Non-paying *No data*													
Poor	2											2	2
Empty	1											1	1
Total Womersley	36	13	3	1		1				1		55	92
Total Osgoldcross	**1609**	**568**	**254**	**155**	**84**	**47**	**22**	**12**	**12**	**26**		**2789**	**5555**
Skyrack Wapentake													
Aberford													
Paying	15	3	6	1			1					26	50
Non-paying	3											3	3
Poor *No data*													
Empty *No data*													
Total Aberford	18	3	6	1			1					29	53
Adel and Eccup													
Paying	48	14	4	4	2					1	[11]	73	125
Non-paying	2											2	2
Poor	2											2	2
Empty	2											2	2
Total Adel and Eccup	54	14	4	4	2					1		79	131

	Number of hearths										List of 10+	Total house-holds	Total hearths
	1	2	3	4	5	6	7	8	9	10+			
Allerton Bywater													
Paying	9	4	5		1		1					20	44
Non-paying *No data*													
Poor	1											1	1
Empty *No data*													
Total Allerton Bywater	10	4	5		1		1					21	45
Alwoodley													
Paying	5	4	3	1				1				14	34
Non-paying *No data*													
Poor	1											1	1
Empty		1	1									2	5
Total Alwoodley	6	5	4	1				1				17	40
Arthington													
Paying	26	11	4	2			1			2	[10, 19]	46	104
Non-paying	3	1										4	5
Poor *No data*													
Empty *No data*													
Total Arthington	29	12	4	2			1			2		50	109
Austhorpe													
Paying	7	3	1	3		1		1				16	42
Non-paying *No data*													
Poor	1											1	1
Empty *No data*													
Total Austhorpe	8	3	1	3		1		1				17	43
Baildon													
Paying	46	18	3	1	1				1			70	109
Non-paying	5	1										6	7
Poor *No data*													
Empty *No data*													
Total Baildon	51	19	3	1	1				1			76	116
Bardsey and East Rigton													
Paying	11	13	4	4				1				33	73
Non-paying		3										3	6
Poor *No data*													
Empty *No data*													
Total Bardsey and East Rigton	11	16	4	4				1				36	79

	Number of hearths										List of 10+	Total house-holds	Total hearths
	1	2	3	4	5	6	7	8	9	10+			
Barwick in Elmet													
Paying	77	33	23	3	2	1			1	2	[10, 19]	142	278
Non-paying	13	3										16	19
Poor	9											9	9
Empty	4	2										6	8
Total Barwick in Elmet	103	38	23	3	2	1			1	2		173	314
Bingley													
Paying	120	56	16	16	6	3		3		1	[18]	221	434
Non-paying	5											5	5
Poor	9											9	9
Empty *No data*													
Total Bingley	134	56	16	16	6	3		3		1		235	448
Bramhope													
Paying	37	5	1		1			1				45	63
Non-paying *No data*													
Poor *No data*													
Empty *No data*													
Total Bramhope	37	5	1		1			1				45	63
Burley													
Paying	33	20	7	2	2		1					65	119
Non-paying	7											7	7
Poor *No data*													
Empty *No data*													
Total Burley	40	20	7	2	2		1					72	126
Carlton													
Paying	6	3	1	2								12	23
Non-paying *No data*													
Poor *No data*													
Empty *No data*													
Total Carlton	6	3	1	2								12	23
Chapel Allerton													
Paying	41	17	6	4	1	1	1	4		1	[10]	76	169
Non-paying	1											1	1
Poor *No data*													
Empty	1											1	1
Total Chapel Allerton	43	17	6	4	1	1	1	4		1		78	171
Collingham													
Paying	12	8	2				1					23	41
Non-paying *No data*													
Poor *No data*													
Empty		1										1	2
Total Collingham	12	9	2				1					24	43

	Number of hearths										List of 10+	Total house-holds	Total hearths
	1	2	3	4	5	6	7	8	9	10+			
East Keswick													
Paying	23	9	2	1	1							36	56
Non-paying *No data*													
Poor *No data*													
Empty *No data*													
Total East Keswick	23	9	2	1	1							36	56
Garforth													
Paying	26	9	2	1	1		1		1			41	75
Non-paying *No data*													
Poor	1											1	1
Empty	1											1	1
Total Garforth	28	9	2	1	1		1		1			43	77
Guisley													
Paying	17	12	2			1						32	53
Non-paying *No data*													
Poor *No data*													
Empty	1											1	1
Total Guisley	18	12	2			1						33	54
Harwood													
Paying	23	17	6		2					1	[18]	49	103
Non-paying	6	3										9	12
Poor *No data*													
Empty	1											1	1
Total Harwood	30	20	6		2					1		59	116
Hawksworth													
Paying	31	12	4							2	[14, 17]	49	98
Non-paying	3											3	3
Poor	1											1	1
Empty *No data*													
Total Hawksworth	35	12	4							2		53	102
Headingley and Burley													
Paying	21	15	11	2				1	1	2	[11, 13]	53	133
Non-paying *No data*													
Poor *No data*													
Empty	1											1	1
Total Headingley and Burley	22	15	11	2				1	1	2		54	134
Horsforth													
Paying	57	24	7	2	3	1	1			2	[10, 11]	97	183
Non-paying	11	5										16	21
Poor	8											8	8
Empty	1		1										3
Total Horsforth	76	29	8	2	3	1	1			2		122	215

	Number of hearths										List of 10+	Total house-holds	Total hearths
	1	2	3	4	5	6	7	8	9	10+			
Ilkley													
Paying	27	14	11	2	2			1				57	114
Non-paying	2	1										3	4
Poor *No data*													
Empty *No data*													
Total Ilkley	29	15	11	2	2			1				60	118
Kippax													
Paying	42	13	6	5	4	1		1		1	[15]	73	155
Non-paying	1	1										2	3
Poor	1											1	1
Empty *No data*													
Total Kippax	44	14	6	5	4	1		1		1		76	159
Leeds													
Paying	206	133	42	28	17	7	3	4	4			444	926
Non-paying *No data*													
Poor	16											16	16
Empty	12	3	2				1					18	31
Total Leeds	234	136	44	28	17	7	4	4	4			478	973
Leeds, Briggate													
Paying	36	18	19	13	10	9	3	8	2	3	[10, 11, 14]	121	423
Non-paying *No data*													
Poor	1											1	1
Empty *No data*													
Total Leeds, Briggate	37	18	19	13	10	9	3	8	2	3		122	424
Leeds, Kirkgate													
Paying	67	37	28	20	5	6	3	1				167	395
Non-paying	1											1	1
Poor	4											4	4
Empty	7	2		1						1	[10]	11	25
Total Leeds, Kirkgate	79	39	28	21	5	6	3	1		1		183	425
Leeds, Mill Hill or Boar Lane													
Paying	79	55	16	3	6	2	2			2	[10, 12]	165	327
Non-paying	9											9	9
Poor *No data*													
Empty	2	2										4	6
Total Leeds, Mill Hill or Boar Lane	90	57	16	3	6	2	2			2		178	342

	Number of hearths										List of 10+	Total house-holds	Total hearths
	1	2	3	4	5	6	7	8	9	10+			
Leeds, The Headrow													
Paying	63	57	41	29	11	5	4	6		3	[10, 11, 12]	219	610
Non-paying	3											3	3
Poor	7											7	7
Empty	5	2	1									8	12
Total Leeds, The Headrow	78	59	42	29	11	5	4	6		3		237	632
Menston													
Paying	27	2		2	1					1	[13]	33	57
Non-paying *No data*													
Poor	2											2	2
Empty *No data*													
Total Menston	29	2		2	1					1		35	59
Morton													
Paying	36	11	6	2					1	1	[16]	57	109
Non-paying *No data*													
Poor	2											2	2
Empty *No data*													
Total Morton	38	11	6	2					1	1		59	111
Otley													
Paying	43	17	26	6	10	1	3			2	[10, 12]	108	278
Non-paying	4											4	4
Poor	6											6	6
Empty	3	1										4	5
Total Otley	56	18	26	6	10	1	3			2		122	293
Parlington													
Paying	10	3	1	1						1	[12]	16	35
Non-paying *No data*													
Poor *No data*													
Empty *No data*													
Total Parlington	10	3	1	1						1		16	35
Poole													
Paying	15	8		2			1					26	46
Non-paying *No data*													
Poor	2											2	2
Empty			1									1	3
Total Poole	17	8	1	2			1					29	51

	Number of hearths										List of 10+	Total house-holds	Total hearths
	1	2	3	4	5	6	7	8	9	10+			
Potter Newton													
Paying	9	6	3	4	1					1	[10]	24	61
Non-paying *No data*													
Poor *No data*													
Empty *No data*													
Total Potter Newton	9	6	3	4	1					1		24	61
Rawdon													
Paying	29	13	7	3					1	1	[10]	54	107
Non-paying	1											1	1
Poor *No data*													
Empty *No data*													
Total Rawdon	30	13	7	3					1	1		55	108
Roundhay													
Paying	11	7	1									19	28
Non-paying *No data*													
Poor	1											1	1
Empty *No data*													
Total Roundhay	12	7	1									20	29
Scarcroft													
Paying	11	4	1			1						17	28
Non-paying	2											2	2
Poor *No data*													
Empty	1											1	1
Total Scarcroft	14	4	1			1						20	31
Seacroft													
Paying	25	15	7	4	2	1			1			55	117
Non-paying *No data*													
Poor	14											14	14
Empty	3											3	3
Total Seacroft	42	15	7	4	2	1			1			72	134
Shadwell													
Paying	17	7	2			1				2	[11, 12]	29	66
Non-paying	1											1	1
Poor *No data*													
Empty *No data*													
Total Shadwell	18	7	2			1				2		30	67
Sturton Grange													
Paying							1					1	7
Non-paying *No data*													
Poor *No data*													
Empty *No data*													
Total Sturton Grange							1					1	7

	Number of hearths										List of 10+	Total house-holds	Total hearths
	1	2	3	4	5	6	7	8	9	10+			
Swillington													
Paying	34	22	7	4	3	3				2	[15, 19]	75	182
Non-paying *No data*													
Poor	9											9	9
Empty	4		1									5	7
Total Swillington	47	22	8	4	3	3				2		89	198
Temple Newsam													
Paying	56	26	10	12	3	1	1			2	[10, 45]	111	269
Non-paying	3											3	3
Poor	6											6	6
Empty	4	2	6	8									
Total Temple Newsam	69	28	10	12	3	1	1			2		126	286
Thorner													
Paying	40	17	10	3								70	116
Non-paying *No data*													
Poor *No data*													
Empty		1										1	2
Total Thorner	40	18	10	3								71	118
Thorpe Stapleton													
Paying					1							1	5
Non-paying *No data*													
Poor *No data*													
Empty *No data*													
Total Thorpe Stapleton					1							1	5
Weardley													
Paying	19	5										24	29
Non-paying *No data*													
Poor *No data*													
Empty *No data*													
Total Weardley	19	5										24	29
Wigton													
Paying	7	4	3									14	24
Non-paying *No data*													
Poor *No data*													
Empty *No data*													
Total Wigton	7	4	3									14	24
Wike													
Paying	4	2	4	1								11	24
Non-paying *No data*													
Poor *No data*													
Empty *No data*													
Total Wike	4	2	4	1								11	24

	Number of hearths										List of 10+	Total house-holds	Total hearths
	1	2	3	4	5	6	7	8	9	10+			
Wothersome													
Paying					1							1	5
Non-paying *No data*													
Poor *No data*													
Empty *No data*													
Total Wothersome					1							1	5
Yeadon													
Paying	45	13	3	3								64	92
Non-paying *No data*													
Poor	1											1	1
Empty *No data*													
Total Yeadon	46	13	3	3								65	93
Total Skyrack	**1892**	**854**	**381**	**197**	**100**	**46**	**30**	**33**	**13**	**37**		**3583**	**7399**
Staincliffe Wapentake													
Addingham													
Paying	58	20	4	2	1							85	123
Non-paying *No data*													
Poor *No data*													
Empty	1											1	1
Total Addingham	59	20	4	2	1							86	124
Airton													
Paying	26	3	1	1								31	39
Non-paying *No data*													
Poor	3											3	3
Empty *No data*													
Total Airton	29	3	1	1								34	42
Appletreewick													
Paying	31	11	2	1			2					47	77
Non-paying *No data*													
Poor	2											2	2
Empty *No data*													
Total Appletreewick	33	11	2	1			2					49	79
Arncliffe													
Paying	11	10	1	1								23	38
Non-paying	1	2										3	5
Poor *No data*													
Empty	1											1	1
Total Arncliffe	13	12	1	1								27	44

	Number of hearths										List of 10+	Total house-holds	Total hearths
	1	2	3	4	5	6	7	8	9	10+			
Bank Newton													
Paying	9	4	4	1		1				1	[12]	20	51
Non-paying *No data*													
Poor	2											2	2
Empty *No data*													
Total Bank Newton	11	4	4	1		1				1		22	53
Barden Forest													
Paying	19	8	1							1	[27]	29	65
Non-paying *No data*													
Poor *No data*													
Empty *No data*													
Total Barden Forest	19	8	1							1		29	65
Barnoldswick													
Paying	40	39	7	2	1			1	1	1	[14]	92	183
Non-paying	1											1	1
Poor	17											17	17
Empty *No data*													
Total Barnoldswick	58	39	7	2	1			1	1	1		110	201
Bashall													
Paying	31	10								1	[14]	42	65
Non-paying	1	1										2	3
Poor *No data*												0	
Empty *No data*													
Total Bashall	32	11								1		44	68
Bolton by Bowland													
Paying	45	22	4	1	1	1						74	116
Non-paying *No data*													
Poor	12											12	12
Empty								1				1	8
Total Bolton by Bowland	57	22	4	1	1	1		1				87	136
Bowland Forest													
Paying	63	20	8			1	1		1	1	[10]	95	159
Non-paying	3											3	3
Poor *No data*													
Empty	4											4	4
Total Bowland Forest	70	20	8			1	1		1	1		102	166
Bracewell													
Paying	7	13	4		1	2						27	62
Non-paying *No data*													
Poor *No data*													
Empty *No data*													
Total Bracewell	7	13	4		1	2						27	62

	Number of hearths										List of 10+	Total house-holds	Total hearths
	1	2	3	4	5	6	7	8	9	10+			
Bradley													
Paying	23	12	4			1						40	65
Non-paying *No data*													
Poor	7											7	7
Empty	1											1	1
Total Bradley	31	12	4			1						48	73
Broughton													
Paying	39	15	3		1					1	[19]	59	102
Non-paying	5	2										7	9
Poor *No data*													
Empty	1											1	1
Total Broughton	45	17	3		1					1		67	112
Buckden													
Paying	39	22	4	1								66	99
Non-paying *No data*													
Poor	2											2	2
Empty *No data*													
Total Buckden	41	22	4	1								68	101
Burnsall													
Paying	25	13	4		1	1						44	74
Non-paying *No data*													
Poor	5											5	5
Empty	1											1	1
Total Burnsall	31	13	4		1	1						50	80
Carleton													
Paying	54	23	6	2	2	2				1	[11]	90	159
Non-paying *No data*													
Poor	12											12	12
Empty *No data*													
Total Carleton	66	23	6	2	2	2				1		102	171
Cawton													
Paying	13	2							1			16	26
Non-paying *No data*													
Poor *No data*													
Empty *No data*													
Total Cawton	13	2							1			16	26
Coniston Cold													
Paying	20	9	2	1								32	48
Non-paying *No data*													
Poor	5											5	5
Empty *No data*													
Total Coniston Cold	25	9	2	1								37	53

	Number of hearths										List of 10+	Total house-holds	Total hearths
	1	2	3	4	5	6	7	8	9	10+			
Conistone													
Paying	21	11	1	1	1	1				1	[10]	37	71
Non-paying *No data*													
Poor	2											2	2
Empty *No data*													
Total Conistone	23	11	1	1	1	1				1		39	73
Cowling Head													
Paying	59	23	5	1								88	124
Non-paying *No data*													
Poor	1											1	1
Empty *No data*													
Total Cowling Head	60	23	5	1								89	125
Cracoe													
Paying	14	6	1									21	29
Non-paying *No data*													
Poor *No data*													
Empty *No data*													
Total Cracoe	14	6	1									21	29
Draughton													
Paying	29	3	1	1								34	42
Non-paying *No data*													
Poor	2											2	2
Empty *No data*													
Total Draughton	31	3	1	1								36	44
Easby													
Paying	10	6	1									17	25
Non-paying	1											1	1
Poor	1											1	1
Empty	1											1	1
Total Easby	13	6	1									20	28
Easington													
Paying	46	11	2	3	1		1					64	98
Non-paying *No data*													
Poor	3											3	3
Empty *No data*													
Total Easington	49	11	2	3	1		1					67	101
East Halton													
Paying	20	8	4	3	3				1			39	84
Non-paying *No data*													
Poor	5											5	5
Empty *No data*													
Total East Halton	25	8	4	3	3				1			44	89

	Number of hearths										List of 10+	Total house-holds	Total hearths
	1	2	3	4	5	6	7	8	9	10+			
Emsley													
Paying	12	7	5	2								26	49
Non-paying	5											5	5
Poor *No data*													
Empty *No data*													
Total Emsley	17	7	5	2								31	54
Eshton													
Paying	16	5					1					22	33
Non-paying *No data*													
Poor	7											7	7
Empty *No data*													
Total Eshton	23	5					1					29	40
Farnhill													
Paying	28	15	4	4								51	86
Non-paying *No data*													
Poor	7											7	7
Empty *No data*													
Total Farnhill	35	15	4	4								58	93
Flasby and Winterburn													
Paying	26	9		1			2			1	[11]	39	73
Non-paying *No data*													
Poor	6											6	6
Empty *No data*													
Total Flasby and Winterburn	32	9		1			2			1		45	79
Gargrave													
Paying	43	16	4		2							65	97
Non-paying *No data*													
Poor	5											5	5
Empty *No data*													
Total Gargrave	48	16	4		2							70	102
Gigleswick													
Paying	46	20	3	7	3	2						81	150
Non-paying *No data*													
Poor	8											8	8
Empty *No data*													
Total Gigleswick	54	20	3	7	3	2						89	158
Gisburne													
Paying	13	12	7	3	4		2		1	1	[11]	43	124
Non-paying *No data*													
Poor	4											4	4
Empty				1								1	4
Total Gisburne	17	12	7	4	4		2		1	1		48	132

	Number of hearths										List of 10+	Total house-holds	Total hearths
	1	2	3	4	5	6	7	8	9	10+			
Gisburne Forest													
Paying	54	11	4									69	88
Non-paying *No data*													
Poor	3											3	3
Empty *No data*													
Total Gisburne Forest	57	11	4									72	91
Gisburne Grainge Mare													
Paying	3	3	1	1	2							10	26
Non-paying *No data*													
Poor *No data*													
Empty *No data*													
Total Gisburne Grainge Mare	3	3	1	1	2							10	26
Glusburne													
Paying	25	4		2		2						33	53
Non-paying *No data*													
Poor	14											14	14
Empty *No data*													
Total Glusburne	39	4		2		2						47	67
Grassington													
Paying	33	13	4									50	71
Non-paying *No data*													
Poor *No data*													
Empty *No data*													
Total Grassington	33	13	4									50	71
Great Mitton													
Paying	21	8	3	1	1							34	55
Non-paying *No data*													
Poor *No data*													
Empty	1											1	1
Total Great Mitton	22	8	3	1	1							35	56
Grindleton													
Paying	43	14										57	71
Non-paying *No data*													
Poor	8											8	8
Empty		3										3	6
Total Grindleton	51	17										68	85
Hanlith													
Paying	19	2										21	23
Non-paying *No data*													
Poor *No data*													
Empty *No data*													
Total Hanlith	19	2										21	23

	Number of hearths										List of 10+	Total house-holds	Total hearths
	1	2	3	4	5	6	7	8	9	10+			
Hartlington													
Paying	32	3										35	38
Non-paying *No data*													
Poor *No data*													
Empty	1											1	1
Total Hartlington	33	3										36	39
Hawkswick													
Paying	12	5	1	1								19	29
Non-paying *No data*													
Poor *No data*													
Empty *No data*													
Total Hawkswick	12	5	1	1								19	29
Hebden													
Paying	25	11										36	47
Non-paying *No data*													
Poor	1											1	1
Empty *No data*													
Total Hebden	26	11										37	48
Hellifield													
Paying	20	8								1	[10]	29	46
Non-paying *No data*													
Poor	10											10	10
Empty *No data*													
Total Hellifield	30	8								1		39	56
Hetton and Bordley													
Paying	34	10		1								45	58
Non-paying	3	1										4	5
Poor	2											2	2
Empty *No data*													
Total Hetton and Bordley	39	11		1								51	65
Horton													
Paying	7	9					1					17	32
Non-paying *No data*													
Poor *No data*													
Empty *No data*													
Total Horton	7	9					1					17	32
Keighley													
Paying	157	57	20	9	3	2	2			1	[12]	251	420
Non-paying	2											2	2
Poor	1											1	1
Empty	1											1	1
Total Keighley	161	57	20	9	3	2	2			1		255	424

	Number of hearths										List of 10+	Total house-holds	Total hearths
	1	2	3	4	5	6	7	8	9	10+			
Kettlewell													
Paying	46	25	3									74	105
Non-paying	5											5	5
Poor	7											7	7
Empty *No data*													
Total Kettlewell	58	25	3									86	117
Kildwick													
Paying	14	4	2				1			2	[10, 14]	23	59
Non-paying *No data*													
Poor	1											1	1
Empty	1	1										2	3
Total Kildwick	16	5	2				1			2		26	63
Kirkby Malham													
Paying	20	5	1									26	33
Non-paying *No data*													
Poor	2											2	2
Empty *No data*													
Total Kirkby Malham	22	5	1									28	35
Langcliffe													
Paying	12	3	4		2							21	40
Non-paying *No data*													
Poor	9											9	9
Empty	1											1	1
Total Langcliffe	22	3	4		2							31	50
Linton													
Paying	10	9		2								21	36
Non-paying *No data*													
Poor *No data*													
Empty *No data*													
Total Linton	10	9		2								21	36
Litton													
Paying	26	18	3	1								48	75
Non-paying *No data*													
Poor *No data*													
Empty *No data*													
Total Litton	26	18	3	1								48	75
Long Preston													
Paying	51	18	1	1								71	94
Non-paying *No data*													
Poor	17											17	17
Empty	1											1	1
Total Long Preston	69	18	1	1								89	112

	Number of hearths										List of 10+	Total house-holds	Total hearths
	1	2	3	4	5	6	7	8	9	10+			
Malham													
Paying	29	16	2	1								48	71
Non-paying *No data*													
Poor *No data*													
Empty	1											1	1
Total Malham	30	16	2	1								49	72
Malham Moor													
Paying	12	14	3	3		1						33	67
Non-paying *No data*													
Poor *No data*													
Empty *No data*													
Total Malham Moor	12	14	3	3		1						33	67
Marton													
Paying	16	14	6	1	2					1	[12]	40	88
Non-paying	3	1										4	5
Poor	2											2	2
Empty *No data*													
Total Marton	21	15	6	1	2					1		46	95
Middop													
Paying	2	6	4			1						13	32
Non-paying *No data*													
Poor *No data*													
Empty *No data*													
Total Middop	2	6	4			1						13	32
Nappa													
Paying	8	1		1								10	14
Non-paying *No data*													
Poor *No data*													
Empty *No data*													
Total Nappa	8	1		1								10	14
Newsholme													
Paying	5	8										13	21
Non-paying *No data*													
Poor *No data*													
Empty *No data*													
Total Newsholme	5	8										13	21

	Number of hearths										List of 10+	Total house-holds	Total hearths
	1	2	3	4	5	6	7	8	9	10+			
Newton formerly Newton in Bowland													
Paying	42	13	2	2				1				60	90
Non-paying	1											1	1
Poor	3											3	3
Empty	1											1	1
Total Newton formerly Newton in Bowland	47	13	2	2				1				65	95
Otterburn													
Paying	9	1					1					11	18
Non-paying *No data*													
Poor	6											6	6
Empty	1											1	1
Total Otterburn	16	1					1					18	25
Paythorne													
Paying	16	12			1							29	45
Non-paying *No data*													
Poor	7											7	7
Empty *No data*													
Total Paythorne	23	12			1							36	52
Rathmell													
Paying	29	10	8	1	1		1					50	89
Non-paying *No data*													
Poor	7											7	7
Empty	2											2	2
Total Rathmell	38	10	8	1	1		1					59	98
Rimington													
Paying	36	22	5	2						1	[16]	66	119
Non-paying *No data*													
Poor	5											5	5
Empty *No data*													
Total Rimington	41	22	5	2						1		71	124
Rylstone													
Paying	32	3	1			1						37	47
Non-paying *No data*													
Poor	1											1	1
Empty	1											1	1
Total Rylstone	34	3	1			1						39	49

	Number of hearths										List of 10+	Total house-holds	Total hearths
	1	2	3	4	5	6	7	8	9	10+			
Sawley and Tosside													
Paying	49	15	3	1	1							69	97
Non-paying *No data*													
Poor	2											2	2
Empty *No data*													
Total Sawley and Tosside	51	15	3	1	1							71	99
Scosthrop													
Paying	12	4										16	20
Non-paying *No data*													
Poor	4											4	4
Empty	1											1	1
Total Scosthrop	17	4										21	25
Settle													
Paying	35	27	23	3	3	1	1			1	[10]	94	208
Non-paying *No data*													
Poor	6											6	6
Empty	1		1									2	4
Total Settle	42	27	24	3	3	1	1			1		102	218
Silsden													
Paying	81	41	9		2			1				134	208
Non-paying		1										1	2
Poor	6											6	6
Empty	1											1	1
Total Silsden	88	42	9		2			1				142	217
Skipton													
Paying	42	24	16	12	7	6	1	4		3	[10, 11, 60]	115	377
Non-paying *No data*													
Poor	29											29	29
Empty	5											5	5
Total Skipton	76	24	16	12	7	6	1	4		3		149	411
Slaidburn													
Paying	39	9	10	3								61	99
Non-paying *No data*													
Poor	9											9	9
Empty		1										1	2
Total Slaidburn	48	10	10	3								71	110
Stainforth													
Paying	18	17	9	2		1						47	93
Non-paying	1											1	1
Poor	2											2	2
Empty *No data*													
Total Stainforth	21	17	9	2		1						50	96

	Number of hearths										List of 10+	Total house-holds	Total hearths
	1	2	3	4	5	6	7	8	9	10+			
Steeton													
Paying	28	13	2	2				1				46	76
Non-paying *No data*													
Poor *No data*													
Empty *No data*													
Total Steeton	28	13	2	2				1				46	76
Stirton													
Paying	21	7										28	35
Non-paying *No data*													
Poor	4											4	4
Empty *No data*													
Total Stirton	25	7										32	39
Sutton													
Paying	25	19	4	2			1					51	90
Non-paying *No data*													
Poor	2											2	2
Empty *No data*													
Total Sutton	27	19	4	2			1					53	92
Swinden													
Paying	3	3	1	1		2						10	28
Non-paying *No data*													
Poor	3											3	3
Empty *No data*													
Total Swinden	6	3	1	1		2						13	31
Thornton in Craven													
Paying	52	42	6	3		1						104	172
Non-paying *No data*													
Poor	4											4	4
Empty	1											1	1
Total Thornton in Craven	57	42	6	3		1						109	177
Threshfield													
Paying	22	15		1				1				39	64
Non-paying *No data*													
Poor *No data*													
Empty *No data*													
Total Threshfield	22	15		1				1				39	64
Waddington													
Paying	38	8	1		1			1				49	70
Non-paying	7	2										9	11
Poor	2											2	2
Empty	1											1	1
Total Waddington	48	10	1		1			1				61	84

	Number of hearths										List of	Total house-	Total hearths
	1	2	3	4	5	6	7	8	9	10+	10+	holds	
West Bradford													
Paying	22	11	3	1	1							38	62
Non-paying *No data*													
Poor	1											1	1
Empty	1											1	1
Total West Bradford	24	11	3	1	1							40	64
West Halton													
Paying	17	7	1	1								26	38
Non-paying *No data*													
Poor	4											4	4
Empty	1											1	1
Total West Halton	22	7	1	1								31	43
Wigglesworth													
Paying	31	24	5	1						1	[12]	62	110
Non-paying *No data*													
Poor	1											1	1
Empty *No data*													
Total Wigglesworth	32	24	5	1						1		63	111
Total Staincliffe	**2747**	**1069**	**269**	**103**	**49**	**30**	**18**	**11**	**5**	**21**		**4322**	**7104**
Staincross Wapentake													
Ardsley													
Paying	19	11	3		1	1		1				36	69
Non-paying		1										1	2
Poor	7											7	7
Empty *No data*													
Total Ardsley	26	12	3		1	1		1				44	78
Barnsley													
Paying	24	27	19	23	9	11	3	1	2	1	[10]	120	395
Non-paying	5	1										6	7
Poor	13											13	13
Empty	1	2	1		1							5	13
Total Barnsley	43	30	20	23	10	11	3	1	2	1		144	428
Barugh													
Paying	22	5	3	3	1							34	58
Non-paying *No data*													
Poor *No data*													
Empty *No data*													
Total Barugh	22	5	3	3	1							34	58

	Number of hearths										List of 10+	Total house-holds	Total hearths
	1	2	3	4	5	6	7	8	9	10+			
Bretton (West Bretton)													
Paying	9	1								1	[13]	11	24
Non-paying *No data*													
Poor *No data*													
Empty *No data*													
Total Bretton (West Bretton)	9	1								1		11	24
Brierley													
Paying	13	10	10	2	1					1	[13]	37	89
Non-paying *No data*													
Poor	4											4	4
Empty *No data*													
Total Brierley	17	10	10	2	1					1		41	93
Carlton													
Paying	13	12	3	1			1			1	[14]	31	71
Non-paying	1											1	1
Poor *No data*													
Empty *No data*													
Total Carlton	14	12	3	1			1			1		32	72
Cawthorne													
Paying	22	17	10	8	4	3			1			65	165
Non-paying *No data*													
Poor *No data*													
Empty *No data*													
Total Cawthorne	22	17	10	8	4	3			1			65	165
Chevet													
Paying										1	[33]	1	33
Non-paying *No data*													
Poor *No data*													
Empty *No data*													
Total Chevet										1		1	33
Clayton West													
Paying	13	7	4	1	2				1	1	[11]	29	73
Non-paying *No data*													
Poor	9											9	9
Empty *No data*													
Total Clayton West	22	7	4	1	2				1	1		38	82

	Number of hearths										List of 10+	Total households	Total hearths
	1	2	3	4	5	6	7	8	9	10+			
Cudworth													
Paying	21	12	3	1		1						38	64
Non-paying	3											3	3
Poor	1											1	1
Empty *No data*													
Total Cudworth	25	12	3	1		1						42	68
Cumberworth													
Paying	14	11	6	1	1							33	63
Non-paying *No data*													
Poor *No data*													
Empty		1										1	2
Total Cumberworth	14	12	6	1	1							34	65
Darton													
Paying	30	13	9	2	2		1					57	108
Non-paying *No data*													
Poor	5											5	5
Empty		1										1	2
Total Darton	35	14	9	2	2		1					63	115
Denby													
Paying	26	8	9	2	5	1	1					52	115
Non-paying	1											1	1
Poor *No data*													
Empty *No data*													
Total Denby	27	8	9	2	5	1	1					53	116
Dodworth													
Paying	19	11	3		1	4		1	2			41	105
Non-paying *No data*													
Poor	1											1	1
Empty *No data*													
Total Dodworth	20	11	3		1	4		1	2			42	106
Gunthwaite													
Paying	1	3	1							1	[12]	6	22
Non-paying *No data*													
Poor *No data*													
Empty *No data*													
Total Gunthwaite	1	3	1							1		6	22
Havercroft													
Paying	4	2	2				1					9	21
Non-paying *No data*													
Poor *No data*													
Empty *No data*													
Total Havercroft	4	2	2				1					9	21

	Number of hearths										List of 10+	Total house-holds	Total hearths
	1	2	3	4	5	6	7	8	9	10+			
Hemsworth													
Paying	21	21	8	6	2	4	1	1				64	160
Non-paying *No data*													
Poor	8											8	8
Empty *No data*													
Total Hemsworth	29	21	8	6	2	4	1	1				72	168
High Hoyland													
Paying	15	5	2	3	3							28	58
Non-paying *No data*													
Poor *No data*													
Empty *No data*													
Total High Hoyland	15	5	2	3	3							28	58
Hoyland Swaine													
Paying	25	5	6	1				1				38	65
Non-paying	1											1	1
Poor *No data*													
Empty *No data*													
Total Hoyland Swaine	26	5	6	1				1				39	66
Hunshelf													
Paying	18	12	3	2	1	1	1					38	77
Non-paying *No data*													
Poor	1											1	1
Empty	1											1	1
Total Hunshelf	20	12	3	2	1	1	1					40	79
Ingbirchworth													
Paying	2	4	1	4	1							12	34
Non-paying *No data*													
Poor *No data*													
Empty *No data*													
Total Ingbirchworth	2	4	1	4	1							12	34
Kexbrough													
Paying	17	8	4	2	1		1	1				34	73
Non-paying *No data*													
Poor	2											2	2
Empty *No data*													
Total Kexbrough	19	8	4	2	1		1	1				36	75
Langsett													
Paying	31	3	5	2								41	60
Non-paying *No data*													
Poor *No data*													
Empty *No data*													
Total Langsett	31	3	5	2								41	60

	Number of hearths										List of 10+	Total households	Total hearths
	1	2	3	4	5	6	7	8	9	10+			
Monk Bretton													
Paying	16	6	10		4		1	1	1		39	102	
Non-paying *No data*													
Poor	4											4	4
Empty *No data*													
Total Monk Bretton	20	6	10		4		1	1	1			43	106
Nostall													
Paying	1		1							1	[24]	3	28
Non-paying *No data*													
Poor *No data*													
Empty *No data*													
Total Nostall	1		1							1		3	28
Notton													
Paying	17	7	4	2								30	51
Non-paying *No data*													
Poor *No data*													
Empty *No data*													
Total Notton	17	7	4	2								30	51
Oxspring													
Paying	16	4	2	1								23	34
Non-paying *No data*													
Poor *No data*													
Empty *No data*													
Total Oxspring	16	4	2	1								23	34
Penistone													
Paying	13	9	2	1	2		1					28	58
Non-paying *No data*													
Poor *No data*													
Empty *No data*													
Total Penistone	13	9	2	1	2		1					28	58
Royston													
Paying	18	8	2	2		1						31	54
Non-paying	2	1										3	4
Poor *No data*													
Empty *No data*													
Total Royston	20	9	2	2		1						34	58
Ryhill													
Paying	12	7	4	3		1						27	56
Non-paying		1										1	2
Poor *No data*													
Empty *No data*													
Total Ryhill	12	8	4	3		1						28	58

	Number of hearths										List of 10+	Total house-holds	Total hearths
	1	2	3	4	5	6	7	8	9	10+			
Shafton													
Paying	9	7	4		2							22	45
Non-paying *No data*													
Poor *No data*													
Empty *No data*													
Total Shafton	9	7	4		2							22	45
Silkestone													
Paying	20	6	6	7	1	2	1					43	102
Non-paying *No data*													
Poor	1											1	1
Empty *No data*													
Total Silkestone	21	6	6	7	1	2	1					44	103
South Hiendley													
Paying	23	7	3	1						1	[12]	35	62
Non-paying *No data*													
Poor *No data*													
Empty	2											2	2
Total South Hiendley	25	7	3	1						1		37	64
Stainborough													
Paying	12	3	1	2	1	1	1					21	47
Non-paying		1										1	2
Poor *No data*													
Empty *No data*													
Total Stainborough	12	4	1	2	1	1	1					22	49
Tankersley													
Paying	16	9	6	2	1					1	[25]	35	90
Non-paying *No data*													
Poor *No data*													
Empty *No data*													
Total Tankersley	16	9	6	2	1					1		35	90
Thurgoland													
Paying	28	11	2	1	1			1	1			45	82
Non-paying *No data*													
Poor	2											2	2
Empty			1									1	3
Total Thurgoland	30	11	3	1	1			1	1			48	87
Thurlstone													
Paying	44	9	8	1	2	1						65	106
Non-paying *No data*													
Poor *No data*													
Empty *No data*													
Total Thurlstone	44	9	8	1	2	1						65	106

	Number of hearths										List of 10+	Total house-holds	Total hearths
	1	2	3	4	5	6	7	8	9	10+			
Wintersett													
Paying	10	3	1	3								17	31
Non-paying *No data*													
Poor *No data*													
Empty			1									1	3
Total Wintersett	10	3	2	3								18	34
Woolley													
Paying	22	11	4	4	1	2	1	1		1	[13]	47	117
Non-paying	2	3										5	8
Poor *No data*													
Empty *No data*													
Total Woolley	24	14	4	4	1	2	1	1		1		52	125
Worsborough													
Paying	39	21	14	11		1		2	1	3	[11, 11, 13]	92	233
Non-paying	5											5	5
Poor *No data*													
Empty *No data*													
Total Worsborough	44	21	14	11		1		2	1	3		97	238
Wortley													
Paying	37	30	7	6	2	1				1	[18]	84	176
Non-paying	2											2	2
Poor *No data*													
Empty	1											1	1
Total Wortley	40	30	7	6	2	1				1		87	179
Total Staincross	**817**	**378**	**198**	**111**	**53**	**36**	**15**	**11**	**9**	**15**		**1643**	**3599**
Strafforth and Tickhill Wapentake													
Adwick le Street													
Paying	25	8	5	2						1	[16]	41	80
Non-paying	1											1	1
Poor	3											3	3
Empty *No data*													
Total Adwick le Street	29	8	5	2						1		45	84
Adwick upon Dearne													
Paying	13	6	1									20	28
Non-paying *No data*													
Poor	1											1	1
Empty *No data*													
Total Adwick upon Dearne	14	6	1									21	29

	Number of hearths										List of 10+	Total house-holds	Total hearths
	1	2	3	4	5	6	7	8	9	10+			
Aldwarke													
Paying										1	[17]	1	17
Non-paying *No data*													
Poor *No data*													
Empty *No data*													
Total Aldwarke										1		1	17
Anston													
Paying	36	12	4	2	1		1	1		1	[11]	58	111
Non-paying *No data*													
Poor	10											10	10
Empty	1	1										2	3
Total Anston	47	13	4	2	1		1	1		1		70	124
Armthorp													
Paying	20	6	3		2							31	51
Non-paying *No data*													
Poor	7											7	7
Empty	2											2	2
Total Armthorp	29	6	3		2							40	60
Aston cum Aughton													
Paying	23	13	6	2		2	1	2		1	[27]	50	137
Non-paying *No data*													
Poor	11											11	11
Empty	1											1	1
Total Aston cum Aughton	35	13	6	2		2	1	2		1		62	149
Attercliffe and Darnall													
Paying	44	24	16	6		2	2			3	[11, 11, 17]	97	229
Non-paying	10	5	3									18	29
Poor	5											5	5
Empty	3			1								4	7
Total Attercliffe and Darnall	62	29	19	7		2	2			3		124	270
Auckley													
Paying	9	5	2									16	25
Non-paying *No data*													
Poor *No data*													
Empty *No data*													
Total Auckley	9	5	2									16	25

	Number of hearths										List of 10+	Total house-holds	Total hearths
	1	2	3	4	5	6	7	8	9	10+			
Austerfield													
Paying	15	11	2		1							29	48
Non-paying *No data*													
Poor	4											4	4
Empty	3											3	3
Total Austerfield	22	11	2		1							36	55
Barnburgh													
Paying	23	5	5	2		1		1		1	[16]	38	86
Non-paying *No data*													
Poor	4											4	4
Empty	1											1	1
Total Barnburgh	28	5	5	2		1		1		1		43	91
Barnby Dun													
Paying	28	22	5	2	3					2	[10, 13]	62	133
Non-paying *No data*													
Poor	6											6	6
Empty	4	1										5	6
Total Barnby Dun	38	23	5	2	3					2		73	145
Bawtry													
Paying	7	13	12	10	3	3	1		1	3	[10, 12, 14]	53	194
Non-paying *No data*													
Poor *No data*													
Empty			1									1	3
Total Bawtry	7	13	13	10	3	3	1		1	3		54	197
Bentley and Arksey													
Paying	46	16	16	11	3	1	4	2	1			100	244
Non-paying	16	2										18	20
Poor	2											2	2
Empty		3	1									4	9
Total Bentley and Arksey	64	21	17	11	3	1	4	2	1			124	275
Bilham													
Paying	6	3	1			1						11	21
Non-paying *No data*													
Poor	1											1	1
Empty		1										1	2
Total Bilham	7	4	1			1						13	24
Billingley													
Paying	14	5				1						20	30
Non-paying *No data*													
Poor	1											1	1
Empty *No data*													
Total Billingley	15	5				1						21	31

	Number of hearths										List of 10+	Total house-holds	Total hearths
	1	2	3	4	5	6	7	8	9	10+	10+		
Blaxton													
Paying	13	1		1								15	19
Non-paying *No data*													
Poor	3											3	3
Empty	1											1	1
Total Blaxton	17	1		1								19	23
Bolton upon Dearne													
Paying	30	12	10	5								57	104
Non-paying	1	2										3	5
Poor	4											4	4
Empty *No data*													
Total Bolton upon Dearne	35	14	10	5								64	113
Bradfield, including Stannington, Waldeshelf and Westnall													
Paying	247	78	39	12	6	5	1	1				389	643
Non-paying	6											6	6
Poor	2											2	2
Empty	3		1									4	6
Total Bradfield, including Stannington, Waldeshelf and Westnall	258	78	40	12	6	5	1	1				401	657
Braithwell													
Paying	34	11	2	4	1			2				54	99
Non-paying *No data*													
Poor	1											1	1
Empty	1	1	1									3	6
Total Braithwell	36	12	3	4	1			2				58	106
Bramley													
Paying	12	6	3						1	1	[11]	23	53
Non-paying *No data*													
Poor *No data*													
Empty			1									1	3
Total Bramley	12	6	4						1	1		24	56

	Number of hearths										List of 10+	Total households	Total hearths
	1	2	3	4	5	6	7	8	9	10+			
Brampton Bierlow													
Paying	34	12	5	6	1		1					59	109
Non-paying *No data*													
Poor	8											8	8
Empty	2		1									3	5
Total Brampton Bierlow	44	12	6	6	1		1					70	122
Brampton en le Morthen													
Paying	13	2	1			1		1	1			19	43
Non-paying *No data*													
Poor	3											3	3
Empty *No data*													
Total Brampton en le Morthen	16	2	1			1		1	1			22	46
Brightside Bierlow													
Paying	34	21	12	4	5	2	1					79	172
Non-paying	5											5	5
Poor	24											24	24
Empty	1	1		1								3	7
Total Brightside Bierlow	64	22	12	5	5	2	1					111	208
Brinsworth													
Paying	7	5	3						1	1	[11]	17	46
Non-paying *No data*													
Poor	5											5	5
Empty *No data*													
Total Brinsworth	12	5	3						1	1		22	51
Brodsworth and Pickburn													
Paying	30	7	1	1	2	1				1	[12]	43	79
Non-paying *No data*													
Poor	7											7	7
Empty	1	1										2	3
Total Brodsworth and Pickburn	38	8	1	1	2	1				1		52	89
Cadeby													
Paying	10	6	3									19	31
Non-paying *No data*													
Poor	2											2	2
Empty *No data*													
Total Cadeby	12	6	3									21	33

	Number of hearths										List of 10+	Total house-holds	Total hearths
	1	2	3	4	5	6	7	8	9	10+			
Cantley													
Paying	28	17	2	5								52	88
Non-paying *No data*													
Poor *No data*													
Empty *No data*													
Total Cantley	28	17	2	5								52	88
Clayton with Frickley													
Paying	18	7	2	2						1	[10]	30	56
Non-paying *No data*													
Poor	2											2	2
Empty	1											1	1
Total Clayton with Frickley	21	7	2	2						1		33	59
Conisbrough													
Paying	28	26	8	8	3		1	1				75	166
Non-paying *No data*													
Poor	6											6	6
Empty	5											5	5
Total Conisbrough	39	26	8	8	3		1	1				86	177
Dalton													
Paying	12	7	1	2		1						23	43
Non-paying *No data*													
Poor	4											4	4
Empty *No data*													
Total Dalton	16	7	1	2		1						27	47
Darfield													
Paying	15	8	6	5			1	1	2	1	[10]	39	112
Non-paying *No data*													
Poor	5											5	5
Empty	1	1	1									3	6
Total Darfield	21	9	7	5			1	1	2	1		47	123
Denaby													
Paying	6	7	1	1						1	[11]	16	38
Non-paying *No data*													
Poor	3											3	3
Empty	1											1	1
Total Denaby	10	7	1	1						1		20	42
Dikes Marsh													
Paying	12	11	5	2	1				1			32	71
Non-paying	36	2										38	40
Poor	6											6	6
Empty	4	1		2								7	14
Total Dikes Marsh	58	14	5	4	1				1			83	131

	Number of hearths										List of 10+	Total house-holds	Total hearths
	1	2	3	4	5	6	7	8	9	10+			
Dinnington													
Paying	10	9	4	1								24	44
Non-paying *No data*													
Poor	4											4	4
Empty	1											1	1
Total Dinnington	15	9	4	1								29	49
Doncaster, Baxter Gate													
Paying	10	1	2	4	3	2	1	1				24	76
Non-paying *No data*													
Poor	1											1	1
Empty	2											2	2
Total Doncaster, Baxter Gate	13	1	2	4	3	2	1	1				27	79
Doncaster, Fisher Gate													
Paying	6	3	3	2	2	3	1		1			21	73
Non-paying *No data*													
Poor	1											1	1
Empty	1											1	1
Total Doncaster, Fisher Gate	8	3	3	2	2	3	1		1			23	75
Doncaster, French Gate													
Paying	17	9	15	12	5		1	3		5	[12, 14, 16, 18, 18]	67	262
Non-paying *No data*													
Poor	4											4	4
Empty	1		2	1								4	11
Total Doncaster, French Gate	22	9	17	13	5		1	3		5		75	277
Doncaster, Hall Gate													
Paying	11	4	2	1	1	1	1	1		1	[11]	23	66
Non-paying *No data*													
Poor	15											15	15
Empty	4				1							5	9
Total Doncaster, Hall Gate	30	4	2	1	2	1	1	1		1		43	90

	Number of hearths										List of 10+	Total house-holds	Total hearths
	1	2	3	4	5	6	7	8	9	10+			
Doncaster, High Street and Scot Lane													
Paying	16	9	8	6	5	4		1		1	[17]	50	156
Non-paying	4		1									5	7
Poor	7											7	7
Empty						1						1	6
Total Doncaster, High Street and Scot Lane	27	9	9	6	5	5		1		1		63	176
Doncaster, Market Place													
Paying	13	16	22	13	7	5	1	1		2	[10, 13]	80	266
Non-paying	1											1	1
Poor	3											3	3
Empty		1										1	2
Total Doncaster, Market Place	17	17	22	13	7	5	1	1		2		85	272
Doncaster, Marsh Gate													
Paying	1	10	3	1		1				1	[10]	17	50
Non-paying	3	1										4	5
Poor	4											4	4
Empty	1											1	1
Total Doncaster, Marsh Gate	9	11	3	1		1				1		26	60
Doncaster, St George Gate													
Paying	5	5	5		1				1	1	[10]	18	54
Non-paying *No data*													
Poor	2											2	2
Empty *No data*													
Total Doncaster, St George Gate	7	5	5		1				1	1		20	56
Doncaster, St Sepulchre Gate													
Paying	11	6	4	2	8	2			1			34	104
Non-paying	23	1										24	25
Poor	10											10	10
Empty	3			1								4	7
Total Doncaster, St Sepulchre Gate	47	7	4	3	8	2			1			72	146

	Number of hearths										List of 10+	Total house-holds	Total hearths
	1	2	3	4	5	6	7	8	9	10+			
Ecclesall													
Paying	46	25	20	15	4	2	2			1	[11]	115	273
Non-paying	11	2										13	15
Poor *No data*													
Empty	2		1									3	5
Total Ecclesall	59	27	21	15	4	2	2			1		131	293
Ecclesfield													
Paying	122	74	42	14	6	5	1		2	1	[10]	267	547
Non-paying *No data*													
Poor	38											38	38
Empty	3		1		1							5	11
Total Ecclesfield	163	74	43	14	7	5	1		2	1		310	596
Edlington													
Paying	7	2	1	1	1	1				1	[21]	14	50
Non-paying *No data*													
Poor	5											5	5
Empty										1	[12]	1	12
Total Edlington	12	2	1	1	1	1				2		20	67
Firbeck													
Paying	7	10		1				1		1	[15]	20	54
Non-paying *No data*													
Poor	2											2	2
Empty *No data*													
Total Firbeck	9	10		1				1		1		22	56
Fishlake													
Paying	55	36	7	8			1			1	[10]	108	197
Non-paying	5											5	5
Poor	2											2	2
Empty	3	1										4	5
Total Fishlake	65	37	7	8			1			1		119	209
Greasbrough													
Paying	25	20	13	3	3					1	[19]	65	150
Non-paying *No data*													
Poor	20											20	20
Empty	1	1										2	3
Total Greasbrough	46	21	13	3	3					1		87	173
Great Houghton													
Paying	17	4	1	1		1				1	[13]	25	51
Non-paying *No data*													
Poor *No data*													
Empty *No data*													
Total Great Houghton	17	4	1	1		1				1		25	51

	Number of hearths										List of 10+	Total house-holds	Total hearths
	1	2	3	4	5	6	7	8	9	10+			
Hamphall Stubbs													
Paying		2	1			1		1	1			6	30
Non-paying *No data*													
Poor *No data*													
Empty *No data*													
Total Hamphall Stubbs		2	1			1		1	1			6	30
Handsworth													
Paying	46	21	13	5	5	3	1	1				95	205
Non-paying	4											4	4
Poor	1											1	1
Empty	2	1	1	1								5	11
Total Handsworth	53	22	14	6	5	3	1	1				105	221
Harthill & Woodall													
Paying	38	21	4	1				1	1	1	[26]	67	139
Non-paying	10		1									11	13
Poor	2											2	2
Empty	2											2	2
Total Harthill & Woodall	52	21	5	1				1	1	1		82	156
Hatfield													
Paying	49	37	11	7		3	2		1	4	[10, 11, 13, 15]	114	274
Non-paying	2											2	2
Poor	17											17	17
Empty	2	1	1									4	7
Total Hatfield	70	38	12	7		3	2		1	4		137	300
Hatfield Woodhouse													
Paying	39	24	4	3								70	111
Non-paying *No data*													
Poor	8											8	8
Empty	3	2	1									6	10
Total Hatfield Woodhouse	50	26	5	3								84	129
Hexthorpe and Balby													
Paying	12	5	8	1								26	50
Non-paying	4											4	4
Poor *No data*													
Empty	3											3	3
Total Hexthorpe and Balby	19	5	8	1								33	57

	Number of hearths										List of 10+	Total house-holds	Total hearths
	1	2	3	4	5	6	7	8	9	10+			
Hickleton													
Paying	9	3	4							1	[32]	17	59
Non-paying *No data*													
Poor	1											1	1
Empty *No data*													
Total Hickleton	10	3	4							1		18	60
High Melton													
Paying	10	8	1	1				1		1	[12]	22	53
Non-paying	1											1	1
Poor	3											3	3
Empty				1		1						2	10
Total High Melton	14	8	1	2		1		1		1		28	67
Hooton Pagnell													
Paying	16	11	6	2		1				1	[23]	37	93
Non-paying *No data*													
Poor	3											3	3
Empty *No data*													
Total Hooton Pagnell	19	11	6	2		1				1		40	96
Hooton Roberts													
Paying	6	6	2	1						1	[14]	16	42
Non-paying *No data*													
Poor	10											10	10
Empty *No data*													
Total Hooton Roberts	16	6	2	1						1		26	52
Hoyland													
Paying	27	6	5		1		1	1		1	[16]	42	90
Non-paying *No data*													
Poor	11											11	11
Empty	1	1										2	3
Total Hoyland	39	7	5		1		1	1		1		55	104
Kimberworth													
Paying	40	32	15	4	3							94	180
Non-paying	6	1										7	8
Poor	16											16	16
Empty *No data*													
Total Kimberworth	62	33	15	4	3							117	204
Kirk Sandall													
Paying	8	9	3	2						2	[11, 12]	24	66
Non-paying *No data*													
Poor *No data*													
Empty	1	1										2	3
Total Kirk Sandall	9	10	3	2						2		26	69

	Number of hearths										List of 10+	Total house-holds	Total hearths
	1	2	3	4	5	6	7	8	9	10+			
Langthwaite and Tilts													
Paying	1											1	1
Non-paying *No data*													
Poor *No data*													
Empty *No data*													
Total Langthwaite and Tilts	1											1	1
Laughton en le Morthen													
Paying	52	10	9	8	4	4				3	[10, 12, 14]	90	211
Non-paying	6	1										7	8
Poor	3											3	3
Empty	1				1							2	6
Total Laughton en le Morthen	62	11	9	8	5	4				3		102	228
Letwell													
Paying	3	8	1		1		1			1	[14]	15	48
Non-paying *No data*													
Poor	5											5	5
Empty	1											1	1
Total Letwell	9	8	1		1		1			1		21	54
Little Houghton													
Paying	14	5										19	24
Non-paying *No data*													
Poor *No data*													
Empty *No data*													
Total Little Houghton	14	5										19	24
Loversall													
Paying	17	4	2						1			24	40
Non-paying *No data*													
Poor *No data*													
Empty *No data*													
Total Loversall	17	4	2						1			24	40
Maltby													
Paying	26	10	15	3	3			2		1	[30]	60	164
Non-paying *No data*													
Poor	4											4	4
Empty	1	1										2	3
Total Maltby	31	11	15	3	3			2		1		66	171

	Number of hearths										List of 10+	Total house-holds	Total hearths
	1	2	3	4	5	6	7	8	9	10+			
Marr													
Paying	13	2	1							1	[14]	17	34
Non-paying	5											5	5
Poor	1											1	1
Empty	2											2	2
Total Marr	21	2	1							1		25	42
Mexborough													
Paying	16	12	2		1			2				33	67
Non-paying *No data*													
Poor	6											6	6
Empty	2		1									3	5
Total Mexborough	24	12	3		1			2				42	78
Nether Hallam													
Paying	35	13	2	5	3	1	1					60	115
Non-paying *No data*													
Poor	10											10	10
Empty	2											2	2
Total Nether Hallam	47	13	2	5	3	1	1					72	127
Ravenfield													
Paying	15	6	3	1						1	[12]	26	52
Non-paying *No data*													
Poor *No data*													
Empty	1											1	1
Total Ravenfield	16	6	3	1						1		27	53
Rawmarsh													
Paying	34	14	6	2			2		1			59	111
Non-paying	10	1										11	12
Poor	2											2	2
Empty	3											3	3
Total Rawmarsh	49	15	6	2			2		1			75	128
Rossington													
Paying	7	10	6	1	1							25	54
Non-paying	3											3	3
Poor	4											4	4
Empty *No data*													
Total Rossington	14	10	6	1	1							32	61
Rotherham													
Paying	41	51	40	16	18	9	2	1	5	2	[10, 14]	185	562
Non-paying	4	1										5	6
Poor	35											35	35
Empty	1	3	2		1					1	[10]	8	28
Total Rotherham	81	55	42	16	19	9	2	1	5	3		233	631

	Number of hearths										List of 10+	Total house-holds	Total hearths
	1	2	3	4	5	6	7	8	9	10+			
Sheffield													
Paying	104	111	80	49	29	14	6	4		8	[10, 10, 10, 11, 12, 15, 21, 36]	405	1190
Non-paying	17	6										23	29
Poor	54											54	54
Empty	5	7	1									13	22
Total Sheffield	180	124	81	49	29	14	6	4		8		495	1295
Sprotbrough													
Paying	10	5	5	1	1		1	1		2	[15, 21]	26	95
Non-paying *No data*													
Poor *No data*													
Empty *No data*													
Total Sprotbrough	10	5	5	1	1		1	1		2		26	95
Stainford and South Bramwith													
Paying	25	18	8	4			1			1	[12]	57	120
Non-paying	1											1	1
Poor	3											3	3
Empty	3					1						4	9
Total Stainford and South Bramwith	32	18	8	4		1	1			1		65	133
Stainton cum Hillaby													
Paying	9	4	3	2				3				21	58
Non-paying *No data*													
Poor *No data*													
Empty *No data*													
Total Stainton cum Hillaby	9	4	3	2				3				21	58
Stansell cum Willingley													
Paying	6	1	1	2	1							11	24
Non-paying *No data*													
Poor	1											1	1
Empty *No data*													
Total Stansell cum Willingley	7	1	1	2	1							12	25

	Number of hearths										List of 10+	Total house-holds	Total hearths
	1	2	3	4	5	6	7	8	9	10+			
Stotfold													
Paying						1						1	6
Non-paying *No data*													
Poor *No data*													
Empty *No data*													
Total Stotfold						1						1	6
Swinton													
Paying	24	11		1		1		1				38	64
Non-paying *No data*													
Poor	1											1	1
Empty *No data*													
Total Swinton	25	11		1		1		1				39	65
Sykehouse													
Paying	41	18	6	3	2	3		1	1			75	152
Non-paying	9	2										11	13
Poor	4											4	4
Empty	5	2										7	9
Total Sykehouse	59	22	6	3	2	3		1	1			97	178
Thorne													
Paying	68	44	22	13	3	3	2			1	[10]	156	331
Non-paying *No data*													
Poor *No data*													
Empty *No data*													
Total Thorne	68	44	22	13	3	3	2			1		156	331
Thorpe Salvin													
Paying	17	6	2					1		1	[20]	27	63
Non-paying	1											1	1
Poor	2											2	2
Empty	1											1	1
Total Thorpe Salvin	21	6	2					1		1		31	67
Thrybergh													
Paying	16	7	2	1			1			1	[22]	28	69
Non-paying *No data*													
Poor	3											3	3
Empty *No data*													
Total Thrybergh	19	7	2	1			1			1		31	72
Thurnscoe													
Paying	15	3	1	1	3							23	43
Non-paying *No data*													
Poor	1											1	1
Empty *No data*													
Total Thurnscoe	16	3	1	1	3							24	44

	Number of hearths										List of 10+	Total house-holds	Total hearths
	1	2	3	4	5	6	7	8	9	10+			
Tickhill Westgate													
Paying	20	17	5	5			1	1		1	[24]	50	128
Non-paying	1	1										2	3
Poor	2											2	2
Empty	4					1						5	10
Total Tickhill Westgate	27	18	5	5		1	1	1		1		59	143
Tickhill, Northgate													
Paying	24	16	9	4	4	1				1	[11]	59	136
Non-paying *No data*													
Poor	1											1	1
Empty	1											1	1
Total Tickhill, Northgate	26	16	9	4	4	1				1		61	138
Tickill Sunderland													
Paying	29	15	10	4								58	105
Non-paying *No data*													
Poor	1											1	1
Empty	2											2	2
Total Tickill Sunderland	32	15	10	4								61	108
Tinsley													
Paying	23	10	6	1	1	2						43	82
Non-paying *No data*													
Poor	3											3	3
Empty		1		1								2	6
Total Tinsley	26	11	6	2	1	2						48	91
Todwick													
Paying	9	8	1	1		1	1					21	45
Non-paying *No data*													
Poor *No data*													
Empty *No data*													
Total Todwick	9	8	1	1		1	1					21	45
Treeton													
Paying	21	5	6	2	2			1				37	75
Non-paying *No data*													
Poor	8											8	8
Empty	1	1										2	3
Total Treeton	30	6	6	2	2			1				47	86

	Number of hearths										List of 10+	Total house-holds	Total hearths
	1	2	3	4	5	6	7	8	9	10+			
Ulley													
Paying	11	7		1	1							20	34
Non-paying *No data*													
Poor *No data*													
Empty			1									1	3
Total Ulley	11	7	1	1	1							21	37
Upper Hallam													
Paying	48	17	8	3			1	1				78	133
Non-paying *No data*													
Poor	6											6	6
Empty *No data*													
Total Upper Hallam	54	17	8	3			1	1				84	139
Wadworth													
Paying	38	6	3	2		1		1		1	[18]	52	99
Non-paying	8	1										9	10
Poor	1											1	1
Empty	1							1				2	9
Total Wadworth	48	7	3	2		1		2		1		64	119
Wales													
Paying	18	12	3	2	1	1						37	70
Non-paying	3	1										4	5
Poor	3											3	3
Empty *No data*													
Total Wales	24	13	3	2	1	1						44	78
Warmsworth													
Paying	14	4	4	1	3					2	[12, 12]	28	77
Non-paying *No data*													
Poor *No data*													
Empty *No data*													
Total Warmsworth	14	4	4	1	3					2		28	77
Wath upon Dearne													
Paying	21	12	6	3	1		1					44	87
Non-paying *No data*													
Poor *No data*													
Empty	2											2	2
Total Wath upon Dearne	23	12	6	3	1		1					46	89
Wentworth													
Paying	31	18	8	4		2				2	[10, 43]	65	172
Non-paying *No data*													
Poor	5											5	5
Empty	2											2	2
Total Wentworth	38	18	8	4		2				2		72	179

	Number of hearths										List of 10+	Total house-holds	Total hearths
	1	2	3	4	5	6	7	8	9	10+			
Wheatley & Sandall													
Paying	3	6	1					1		1	[11]	12	37
Non-paying *No data*													
Poor	2											2	2
Empty	1											1	1
Total Wheatley & Sandall	6	6	1					1		1		15	40
Whiston													
Paying	30	14	9	3	1	2	2	1	1	1	[11]	64	156
Non-paying *No data*													
Poor	3											3	3
Empty *No data*													
Total Whiston	33	14	9	3	1	2	2	1	1	1		67	159
Wickersley													
Paying	11	6	5	4		1						27	60
Non-paying *No data*													
Poor	1											1	1
Empty *No data*													
Total Wickersley	12	6	5	4		1						28	61
Wombwell													
Paying	34	25	11	1		2				1	[10]	74	143
Non-paying *No data*													
Poor	4											4	4
Empty	1											1	1
Total Wombwell	39	25	11	1		2				1		79	148
Woodsetts and Gildingwells													
Paying	6	6	2	2	1							17	37
Non-paying	3											3	3
Poor	3											3	3
Empty			1									1	3
Total Woodsetts and Gildingwells	12	6	3	2	1							24	46
Total Strafforth and Tickhill	**3418**	**1463**	**750**	**372**	**176**	**109**	**50**	**48**	**25**	**84**		**6495**	**13807**
Total West Riding	**22523**	**8961**	**3590**	**1876**	**888**	**481**	**272**	**219**	**118**	**339**		**39267**	**75725**

APPENDIX I: ADMINISTRATION OF THE HEARTH TAX

By Elizabeth Parkinson

The hearth tax was first levied in 1662 to provide King Charles II with some much-needed money. The Act introducing the tax stated that 'every dwelling and other House and Edifice. . . . shall be chargeable. . . . for every Fire hearth and Stove. . . . the sum of Twoe shillings by the yeare'.[1] The money was to be paid in two equal instalments at Michaelmas (29 September) and Lady Day (25 March). Payment was to be made by the occupier or, if the house was empty by the owner according to a list of named householders with the number of their hearths. Exemption from payment was allowed for certain properties. Throughout the twenty-seven years of its life from 1662 to 1689 several different administrative systems were tried, some more than once in order to improve the yield. These included unpaid local government officials headed by the sheriffs, professional tax collectors, private agents or farmers and finally a central commission.[2]

Under the initial administration of the sheriffs, the lowest official the petty constable was responsible for notifying the householders within his jurisdiction that they had to provide a return of the number of hearths in their occupation.[3] From these self-assessments the petty constables compiled a list of all the **liable** hearths with the names of the occupiers and those of the owners if the property was empty, and delivered it to the next meeting of the Quarter Sessions. Here the clerk of the peace was responsible for collating the constables' returns into a single county list to be inspected by three justices and enrolled in duplicate. One copy was returned to the Exchequer as the record for collection while the other was retained locally to serve as a check on the money collected. Provision was also made for the recording and enrolment of any change in hearth numbers in the subsequent collections. As to collection of the money, strict time limits were laid down for each stage of the process from taxpayer to petty constable to high constable to sheriff and finally to the Exchequer, amounting to sixty days in all, for which expenses were allowed. In reality less than one fifth of the assessed total

1 Details of the acts of parliament can be found in *Statutes of the Realm*, (1810–28). The specific reference to the 1662 Act is 14 Car.II c.10

2 C.A.F. Meekings was the first to identify the different administrative periods as outlined in his *The Hearth Tax 1662–89: Exhibition of Records*, Public Record Office (London, 1962); T. Arkell gives a clear description of the legislation in 'Printed instructions for administering the hearth tax' in K. Schürer and T. Arkell, eds, *Surveying the People: the interpretation and use of document sources for the study of population in the later seventeenth century* (Oxford, 1992), 38–64.

3 A collection of signed returns from 23 parishes in the Upper Division of Barkston Ash Wapentake is preserved in the BL Add MS 38,0912.

revenue for the first collection reached the Exchequer within this time whilst the proceeds of the Lady Day 1663 collection took even longer. Parliament felt that the slow return of the money was due to slack assessing so passed a revising act in July 1663 that concentrated on tightening up the assessment procedure.[4] Now not only had the petty constable to check each assessment with a search of the house with two substantial inhabitants, but he had to record **all** householders, whether liable or not. This list was then subjected to an additional check by the high constable and two justices before being returned to the clerk of the peace for enrolment at the Quarter Sessions. The revision of 1663 had hardly been introduced before the Lord Treasurer Southampton realised that it was unlikely to improve matters. A second revising act was passed in May 1664 which took effect from the Michaelmas 1664 collection.[5] Under it the amateur local government officials were replaced by a centralised system of county receivers appointed by the king who managed teams of sub-collectors or chimney men. The receivers had to provide sureties so ensuring some Exchequer control over them. They were issued with copies of the 1662 assessments and instructions as to how they should compile their lists. They were also issued with commissions to collect the arrears from the sheriffs' time. Two receivers were appointed for Yorkshire, one for the North and East Ridings and one for the West Riding and York. The receiver for the West Riding and York was Lt. Col. Joshua Greathead of Gildersome (called 'John' on p. 249 with six hearths).[6]

By the spring of 1666 the government's need for money was dire as the war with the Dutch was not going well. To obtain instant cash the receivers were hastily dismissed and the tax was farmed to a consortium of London merchants for an advance of £250,000 and at a rent of £145,000 out of which most of the advance and rent would be recouped. The farm was due to start at Michaelmas 1666 but the farmers agreed to take over the Lady Day 1666 collection which in some counties had already been started by the receivers. Thus across the country this collection was either shared by farmers and receivers or managed solely by farmers, all of whom were responsible to the Exchequer. The farmers' contract was for a period of seven years with an option to surrender after three, during which time the Exchequer was not involved in the management.[7] The country was divided into appropriate sub-units which were managed by sub-farmers. In

4 15 Car. II c.13.

5 16 Car. II c.3.

6 As Major Greathead, he had acted as an informer and a key prosecution witness in the prosecution of those involved in the Northern or Farnley Wood Plot. On 21 Dec 1663 he petitioned for 'a Grant of the Collectorship of Excise in Yorkshire as he did good service in discovery of the late plot and that he should have an interest in the collectorship when the present farm is expired' As well as becoming receiver for the Hearth Tax for the West Riding and York, he was also given £100 as a free gift out of the King's £2,000 for Secret Service, a free pardon, and patently promotion to Lt.Col. *Calendar of State Papers Domestic, 1663–4,* 383, 387, 417, also J.D. Purdy, *Yorkshire Hearth Tax Returns,* (Hull, 1991), 9 relying on Browning, *Memoirs of Sir John Reresby,* 47.

7 C.D. Chandaman, *The English Public Revenue1660–1688* (Oxford, 1975), 92–5.

Yorkshire it was managed initially by the sub-farmer Toby Humphrey.[8] However by the spring of 1668 there were different men involved. On 28 April Joshua Greathead handed over a copy of his Lady Day 1666 assessments for the wapentakes of Claro and Skyrack to Colonel Robert Brandling and his partners, sub-farmers for Yorkshire to use for their collection.[9] Outside circumstances did not help the farmers, for the Fire of London in September 1666 both destroyed their office and many of the buildings, thus reducing the receipts in the capital. Nation-wide the taxpayer was also less keen to oblige the tax collector for he now had to open his door to yet another unfamiliar set of officials and there was talk around the country about removal of the tax. As a result the farmers soon found that collecting the tax was not profitable enough to compensate for the work involved so in November 1668 they gave notice that they would revoke their contract after the Lady Day 1669 collection.

It was not until the spring of 1670 that a second receivers' administration was set up. Unlike the first receivers, the new officials were managed by a central Hearth Tax Office, although they were still ultimately responsible to the Exchequer. In May 1670 Walter Strickland of Ripon received his patent as receiver of Hearth Tax and Aid for the West Riding and York, charged with collecting the tax from Michaelmas 1669 onwards. He died before the Lady Day 1671 collection, which left his widow Barbara to account for the three half-years from Michaelmas 1669 to Michaelmas 1670. She was not able to settle the account until February 1676.[10] She is listed in Lady Day 1672 in Allhallowgate in Ripon with twelve hearths. For the Lady Day 1672 collection, the principal one printed here, the receiver was Walter Strickland's successor James Collins.[11] Fresh instructions were issued in 1670 as to how to compile the lists, but unfortunately no copy has survived. Most of the county returns for Michaelmas 1670 to Lady Day 1674, as opposed to the schedules of variation merely recording changes since the last return, have a similar format noting both chargeable and not chargeable but the latter are not recorded in a consistent way.[12]

In spite of increasing yield, Lord Treasurer Danby, who as Sir Thomas Osborne had been the sheriff responsible for the first collection of the hearth tax in Yorkshire, decided to farm the tax from Michaelmas 1674 because he wanted to achieve some certainty in the return from the tax. Two successive five-year

[8] C.A.F. Meekings, *Analysis of Hearth Tax Accounts 1666–1689*, List and Index Society,163 (London, 1980), 417. Tobias Humphris, was still called collector for firehearths, in a receipt for £50 on 20 May 1667, now filed with exemption certificates in TNA E179/350/2/574.

[9] TNA E179/262/11 and E179/210/421.

[10] *Calendar of Treasury Books, 1669–72*, 360.

[11] Described as 'his Ma[jes]ties Collector and Receiver of his Revenues of Hearth money' at the head of the first membrane of the return, p. 137 above. At Lady Day 1672 he was himself taxed in Crux parish, York, on 10 hearths, 'one of these newly built', according to the sheriff's copy of the return.

[12] E Parkinson, 'Understanding the Hearth Tax Returns, Historical and Interpretative Problems' in Barnwell and Airs, eds, *Houses and the Hearth Tax*, 15.

contracts were negotiated with different bankers at different rents. The 1674 farmers immediately advanced £125,000 to Danby, and paid themselves interest on it, at 6 per cent per annum, out of the hearth tax until they had recovered their capital. Unlike the first farm, there was no sub-farming, so there was no specific person charged with the West Riding. All farmers were managed centrally, with a proviso that the records were made available to the government. In 1684, after it was discovered that the third farm had raised much more money than it paid to the Exchequer, the administration was handed over to salaried commissioners who also managed the excise.[13] For these purposes the country was divided into huge areas. The four northern counties formed one such area. To the south of them all the Ridings of Yorkshire, were linked together with Lancashire, Lincolnshire Nottinghamshire and Rutland under the charge of Andrew Broughton. Andrew Broughton served from Michaelmas 1684 to Lady Day 1686, he was followed for Michaelmas 1686, and presumably also Lady Day 1687 by Maurice Trant (although no accounts survive for that collection). In July 1687 Matthew Hammarton petitioned for the 'place of receiver-general of Hearth Money for co.York and adjacent counties, which Maurice Trant will not long be able to discharge'. He was not successful, George Blackburne accounted for the collections from Michaelmas 1687 and Lady Day 1688, and again for the final collection at Lady Day 1689, after Thomas Brabin had managed the Michaelmas 1688 collection rather badly.[14] The Commission was the last administration of the Hearth Tax, for William and Mary in 1689 repealed the tax as a means of gaining popularity.[15]

Exemption

Initially the clauses of the 1662 Bill made no mention of exemption but conditions for non-liability were added as amendments during the Bill's passage through parliament. Three exemption clauses were included in the 1662 Act. The first exempted any householder already excluded from paying the local rates to church and poor where such non-payment was 'by reason of his poverty or smallness of his estate' and not because the landlord paid the rates for his tenant. The second clause exempted those houses whose rentable value at market rates was twenty shillings a year or less and whose occupiers did not have or use any 'Lands Tenements Goods or Chattels of the value of ten pounds in their owne possession or in the possession of any other in trust for them'. Anyone in this category required a certificate signed by the minister and at least one of the churchwardens or overseers of the poor of their parish and certified by two justices. These certificates were valid for one year or two collections. In practice there was much overlap

13 Chandaman, *English Public Revenue*, 101–5.

14 Meekings, *Analysis of Hearth Tax Accounts 1666–1689*, 142, 145, 148, 152, 155, 157, 159, 161, 167; *Calendar of State Papers Domestic*, 1687–9, (HMSO, London, 1972), item no. 178.

15 1 Wm and Mary c.10.

between these two categories of exemption causing confusion as to who required a certificate. In addition, the involvement of parochial officials introduced a second group of administrators whose areas of jurisdiction did not always match those of the payers in the county lists. The taxation units in the north were generally the townships, whereas the exemption units were normally the much larger parishes. The third clause excluded three different types of hearth, namely those hearths in any hospital or almshouse (except those with an annual income over one hundred pounds a year), those in any 'Blowing house and Stampe, Furnace or Kiln', and any private ovens. Again poor drafting of this clause did not make it clear that smiths' forges and bakers' ovens were liable thus creating a fertile area for dispute. The conditions for non-liability were tightened in the 1664 Act whereby any dwelling which was previously assessed as chargeable, nor one with more than two hearths, could be exempted unless it became ruinous. Also, those landlords who subdivided properties after 1663 so as to reduce the rental below the twenty shillings threshold for exemption were themselves made liable for the tax. Although no copy of the 1670 instructions has survived it is probable that the clause 'living in property with a rental not greater than 20s a year' was intended now to be the sole criterion for exemption.[16] At local level this caused much confusion and as a result the recording of them on the surviving county lists of Michaelmas 1670 to Lady Day 1674 varies even within a county. Some are described as 'discharged by legal certificate', 'under the value and poor', 'not liable', 'paupers', 'non-solvent', 'receiver of alms of the parish', or 'takes collection'. In other cases they are only noted in numerical terms.[17] Furthermore those who administered the hearth tax in the West Riding of Yorkshire were inexplicably far more reluctant than anywhere else in the country to record on the duplicate those exempted by certificate. For the West Riding in 1669–70 there were only 978 hearths exempted out of 68,098 (under 1.5 per cent). The only county with fewer exempt was Rutland, with 829, but that was out of 5,525 (15 per cent). A county with a comparable number of hearths, Surrey, with 68,852, had 14,948 exempt (22 per cent). It is not that the whole of Yorkshire was peculiar in this respect, it was just the West Riding. Even the East and North Ridings (with which Hull was joined) had 8,331 exempt out of 48,423 hearths (17 per cent). This disparity is very striking, and as yet unaccounted for.[18]

The yield of the tax

The complicated history of management was the result of the government's urgent need to increase the receipts of the tax. Initially the tax was anticipated to yield about £300,000 but this was a hopeless overestimate as shown in the

16 Arkell, 'Understanding exemption from the hearth tax', 18–21.
17 Parkinson, 'Understanding the hearth tax returns', 15.
18 Meekings, *Analysis of Hearth Tax Accounts 1666–1689*, 118; Purdy, *Yorkshire Hearth Tax Returns*, 123.

Table 3: Yield of the Hearth Tax under different administrations 1662–1689

Collections	Officials	Net annual yield
1662 Michaelmas [M] to 1664 Lady Day [L]	Sheriffs	£115,000
1664M–1665M	Receivers	£112,500
1666L	Receivers/Farmers	
1666M–1669L	First Farmers	£103,000
1669M–1674L	**Second Receivers**	**£145,000**
1674M–1679L	Second Farmers	£144,500
1679M–1684M	Third Farmers	£157,000
1684M–1689L	Commission	£216,000

The period outlined in bold relates specifically to the time of the transcribed assessment in this volume.

table above. The problem was compounded initially by the passing of three acts within two years which laid a very shaky foundation for the management not helped by the poorly drafted legislation concerning exemptions which was never really properly addressed.

The figures given above show the national net annual yield of the tax under the different administrations but give no indication of the administrative costs or individual county receipts.[19] Lack of space precludes a discussion of the former but the yield of the tax in Yorkshire requires some mention. Initially, yield depended mainly upon the efficiency of the sheriffs and since shrieval appointments were made anually in November, there could be three different sheriffs involved from Michaelmas 1662 to Lady Day 1664 for each county. Some were good financial administrators some were not. For the Michaelmas 1662 collection in Yorkshire, Sir Thomas Osborne (appointed sheriff in November1661) was responsible for the entire county excluding the city of York. He showed great financial acumen for in spite of being responsible for one of the largest most distant counties he paid about three quarters of what was due within three months of leaving office. It is not surprising that such expertise led to his appointment as Lord Treasurer in 1673 and elevation as the Earl of Danby in 1674. His two successors were not as efficient, but it was not all their own fault. The disturbances of the anti-royalist Northern Plot of 1663–4 whose intention was to enforce the King's promises made at Breda and also to 'take away excises and chimney money' made collection very difficult. Both Sir Thomas Gower of Stittenham and Sir Roger Langley of Sheriff Hutton were allowed by the Exchequer to use some of the hearth tax receipts to defray expenses involved in

[19] Chandaman, *English Public Revenue*, 90–109.

putting down the plot and trying the perpetrators. As a consequence, the Yorkshire receipts of the tax to the Exchequer, combining the receipts of all three sheriffs was only £9,745, less than half the assessed charge of £21,521.[20]

From Michaelmas 1664 to Michaelmas 1665 under Col. Greathead's administration 3,782 hearths were 'new discovered' on top of the 62,788 hearths declared in 1662 (55,494 in the West Riding and 7,294 in York). Furthermore he was one of the most successful receivers in the country bringing in £10,603 of the £11,256 charge, some 94 per cent of it. In Yorkshire, if not elsewhere, the change to receivers brought improvement.[21] With little data on the first farmers' administration, we move to Walter Strickland's management from Michaelmas 1670 to Lady Day 1674. He increased the taxable hearths in the West Riding to 67,120, with only a further 978 not chargeable hearths.[22] Again there is little information for the years between 1674 to 1684. The Commission saw the highest return of the tax noted by Sir Charles Dering Comptroller of the Hearth Tax Office in 1686 as 'Just Improvement'. For 'Yorke' he reported an increase in hearths from 180,538 at Michaelmas 1684 to 187,611 at Lady Day 1685. This resulted in increasing receipts by Andrew Broughton from £14,188 for the half year Lady Day 1685 to £15,008 to Michaelmas 1685 and finally£16,333 to Lady Day 1686.[23] By 1689 when the tax was repealed it showed its highest return. In the country as a whole it was almost double that of 1662. It is not clear how much the recording of successive increases in the number of taxed hearths in the West Riding reflected a tighter interpretation of the law, a growing efficiency on the part of the collectors or actual increases in the number of hearths due to new building. All three exerted an influence of varying proportions. As Colum Giles has pointed out, there were more new houses with more hearths, and more hearths were added to existing houses in the decades concerned. For example, the sheriff's return for the City of York reports 'one of these newly built' of the hearths in the house of James Collins, himself the receiver of the Lady Day 1672 collection for the West Riding. The 1660s, 1670s and 1680s were a time of considerable building activity in some parts of the West Riding. The Keighley/Addingham area, for example, is one with many dated houses from this period.[24] So an increase in recorded hearths does reflect an increase in real hearths.

[20] *Calendar of Treasury Books 1660–67*, 566; E. Parkinson, *The Administration of the Hearth Tax 1662–1666* (unpublished University of Surrey, Roehampton PhD, 2001), 69. Both were substantial men. Sir Roger Langley at Sherrif Hutton Park in East and West Lillings was listed in the 1673 Hearth Tax returns for the North Riding with 31 hearths.

[21] C.A.F. Meekings, *Analysis of Hearth Tax Accounts 1662–1665*, List and Index Society, 153 (London, 1979), 323.

[22] Meekings, *Analysis of Hearth Tax Accounts 1666–1689*, 91, 118.

[23] *Idem*, pp.145, 148, 152.

[24] Tabulated in C. Giles, *Rural houses of West Yorkshire, 1400–1830*, Royal Commission on Historical Monuments (England)) Supplementary series, 8 (HMSO, London, 1986), 109.

Appendix II: Surviving West Riding Hearth Tax Documents

West Riding hearth tax documents held at the National Archives

Assessments and Returns

1662

E179/210/386: parchment roll of seven membranes. Individual assessments for the Liberty of Ripon first collection of this tax, due at Michaelmas 1662.

E179/262/9: parchment roll of eight membranes. Individual assessments for the borough of Leeds, Michaelmas 1662.

1662–3

E179/354 part 1: large bundle of around five hundred folios and membranes of paper and parchment, includes Yorkshire; part two: one folder, two documents auditors' papers relating to arrears, Yorkshire 1662–3.

1663

E179/210/388B: roll of five membranes. Sums outstanding on the account of Sir Thomas Gower, former sheriff and collector of the hearth tax for the half year ending at for Lady Day 1663 (second collection). The document lists, by wapentake and settlement, the names of defaulters and the amount each owed. The vast majority owed 12*d*., the amount due for a single hearth for each collection. The Second Revising Act, of 17 May 1664, ordered the collection of such arrears.

E179/210/388A: roll of five membranes – same as previous, but for Michaelmas 1663 (the third collection of this grant).

1662–4

E179/321/149: auditor's certificate or report. A single paper sheet, dated October 1666, relating to the sums collected from the counties of Yorkshire and Northumberland, the county palatine of Durham and the cities and towns of York, Hull, Newcastle and Berwick for the first two collections of this tax, and also for the fourth collection, due at Lady Day 1664. It gives the numbers of assessed hearths in each place for these collections (the first two collections are accounted together), and the amounts due. Marginal calculations also give the figures for each of the three Ridings of Yorkshire.

E179/210/394: this rolled file comprises a complicated collection of documents: writs, schedule of payments, schedules of arrears, instructions to collectors and commissioners' certificate, 33 membranes in all. It details the results of an investigation, ordered in June 1666, conducted by Joshua Greathead, receiver general of the hearth tax in the City of York and the West Riding of Yorkshire, into arrears outstanding from the collections due between Michaelmas 1662 and Lady Day 1664 inclusive, the first four collections of this tax. As receiver, Greathead was responsible not only for the collection of the arrears from these first four collections, but also for the collection of the next three payments. Highly likely that the second membrane once formed a covering certificate for roll E179/210/393, next below. It bears the signature and seal of Richard Clapham, the Clerk of the Peace for the West Riding. It bears a confusing heading, claiming to relate to the collection of the receiver Joshua Greathead due at 'Michaelmas 16 Charles II A.D. 1665'. This is contradictory, since Michaelmas 16 Charles II occurred in 1664, but Greathead, as well as being receiver of earlier arrears, was receiver of the three collections due between Michaelmas 1664 and Michaelmas 1665. So it sounds like the cover certificate for the Michaelmas 1664 assessment.

Michaelmas 1664

E179/210/393: parchment roll of 105 membranes. This large document is an individual assessment for the entire West Riding compiled for the Michaelmas 1664 collection (the fifth) and re-used for the next two payments (certainly Joshua Greathead, the receiver, accounted for all three collections together). Notes at the end give the sum total of hearths assessed (48,099). It lacks its heading, but membrane 2, of the collection of arrears schedules in E179/209/394, next above, seems to be the misplaced covering certificate for this assessment. Some settlements have been missed from Barkston Ash wapentake and a separate assessment for them, survives at E179/210/392, next below.

E179/210/392: parchment roll of four membranes. An assessment for part of the wapentake of Barkston Ash in the West Riding of Yorkshire. The heading explicitly states that it forms a supplementary list of places omitted from an earlier assessment for this wapentake, and that it relates to the money due at Michaelmas 1664, the fifth collection towards this grant, i.e. it corrects omissions from E179/210/393, above.

E179/402/3: paper roll of thirteen folios. Auditor's abstract of details taken from E179/210/393, above.

1664–6

E179/361: a large bundle of auditors' papers, around five hundred folios, from miscellaneous counties. A very few relate to the West Riding. A note of money received and not accounted for Lady Day 1666 from places in the West Riding, possibly for the farmers' first period of administration, and one folder, containing four 'castings' or abstracts of returns, for places in the East, North and West

Ridings of Yorkshire and in county Durham; the first document contains columns headed 'Michaelmas 1664' and 'Lady Day 1665'.

E179/210/420 part 3: paper bundle of seven membranes of accounting documents relating to the work of Joshua Greathead, gent., receiver of the hearth tax in the West Riding and the city of York for the one and half years up to Michaelmas 1665 (the fifth, sixth and seventh collections of this tax), and also of arrears pending on the accounts for the two years up to Lady Day 1664 (the first four collections). The first two membranes are stitched together to form a compotus for Greathead's collections, while the remaining membranes comprise four separate states of account. A note on membrane 6 refers to interest due between July 1668 and 1 May 1669, thus suggesting that that piece was compiled at some point after the latter date. It is impossible to give any precise dates for these pieces, each was compiled at a different stage in what was evidently a long and complicated accounting process.

E179/355: very large bundle of around a thousand parchment membranes and paper folios for miscellaneous counties. It includes twelve documents of auditor's reckonings for the hearth tax for various parts of Yorkshire 1662–1666.

E179/354 part 1: large bundle of around five hundred parchment and paper membranes and folios for miscellaneous counties, including for Yorkshire: one folder containing a single document: receiver general's receipt for West Riding, 1666; and another folder, containing three documents of auditors' papers relating to the collection for Lady Day, 1666.

1666 assessments for 1668 collection.

E179/262/11: paper book of 66 pages. Individual assessment for the wapentake of Claro for the Lady Day 1666 collection of the hearth tax, the eighth collection of this tax. The note recording the book's delivery by Joshua Greathead, the collector, to Colonel Robert Brandling and his partners, sub-farmers for Yorkshire, is dated 24 April 1668. An equivalent document for Skyrack wapentake also survives at E179/210/421, next below.

E179/210/421: paper book of 41 folios. An individual assessment for the wapentake of Skyrack relating to the Lady Day 1666 collection of the hearth tax. It was written in the same hand as the book for Claro wapentake, next above, and was also delivered by Joshua Greathead, the collector, to Colonel Robert Brandling and his partners, sub-farmers for Yorkshire, on 24 April 1668.

E179/210/394: paper book of 111 folios. A copy of an assessment (individuals) for the wapentakes of Agbrigg and Morley, for the collection due at Lady Day 1666. Similar books survive for Claro and Skyrack wapentakes, E179/262/11 and E179/210/421, next above, but this book was delivered to a different sub-farmer, presumably also in April 1668.

1669–70

E179/210/396: roll of 4 membranes. A record of the sums paid by the cutlers and smiths in the parish of Sheffield towards the three half-years' collections ending at Michaelmas 1670 (i.e. the collections due at Michaelmas 1669, and Lady Day and Michaelmas 1670, the fifteenth, sixteenth and seventeenth collections of this tax), which records the names of the cutlers and smiths within the town of Sheffield and its outlying townships, the numbers of hearths or furnaces each possessed, and the amount of tax paid, at 1s per hearth for each collection. Many of the entries are annotated, stating that certain individuals only paid for one or two collections (presumably relating to hearths built or dismantled during this period).

E179/210/411: parchment roll of 53 membranes. An assessment of individuals. Unfortunately there is no detailed heading and no surviving indication of the collection(s) to which the document relates. According to the note on the dorse of m.52, the document was delivered to the Exchequer on 7 July 1671 by the Clerk of the Peace, John Peables. C.A.F. Meekings, through his extensive research on the Hearth Tax accounts, suggested that it covered the one and a half years up to Michaelmas 1670, thus relating it to the collections at Michaelmas 1669, Lady Day 1670 and Michaelmas 1670. The place names within the present piece appear in almost precisely the same order as those in E179/210/399, see below. This would tend to back Meekings' dating for the present piece, since it is highly likely that E179/210/399 was compiled through comparison of the assessment for the 1671 collection with that from an earlier collection. The earlier roll could indeed have been this present assessment (or more probably a duplicate or perhaps a slightly later roll copied from it). Although a large amount of the document survives here, it is very incomplete. Many of the membranes have suffered a degree of damage, and some are almost entirely missing, and large parts of this roll have clearly become detached. However, almost all have been discovered elsewhere within the E 179 series. Three membranes now form the piece at E179/210/414, and, as the contemporary numbering on each clearly shows, these once formed the detached portions of membranes 35, 49 and 51 of the present piece. However, the pieces do not fit exactly against the sections surviving within the present piece, and small sections of each membrane have clearly been lost. Similarly, thirteen further fragments appear within the piece at E179/262/17 part 10 (forming the missing sections of membranes 36–39, 41–48 and rot .50), and two more at E179/368/8 part 6 (membranes 34 and 52). It is unclear whether any more are missing. Clearly extensive conservation treatment is necessary.

E179/262/17 part 10: a bundle of fragments of thirteen parchment membranes detached from E179/210/411 see above; an assessment probably relating to the three collections due at Michaelmas 1669, Lady Day 1670 and Michaelmas 1670, the fifteenth, sixteenth and seventeenth collections of this tax.

E179/210/414: three fragments from the damaged hearth tax roll now at E179/210/411, see above, an assessment for the entire West Riding, probably relating to the one-and-a-half years up to Michaelmas 1670.

E179/368/8 part 6: two fragmentary membranes from a hearth tax assessment for the West Riding. They once formed parts of the roll now at E179/210/411, see above, an assessment probably compiled for the collections due at Michaelmas 1669 and Lady Day and Michaelmas 1670 (the fifteenth, sixteenth and seventeenth collections of this grant).

E179/262/12: parchment roll of 29 membranes A list both of the empty houses and the individuals exempt by certificate within the West Riding for the three half years' payments ending at Michaelmas 1670 (the fifteenth, sixteenth and seventeenth collections of that grant). The schedule of non-payers also includes the wapentake of The Ainsty, within the county of the City of York. The present piece is in the same hand and style as the Lady Day 1672 assessment, below, suggesting that both documents may have been produced at the same time. They may both have been produced in 1675 during a concerted effort to clear the accounts.

1671–2

E179/210/399: parchment roll of 39 membranes. The majority of the document records the changes in the assessment for the West Riding for the year 1671 (presumably the collections due at Michaelmas 1671 and Lady Day 1672, the nineteenth and twentieth collections of this grant), and lists the increases and decreases in the taxable hearths in each settlement. In addition, membranes 6v.-9 comprise a complete assessment for the parish of Sheffield, listing all the individuals liable to pay.

Lady Day 1672

A large roll for the collection due at Lady Day 1672, has been broken up into a number of separate rolls:

E179/210/400: parchment roll, 81 membranes. Individual assessment for the wapentake of Claro.

E179/210/412: parchment roll, 29 membranes. Individual assessment for the wapentake of Staincross.

E179/210/413: parchment roll, 169 membranes. Individual assessment for the wapentakes of Agbrigg and Morley.

E179/210/415: parchment roll, 26 membranes. A badly damaged and fragmented assessment for Osgoldcross wapentake.

E179/210/417: parchment roll, 51 membranes. Individual assessment for the wapentake of Skyrack;

E179/210/418: parchment roll, 84 membranes. Individual assessment for the wapentakes of Staincliffe and Ewcross.

E179/262/14: parchment roll, 30 membranes. Individual assessment for the wapentake of Barkston Ash.

E179/262/15 parchment roll, 107 membranes. Individual assessment for the wapentake of Strafforth and Tickhill.

These are the basis for the text printed in this volume, and are discussed at greater length by Duncan Harrington in 'The documents used in this edition', above pp. 80–84.

As well as these eight separate rolls there are also a number of fragments which have been separated from them.

Detached from the Claro roll is E179/368/8 part 7, the missing section of membrane 47 of the roll now at E 179/210/400.

Detached from the Osgoldcross roll, which is in very poor condition, are E179/262/17 part 9, seven of the missing membranes; E179/368/8 part 8, three more of the missing membranes; E179/209/373 part 4, a single further missing membrane; E179/368/6 part 5 part of a further missing membrane. However, the sections of the original roll which lay immediately before m 3, between m 3 and m 4, and between m 6 and the assessment for Heck, are still missing. Clearly extensive conservation treatment is necessary.

Detached from the Skyrack roll E179/368/8 part 9, a single membrane, which once formed part of the assessment for Bingley, and lay between the membranes currently forming mm. 6–7 of the Skyrack roll.

Lady Day 1673 Assessment for 1673–4 Collections

E179/262/13: parchment roll of 125 membranes. Assessment of individuals for the collections due at Lady Day 1673, Michaelmas 1673 and Lady Day 1674, the 21st, 22nd and 23rd collections. Because of the poor condition of the Osgoldcross section of the Lady Day 1672 roll, the Osgoldcross section of this roll has been published here. See 'The Documents Used in this Edition' above p. 83.

Undateable

E179/368/9: bundle of 14 fragmentary parchment membranes. The fragments have been arranged in an approximation of their original order, but clearly these form only fourteen membranes of an assessment roll of possibly around 150 membranes. Most membranes (eleven) relate to the wapentake of Morley, while two relate to Barkston Ash wapentake, and one to Agbrigg wapentake. Analysis of the names suggests that it probably relates to an early collection. Two further membranes, both also from the Morley assessment, now form part 4 of E179/262/17, below.

E179/262/17 part 4: consists of two fragmentary membranes from E 179/368/9, above.

E179/241/352 part 17: not really identifiable. This is a bundle of two fragments of parchment membranes containing parts of assessments for the hearth tax for Yorkshire, possibly from the West Riding.

E179/262/17 part 3: two paper folios relating to an unknown hearth tax collection in the wapentake of Strafforth and Tickhill. It bears no heading beyond the simple words 'to be added to the engrossed schedule', suggesting that it contains the names of individuals omitted from an earlier assessment for a particular collection.

E179/320/40: this single sheet of paper seems to be a jottings sheet, produced by an Exchequer clerk during the accounting process for an unknown hearth tax collection in the West Riding, containing a number of notes made as he checked through an assessment roll or rolls for the West Riding. Headings appear for the wapentakes of Staincliffe and Ewcross, Agbrigg, Morley and Strafforth and Tickhill, and are followed by a variety of notes recording things such as the number of liable people who had not paid, and clerical errors in the assessment such as numbers omitted or names missing. On the dorse are a number of indecipherable calculations.

E179/368/8 part 3: this single sheet of paper appears to be an auditor's working document relating to a hearth tax collection in Skyrack wapentake, but there is no indication of which.

Exemption Certificates

All the certificates of exemption relating to the West Riding have been listed. A list of these appears in the following exemption certificate appendix, arranged alphabetically by township.

1670–4

E179/325: paper bundle of 473 certificates of exemption, 1670–4. Only six certificates come from the West Riding of Yorkshire.

E179/349: three boxes containing 1,229 certificates of exemption, 1670–4, from all three Ridings of Yorkshire and the city of York. The certificates in Box 2 mainly come from the West Riding.

E179/350: three boxes containing 1604 certificates of exemption, 1670–4, from all three Ridings of Yorkshire and the city of York.

E179/355: a box containing 321 certificates of exemption, 1672, mainly from the East and North Ridings.

At some future date the National Archives intends to sort and re-arrange the 2833 certificates in the six boxes of E179/349 and 350 together with those from E179/355.

1680
E179/354 part 1 of 8: a bundle of around five hundred certificates of exemption; some parchment and some paper, for various counties. They include at Yorkshire 3), three certificates of exemption for the West Riding 1680.

Additional Documents are constantly being identified in the National Archives. For the latest list of Hearth Tax documents for the West Riding see the web-site <www.nationalarchives.gov.uk/E179/>.

West Riding hearth tax documents held at the British Library

Amongst the additional manuscripts at the British Library (Add MS 38,0912) are some constables returns for the Upper Division of Barkston Ash Wapentake, Thomas Osborne sheriff, for the Michaelmas 1662 return, presented to the library by the Duke of Leeds. These signed returns are of great interest because of their poor rate of survival. The collection contains returns from 23 parishes, with 1,393 signatures and the amount of money due, together with two exemption certificates.

Wakefield Metropolitan District Council Library

Balne Lane Library (special collections), Wakefield
Nomina Villarum hearth tax return, being the sheriff's copy of the Lady Day 1672 return in the possession of Wakefield Metropolitan District Council Library. This is a document from which the National Archives Lady Day 1672 return may have been compiled, although in the sheriff's copy some of the settlements appear in different places, and some with different headings. The assessments themselves appear to be identical, with the exception of those individuals whose hearths had been exempted or destroyed. These individuals are named as such in the document in Wakefield, whereas, in the Exchequer copy, they are omitted and a sum total of all such non-taxable hearths given at the end of each settlement's assessment.

West Riding hearth tax documents held at the Leeds District Archives

Leeds 1663 in Leeds Corporation Court Book, LCM1, 212ff.

Appendix III: Exemption Certificates

The large group of exemption certificates for the West Riding are in many ways disappointing, after the exemption certificates for County Durham where there were exemption certificates for all but six townships with no non-payers in the main return that we printed.[1] In the West Riding, despite the huge number of surviving certificates, listed below pp. 569–88, there were none surviving for very many places with no record of non-payers from the main roll of Lady Day 1672. It was therefore impossible to fill the gaps in the roll as we had done in County Durham.

It is true that there were some outstanding examples of exemption certificates which added greatly to the material on particular settlements. Above all the character of Halifax was changed by the exemption certificates. In the return for Lady Day 1672 itself, Halifax had 313 payers and 39 non-payers.[2] In the exemption certificates for October 1670 (printed below pp. 589–91), Halifax had 179 exempt. In the exemption certificate for March 1673 (printed below pp. 591–2) Halifax had 143 exempt, plus one crossed out (disallowed). However there is some confusion in 1672. The sheriff's copy of the return for Lady Day has 37 people exempt with a certificate, and 71 further people simply recorded as 'poor'. Unfortunately, this confusion between those exempted by certificate, and those recorded as 'poor' rather than as 'non-payers' was widespread in the West Riding. There were some examples of settlements where the distinction between those who received relief and those 'omitted by reason of poverty' was exactly made. Professor Hey cites Hutton Wandesley and Rawcliffe amongst those.[3] But the largest group of returns from townships and villages demonstrated *either* ignorance of the legal distinction between those on parish relief and those living in houses with a rental of under £1 a year or with less than £10 in goods or land, *or* a complete lack of care in making the distinction.[4] Sometimes the words 'non-paying' and 'poor' seem interchangeable. This was true in all the wapentakes. In Selby in Barkston Ash, there were 35 certified in 1674, and 35 poor in the 1672 return. In Wheatley and Sandall, in Strafforth wapentake, there were 2 certified in 1673, and 2 poor in the return the previous year. Osgoldcross wapentake had Ackworth, where 21 people were certified in 1672, and in the 1673–4 return 20 were written down as 'poor'. In other cases the same total of certificated and

1 *Durham*, pp. lxiii–lxiv.
2 David Hey, 'The West Riding in the Late Seventeenth Century', pp. 16–17 above, and other e.g.s pp. 15–16.
3 Hey, 'West Riding', above p. 15.
4 *Loc.cit.*

poor was found, but the total was made up differently in different documents. Newton in Bowland had 4 people certificated in 1672, but in the return of that year one was a non-payer and three were 'poor'. The biggest example is of course Halifax itself, The West Riding had very few examples of the complete change in our understanding of the social structure of a community by the exemption certificates, which added so many on certificate and thereby changed the size and nature of a community visible only in the official return, as at Barnard Castle in County Durham. The conclusion seems to be that in the West Riding at least it is not safe to use either the figures for a settlement given in the official roll, or those on a certificate, without consulting the other. The absence of so many certificates means much less illumination is thrown on the official return by them. The following table gives some idea of the necessity of using return and certificates together.

Table 4: Townships with significantly different data for non-chargeable households in the 1672 return and in exemption certificates.

Exemption certificates with only a single name have not been included, even when there is no data for either non-payers or poor in the return.

Township or other tax unit	Wapentake	1670 Certs.	1671 Certs	**Lady Day 1672 Paying**	**Lady Day 1672 non-paying**	**Lady Day 1672 poor**	1672 Certs	1673 Certs	1674 Certs
Acomb	Ainsty		6*	**40**	**4**	**no data**	5*		
Attercliffe with Darnell	Strafforth	31		**97**	**18**	**5**	33*		
Bramley	Strafforth	4		**23**	**no data**	**no data**			
Cantley	Strafforth	2		**52**	**no data**	**no data**			
Darrington	Osgoldcross		9	**37**	**no data**	**2**			
Halifax	Morley	179		**313**	**39**	**111**		143	
Hampsthwaite	Claro	2		**36**	**no data**	**no data**			
Hartshead cum	Morley	7		**84**	**no data**	**no data**			
Headingly and	Skyrack	3		**53**	**no data**	**no data**			
Hook	Osgoldcross	2		**54**	**no data**	**no data**	6*		
Knaresborough	Claro	25		**166**	**no data**	**15**			
Penistone	Staincross	3		**28**	**no data**	**no data**			
Rawdon	Skyrack	33		**54**	**1**	**no data**	11*		
Sawley	Claro	14		**69**	**no data**	**7**			
Swinton	Strafforth		11*	**38**	**no data**	**1**			
Thorne	Strafforth			**156**	**no data**	**no data**	37*		37
Wales	Strafforth			**37**	**4**	**3**	24*		
Weardley	Skyrack	3		**24**	**no data**	**no data**			
Worsborourgh	Staincross		23*	**92**	**5**	**no data**	5*		

Most, but far from all of these exemption certificates are on printed paper forms. Printed certificates survive generally from June 1670 until Lady Day 1674, during the period when the 'second Receivers' were administering the Hearth Tax. They ceased, or ceased to survive after the Hearth tax was farmed out for the second time. The normal wording for these forms was as follows:

WEE the Minister of the Parish of

of the said Parish

doe hereby Certifie unto his Majesties Justices of the Peace for the said

That we doe believe That the

respective

Houses wherein the persons hereunder named doe Inhabit are not ofgreater vallue than twenty shillings *per annum* upon the full Im-proved rent, And that neither the Person so inhabiting, nor any other using the same Messuages hath, useth, or Occupieth any Lands or Tenements of their own or others of the yearly vallue of Twenty shillings *per annum,* Nor hath any Lands, Tenements, Goods or Chattels of the vallue of Ten pounds in their own Possession, or in the Possession of any other in trust for them. And that the said houses have not above two Chimbneys, Fire-hearthes and Stoves in them respectively. Northat the said houses nor any ofthem have been divided into severall Tenements, or from the grounds formerly in-joyed with them, since the time limited in the Act of Parliament. Witness our hands this day of

One of these forms is reproduced on p. 568

The Yorkshire exemption certificates are mostly concentrated in seven boxes in the National Archives, three boxes each under the call numbers E179/349 and E179/350, and a further box under the call number E179/355. It is the long term intention of the National Archives to re-order the 3154 certificates in these boxes. In the meanwhile Mr Duncan Harrington, FSA, working for the British Academy Hearth Tax Project has made working lists of the contents of each box, giving each certificate a pencil number. The West Riding certificates are concentrated in E179/349 boxes 2 and 3, and E179/350 boxes 2 and 3. There are only small numbers in the other boxes, and there is also a handful more in E179/325. There are probably also stray Yorkshire certificates mixed in with those from other counties which have not yet been listed, just as there are stray certificate from other counties in the Yorkshire boxes. The following list of those from the West Riding and the Ainsty of York has been abstracted from Mr Harrington's lists of the individual boxes, and re-arranged alphabetically by township. He has further transcribed a large number of these certificates for the Project and these are marked with an asterisk in the following list. They are at the British Academy Hearth Tax Project at Roehampton University. It is intended that they will eventually be put on their web-site. Those certificates marked with a P are printed in this volume, below, pp. 589–98.

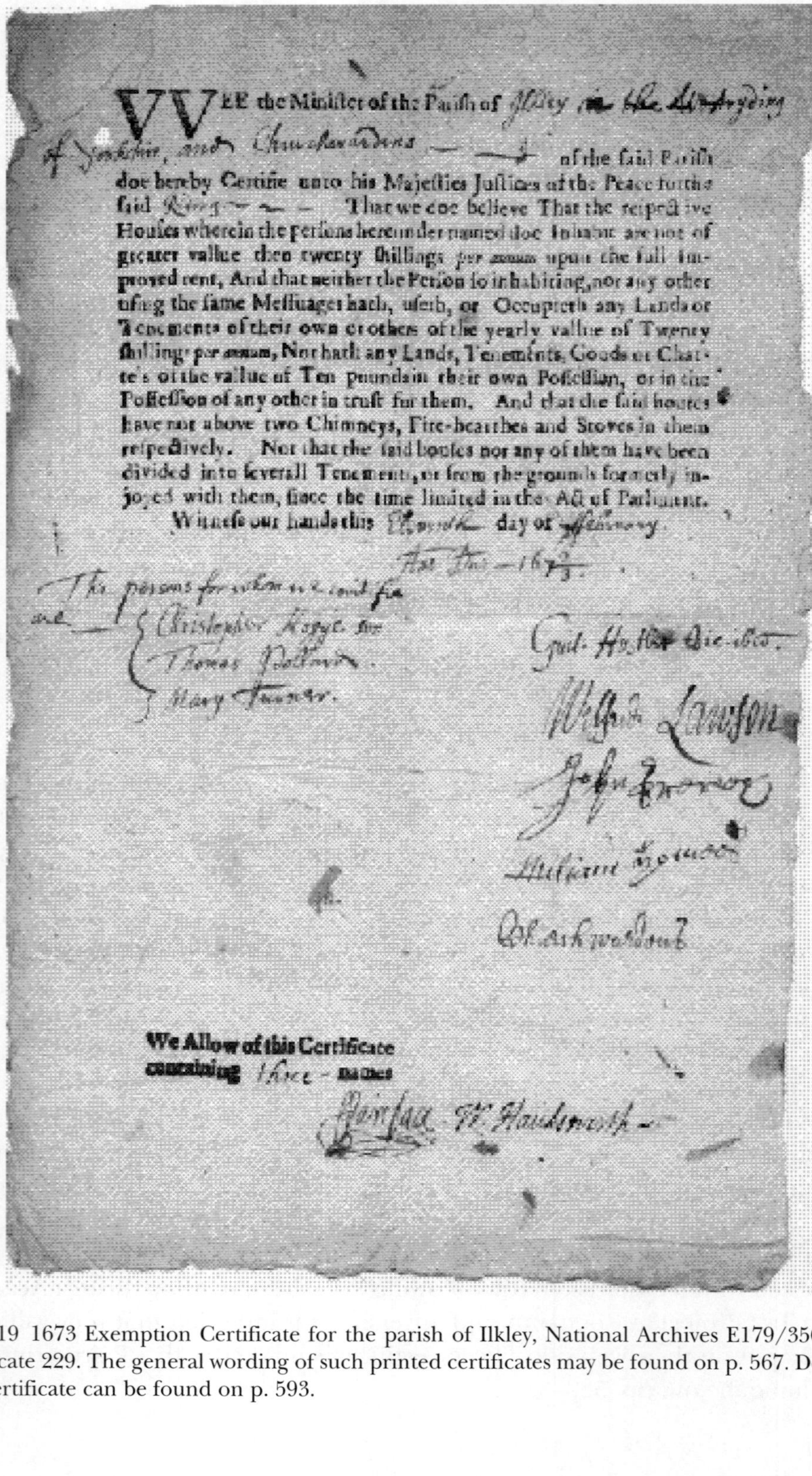

WEE the Minister of the Parish of Ilkley in the Westryding of Yorkshire, and Churchwardens of the said Parish doe hereby Certifie unto his Majesties Justices of the Peace for the said Riding That we doe believe That the respective Houses wherein the persons hereunder named doe Inhabit are not of greater vallue then twenty shillings *per annum* upon the full improved rent, And that neither the Person so inhabiting, nor any other using the same Messuages hath, useth, or Occupieth any Lands or Tenements of their own or others of the yearly vallue of Twenty shillings *per annum*, Nor hath any Lands, Tenements, Goods or Chattels of the vallue of Ten pounds in their own Possession, or in the Possession of any other in trust for them. And that the said houses have not above two Chimneys, Fire-hearthes and Stoves in them respectively. Nor that the said houses nor any of them have been divided into severall Tenements, or from the grounds formerly injoyed with them, since the time limited in the Act of Parliament.

Witness our hands this Eleventh day of February

Ano Dni – 1672/3.

The persons for whom we certifie are –
Christopher Knype sen
Thomas Dollman
Mary Turner.

Guil. Hustler Vic. ibm.
William Lawson
John Turner
William Turner
Churchwardens

We Allow of this Certificate containing three – names

Fairfax W. Hawksworth

Plate 19 1673 Exemption Certificate for the parish of Ilkley, National Archives E179/350 box 2 certificate 229. The general wording of such printed certificates may be found on p. 567. Details of this certificate can be found on p. 593.

Table 5: Consolidated list of surviving West Riding Hearth Tax Exemption Certificates

TNA reference	See p. 567	Township	No. exempted	Date
E179/325/6	*	Abberforth [Aberford]	3	1672, 29 Jun
E179/350/3/349	*	Ackworth	7	1671, 18 Jul
E179/350/2/227	*	Ackworth	21	1672, 09 Nov
E179/350/3/335	* P	Acombe [Acomb]	1	1671, 01 Mar
E179/350/3/322	* P	Acombe [Acomb]	5	1672, 15 Oct
E179/350/3/333	* P	Acombe [Acomb]	5	1671, 20 Dec
E179/325/11	*	Addle (cum Eccopp) [Adel cum Eccup]	2	1672, 09 Nov
E179/350/2/379	*	Adle [Adel] Kirskill [Creskeld hall]	1	1672, 00 000
E179/350/2/247	*	Adwick upon Street [Adwick le Street]	6	1672, 30 Jan
E179/350/2/230	*	[Airmyn] Chapel of Armyn in Snaith	7	1672, 23 May
		Aismunderby see Ripon, Bondgate		
E179/350/3/391	*	Aldbrough [Aldborough]	3	1670, 26 Aug
E179/349/2/299	*	Aldburgh [Aldborough]	3	1672, 04 Jun
		Allerton, Chapelry of see Chapel Allerton		
E179/350/3/385	*	Allerton Maleverer, Hopperton [Allerton Mauleverer]	1	1671, 00 Jul
E179/349/2/222	*	Almonbury [Almondbury]	1	1670, 14 Sep
E179/349/2/303	*	Almondberry [Almondbury]	8	1674,13 May
E179/349/2/220A	*	Almondberry [Almondbury]	9	1670, 22 Sep
E179/349/2/223	*	Almondbury	2	1670, 09 Sep
E179/349/2/306		Almonbury township Southcrosland [Almondbury]	1	1674, 13 May
E179/349/2/304		Almonbury Southcrosland [Almondbury]	1	1674, 25 May
E179/349/2/285		Appletrewick, in Burnsall	1	1670, 23 Nov
E179/349/2/319		Darfeild, dorse Ardsley [Ardsley]	1	1672/3, 11 Mar
E179/350/3/351	*	Darfield, Ardsley [Ardsley]	1	1672, 22 Mar
E179/349/2/257	*	Arkendale [in] psh Knaresbrough	4	1672, 09 Apr
		Arksey see Bentley and Arksey		
E179/349/2/189	*	Arncliffe	1	1672, 10 Apr
E179/349/2/219		Arncliffe in Littondale in Craven	1	no date ?1670
E179/349/2/220		Arncliffe in Littondale in Craven	2	no date ?1670
E179/349/2/194	*	Arnecliffe [Arncliffe]	1	1672, 10 Apr
E179/349/2/193	*	Arnecliffe [Arncliffe]	1	1672, 10 Apr
E179/325/9	*	Arthington	1	1672, 01 Dec
E179/349/2/51		Adle (dorse 'Arthington') [Arthington]	4	1670, 20 Sep
E179/349/2/106		Weston cum Askwith (dorse Askwith) [Askwith]	3	1670, 27 Aug
E179/350/2/410		Aston, dorse Ashton cum Aughton	7	1674, 13 Apr
E179/349/2/218		Attercliffe cum Darnall, Chapelry & township of	31	1670, 21 Nov

E179/350/2/396	* P	Sheffield constab. Attercliffe [Attercliffe and Darnall] some entries annotated to the effect they are liable	33	1672, 20 Apr
E179/349/2/217		Austerfield	1	1670,16 Mar
E179/349/2/215		Austerfield	1	1670, 17 Aug
E179/349/2/216		Austerfield	1	1670, 17 Aug
E179/349/2/214A		Austerfield	1	1670, 06 Nov
E179/349/2/49		Bayldon [Baildon], Chapelry in the psh Otley	6	1670, 07 Oct
E179/350/2/214	*	Baildon	6	1672, 23 Dec
		Balby see Hexthorpe and Balby		
E179/349/2/50		Bardsey, dorse Bardsey cum Rigton [Bardsey and East Rigton]	3	1670, 16 Sep
E179/349/2/167	*	Bardsey, dorse Bardsey and Righton	3	1672, 29 Nov
E179/350/3/375	*	Shereburne, Barkston [Barkston]	6	1671, 19 Aug
E179/350/2/407		Barmbrough [Barnburgh]	3	1674, 10 Apr
E179/350/2/406		Barmby upon Dunn [Barnby upon Don]	1	1673, 04 Oct
E179/349/3/78	* P	Barnesley [Barnsley]	6	1672, 07 Dec
E179/350/2/269	*	Barnesley [Barnsley]	1	1672, 07 Dec
E179/349/2/242	*	Barnoldswicke [Barnoldswick]	1	1672, 17 Oct
E179/349/2/293		[Barugh] Bargh, dorse Barugh	1	1670, 11 Dec
E179/349/2/45		Barwick in Elmet	1	1670, 19 May
E179/349/2/44		Barwick in Elmet	1	1670, 23 May
E179/349/2/43		Barwick in Elmet	1	1670, 10 Nov
E179/350/3/370	*	Barwick in Elmet	14	1671, 30 Nov
E179/350/2/225	*	Barwick in Elmet	23	1671, 23 Dec
E179/349/2/241	*	Bashall [Bashaw], parish Mitton	3	1672, 11 Apr
E179/350/3/360	*	Batley	1	1671, 20 Jul
E179/349/2/333	*	Batley	15	1672, 05 Sep
E179/350/2/211	*	Beaghall [Beal], township in psh Kellington	2	1672, 03 May
E179/350/3/345	*	Beaghall, [Beal] Kellington	2	1671, 19 Jul
E179/350/3/363	*	Beeston in Leeds	7	1671, 00 000
E179/349/2/19		Beston [Beeston] in the psh Leeds	1	1674, 24 Apr
E179/350/2/248	*	Arksey dorse Arksey cum Bentley [Bentley and Arksey]	21	1672, 06 Jun
E179/350/3/321	*	Bickerton in Bilton,	1	1672, 13 Oct
E179/350/3/331	*	Bilbrough	6	1671, 19 Jan
E179/350/3/330	*	Bilbrough dorse Bilton	2	1671, 08 Oct
E179/350/3/329	*	Bilton	1	1672, 18 Oct
E179/350/3/328	*	Bilton	1	1672, 19 Oct
		Bilton, see also Bickerton, Bilbrough, Tockwith		

E179/350/2/216	*	Bingley	6	1672, 10 Mar
E179/349/2/47		Bingley	12	1670, 03 Oct
E179/350/3/366	*	Bingley	2	1671, 24 Oct
		Bingley see also Morton		
E179/349/2/337		Birstall	2	1672/3, 03 Jan
		Birstall, see also Cleckheaton, Gomersall		
E179/350/3/334	*	Bishopthorpe	1	no date [1671–2]
E179/350/3/332	*	Bishopthorpe	4	1671, 27 Jul
E179/349/2/256	*	Constab Bishopton Sutton cum	1	1672, 11 Dec
		Clotheram, psh Ripon [Bishopton and Clotherholme]		
E179/350/3/379	*	Bishopton with Sutton psh Ripon [Bishopton and Clotherholme]	1	1672, 06 Jun
E179/350/3/380	*	Clotherham psh Ripon [Bishopton and Clotherholme]	1	1671, 26 Jun
E179/350/3/388	*	Sutton Grange in Bishopton [Bishopton and Clotherholme]	1	1671, 29 Jun
E179/349/2/292		Regillmosse in psh Bolton iuxta Bolland [Bolton by Bowland]	1	1668/9, 06 Jan
E179/349/2/290		Reyhead psh Bolton nigh Bolland [Bolton by Bowland]	1	1669, 05 Aug
E179/349/2/291		Reyhead psh Bolton nigh Bolland [Bolton by Bowland]	1	1669, 30 Aug
E179/350/2/408		Boulton upon Dearne [Bolton upon Dearne]	7	1673, 24 Oct
E179/350/2/249	*	Boltion upon Dearne [Bolton upon Dearne]	3	1672, 26 Jan
E179/350/3/377	*	Burrowbridge [Boroughbridge]	3	1671, 07 Jun
E179/349/2/224		Burrowbridge psh Oldbrough [Boroughbridge]	6	1670, 18 Aug
E179/349/2/243	*	Bolland Forest [Bowland Forest]	3	1672, 28 Jul
E179/350/2/256	*	Bradfeild [Bradfield]	7	1672, 01 Aug
E179/349/2/335	*	Bradford, Bowling [Bowling]	3	1672, 20 Apr
E179/349/2/23		Bradford, const Bowling [Bowling]	5	1674, 28 Apr
E179/349/2/22		Bradford	1	[1674]
E179/349/2/332	*	Bradford	1	1672,
E179/349/2/18		Bradford	3	1674, 11 May
E179/349/2/21		Bradford	2	1674, 23 May
E179/349/2/20		Bradford	1	1674, 25 May
E179/349/2/288		Bradford,	30	1670?
E179/350/3/362	*	Bradford	1	1671, 06 Feb
E179/349/2/289		Bradford, Kirkgate	21	1670, Sep

E179/349/2/31		Eccleshill in psh Bradford. [Bradford]	1	1674, 08 May
E179/349/2/254	*	Bramham	2	1672, 05 Aug
E179/349/2/253	*	Bramham, Cliffend [Bramham]	2	1672, 14 Oct
E179/349/3/172		Leeds, Bramley [Bramley]	4	1670, 12 Sep
E179/349/2/343	*	Brayton	3	1672, 02 Dec
		Bridge Hewick see Copt Hewick		
E179/349/2/280		Brearley within psh.Felchurch [Brierley]	5	1670, 07 Dec
E179/350/2/395	*	Sheffield dorse Brightside Bierlow [Brightside Bierlow]	16	1672, 03 Apr
E179/350/3/355	*	Sheffield dorse Brightside Brierley [Brightside Bierlow]	17	1671, 31 Oct
E179/350/3/352	*	Brosworth with Pigburn [Brodsworth and Pickburn]	5	1671, 02 Nov
E179/349/2/284		Brotherton, Barkston Ash wap:	1	1670?
E179/349/2/240	*	Broughton	8	1672, 27 Mar
E179/350/2/360	*	Burley [Burley in Wharfedale]	7	1672, 04 Dec
E179/349/2/46		Warley (dorse Burley in Wharfdale) [Burley in Wharfedale]	7	1670/1, 25 Jan
E179/350/2/318	*	Burnsall	5	1671, 11 Jul
		Burnsall see also see Appletreewick and Hetton with Bordley		
E179/349/2/122		Burton in Lonsdale in the psh Thorneton	3	1670, 05 Dec
E179/349/2/123		Burton in Lonsdale in the psh Thorneton	11	1670, 05 Dec
E179/349/2/124		Burton in Lonsdale in the psh Thorneton	1	1669, 20 Dec
E179/349/2/296	*	Burton Leonard	?3	1672, 19 Apr
E179/349/2/318	*	Burton Leonard	1	1672, 22 Apr
E179/350/3/378	*	Burton Leonard	1	1671, 23 Jun
		Burton see also Monk Bretton		
E179/349/2/17		Calverley [Calverley with Farsley]	10	1673, 13 Oct
E179/349/2/212		Calverley cum Farsley	1	no date ?1670
E179/349/2/331		Calverley cum Farsley	11	1673, 18 Feb
E179/349/2/211		Cantley	1	1670, 20 Oct
E179/349/2/210		Cantly [Cantley]	1	1670, 20 Oct
E179/350/3/276	*	Carleton in psh of Royston [Carlton] (Staincross)	1	1672, 07 Dec
E179/350/3/374	*	Carlton in the parish of Snaith [Carlton] (Osgoldcross)	1	1671, 07 Dec
E179/350/3/347	*	Castleford	1	1671, 05 Oct
E179/349/2/209		Castly [Castley] in parish of Leathley	1	1670, 27 Aug
E179/350/3/386	*	Leathley, constab Castley	1	1671, 24 May

E179/349/2/105		Cawood	28	no date ?1670
E179/349/2/342	*	Cawood	20	1672, 14 Oct
E179/349/2/67	*	[Chapel Allerton] Borough of Leeds, Chapelry of Allerton	1	1672,
E179/349/3/159		Kirke Fenton [Church Fenton]	1	1670, 04 Nov
E179/349/2/89	*	Kirk Fenton [Church Fenton]	1	1672, 22 Oct
E179/350/2/381		Clayton cum Frickley [Clayton with Frickley]	1	1674,04 May
E179/350/3/354	*	Frickley cum Clayton [Clayton with Frickley]	1	1671, 25 Mar
E179/349/2/334	*	Birstall, dorse Cleckheaton [Cleckheaton]	2	1672, 03 Sep
		Clotherholme see Bishopton and Clotherholme		
E179/350/3/353	*	Conisborough [Conisbrough]	1	1671, 15 Oct
E179/349/2/264		Connystropp in the parish of Goldsbrough [Coneythorpe]	1	1670/1, 19 Jan
E179/349/2/263		Goldsbrough dorse Connystropp [Coneythorpe]	2	1670, 25 Aug
E179/349/2/258		Liberty of Ripon. Dorse Copt Hewick & Hewick on the Bridge [Copt Hewick, Bridge Hewick separately listed]	4	1672, 25 Jun
E179/349/1/97		Cowick, in psh Snaith,	3	1674, 14 Apr
E179/349/2/305		Cowick, in psh Snaith,	1	1674, 6 May
E179/349/2/208		Cowlthroppe [Cowthorpe]	2	1670, 25 Aug
E179/349/3/169	*	Cowthrop [Cowthorpe]	1	1672, 03 Jun
E179/349/3/170	*	Cowthrop [Cowthorpe]	1	1672, 03 Jun
E179/349/2/300		Cowthrop [Cowthorpe]	2	1673, 10 Nov
E179/349/2/16		Crofton	12	1674, 5 May
E179/349/2/207		Cudworth	3	no date ?1670
E179/350/3/274	*	Royston, dorse Cudworth	3	1672, 17 May
E179/349/2/206		Darrington	9	1671, 12 Jan
E179/349/2/205		Darton	1	1669, 14 Oct
E179/349/2/203		Darton	1	1670, 07 Dec
E179/349/2/204		Darton	1	1670, 07 Dec
E179/349/2/205A		Darton, Maplewell	1	1670, 17 Dec
E179/350/2/403		Mexbrough dorse Denaby [Denaby]	3	1674, 27 Apr
E179/349/2/188	*	Dent	2	1672, 10 Jul
E179/349/2/201		Dent	1	1670, 08 Dec
E179/349/2/202		Dent [on the reverse a list of 29 names and sums of money]	1	1670, 08 Dec
E179/350/2/390		Thorne, Dikes marsh [Dikes Marsh]	37	1674,

E179/349/3/178		Silkestone township of Dodworth [Dodworth]	1	1674, 27 Apr
E179/350/2/253	*	Doncaster	1	1672, 25 Jan
E179/350/2/243	*	Doncaster	3	1672, 18 Feb
E179/350/2/244	*	Doncaster	1	1672, 22 May
E179/350/2/246	*	Doncaster	6	1672, 23 May
E179/349/2/197		Doncaster	1	1670, 1 Nov
E179/349/2/196		Doncaster	2	1670, 12 Nov
E179/350/2/405		Doncaster, Baxtergate	1	1673, 08 Dec
E179/349/2/198		Doncaster, Bowerfold (dorse Market Place)	1	1670, 09 Nov
E179/350/2/250	*	Doncaster, Marshgate	3	1672, 11 Feb
E179/350/2/234	*	Doncaster, Scot Lane	1	1672, 11 Feb
E179/350/2/254	*	Doncaster, Scotlane	5	1672, 11 Feb
E179/349/2/199		Doncaster, St Pulchregate without the Barr [St Sepulchre Gate]	1	1670, 09 Nov
E179/349/2/200		Doncaster, St Pulchregate without the Barr [St Sepulchre Gate]	1	1670, 09 Nov
E179/350/2/251	*	Doncaster, St Pulcher gate without the Barr & Baxtergate[St Sepulchre Gate]	2	1672, 14 Feb
E179/350/2/245	*	Doncaster, St Pulchergate without the Barrs [St Sepulchre Gate]	25	1672, 14 Feb
E179/350/2/315	*	Skipton, Eastby (dorse Emsley & Eastby) [Easby]	1	1670, 02 Sep
E179/349/2/69		Skipton, Eastby (dorse Emsley & Eastby) [Easby]	9	no year 06 Dec
		East Tadcaster see Tadcaster		
E179/349/2/126		Sheffield, in Ecclesall Barlay [Ecclesall Bierlow]	5	1670, 10 Dec
E179/350/2/397	*	Ecclesall in psh Sheffield [Ecclesall Bierlow]	16	1672, 15 Jul
		Ecclesall, or Ecclesall Bierlow, in the psh Sheffield is the Ecclesall in Strafforth wap, not that in Morley wap		
E179/349/2/341	*	Elland [Elland with Greetland]	24	1672, 19 Aug
E179/349/2/9		Emley	17	1674, 20 Apr
E179/349/2/144		Skipton, Emsey [Emsley]	1	1670, 17 Jan
E179/349/2/145		Skipton, Emsey [Emsley]	1	1671, 06 Nov
		Esholt with Hawksworth see Hawksworth		
E179/349/2/278		Gargrave Psh, Eshton [Eshton]	1	1670, 22 Sep
E179/349/2/97		Hampestwhait (dorse Fellcliffe) [Felliscliffe]	1	1674, 06 Apr
E179/350/3/346	*	Ferry Freiston [Ferry Fryston]	1	1671, 13 Jul

E179/350/2/213	*	Fetherstone [Featherstone],	3	1672, 13 Apr
E179/350/2/263	*	Fishlake	13	1672, 27 Jan
E179/349/2/120		Thornhill, Flockton Over	1	1670, 09 Sep
E179/349/2/279		Follifoot	1	1670, 20 Aug
E179/349/2/298	*	Follifoot Mooreside, in psh Spofforth	1	1672, 01 Jun
E179/349/2/274		Gargrave	1	1670, 22 Sep
E179/349/2/275		Gargrave	1	1670, 22 Sep
E179/349/2/276		Gargrave	1	1670, 22 Sep
E179/349/2/277		Gargrave	1	1670, 22 Sep
E179/349/3/350		Gisburn [Gisburne]	5	1674, 16 Apr
E179/349/2/268		Gisburne	1	1670, ? Nov
		Goole, see Hook		
E179/349/2/137		Rippon, Grantley cum Everson [Grantley and Eavestone]	1	1670, 17 Aug
E179/349/2/138		Rippon, Grantley cum Everson [Grantley and Eavestone]	1	1670, 17 Aug
E179/349/2/139		Rippon, Grantley cum Everson [Grantley and Eavestone]	1	1670, 17 Aug
E179/349/3/145		Mitton repaired with a sheet of paper having places and sums, people and money [Great Mitton]	5	1670, 03 Dec
E179/349/2/250		Usburne Magna [Great Ouseburn]	5	1670/1, 28 Jan
E179/349/2/115		Usburne Magna [Great Ouseburn]	5	1670, 25 Aug
E179/350/3/390	*	Kirkby Malzard, Grewillthorp [Grewelthorpe]	12	1671, 08 Oct
E179/349/2/226	*P	Halifax	10	1670, 10 Oct
E179/349/2/227	*P	Halifax	12	1670, 13 Oct
E179/349/2/228	*P	Halifax	157	1670, 13 Oct
E179/349/2/344	*P	Halifax	143	1673, 3 Mar
		Hallam see Nether Hallam		
E179/349/3/187		Hamlington [Hambleton psh Brayton]	1	1670, 28 Apr
E179/349/3/186		Hamlinton [Hambleton psh Brayton]	1	1668, 11 Jul
E179/349/3/150		Hampsthwaite	2	1670, 01 Sep
E179/350/2/572	*	Hansworth [Handsworth]	5	1672, 12 Feb
E179/350/2/258	*	Hartehill [Harthill & Woodall]	1	1672, 30 Jan
E179/350/2/257	*	Hartehill [Harthill & Woodall]]	13	1672, 30 Jan
E179/349/3/185		Hartshead	7	1670, 15 Sep
E179/349/2/66	*	Harwood	9	1672, 01 Dec
E179/349/2/42		Harwood (dorse Harwood)	9	1670/1, 06 Feb
E179/349/2/100		Hatfield, Dunscroft	3	1670, 14 Oct
E179/350/2/571	*	Hatfield	4	1672, 04 Feb
E179/350/2/262	*	Hatfeild, Stainforth [Hatfield]	1	1672, 06 Apr

E179/350/3/271	*	Cold Hiendley, psh Felkirk [Havercroft with Cold Hiendley]	1	1672, 08 Dec
E179/349/2/76		Otley, hamlet of Eshoult and township of Hawksworth [Hawksworth]	1	1670?
E179/349/2/77		Otley, hamlet of Eshoult and township of Hawksworth [Hawksworth]	1	1670?
E179/349/2/75		Ottley, Hawksworth	3	1670, 18 Sep
E179/350/2/359	*	Hawksworth	3	1672, 30 Nov
E179/349/2/99		Haworth	2	1670, 13 Sep
E179/349/2/78	*	Leeds (dorse Headingley cum Burley) [Headingley with Burley]	1	1670, 01 Sep
E179/349/2/79		Headingley cum Burley Borough of Leeds,	1	1670,
E179/349/2/80		Headingley cum Burley Borough of Leeds,	1	1670?
E179/349/2/336	*	Heaton hamlet in Bradford psh	14	1672, 10 Nov
E179/349/3/173		Henshall in psh Snaith [Hensall]	1	1670/1, 2 Jan
E179/349/3/174		Henshall psh Snaith [Hensall]	1	1670/1, 2 Jan
E179/349/2/282		Burnsall, Hetton chaplery Rilston (dorse Hetton cum Boardley) [Hetton and Bordley]	4	1670, 10 Dec
E179/349/2/283		Burnsall, Hetton chaplery Rilston (dorse Hetton cum Boardley) [Hetton and Bordley]	3	1670, 10 Dec
E179/350/2/318	*	Hetton, Burnsall [Hetton and Bordley]	5	1671, 11 Jul
E179/350/2/402		Balby in psh Doncaster [Hexthorpe and Balby]	1	1674, 25 Apr
E179/350/2/573	*	Hextrop in psh Doncaster [Hexthorpe and Balby]	1	1672, 31 May
E179/350/2/242	*	Hextropp in psh Doncaster [Hexthorpe and Balby]	1	1672, 10 Feb
E179/350/2/241	*	Hextropp in psh Doncaster [Hexthorpe and Balby]	1	1672, 30 May
E179/350/2/252	*	Hextropp in psh Doncaster [Hexthorpe and Balby]	1	1672, 31 May
E179/350/2/240	*	High Melton	1	1672, 20 Jan
E179/349/2/98		Hipperholme, Township of (dorse Hipperholme cum Brighouse)	9	1670, 14 Sep
E179/349/3/164		Leeds, Holbeck [Holbeck]	1	1671, 08 Feb
E179/349/3/175		Leeds, Holbeck [Holbeck]	1	1671, 13 Feb
E179/349/2/27		Chapel Houlbecke in the psh Leeds [Holbeck]	16	1674, 12 May
E179/349/2/29		Holmefirth Constab. [Holme]	3	1674, 02 Apr

E179/349/2/134		Holmeforth [Holme]	2	1670, 19 Sep
E179/349/2/72		Holmfirth in psh Almondbury [Holme]	2	1670, 19 Sep
E179/349/2/135		Holmfrith [Holme]	1	1670, 26 Sep
E179/349/2/221		Honley, in Almonbury [Honley]	14	1670, 17 Sep
E179/349/2/71		Hooke [Hook]	2	1670
E179/350/2/217	*	Hooke & Gowle in Snaith, [Hook] listed separately from [Goole] in return	6	1672, 26 Oct
E179/350/2/400		Hooton [Roberts], same minster as next and also same churchwarden	1	1674, 23 Apr
E179/350/2/401		Hooton Roberts	5	1674, 28 Apr
E179/350/3/359	*	Horbury	1	1671, 03 Feb
E179/350/3/371	*	Guisley, within the town of Horsforth [Horsforth]	6	1671, 18 Oct
E179/350/2/198	*	Horseforth in the psh of Guiesley	1	1672, 00 000
E179/349/2/83		Horsforth	1	1670
E179/350/2/199	*	Horsforth in the psh of Guiseley	6	1672, 00 Dec
E179/350/2/200	*	Horsforth in the psh of Guisley	11	1672, 20 Aug
E179/349/2/81		Horsforth psh Guisley	1	1670
E179/349/2/84		Horsforth psh Guisley	1	1670, 03 Oct
E179/349/2/82		Horsforth, Newlay Bridge [New Laithes]	1	1670
E179/350/2/328	*	Horton in Riblesdale [Horton in Ribblesdale]	1	1672, 24 Apr
E179/349/2/287		Hortons Ambo, Bradford	6	1670
E179/350/3/373	*	Hoyland	2	1671, 14 Aug
E179/350/3/268	*	Silkston, Hoyland Swaine [Hoyland Swaine]	1	1671, 06 Nov
E179/350/3/365	*	Huddersfield	2	1671, 07 Feb
E179/349/2/13		Huddersfield	1	1674, 12 Apr
E179/349/2/324	*	Huddersfield	1	1674, 21 May
E179/349/3/199	*	Huddersfield	13	1670, 19 Sep
E179/349/2/11	*	Huddersfield	1	1673, 24 Oct
E179/349/2/14	*	Huddersfield	1	1673, 24 Oct
E179/350/2/270	*	Hunsingore	1	1672, 20 Jun
E179/350/2/271	*	Hunsingore	1	1671, 24 Jun
E179/349/3/184		Hunsingore	1	1670, 18 Aug
E179/349/3/154		Leeds, Hunslett [Hunslet]	1	1670
E179/349/3/182	*	Hunslet	1	1671, 22 Feb
E179/349/3/183	*	Hunslet	1	1671, 22 Feb
E179/350/3/394	*	Psh Birstall, town Hunsworth	1	1671, 27 Jan
E179/349/2/28		Burstall, township of Hunsworth	7	1674, 08 May
E179/350/3/327	* P	Hoton Wainsley alias Marston [Hutton Wandesley and Angram], in Long Marston	5	1672, 7 Oct

E179/350/3/341	* P	Hoton Wainsley alias Marston, dorse Hutton & Angram [Hutton Wandesley and Angram]	7	1671, 23 Oct
E179/349/2/73		Ilkley	1	1670, 25 Sep
E179/349/2/74		Ilkley	2	1670, 25 Sep
E179/350/2/229	* P	Ilkley	3	1673 11 Feb
E179/349/3/180		Ingleton [psh Bentham]	1	1670
E179/349/3/179		Ingleton [psh Bentham]	2	1670
E179/349/2/114		Winterskill in the chapelry of Ingleton [Ingleton]	1	1670, 22 Nov
E179/350/2/320	*	dorse Keighley	1	1672, 12 Apr
E179/350/2/321	*	Keighley	1	1672, 12 Apr
E179/350/2/322	*	Kettlewell	5	1671, 20 Oct
E179/349/3/162		Kettlewell	4	1670, 08 Dec
E179/349/3/163		Kettlewell [same vicar different churchwardens]	1	no date?1670–1
E179/349/3/181		Kettlewell, Starbottom [Starbotton] returned in Kettlewell	1	no date ?1670
E179/349/3/157		Kimberworth in psh Rotherham	1	1670, 01 Nov
E179/349/3/158		Kimberworth psh Rotherham	9	1670, 09 Nov
E179/350/2/255	*	Rotherham dorse Kimberwell & Redwell [Kimberworth?]	27	1672, 23 Sep
E179/350/2/231	*	Kippax	2	1672, 30 Nov
E179/349/3/153		Kirkby Hall psh Little Ouseburn [Kirby Hall] 5 further names scored through	1	1670, 26 Aug
E179/349/3/149		Kir Dighton [Kirk Deighton]	1	1670, 22 Aug
E179/349/3/270		Kirkeby Malhamdale in Craven [Kirkby Malham]	4	1674, 28 Apr
E179/349/2/180	*	Kirkhammerton	2	1672, 10 Apr
E179/349/2/338	*	Kirkheaton	3	1672, 20 Aug
E179/349/3/160		Knaresborough	14	1670, 04 Oct
E179/349/3/161		Knaresborough	11	1670, 04 Oct
		Knaresborough see also Arkendale		
E179/349/3/121		Knottingley in psh Pontefract	2	1670, 13 Apr
E179/350/3/350	*	Pontefract, Knottingley	9	1671, 10 Oct
E179/350/2/197	*	Knottingly, Pontefract	2	1672, 21 Oct
E179/350/2/212	*	Pontefract, Knottingley	2	1672, 06 Nov
E179/350/2/568	*	Laughton in le Morthing [Laughton en le Morthen]	4	1672, 30 Jan
E179/350/2/569	*	Laughton in le Morthing [Laughton en le Morthen]	1	1672, 01 Feb

E179/350/2/570	*	Laughton in le Morthing, Sladehooton [Laughton en le Morthen]	2	1672, 05 Feb
E179/349/3/146		Laughton in le Morthing [Laughton en le Morthen]	1	1670, 24 Nov
E179/350/2/399		Laughton in the Morthing [Laughton en le Morthen]	6	1674,
E179/349/3/207	*	Leathley	3	1672, 02 Jun
E179/349/3/148		Ledston, Charles Hammond vicar	1	no date
E179/349/3/147		Ledstone Thomas Hunt vicar	1	1670, 01 Nov
E179/350/2/361	*	Leeds	1	1672,
E179/349/2/54	*	Leeds	7	1671, 7 Feb
E179/349/2/58	*	Leeds	1	1671, 8 Feb
E179/349/2/56	*	Leeds	1	1670, 23 Sep
E179/349/2/53		Leeds (dorse Leeds)	13	1670/1, 07 Feb
E179/349/2/52		Leeds (dorse Leeds)	22	1670, 20 Sep
E179/350/3/368	*	Leeds	1	1671, 29 Nov
E179/350/2/218	*	Leeds dorse Headrow [Leeds, The Headrow]	2	1672, 30 Jan
E179/349/2/57		Leeds, Kirkgate [Leeds, Kirkgate]	1	1670/1?
E179/349/2/59		Leeds, Kirkgate	1	1670, 5 Jul
E179/349/2/88		dorse Leeds, Mill Hill [Leeds, Mill Hill or Boar Lane]	6	1670/1, 07 Feb
E179/350/2/224	*	Leeds, Milne Hill or Boares Lane	11	1672, 27 Jan
E179/349/2/55	*	Leeds, dorse East part of the maine?ryd?emy [Leeds]	16	1670/1, 26 Jan
E179/350/2/219	*	Leeds, March Lane, dorse East part of Mainridding [Leeds]	1	1672,
E179/349/2/238		Kirkheaton dorse Lepton [Lepton]	10	1672, 07 Feb
E179/349/2/26		Kirkheaton, Lepton [Lepton]	1	1674, 04 May
E179/349/2/25		Township of Lepton	10	1674, 01 May
E179/350/2/259	*	Letwell	1	1674, 27 Apr
E179/349/2/15	*	Huddersfield, Quarmby [Lindley cum Quarmby]	1	1673, 25 Oct
E179/349/2/61	*	Huddersfield, Quarmby [Lindley cum Quarmby]	1	1673, 01 Nov
E179/349/3/152		Lynton [Linton]	2	1669, 03 Sep
E179/350/3/387	*	Spofforth psh, Larton [Linton]	1	no date
E179/349/2/153	*	Spofforth, Ribston Parva [Little Ribston]	1	1672, 25 Nov
E179/349/2/152	*	Spofforth, Ribston Parva	3	1672, 1 Jun
E179/349/2/10		Liversie in the parish of Birstall [Liversedge]	5	1673, 12 Apr
E179/349/3/156		Long Preston	8	1670, 30 Nov

E179/349/3/155		Long Preston, names and numbers on reverse	1	1670, 22 Nov
		Long Sandall see Wheatley and Sandall		
E179/349/3/171	*	Markinton [Markington with Wallathwate]	1	1672, 29 Jun
E179/349/2/246		Markinton, Ripon parish [Markington with Wallathwate]	1	1674
E179/349/2/247		Markinton, Ripon parish [Markington with Wallathwate]	1	1674
E179/350/2/564	*	Marr	2	1672, 20 Jan
E179/350/2/566	*	Marr	2	1672, 20 Jan
E179/350/2/567	*	Marr	2	1672, 20 Jan
E179/350/2/565	*	Marr	2	1672, 27 Jan
E179/349/3/141		Marton	1	1670, 23 Nov
E179/350/2/317	*	Marton Psh [Marton]	12	1672, 20 Jul
E179/349/3/142		East Marton [Marton]	1	1670, 22 Nov
E179/349/3/143		Marton West [Marton]	1	1670, 24 Nov
E179/349/3/144		Marton West [Marton]	1	1670, 24 Nov
E179/349/3/139		Marton West psh Marton [Marton]	1	1670, 01 Nov
E179/349/3/140		Marton West psh Marton [Marton]	1	1670, 01 Nov
		Melton see High Melton		
E179/349/2/85		Otley, Menstone [Menston]	1	1670/1, 25 Jan
E179/349/3/151		Hampsthwaite constab. Menwith and Darley, [Menwith cum Darley]	1	no date ?1670
E179/350/2/398		Mexbrough [Mexborough]	4	1674, 30 May
E179/349/3/137		Mexbrough [Mexborough]	8	1670, 10 Nov
E179/349/2/339	*	Luddingden town Midgley [Midgley]	20	1672, 10 Nov
E179/349/2/24		Mirfeild [Mirfield]	5	1674, 17 May
E179/349/3/145		Mitton repaired with a sheet of paper having places and sums, people and money [Great Mitton]	5	1670, 03 Dec
E179/349/3/138		Burton alias Munck [Monk Bretton]	2	1670, 21 Mar
E179/350/3/326	*	Moor Munckton [Moor Monkton]	7	1672, 21 Oct
E179/350/3/343	*	Moore Munckton [Moor Monkton]	6	1671, 15 Dec
E179/349/2/48		Morton in Bingley [Morton]	1	1670?
E179/349/2/125		Sheffield, Heeley in constab. Hallam cum Ecclesall [Nether Hallam]	1	1670, 22 Nov
E179/349/3/188		Sheffield, Lower Hallam [Nether Hallam]	1	1670, 17 Dec
E179/349/3/189		Sheffield, Lower Hallam [Nether Hallam]	1	1670, 18 Dec
E179/349/3/135		Otley, Newhall cum Cliffton [Newell with Clifton]	1	1670, 27 Aug

E179/350/2/413	*	Newton [Newton in Bowland]	4	1672, 20 Jul
E179/349/1/287		Newtone in the West Riding (Cornelius Cockburne curate) [too many Newtons to identify which, apart from curate's name]	1	1674, 7 Jun
E179/350/2/365		Normanton	1	1666, 22 Apr
E179/350/2/203	*	Norton in Campsal	3	1672, 25 Oct
E179/349/3/113		Notton Town of and psh of Royston	1	1670, 09 Dec
E179/325/7	*	Otley	6	1672, 29 May
E179/350/3/369	*	Otley	7	1671, 30 Jun
E179/349/3/134		Otley	1	1670, 28 Aug
E179/349/2/86		Otley [primitive repair using another form]	8	1670/1, 25 Jan
E179/349/3/136		Otterborne[Otterburn]	5	1670, 22 Oct
		Ouseburn see Great Ouseburn		
E179/349/2/12		Town of Ovenden	4	1674, 10 May
E179/350/3/389	*	Paiteleybriggs [Pateleley Bridge] dorse Bishopside	3	1671, 13 Nov
E179/349/2/168	*	Pannall [Pannal]	6	1672, 3 Jul
E179/349/3/119		Pannall [Pannal]	1	1670, 13 Oct
E179/349/2/266		Gisborne, Paythorne [Paythorne]	1	1670, 26 Nov
E179/349/2/267		Gisborne, Paythorne [Paythorne]	1	1670, 26 Nov
E179/349/3/120		Penistone	2	1670, 03 Apr
E179/350/3/270	*	Denby Milne, Penistone	1	1672, 12 Oct
E179/350/3/393	*	Plomton [Plompton]	1	1671, 03 Jun
E179/349/2/295	*	Spofford, dorse Plumpton [Plompton]	2	1672, 08 Jun
E179/349/2/142		Pollington in Snaith	10	1670, 22 Oct
E179/349/3/127		Pontefract	1	1670?
E179/349/3/118		Pontefract	1	1671, 2 Jan
E179/349/3/123		Pontefract	5	1671, 2 Jan
E179/349/3/116		Pontefract	1	1671, 13 Jan
E179/349/3/124		Pontefract	10	1671, 13 Jan
E179/349/3/128		Pontefract	2	1670, 30 Dec
E179/349/3/132		Pontefract	1	1670, 31 Dec
E179/349/3/117		Pontefract Burrough	4	1671, 11 Jan
E179/350/2/207	*	Pontefract Bailygate [Pontefract, Bailey Gate]	3	1672, 15 Nov
E179/350/2/364	*	Pontefract dorse Bailygate	1	1672, 22 Nov
E179/350/2/363	*	Pontefract dorse Neat Market	3	1672, 25 Oct
		[Pontefract, Neate Market]		
E179/349/3/131		Pontefract dorse New Market & Neatmarket	2	1670?

E179/349/3/122		Pontefract, Nautmarket [Pontefract, Neate Market]	3	1670/1, 16 Jan
E179/350/2/209	*	Pontefract, dorse Ropegate [Pontefract, Roper Gate]	4	1672, 26 Oct
E179/349/3/125		Pontefract, Gilliegate & Baxtergate	3	1670, 30 Dec
E179/350/2/210	*	Pontefract, Mickellgate [Pontefract, Micklegate]	1	1672, 26 Oct
E179/349/3/126		Pontefract, Micklegate	1	1670?
E179/349/3/130		Pontefract, Munckhill	1	1670?
E179/349/3/129		Pontefract, Munckhill [Monk Hill]	1	1670?
E179/349/3/133		Pontefract, Newgate	2	1670, 16 Jun
E179/350/3/361	*	Pudsey in the psh Claverley	11	1671, 06 Nov
E179/350/2/201	*	Purston Jaglin, in Fetherstone	7	1672, 05 Nov
E179/349/3/112		Chapelry of Rastricke within the psh of Elland [Rastrick]	11	1670, 14 Sep
E179/350/2/222	* P	Rawcliffe	17	1672, 01 Nov
E179/350/3/344	* P	Rawcliffe,	52	1671, 00 000
E179/349/2/302		Rawkcliffe, dorse Osgoldcross wap: [Rawcliffe]	39	1674, 12 Apr
E179/349/2/87		Guisley, Rawden [Rawdon]	33	1670, 03 Oct
E179/350/2/226	*	Rawdon, Psh Guslay	11	1672, 30 Aug
E179/350/2/393		Rawmarsh	35	1674, 04 Jun
E179/350/2/221	*	Reedness, in Whitgift Psh	2	1672, 17 Oct
		Ribston see Little Ribston		
E179/349/2/271		Gisborne dorse Remington [Rimington]	2	1670, 26 Nov
E179/349/2/265		Gisburne, township Rimington	3	1670, 28 Nov
E179/349/1/9	*	Ripon	1	1672,
E179/349/2/177	*	Ripon	1	1672, 03 Jun
E179/349/2/252	*	Ripon	2	1672, 20 Oct
E179/349/2/176		Ripon	1	1671, 30 Nov
E179/349/2/155	*	Ripon Town of [John Milner mayor]	1	1672?
E179/349/3/99		Ripon Agnesgate [in Allhallowgate]	1	1670, 17 Aug
E179/349/2/140		Ripon Town of, Agnesgate	2	1670/1, 16 Jan
E179/349/3/94		Ripon Alhallowgate	1	1670, 16 Aug
E179/349/3/101		Ripon Alhallowgate	1	1670, 17 Aug
E179/349/3/109		Ripon Allhallowgate	1	1670, 17 Aug
E179/350/3/384	*	Ripon, Alhallowgate,	1	1671, 07 Dec
E179/349/2/173	*	Ripon, Allhallowgate	1	1672, 01 Jun
E179/350/3/381	*	Ripon, Allhallowgate,	5	1671, 19 Jan
E179/350/3/382	*	Ripon [the same person on cert E179/350/3/381]	1	1671, 17 Jan
E179/349/2/172		Ripon, Stamergate: constab. Allhallowgate, Stamergate & Agnesgate	1	no date ?1672

E179/349/3/111		Ripon Bondgate	1	1670, 16 Aug
E179/349/3/91		Ripon Bondgate	1	1670, 16 Aug
E179/349/2/136		Bondgate near Ripon	1	1670, 16 Aug
E179/349/2/244		Bondgate, Ripon	1	1674, 10 May
E179/349/2/245		Bondgate, Ripon, dorse Osmonderly [Aismunderby] cum Bondgate	1	1674, 10? May
E179/349/2/154	*	Crosgate in Ripon,	1	1671, 27 Jun
E179/349/2/170	*	Ripon, Horsefair	1	1672, 03 Jun
E179/349/2/178	*	Ripon, Horsefaire	1	1672, 03 Jun
E179/349/2/179	*	Ripon, Horsefaire	1	1672, 03 Jun
E179/349/1/8	*	Ripon, Horsefaire in	1	1672, 4 Jun
E179/349/2/251	*	Ripon, Horsefaire in	1	1672, 5 Jun
E179/349/2/174	*	Ripon, Skelgate [Skellgate]	1	1672, 02 Apr
E179/349/3/104		Ripon Skelgaite [Skellgate]	1	1670, 07 Aug
E179/349/3/105		Ripon Skelgate [Skellgate]	1	1670, 19 Aug
E179/349/3/102		Ripon Stannergate [in Allhallowgate]	1	1670, 19 Apr
E179/349/3/106		Ripon Stannergate	1	1670, 16 Aug
E179/349/3/107		Ripon Stannergate	1	1670, 16 Aug
E179/349/3/108		Ripon Stannergate	1	1670, 16 Aug
E179/349/3/93		Ripon Stannergate	1	1670, 16 Aug
E179/349/3/96		Ripon Stannergate	1	1670, 16 Aug
E179/349/3/97		Ripon Stannergate	1	1670, 16 Aug
E179/349/3/98		Ripon Stannergate	1	1670, 16 Aug
E179/349/3/100		Ripon Stannergate	1	1670, 17 Aug
E179/349/3/92		Ripon Stannergate	1	1670, 18 Aug
E179/349/3/95		Ripon Stannergate	1	1670, 18 Aug
E179/349/3/110		Ripon Stannergate, but AllHallowgate in text	1	1670, 17 Aug
E179/350/3/383	*	Ripon, Stainergate	1	1671, 08 Jul
E179/349/2/171	*	Ripon, Stammergate	1	1672, 03 Jun
E179/349/2/175	*	Ripon, Stammergate	1	1672, 04 Jun
E179/349/1/3		Standergate in Ripon	1	1671, 20 Jun
E179/349/2/249	*	Stannergate, Ripon	1	1672, 20 Jun
E179/349/2/248		Ripon Westgate,	?5	1673, 30 Apr
E179/349/3/103		Ripon town dorse Westgate	3	1670, 19 Aug
E179/350/2/237	*	Rossington	3	1672, 08 Feb
E179/350/2/392		Rossington	1	1674, 18 Apr
E179/350/2/238	*	Rotherham	9	1672, 17 Feb
E179/350/2/404		Rotherham	9	1673, 17 Mar
E179/350/2/391		Rotherham	1	1673, 15 Dec
E179/349/3/115		Royston	1	1670, 12 Nov
E179/350/3/273	*	Royston	3	1672, 20 Nov

E179/349/3/114		Royston dorse a note about one of those listed 'Ann watts house is lyable land being taken from it but a yeare a goe.'	4	1670, Nov
E179/350/3/325	* P	Rufforth	5	1672, 27 Mar
E179/350/3/342	* P	Rufforth	5	1671, 02 Apr
		Sandall see Wheatley		
E179/349/2/146		Sawlay & Tossyde [Sawley and Tosside] (Staincliff wap)	1	1670?
E179/349/2/4		Sawley, Chapelry of in psh Ripon (Claro wap)	14	1670, 19 Aug
E179/350/2/436		Saxton	9	1674, 14 May
E179/349/2/130		Saxton	7	1670, 31 Oct
E179/350/2/232	*	Scarecroft in the psh Thorner [Scarcroft]	1	1672, 07 Jun
E179/350/2/233	*	Scarecroft in the psh Thorner [Scarcroft]	1	1672, 30 Nov
E179/349/2/34		Seacrofte in Whitkirke [Seacroft]	2	1670, 29 Sep
E179/349/2/35		Seacrofte, Whitkirke	2	1670, 29 Sep
E179/349/2/36		Whitchurch, Seacroft	1	1670, 29 Sep
E179/349/2/151		Seberge, Martwhaite [Sedburgh Marthwaite]	1	1670, 01 Dec
E179/349/2/148		Sedberge, hamlet Marrtwhaite [Sedburgh Marthwaite]	1	1670, 01 Dec
E179/349/2/147		Sedberge hamlet Marthwait [Sedburgh Marthwaite]	1	1670, 02 Dec
E179/349/2/150		Sedbergh, Marthwayte	1	1670, 03 Dec
E179/349/2/149		Sedbergh, Custley in Bland (Long explanation about a furnace removed)	1	1670, 03 Dec
E179/350/3/376	*	Selby	2	1671, 16 Jun
E179/350/2/435		Selbye dorse Barston Ash	35	1674, 14 Apr
E179/349/2/273		Giggleswick, constab. Settle [Settle]	5	1670, 28 Nov
E179/349/2/32		Thorner, Shadwell [Shadwell]	1	1670, 16 Sep
E179/325/10	*	Thorner dorse Shadwell	1	1672/3, 31 Jan
E179/349/2/132		Sharoe in psh Rippon, Claro wap: [Sharow]	2	1670, 1[?7] Aug
E179/349/2/96		Sharowe (dorse Sharo) [Sharow]	1	1673, 14 Nov
E179/350/2/394	*	Sheffield	50	1672, 28 Feb
E179/350/2/292	*	Sheffield	61	1674, 31 Mar
E179/349/2/127	*	Sheffield	27	1670, 12 Dec
		Sheffield see also Attercliffe and Darnall, Brightside Bierlow, Ecclesall Bierlow, Nether Hallam		

E179/349/2/345	*	Sherburn also mentions Newthorp in the same parish [Sherburn in Elmet]	18	1672, 16 Oct
E179/349/2/128		Shereburn, Lotherton cum Abberforth [Sherburn in Elmet]	5	1670, 31 Oct
E179/349/2/129	*	Shereburn, Milforth [Sherburn in Elmet]	5	1670, 31 Oct
E179/349/2/131		Shereburn, Shereburn constab. [Sherburn in Elmet]	16	1670, 31 Oct
E179/349/2/259	*	Sicklinghall in Kirkby	1	1672, 11 Jun
E179/350/3/267	*	Silkston [Silkeston]	1	1672, 12 Dec
E179/350/2/315	*	Silsden in psh Kildweeke [Silsden]	1	1672, 24 Apr
E179/349/2/133		Skelton in the psh Rippon	3	1670, 17 Aug
E179/349/2/6		Sladeburne (dorse Slaydburne) [Slaidburn]	1	167[?0], 1 Dec
E179/349/2/8		Slaidburne constab. Slaidburne	1	1670, 28 Nov
E179/349/2/7		Slaydburne [Slaidburn] all of Batteris within the Forest [Battersby]	3	1670, 13 Dec
E179/349/3/168		Snaith	2	1674, 14 Apr
E179/349/2/301		Snaith	1	1674, 16 Apr
E179/350/2/206	*	Snaith	1	1672, 02 May
E179/325/8	*	Snaith	9	1672, 14 Oct
E179/350/2/228	*	Snaith	1	1672, 16 Oct
E179/349/2/143		Snaith	3	1670, 24 Oct
E179/350/2/208	*	Snaith	1	1672, 04 Nov
		Snaith, see also Airmyn		
E179/349/2/62		Soothill Township of	1	1674, 04 May
E179/350/3/348	*	South Elmsall in psh South Kirkeby [South Elmsall]	1	1671, 10 Oct
E179/349/2/141		South Kirkby [South Kirkby]	2	1670?
E179/350/2/205	* P	South Kirkeby	1	1672, 22 Nov
E179/350/2/204	* P	South Kirkeby	4	1672, 21 Nov
E179/349/2/328	*	South Milford, psh Sherburne [South Milford]	7	1672, 16 Oct
E179/349/2/3		Spawforth (dorse Spofforth)	4	1670, 23 Aug
E179/349/2/297	*	Spofford	5	1672, 28 Mar
E179/349/2/1		Spofforth [Spofforth]	1	1669/0, 20 Mar
E179/349/2/145		Silkton, township of Stainebrough [Stainborough]	1	1670, 02 Sep
E179/350/2/316	*	Stainforth in Gigleswicke [Stainforth] (Staincliffe wap)	1	1672, 16 Apr
E179/350/3/364	*	Stainland	6	no date ?1671
E179/349/2/5		Outwoodside in Stanley [Stanley]	1	1670, 16 Sep
E179/349/2/103		Wakefield (dorse Stanley) [Stanley]	1	1671, 13 Mar

E179/349/2/60		Wakefield (dorse Stanley) [Stanley]	1	1674, 27 Apr
E179/350/3/392	*	Ramsgill in Steanbeck Down [Stonebeck Down]	1	1671, 27 May
E179/349/2/272		Gisborne, Swinden [Swinden]	4	1670, 25 Nov
E179/349/3/208	*	Swimfleet dorse Swynfleet [Swinefleet]	2	1672 , 4 Apr
E179/349/2/181	* P	Swinton	11	1671, 17 Nov
E179/350/2/264	*	Fishlake dorse Sykehouse [Sykehouse]	12	1672, 25 Jan
E179/349/2/119		Tadcaster	1	1670?
E179/350/3/324	* P	Tadcaster	2	1672, 16 Oct
E179/350/3/340	* P	Tadcaster [East]	1	1671, 06 Dec
E179/350/3/337	* P	Tadcaster East 'bowells of compassion'	1	1671, 06 Dec
E179/350/3/336	* P	Tadcaster East part of	1	1671, 06 Dec
E179/349/2/39		Whitkirke constab Temple Newsam [Temple Newsam]	3	1670/1, 01 Feb
E179/349/2/37	*	Whitechurch (dorse Temple Newsom) [Temple Newsam]	9	1672?
E179/350/2/235	*	Whitkirke dorse Temple Newsam [Temple Newsam]	1	1674, 06 Apr
E179/349/2/38		Whitkirke, Temple Newsam	5	1670, 26 Sep
E179/350/2/236	* P	Thorne	37	1672, 08 Feb
E179/349/2/33		Thorner	1	1670, 28 Jan
E179/350/3/367	*	Thorner	1	1671, 20 Apr
E179/349/3/264		Thorneton (there is no way of telling whether these are Thornton in Ewcross wap or Thornton in Morley wap)	1	1674, 20 Apr
E179/349/3/267		Thorneton	1	1674, 20 Apr
E179/349/2/121		Thornton	5	1670, 23 Nov
E179/350/3/323	*	Thorp Arch	1	1672, 02 Apr
E179/350/3/338	*	Thorparch Thorp Arch]	1	1671, 15 May
E179/350/2/239	*	Tickhill	2	1672, 14 Jul
E179/350/3/339	*	Tockwith in Bilton [Tockwith]	1	1671, 09 Aug
E179/349/2/116		Todwick	3	1670, 07 Nov
E179/349/2/118		Treaton [Treeton]	1	1670, 20 Nov
E179/349/2/117		Treeton	1	1670, 14 Nov
E179/350/2/319	*	Waddington dorse & West Bradforth [Waddington]	11	1672, 25 Jul
E179/349/2/286		Bradford constab.Wadington [Waddington]	10	1670, 30 Nov
E179/350/2/260	*	Wadworth	11	1672, 21 Jan
E179/350/2/267	*	Wadworth	2	1672, 22 Jan
E179/349/2/340	*	Wakefield Kirkgate	13	no date
E179/349/2/108		Wakefield, Kirkegate	40	1670?, 8 Sep
E179/349/2/110		Wakefield, Kirkgate	1	1670?

E179/349/2/109		Wakefield, Northgate	18	1670, 28 Sep
E179/349/2/64		Wakefield Northgate	3	1674, 01 May
E179/349/2/107		Wakefield, Overpott Ovens [Outwood] (dorse Aygbrigg & Morley wap:)	1	1670,
E179/350/2/378	* P	Wales	24	1672, 29 Sep
E179/349/2/68	*	Hallifax, town of Warley [Warley]	1	1673, 06 Dec
E179/350/3/357	*	Warmefield, (1 from Sharleston) [Warmfield cum Heath]	11	1671, 06 Nov
E179/350/3/358	*	Warmfield dorse with Heath	31	1671, 07 Nov
		[Warmfield cum Heath]		
E179/350/2/385		Warmsworth	1	1673, 04 Oct
E179/349/2/2	*	Wasshford	1	1672,
E179/350/2/389	*	Wath upon Dearne	1	no date ?1673–4
E179/349/2/41		Harwood (dorse Weardley) [Weardley]	3	1670, 00 Sep
E179/349/2/104		Weatherby Bridgend & Clifford [Wetherby]	3	1670, 31 Oct
E179/349/2/102		Wath, Wentworth [Wentworth]	1	1670, 29 Sep
E179/349/2/101		Wath, Wentworth and on dorse [Wentworth]	1	1670, 29 Sep
E179/349/2/260	*	Harwood, Weeton cum Hewby [Weeton and Huby]	5	1672, 02 Jun
E179/349/2/255	*	Weston cum Askwith	3	1672, 19 Jun
E179/350/2/386		Wheatley, in psh Doncaster [Wheatley and Sandall]	1	1673, 04 Oct
E179/350/2/388		Doncaster (dorse Wheatley and Sandall) [Wheatley and Sandall]	1	1673, 15 Nov
E179/350/2/387		Long Sandall, in psh Doncaster [Wheatley and Sandall]	1	1674, 18 May
E179/350/2/268	*	Whitkirk	1	1672, 18 Jan
E179/349/2/63		Thornhill, township of Whittley [Whitley] (Agbrigg wap)	7	1674, 16 May
E179/350/3/356	*	Whitley in the psh Kirkheaton [Whitley] (Osgoldcross wap)	1	1671, 16 Feb
E179/350/2/223	*	Whitley, Kellington	5	1672, 21 Oct
E179/350/2/261	*	Gildingwells [Woodsetts and Gildingwells]	2	1672, 01 Feb
E179/350/2/266	*	Woodsetts, in psh Anston, dorse Woodsetts with Gildingwells	1	1672, 12 Nov
E179/349/2/214		Woodsetts in Anston,	1	no date
E179/350/2/383		Woodsetts, Anston,	1	1674, 01 May
E179/350/2/384		Woodsetts, Anston,	1	1674, 27 May
E179/350/2/325		Woolley	5	1674, 30 Mar
E179/350/3/269	*	Woolley	3	1672, 06 Dec

E179/350/3/266	*	Woolley	2	1672, 10 Dec
E179/349/2/113		Woolley Town of	1	1670, 08 Dec
E179/349/2/112		Woolley Town of	3	1670, 09 Dec
E179/349/2/111		Woolley Town of	1	1670, 12 Dec
E179/350/3/275	* P	Worsbrough in psh Darfeilde [Worsborough]	5	1672, 09 Dec
E179/350/3/372	* P	Worsbrough in the parish of Darfield	23	1671, 02 Nov
E179/350/3/272	*	Wortley, in Tankersley [Wortley]	2	1672, 12 Dec
E179/349/2/40		Guiesley and township of Yeadon [Yeadon]	1	1670?

In the National Archives, as well as these certificates, there is E179/262/12, which does not contain certificates, but is a parchment roll of 29 membranes, described above p. 561, giving the names of those exempted by certificate for Michaelmas 1669, Lady Day 1670, and Michaelmas 1670. It is just possible that this roll might correct some of the deficiencies in the surviving exemption certificates from the West Riding themselves, especially as it is written in the same hand and style, and probably at the same date, as the Lady Day 1672 assessment printed in this volume. However, even in an eighteen month period there could be a considerable turnover in population, both from death and mobility, particularly at this level in society. Nevertheless the total of 902 exempted hearths returned to the Exchequer in 1672 (1.2% of the whole number) was only slightly fewer than the 978 returned in 1669–70 (1.5% of the whole).

Transcribed Certificates

The certificates chosen for publication include both manuscript certificates and those on printed forms. Whether manuscript or printed is indicated at the head of each. Spelling is as found on the document but capital letters are as in modern usage. Expansion of contractions that cannot be reproduced in print are shown in brackets. The names crossed out are thus in the original, presumably implying that their exemption was not allowed. Only in the 1672 certificate for Attercliffe are the reasons given, below p. 594.

From: E179/349 box 2
This box contains 345 Yorkshire Exemption Certificates, mostly from the West Riding, many from 1670.

No. 181 Printed
Parish of SWINTON
17 November 1671

Henr: Jackson
Wm Burnitt
Ellin Jobson
Rd: Ward
Geo Ward
Wm Auton/Anton
Tho: Smith
Rd: Whitelock
Widd. Baker
Tho: Bodey
Chr: Oliver

D. Saunears/Saundars/Samwears Rector
John Bowis churchwarden
JPs: Will Dalton, Rich: Grahme

No. 226. Manuscript
Parish of HALIFAX
10 October 1670
John Hall
John Norcliffe
Widow Nicol
Henry Podrow
Widow Jackson
Robt Davy
Widow Mawde
Matthew Wigney
John Riddihough
John Benton

'and doe further certify yt none of these persons have ever paid their Easter dues'
Ri: Hooke vic. of Halyfax
Samll Hartley, Richard Jackson churchwardens
JPs: Will: Farrer, Wm Batte

No. 227 Manuscript
Parish of HALIFAX
13 October 1670

George Story
John Stockes
Mary Bentley widow
Samuell Ward
Richard Hoile
Lawrence Watmough
William Hirst
Hugh Robinson
James Wardle
James Cockson
Robert Mitchell
Thomas Mitchell butcher

Ri: Hooke vic. of Halyfax
Samuell Hartley, Rich: Jackson churchwardens
JPs: Will: Farrer, Wm Batte

No. 228 Manuscript
Parish of Hallifax
13 October 1670
William Wraye
Richard Pacocke
Nicholas Lee
Samuel Jackson
Rolland Holdsworth
Henry Elliott
Daniel Broadley iun
Anne Farrer
Anne Croft vid
Mary Lister vid
Michael Bairstow
Mary Deane
Anne Barrocke
James Grenewod
Cuthbert Hanson

Thomas Walker
Edward Beverley
Michael Grenewod
William Midley
John Shawe
John Beverley
Mary Walker
Thomas Bairstow
Sara Rideinge
James Ewen
Nicholas Scawsby
Thomas Sattersfeild
Luke Horsfall
Mathew Wigney
Marye Pearson
John Walker
Garret Denton
John Walton
Thomas Watson
Timothy Learoid
Isaac Walton
John Robinson
Michael Bairstow
Grace Stocke
Henry Coe
Samuel Aikroid
John Butterfeild
Henry Watson
George Lister
Michael Hodgson
Willm Dixon
Anthony Newton
John Tristram
Anthony Bairstow
Isaac Clarke
Thomas Gaskin
Effan Burton
George Storye
John Whiteley
Widdow Hanson
Widdow Tayler
John Wilkinson
Richard Wilkinson
John Duckworth
Lawrence Watmough
James Coxon
James Wardle
John Whiteley
Widdow Lawson
Willm Hirst
John Wilson
John Holdsworth
John Nicholl
John Earby
Joseph Firth
John Garnet
Samuel Lister
Samuel Whiteley
Richard Ramsden
Willm Stockes
John Gleidhill
Richard Wilkinson
Widdow Woodhead
Anne Lawrence
John Hanson
Thomas Foard
Martha Turner
Elizabeth Drake
Abraham Tetlow
Ephan Gorton
John Walshaw
Nicholas Holegate
Margrett Pearson
Willm Scott
John Sutcliffe
Marye Hailey
Xpofer Clarkson
Robert Harper
Grace Thomas
Widdow Morris
John Hoyle
Richard ~~Hoyle~~ Firth
Henry Ramsden
Judith Harper
Anne Scholefeild
Vid Wood
Joseph Thicker
John Itchinge
Richard Watson
James Dickinson
George Holmes
Samuel Hilhouse
Widdow Lake
Abraham Law
Mary Sponer
Willm Newell
Thomas Firth
Timothy Stockes
Joseph Grimeshaw
Anne Hoile vid
James Crabtree
Widdow Ingham
Dinah Marshall
Wilmer Harper
Dorothy Robert
Vid Smith
Samuel Lister
George Leach
Vid Bullett
Thomas Duckworth
Sara Cooke
Sara Midgley
George Scott
George Whiteley
Willm Swifte
Willm Clough
Abraham Lelliwell
Thomas Mitchell
Vid Woodhead
Michael Greenwood
Edward Scholefeild
Mathew Wadsworth
Samuel Bowker
Thomas Chew
John Sutcliffe
Nathaniel Farnside
Joseph Walshaw
James Farrer
Mary Laughton
Willm Stocke
John Berrey
Edward Marshall
John Addison
Henry Swifte
Richard Horraby

Mary Blackburne
Mary Pellington
George Lister
Robert Horraby
Vid Hindle
Jeremy Midley
Thomas Loncaster

Ri: Hooke vic. of Halyfax
Samuel X Hartley, Richard Jackson churchwardens
JPs: Will: Farrer, Wm Batte

No. 344. Manuscript
Parish of HALIFAX
3 March 22th Charles II 1672 [sic = 1673n.s.]

A
George Armitage
Richard Askew

B
John Barbar
Ralph Bowes
John Burton
Brian Bentley
Willm Baker
Richard Bentom
Mary Bentom
John Beverley
Tho: Bairstow
Anth: Bairstow
John Brown the tinker
Henry Brommett
Mich Broadley
Dan Broadley
Widow Blackburn
Judith Benson
Ric Bairstow
Margrett Brown
Jer Bairstow
Jonas Bates
John Asden

C
Mary Coardley
John Cowburn
Henry Coor
Isaac Clark
Anne Croft
Grace Clay
James Cocks
Mary Cooper

D
Willm Dickson
Jarrett Denton
Anne Drake

E
Mary Earnshey
James Evans

F
Widd Fox
Joseph Firth
John Fisher
John Firth
Richard Firth
Elizabeth Firth
Thomas Firth
Mary Firth

G
Jarrett Goodburn
Robert Gledhill the collier
Thomas Gorston
Ephan Gorton
Mich Greenwood
Widow Gorton

H
Luke Horsfall
Ric Huntington
Widow Hoyle
Ric Horrabey
Richard Hoyle
John Hoyle
Thomas Heaton
Michaell Hodgson
John Hall
John Hanson
Willm Huett

J
Susan Johnson
John Jewett
John Jagger the butcher
Thomas Jepson junior

L
Martha Leroid
George Lister
Mary Lister
Sand Longbothom
Henry Lumm
Anne Lawrence
Judith Lambert
Sam Lister
George Leach
Isabell Longbothom
Abr Lumbe

M
Henry Mawde
Margrett Milner
Sara Midgley
Edward Milner
Thomas Mitchell
Widow Mawde

N
Mary Nicolls
Anthony Newton
Willm Nowell
Ambrose Naylor
Anthony Newton

P
George Page
John Paulden
John Pellington
David Pilling
Edward Pellington

Mary Pearson
~~Samuell Paulden~~
Margret Pearson

R
Jonathan Robertshey
Sara Riding
Richard Ramsden
Thomas Riding
Jonas Ridihough
Martha Royd

S
Samuell Slater
Isaac Stocke
Edward Smith
Ambrose Smith
Widow Mary Smith
Alice Sladen
John Shawe
George Story
Nic Sewbey
Sam Shepherd
Timothy Stocke
John Stocke
Willm Sw…?de
Tobyas Saltonstall
Martha Seed

T
Abraham Tetlawe
Jonas Turner
John Turner
Widow Tires
Widow Turner

V
George Urrin

W
Thomas Watson
Willm Wrey
Widow Watson
Henry Watson
John Walbanke
Samuell Whiteley
Anne Wilson
Gyles Whittikar
James Wardle
Widow Walker
Thomas Walker
John Walker
Richard Wilkinson
Widow Watmough
Joshua Wilson
Widow Woodhead
Widow Whittles
Dorothy Whitehead
Margrett Wardle & Mary Ottywell
John Whiteley
John Walshey

Ri: Hooke vic of Halyfax
Jno X Ingham overseer
Ralph Crosbie
John Learoyd overseer
Jonathan Oldfeild churchwarden
JPs: Will: Farrer, Wm. Batte

From E179/349 box 3
This box contains 365 Yorkshire Exemption Certificates, from the City of York and from the North and West Ridings, mostly from 1670 and 1671.

No. 78. Printed
BARNESLEY
7 Dec 1672

Ye inhabitants of ye cottages are these yt follow
Robert Shepherd
Jane Hall
Richard Willey
John Senior
William Fostard
Geo: Clugh
[6]

Thomas Clarke curat
Tho: Brownley, Thomas Heley, churchwardens
JPs: H Edmundes, J. Wentworth

From E179/350 box 2
This box contains 576 Yorkshire Exemption Certificates, from all three Ridings, mostly from 1672–4.

No. 204 Manuscript
Parish of South Kirkeby [Kirkby]
21 November 1672

~~William ?M..than~~
William Hodder
Edward Cliffe
John Beethon
Anne Barber
5 altered to 4

Tho: Peighen vicar
Richard Parkin overseare of the pore
John Marriott cherch warner
JPs: Tho: Yarburgh, Fra: Whyte

No. 205 Manuscript
Parish of SOUTH KIRKEBY [South Kirkby]
22 November 1672

William Machin 'of South Kirkby aforesaid hath a

wife and six chiuldren, being a very poore man, lives in a roome of Kirkby Hall upon the charity of Sir John Digby and others without paying any rent'

Tho: Peighen vicar
John Marriott church warden
Richard Parkin oversea[r]e of the pore
JPs: Tho: Yarburgh, Fra: Whyte

No. 222 Manuscript
RAWKCLIFFE
1 November 1672

John Browne
Wm Cocke
Uxr Coventree
John Bigley
Wm Atkinson
Edw. Taylor
Uxr Fingley
Uxr Atkinson
Edw. Aumler
Ant: Aumler
Robt Stephenson
George Eratt
Wm Cooper
Franc: Hollings
John Fleming
Robt Meggott
Thos Hutchinson

John Fenton minister
Joseph X Topliffe church-maistr, William X Martindale overseere
JPs: Jo Dawnay, Tho: Yarburgh

No. 229 Printed (see Plate 19 p. 568)
Parish of ILKLEY
11 February 1672/3

Christopher Hogge sen.
Thomas Pollard
Mary Turner

Guil: Hustler vic. ibid.[5]
Wilfred Lawson, John Brerey[6], Wiliam Homees churchwardens
JPs: Fairfax[7], W. Hauksworth

No. 236 Printed
THORNE parish
8 February 1672/3

Edw Rodwell
John Twingatte
John Sikes
Edw Casling
Geo Midlebrooke
Will Chancey
Robt Tayngate
Will Watson
John Heaton
Wido Blackeburne
Will Willbarne
John Loft
Nickls Clarke
Will West
John Hall
Will Jackeson
Tho: Bell
Simon Greene
Tho: Greene
Geo: Beatye
Will: Spinke
Wido Britton
Thos Watking
Edw Hanson
Christr Cade
Will Graves
Thos Burgis
John Sutton
Richard Cooke
Will Watson
Will Bilton
Will Bladworth
Tho Wilburne
John Eckles
Wido Midlebrooke
Richard Bedson
Thos Pooles

John Howard Minister
Eel: Canby churchwarden
JPs: John Boynton, Godf: Copley

No. 378 Manuscript
Parish of WALES
29 September 1672
Margret Calver
Robt: Fox
Robt Smith
Alice ~~Smith~~ Stace
John Hudson
John Clarke jun
Henry Walker
Gilberd Barlow
John Bradshaw
Frances Rollinson

[5] See Cambridge Alumni. Was Vicar of Ilkley 1665–1703 until his death, where he also kept school. Note that he is given as Mr Hastler in Thoresby Society vol. i (1891) p. 197.
[6] This signature is almost indecipherable he is given as Constable but not in list of those paying the Hearth Tax.
[7] Query Charles Fairfax Esq. 13 hearths at Menston.

Elizabeth Harpham
Janne Greasby
Christopher Rollinson
Francis Stacy
Isabell Willinton
Anthony Stones
John Jackson
Henry Stacy
Elizabeth More
Edward Faulden
Dorothy Faulden
Ottiwell Bawden
Henry Stacy
Nicholas Clarke jun

Willm Radcliffe minister
William Linlay, Edward Hill churchwardens
JPs: Conyers Darcy,[8] Cha: Osborne

No. 396 Printed
Sheaffeeild [Sheffield], ATTERCLIFF CUM DARNALL Constablery
30 April 1672
Godfry Bright
Thomas Soursby
Rodger Ausborne
John Johnson
Thomas Parramore
Thomas Law
Thomas Oakes
William Hoole
Richard Austike
Joseph Wallton
Howmphree Godthard
Thomas Naw
William Woodhouse
Thomas Unwin
Wid Beighton (*margin* above 20s per annum)
Wid Longley
John Godthard (*margin* 22s per annum)
George Parkin
Nicolas Smith
James Newbauld se[n]
John Stacy
Thomas Stacy
Wid Brodbent (*margin* house her owne cost 19li)
Wid Stainforth
John Stainforth
John Holland (*margin* 26s per annum)
Thomas Pearson (*margin* lyable house his owne)
Wid Parkin
Robert Steele (*margin* is lyable it is ye farme house)
William Penistone
William Ashforth
James Howmes (*margin* house his owne cost 30 li & keepes a cowe)
Wid ~~Cowper~~ Stainforth (*margin* a house devided allwaies lyable
Cuthbert Browne minist ibid
Samuel Chadwick church-warden
JPs: J ?Keresby, R[alph] Knight

From E179/350 Box 3
This box contains 416 Yorkshire Exemption Certificates, from the City of York and all three Ridings, mostly from 1671 and 1672.

No. 275 Manuscript
WORSBROUGH in the parish of Darfeilde
9 December 1672

John Turton
John Woodhead
William Mellard
Thomas Shaw
John Tottington

Tho: Woodfen Lectr
Robert Tottington, Edward Rock churchwardens
JPs: H Edmunds, J. Wentworth

No. 322 Printed

Parish of ACOMBE
15 October 1672

George Jilburne
John Chapman
Richard Shipton
Alice Chapman widdow
Peter Jibbe poore folkes all

John Bowcocke minister
Robert Sceedkocke, Richard Boumforth churchwardense alias Guardians of Acombe
JPs: [Geo. Manck]lins[9] [Tho: Bautr]y

Written on the dorse: 'Remembr Richd Tilburne'

No. 324 Printed
TADCASTER
16 October 1672

Antho: Wise
Mary Langton widdow

[8] *Justices of the Peace 1642–1700,* Yorkshire West Riding Conyers Dracy Esq., Jan 1670/1 C231/7 page 384.
[9] *Register of the Freemen of the City of York* Vol II 1559–1759 (1900) p. 130 Mayor 1665. [other references not noted].

Thomas Croft Officiall ibid:
Nicholas Pennington
JPs: Hen: Thomson,[10] Geo: Lamplugh[11]

No. 325 Printed
RUFFORTH
27 March 1672

Names of the poore
George Cowpland
John Catterton
Robte Smyth
Anne Richison
Alice Johnson vid

John Bowcocke minister
Henry X Cartwright, John X Wilson churchwardens
JPs: Hen: Tireman[12], Willm Richardson

No. 327 Manuscript
Hoton Wainsley alias Marston [HUTTON WANDESLEY]
7 October 1672

Thomas Vary
Robert Bootland
Elizabeth Bentley
Mary Acome widdow
John Wright the elder all receive relief out of the poor mans boxe

We also certifie the same concerninge [the following whose rents under £1 and do not receive relief]
Jane Bashlour
An Abbey
An Shau
Jane Cartwright
John Wright the younger

F Micklethwait
John X Fawcit, John Wheatlay, John Acom
JPs: Geo: Mancklins, Tho: Williamson

No. 333 Printed
Parish of ACOMBE
20 December ~~16720~~ 1671

Richard Shipton
Alice Chapman wid.
John Chapman

George Jibburne
Peeter Jibb all poore people
John Bowcocke minister[13]
William Mealbye, George Kilbanke
JPs: Willm Richardson maior, Hen: Tireman

No 335 Printed
Parish of ACOMBE
1 March ~~1670~~ 1671

Alice Rogison
John Bowcocke minister
Thomas Darwen
George X Gilbancke, William Mealbye churchwardens
JPs: William Richardson maior, Hen: Tireman

No 336. Manuscript
[EAST TADCASTER]
"To the right honorble the Lord Maior of the Citty of Yorke
Att the request of the bearrer hearof Anthony Wisse of the East Part of Tadcaster for certefying the true vallue of what he farmeth: we do humbly certefy that he is a poore man and that the poore cottadge he lives in which is all that ever he farmes in all the world is but six shillings eight pence per annum: and being of lait charged with the duty of Harth mony: contrary to the Actt in that behalph he humbly beggs your lordships best help and assistance for acquitinge him heareof and he will as in duty bound ever to pray for you: to the truth hearof we set to our hands this sixth of Decemr 71

10 *Register of the Freemen of the City of York* Vol II 1559–1759 (1900) p. 126 Henry Thompson Mayor 1662 [other references not noted].
11 *Register of the Freemen of the City of York* Vol II 1559–1759 (1900) p. 125 Mayor 1661 [other references not noted].
12 *Register of the Freemen of the City of York* Vol II 1559–1759 (1900) p. 133 Mayor 1667 [other references not noted].
13 *Cambridge Alumni*: Adm. pens. at CLARE, Apr. 3, 1658. B. in London. ' Matric. 1658; B.A. 1661.

Thomas Croft officiall ibid:
(signatures) John Lovell, Robt Morley, John Adcocke church warden, John Ryther church warden, Tho: Gelsthorpe

Wee doe beleeve the person abovesaid to be incapable of paying hearth money and therefore recomend him to be discharged thereof
Willm Richardson maior, Tho: Bautry

No 337. Manuscript
[EAST TADCASTER]
"To the right honorble the Lord Maior of the Citty of Yorke
We whose names are hear subscribed out of bowell of compassion in the behalph of one widdow Langton within that part of Tadcaster within your lordships libertee being a verry poore woman having eight small children: seaven whearof not caipable of releveing themselves: but laime and distempered in boddy so that we are forst to releve them by a weekly allowance out of the poore mans box: yet not with standing the Act for payment of harth mony do acquitt such from paying: yet of laitt in her husbands time the collectors forst him to pay allthough the cottadge she lives in is but eight shillings yearly rent and being all that ever she farmes in all the world: we humblybegg in her behalph: for she is not able to came her selfe that your lordship would be graiously pleased to afford her your helpe in obtaing the bennifitt of the Actt and she will be ever bound in duty to pray for you; to the truth hearof we set to our hands this 6th of Decmr 71

Thomas Croft officiall ibid:[14]
(signatures) Robt Morley, John Lovell, John Adcocke churchwarden, John Ryther church warden, Tho: Gelsthorpe
Wee doe beleeve the person abovesaid not liable to pay hearth money
Willm Richardson maior, Geo: Lamplugh

No. 340 Manuscript
[EAST TADCASTER]
"To the right honorble the Lord Maior of the City of Yorke
"May it please youre lordship the bearer hearof John Howden of that p[ar]t of Tadcaster within your lordships libbertee ... he has of laite beene distrest upon by the collector for that use: ... 6th of Decemr 1671

Thomas Croft officiall ibid:
(signatures) John Lovell, Robt Morley, John Adcocke church warden, John Ryther church warden, Tho: Gelsthorpe
Wee doe beleeve the person abovesaid not liable to pay hearth money
Willlm Richardson maior, Tho: Bautry

No 341 Manuscript
Hoton Wainsley alias Marston [HUTTON WANDESLEY]
23 October 1671

Thomas Vary
Robert Bootland
Ann Shaw
Elizabeth Bentley
Mary Acome widdow
Laurence Smith

[14] *Cambridge Alumni*: Adm. pens. at JESUS, June 18, 1664. Of Leeds, Yorks. S. of James. ' Matric. 1664; Scholar, 1667; B.A. 1667–8; M.A. 1671. Ord. deacon (Ely) Sept. 24, 1670. R. of Broughton, Lincs. Died 1693. Father of Thomas (1684). (Burke, L.G.)

John Wright the elder all receive relief

also Jane Baslour
Jane Cartwright
An Abbey
An Shaw
John Wright the younger and Edward Wood last two do not receive relief
E. Micklethwait rector[15]
John Williamson John X Shaun Jo: Taylor
JPs: Cressy Burnett, Willm Richardson maior

No. 342 Printed
RUFFORTH
2 Aprill 1671

George Coupland
John Catterton
Robte Smith
Anne Richison widdow
Alice Johnson widdow

John Bowcocke minister
Quintin Clay, Thomas X Kidson churchwardens
JPs: William Richardson maior, George Lamplugh

No. 344 Manuscript
[RAWCLIFFE]
1671

Ux Bigley
Tho. Maples
Nic: Colterd
Mar. Hollings
Wm. Speighte
Jam. Bancks
Jo. Ambler
ux. Margison junr
Tho. Crocker
Wm. Cocke
Bry: Arsdall
Wm. Cooper
Fra. Hollings
Jo. Fleeman
Ux Hembrough
Ux Towtan
Fr. Balmforth
Rog. Pickhaver
Wm Fearne
Ant. Bowland
Jo. Lightefoote
Wm Hodgson
Tho. Hutcheson
Geo. Walker
Rob. Stephenson
Geo. Sutton
Jo. Cocke
Ux. Nixon
Jo. Woodhouse
Wm. Hollings
Susan Ambler
Tho. Reedness
Hen. Pinder
Edw. Eratt
Wm. Martindall
Eliz. Harte
Tho. White
Sarah Taylor
Tho. Acklam
Samson Mangall
Ux. Wilson
Rob. Megott
Rob. Bigley
Han. Harte
Chr. Jenson
Wm. Rusholme
Uxr Coventree
Geo. Jackson
Tho. Pickhaver
Thos Newse
Uxr Hall
Rich. Newse
". . . the persons above named and every of them with divers other beggars in our town are exempted from usuall taxes . . ."

Patrick Jacks[on] minister
Will Knipe, Javis Granger, Robert Crabtre & Francis Leavens churchwardens

Allowed by Jo Hawnay Thomas Harburgh

No. 372 Manuscript
Chapelry of WORSBROUGH in the parish of Darfeilde
2 November 1671

John Turton
Michaell Leich
Izabell Lee
~~?Sander Casson~~
John Hawksworth
Thomas Moor
Edward Cutt
Alexander Casson

15 *Cambridge Alumni*: Adm. pens. (age 17) at SIDNEY, Nov. 23, 1642. S. of Mark (1613), R. of Marston, Yorks. Bapt. there, Feb. 14, 1625–6. Schools, York and Coxwold (Mr Wm. Smelt). B.A. 1646; M.A. 1650. R. of Marston; Preb. of York, 1670–81. Married Margaret, dau. of Thomas Levens, of Rusholme, Yorks. Died Jan. 28, 1681–2. Buried at Marston. Father of the next and of Mark (1669). (Vis. of Yorks., 1666; Foster, Yorks. Pedigrees.)

Francis Secker
William Moorhouse
Thomas Cudworth
Sarah Hampton widow
John Marshall
Margarett Tottington widdow
Richard Eatton
~~William ?Neale~~
Mathew Smitjh
John Woodheade
Ann Roydes widow
~~Thomas Wood~~
Elizabeth Hawksworth widow
William Longley
Danyell Oates
Thomas Fisher
William Meller
John Tottinton

Dorse: Stainecrosse certificates added pro 1671 Exr per J Moore Memorand' these certificates are over and above those for ye 3 halfe yeares ended at Lady day 1670 those being the same for this yeare and these are added

Tho: Woodfen Lectr
Richard Wildsmith and Jonathan Reanar churchwardens
JPs: H Edmunds, J Wentworth

ABBREVIATIONS

Borthwick	Borthwick Institute for Archives, University of York
BL	British Library, London
HMSO	Her Majesty's Stationery Office, London
RCHME	Royal Commission on the Historical Monuments of England
TNA	The National Archives
WMDL	Wakefield Metropolitan District Library, Wakefield
WYA	West Yorkshire Archives, Wakefield

BIBLIOGRAPHY

Manuscript sources

Documents listed in Appendix II Surviving West Riding Hearth Tax Documents and Table 5 in Appendix III Exemption Certificates, are not repeated here. Other National Archive documents consulted have been.

BL, Lansdowne MS, 898

Borthwick, inventories of Daniel Thorpe, Sharlston, and John Hanson, Warley, Pontefract Deanery, December 1693, August 1693

Borthwick, inventory of Michael Graggs, Knottingley, Pontefract Deanery, June 1693

Borthwick, inventory of Ralph Roades, Thornhill, Pontefract Deanery, May 1689

Borthwick, R.VI.E.2

Borthwick, inventory of Thomas Brook, Edderscliffe, Liversedge, Pontefract Deanery, May1693

Borthwick, inventory of Timothy Sutcliffe, Northowram, Pontefract Deanery, June 1689

Lichfield Joint Record Office, Archdeaconry of Derby, wills and inventories

Sheffield Archives, ACM S60

TNA, C5/448/19

TNA, E179/210/400

TNA, E 179/210/412
TNA, E179/210/413
TNA, E179/210/415
TNA, E 179/210/417
TNA, E179/210/418
TNA, E179/262/13
TNA, E179/262/14
TNA, E179/262/15
TNA, E179/349/322
TNA, E179/350/78
TNA, E179/350/205
TNA, E179/350/264
TNA, E179/350/325
TNA, E179/350/327
TNA, E179/350/336
TNA, E179/350/337
TNA, E179/350/372
TNA, E179/350/394
TNA, E179/350/2/292
TNA, E179/350/3/344
TNA, E179/354/4
TNA, E179/359
TNA, E179/3544
TNA PC2/59
TNA, WO 30/48

WMDL, Wakefield Hearth Tax Return for 1672

WYA, quarter sessions records

Printed primary sources

An Exact and Perfect Survey and View of the Manor of Sheffield, with other Lands, by John Harrison, 1637, ed. J.G. Ronksley, 1908 (Sheffield)

Britain, or, a Chorographicall Description of the most flourishing Kingdomes, England, Scotland, and Ireland … Written first in Latine by W. Camden … translated newly into English by Philemon Holland … Finally revised, amended, and enlarged with sundry additions, ed. W. Camden, 1610 (London)

Britain, or A chorographicall description of the most flourishing kingdomes, England, Scotland, and Ireland, and the Islands adjoyning, out of the depth of antiquitie: beautified with mappes of the severall shires of England, ed. W. Camden 1637 (London)

Ogilby, J., *Britannia, or an Illustration of the Kingdom of England and Dominion of Wales*, 1675 (London), Facsimile Reprint, 1939 (London)

Britannia depicta: or, Ogilby improved, 1st ed., 1720 (London, Tho. Bowles), Facsimile reprint, 1970 (Newcastle upon Tyne)

Calendar of State Papers: Domestic Series, Charles II, 1660–1685, 28 vols., 1860–1947 (HMSO, London)

Calendar of State Papers Domestic, 1687–9, 1972 (HMSO, London)

Calendar of Treasury Books, 1660–1718, prepared by W.A. Shaw, 1904–57 (HMSO, London)

Davenant, Charles, 1695, *Essay after the Ways and Means of Supplying the War* (London)

Defoe, D., *A Tour through the Whole Island of Great Britain*, 1724–7 (London), numerous reprints.

Fuller's Worthies: Selected from The Worthies of England by Thomas Fuller, ed. R. Barber, 1987 (London)

Houghton, John, 1693, *An Account of the Acres and Houses with The Proportional Tax, etc., of Each County in England and Wales* (London)

Samuel Buck's Yorkshire Sketchbook: reproduced in facsimile from Lansdowne MS 914 in the British Library, with an introduction by Ivan Hall, 1979 (Wakefield)

The Compton Census of 1676: A Critical Edition, ed. A. Whiteman, British Academy, Records of Social and Economic History, N.S. 10, 1986 (London)

The Hearth Tax Returns for South Yorkshire, Lady Day 1672, ed. D. Hey, 1991 (Division of Continuing Education, University of Sheffield)

The Hearth Tax List for the West Riding of Yorkshire 1672 Lady Day, ed. J. Hebden, 1990–4 (Ripon Historical Society and Ripon, Harrogate and District Family History Group, Ripon)

'Return of the Hearth Tax for the Wapentake of Skyrack, 1672', ed. J. Stansfield, Thoresby Society, *Miscellanea*, vol 2, part 3, 1891, 180–204 and vol 4, part 1, 1892, 17–36

The Illustrated Journeys of Celia Fiennes, c.1682–c.1712, ed. C. Morris, 1984 (London)

The Memoirs of Sir John Reresby, ed. A. Browning, 1936 (Glasgow)

Secondary sources

Alcock, N. W., 1993, *People at Home: Living in a Warwickshire Village 1500–1800* (Chichester)

Ambler, L., 1913, *The Old Halls and Manor Houses of Yorkshire* (London)

Arkell, T., 'Printed instructions for administering the hearth tax' in K. Schürer and T. Arkell, eds, *Surveying the People: the interpretation and use of document sources for the study of population in the later seventeenth century* (Oxford, 1992), 38–64

Arkell, T., 2003, 'Identifying Regional Variations from the Hearth Tax', *The Local Historian* 33, 148–74

Ashurst, D., n.d., *The History of South Yorkshire Glass* (Department of Archaeology & Prehistory, University of Sheffield)

Baildon, W. P., 1913, *Baildon and the Baildons*, 3 vols, privately printed

Barnwell, P. S., 2006, 'Houses, Hearths and Historical Inquiry', in Barnwell and Airs, eds, *Houses and the Hearth Tax*, 177–83

Barnwell, P.S., and M. Airs, eds, 2006, *Houses and the Hearth tax: the later Stuart house and society*, Council for British Archaeology Research Report 150

Beresford, M. W., 1988, 'East End, West End: the face of Leeds during urbanisation 1684–1842' *Publications of the Thoresby Society*, 50–1 (nos. 131–2)

Binfield, C., and D. Hey, eds, 1997, *Mesters to Masters: A History of the Company of Cutlers in Hallamshire* (Oxford)

Braddick, M. J., 1994, *Parliamentary Taxation in Seventeenth-Century England* (Woodbridge)

Buckatzsch, E. J., 1950, 'Places of Origin of a Group of Immigrants into Sheffield, 1625–1799', *Economic History Review*, 2nd ser., 2, 303–6

Cameron, K., 1996, *English Place-Names* (London)

Chandaman, C. D., 1975, *The English Public Revenue 1660–1688* (Oxford)

Cliffe, J. T., 1969, *The Yorkshire Gentry from the Reformation to the Civil War* (London)

Cooper, N., 1999, *The Houses of the Gentry 1400–1680* (New Haven & London)

Duckham, B.F., 1967, *The Yorkshire Ouse: The History of a River Navigation* (Newton Abbot)

Fraser D., 1980, ed., *A History of Modern Leeds* (Manchester)

Giles, C., 1986, *Rural houses of West Yorkshire, 1400–1830*, Royal Commission on Historical Monuments (England) Supplementary series, 8 (HMSO, London)

Giles, C., 'The West Riding Hearth tax Returns of 1672: what do they tell us about the Great Rebuilding?', in Barnwell and Airs, eds, *Houses and the Hearth Tax*, 132–43

Girouard, M., 1983, *Robert Smythson and The Elizabethan Country House* (New Haven & London)

Glass, D.B. and Eversley, D.E.C. eds, 1965, *Population and History* (London)

Hargreaves, J., 1999, *Halifax* (Lancaster)

Harvey, J., 1975, *York* (London)

Heaton, H., 1965, *The Yorkshire Woollen and Worsted Industries from the Earliest Times up to the Industrial Revolution* (Oxford, 2nd edn)

Hey, D., 1973, 'The Pattern of Nonconformity in South Yorkshire, 1660–1851', *Northern History* 8, 86–119

Hey, D., 1984, 'Yorkshire and Lancashire' in *The Agrarian History of England and Wales, V:I*, ed. Thirsk, 59–88

Hey, D., 1991, *The Fiery Blades of Hallamshire: Sheffield and its neighbourhood, 1660–1740* (Leicester)

Hey, D., 2005, 'The South Yorkshire Steel Industry and the Industrial Revolution', *Northern History* 42, 91–6

Hey, D., and G. Redmonds, 2002, *Yorkshire Surnames and the Hearth Tax Returns of 1672–73,* University of York Borthwick Paper 102

Hoskins, W. G., 1953, 'The Rebuilding of Rural England 1570–1640', *Past and Present,* 4, 44–59

Hudson, P., 1986, *The Genesis of Industrial Capital: a Study of the West Riding Wool Textile Industry, c.1750–1850.* Cambridge University Press

Linstrum, D., 1978, *West Yorkshire, Architects and Architecture* (London)

Marshall, L. M., 1936, 'The Levying of the Hearth Tax', *English Historical Review,* 51, 628–646

Moorhouse, S. A., 1981, 'Communications', in M. I. Faull and S. A. Moorhouse, eds, *West Yorkshire: an Archaeological Survey to A D 1500, Volume 3 The Rural Medieval Landscape* (Wakefield)

Meekings, C. A. F., 1962, *The Hearth Tax 1662–89: Exhibition of Records*, Public Record Office (London)

Meekings, C.A.F., 1979, *Analysis of Hearth Tax Accounts 1662–1665,* List and Index Society, 153 (London)

Meekings, C.A.F., 1980, *Analysis of Hearth Tax Accounts 1666–1689,* List and Index Society, 163 (London),

Murray, H., 1997, *Scarborough, York and Leeds: the Town Plans of John Cossins 1697–1743* (York)

Overton, M., *et al,* 2004, *Production and Consumption in English Households 1600–1750* (London)

Parkinson, E., 2006, 'Understanding the Hearth Tax Returns, Historical and Interpretative Problems' in Barnwell and Airs, eds, *Houses and the Hearth Tax,* 7–17

Palliser, D. M., 1979, *Tudor York* (Oxford)

Pickles, M. F., 1996, 'Labour migration: Yorkshire, c. 1670–1743', *Local Population Studies,* 57, 29–49

Purdy, J. D., 1991, *Yorkshire Hearth Tax Returns,* Centre for Regional and Local History, University of Hull, Studies in Regional and Local History 7 (Hull)

Redmonds, G., *The Making of Huddersfield* (Barnsley, 2003)

Roebuck, P., 1980, *Yorkshire Baronets 1640–1760: Families, Estates and Fortunes* (Oxford)

RCHME, 1972, *An Inventory of the Historical Monuments in the City of York: Vol III, South-West of the Ouse,* HMSO (London)

RCHME, 1981, *An Inventory of the Historical Monuments in the City of York: Vol V, The Central Area,* HMSO (London)

RCHME, 1986, *Rural Houses of West Yorkshire 1400–1830,* HMSO (London)

Schürer, K., and T. Arkell, eds, 1992, *Surveying the people: the interpretation and use of document sources for the study of population in the later seventeenth century* (Oxford)

Shaw-Taylor, Leigh, 2005, 'Family farms and capitalist farms in mid nineteenth century England' *Agricultural History Review,* 53, 158–91

Sheeran, G., 1998, *Medieval Yorkshire Towns: People, Buildings and Spaces* (Edinburgh)

Smith, D. E., 1980, 'Otley: a study of a market town during the late seventeenth and eighteenth centuries', *Yorkshire Archaeological Journal*, 52, 153–6

Smith, R.B., 1970, *Land and Politics in the England of Henry VIII: The West Riding of Yorkshire, 1530–1546* (Oxford)

Spufford, M., 1962, 'The Significance of the Cambridgeshire Hearth Tax', *Proceedings of the Cambridge Antiquarian Society*, 55, 53–64

Spufford, M., 2000, 'The scope of Local History, and the potential of the Hearth Tax Returns', *The Local Historian*, 30, 202–221 [The 2000 Phillimore Lecture reprinted separately as *The Potential of the Hearth Tax*, 2000].

Spufford, M., 2006,'Chimneys, Wood and Coal', in Barnwell and Airs, eds, *Houses and the Hearth Tax*, 22–32

Thirsk, J., ed., 1967, *The Agrarian History of England and Wales, IV: 1540–1640* (Cambridge)

Thirsk, J., ed., 1984, *The Agrarian History of England and Wales, V:I: 1640–1750* (Cambridge)

Weatherill, L., 1997, *Consumer Behaviour and Material Culture in Britain 1660–1760* (London, 2nd edn)

Wrightson, K., 2002, *Earthly Necessities: Economic Lives in Early Modern Britain 1470–1750* (London, 2nd edn)

Wrigley, E.A. and Schofield, R.S., 1981, *The Population History of England 1541–1871* (London)

Unpublished doctoral dissertations

Ashurst, D., 'Worsbrough: Change and Continuity in the Society, Economy and Buildings of a South Yorkshire Township, 1600–1851' (University of Sheffield, 1994)

Parkinson, E., 'The Administration of the Hearth Tax, 1662–1666' (University of Surrey Roehampton, 2001). Revised version in preparation for publication by List and Index Society, 2008.

Unwin, M. J., 'The Hallamshire Cutlery Trades in the late seventeenth century: a study of the hearth tax returns and the records of the Cutlers' Company' (University of Sheffield, 2002)

Electronic sources

<www.nationalarchives.gov.uk/E179/>

Personal Name Index

Please note. We have NOT, in this index, run together variant spellings of the same surname, because of the danger of making false assumptions. Murgatroyds, for instance, are spelled Murgatroide, Murgetroyd, Murgotroyd. Although close together, they are not combined, and the seeker has to look for them. Other names are not necessarily close together alphabetically, and therefore demand more labour, Sykes and Sikes are a long way apart, as are Holdsworth and Houldsworth. Furbisher, Frubisher and Frobisher also demand a hunt, so the family historian needs to have a vivid orthographic imagination. Christian names, however, have generally been modernised and extended. Names of modern persons have not been indexed.

G

I

J

K

L

M

N

P

T

Y

Place Name Index

Subject Index

Key to Map of Townships on End Paper

NUMBER	TOWNSHIP	WAPENTAKE
1	Aberford	Skyrack
2	Acaster Malbis	Ainsty
3	Acaster Selby	Ainsty
4	Ackton	Osgoldcross
5	Ackworth	Osgoldcross
6	Acomb	Ainsty
7	Addingham	Staincliffe
8	Adel cum Eccup	Skyrack
9	Adlingfleet	Osgoldcross
10	Adwick le Street	Lower Strafforth
11	Adwick upon Dearne	Lower Strafforth
12	Airmyn	Osgoldcross
13	Airton	Staincliffe
14	Aismunderby with Bondgate	Claro
15	Aldborough	Claro
16	Aldfield	Claro
17	Aldwark	Upper Strafforth
18	Allerton and Wilsden	Morley
19	Allerton Bywater	Skyrack
20	Allerton Mauleverer with Flaxby	Claro
21	Almondbury	Agbrigg
22	Altofts	Agbrigg
23	Alwoodley	Skyrack
24	Angram and Hutton	Ainsty
25	Anston	Strafforth & Tickhill
26	Appleton Roebuck	Ainsty
27	Appletreewick	Staincliffe
28	Ardsley	Staincross
29	Arkendale	Claro
30	Armley	Morley
31	Armthorpe	Lower Strafforth
32	Arncliffe	Staincliffe
33	Arthington	Skyrack
34	Askham Bryan	Ainsty
35	Askham Richard	Ainsty
36	Askwith	Claro
37	Aston with Aughton	Upper Strafforth
38	Attercliffe with Darnall	Upper Strafforth
39	Aukley	Lower Strafforth
40	Austerfield	Lower Strafforth
41	Austhorpe	Skyrack
42	Austwick	Ewcross
43	Azerley	Claro
44	Baildon	Skyrack
45	Balby with Hexthorpe	Lower Strafforth
46	Balne	Osgoldcross
47	Bank Newton	Staincliffe
48	Barden	Staincliffe
49	Bardsey cum Rigton	Skyrack

NUMBER	TOWNSHIP	WAPENTAKE
50	Barkisland	Morley
51	Barkston	Barkston Ash
52	Barlow	Barkston Ash
53	Barnbrough	Lower Strafforth
54	Barnby upon Dun	Lower Strafforth
55	Barnoldswick	Staincliffe
56	Barnsley	Staincross
57	Barugh	Staincross
58	Barwick	Skyrack
59	Bashall Eaves	Staincliffe
60	Batley	Agbrigg
61	Bawtry	Lower Strafforth
62	Beal	Osgoldcross
63	Beamsley	Claro
64	Beeston	Morley
65	Bentham	Ewcross
66	Bentley with Arksey	Lower Strafforth
67	Bewerley	Claro
68	Bickerton	Ainsty
69	Bilbrough	Ainsty
70	Bilham	Lower Strafforth
71	Billingley	Lower Strafforth
72	Bilton	Ainsty
73	Bingley	Skyrack
74	Birkin	Barkston Ash
75	Birstwith	Claro
76	Bishop Monkton	Claro
77	Bishop Thornton	Claro
78	Bishopside	Claro
79	Bishopthorpe	Ainsty
80	Bishopton with Clotherholme	Claro
81	Blaxton	Lower Strafforth
82	Blubberhouse	Claro
83	Bolton	Morley
84	Bolton by Bowland	Staincliffe
85	Bolton Percy	Ainsty
86	Bolton upon Dearne	Lower Strafforth
87	Boroughbridge	Claro
88	Bowland Forest	Staincliffe
89	Bowling	Morley
90	Bracewell	Staincliffe
91	Bradfield	Upper Strafforth
92	Bradfield Stannington	Upper Strafforth
93	Bradfield Waldershelf	Upper Strafforth
94	Bradfield Westnall	Upper Strafforth
95	Bradford	Morley
96	Bradford West	Staincliffe
97	Bradley	Staincliffe
98	Braithwell	Upper Strafforth
99	Bramham	Barkston Ash
100	Bramhope	Skyrack
101	Bramley	Upper Strafforth
101	Bramley	Morley
103	Brampton on le Morthen	Upper Strafforth

NUMBER	TOWNSHIP	WAPENTAKE
104	Brayton	Barkston Ash
105	Brearton	Claro
106	Bridge Hewick	Claro
107	Brierley	Staincross
108	Brightside Bierlow	Upper Strafforth
109	Brinsworth	Upper Strafforth
110	Brodsworth with Pickburn	Lower Strafforth
111	Brampton Bierlow	Upper Strafforth
112	Brotherton	Barkston Ash
113	Broughton	Staincliffe
114	Buckden	Staincliffe
115	Burghwallis	Osgoldcross
116	Burley in Wharfedale	Skyrack
117	Burn	Barkston Ash
118	Burnsall	Staincliffe
119	Burton in Lonsdale	Ewcross
120	Burton Leonard	Claro
121	Burton Salmon	Barkston Ash
122	Byron with Pool	Barkston Ash
123	Cadeby	Lower Strafforth
124	Calton	Staincliffe
125	Calverly cum Farsley	Morley
126	Camblesforth	Barkston Ash
127	Campsall	Osgoldcross
128	Cantley	Lower Strafforth
129	Carleton	Barkston Ash
129	Carleton	Staincliffe
131	Carlton	Staincross
131	Carlton	Skyrack
133	Castleford	Osgoldcross
134	Castley	Claro
135	Cattal	Claro
136	Catterton	Ainsty
137	Cawood	Barkston Ash
138	Cawthorne	Staincross
139	Chapel Allerton	Skyrack
140	Chapel Haddlesey	Barkston Ash
141	Chevet	Staincross
142	Church Fenton	Barkston Ash
143	Churwell	Morley
144	Clapham and Newby	Ewcross
145	Clayton	Morley
146	Clayton West	Staincross
147	Clayton with Frickley	Lower Strafforth
148	Cleckheaton	Morley
149	Clifford	Barkston Ash
150	Clifton cum Hartshead	Morley
151	Clifton with Norwood	Claro
152	Clint	Claro
153	Collingham	Skyrack
154	Colton	Ainsty
155	Coneythorpe	Claro
156	Conisbrough	Upper Strafforth
157	Coniston Cold	Staincliffe

NUMBER	TOWNSHIP	WAPENTAKE
158	Conistone	Staincliffe
159	Copgrove	Claro
160	Copmanthorpe	Ainsty
161	Copt Hewick	Claro
162	Cowick	Osgoldcross
163	Cowling	Staincliffe
164	Cowthorpe	Claro
165	Cracoe	Staincliffe
166	Cridling Stubbs	Osgoldcross
167	Crigglestone	Agbrigg
168	Crofton	Agbrigg
169	Cudworth	Staincross
170	Cumberworth	Staincross
171	Cumberworth half	Agbrigg
172	Dacre	Claro
173	Dalton	Upper Strafforth
173	Dalton	Agbrigg
175	Darfield	Lower Strafforth
176	Darrington	Osgoldcross
177	Darton	Staincross
178	Denaby	Upper Strafforth
179	Denby	Staincross
180	Dent	Ewcross
181	Denton	Claro
182	Dewsbury	Agbrigg
183	Dikes Marsh	Lower Strafforth
184	Dinnington	Upper Strafforth
185	Dodworth	Staincross
186	Doncaster	Lower Strafforth
187	Draughton	Staincliffe
188	Drax with Newland	Barkston Ash
189	Drighlington and Adwalton	Morley
190	Dringhouses	Ainsty
191	Dunkeswick	Claro
192	Dunsforth	Claro
193	Easington	Staincliffe
194	East Ardsley	Agbrigg
195	East Keswick	Skyrack
196	Ecclesall Bierlow	Upper Strafforth
197	Ecclesfield	Upper Strafforth
198	Eccleshill	Morley
199	Edlington	Upper Strafforth
200	Eggborough	Osgoldcross
201	Elland with Greetland	Morley
202	Embsay	Staincliffe
203	Emley	Agbrigg
204	Erringden	Morley
205	Eshton	Staincliffe
206	Fairburn	Barkston Ash
207	Farnham	Claro
208	Farnhill with Cononly	Staincliffe
209	Farnley	Morley
209	Farnley	Claro
211	Farnley Tyas	Agbrigg

NUMBER	TOWNSHIP	WAPENTAKE
212	Featherstone	Osgoldcross
213	Felliscliffe	Claro
214	Fenwick	Osgoldcross
215	Ferrensby	Claro
216	Ferry Fryston and Ferrybridge	Osgoldcross
217	Fewston and Timble	Claro
218	Firbeck	Upper Strafforth
219	Fishlake	Lower Strafforth
220	Flasby with Winterburn	Staincliffe
221	Flockton	Agbrigg
222	Fockerby	Osgoldcross
223	Follifoot	Claro
224	Fountains Abbey	Claro
225	Fountains Earth	Claro
226	Garforth	Skyrack
227	Gargrave	Staincliffe
228	Gateforth	Barkston Ash
229	Giggleswick	Staincliffe
230	Gildersome	Morley
231	Gildingwells and Woodsetts	Upper Strafforth
232	Gisburn	Staincliffe
233	Gisburn Forest	Staincliffe
234	Givendale	Claro
235	Glass Houghton	Osgoldcross
236	Glusburn	Staincliffe
237	Golcar	Agbrigg
238	Goldsborough	Claro
239	Gomershall	Morley
240	Goole	Osgoldcross
241	Gowdall	Osgoldcross
242	Grantley	Claro
243	Grassington	Staincliffe
244	Greasbrough	Upper Strafforth
245	Great Houghton	Lower Strafforth
246	Great Ouseburn	Claro
247	Great Ribston with Walshford	Claro
248	Green Hammerton	Claro
249	Grewelthorpe	Claro
250	Grimston	Barkston Ash
251	Grindleton	Staincliffe
252	Guiseley	Skyrack
253	Gunthwaite	Staincross
254	Haldenby and Eastoft	Osgoldcross
255	Halifax	Morley
256	Halton East	Staincliffe
257	Halton West	Staincliffe
258	Hambleton	Barkston Ash
259	Hampole with Stubbs	Lower Strafforth
260	Hampsthwaite	Claro
261	Handsworth	Upper Strafforth
262	Hanlith	Staincliffe
263	Harewood	Skyrack
264	Harrogate	Claro
265	Harthill with Woodhall	Upper Strafforth

NUMBER	TOWNSHIP	WAPENTAKE
266	Hartlington	Staincliffe
267	Hartwith cum Winsley	Claro
268	Hatfield and Hatfield Woodhouse	Lower Strafforth
269	Haveram Park E.P.	Claro
270	Havercroft	Staincross
271	Hawkswick	Staincliffe
272	Hawksworth	Skyrack
273	Haworth	Morley
274	Headingley and Burley	Skyrack
275	Healaugh	Ainsty
276	Heaton with Clayton	Morley
277	Hebden	Staincliffe
278	Heck	Osgoldcross
279	Heckmondwike	Morley
280	Hellifield	Staincliffe
281	Hemsworth	Staincross
282	Hensall	Osgoldcross
283	Heptonstall	Morley
284	Hessay	Ainsty
285	Hetton with Bordley	Staincliffe
286	Hickleton	Lower Strafforth
287	High Hoyland	Staincross
288	High Melton	Lower Strafforth
289	Hillam	Barkston Ash
290	Hipperholme with Brighouse	Morley
291	Hirst Courtney	Barkston Ash
292	Holbeck	Morley
293	Holgate	Ainsty
294	Holm	Agbrigg
295	Honley	Agbrigg
296	Hook	Osgoldcross
297	Hooton Pagnell	Lower Strafforth
298	Hooton Roberts	Upper Strafforth
299	Horbury	Agbrigg
300	Horsforth	Skyrack
301	Horton	Staincliffe
301	Horton	Morley
303	Horton in Ribblesdale	Ewcross
304	Hoyland	Strafforth & Tickhill
305	Hoyland Swaine	Staincross
306	Huddersfield	Agbrigg
307	Huddleston cum Lumby	Barkston Ash
308	Humberton cum Milby	Claro
309	Hunshelf	Staincross
310	Hunsingore	Claro
311	Hunslet	Morley
312	Hunsworth	Morley
313	Idle	Morley
314	Ilkley	Skyrack
315	Ingbirchworth	Staincross
316	Ingerthorpe	Claro
317	Ingleton	Ewcross
318	Keighley	Staincliffe
319	Kellington	Osgoldcross

NUMBER	TOWNSHIP	WAPENTAKE
320	Kettlewell	Staincliffe
321	Kexbrough	Staincross
322	Kildwick	Staincliffe
323	Killinghall	Claro
324	Kimberworth	Upper Strafforth
325	Kippax	Skyrack
326	Kirby Hall	Claro
327	Kirk Bramwith	Osgoldcross
328	Kirk Deighton	Claro
329	Kirk Hammerton	Claro
330	Kirk Sandal	Lower Strafforth
331	Kirk Smeaton	Osgoldcross
332	Kirkburton	Agbrigg
333	Kirkby Malham	Staincliffe
334	Kirkby Malzeard	Claro
335	Kirkby Overblow	Claro
336	Kirkby Wharfe	Barkston Ash
337	Kirkby with Netherby	Claro
338	Kirkheaton	Agbrigg
339	Knapton	Ainsty
340	Knaresborough	Claro
341	Knaresborough Tendergate	Claro
342	Knottingley	Osgoldcross
343	Langcliffe	Staincliffe
344	Langfield	Morley
345	Langsett	Staincross
346	Laughton en le Morthen	Upper Strafforth
347	Laverton	Claro
348	Leathley	Claro
349	Ledsham	Barkston Ash
350	Ledston	Barkston Ash
351	Leeds and Leeds East Division	Skyrack
352	Lepton	Agbrigg
353	Letwell	Upper Strafforth
354	Lindley	Claro
355	Lindley cum Quarmby	Agbrigg
356	Linton	Claro
356	Linton	Staincliffe
358	Little Fenton	Barkston Ash
359	Little Houghton	Lower Strafforth
360	Little Ouseburn	Claro
361	Little Ribston	Claro
362	Little Smeaton	Osgoldcross
363	Little Timble	Claro
364	Litton	Staincliffe
365	Liversedge	Morley
366	Long Marston	Ainsty
367	Long Preston	Staincliffe
368	Langthwaite with Tilts	Lower Strafforth
368	Langthwaite with Tilts	Lower Strafforth
370	Longwood	Agbrigg
371	Loversall	Lower Strafforth
372	Malham	Staincliffe
373	Malham Moor	Staincliffe

NUMBER	TOWNSHIP	WAPENTAKE
374	Maltby	Upper Strafforth
375	Manningham	Morley
376	Markington with Wallerthwaite	Claro
377	Marr	Lower Strafforth
378	Marsden	Agbrigg
379	Marton	Staincliffe
380	Claro	
381	Meltham	Agbrigg
382	Menston	Skyrack
383	Menwith cum Darley	Claro
384	Methley	Agbrigg
385	Mexborough	Upper Strafforth
386	Micklefield	Barkston Ash
387	Middlethorpe	Ainsty
388	Middleton and Stockill	Claro
389	Middleton and Thorpe	Agbrigg
390	Middop	Staincliffe
391	Midgley	Morley
392	Minskip	Claro
393	Mirfield	Agbrigg
394	Mitton	Staincliffe
395	Monk Bretton	Staincross
396	Monk Fryston	Barkston Ash
397	Moor Monkton	Ainsty
398	Morley	Agbrigg
399	Morton	Skyrack
400	Moss	Osgoldcross
401	Nesfield	Claro
402	Nether Hallam	Upper Strafforth
403	Nether Poppleton	Ainsty
404	Newall with Clifton	Claro
405	Newby with Mulwith	Claro
406	Newsholme	Staincliffe
407	Newthorpe	Barkston Ash
408	Newton	Staincliffe
409	Newton Kyme cum Toulston	Barkston Ash
410	Nidd	Claro
411	Norland	Morley
412	Normanton	Agbrigg
413	North Bierley	Morley
414	North Crosland	Agbrigg
415	North Deighton	Claro
416	North Elmsall	Osgoldcross
417	North Owram	Morley
418	North Stainley with Sleningford	Claro
419	Norton	Osgoldcross
420	Nostell	Staincross
421	Notton	Staincross
422	Nun Monkton	Claro
423	Nunwick with Howgrave	Claro
424	Ossett	Agbrigg
425	Otley	Skyrack
426	Otterburn	Staincliffe
427	Ovendon	Morley

NUMBER	TOWNSHIP	WAPENTAKE
428	Owston	Osgoldcross
429	Oxspring	Staincross
430	Oxton and Owston	Ainsty
431	Pannal	Claro
432	Parlington	Skyrack
433	Paythorne	Staincliffe
434	Penistone	Staincross
435	Plompton	Claro
436	Pollington	Osgoldcross
437	Pontefract	Osgoldcross
438	Pontefract Park	Osgoldcross
439	Poole	Skyrack
440	Potter Newton	Skyrack
441	Pudsey	Morley
442	Purston Jaglin	Osgoldcross
443	Quick	Agbrigg
444	Rastrick	Morley
445	Rathmell	Staincliffe
446	Ravenfield	Upper Strafforth
447	Rawcliffe	Osgoldcross
448	Rawdon	Skyrack
449	Rawmarsh	Upper Strafforth
450	Reedness	Osgoldcross
451	Rigton	Claro
452	Rimmington	Staincliffe
453	Ripley	Claro
454	Ripon	Claro
455	Rishworth	Morley
456	Roecliffe	Claro
457	Rossington	Lower Strafforth
458	Rotherham	Upper Strafforth
459	Rothwell	Agbrigg
460	Roundhay	Skyrack
461	Royston	Staincross
462	Rufforth	Ainsty
463	Ryhill	Staincross
464	Rylstone	Staincliffe
465	Ryther with Ozendike	Barkston Ash
466	Sandal Magna	Agbrigg
467	Sawley	Claro
468	Sawley and Tossett E.P.	Staincliffe
469	Saxton cum Scarthingwell	Barkston Ash
470	Scammonden	Agbrigg
471	Scarcroft	Skyrack
472	Scothrop	Staincliffe
473	Scotton	Claro
474	Scriven	Claro
475	Seacroft	Skyrack
476	Sedbergh	Ewcross
477	Selby	Barkston Ash
478	Settle	Staincliffe
479	Shadwell	Skyrack
480	Shafton	Staincross
481	Sharlston	Agbrigg

NUMBER	TOWNSHIP	WAPENTAKE
482	Sharow	Claro
483	Sheffield	Upper Strafforth
484	Shelf	Morley
485	Shelley	Agbrigg
486	Shepley	Agbrigg
487	Sherburn	Barkston Ash
488	Shipley	Morley
489	Shitlington	Agbrigg
490	Sicklinghall	Claro
491	Silkstone	Staincross
492	Silsden	Staincliffe
493	Skelbrooke	Osgoldcross
494	Skelton	Claro
495	Skipton	Staincliffe
496	Skircoat	Morley
497	Slaidburn	Staincliffe
498	Slaithwaite	Agbrigg
499	Snaith	Osgoldcross
500	Snydale	Agbrigg
501	Soothill	Agbrigg
502	South Crosland	Agbrigg
503	South Elmsall	Osgoldcross
504	South Hiendley	Staincross
505	South Kirkby	Osgoldcross
506	South Milford	Barkston Ash
507	South Owram	Morley
508	South Stainley with Cayton	Claro
509	Sowerby	Morley
510	Spofforth	Claro
511	Sprotborough	Lower Strafforth
512	Stainborough	Staincross
513	Stainburn	Claro
514	Stainforth	Staincliffe
515	Stainforth and Bramwith	Lower Strafforth
516	Stainland	Morley
517	Stainton with Hellaby	Upper Strafforth
518	Stancil with Wellingley	Lower Strafforth
519	Stanesfield	Morley
520	Stanley	Agbrigg
521	Stapleton	Osgoldcross
522	Staveley	Claro
523	Steeton	Staincliffe
523	Steeton	Ainsty
525	Stirton	Staincliffe
526	Stonebeck Down	Claro
527	Stonebeck Up	Claro
528	Stotfold	Lower Strafforth
529	Studley Roger	Claro
530	Sturton Grange	Skyrack
531	Sutton	Staincliffe
532	Sutton Askern	Osgoldcross
533	Stutton with Hazlewood	Barkston Ash
534	Swillington	Skyrack
535	Swinden	Staincliffe

NUMBER	TOWNSHIP	WAPENTAKE
536	Swinefleet	Osgoldcross
537	Swinton	Upper Strafforth
538	Sykehouse	Lower Strafforth
539	Tadcaster	Barkston Ash
540	Tadcaster East	Ainsty
541	Tankersley	Staincross
542	Tanshelf	Osgoldcross
543	Temple Newsam	Skyrack
544	Templehirst	Barkston Ash
545	Thorne	Lower Strafforth
546	Thorner	Skyrack
547	Thornhill	Agbrigg
548	Thornton	Morley
549	Thornton in Craven	Staincliffe
550	Thornton in Lonsdale	Ewcross
551	Thorp Arch	Ainsty
552	Badsworth	Osgoldcross
552	Thorpe Audlin	Osgoldcross
553	Thorpe Salvin	Upper Strafforth
554	Thorpe Stapleton	Skyrack
555	Thorpe Willoughby	Barkston Ash
556	Threshfield	Staincliffe
557	Thribergh	Upper Strafforth
558	Thruscross	Claro
559	Thurgoland	Staincross
560	Thurlstone	Staincross
561	Thurnscoe	Lower Strafforth
562	Thurstonland	Agbrigg
563	Tickhill	Lower Strafforth
564	Tinsley	Upper Strafforth
565	Tockwith	Ainsty
566	Todwick	Upper Strafforth
567	Tong	Morley
568	Towton	Barkston Ash
569	Treeton	Upper Strafforth
570	Ulleskelf	Barkston Ash
571	Ulley	Upper Strafforth
572	Upper Hallam	Upper Strafforth
573	Upper Poppleton	Ainsty
574	Upton	Osgoldcross
575	Waddington	Staincliffe
576	Wadsworth	Morley
577	Wadworth	Lower Strafforth
578	Wakefield	Agbrigg
579	Walden Stubbs	Osgoldcross
580	Wales	Upper Strafforth
581	Walton	Ainsty
582	Walton and West Bretton	Agbrigg
583	Warley	Morley
584	Warmfield with Heath	Agbrigg
585	Warmsworth	Lower Strafforth
586	Wath upon Dearne	Lower Strafforth
587	Weardley	Skyrack
588	Weeton	Claro

NUMBER	TOWNSHIP	WAPENTAKE
589	Wentworth	Upper Strafforth
590	West Bretton	Staincross
591	West Ardsley	Agbrigg
592	West Haddlesey	Barkston Ash
593	Weston	Claro
594	Westwick	Claro
595	Wetherby	Claro
596	Wheatley & Sandall	Strafforth & Tickhill
597	Whiston	Upper Strafforth
598	Whitcliff with Thorpe	Claro
599	Whitgift	Osgoldcross
600	Whitley	Agbrigg
600	Whitley	Osgoldcross
602	Whitwood	Agbrigg
603	Whixley	Claro
604	Wickersley	Upper Strafforth
605	Wigglesworth	Staincliffe
606	Wighill	Ainsty
607	Wigton	Skyrack
608	Wike	Skyrack
609	Wilstrop	Ainsty
610	Wintersett	Staincross
611	Wistow	Barkston Ash
612	Wombwell	Upper Strafforth
613	Womersley	Osgoldcross
614	Woolley	Staincross
615	Worsborough	Staincross
616	Wortley	Staincross
616	Wortley	Morley
618	Wothersome	Skyrack
619	Wyke	Morley
620	Yeadon	Skyrack

WEST RIDING

Townships